ETHICS AND THE PRACTICE OF LAW

DAVID E. SCHRADER

Austin College

PRENTICE HALL, Englewood Cliffs, New Jersey 07632

Library of Congress Cataloging-in-Publication Data

Schrader, David E.,
   Ethics and the practice of law.

   Includes index.
   1. Legal ethics—United States—Cases. I. Title.
KF306.A4S36 1988   174'.3'0973   87-12644
ISBN 0-13-290636-8

Editorial/production supervision
   and interior design: Robert DeGeorge
Cover design: Edsal Enterprises
Manufacturing buyer: Margaret Rizzi

To Sandy, Sara, and Tami

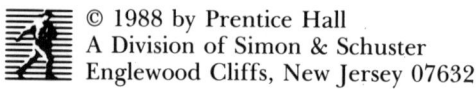
Printed in the United States of America

10   9   8   7   6   5   4   3   2   1

ISBN 0-13-290636-8   01

PRENTICE-HALL INTERNATIONAL (UK) LIMITED, *London*
PRENTICE-HALL OF AUSTRALIA PTY. LIMITED, *Sydney*
PRENTICE-HALL CANADA INC., *Toronto*
PRENTICE-HALL HISPANOAMERICANA, S.A., *Mexico*
PRENTICE-HALL OF INDIA PRIVATE LIMITED, *New Delhi*
PRENTICE-HALL OF JAPAN, INC., *Tokyo*
SIMON & SCHUSTER ASIA PTE. LTD., *Singapore*
EDITORA PRENTICE-HALL DO BRASIL, LTDA., *Rio de Janeiro*

CONTENTS

PREFACE

This book is about lawyers' ethics. Its purpose is not to tell unethical lawyers how to become ethical. Rather its purpose is to help ethical people, whether lawyers, prospective lawyers, or interested lay persons, to understand better the ethical issues involved in the practice of law.

The legal profession is unique among professions in the way in which ethical concerns define its entire context. The legal system, which creates the role of the attorney, exists to promote and enforce our society's conception of justice. Thus, whatever may be said about the purposes of other professions, the purpose of the legal profession is bound up from the beginning with questions of social morality.

Yet the question of what constitutes ethical behavior in the legal profession cannot simply be reduced to the goal of promoting justice in society. The individual attorney is not, after all, a "lone ranger" in pursuit of the public's vision of justice. Rather, the individual lawyer is part of a system of justice. Thus, the ethical constraints on that attorney's behavior are in large measure determined by the role that he or she plays within that system. It is this role and the particular ways in which it shapes what the ethical lawyer ought to do that have been the source of tremendous confusion about the moral obligations of attorneys, among those within the profession and those outside of it.

The first three chapters of this book are designed to help the reader gain an understanding of the adversary system of justice as it operates in the United States and the role the individual attorney is supposed to play within that system. The introductory chapter gives a very brief sketch of two viable approaches to ethical theory for people living in the late twentieth century in the United States: utilitarianism and the approach to ethical theory that developed out of the work of Immanuel Kant. The second chapter offers some attempts to extend ethical theory into the area of social justice. The readings in that chapter address the issue of what we should expect a judicial system to take as its ethical guidelines. Chapter Three examines the adversarial system of justice, looking at the question of how well adversarial proceedings serve the end of accomplishing justice and at the extent to which the individual attorney bears responsibility for the results that he or she helps to accomplish within that system.

The two last (and largest) chapters of the book look at the more particular obligations under which the legal profession collectively and the attorney individually operate. Chapter Four examines those responsibilities of the attorney and the legal profession that are most directly obligations to the system of justice. The topics around which this chapter is organized are: the duty to make legal services broadly available, the duty to represent competently, and the duty to deal with others in the system honestly. Chapter Five, by contrast, examines those responsibilities of the attorney that are most directly obligations to the client, who is after all the one with whom the attorney deals most intimately. The topics around which this chapter is organized are: loyalty to the client, protecting the client's confidences, and serving the client with competence.

These subdivisions within the fourth and fifth chapters should help the reader gain a clearer understanding of the ways in which attorneys' obligations sometimes conflict with one another. While this presentation will not provide any easy recipe for the resolution of those conflicts, still a clearer identification of the obligations that generate the conflicts may provide attorneys, or those who deal with them, with some analytical tools that may help in the process of resolving such conflicts.

Like any book, this one has come about because of the efforts of a great many people. Above all, I must thank my good friend and colleague, Lee Van Zant. Professor Van Zant encouraged me to work in the area of applied ethics nearly ten years ago. Since that time, he and I have jointly taught a course in business ethics. It was largely as a result of that effort that I developed the interest in legal ethics that has led to this book. Furthermore, Professor Van Zant read and commented on early drafts of several of the introductions that are included in this book.

My attorney, Roger D. Sanders, also read early drafts of my introductions and provided me with a lawyer's eye response that proved very helpful to me.

The entire work was read by the students in my Fall 1985 course in legal ethics: Lee Bash, Tab Bingamon, Mike Eliasson, John Heimsath, Sean Ibison, Keith Jeffers, Kirk Justus, Eric Ostrom, Rodney Roe, and Kimberly White. They gave me valuable feedback on the suitability of these materials, as well as some not included here, for classroom use.

Attorneys Robert Richardson and David Stagner also helped by making me aware of material that I would otherwise have ignored.

Austin College provided financial assistance with the typing of certain portions of the manuscript.

Finally, my wife, Sandy, and my daughters, Sara and Tami, contributed greatly to this work by providing a home environment in which I could carry on both research and manuscript preparation. They also helped more than they can possibly realize with their constant reassurances that what I was doing was worth the effort.

chapter one

INTRODUCTION

This is a book about ethics in the legal profession. The legal profession is perhaps unique among the professions, both in the amount of discussion carried on by organized groups within the profession regarding its ethical responsibilities, and in the pervasiveness outside the profession of the impression that it is wholly amoral. It is my hope that this book will help those who look at the legal profession from the outside to realize that it exists in anything but a moral vacuum, and my hope also that it will help those who work or plan to work within the legal profession to gain a clearer perspective from which to grapple with the numerous moral dilemmas that confront the attorney.

Among practicing attorneys, discussions of professional ethics generally start with, and lamentably often also end with, the American Bar Association's "Code of Professional Responsibility"; its predecessor, the "Canons of Professional Ethics"; or perhaps the new "Model Rules of Professional Conduct." The fact that the Canons were first adopted by the ABA in 1908 shows quite clearly that the organized bar has long acknowledged the necessity of dealing explicitly with the ethical problems arising in the practice of law. While this long-standing acknowledgement is in itself laudable, limiting a discussion of legal ethics to those documents would surely be unfortunate. The ABA's various codes are, like most attempts at professional self-regulation, combinations of legitimate ethical concern,

concern with professional etiquette, and concern to protect the economic status of the profession. This combination makes it difficult to disentangle the several strands that comprise these codes, to distinguish among matters of ethics, courtesy, and self-interest.

A second problem is that the codes are not systematic. The CPR is a collection of "Ethical Considerations" and "Disciplinary Rules" which are organized around certain topics, while the Model Code consists of "Rules" and "Comments." They do not, however, contain an overriding rationale that might help the attorney in those cases where two or more rules appear to conflict or where the rules appear to speak but with no clarity. That very distinction between "Ethical Considerations" or "Comments" and "Rules" has the practical effect of leading the practicing attorney to take the "Rules" seriously while disregarding the "Ethical Considerations" or "Comments." It tends to give the CPR even more the character of a list of "Dont's." Such an approach to legal ethics quite naturally leads many lawyers to confuse questions of legal ethics with questions of what the Bar Association will permit them to do.

In spite of these shortcomings, many a law school course in professional responsibility consists in nothing more than memorizing the CPR. The remedy for these shortcomings starts with the recognition that difficult ethical decisions are most fruitfully approached from the perspective of some kind of ethical theory.

This book differs considerably from the traditional law school approach to legal ethics. It starts out by offering some background in ethical theory as well as some examination of the role played by the attorney in an adversarial system of justice. Against this background the reader will better be able to make sense of the discussions of particular issues in legal ethics which comprise the major part of the book.

THE NEED FOR ETHICAL THEORY

Ethical theory is an important starting point for a consideration of legal ethics. Yet people disagree profoundly about ethical theory and, moreover, there are many very fine and decent people who have given virtually no reflection to ethical theory. There are many who, like Cephalus in Plato's *Republic*, seem to have a knack for doing good without having much of an idea what it is that makes what they do good.

What is true of life in general is doubly true of legal practice. Often people find themselves in situations of conflict, where a person is under obligation to two or more people and where those obligations cannot all be fulfilled. This kind of situation is particularly prevalent in legal practice: an attorney may unwittingly step into a situation in which he or she is under obligation to two or more clients whose interests cannot be mutually served, or an attorney's obligation to be a faithful and zealous agent of a client comes into conflict with the attorney's role as an officer of the court. In this kind of situation the person who relies upon such a knack for doing good, following the dictates of a good conscience, or what we might call good moral intuitions, finds him or herself in a quandary. There are clear and legitimate feelings of sympathy with both sides. Moreover, people of good will will find themselves in sharp disagreement.

An ethical theory will not invariably yield a quick and easy answer in such cases. It will not even lead all persons of good will to eventual agreement. What we can expect of an ethical theory is that it will provide a clearer means of focusing on and sorting out the issues at stake. It will provide a general line of justification for each of the competing claims, and this in turn will provide a line of approach to a resolution of those competing claims.

A second area wherein ethical theory offers some advantage over pretheoretical ethical intuitions lies in its capacity to help overcome subjective prejudice and our deeply rooted tendency to judge our own moral case by different standards from those by which we judge the cases of others. Whatever one may say about the subjective factors involved in the genesis of a theory or in an individual's acceptance of a theory, there is still an important sense in which any theory is objective. A theory has logical consequences. An ethical theory, like any other theory, is couched in general terms, but as with all theories, when it is conjoined with descriptions of concrete states of affairs, it will yield some very concrete implications. These implications follow quite apart from whether they will please or displease, benefit or harm the particular agents in question. The person who is willing to assess his or her behavior in terms of some ethical theory has, therefore, the advantage of a standard that is at least to some extent capable of transcending the subjective prejudices and self-deceptions that tend to beset all of us.

This element of objectivity is particularly crucial because it opens the way to reasoned discussion and criticism in regard to both self and others— of the moral standards which we bring to bear on the behavior of both ourselves and others.

KINDS OF ETHICAL THEORY

There are, I believe, two basic approaches to ethical theory which constitute live theoretical options for people in the late twentieth century: utilitarian theories and those theories that follow the basic lines laid out in the ethical writings of Immanuel Kant.[1] Moreover, these two approaches to ethical theory, utilitarian and Kantian, fall one on each side of the major division that most writers recognize as separating the two possible modes of analysis in ethical theorizing, the division between teleological and deontological approaches to ethical theory. *Teleological* theories of ethics are theories that assess human behavior in terms of its accomplishment of or tendency to accomplish certain desired ends or goals. *Deontological* theories of ethics, on the other hand, assess human behavior in terms of the principles in accordance with which the agent determined his or her behavior. It is apparent that, whatever similarities or differences in the kinds of behavior advocated by teleological and deontological theories, the two approaches differ radically in the ways in which they analyze human behavior.

UTILITARIAN THEORIES

I speak of utilitarian theor*ies* because utilitarianism is not simply one theory. The one-line description of the goal of utilitarianism is "the greatest good for the greatest number." This brief characterization of utilitarianism helps us to focus on the two central features that identify a theory of ethics as utilitarian. A utilitarian ethical theory holds that (1) there is some intrinsic good, something held to be good in and of itself; and that (2) this good, whatever it is, is measurable and hence maximizable. Essentially, different varieties of utilitarianism are distinguishable in terms of what they hold to be intrinsically good and how they propose to measure that good. Of course, how a theory proposes to measure the good must itself be determined in the light of what it takes to be the good.

A number of distinct varieties of utilitarian moral theory have been developed, two of which will be presented in Chapter Two. In addition to the varieties of traditional utilitarianism developed by moral theorists such as Jeremy Bentham and John Stuart Mill, there has also been the currently influential "subjective preference" type of utilitarianism which takes each person's good to be the object of his or her desires, and which underlies much of contemporary economic theory.

While it may be interesting to look at the general lines along which one might develop some form of utilitarian ethical theory, such an exposition has little point if we do not look at the question of the strengths and weaknesses of utilitarianism. Why might one wish to hold some form of utilitarianism? Why might one wish to reject utilitarianism in any or all of its forms?

There are three features of utilitarianism that have made it a broadly attractive position over the past 150 years. First, utilitarianism has a strongly empirical flavor. I use the term "flavor" here quite self-consciously. By its nature, ethical theory cannot be empirical in the same sense as can physics. Ethical theory, after all, is prescriptive, not descriptive. It tells what we ought to do, not what we do in fact do. If some ethical theory tells us that some particular agent in some particular set of circumstances ought to do A, and that agent then does B, that action does not count against the theory. Rather it tells us that, according to that theory, the agent acted wrongly. The implications of ethical theories are prescriptions, not predictions. Nevertheless, utilitarianism does have a particularly appealing kind of connection with experience. The several varieties of utilitarianism identified above all start out with a conception of the intrinsic good that appears to be testable in human experience. Bentham gave us pleasure, which is a quality attaching to experience. Mill gave us a broader notion of human happiness, still a quality of our experience. The subjective preference utilitarian gave us preference, again apparently rooted in experience. To the average person of the twentieth century this connection with experience constitutes an appearance of scientific rigor which tends to lend stature to utilitarianism.

A second appealing feature of utilitarianism is its promise of a neat decision procedure. With its concern for the maximization of utility, utilitarianism presupposes some kind of numerical measurement of utility. Once that measurement is found, all we have to do is be able to distinguish more from less. Once we have found the appropriate moral calculus, it would seem to be a short step to the development of a moral calculator that would make all of our decisions for us on a purely mechanical basis. From the perspective of subjective preference utilitarianism, there are a good many economists who think that neoclassical microeconomic theory offers us precisely that calculator.

The final feature of utilitarianism which has been a great source of attraction since the beginnings of utilitarianism is its basic egalitarian thrust. Particularly in the hands of Bentham and Mill, utilitarianism provided a radical new approach to social issues according to which the happiness or pleasure of the poorest beggar in London counted for precisely the same, no more and no less, as that of Queen Victoria. The utilitarian approach proved to be a significant force in the direction of social justice in the nineteenth century. Subjective preference utilitarianism, the major twentieth-century descendant of Bentham and Mill, has been much more ambiguous on this point. At least to the extent that the greatest good comes to be measured by aggregate market demand, the twentieth-century utilitarians, at least those of an economic stripe, have moved away from the earlier egalitarianism back to a much more plutocratic vision of social decision.

On the other side of the coin, there are two central problems which work against the acceptability of utilitarianism. The first is strictly an internal problem, one that is generated by the shape of utilitarianism itself. This is the problem of measurement. I have just said that one of the attractive features of utilitarianism is that it promises a neat and systematic decision procedure. Such a procedure is based upon the notion that the good, whatever it is taken to be, can be measured. For the utilitarian, problems in measuring the good translate into problems in delivering on that promise of a decision procedure. As must be clear from what has been said about utilitarianism thus far, every variety of utilitarianism has its own unique problem of measurement. To date, no variety of utilitarianism has put forward a problem-free approach to measurement of the good. To say this much, however, is not to say that the problem of measurement ought to force one to abandon utilitarianism. Rather, it is to set one of the ongoing challenges to the future development of utilitarian moral theory. It is clearly a challenge that the utilitarian cannot ignore, given the centrality of measurement to the utilitarian approach to ethics.

The second problem is an external one. It is generated not by the constraints that utilitarianism places on itself, but rather by constraints placed on any attempt at ethical theorizing by collective human moral experience. This is the problem of unjust consequences. It is at least a presumptive problem for an ethical theory if it leads to consequences, to ethical decisions, that run counter to our pretheoretical sense of justice. Utilitarianism, with its concern for the greatest good for the greatest number, appears to require that the rights and legitimate interests of the minority on occasion be sacrificed unjustly for the greater benefit of the majority. This appears to be so in the case of both distributive justice and retributive justice.

In the distributive area, for example, it is not at all clear that utilitarian considerations would rule out a society in which, say, twenty percent of the population served as slaves for the remaining eighty percent, at least as long as that twenty percent were carefully trained (brainwashed) to believe that they were not entitled to the same expectations as others and they were basically well cared for. The utilitarian will respond with the alleged "law" of diminishing marginal utility, the claim that at a certain point each successive unit of a commodity consumed produces less per-unit utility than the previous unit. Similarly, the utilitarian may respond that relative distributional equity serves to promote social stability and, thereby, higher utility. These responses may or may not prove adequate. What is crucial to note at this point is that each of them depends upon empirical claims about social order and the shape of individual human preference schedules that are at the very least subject to dispute.

The problem in the area of retributive justice is perhaps even more difficult. The problem for the utilitarian is how to draw the connection between real, as opposed to perceived, guilt and punishment. If we look at punishment from a purely utilitarian point of view, we are, of course, drawn irresistibly to a deterrence approach to punishment. So long as our guiding concern is to generate the greatest good for the greatest number, our concern will be with punishing in such a manner as to diminish the total disutility brought into society by crime. Unfortunately, the deterrent value of punishing an innocent person whom everyone believes to be guilty is precisely the same as the deterrent value of punishing a person who is actually guilty.

Perhaps a variety of utilitarianism is available to us that can circumvent the problem of unjust consequences as outlined above. On the other hand, the problem may prove intractable to utilitarianism. In either event, it is one of the two significant problems that face the utilitarian moral theorist.

No variety of utilitarianism can be acceptable without at least some serious attempt to come to grips with both the problem of measurement and the problem of unjust consequences.

KANTIAN THEORIES

The claim that the end justifies the means is obviously an ethically controversial claim. While the utilitarian justifies all action in terms of the ends brought about by that action, the Kantian approach to ethics clearly rejects the justification of action solely in terms of ends. Rather it regards principle as the distinguishing mark of moral action.

There are three fundamental propositions set forward in Kant's *Groundwork of the Metaphysics of Morals* that provide the point of departure for Kantian approach to ethical theory:

1. "It is precisely in this that the worth of character begins to show . . ., that he does good, not from inclination, but from duty."[2]

2. "An action done from duty has its moral worth, not in the purpose to be attained by it, but in the maxim in accordance with which it is decided upon."[3]
3. "Duty is the necessity to act out of reverence for the moral law."[4]

The second of Kant's three propositions, of course, is simply Kant's statement of what I noted in introducing this section: that action is justified not by the end (purpose) that it is supposed to accomplish, but rather by the rule or principle of action (maxim) that led the agent to act as he or she did. Kant's first proposition has already given us all of this by implication in telling us what kind of intentions, what kind of rules of action, give an action moral worth. Actions are good to the extent that they spring from intentions directed to the pursuit of duty rather than from intentions directed to the pursuit of inclination or passion. An example should serve to illustrate the distinction that Kant wants to draw here. Consider a shopkeeper who scrupulously and invariably returns correct change to customers. There are at least three possible motivational bases for such behavior. The first possibility is that the shopkeeper gives correct change because, after all, business is business. The shopkeeper wants to produce large profits and knows that customers are more likely to return when they can count on receiving correct change. Correct change serves as an indication of honesty in business relationships and honesty, in the end, pays off. A second possibility is that the shopkeeper gives correct change because of some inner compulsion for correctness. The shopkeeper enjoys the feeling of satisfaction that comes at the end of each business day when the count of the day's receipts agrees to the penny with the closing tally on the cash register tape. Clearly there are people who get precisely this kind of satisfaction from mathematical correctness. A third possibility is that the shopkeeper gives correct change because it is his or her duty (whatever that means) to do so. According to a Kantian analysis, it is only in this last case that the action of giving correct change has any moral worth. In each of the two earlier cases, the shopkeeper gave correct change because of what was in it for him or her. In those two cases the shopkeeper's action was ruled by subjective inclination. Only in the last case did the shopkeeper's action follow the rule of objective duty.

An obviously unanswered question at this point is what Kant means by "duty." Kant's third proposition supplies the answer. "Duty is the necessity to act out of reverence for the moral law." To follow the rule of duty, therefore, is to follow the rule of moral law—not merely to *act* as the moral law commands, but to do what one does simply *because* the moral law commands it. From this proposition it follows that the possibility of acting on the basis of an objective duty rests on the possibility of there being such a moral law. Moreover, the moral force of the command to act from duty depends, in precisely the same manner, on the basis upon which such a law is to be justified.

The moral law, for Kant, is a law of reason. The shape and content of the moral law are determined by the character of law generally and, more specifically, by a couple of important facts about human beings. Law, simply by virtue of its character as law, must be universal. The laws of nature, for example, cover the workings of all physical objects. The moral law then, if it is genuinely to be law rather than mere general custom or courtesy, must cover all human behavior. If it is any narrower in scope, it cannot be law. If there is nothing of that breadth of scope, then there is no moral law. This much is fundamental to Kant.

The fact that law must necessarily be universal leads to several of Kant's formulations of the moral law:

K1:   "Act only on that maxim through which you can at the same time will that it should become a universal law."[5]

K2:   "Act as if the maxim of your action were to become through your will a universal law of nature."[6]

K4:   Act in conformity with "the Idea of the will of every rational being as a will which makes universal law."[7]

Kant's basic contention here is that to act out of reverence for the moral law is to act on the basis of principles of behavior which one would be willing to have held as universal principles of human behavior. Act as you would have others act. Kant illustrates this approach most clearly with the example of deceptive promising. Making deceptive promises would violate the moral law precisely because the principle of making deceptive promises could not be maintained as a universal principle of behavior. If the making of deceptive promises were to be made universal, the very institution of promising could no longer be maintained. Promising, after all, depends on a general presumption that promises are kept.[8]

Of course a moral law is a law for moral agents. Human beings are moral agents. If there are other beings in the universe capable of rational activity, they also would be moral agents. What is distinctive of rational agents is that they are capable of framing ends for themselves and then acting in pursuit of those ends. As an extension of this, they are capable of developing long-range plans for their lives and attempting to realize those plans. Inanimate objects, on the other hand, can clearly have no ends. They are characteristically simply used as means to the ends of rational agents. Finally, while we might argue over the propriety of speaking of lower animals as having ends, there is little controversy in the claim that such animals are not capable of choosing their own ends. Whatever appreciation we may have for the behavior of the mother bird as she decoys a predator away from her nest and young, we may clearly not say that she chose the survival of her young as a deliberate alternative to some other end.

The fact that rational agents are unique in being capable of choosing their own ends leads to quite a different formulation of the moral law:

K3:   "Act in such a way that you always treat humanity, whether in your own person or in the person of any other, never simply as a means, but always at the same time as an end."[9]

The word "simply" is crucial here. The moral law does not prohibit me from using another person as a means to some end of mine. If it were to do that, I would be morally prohibited from asking my neighbor to give me a ride to work when my car was in the shop for repair. Rather what the moral law requires is that, in dealing with any human being, myself or another, we acknowledge that that person is also a rational agent. We must acknowledge, in particular, that others have their own ends, and that we violate their humanity if we use them in pursuit of our ends without also paying heed to their ends. Again, Kant illustrates this law with the case of making a deceptive promise in order to obtain a loan.[10] If I were to secure a loan of ten dollars from you on the basis of a promise that I would repay you on Tuesday while in fact I had no intention whatsoever of repaying you at that time, I would be treating you not as a human being, but rather as something akin to a cash machine. I would be failing to acknowledge that you might have purposes of your own to which you planned to put the ten dollars on Wednesday. I would, in sum, be treating you merely as a means to my own ends, failing to acknowledge you at the same time as a framer of your own ends.

While Kant held that his several formulations of the moral law were all equivalent, it is clear that there are two quite distinct emphases in the different formulations. On the one hand, we see an emphasis on universalizability. Act as you would have others act. Do unto others as you would have everyone do unto everyone else. On the other hand, we also see an emphasis on the dignity of the human individual. Treat people as people, not mere objects. Don't simply use people.

Whether or not Kant was right about the equivalence of his several formulations of the moral law, the two different emphases noted above have served to inspire the development of two quite different approaches to the problems of social ethics. The emphasis on universalizability has given rise to a clearly egalitarian approach to theories of social ethics, while the emphasis on the dignity of the human individual has given rise to a far more individualistic approach.

It is apparent then that, just as there is a considerable variety of types of ethical theory that fall under the rubric of utilitarianism, there is also a broad variety that spring from the basic approach set forward by Kant. Again, it is important to note Kant may or may not be correct in claiming that the various formulations of the moral law are all equivalent. In either case, it is clear that the different emphases drawn by the different formulations can lead to differences in perspective on the moral law. These, in turn, can lead to the development of quite different varieties of basically Kantian ethical theories.

Like utilitarianism, the Kantian approach to ethical theory has both its strengths and its weaknesses. The chief strength of Kant's approach is the high level of accord it has with some of our most basic pretheoretical intuitions regarding the normative evaluation of human behavior. This accord with intuition shows up at several levels. At the grossest level, we might note that most people seem to want to claim that the end doesn't justify the means, that why one does what one does is at least as important as what one actually accomplishes. The claim that the end doesn't justify the means is, of course, one way of expressing a pretheoretical intuition that ethical theory must be nonteleological. While this does not lead one to anything like a full-blown Kantian ethical theory, it clearly does move one away from utilitarianism. To the extent that one sees some variety of Kantian ethical theory as the major serious alternative to utilitarianism, the rejection of utilitarianism is a major step in the direction of a Kantian theory.

At a finer level, the various statements of Kant's principle of universalizability give formal expression to a terribly basic and common intuition about the basis of ethical judgment. I suspect that every parent has at one time or another had the experience of having a child mistreat a sibling or playmate. One's daughter throws a toy at a playmate or rips to shreds her sister's birthday cards. At least in the parent's calmer moments, he or she will sometimes say to the daughter, "How would you like it if other children did that to you?" One might call this the kiddy version of the Golden Rule.

Similarly, Kant's insistence that human beings be treated as ends, and not merely as means, also echoes some of our most deeply felt moral intuitions. Often, when a person thinks that he or she has been unfairly taken advantage of by another person, we may expect to hear that person say something like, "I was just being used." "Being used" here amounts to being treated like a mere object, being treated in a manner appropriate to something less than a full-fledged human being. The complaint makes it clear that most people tend to regard such treatment as morally inappropriate.

On the reverse side of the coin, we find two major criticisms lodged against the Kantian approach to ethical theory: that it is too rigid, and that it is so flexible as to have no content at all. While these two criticisms would appear at first blush to be radically different from each other, they are in fact simply two sides of a common problem. The real difficulty for the Kantian ethical theorist is to establish the content of his or her theory.

The fact that Kant's approach could inspire such radically divergent views on social justice as the egalitarianism of John Rawls and libertarianism of Robert Nozick should lead us to a healthy suspicion on precisely this point. The root of the problem lies in the fact that we see such tremendous levels of disagreement about what moral rules people would be prepared to universalize, and about what constitutes treatment of human beings as ends and not as mere means. The mere fact that there are utilitarians should tell us that there are some people who would be not only willing, but eager to universalize the rule, "Act so as to bring about the greatest balance of happiness over unhappiness." By contrast, there are egoists who would want to universalize the rule, "A person should act in pursuit of his or her own self-interest." It has, of course, frequently been pointed out in criticism of Kant's position that a dedicated Nazi would universalize the rule, "One should work for the extermination of the Jewish people." If sufficiently fanatical, that Nazi might even continue to will that rule as universal even upon the discovery that he or she turned out to be a Jew. Similarly, William Tecumseh Sherman surely had what he took to be a universalizable rule in mind when he said, "The only good Indian is a dead Indian." Finally we might imagine that I should be willing to universalize the rule, "People should work to promote the interests of David Schrader." It begins to look as though anyone can, given the proper set of descriptions, find some set of rules which he or she would be willing to universalize and which would legitimize whatever he or she wished to do. Whether this is indeed the case, it appears that, however we set about constructing an ethical theory based on a Kantian approach, the problem of clarity of content will arise to some significant extent.

As we look at ethical theory, we find that ethics is very much like any area in which there are significant rival approaches. Both of the major approaches to ethical theory are based on strongly rooted and natural intuitions about what constitutes right behavior. There are strong initial reasons to be inclined toward a utilitarian approach, just as there are strong initial reasons to be inclined toward a Kantian approach. Yet at the same time there are difficulties with both approaches. Most of us, as we set about making some of the hard ethical choices tht confront us from time to time in both our private and professional lives, find ourselves adopting a utilitarian approach, or perhaps a Kantian approach, or perhaps some combination of the two. Thus it becomes important to be aware of the shortcomings of the approaches we choose. To the extent that we employ utilitarian considerations in our decision making, we must be prepared to respond to the problems of measurement and unjust consequences. To the extent that we employ Kantian considerations, we must be aware of the problem of unclarity or arbitrariness of content. For all of these difficulties, however, the one option that is never open to us is the abandonment of theory altogether. In the practical business of decision making, just as in the practical business of bridge building, theoretical considerations are the major helps we have in crossing unfamiliar chasms in the terrain.

LAWYERS AND SYSTEMS OF JUSTICE

When we are concerned with ethical decision making within the context of legal practice, we must face additional considerations. The ordinary day-to-day ethical obligations we have toward others may be somewhat different from those under which we find ourselves in particular professional contexts. The police officer, for example, is permitted to hit or shoot someone in some contexts in which such acts would obviously be forbidden to the rest of us. The lawyer too, in his or her professional life, seems to be exempt from certain obligations which are binding upon the rest of us. More than that, the lawyer at times would seem to have obligations that run directly counter to obligations binding the rest of us.

Perhaps the most common defense of the claim that professional roles carry with them their own set of obligations is that each profession serves some particular purpose and that those in the profession acquire obligations leading to the successful accomplishment of that purpose. This line of justification clearly will not do. To illustrate, note that this approach might lead us to hold that a hit-person is obligated to be a good shot. The point is that if a professional role is not itself a part of a morally acceptable way of life, then it cannot generate obligations for those who occupy such roles. To show that a professional role does impose obligations different from or contrary to our everyday obligations, one must first show that the profession itself is morally justifiable. General Sherman would need to show that there are just wars. People have in fact argued for such a claim.

Applying all of this to the lawyer, to understand and to justify the various obligations that devolve upon the lawyer by virtue of his or her professional role, we need to understand the role that the attorney plays in the adversary system of justice, and we need to see the grounds on which one might argue that this adversary system functions as a part of a just social order.

A judicial system is surely one of the most essential elements in civil society. It functions to provide just adjudication of the civil disputes that inevitably arise when people interact with one another, and to identify and punish those in society who violate either other members of society or the very fabric of society itself. While it is a society's laws that tell us what a society determines to constitute just resolution of conflicts within that society, and what a society determines to constitute punishable wrongs, it is the society's judicial system that gives the set of procedures that that society has adopted to determine whether and how the particular acts and disputes of concrete individuals fall under those laws. Generally, a society's laws give us that society's concept of substantive justice, while its judicial system gives us at least an important part of its concept of procedural justice.

In distinguishing between substantive justice and procedural justice, we are distinguishing between those states of affairs that constitute just social arrangements—such as criminals being convicted and punished—and the best procedures for accomplishing those ends. Procedural justice, normally at least,[11] will thus be dependent upon the antecedent acceptance of some prior notion of substantive justice. In cases in which we can identify a procedure that is guaranteed to produce or identify substantive justice, we shall say that we have perfect procedural justice. In all likelihood, the discovery of perfect procedural justice, in those cases in which it is to be had, is a matter of technical ingenuity. In the vast majority of cases, however, we must be content with imperfect procedural justice, procedures that do not guarantee a just result but presumably give us the best attainable approximation to substantive justice. Judicial procedures are obviously of this latter kind. Criminal justice gives us the clearest case. Clearly substantive justice would be achieved if the guilty were always convicted and punished while the innocent were always acquitted. Unfortunately, no human system is devisable that would invariably be able to distinguish correctly between the guilty and the innocent. Therefore we must develop our judicial procedures in such a way as to achieve the next best result.

The problem we encounter in dealing with imperfect procedural justice is to determine what is the next best result. How are we to resolve the invariable trade-offs which must be made as we consider the various possible candidates for second best? Again in the area of criminal justice, we must note that any procedure that will increase the number of the guilty that we convict will also tend to increase the number of innocent that we convict. Similarly, procedures that will increase the chances that innocent people who have been charged with crimes will be acquitted will increase the number of guilty who are acquitted as well.

Several issues arise as we consider the problem of judicial decision in both civil and criminal law. Upon which party, the state or the defendant, or the plaintiff or the defendant, should the burden of proof lie? What level of proof should be required for a judicial determination: Proof beyond reasonable doubt? A preponderance of evidence? What should be the process of discovery? Should civil procedures be the same as criminal procedures?

It is the character of the process of discovery in particular that defines the role of the lawyer. To look at it in a very general way, there are two basically different kinds of approaches to the process of judicial discovery. This is not, of course, to suggest that either of them does or should exist in a pure form. These two "systems," the adversary system and the inquisitorial system, involve very different roles for the attorney. The *adversary* system features the attorneys for the contending parties as adversaries in the arena of the court, each representing the interests of his or her client, with the judge (and jury) as impartial arbiters. The *inquisitorial* system, by contrast, features the court, judge, and attorneys, as an investigative team, carrying out an impartial search for the truth. Again, to speak very generally, the adversary system has tended to dominate in those countries with a common law tradition (particularly the English-speaking world), while the inquisitorial system has dominated those countries with a civil law tradition (such as France and Germany) and those in the Communist world.

The differences between the two systems may be characterized in a great many different ways, most of which serve to suggest the superiority of the inquisitorial system. I suspect that the words that stood out as you read the initial characterizations of the two systems in the last paragraph were "arena" and "truth." This kind of emphasis makes it appear that the inquisitorial system is primarily concerned with truth while the adversary system is primarily concerned with theatrics. This is surely the understanding (or misunderstanding) of the two systems that underlies much of the criticism of our legal system and of the legal profession that one encounters in public conversation on judicial process. Similarly, the adversary system is sometimes claimed, to its obvious disadvantage, to have its roots in the medieval "trial by combat."[12]

There are, of course, a number of ways in which we might look at adversarial proceedings: as theater, as combat, or even as a search for the truth. The adversary system functions as a search for truth by beginning with the acknowledgement that the same evidence may sometimes lead us to different conclusions if we view it with different biases. The job of the opposing attorneys, therefore, is to examine the evidence and the law bearing on the case from opposing biases. This is true for both criminal and civil proceedings. The judge and jury meanwhile are to sit as impartial arbiters between the two constructions of the facts and law. Note that an adversarial proceeding is designed to provide every possible guarantee of the impartiality of the judge and jury. Judges may be required to remove themselves from particular cases. Prospective jurors may be "bumped" for even the slightest suspicion of prejudice. Usually an attorney is allowed to bump a restricted number of prospective jurors on the basis of nothing but subjective hunch. In the extreme case, a change of venue may be requested where the attorney believes that an impartial trial is impossible in a given location.

The adversary system is not, of course, without its faults. If, for example, we combine the adversary system of justice with a legal profession that allocates its services on the basis of a substantially free market economy, there is strong reason to think that the resulting judicial system will have a pronounced bias in favor of the claims of the wealthy. Such a bias would clearly run counter to sound principles of procedural justice. It is important to note, however, that such a bias may not necessarily be endemic to the adversary system of justice.

It is also arguable that an adversary system of justice tends to spawn a good deal of needless, time-consuming litigation and that it is therefore a very inefficient system. Similarly, it is arguable that there are significant areas of civil law in which conflict may not be most suitably resolved by adversarial procedures. This would be particularly true where the conflict involves important third-party interests, such as the interests of children in a great many divorce settlements. Other cases where this might be true would be those in which the parties, despite their conflicts, may have substantially convergent interests, as is the case in many estate settlements.

The weight of these various criticisms of the adversary system of justice will be examined in a later chapter. For the present, the important point is that the adversary system assigns a particular role to the attorney in the quest for justice. This role is a peculiar one, requiring specific and systematic biases which obligate the attorney to act at times in ways that would clearly be forbidden to anyone who was not playing such a role in such a system.

Given the fact that the peculiar duties of the attorney are justified only by virtue of the attorney's role in the (presumably) just adversary system of justice, it follows that those duties are, at bottom, duties to the system of justice. The duties that the attorney has to his or her client rest upon the attorney's duty to help in the accomplishment of justice. The attorney has obligations to the client, obligations to the court, obligations to the legal profession, and obligations to third parties. All of these are simply different parts of the attorney's obligation to help bring about justice.

PLAN OF THE BOOK

In the study of legal ethics we are concerned with seeing how the attorney's obligation to help bring about justice through the particular institutions of the adversary system shape the various derivative obligations noted above. What is the character of the attorney's obligation to the client? What is the character of the attorney's obligation to the court? To the legal profession? To third parties? Perhaps most important of all, how is the attorney to go about resolving the obvious and inevitable conflicts that will arise among the variously directed obligations that are imposed by his or her professional position?

The remainder of this book will help the reader to develop a perspective from which to examine the various obligations which circumscribe the work of the attorney, and then will provide an examination of the most central of those obligations. Initially we will look at perspectives on the moral context of legal practice. First, Chapter Two will focus on ethical theories and theories of justice, and Chapter Three will give some perspectives on the adversary system of justice, looking at both sympathetic and critical views of that system.

The book will then examine the major kinds of ethical issues which arise in the practice of law. Chapter Four will focus on those obligations of the attorney and of the legal profession collectively that are most centrally obligations to the system of justice itself. First and foremost among these obligations are those relating to the availability of legal services. A natural place to start is with the whole issue of the openness of the legal profession. There has been a long tendency for the legal profession to function as something of a club with membership open only to people like those who already belong. In many states women were formally barred from the legal profession for much of the nineteenth century. Even in our own day it is of some significance that Supreme Court Justice Sandra Day O'Connor, upon graduating third in her class from the Stanford University School of Law, could find a job only as a legal secretary. Similarly, until quite recently law schools have been no different from other American institutions in discriminating against members of minority groups. These restrictions have naturally tended to make legal services less available to significant groups of people in society. Yet presumably the adversary system can operate as it should only if legal services are widely available. Additional areas of considerable controversy impinging upon the availability of legal services surround the representation of the unpopular and those who are widely believed to be guilty. It is patently obvious that the representation of such clients has subjected lawyers to considerable public criticism and, on more than one occasion, has significantly damaged the practices of attorneys who have undertaken such representation. A final area that affects the availability of legal services in a society in which the legal profession is a part of a market economy is the cost of legal services, the problem of representation of those who cannot afford the fees lawyers customarily charge. The other two areas with which Chapter Four will be concerned are competence and honesty.

Chapter Five will concern itself with the attorney's obligations to his or her client, in particular, loyalty, confidentiality, and, again, competence. The attorney's obligation to be loyal to the client's interests raises a variety of complex issues. In a number of contexts of legal practice, particularly family practice, corporate practice, and governmental practice, loyalty raises particularly troublesome issues as the attorney is faced with unique difficulties in determining what exactly are the interests to which he or she is to be loyal. One of the elements of loyalty that warrants separate treatment is confidentiality. In this area a particularly difficult ethical problem arises in what Monroe Freedman calls "the criminal defense lawyer's trilemma,"[13] the apparent conflict among the attorney's obligation to learn all the facts relevant to the client's case, the obligation to protect the confidences of the client, and the obligation to be candid with the court. The final issue presented in Chapter Five concerns the obligation of the attorney to do a competent job of handling the affairs of his or her client and the attorney's liability to the client for failure to do so.

Each chapter, except for Chapter Two, will include both selected legal opinions and systematic ethical readings. While this volume does not pretend to give an exhaustive treatment of all the ethical questions that arise in the practice of law, it nevertheless offers a set of diverse perspectives on the major problem areas in legal ethics that should provide the reader with material for additional reflection.

NOTES

1. The primary of these writings are Immanuel Kant, *Critique of Practical Reason*, trans. Lewis White Beck (Indianapolis: Bobbs-Merrill Company, Inc., 1956); and Immanuel Kant, *Groundwork of the Metaphysics of Morals*, trans. H. J. Paton (New York: Harper and Row, Publishers, 1964).

2. Kant, *Groundwork of the Metaphysics of Morals*, p. 66.

3. Ibid., pp. 67f.

4. Ibid., p. 68.

5. Ibid., p. 88.

6. Ibid., p. 89.

7. Ibid., p. 98.

8. Ibid., pp. 89f.

9. Ibid., p. 96.

10. Ibid., p. 97.

11. If the notion of "pure procedural justice," as developed, for example in John Rawls, *A Theory of Justice* (Cambridge, MA: Harvard University Press), 1971, pp. 85ff., is cogent, then there will be at least some situations in which procedural justice will not be dependent on any antecedent vision of substantive justice.

12. See Geoffrey C. Hazard, Jr. *Ethics in the Practice of Law* (New Haven, CT: Yale University Press, 1978), p. 120.

13. This term is introduced in Monroe H. Freedman, *Lawyers' Ethics in an Adversary System* (Indianapolis: Bobbs-Merrill Company, Inc., 1975), pp. 27–42.

chapter two

ETHICS AND JUSTICE

INTRODUCTION

At the very outset of the introductory chapter I noted the importance of recognizing that difficult ethical decisions are most fruitfully approached from the perspective of some kind of ethical theory. It would follow from this that the first chapter of readings in this book should offer some examples of such theoretical perspectives. I also claimed that there were, for the reflective citizen of the United States in the twentieth century, two viable approaches to ethical theory, utilitarian and Kantian approaches. That claim is embodied in the selection of material for this chapter.

The three selections in this chapter represent three very different approaches to the issue of justice. John Rawls's "The Rule of Law" is a section from his very important work, *A Theory of Justice*. Rawls develops in that work a substantially egalitarian view of justice which works out of the Kantian tradition of ethical theory. His methodological starting point is his "original position," a hypothetical situation wherein the individual abstracts away everything that distinguishes him or her as a particular, concrete individual with particular subjective interests. Rawls maintains that individuals in the original position should be able to come to unanimous agreement (since they would lack clashing personal interests) about the principles and institutions of justice that would govern society. Rawls argues that the individuals in the original position would adopt two principles of justice. As given their final formulation in section 46 of *A Theory of Justice*, they are:

1. Each person is to have an equal right to the most extensive total system of equal basic liberties compatible with a similar system of liberty for all.
2. Social and economic inequalities are to be arranged so that they are both (a) to the greatest benefit of the least advantaged, consistent with the just savings principle, and (b) attached to positions open to all under conditions of fair equality of opportunity.

Rawls sees the rule of law as being intimately connected with the first principle of justice. Law sets the boundaries around people's liberties. A just set of laws enables people to frame legitimate expectations in the course of their interactions with other people. Among the implications Rawls draws from these points, several are relevant to our present concerns. In particular, Rawls notes the necessity of treating similar cases similarly. The results one gets from the rule of law should turn on what one has done or what has been done to a person, not on the person's status, wealth, or connections. Moreover, Rawls argues that the rule of law implies the existence of "rational procedures of inquiry . . . reasonably designed to ascertain the truth." (Keep this in mind as you read the discussions of the adversary system of justice in Chapter Three.) Finally, and this is of particular significance as it relates to the remaining readings in this chapter, Rawls explicitly denies that the just rule of law involves either balancing the greater good of some against the lesser good of others (utilitarianism) or sacrificing liberty for the sake of greater economic or other social benefits.

In "The Just Society," Rolf Sartorius presents a utilitarian account of justice. Like Mill, Sartorius is a qualitative utilitarian, recognizing that human satisfactions differ not only in quantity of happines but also in quality. Some kinds of happiness are simply more human than others. Unlike Mill, however, Sartorius wants to maintain a variety of act-utilitarianism. That is, Sartorius's variety of utilitarianism is not aimed at justifying rules of behavior that will tend to maximize happiness but at the justification of particular human acts. As a result, Sartorius spends the first part of "The Just Society" showing how an act-utilitarian can take general rules with sufficient seriousness to make sense of a rule of law. The second section included here (Sartorius's section 5, "Retributive Justice") is substantially an attempt to show that some of our central concerns about justice can be accommodated by Sartorius's version of act-utilitarianism. Most central to Sartorius's analysis is his claim, shared with Rawls, that above all a system of retributive justice must function as a guide on the basis of which individuals may form legitimate expectations in their social interactions. Sartorius views this function of rules, however, in a strictly utilitarian manner. Individuals should be able to use a system of laws as a basis for forming rational expectations about the consequences of their voluntary acts and the voluntary acts of others. The system of laws is supposed to act as something of a price system for channeling human behavior. Its penalties serve to make certain forms of behavior too expensive, generative of an overall balance of pain over pleasure.

It is well worth noting that Sartorius explicitly takes up the challenge to utilitarian theories laid out in the introductory chapter to the effect that actual guilt is irrelevant to a utilitarian analysis of retributive justice. Sartorius argues that the utilitarian has considerable resources for denying that criticism, but he does acknowledge that it is at least possible that a point may be reached where utilitarian principles of justice would require the punishment of an innocent for the general good. The reader is urged to consider Sartorius's defense at that point with a great deal of care.

The final reading in this chapter offers a contemporary economic-utilitarian treatment of justice. Richard Posner's "The Market and the Adversary System as Methods of Resource Allocation" is taken from a chapter of his *Economic Analysis of Law*. In that work Posner advocates viewing the law as a vehicle for maximizing the economic efficiency of the allocation of society's resources. Normally, of course, market-oriented economists tend to see the free operation of economic markets as the vehicle for bringing about the most efficient allocation of resources. As Posner notes at the outset of this selection, however, there are circumstances under which the costs of market determination may make that mode of determination actually more expensive (and thus less efficient) than a legal determination. In those cases, a legal determination may well bring about a greater overall level of efficiency. Posner devotes the first two sections of this reading to first comparing legal allocation with market allocation, then comparing judicial and legislative allocation as the two different aspects of legal allocation. Posner then, in the remainder of the reading, shows how the independence of the judiciary serves the ends of economic efficiency, and how the structure of the judicial system bends the individual utility functions of judges to the service of overall economic efficiency.

Let me close this chapter introduction with a reminder to the reader that these three readings on ethical theories and theories of justice (particularly retributive justice) should serve to provide a framework from which the issues treated in the remainder of the book can be rendered more coherent. Questions such as how well the adversary system serves the ends of justice, and how well particular forms of behavior on the part of attorneys serve those same ends, can surely be most clearly addressed from the perspective of some coherent idea of what constitutes that justice the system is to serve.

The Rule of Law

JOHN RAWLS

I now wish to consider rights of the person as these are protected by the rule of law.[20] As before, my intention is not only to relate these notions to the principles of justice but to elucidate the sense of the priority of liberty. I have already noted (s. 10) that the conception of formal justice, the regular and impartial administration of public rules, becomes the rule of law when applied to the legal system. One kind of unjust action is the failure of judges and others in authority to apply the appropriate rule or to interpret it correctly. It is more illuminating in this connection to think not of gross violations exemplified by bribery and corruption, or the abuse of the legal system to punish political enemies, but rather of the subtle distortions of prejudice and bias as these effectively discriminate against certain groups in the judicial process. The regular and impartial, and in this sense fair, administration of law we may call "justice as regularity." This is a more suggestive phrase than "formal justice."

Now the rule of law is obviously closely related to liberty. We can see this by considering the notion of a legal system and its intimate connection with the precepts definitive of justice as regularity. A legal system is a coercive order of public rules addressed to rational persons for the purpose of regulating their conduct and providing a framework for social cooperation. When these rules are just they establish a basis for legitimate expectations. They constitute grounds upon which persons can rely on one another and rightly object when their expectations are not fulfilled. If the bases of these claims are unsure, so are the boundaries of men's liberties. Of course, other rules share many of these features. Rules of games and of private associations are likewise addressed to rational persons in order to give shape to their activities. Given that these rules are fair or just, then once men have entered into these arrangements and accepted the benefits that result, the obligations which thereby arise constitute a basis for legitimate expectations. What distinguishes a legal system is its comprehensive scope and its regulative powers with respect to other associations. The constitutional agencies that it defines generally have the exclusive right to

A Theory of Justice (Cambridge, MA: Harvard University Press, 1971), pp. 235–43. © 1971 by The President and Fellows of Harvard College. Reprinted by permission of Harvard University Press and Oxford University Press.

[20][To avoid confusion, original footnote numbers will be retained throughout this text for those readers who may wish to refer to the original sources for additional information]. For a general discussion, see Lon Fuller, *The Morality of Law* (New Haven, Yale University Press, 1964), ch. II. The concept of principled decision in constitutional law is considered by Herbert Wechsler, *Principles, Politics, and Fundamental Law* (Cambridge, Harvard University Press, 1961). See Otto Kirchenheimer, *Political Justice* (Princeton, Princeton University Press, 1961), and J. N. Shklar, *Legalism* (Cambridge, Harvard University Press, 1964), pt. II and for the use and abuse of judicial forms in politics. J. R. Lucas, *The Principles of Politics* (Oxford, The Clarendon Press, 1966), pp. 106–143, contains a philosophical account.

at least the more extreme forms of coercion. The kinds of duress that private associations can employ is strictly limited. Moreover, the legal order exercises a final authority over a certain well-defined territory. It is also marked by the wide range of the activities it regulates and the fundamental nature of the interests it is designed to secure. These features simply reflect the fact that the law defines the basic structure within which the pursuit of all other activities takes place.

Given that the legal order is a system of public rules addressed to rational persons, we can account for the precepts of justice associated with the rule of law. These precepts are those that would be followed by any system of rules which perfectly embodied the idea of legal system. This is not, of course, to say that existing laws necessarily satisfy these precepts in all cases. Rather these maxims follow from an ideal notion which laws are expected to approximate, at least for the most part. If deviations from justice as regularity are too pervasive, a serious question may arise whether a system of law exists as opposed to a collection of particular orders designed to advance the interests of a dictator or the ideal of a benevolent despot. Often there is no clear answer to this question. The point of thinking of a legal order as a system of public rules is that it enables us to derive the precepts associated with the principle of legality. Moreover, we can say that, other things equal, one legal order is more justly administered than another if it more perfectly fulfills the precepts of the rule of law. It will provide a more secure basis for liberty and a more effective means for organizing cooperative schemes. Yet because these precepts guarantee only the impartial and regular administration of rules, whatever these are, they are compatible with injustice. They impose rather weak constraints on the basic structure, but ones that are not by any means negligible.

Let us begin with the precept that ought implies can. This precept identifies several obvious features of legal systems. First of all, the actions which the rules of law require and forbid should be of a kind which men can reasonably be expected to do and to avoid. A system of rules addressed to rational persons to organize their conduct concerns itself with what they can and cannot do. It must not impose a duty to do what cannot be done. Secondly, the notion that ought implies can conveys the idea that those who enact laws and give orders do so in good faith. Legislators and judges, and other officials of the system, must believe that the laws can be obeyed; and they are to assume that any orders given can be carried out. Moreover, not only must the authorities act in good faith, but their good faith must be recognized by those subject to their enactments. Laws and commands are accepted as laws and commands only if it is generally believed that they can be obeyed and executed. If this is in question, the actions of authorities presumably have some other purpose than to organize conduct. Finally, this precept expresses the requirement that a legal system should recognize impossibility of performance as a defense, or at least as a mitigating circumstance. In enforcing rules a legal system cannot regard the inability to perform as irrelevant. It would be an intolerable burden on liberty if the liability to penalties was not normally limited to actions within our power to do or not to do.

The rule of law also implies the precept that similar cases be treated similarly. Men could not regulate their actions by means of rules if this precept were not followed. To be sure, this notion does not take us very far. For we must suppose that the criteria of similarity are given by the legal rules themselves and the principles used to interpret them. Nevertheless, the precept that like decisions be given in like cases significantly limits the discretion of judges and others in authority. The precept forces them to justify the distinctions that they make between persons by reference to the relevant legal rules and principles. In any particular case, if the rules are at all complicated and call for interpretation, it may be easy to justify an arbitrary decision. But as the number of cases increases, plausible justifications for biased judgments become more difficult to construct. The requirement of consistency holds of course for the interpretation of all rules and for justifications at all levels. Eventually reasoned arguments for discriminatory judgments become harder to formulate and the attempt to do so less persuasive. This precept holds also in cases of equity, that is, when an exception is to be made when the established rule works an unexpected hardship. But with this proviso: since there is no clear line separating these exceptional cases, there comes a point, as in matters of interpretation, at which nearly any difference will make a difference. In these instances, the principle of authoritative decision applies, and the weight of precedent or of the announced verdict suffices.[21]

The precept that there is no offense without a law (*Nulla crimen sine lege*), and the requirements it implies, also follow from the idea of a legal system. This precept demands that laws be known and expressly promulgated, that their meaning be clearly defined, that statutes be general both in statement and intent and not be used as a way of harming particular individuals who may be expressly named (bills of attainder), that at least the more severe offenses be strictly construed, and that penal laws should not be retroactive to the disadvantage of those to whom they apply. These requirements are implicity in the notion of regulating behavior by public rules. For if, say, statutes are not clear in what they enjoin and forbid, the citizen does not know how he is to behave. Moreover, while there may be occasional bills of attainder and retroactive enactments, these cannot be pervasive or characteristic features of the system, else it must have another purpose. A tyrant might change laws without notice, and punish (if that is the right word) his subjects accordingly, because he takes pleasure in seeing how long it takes them to figure out what the new rules are from observing the penalties he inflicts. But these rules would not be a legal system, since they would not serve to organize social behavior by providing a basis for legitimate expectations.

Finally, there are those precepts defining the notion of natural justice. These are guidelines intended to preserve the integrity of the judicial process.[22] If laws are the directives addressed to rational persons for their

[21]See Lon Fuller, *Anatomy of the Law* (New York, The New American Library, 1969), p. 182.

[22]This sense of natural justice is traditional. See H. L. A. Hart, *The Concept of Law* (Oxford, The Clarendon Press, 1961), pp. 156, 202.

guidance, courts must be concerned to apply and to enforce these rules in an appropriate way. A conscientious effort must be made to determine whether an infraction has taken place and to impose the correct penalty. Thus a legal system must make provisions for conducting orderly trials and hearings; it must contain rules of evidence that guarantee rational procedures of inquiry. While there are variations in these procedures, the rule of law requires some form of due process: that is, a process reasonably designed to ascertain the truth, in ways consistent with the other ends of the legal system, as to whether a violation has taken place and under what circumstances. For example, judges must be independent and impartial, and no man may judge his own case. Trials must be fair and open, but not prejudiced by public clamor. The precepts of natural justice are to insure that the legal order will be impartially and regularly maintained.

Now the connection of the rule of law with liberty is clear enough. Liberty, as I have said, is a complex of rights and duties defined by institutions. The various liberties specify things that we may choose to do, if we wish, and in regard to which, when the nature of liberty makes it appropriate, others have a duty not to interfere.[23] But if the precept of no crime without a law is violated, say by statutes being vague and imprecise, what we are at liberty to do is likewise vague and imprecise. The boundaries of our liberty are uncertain. And to the extent that this is so, liberty is restricted by a reasonable fear of its exercise. The same sort of consequences follow if similar cases are not treated similarly, if the judicial process lacks its essential integrity, if the law does not recognize impossibility of performance as a defense, and so on. The principle of legality has a firm foundation, then, in the agreement of rational persons to establish for themselves the greatest equal liberty. To be confident in the possession and exercise of these freedoms, the citizens of a well-ordered society will normally want the rule of law maintained.

We can arrive at the same conclusion in a slightly different way. It is reasonable to assume that even in a well-ordered society the coercive powers of government are to some degree necessary for the stability of social cooperation. For although men know that they share a common sense of justice and that each wants to adhere to the existing arrangements, they may nevertheless lack full confidence in one another. They may suspect that some are not doing their part, and so they may be tempted not to do theirs. The general awareness of these temptations may eventually cause

[23]It may be disputed whether this view holds for all rights, for example, the right to pick up an unclaimed article. See Hart in *Philosophical Review*, vol. 64, p. 179. But perhaps it is true enough for our purposes here. While some of the basic rights are similarly competition rights, as we may call them—for example, the right to participate in public affairs and to influence the political decisions taken—at the same time everyone has a duty to conduct himself in a certain way. This duty is one of fair political conduct, so to speak, and to violate it is a kind of interference. As we have seen, the constitution aims to establish a framework within which equal political rights fairly pursued and having their fair value are likely to lead to just and effective legislation. When appropriate we can interpret the statement in the text along these lines. On this point see Richard Wollheim, "Equality," *Proceedings of the Aristotelian Society*, vol. 56 (1955–1956), pp. 29lff. Put another way, the right can be redescribed as the right to try to do something under specified circumstances, these circumstances allowing for the fair rivalry of others. Unfairness becomes a characteristic form of interference.

the scheme to break down. The suspicion that others are not honoring their duties and obligations is increased by the fact that, in the absence of the authoritative interpretation and enforcement of the rules, it is particularly easy to find excuses for breaking them. Thus even under reasonably ideal conditions, it is hard to imagine, for example, a successful income tax scheme on a voluntary basis. Such an arrangement is unstable. The role of an authorized public interpretation of rules supported by collective sanctions is precisely to overcome this instability. By enforcing a public system of penalties, government removes the grounds for thinking that others are not complying with the rules. For this reason alone, a coercive sovereign is presumably always necessary, even though in a well-ordered society sanctions are not severe and may never need to be imposed. Rather, the existence of effective penal machinery serves as men's security to one another. This proposition and the reasoning behind it we may think of as Hobbes's thesis[24] (s. 42.)

Now in setting up such a system of sanctions the parties in a constitutional convention must weigh its disadvantages. These are of at least two kinds: one kind is the cost of maintaining the agency covered say by taxation; the other is the danger to the liberty the representative citizen measured by the likelihood of that these sanctions will wrongly interfere with his freedom. The establishment of coercive agency is rational only if these disadvantages are less than the loss of liberty from instability. Assuming this to be so, the best arrangement is one that minimizes these hazards. It is clear that, other things equal, the dangers to liberty are less when the law is impartially and regularly administered in accordance with the principle of legality. While a coercive mechanism is necessary, it is obviously essential to define precisely the tendency of its operations. Knowing what things it penalizes and knowing that these are within their power to do or not to do, citizens can draw up their plans accordingly. One who complies with the announced rules need never fear an infringement of his liberty.

It is clear from the preceding remarks that we need an account of penal sanctions, however limited, even for ideal theory. Given the normal conditions of human life, some such arrangements are necessary. I have maintained that the principles justifying these sanctions can be derived from the principle of liberty. The ideal conception shows in this case anyway how the nonideal scheme is to be set up; and this confirms the conjecture that it is ideal theory which is fundamental. We also see that the principle of resonsibility is not founded on the idea that punishment is primarily retributive or denunciatory. Instead it is acknowledged for the sake of liberty itself. Unless citizens are able to know what the law is and are given a fair opportunity to take its directives into account, penal sanctions should not apply to them. This principle is simply the consequence of regarding a legal system as an order of public rules addressed to rational persons in order to regulate their cooperation, and of giving the appropriate weight to liberty. I believe that this view of responsibility enables us to

---

[24]See *Leviathan*, chs. 13–18. And also Howard Warrender, *The Political Philosophy of Hobbes* (Oxford, The Clarendon Press, 1957), ch. III: and D. P. Gauthier, *The Logic of Leviathan* (Oxford, The Clarendon Press, 1969), pp. 76–89.

explain most of the excuses and defenses recognized by the criminal law under the heading of *mens rea* and that it can serve as a guide to legal reform. However, these points cannot be pursued here.[25] It suffices to note that ideal theory requires an account of penal sanctions as a stabilizing device and indicates the manner in which this part of partial compliance theory should be worked out. In particular, the principle of liberty leads to the principle of responsibility.

The moral dilemmas that arise in partial compliance theory are also to be viewed with the priority of liberty in mind. Thus we can imagine situations of an unhappy sort in which it may be permissible to insist less strongly on the precepts of the rule of law being followed. For example, in some extreme eventualities persons might be held liable for certain offenses contrary to the precept ought implies can. Suppose that, aroused by a sharp religious antagonisms, members of rival sects are collecting weapons and forming armed bands in preparation for civil strife. Confronted with this situation, the government may enact a statute forbidding the possession of firearms (assuming that possession is not already an offense). And the law may hold that sufficient evidence for conviction is that the weapons are found in the defendant's house or property, unless he can establish that they were put there by another. Except for this proviso, the absence of intent and knowledge of possession, and conformity to reasonable standards of care, is declared irrelevant. It is contended that these normal defenses would make the law ineffective and impossible to enforce.

Now although this statute trespasses upon the precept ought implies can, it might be accepted by the representative citizen as a lesser loss of liberty, at least if the penalties imposed are not too severe. (Here I assume that imprisonment, say, is a drastic curtailment of liberty, and so the severity of the contemplated punishment must be taken into account.) Viewing the situation from the legislative stage, one may decide that the formation of paramilitary groups, which the passing of the statute may forestall, is a much greater danger to the freedom of the average citizen than being held strictly liable for the possession of weapons. Citizens may affirm the law as the lesser of two evils, resigning themselves to the fact that while they may be held guilty for things they have not done, the risks to their liberty on any other course would be worse. Since bitter dissensions exist, there is no way to prevent some injustices, as we ordinarily think of them, from occurring. All that can be done is to limit these injustices in the least unjust way.

The conclusion once again is that arguments for restricting liberty proceed from the principle of liberty itself. To some degree anyway, the priority of liberty carries over to partial compliance theory. Thus in the situation discussed the greater good of some has not been balanced against the lesser good of others. Nor has a lesser liberty been accepted for the sake of greater economic and social benefits. Rather the appeal has been to the common good in the form of the basic equal liberties of the representative citizen. Unfortunate circumstances and the unjust designs of some necessi-

---

[25]For these matters, consult H. L. A. Hart, *Punishment and Responsibility* (Oxford, The Clarendon Press, 1968), pp. 173–183, whom I follow here.

tate a much lesser liberty than that enjoyed in a well-ordered society. Any injustice in the social order is bound to take its toll; it is impossible that its consequences should be entirely cancelled out. In applying the principle of legality we must keep in mind the totality of rights and duties that defines the liberties and adjust its claims accordingly. Sometimes we may be forced to allow certain breaches of its precepts if we are to mitigate the loss of freedom from social evils that cannot be removed, and to aim for the least injustice that conditions allow.

The Just Society

ROLF E. SARTORIUS

A stable social order in large part depends upon a common conviction that basic social institutions—economic, political, educational, etc.—are just. But one of the most persistent complaints against act-utilitarianism is that it is unable to account for our considered moral judgments concerning social justice. The fundamental principles of a just moral and political order, it is contended, demand that utilitarian considerations sometimes be subordinated to individual claims of entitlement based upon principles of just desert. Whether it be political liberty, economic benefits, or personal freedom that is involved, it is contended that act-utilitarianism would override the morally legitimate claims of the individual as a means of furthering the common good. If men are to be treated as moral ends rather than as mere means to the satisfaction of the interests of others, and are to be secure in their expectations that they will receive from their social institutions that which they are due, principles of distributive and retributive justice which are independent of, and absolute with respect to, the principle of utility must, it is claimed, prevail.

1. UTILITARIAN PRINCIPLES OF JUSTICE

The approach which I shall adopt is in large part dictated by the general account of individual conduct and social norms developed in Chapters 4 and 5. Let me sketch it here, and reply to the charge that it is inconsistent with act-utilitarianism.

Principles of distributive and retributive justice serve primarily as criteria for evaluating the design and operations of those social institutions which determine the pattern of expectations within a community as to how the primary objects of human desire will be distributed and what kinds of

Individual Conduct and Social Norms © 1975, Dickenson Publishing Company, pp. 117–20 and 133–38. Reprinted by pemission of Wadsworth, Inc.

claims upon them will be recognized as legitimate. An economic system with its associated wage, price, and tax mechanisms; a political constitution; legal rules concerning private property; a penal code—all are institutional vehicles for determining how the primary goods of self-esteem, the means of material well-being, political power, personal liberty, and social opportunity will be distributed amongst the members of society.[1] Although individual acts and agents may be spoken of as just and unjust, thus suggesting that there are quite general principles of justice with a very wide range of application, the institutional application is nonetheless primary. Indeed, the just act is often simply that which is required by the constitutive rules of a just institution.

Previous chapters have argued that act-utilitarians might often recognize the need for, and thus rationally participate in the creation and support of, conventional moral norms which bar direct appeals to utility. Such are rational means for directing behavior into desirable channels that it would otherwise not take, and their existence is the basis for many of the secure expectations that an individual may have as to how members of his community will behave. On the basis of such expectations, plans may be made and coordinated in advance, and the individual can predict the consequences of his voluntary acts with reliability which otherwise would fail to obtain.

The principles of social justice, in my view, are the most fundamental guidelines for the design and operation of those social institutions which generate individuals' expectations about what claims they will be recognized as having on the distribution of those primary goods which virtually all men desire. With regard to both distributive and retributive justice, I shall argue that there are certain salient features of man and his world which provide the best reasons for act-utilitarians to establish and support institutions which conform to familiar liberal notions of social justice. Furthermore, I shall contend that there are conditions under which it is reasonable for some principles of justice to be given the status of conventional moral norms which bar direct appeals to utility and not merely that of rules of thumb for institutional design.

John Rawls has recently contended that the choice and public acceptance of principles of justice by the members of a hypothetical community of rational utilitarians would be tantamount to their abandonment of utilitarianism as a moral theory. If it is believed that the direct employment of the act-utilitarian principle itself in the distribution of primary goods would have undesirable consequences, and if principles of justice which are absolute with respect to considerations of utility are instead chosen as the basis for designing and criticizing institutions created for that purpose, utilitarianism, it is claimed, has been rejected.[2]

A major purpose of this essay has been to demonstrate how and why just this kind of claim is radically mistaken.

Do Hobbesian individuals, creating and supporting institutions and social (primarily legal) norms which penalize otherwise self-interested

---

[1] The notion of primary goods is from Rawls, *Theory of Justice*, 62 and following pages.
[2] Rawls, *Theory of Justice*, 181–182, 502.

behavior, abandon either psychological or ethical egoism? By establishing rules of justice do they thereby become just in some sense which is inconsistent with them continuing to act solely on the basis of the maxims of rational prudence? The answer, quite clearly, is that they do not. As we have seen, they have merely restructured (out of self-interest) the set of considerations of future consequences of which they—continuing to act always and only on the basis of self-interest—will have to take account.

Likewise, act-utilitarians remain act-utilitarians as long as it is only the act-utilitarian principle which they recognize as the ultimate prescriptive criterion for individual moral choice. If they choose to support a conventional moral norm concerning the making and keeping of promises which bars direct appeals to utility, they have not thereby abdicated the right to decide each case on its direct utilitarian merits, but merely restructured (in a radical way, to be sure) the set of consequentialist considerations which will determine where the merits lie. If they support a constitutional democracy and adopt majority rule as a social decision procedure, what is in question are the atomic although coordinated individual acts of individual agents each of which may be justified on direct act-utilitarian grounds. They are not to be understood as having adopted the view that what the majority decides, rather than what the act-utilitarian principle determines, is the ultimate arbiter of what is morally right, nor have they incurred even a prima facie obligation to obey the laws enacted by the majority.

Similarly, support of principles of justice which bar direct appeals to utility, and active participation in the creation and maintenance of institutions which satisfy those principles, in no manner imply that the act-utilitarian principle has been abandoned. Each individual remains free to decide each case on its direct utilitarian merits, but where the merits lie will depend in large part upon the institutional framework within which individual choices are made. Although the design of that framework may be guided by principles of justice which bar direct appeals to utility, the theory remains an act-utilitarian one if the choice of those principles is itself based on direct utilitarian considerations.

I conclude, then, that the act-utilitarian can seriously and consistently consider concrete proposals for principles of social justice, viewing them either as possible constitutional limits on legislation, more specific legal norms, conventional moral rules, or merely rules of thumb as guides to institutional design. Whatever the principles of justice which he adopts, and whatever the manner in which he adopts them, his grounds for doing so will be direct utilitarian ones which he by no means need subsequently abandon as his sole prescriptive guide to individual moral choice.

5. RETRIBUTIVE JUSTICE

The generic notion of retributive justice subsumes both legal and moral responsibility. Although I shall confine my remarks primarily to the legal case, they are intended to apply, *mutatis mutandis*, to morality as well.

Few today would deny that the institutional goals which justify the enormous expense to which society goes to inflict suffering on people in the name of the law are utilitarian in character. Deterrence, reform and rehabilitation, and the prevention of resort to self-help are generally acknowledged as the primary reasons for maintaining a system of legal punishment.[18] Likewise, there is widespread agreement that a utilitarian account of the severity of the legal sanctions attached to various offenses is also plausible.[19] Even those who wish to retain capital punishment as a maximum or mandatory sentence for certain offenses (kidnapping, air highjacking, murder of police officers) are inclined to argue in terms of the need for stronger deterrents, rather than retributively in terms of what the criminal has coming in virtue of the moral turpitude of his offense.[20]

Where retributive theory continues to thrive is with respect to questions of responsibility. Who is to be punished? Only those, it is answered, who have broken the law and are responsible for so doing. Neither the innocent, nor those who are not responsible for their acts, may ever justly be punished. But, it is contended, the act-utilitarian might justify precisely such injustices in terms of consequentialist considerations. Legal officials acting on act-utilitarian grounds might conspire to frame and severely punish an innocent man in order to "set an example" during a crime wave where none of the real culprits have been apprehended. The criminal law might have a greater deterrent effect if certain traditional excusing or mitigating conditions, such as insanity, which some break the law in hope of shamming if apprehended, were eliminated altogether. These, genuine possibilities on act-utilitarian grounds, would be absolutely prohibited by the deontologist's principles of justice, whether or not he be a retributivist.[21]

Rule-utilitarianism, it has been claimed, is the only form of utilitarianism which can account for our intuitive conviction that there is something unjust about "punishing" either the innocent or those who are not responsible for their acts.[22] The rules constitutive of the institution of criminal punishment are to be justified on utilitarian ground, but the specific acts of those charged with enforcing and applying the law are not. Rather, their acts are to be justified in terms of the rules in question, and any discretion which they have to appeal to direct utilitarian considerations must be one which is granted to them by those rules. There are obvious utilitarian reasons, it is contended, for framing the institutions of the criminal law in terms of rules which deny officials the discretion ever to consider "punishing" the innocent, and which retain as well the traditional battery of legal excuses—infancy, insanity, duress, etc. Basically, these reasons all

[18]The question of just how well the criminal law accomplishes these goals is a difficult and controversial one which fortunately need not be answered here.

[19]Including Rawls, "Two Concepts."

[20]But see the brilliant defense of retributivism in Morris, "Persons and Punishment."

[21]See the essays in Hart, *Punishment and Responsibility*.

[22]Rawls, "Two Concepts," and Brandt, "Utilitarian Theory," are the most notable examples.

revolve around the desirability—indeed, the necessity—of men being able to have secure expectations about what the consequences of their voluntary acts will be. Although legal sanctions may be needed to direct human behavior into channels that it would otherwise not take, the purpose of having them would in large part be defeated if men could not reliably predict that they could voluntarily avoid them by acting in certain ways. The apprehension which one would constantly live under in a Kafkaesque world in which one might be "punished" although innocent or not responsible is so great that it can hardly be imagined. As Rawls has put it,

> [P]unishment works like a kind of price system: by altering the prices one has to pay for the performance of actions it supplies a motive for avoiding some actions and doing others . . . . [A]n institution which is set up to "punish" the innocent, is likely to have about as much point as a price system (if one may call it that) where the prices of things change at random from day to day and one learns the price of something only after one has agreed to buy it.[23]

All of the above points can be accommodated within the framework of *act*-utilitarianism. One of the major themes of this essay has been that the act-utilitarian can consistently participate in the creation and support of structures of social rules which function as more than rules of thumb and, in a sense, bar direct appeals to utility. A system of criminal justice is as clear a case of this as one could hope to find. Not only does it establish a system of "prices" attached to acts which is within the province of the private citizen to perform, it also controls the behavior of those officials who are charged with the enforcement of the criminal law by attaching "prices" to their acts as well. Far from granting officials the discretion to "punish" innocent men, the hazards associated with unpredictable behavior on the part of legal officials are so great that they will be avoided by making those officials liable to severe legal penalties for such things as false arrest, interference with a citizen's civil rights, perjury, etc. Indeed, laws against entrapment are some evidence that even a minimum of official tampering with the association between fully voluntary conduct and the incidence of the legal sanction is viewed as being so fraught with danger that it is worth paying a high cost (in terms of the acquittal of known criminals) in order to discourage it.

Putative criticisms of act-utilitarianism built upon the familiar theme of punishing the innocent, then, are without foundation at the level of institutional design. All of the dangers supposedly associated with act-utilitarianism simply serve to highlight the importance of certain considerations of which the act-utilitarian is fully capable of taking account. As soon as the critic goes beyond the bare assertion that the act-utilitarian might sometimes find reason to "punish" the innocent to a discussion of what is so wrong with such a possibility, he is to be found appealing to straightforward utilitarian consideration.[24]

The critic will be quick to point out that in my account of individual conduct and social norms all individuals, including legal officials, remain

---

[23]Rawls, "Two Concepts," 12.

[24]As with Rawls, "Two Concepts," and frequently with Hart, *Punishment and Responsibility.*

free to act upon the basis of a direct consideration of utilitarian consequences, whatever the nature of the institutions and social norms which structure such considerations. Although the features of institutional design which I have mentioned may render it quite *unlikely* that legal officials acting on utilitarian (or egotistical) grounds will view the framing of an innocent man as likely to have the best consequences, cases can be imagined where, all things considered, this would appear to be called for by the application of the act-utilitarian principle.

All of this must be admitted. But once a case is convincingly described in which it is clear that the framing of an innocent man *would* have the best consequences, even given due consideration to the likelihood of the subsequent punishment of those who have framed him, the result is one that the act-utilitarian should by no means seek to avoid. Although the importance of such life-boat examples to moral philosophy can be overemphasized, it is an undeniable fact of our moral experience that sometimes it is the lesser of two evils that must be chosen. Avoidable and predictable human suffering is tolerated by almost any familiar social practice which involves the allocation of scarce resources, the only plausible rationale for this being in terms of the maximization of the sum total of human satisfactions. Unless one believes that there is some central moral distinction to be made between the "statistical lives" of the predictable victims of avoidable automobile crashes, industrial accidents, and communicable diseases, on the one hand, and the lives and fortunes of known individuals identifiable by proper name, the suffering of the innocent must be accepted as a virtually unavoidable aspect of human life.[25]

Similar remarks apply to questions of legal responsibility. A systematic and general failure to permit individuals to avoid the incidence of legal sanctions by successfully pleading lack of *mens rea* would produce a level of insecurity and anxiety so intolerable as to virtually militate against the continuation of many socially desirable forms of human interaction. Although the criminal law might have a greater deterrent effect if traditional legal excuses were eliminated altogether, this because there would then be no possibility of shamming them, the price, in utilitarian terms, would simply be too great a one to pay.

Although the general absence of the possibility of appealing to traditional excusing and mitigating conditions as a means of avoiding legal sanctions would surely be intolerable, this is not to say that exceptions do not exist. Strict and vicarious liability are familiar phenomena in the civil and to some degree in the criminal law, and it is clear that a consistent utilitarian rationale can be provided for them. But, in the main, even they do not function so as to make legal sanctions strictly unavoidable, but rather push back to an atypically early stage the point at which voluntary choice must be exercised if certain kinds of consequences of one's acts are to be predictably avoided.[26] One may be strictly liable in the criminal law for selling adulterated food or drugs or serving alcoholic beverages to a minor, for instance, but then one can always get out of the business in question if one thinks that the risks are too great. More problematic is the

---

[25]The notion of statistical lives is from Fried, *Anatomy*, Chapter XII.
[26]The point is well made by Wasserstrom in "Strict Liability."

notion of holding all the members of a group responsible for a wrong committed by one of its members, known or (more typically) unknown. In the normal case, the utilitarian surely will find good reason to reject resort to such practices; but as many elementary school teachers would be quick to suggest, here, too, one can easily conceive of situations in which invoking group responsibility would be the lesser of two evils.

In sum, there are typically the best of reasons for making the incidence of social sanctions, whether legal or moral, contingent upon the performance of prior acts which the individual agent could have voluntarily chosen not to perform. As with the practice of promising, retributive justice is structured in large part in terms of retrospective rather than prospective considerations, although the rationale for both is nonetheless a direct utilitarian one. In both cases, too, the practice may be viewed as aimed at giving the individuals as firm a basis as possible for forming rational expectations about what the consequences of their voluntary acts and those of others are likely to be. To this end, social norms constitutive of the practice of promising bar direct appeals to utility as grounds for the breaking of a promise, and these norms make a difference in the nature of rational expectations because they are backed up by social sanctions. Similarly, legal sanctions, in order to be able to function as a sort of price system effectively channeling voluntary choice behavior into lines that it would otherwise not take, must in the main be withheld from the innocent and those who are in some manner not responsible for what they do. In the interstices of such practices, though, there is room for each individual to decide each case on its merits on direct utilitarian grounds. All things considered, including the demands of social norms and institutional practices worthy of the act-utilitarian's support, promises must sometimes be broken, and the innocent sometimes made to suffer.

The Market and the Adversary System as Methods of Resource Allocation

RICHARD A. POSNER

§19.1 LEGAL AND MARKET ALLOCATION COMPARED

We have seen that the ultimate question for decision in many lawsuits is what allocation of resources would maximize efficiency. The market normally decides this question, but is is given to the legal system to decide in situations where the costs of a market determination would exceed those of

Economic Analysis of Law, 2nd ed. (Boston: Little, Brown and Company, 1977), pp. 399–405, 409–11, and 412–17. Reprinted by permission.

a legal determination. The criteria of decision are often the same, but what of the decision-making process? Here we find some surprising parallels, together with significant differences.

Like the market (although less extensively), the law uses prices equal to opportunity costs to induce people to maximize efficiency. Where compensatory damages are the remedy for a breach of legal duty, the effect of liability is not to compel compliance with law but to compel the violator to pay a price equal to the opportunity costs of the violation. If that price is lower than the value he derives from the unlawful act, then efficiency is maximized if he commits it, and the legal system encourages him to do so; if higher, efficiency requires that he not commit the act and again the damage remedy provides the correct incentive. Like the market, the legal system confronts the individual with the costs of his acts but leaves the decision whether to incur those costs to him.

To command obedience to the legal precept under pain of penalties greater than the actual social costs of disobedience may seem to abandon the market analogy; and penalties of that kind are sometimes prescribed by the legal system—but in circumstances, as we have seen,[1] normally consistent with the creation of the correct economic incentives.

Again like the market, the legal process relies for its administration primarily on private individuals motivated by economic self-interest rather than on altruists or officials. Although it may seem immaterial, from the standpoint of imparting correct economic incentives to defendants and potential defendants, who receives the damages that are assessed—the price of the unlawful conduct is unaffected[2]—payment of the damages to the person injured by the unlawful act is necessary to give him an incentive to shoulder the principle burdens involved in the enforcement of law. Through the lawyer that he hires, the victim of conduct that may be unlawful (inefficient) investigates the circumstances surrounding the allegedly unlawful act, organizes the information obtained by the investigation, decides whether to activate the machinery of legal allocation, feeds information in digestible form to that machinery, checks the accuracy of the information supplied by the defendant, presses if necessary for changes in the rules of allocation followed by the courts, and sees to the collection of the judgment. The state is thereby enabled to dispense with a police force to protect people's common law rights, public attorneys to enforce them, and other bureaucratic personnel to operate the system. These functionaries would be less highly motivated than a private plaintiff, since their economic self-interest would be affected only indirectly by the outcomes of particular cases. The number of public employees involved in the protection of private rights of action is remarkably small considering the amount of activity regulated by the laws creating those rights, just as the number of public employees involved in the operation of the market is small relative to the activity organized by the market.

A closely related point is that the legal process, like the market, is competitive. The adversary system places the tribunal in the position of a

[1] In §7.2 *supra.*
[2] But see §6.12 note 2 *supra.*

consumer forced to decide between the similar goods of two fiercely determined salesmen. To be sure, most cases are settled before trial, but those cases do not enter into the process by which legal rules are created and modified.[3] The critical stage of the legal allocation process is dominated by the competition between plaintiff and defendant for the favor of the tribunal.

Finally, law resembles the market in its impersonality—in economic terms its subordination of distributive considerations. The invisible hand of the market has its counterpart in the aloof disinterest of the judge. The method by which judges are compensated and the rules of judicial ethics are designed to assure that the judge will have not financial or other interest in the outcome of a case before him, no responsibility with respect to the case other than to decide issues tendered by the parties, and no knowledge of the case other than what the competition of the parties conveys to him about it. Jurors are similarly constrained. The disappointed litigant will rarely have grounds for a personal animus against the tribunal, just as the consumer who does not find a product he wants at a price he is willing to pay will rarely have grounds for a personal animus against a seller.

Judicial impersonality is reinforced by the rules of evidence, which exclude as irrelevant considerations that go not to the conduct of the parties but to their relative deservedness. The poor man may not advance poverty as a reason why he should be excused from liability or the wealthy man appeal to the judge's sense of class solidarity. These distributive factors cannot be entirely banished from the courtroom, but they may be sufficiently muted to shift the focus of attention to allocative considerations. Similarly, in the market sellers have a strong incentive to ignore distributive considerations and thereby maximize efficiency. The allocation of resources in accordance with the criterion of efficiency, whether done by the law or by the market, affects the distribution of income and wealth. But in both methods of allocation it is the criterion of efficiency rather than of distributive justice that primarily guides decision.

Our emphasis on the allocative function of the legal system suggests a possible economic justification for government's defraying a portion of the cost of the sytem (judge's salaries, the cost of building and maintaining court houses, etc.). If the function of the legal system were solely to settle disputes, it would be appropriate to impose the entire costs of the system on the disputants. But that is not its only function. It establishes rules of conduct designed to shape future conduct, not only the present disputants' but also other people's. Since the social benefits of a litigation may exceed the private benefits to the litigants, the amount of litigation might be too small if the litigants had to bear the total costs of the suit.[4] The governmental subsidy to litigation is modest. The main expenses—attorneys' fees—are defrayed entirely by the litigants.

The fundamental difference between law and the market as methods of allocating resources is that the market is a much more efficient mechanism of valuing competing uses. In the market people have to back up their

---

[3] See §20.2 *infra*.

[4] On the demand for and supply of legal rules see further §20.2 *infra*.

value assertions with money (or some equivalent sacrifice of alternative opportunities). Willingness to pay imparts greater credibility to a claim of superior value than forensic energy does.

The difficulties of legal determination of preferences or relative values may explain the tendency of common law courts to avoid major allocative judgments. The treatment of custom as a defense to negligence is a good example. In principle it is not a defense, and this, as we saw in the chapter on torts, is economically correct.[5] But in practice, conduct sanctioned by the custom of the defendant's industry is rarely adjudged negligent. The reluctance of the courts to condemn customary practice reflects the difficulty of determining value forensically. The plaintiff's lawyer may argue vigorously and persuasively that the gain in accident cost reduction from installation of a 24-inch rubber bumper on every new automobile produced will exceed the cost of the bumper. But since no manufacturer at present produces a car with such a bumper, the estimate of costs will be conjectural and the defendant will be able to argue plausibly for a higher estimate. Nor will there be experience with the effects of such bumpers on the severity of accidents, other than experimental evidence that will inevitably be vulnerable to contentions that it does not accurately predict the effects of real-world usage. The vogue of cost-benefit analysis has created inflated notions of the effectiveness of analytical techniques in resolving questions of cost and demand. It is not surprising that judges should view with skepticism arguments so difficult to validate in the absence of willingness to pay for upsetting a customary practice. The cost of overcoming this skepticism is likely to exceed the plaintiff's stake in the outcome of the case.

Another consequence of the inability of law to measure preferences accurately is a tendency of the legal process to suppress variances in value. Many people place a value on their homes that exceeds its market price. But a standard of subjective value in eminent domain cases, while the correct standard as a matter of economic principle, would be virtually impossible to administer because of the difficulty of proving (except by evidence of refusal to accept a bone fide offer just below the owner's valuation) that the house was worth more to the owner than the market price.[6]

The problem of valuation is acute with respect to damages for pain and suffering, which encompass disfigurement and other real, but ordinarily not pecuniary (unless an impairment of earning capacity results), costs of accidents. People's sensitivity to this type of loss must vary widely, but proof of above- or below-average sensitivity is virtually impossible, so the tendency is to award a standard or average figure (perhaps the average of the jurors' sensitivities).

Still another example of the difficulty in simulating the market through legal decisions is presented by the impossibility doctrine, under which, as we saw, the courts try to decide which of the parties to the contract was the superior risk bearer ex ante, and assigns the entire loss to him.[7] Observe the dichotomous character of the legal outcome: either A is

[5]See §6.5 *supra*.
[6]See §3.5 *supra*.
[7]See §4.5 *supra*.

made to bear the entire risk, or B is. Yet in markets we frequently observe risk sharing: coinsurance and deductibles in insurance contracts and share-cropping are some examples. But to attempt this sort of thing in a law case would require a degree of fine tuning that courts are probably incapable of attaining at reasonable cost.

The deficiencies of legal as compared with market allocation have two implications for policy. The first is that it is desirable, so far as is consistent with achieving efficient use of resources, to minimize the necessity for broad cost-benefit analysis in legal decisions. But it is not always possible. The problem of custom could be attacked by substituting a rule of strict liability for one of negligence liability. The accident costs that could be prevented by a change in customary practices would be made costs to the industry, whose firms would then decide for themselves whether the costs of changing the customary practices would yield a greater accident cost reduction. But such a rule would eliminate the incentive of accident victims under a negligence standard to investigate the value, in reduced accident costs, of changing their customary modes of behavior.[8] Another step is necessary in order to evaluate such a rule: an inquiry into whether the victims' custom is more likely than the injurers' to be inefficient. But this is just another legal cost-benefit analysis.

The second implication, one by now familiar to the reader, is that people should be prevented from transforming market transactions into legal transactions unless the costs of market transactions are very high, for the legal substitute is a poor one. This is the economic justification for punishing theft even where the probability of apprehension is unity.[9]

§19.2 JUDICIAL AND LEGISLATIVE ALLOCATION COMPARED

While many of the legal rules discussed in previous chapters of this book seem designed to promote efficiency, many others, such as the minimum wage, auto safety legislation, and restrictions on competition in banking—to name just a few—do not. The list of inefficient rules discussed in this book could be extended enormously, to cover much of the nation's statute law and administrative regulations.[1] Although the correlation is far from perfect, judge-made rules tend to be efficiency promoting[2] while those

---

[8]Cf. §6.11 *supra.*

[9]See §6.1 *supra.*

§19.2 [1]See, e.g., William F. Baxter, "NYSE Fixed Commission Rates: A Private Cartel Goes Public," 22 *Stan. L. Rev.* 675 (1970); Cabinet Task Force on Oil Import Control, *The Oil Import Question* (Govt. Printing Office 1970); George W. Hilton, "The Consistency of the Interstate Commerce Act," 9 *J. Law & Econ.* 87 (1966); William A. Jordan, *Airline Regulation in America: Effects and Imperfections* (1970); Edmund W. Kitch, Marc Isaacson, and Daniel Kasper, "The Regulation of Taxicabs in Chicago," 14 *J. Law & Econ.* 167 (1971); and, for a general (though already somewhat dated) survey of the literature, William A. Jordan, "Producer Protection, Prior Market Structure and the Effects of Government Regulation," 15 *J. Law & Econ.* 151 (1972).

[2]Rules of the common law, not rules interpreting statutes.

made by legislatures tend to be efficiency reducing.[3] How is this important difference in the character of judicial and legislative law to be explained?[4]

One possible explanation lies in the differences in the procedures by which rules of law are formulated by judges on the one hand and legislatures on the other. A judge, especially of an appellate court, which is where the most important judge-made rules are fashioned, is unlikely to decide a case on the basis of which of the parties is the "better" person. He knows the parties even less well than the trial judge and, as we have already discussed, considerations pertaining to their relative deservedness (wealth, poverty, good breeding, etc.) are suppressed. Moreover, a judgment based on such considerations would be difficult to rationalize in a judicial opinion, or, stated otherwise, to generalize in a rule. Almost by default the judge is compelled to view the parties as respresentatives of activities— owning land, growing tulips, walking on railroad tracks, driving cars. The methods of judicial compensation and the rules governing conflicts of interest exclude a choice among the competing activities based on the judge's narrowly economic self-interest. In these circumstances, it is natural if not inevitable that he should ask which of the competing activities is more valuable in the economic sense.

The legislative process presents a marked contrast to the judicial. There is no rule against the admission of considerations relating to the relative deservedness of the people affected by proposed legislation. The adversary system, with its comparison of concrete interfering activities that assures that questions of relative costs are always close to the surface of the controversy, is not employed. Also, legislative tools for redistributing wealth are much more flexible and powerful than the judicial. Ordinarily, the only way a court can redistribute wealth is by means of (in effect) an excise tax on the activity involved in the suit.[5]

§19.6 THE RELATIONSHIP OF THE INDEPENDENT JUDICIARY TO INTEREST-GROUP POLITICS

The federal and to a lesser degree state judiciaries enjoy a considerable independence from the interest-group pressures that play about legislators and other elected officials and the executive officers who serve at the pleasure of elected officials. This results not merely from the rules of judicial procedure[1] but also from the rules governing judicial tenure and compensation.[2] Yet how is the independence of the judiciary to be reconciled with

[3]Excluding legislative rules codifying common law principles (e.g., forbidding murder).

[4]Administrative regulation is discussed in Chapter 23. On the reasons for the common law tendency toward efficiency see also §§19.7, 21.4 *infra*.

[5]See §16.8 *supra*.

§19.6 [1] E.g., forbidding ex parte contacts, refusing to accord standing to interest groups as distinct from individuals or firms actually injured by a claimed invasion of right, and excluding evidence unrelated to the legal merits of the claim (see §19.2 *supra*).

[2]Federal judges, for example, have lifetime tenure and their salaries cannot be reduced during their terms of office.

an interest-group view of the governmental process, such as that developed in the previous section? It is not enough to say that there must be an independent judiciary to enforce the Constitution; that does not explain why the independent judiciary has been given the nation's nonconstitutional judicial business as well as the consitutional and why countries, like England, that have no constitutional review of legislation nonetheless have an independent judiciary. The answer suggested here is that an independent judiciary is necessary to make an interest-group system work with maximum effectiveness.[3]

We have seen that legislation is in effect "sold" by legislatures to politically effective interest groups. And we know from Chapter 4 that, in the case of private sales or contracts, at least where performance is not simultaneous on both sides of the bargain and where desire for future business cannot be relied upon to assure faithful performance, the contracting parties will insist that there be a court or arbitrator—an independent third party—to turn to for enforcement of the contract. But there is no legal enforcement mechanism for applying sanctions to the legislature that fails to carry out its "bargain" with an interest group. If, for example, the airline industry obtains from Congress (as apparently it did in 1938) legislation designed to foster monopoly pricing while preventing the entry of new competitors that such pricing would ordinarily attract, the enacting Congress cannot prevent a subsequent Congress from amending the legislation in a way unfavorable to the airlines, or indeed from repealing it altogether. To be sure, congressional bad faith of this sort would reduce the present value of legislative protection to interest groups in the future, and hence congressmen's future welfare. But for many individual congressmen, especially those who did not expect to remain in Congress for long, the benefits from repudiating a previous Congress's "deal" might outweigh the costs. Moreover, in any case where the initial vote enacting the legislation was close, the defection from the winning coalition of only a few congressmen, as a result of retirement or defeat at the polls, might lead to a repeal in the next session of Congress; the newly elected congressmen would have no commitments to honor the "deals" of their predecessors.

The stability necessary to enable long-term legislative deals is supplied by (1) the procedural rules of the legislature and (2) the independent judiciary. . . .

Legislation is not self-enforcing. If the people subject to a law refuse to obey it, recourse to the courts is necessary. A judiciary that was subservient to the current membership of the legislature could effectively nullify legislation enacted in a previous legislature. The limits of human foresight, the ambiguities of language, and the high cost of legislative deliberation combine to assure that most legislation will be enacted in a seriously incomplete form, with many areas of uncertainty left to be resolved by the courts. Insofar as judges are merely agents of the current legislature, they will utilize their considerable interpretive leeway to rewrite previously enacted legislation in conformity with the views of the current rather than

---

[3]See William M. Landes and Richard A. Posner, "The Independent Judiciary in an Interest-Group Perspective, 18 *J. Law & Econ.* 875 (1975), on which this section draws heavily.

the enacting legislature and they will thereby impair the "contract" between the enacting legislature and the group that procured the legislation.

If we assume that an independent judiciary would, in contrast, enforce the legislation according to the original understanding (an assumption examined in the next section), it follows that an independent judiciary facilitates—rather than, as conventionally believed, limits—the practice of interest-group politics. To be sure, being independent, the judges may (directly or indirectly) refuse to enforce legislation that they do not like and this possibility reduces the value of legislation to the group seeking it . . . . But that is a necessary price to pay for a system in which interest groups will have incentives to invest in legislation that yields benefits over an extended period of time.

The theory of judicial independence sketched above has a number of implications with respect to the structure of the legal system . . . . Here some implications regarding (1) the form of interest-group legislation and (2) the determinants of judicial tenure are presented.

1.   Above, the legislative act was treated as complete at the time of enactment—all of the benefits of the legislation were assumed to flow without subsequent legislative action. Yet some legislation is ineffective without substantial annual appropriations by the legislature, either to pay a periodic subsidy or to defray the expenses of a public agency charged with enforcing the statute. Legislation incomplete in this sense at the time of enactment is much less valuable to its beneficiaries than legislation that is complete when enacted; in the first case, the beneficiaries may have to "buy" the legislation anew every year. Hence we would expect—and we find—that interest-group legislation is typically cast in a form that avoids the necessity for substantial annual appropriations. Legislation setting up regulatory agencies that use power over rates and entry to redistribute wealth is an important example: the annual budgets of these agencies are very small in relation to the redistributions that they effect. Not only is regulation used much more often than direct subsidization to benefit interest groups, but when direct subsidies are used their funding is often made independent of further legislative action by the device of the earmarked tax, as in the interstate highway and social security programs.

The problem of legislation that requires substantial annual appropriations to maintain its effectiveness is illustrated by the experience with Prohibition. The supporters of Prohibition were able to obtain a constitutional amendment—normally a particularly durable form of interest-group legislation. However, prohibiting the sale of alcoholic beverages required a massive law enforcement effort. Subsequent Congresses were unwilling to appropriate the sums necessary to increase the number of federal judges, prosecutors, customs inspectors, etc. to levels at which Prohibition would have been effectively enforced. The result was that the constitutional amendment was effectively nullified, and it was repealed in 1933 after having been in effect for only 13 years. Constitutional amendments that do not require substantial annual appropriations to enforce, such as the First Amendment, have proved much more durable.

2.   The value of judical independence is a function of the number of periods over which the returns from special-interest legislation accrue. Since an independent judiciary is, as we have seen, a source of costs as well as benefits to the legislature, we would expect the judiciary to be given less independence the shorter the expected duration of special-interest legislation. This may explain why, as we move down the ladder from the federal to the state to the local government level, we find in general shorter terms for judges and greater reliance on election rather than appointment as the method of selecting them. This pattern is consistent with the fact that, the more confined or local is the jurisdiction of a legislature, the less scope it has for enacting protective legislation.[6] There is more competition for residents among cities and towns than among states, and among states than among countries, because from the resident's standpoint different cities are better substitutes for one another than different states, and different states better substitutes then different countries. This limits the effectiveness of schemes of redistributing wealth from one group of residents to another at the state and local levels. Also, the regulation of a product or service is less effective the more limited the jurisdiction of the regulatory authority, because the providers are more mobile within a more limited area.

Thus it is hardly surprising that many federal regulatory schemes, such as railroad regulations, arose from the debris of state regulatory attempts and that much state regulation emerged from the failures of regulation at the municipal level. But this means that the importance of an independent judiciary to the practice of interest-group politics declines as we move from regulation that is less local to regulation that is more local. The interest groups will not seek durable compacts from state and local legislatures anyway, so why should the political branches pay the price of an independent judiciary.

§19.7 WHAT DO JUDGES MAXIMIZE?

We have assumed in the previous sections of this chapter that (1) when judges are the makers of substantive law the rules of law will tend to be consistent with the dictates of efficiency, and (2) when judges are applying statutes they will do so in accordance with the terms of the original "deal" between the enacting legislature and the beneficiaries of the legislation. This section attempts to sketch a theory of judicial incentives that will reconcile these assumptions.

Presumably judges, like the rest of us, seek to maximize a utility function that includes both monetary and nonmonetary elements (the latter including leisure, prestige, and power). As noted earlier, however, the rules of the judicial process have been carefully designed both to prevent the judge from receiving a monetary payoff from deciding a particular case one way or the other and to minimize the influence of politically effective

---

[6]See Chapter 26 for further analysis of this point.

interest groups on his decisions. To be sure, the effectiveness of these insulating rules is sometimes questioned. It is often argued, for example, that the judge who owns land will decide in favor of landowners, the judge who walks to work in favor of pedestrians, the judge who used to be a corporate lawyer in favor of corporations. However, where a particular outcome would promote the interests of a group to which the judge no longer belongs (our last example), it is difficult to see how the judge's self-interest is advanced by selecting that outcome, although the judge's previous experience might lead him to evaluate the merits of the case differently from judges of different backgrounds. As for any increase in a judge's income from a ruling in favor of a broad group, such as pedestrians or homeowners, to which he still belongs, it will usually be so trivial as to be outweighed by the penalties, mild as they are (professional criticism, reversal by a higher court, etc.), for deciding a case in a way perceived to be unsound or biased. Even at the level of the United States Supreme Court, the number of decisions that change more than incrementally the fortunes of a particular industry or activity is trivial. It is not surprising that attempts to link judicial policies and outcomes to the personal economic interests of the judges have foundered.[1]

A somewhat more plausible case can be made that judges might slant their decisions in favor of powerful interest groups in order to increase the prospects of promotion to higher office, judicial or otherwise. This may be a factor in the behavior of some lower court judges, but their behavior is held in check by appellate review; and state and federal supreme court judges (especially the latter) in general do not seek promotion. This is true even at the intermediate federal appellate level: virtually no federal court of appeals judge leaves office save by death or retirement.

It would seem, therefore, that the explanation for judicial behavior must lie elsewhere than in pecuniary or political factors. That most judges are leisure maximizers is an assumption that will not survive even casual observation of judicial behavior. A more attrative possibility, yet still one thoroughly consistent with the ordinary assumptions of economic analysis, is that judges seek to impose their preferences, tastes, values, etc. on society. This may explain judges' extreme sensitivity to reversal by a higher court: the reversal wipes out the effect of the judge's decision both on the parties to the immediate case and on others, similarly situated, whose behavior might be influenced by the rule declared by the judge. As we shall see in the next chapter, the assumption that judges seek to impose their preferences on society may explain the role of precedent in judicial decisions; decision by precedent is a method of imparting durability to judicial rulings.

Decision according to the original tenor of legislation is explicable in similar terms. If judges did not enforce statutes in this way, the independence of the judiciary would cease to perform an essential function in the interest-group system: legislatures would reduce the independence of the

§19.7 [1]See Roscoe Pound, "The Economic Interpretation and the Law of Torts," 53 *Harv. L. Rev.* 365 (1940).

judiciary (that independence being, as we have seen, costly); and judges would lose some or all of the power and autonomy that judicial independence confers.[2]

The explanation for the other datum with which we began, the implicit economic content of the common law, seems straightforward with regard to those areas—contracts mainly, but also large stretches of property and torts—where transaction costs are low. In such areas, as we know from Part II, inefficient rules of law will be nullified by express agreement of the parties, while persistent judicial defense of economic logic will simply induce contracting parties to substitute private arbitration for judicial resolution of contract disputes. In areas where there is no preexisting voluntary relationship between the disputants (for example, accidents between strangers, common law crimes), the courts are not subject to the same competitive constraints. But these are areas where there is a strong social consensus in favor of the use of the efficiency criterion—else the criterion would long ago have given way to some distributive principle sought by a politically effective interest group (for example, that black income tax evaders should be punished less severely than whites). If courts in these circumstances refuse to enforce the efficiency criterion—for instance, failed to punish the murderer, or impose damages on the careless driver—the likely consequence would be legislative preemption of a major sphere of judicial autonomy—the fashioning of common law rules and doctrines.[3]

[2]Whether such a concern on the part of judges is plausible, given free-rider problems (what free-rider problems?), is discussed in §20.2 *infra*.

[3]A reason for the common law's tendency to efficiency that is unrelated to judicial incentives is suggested in §21.4 *infra*.

chapter three

THE ADVERSARY SYSTEM OF JUSTICE

INTRODUCTION

This chapter is about the adversary system of justice and the roles that it creates for attorneys. As was noted in Chapter One, the adversary system places the attorney in a role which requires that he or she assume a particular and systematic set of biases in the conduct of a case. This position has led to a popular perception of the attorney as something akin to a "hired gun," a specialized kind of bodyguard. This is all fine as long as the situation is like that of Perry Mason, whose every client is really innocent. It is also fine as long as the lawyer is working in defense of the defenseless and the downtrodden.

When the lawyer plies his or her trade on behalf of the slumlord, the organized crime boss, the corrupt politician, or even the local thug whom everyone knows mugged the poor old lady on her way home from church, then that attorney's role is regularly seen by the popular eye as an impediment to the accomplishment of justice, rather than as an integral part of that process. Similarly, in the area of civil litigation we sometimes speak of the "ambulance chaser," the lawyer who tries to convince people that they have been wronged and that they are entitled to some form of relief, of which the lawyer receives a healthy cut for his or her services. We often suspect the insurance company attorney of being a specialist at preventing people from getting what they deserve. All of these kinds of cases lead people to question whether the role of the attorney in an adversarial system of justice is an ethically defensible role at all.

The absolutely crucial role played by the attorney in adversarial proceedings is well illustrated in Mr. Chief Justice Burger's opinion for the Court in *Bronston v. United States.* In that case the fundamental issue is "whether a witness may be convicted of perjury for an answer, under oath, that is literally true but not responsive to the question asked and arguably misleading by negative implication." The Chief Justice gives an unequivocally negative answer, at least so far as we are dealing with federal perjury statutes. It is, of course, the reason for Mr. Chief Justice Burger's negative answer that is important to the purposes of this chapter. The Court holds that it is the sole responsibility of the questioning attorney to make sure that a witness answers responsively. In effect, the Court is holding that the attorney cannot expect perjury statutes to make up for sloppy cross-examination. The adversary system places the responsibility for placing information before the court solely on the shoulders of the attorney. To the extent that the attorney performs that function well, justice tends to be served well also. To the extent that the attorney performs that function sloppily or ineptly, miscarriage of justice may well be the result.

Judge Marvin Frankel's "The Search for Truth: An Umpireal View" has been one of the most powerful criticisms of the adversarial approach to justice presented to date. A part of the reason that that article has constituted such a powerful critique of our system of justice is that it was lodged by a distinguished federal Judge. Judge Frankel's criticisms of the adversary system of justice have developed, moreover, as a result of the judge's years of service on the federal bench. His central contention is that the adversary system places too low a premium on truth. He maintains that the kind of assignment of roles that takes place in the adversary system, passive judge and adversarial counsels, tends with far too great a regularity to lead to results that are precisely the opposite of what justice would dictate.

Judge Frankel's proposed solution to the problems he sees with our system of justice is not a wholesale abandonment of the adversary system, but rather a major and far-reaching modification of it. Frankel, assuming that truth is not in fact the basic objective of the adversary system, at least as it functions in the American legal system, argues that truth should be the paramount objective of such a system. He then goes on to claim that the pursuit of truth should therefore be the central concern of counsels working within the system of justice. It is crucially important to note at this juncture that the claim that the *system* of justice should be devoted to the pursuit of truth is not the same as, nor does it imply, the claim that the various *agents* that function *within* the system of justice should take it upon themselves to devote their individual efforts to the pursuit of truth. Judge Frankel, however, clearly intends to put forward both claims. He holds, moreover, that the former claim does imply the latter.

The concrete implications of this modification of the focus of counsel's duty are most centrally a reduction of the attorney's duty of confidentiality to his or her client, and an expansion of counsel's duty to reveal information at his or her disposal to the court. While Judge Frankel is clearly concerned that the adversary system not be modified to the extent of making the attorney "too conformist, too 'governmental,' " his article leaves no doubt that he believes that the role of the attorney as presently constituted lies too far in the opposite direction.

In the issue of the *University of Pennyslvania Law Review* in which Judge Frankel's article first appeared, it was followed by a critical response by Dean Monroe Freedman, one of today's strongest defenders of the attorney's taking a strongly adversarial stance. Dean Freedman proffers two lines of defense for the adversarial approach to lawyering. In the first instance, Freedman argues that, contrary to the claim of Judge Frankel, something akin to the adversarial approach is used in virtually all areas wherein people are concerned with discovering the truth. He argues that both scientific and historical research are conducted by a process in which the examiner starts out by looking at the cases that can be put forward on behalf of the varied and opposing accounts that have been developed to account for the evidence bearing on the question before the investigation. This leads Freedman to the conclusion that the adversary system places a far higher premium on truth than Judge Frankel claims it to do. In fact, Freedman claims that an adversarial approach is precisely that approach that will give us the most reliable method of arriving at the truth.

Freedman's second line of defense is more ideological than epistemological. He notes that our political system is premised upon a belief in certain fundamental individual rights. The recognition of the dignity of the individual citizen requires above all that the awesome power of the state not be able to be directed against the individual without that individual's having some recourse to a means of defense. It is precisely the defense attorney who provides that means of defense in a criminal trial. The defense attorney, notes Freedman, is the one and sole shield standing between the individual and the marshalled powers of civil society. Freedman claims, then, that this additional ideological purpose of the adversary system of justice may well warrant that system even apart from any truth-regarding considerations. Given that Freedman would also claim that the adversary system is defensible on truth-regarding grounds as well as on grounds of political ideology, he is led to conclude that the adversarial system, along with the unrestrainedly adversarial role of the attorney as it is presently constituted, is more than amply justified.

It is important to note here that Freedman's ideological defense of the adversary approach to justice was based on the character of criminal proceedings, the State v. Jane Q. Citizen. A question that must be asked at this point is this: even if a strongly adversarial approach is the most appropriate for criminal proceedings, is it equally suitable in civil proceedings? In his article, "The Zeal of the Civil Advocate," Murray L. Schwartz attempts to disentangle the truth-regarding line of defense of adversarial proceedings from that defense based on political ideology. Schwartz argues that there is a fundamental difference between criminal proceedings and civil proceedings, and that, moreover, criminal proceedings turn out to be atypical with respect to the most central postulates of the adversary system, the Postulate of Equal Competence and the Postulate of Equal Adversariness. Schwartz argues that what makes the kind of strongly adversarial stance of the criminal defense lawyer appropriate is the basic fact that the criminal defendant must stand before the amassed power of the state. The position of the criminal defense lawyer is warranted by concerns of political liberty. Any concern for truth must occupy a strictly subsidiary status. By contrast, the context of the civil trial does embody, at least to a good level of approximation, the two postulates that are an integral part of the traditional justifications of the adversary system. Schwartz's surprise result, however, is that the rules of conduct proposed by Judge Frankel are in fact more appropriate to the kind of adversarial proceeding that has the pursuit of truth its primary goal. In this, Schwartz pulls an interesting switch on Freedman's position. Schwartz argues that Freedman's position may well be correct for criminal proceedings, but that it is so not because of the adversarial character of such proceedings, but rather because of the ways in which such proceedings depart from genuine adversary proceedings. The civil court, on the other hand, Schwartz takes to be the more properly adversarial kind of proceeding, and in that kind of proceeding a good deal more candor is warranted on the part of opposing counsel in order to make the adversarial ideal work as it is supposed to. Finally, Schwartz argues that the attorney in a civil proceeding bears a moral responsibility for the results achieved on his or her client's behalf in a way that is both unlike the situation of the criminal trial and unlike the view of moral responsibility traditionally held by the organized bar.

Bronston v. United States

Supreme Court of the United States, 1973.
409 U.S. 352, 93 S.Ct. 595, 34 L.Ed.2d 568.

Mr. Chief Justice Burger delivered the opinion of the Court.

We grant the writ in this case to consider a narrow but important question in the application of the federal perjury statute, 18 U.S.C.A. §1621:[1] whether a witness may be convicted of perjury for an answer, under oath, that is literally true but not responsive to the question asked and arguably misleading by negative implication.

Petitioner is the sole owner of Samuel Bronston Productions, Inc., a company that between 1958 and 1964, produced motion pictures in various European locations. For these enterprises, Bronston Productions opened bank accounts in a number of foreign countries; in 1962, for example, it had 37 accounts in five countries. As president of Bronston Productions, petitioner supervised transactions involving the foreign bank accounts.

[1]Statement of federal perjury statute, 18 U.S.C.A. §1621, omitted.]

In June 1964, Bronston Productions petitioned for an arrangement with creditors under Chapter XI of the Bankruptcy Act, 11 U.S.C.A. §701 et seq. On June 10, 1966, a referee in bankruptcy held a §21(a) hearing to determine, for the benefit of creditors, the extent and location of the company's assets. Petitioner's perjury conviction was founded on the answers given by him as a witness at that bankruptcy hearing, and in particular on the following colloquy with a lawyer for a creditor of Bronston Productions:

> "Q. Do you have any bank accounts in Swiss banks, Mr. Bronston?
> "A. No, sir.
> "Q. Have you ever?
> "A. The company had an account there for about six months, in Zurich.
> "Q. Have you any nominees who have bank accounts in Swiss banks?
> "A. No, sir.
> "Q. Have you ever?
> "A. No, sir."

It is undisputed that for a period of nearly five years, between October 1959 and June 1964, petitioner had a personal bank account at the International Credit Bank in Geneva, Switzerland, into which he made deposits and upon which he drew checks totaling more than $180,000. It is likewise undisputed that petitioner's answers were literally truthful. (a) Petitioner did not at the time of questioning have a Swiss bank account. (b) Bronston Production, Inc. did have the account in Zurich described by petitioner. (c) Neither at the time of questioning nor before did petitioner have nominees who had Swiss accounts. The Government's prosecution for perjury went forward on the theory that in order to mislead his questioner, petitioner answered the second question with literal truthfulness but unresponsively addressed his answer to the company's assets and not to his own—thereby implying that he had no personal Swiss bank account at the relevant time.

* * *

There is, at the outset, a serious literal problem in applying §1621 to petitioner's answer. The words of the statute confine the offense to the witness who "willfully * * * states * * * any material matter which he does not believe to be true." Beyond question, petitioner's answer to the crucial question was not responsive if we assume, as we do, that the first question was directed at personal bank accounts. There is, indeed, an implication in the answer to the second question that there was never a personal bank account; in casual conversation this interpretation might reasonably be drawn. But we are not dealing with casual conversation and the statute does not make it a criminal act for a witness to willfully state any material matter that *implies* any material matter that he does not believe to be true.[4]

---

[4]Petitioner's answer is not to be measured by the same standards applicable to criminally fraudulent or extortionate statements. In that context, the law goes "rather far in punishing intentional creation of false impressions by a selection of literally true representations, because the actor himself generally selects and arranges the representations." In contrast, "under our system of adversary questioning and cross-examination the scope of disclosure is largely in the hands of counsel and presiding officers." A.L.I.Model Penal Code §208.20, Comment (Tent. Draft No. 6, 1957, p. 124).

The government urges that the perjury statute be construed broadly to reach petitioner's answer and thereby fulfill its historic purpose of reinforcing our adversary factfinding process. We might go beyond the precise words of the statute if we thought they did not adequately express the intention of Congress, but we perceive no reason why Congress would intend the drastic sanction of a perjury prosecution to cure a testimonial mishap that could readily have been reached with a single additional question by counsel alert—as every examiner ought to be—to the incongruity of petitioner's unresponsive answer. Under the pressures and tensions of interrogation, it is not uncommon for the most earnest witness to give answers that are not entirely responsive. Sometimes the witness does not understand the question, or may in an excess of caution or apprehension read too much or too little into it. It should come as no surprise that a participant in a bankruptcy proceeding may have something to conceal and consciously tries to do so, or that a debtor may be embarrassed at his plight and yield information reluctantly. It is the responsibility of the lawyer to probe; testimonial interrogation, and cross-examination in particular, is a probing, prying, pressing form of inquiry. If a witness evades, it is the lawyer's responsibility to recognize the evasion and to bring the witness back to the mark, to flush out the whole truth with the tools of adversary examination.

* * *

Though perhaps a plausible argument can be made that unresponsive answers are especially likely to mislead,[5] any such argument must, we think, be predicated upon the questioner's being aware of the unresponsiveness of the relevant answer. Yet, if the questioner is aware of the unresponsiveness of the answer, with equal force it can be argued that the very unresponsiveness of the answer should altert counsel to press on for the information he desires. It does not matter that the unresponsive answer is stated in the affirmative, thereby implying the negative of the question actually posed; for again, by hypothesis, the examiner's awareness of unresponsiveness should lead him to press another question or reframe his initial question with greater precision. Precise questioning is imperative as a predicate for the offense of perjury.

It may well be that petitioner's answers were not guileless but were shrewdly calculated to evade. Nevertheless, we are constrained to agree with Judge Lumbard, who dissented from the judgment of the Court of Appeals, that any special problems arising from the literally true but unresponsive answer are to be remedied through the "questioner's acuity" and not by a federal perjury prosecution.

Reversed.

[5][Omitted.]

The Search for Truth: An Umpireal View

MARVIN E. FRANKEL

What I have written for the thirty-first Benjamin N. Cardozo Lecture makes no pretense to be polished or finished wisdom. In the words of an imposingly great predecessor, Judge Charles E. Clark, beginning the fifth of these lectures in 1945, I propose "to suggest problems and raise doubts, rather than to dispense legal or moral truth."[1] Probably more rash than Judge Clark, I do not experience "trepidation"[2] for offering questions rather than answers; honest exploration in any province of the law is surely no dishonor to the questing spirit of Judge Cardozo.

My questions, briefly stated, have to do with some imperfections in our adversary system. My purposes are to recall some perennial problems, to touch upon one or two familiar ideas for improvement, and to sketch some tentative lines along which efforts to reform our law might proceed.

Because I plan to focus on recurrent criticisms of the activity to which my professional life is and has been devoted, I find it fortifying and prudent, if not heroic, to extend this introduction with a few deprecatory words. The business of the American trial courtroom seems to me in many ways to be instructive, creative, and sometimes even noble. As for the task of judging, it is nearly always a rich and satisfying challenge. The work produces fascinations and rewards that my imagination had failed to picture in advance. The trial court is a scene of drama, wit, humor, and humanity, along with sorrows and the stretches of boredom. Even the periods of tedium are charged with the awareness of important stakes. There are daily choices that compel the judge to confront himself or herself, not less than those who will be affected, in stark and moving ways. There is power and there is, often more satisfying, the opportunity to forego the exercise of power.[3]

If I question the adequacy of our trial processes, it is not to serve the judges. It is to serve the ends of justice, for the furtherance of which all in our profession are commissioned. As is so often the case, Holmes said it better:

> I take it for granted that no hearer of mine will misinterpret what I have to say as the language of cynicism . . . . I trust that no one will understand me to be speaking with disrespect of the law, because I criticise it so freely. I venerate the law, and especially our system of law, as one of the vastest products of

University of Pennsylvania Law Review, 123, No. 5 (May 1975), sections I, II, and IV, 1032–41 and 1052–59 (delivered as the 31st Annual Benjamin Cardozo Lecture, before the Association of the Bar of the City of New York, December 16, 1974). Reprinted by permission.

[1]Clark, "State Law in the Federal Courts: The Brooding Omnipresence of Erie v. Tompkins," 55 *Yale L. J.* 267, 268–69 (1946).

[2]Id. 268.

[3]Cf. C. Bok, *I Too, Nicodemus* 330 (1946).

the human mind . . . . But one may criticise even what one reveres. Law is the business to which my life is devoted, and I should show even less than devotion if I did not do what in me lies to improve it . . . .[4]

I. THE JUDICIAL PERSPECTIVE

My theme, to be elaborated at some length, is that our adversary system rates truth too low among the values that institutions of justice are meant to serve. Having worked for nine years at judging, and having evolved in that job the doubts and questions to be shared with you, I find it convenient to move into the subject with some initial reminders about our judges: who they are, how they come to be, and how their arena looks to them.

Except when we rely upon credentials even more questionable, we tend to select our trial judges from among the people with substantial experience as trial lawyers. Most of us have had occasion to think of the analogy to the selection of former athletes as umpires for athletic contests. It may not press the comparison too hard to say it serves as a reminder that the "sporting theory"[5] continues to infuse much of the business of our trial courts. Reflective people have suggested from time to time that qualities of detachment and calm neutrality are not necessarily cultivated by long years of partisan combat.[6] Merely in passing, because it is not central to my theme, I question whether we are wise to have rejected totally the widespread practice in civil law countries of having career magistrates, selected when relatively young to function in the role of impartial adjudicators. Reserving a fuller effort for another time, I wonder now whether we might benefit from some admixture of such magistrates to leaven or test our trial benches of elderly lawyers.

In any event, our more or less typical lawyer selected as a trial judge experiences a dramatic change in perspective as he moves to the other side of the bench. It is said, commonly by judges, that "[t]he basic purpose of a trial is the determination of truth . . . ."[7] Justice David W. Peck identified "truth and . . . the right result" as not merely "basic" but "the sole objective of the judge . . . ."[8]

[4]O. W. Holmes, "The Path of the Law," in *Collected Legal Papers* 167, 194 (1920). The quotation was used in a similar setting by Judge Jerome Frank. J. Frank, *Courts on Trial* 3 (1950). As will be seen, this lecture follows in more pervasive respects positions urged in that engaging and valuable book. That the positions have not prevailed might discourage people more impatient than those who believe in the possibility of law reform.

[5]The phrase was undoubtedly a cliché when Roscoe Pound used it in a famous address in 1906. Pound, "The Causes of Popular Dissatisfaction with the Administration of Justice," 29 *ABA Rep.* 395, 404 (1906). Like other clichés, it still tells an important story. It also shares with many clichés the quality of referring to a widely known, deeply troublesome problem which has become entombed in a phrase so that it does not seem to require much active attention as a live concern.

[6]See, e.g., B. Shientag, *The Personality of the Judge* 19 (1944) (3rd Annual Benjamin N. Cardozo Lecture).

[7]*Tehan v. United States ex rel. Shott* U.S. 406, 416 (1966).

[8]D. Peck, *The Complement of Court and Counsel* 9 (1954) (13th Annual Benjamin N. Cardozo Lecture).

These are not questionable propositions as a matter of doctrine or logic. Trials occur because there are questions of fact. In principle, the paramount objective is the truth. Nevertheless, for the advocate turned judge this objective marks a sharp break with settled habits of partisanship. The novelty is quickly accepted because it has been seen for so long from the other side. But the novelty is palpable, and the change of role may be unsettling. Many judges, withdrawn from the fray, watch it with benign and detached affection, chuckling nostalgically now and then as the truth suffers injury or death in the process.[9] The shop talk in judge's lunchrooms includes tales, often told with pleasure, of wily old advocates who bested the facts and prevailed. For many other judges, however, probably a majority at one time or another, the habit of adversariness tends to be rechanneled, at least in some measure, into a combative yearning for truth. With pehaps a touch of the convert's zeal, they may suffer righteously when the truth is being blocked or mutilated, turn against former comrades in the arena, feel (and sometimes yield to) the urge to spring into the contest with brilliant questions that light the way.

However the trial judge reacts, in general or from time to time, the bench affords a changed and broadened view of the adversary process. "Many things look different from the bench. Being a judge is a different profession from being a lawyer."[10] In the strictest sense I can speak only for myself, but I believe many other trial judges would affirm that the different perspective helps to arouse doubts about a process that there had been neither time nor impetus to question in years at the bar. It becomes evident that the search for truth fails too much of the time. The rules and devices accounting for the failures come to seem less agreeable and less clearly worthy than they once did. The skills of the advocate seem less noble, and the place of the judge, which once looked so high, is lowered in consequence. There is, despite the years of professional weathering that went before the assumption of the judicial office, a measure of disillusionment.

The disillusionment is, as I indicated at the outset, only a modest element of the judicial experience. It is relevant here, however. It accounts for recurrent judicial expressions that seem critical of the bar when they probably stem from more basic dissatisfactions. In any event, it is undoubtedly part of the genesis of this essay.

II. THE ADVERSARIAL POSTURE

The preceding comments on the transition from bar to bench have touched explicitly upon the role of the advocate. That role is not, however,

---

[9] As in the sentence just ended, this essay will be laced with general statements about matters of fact that are neither quantified nor tightly documented. These rest variously upon introspection, observation, reading, and conversations with fellow judges. They are believed to be accurate, but they are undoubtedly debatable in many instances.

[10] H. Lummus, *The Trial Judge* 39 (1937). See also Medina, "Some Reflections on the Judicial Function: A Personal Viewpoint," 38 *A.B.A.J.* 107 (1952).

a matter of sharp and universally agreed definition. The conception from which this paper proceeds must now be outlined.

In a passage partially quoted above, Presiding Justice David W. Peck said:

> The object of a lawsuit is to get at the truth and arrive at the right result. That is the sole objective of the judge, and counsel should never lose sight of that objective in thinking that the end purpose is to win for his side. Counsel exclusively bent on winning may find that he and the umpire are not in the same game.[11]

Earlier, stating his theme that court and counsel "complement" each other, Justice Peck said:

> Unfortunately, true understanding of the judicial process is not shared by all lawyers or judges. Instead of regarding themselves as occupying a reciprocal relationship in a common purpose, they are apt to think of themselves as representing opposite poles and exercising divergent functions. The lawyer is active, the judge passive. The lawyer is partisan, the judge neutral. The lawyer imaginative, the judge reflective.[12]

Perhaps unfortunately, and certainly with deference, I find myself leaning toward the camp the Justice criticized. The plainest thing about the advocate is that he is indeed partisan, and thus exercises a function sharply divergent from that of the judge. Whether or not the judge generally achieves or maintains neutrality, it is his assigned task to be nonpartisan and to promote through the trial an objective search for the truth. The advocate in the trial courtroom is not engaged much more than half the time—and then only coincidentally—in the search for truth. The advocate's prime loyalty is to his client, not to truth as such. All of us remember some stirring and defiant declarations by advocates of their heroic, selfless devotion to The Client—leaving the nation, all other men, and truth to fend for themselves. Recall Lord Brougham's famous words:

> [A]n advocate, in the discharge of his duty, knows but one person in all the world, and that person is his client. To save that client by all means and expedients, and at all hazards and costs to other persons, and, among them, to himself, is his first and only duty; and in performing this duty he must not regard the alarm, the torments, the destruction which he may bring upon others. Separating the duty of a patriot from that of an advocate, he must go on reckless of consequences, though it should be his unhappy fate to involve his country in confusion.[13]

Neither the sentiments nor even the words sound archaic after a century and a half. They were invoked not longer than a few months ago by a thoughtful and humane scholar answering criticisms that efforts of counsel

[11]D. Peck, *supra* note 8, at 9.
[12]Id. 7.
[13]2 *Trial of Queen Caroline* 8 (J. Nightingale ed. (1821).

for President Nixon might "involve his country in confusion."[14] There are, I think, no comparable lyrics by lawyers to The Truth.

This is a topic on which our profession has practiced some self-deception. We proclaim to each other and to the world that the clash of adversaries is a powerful means for hammering out the truth. Sometimes, less guardedly, we say it is "best calculated to getting out all the facts . . . ."[15] That the adversary technique is useful within limits none will doubt. That it is "best" we should all doubt if we were able to be objective about the question. Despite our untested statements of self-congratulation, we know that others searching after facts—in history, geography, medicine, whatever—do not emulate our adversary system. We know that most countries of the world seek justice by different routes. What is much more to the point, we know that many of the rules and devices of adversary litigation as we conduct it are not geared for, but are often aptly suited to defeat, the development of truth.

We are unlikely ever to know how effectively the adversary technique would work toward truth if that were the objective of the contestants. Employed by interested parties, the process often achieves truth only as a convenience, a byproduct, or an accidental approximation. The business of the advocate, simply stated, is to win if possible without violating the law. (The phrase "if possible" is meant to modify what precedes it, but the danger of slippage is well known.) His is not the search for truth as such. To put that thought more exactly, the truth and victory are mutually incompatible for some considerable percentage of the attorneys trying cases at a given time.

Certainly, if one may speak the unspeakable, most defendants who go to trial in criminal cases are not desirous that the whole truth about the matters in controversy be exposed to scrutiny. This is not to question the presumption of innocence or the prosecution's burden of proof beyond reasonable doubt. In any particular case, because we are unwilling to incur more than a minimal risk of convicting the innocent, these bedrock principles must prevail. The statistical fact remains that the preponderant majority of those brought to trial did substantially what they are charged with. While we undoubtedly convict some innocent people, a truth horrifying to confront, we also acquit a far larger number who are guilty, a fact we bear with much more equanimity.[16]

[14]Freedman, "The President's Advocate and the Public Interest," *N.Y.L.J.*, Mar. 27, 1974, at 1, col. 1. Dean Freedman went on to explain that the system contemplates an equally single-minded "advocate on the other side, and an impartial judge over both." Id 7, col. 2.

[15]D. Peck, *supra* note 8, at 9.

[16]One of our greatest jurists has observed:

"What bothers me is that almost never do we have a genuine issue of guilt or innocence today. The system has so changed that what we are doing in the courtroom is trying the conduct of the police and that of the prosecutor all along the line. Has there been a misstep at this point? At that point? You know very well that the man is guilty; there is no doubt about the proof. But you must ask,

One reason we bear it so well is our awareness that in the last analysis truth is not the only goal. An exceedingly able criminal defense lawyer who regularly serves in our court makes special point of this. I have heard him at once defy and cajole juries with the reminder that the question is not at all "guilt or innocence," but only whether guilt has been shown beyond a reasonable doubt. Whether that is always an astute tactic may be debated. Its doctrinal soundness is clear.

Whatever doctrine teaches, it is a fact of interest here that most criminal defense counsel are not at all bent upon full disclosure of the truth. To a lesser degree, but stemming from the same ethos, we know how fiercely prosecutors have resisted disclosure, how often they have winked at police lapses, how mixed has been their enthusiasm for the principle that they must seek justice, not merely convictions.[17] While the patterns of civil cases are different, and variable, we may say that it is the rare case in which either side yearns to have the witnesses, or anyone, give *the whole truth*. And our techniques for developing evidence feature devices for blocking and limiting such unqualified revelations.

The devices are too familiar to warrant more than a fleeting reminder. To begin with, we leave most of the investigatory work to paid partisans, which is scarcely a guarantee of thorough and detached exploration. Our courts wait passively for what the parties will present, almost never knowing—often not suspecting—what the parties have chosen not to present. The ethical standards governing counsel command loyalty and zeal for the client, but no positive obligation at all to the truth. Counsel must not knowingly break the law or commit or countenance fraud. Within these unconfining limits, advocates freely employ time-honored tricks and stratagems to block or distort the truth.

As a matter of strict logic, in the run of cases where there are flatly contradictory assertions about matters of fact, one side must be correct, the other wrong. Where the question is "Did the defendant pass the red light?" or "Does the plaintiff have a scarred retina?" or "Was the accused warned of the reasons why anyone of sound mind would keep quiet and did he then proceed nevertheless like a suicidal idiot to destroy himself by talking?" the "facts" are, or were, one way or the other. To be sure, honest people may honestly differ, and we mere lawyers cannot—actually, must

---

for example: Was there something technically wrong with the arrest? You're always trying something irrelevant. The case is determined on something that really hasn't anything to do with guilt or innocence. To the extent you are doing that to preserve other significant values, I think it is unobjectionable and must be accepted. But with a great many derailing factors there is either no moral justification or only a very minimal justification."

McDonald, "A Center Report: Criminal Justice," *The Center Magazine*, Nov. 1968, at 69, 76 (remarks of Judge Walter V. Schaefer).

[17]Among the most recent and highly publicized examples of prosecutors subordinating truth and fairness to the lust after victory are the dismissals of indictments in the Wounded Knee and Ellsberg cases. *United States v. Banks*, 383 F. Supp. 389 (D.S.D. 1974); *United States v. Russo*, No 9373-CD-WMB (C.D. Cal., May 11, 1973).

not—set ourselves up as judges of the facts. That is the great release from effective ethical inhibitions. We are not to pass judgment, but only to marshall our skills to present and test the witnesses and other evidence—the skills being to make the most of these for our side and the least for the opposition. What will out, we sometimes tell ourselves and often tell others, is the truth. And, if worse comes to worst, in the end who really knows the truth?

There is much in this of cant, hypocrisy, and convenient overlooking. As people, we know or powerfully suspect a good deal more than we are prepared as lawyers to admit or explore further. The clearest cases are those in which the advocate has been informed directly by a competent client, or has learned from evidence too clear to admit of genuine doubt, that the client's position rests upon falsehood. It is not possible to be certain, but I believe from recollection and conversation such cases are far from rare. Much more numerous are the cases in which we manage as counsel to avoid too much knowledge. The sharp eye of the cynical lawyer becomes at strategic moments a demurely averted and filmy gaze. It may be agreeable not to listen to the client's tape recordings of vital conversations that may contain embarrassments for the ultimate goal of vindicating the client. Unfettered by the clear prohibitions actual "knowledge" of the truth might impose, lawyers may be effective and exuberant in employing the familiar skills: techniques that make a witness look unreliable although the look stems only from counsel's artifice, cunning questions that stop short of discomfiting revelations, complaisant experts for whom some shopping may have been necessary. The credo that frees counsel for such arts is not a doctrine of truth-seeking.

The litigator's devices, let us be clear, have utility in testing dishonest witnesses, ferreting out falsehoods, and thus exposing the truth. But to a considerable degree these devices are like other potent weapons, equally lethal for heroes and villains. It is worth stressing, therefore, that the gladiator using the weapons in the courtroom is not primarily crusading after truth, but seeking to win. If this is banal, it is also overlooked too much and, in any event, basic to my thesis.

Reverting to the time before trial, our unlovely practice of plea bargaining—substantially unique to the United States—reflects as one of its incidents the solemn duty of defense counsel to seek the acquittal of guilty people. Plea negotiations must begin, in principles governing all but some exotic cases, with the understanding that the defendant is guilty. Plea negotiations should not otherwise be happening. But the negotiations break down in many cases, most often because there is no mutually acceptable deal on the sentence, the key concern.[18] When that occurs, the defendant goes to trial, and the usual measures to prevent conviction are to be taken

---

[18]The discussion here applies quite generally, but not universally. "Sentence bargaining," probably a better label, is almost entirely unknown in the Southern District of New York. It happens with varying frequency in other federal courts—the Agnew case comes to mind, cf. Hoffman, "Plea Bargaining and the Role of the Judge," 53 *F.R.D.* 499 (1971)—and appears to be widespread in the state courts of New York and elsewhere.

by his advocate. The general, seemingly principled, view would hold his tendered plea and attendant discussion inadmissible at trial.[19] Does all this make sense? Is it comfortable? All of us in the law have explained patiently to laymen that "guilty" means not simply that "he did it"; it means nothing less than that he has been "found-guilty-beyond-a-reasonable-doubt-by-a-unanimous-jury-in-accordance-with-law-after-a-fair-trial." Despite the sarcastic hyphens, all of us mean that and live by it. But when a fair trial entails a trial so tortured and obstacle-strewn as our adversary process, we make the system barely tolerable, if not widely admired, only by contriving that most of those theoretically eligible get no trial at all. The result suggests we might inquire how things work on the European continent, where the guilty plea, at least in technical strictness, is scarcely known and the plea bargain seems to be truly nonexistent.

Our relatively low regard for truth-seeking is perhaps the chief reason for the dubious esteem in which the legal profession is held. The temptation to quote poetical diatribes is great. Before fighting it off altogether, let us recall only Macaulay on Francis Bacon, purporting not to

> inquire . . . whether it be right that man should, with a wig on his head, and a band round his neck, do for a guinea what, without those appendages, he would think it wicked and infamous to do for an empire; whether it be right that, not merely believing but knowing a statement to be true, he should do all that can be done by sophistry, by rhetoric, by solemn asseveration, by indignant exclamation, by gesture, by play of features, by terrifying one honest witness, by perplexing another, to cause a jury to think that statement false.[20]

Less elegant than Macaulay but also numbered among the laymen who do not honor us for our dealings with the truth are many beneficiaries of such stratagems. One of the least edifying, but not uncommon, of trial happenings is the litigant exhibiting a special blend of triumph, scorn, complicity, and moral superiority when his false position has scored a point in artful cross-examination or some other feat of advocacy. This is a kind of fugitive scene difficult to document in standard ways, but described here in the belief that courtroom habitués will confirm it from their own observations.

I am among those who believe the laity have ground to question our service in the quest for truth. The ranks of lawyers and judges joining in this rueful stance are vast. Many have sought over the years to raise our standards and our functioning, not merely our image. There has been success. Liberalized discovery has helped, though the struggles over that, including the well-founded fears of tampering with the evidence, highlight the hardy evils of adversary management. We have, on the whole, seemed to become better over time, occasional lapses notwithstanding. At any rate, the main object of this talk is not merely to bewail, but to participate in the

---

[19]See *ABA Project on Minimum Standards for Criminal Justice, Pleas of Guilty* § 3.4 (Approved Draft [1968]).

[20]T. Macaulay, *The Works of Lord Macaulay* 135 (H. Trevelyan ed. 1900).

ongoing effort to improve. Modest thoughts on that subject, respectively negative and positive, occupy two sections that follow.

III. TWO UNPROMISING APPROACHES [OMITTED]

IV. SOME PROPOSALS

Having argued that we are too much committed to contentiousness as a good in itself and too little devoted to truth, I proceed to some prescriptions of a general nature for remedying these flaws. Simply stated, these prescriptions are that we should:

1. modify (not abandon) the adversary ideal,
2. make truth a paramount objective, and
3. impose upon the contestants a duty to pursue that objective.

A. Modifying the Adversary Ideal

We should begin, as a concerted professional task, to question the premise that adversariness is ultimately and invariably good. For most of us trained in American law, the superiority of the adversary process over any other is too plain to doubt or examine. The certainty is shared by people who are in other respects widely separated on the ideological spectrum. The august "Code of Professional Responsibility," as has been mentioned, proclaims, in order, the "Duty of the Lawyer to a Client,"[55] then the "Duty of the Lawyer to the Adversary System of Justice."[56] There is no announced "Duty to Truth" or "Duty to the Community." Public interest lawyers, while they otherwise test the law's bounds, profess a basic commitment "to the adversary system itself" as a means of giving "everyone affected by corporate and bureaucratic decisions . . . a voice in those decisions . . . ."[57] We may note similarly the earnest and idealistic scholar who brought the fury of the (not necessarily consistent) establishment upon himself when he wrote, reflecting upon experience as devoted defense counsel for poor people, that as an advocate you must (a) try to detroy [sic] a witness "whom you know to be telling the truth," (b) "put a witness on the stand when you know he will commit perjury," and (c) "give your client legal advice when you have reason to believe that the knowledge you give him will tempt him to commit perjury."[58] The "policies" he found to justify these views, included, as the first and most fundamental, the maintenance

[55][*ABA Code of Professional Responsibility*] (heading preceding EC 7-4).

[56]Id. (heading preceding EC 7-19).

[57] Halpern and Cunningham, "Reflections on the New Public Interest Law," 59 *Geo. L.J.* 1095, 1109 (1971).

[58]Freedman, "Professional Responsibility of the Criminal Defense Lawyer: The Three Hardest Questions," 64 *Mich. L. Rev.* 1469 (1966).

of "an adversary system based upon the presupposition that the most effective means of determining truth is to present to a judge and jury a clash between proponents of conflicting views."[59]

Our commitment to the adversary or "accusatorial" mode is buttressed by a corollary certainty that other, alien systems are inferior. We contrast our form of criminal procedure with the "inquisitorial" system, conjuring up visions of torture, secrecy, and dictatorial government. Confident of our superiority, we do not bother to find out how others work. It is not common knowledge among us that purely inquisitorial systems exist scarcely anywhere; that elements of our adversary approach exist probably everywhere; and that the evolving procedures of criminal justice, in Europe and elsewhere, are better described as "mixed" than as strictly accusatorial or strictly inquisitorial.[60]

In considering the possibility of change, we must open our minds to the variants and alternatives employed by other communities that also aspire to civilization. Without voting firmly, I raise the question whether the virginally ignorant judge is always to be preferred to one with an investigative file. We should be prepared to inquire whether our arts of examining and cross-examining, often geared to preventing excessive outpourings of facts, are inescapably preferable to safeguarded interrogation by an informed judicial officer.[61] It is permissible to keep asking, because nobody has satisfactorily answered, why our present system of confessions in the police station versus no confessions at all is better than an open and orderly procedure of having a judicial officer question suspects.[62]

If the mention of such a question has not exhausted your tolerance, consider whether our study of foreign alternatives might suggest means for easing the unending tension surrounding the privilege against self-incrimination as it frequently operates in criminal trials. It would be prudent at least to study closely whether our criminal defendant, privileged to stay suspiciously absent from the stand or to testify subject to a perjury prosecution or "impeachment" by prior crimes, is surely better off than the European defendant who cannot escape questioning both before and at trial, although he may refuse to answer, but is free to tell his story without either the oath or the impeachment pretext for using his criminal record against him.[63] Whether or not the defendant is better off, the question remains open whether the balance we have struck is the best possible.

To propose only one other topic for illustration, we need to study whether our elaborate struggles over discovery, especially in criminal cases, may be incurable symptoms of pathology inherent in our rigid insistence that the parties control the evidence until it is all "prepared" and packaged

[59]Id. 1470. See also id. 1471, 1477–78, 1482.

[60]W. Schaefer, *The Suspect and Society* 71 (1967); Damaska, "Evidentiary Barriers to Conviction and Two Models of Criminal Procedure: A Comparative Study", 121 *U. Pa. L. Rev.* 506, 557–61, 569–70 (1973).

[61]Cf. Watts v. Indiana, 338 U.S. 49, 54–55 (1949).

[62]See W. Schaefer, *supra* note 60; cf. Friendly, "The Fifth Ammendment Tomorrow: The Case for Constitutional Change," 37 *U.Cin. L. Rev.* 671, 685, 700–01, 713–16 (1968).

[63]See Damaska, *supra* note 60, at 527–28.

for competitive manipulation at the eventual continuous trial. Central in the debates on discovery is the concern of the ungenerous that the evidence may be tainted or alchemized between the time it is discovered and the time it is produced or countered at the trial. The concern, though the debaters report it in differing degrees, is well founded. It is significant enough to warrant our exploring alternative arrangements abroad where investigation "freezes" the evidence (that is, preserves usable depositions and other forms of relatively contemporaneous evidence) for use at trial, thus serving both to inhibit spoilage and to avoid pitfalls and surprises that may defeat justice.[64]

Such illustrative lines of study and comparison are tendered here only as the beginning of a suggested agenda. For myself, I plan to go back to law school with them by proposing their consideration as topics for seminars I shall be privileged to "give" (more aptly, to share) during the coming year. It is my hope that some of those who read this may wish to embark upon comparable efforts.

B. Making Truth the Paramount Objective

We should consider whether the paramount commitment of counsel concerning matters of fact should be to the discovery of truth rather than to the advancement of the client's interest. This topic heading contains for me the most debatable and the least thoroughly considered of the thoughts offered here. It is a brief suggestion for a revolution, but with no apparatus of doctrine or program.

We should face the fact that the quality of "hired gun"[65] is close to the heart and substance of the litigating lawyer's role. As is true always of the mercenary warrior, the litigator has not won the highest esteem for his scars and his service. Apart from our image, we have had to reckon for ourselves in the dark hours with the knowledge that "selling" our stories rather than striving for the truth cannot always seem, because it is not, such

---

[64]In the depths of the cold war, Mr. Justice Jackson reported a comparison that should be no more offensive in a time of even tremulous détente:

> [T]he Soviet Delegation objected to our practice on the ground that it is not fair to defendants. Under the Soviet System when an indictment is filed every document and the statement of every witness which is expected to be used against the defendant must be filed with the court and made known to the defense. It was objected that under our system the accused does not know the statements from accusing witnesses, nor the documents that may be used against him, that such evidence is first made known to him at the trial too late to prepare a defense, and that this tends to make the trial something of a game instead of a real inquest into guilt. It must be admitted that there is a great deal of truth in this criticism. We reached a compromise by which the Nurnberg indictment was more informative than in English or American practice but less so than in Soviet and French practice.

Bull, "Nurnberg Trial," 7 *F.R.D.* 175, 178 (n.d.) (quoting Justice Jackson, source not indicated).

[65]See H. Packer and T. Ehrlich, *New Directions in Legal Education* 33 (1972).

noble work as befits the practitioner of a learned profession. The struggle to win, with its powerful pressures to subordinate the love of truth, is often only incidentally, or coincidentally, if at all, a service to the public interest.

We have been bemused through the ages by the hardy (and somewhat appealing) notion that we are to serve rather than judge the client. Among the implications of this theme is the idea that lawyers are not to place themselves above others and that the client must be equipped to decide for himself whether or not he will follow the path of truth and justice. This means quite specifically, whether in *Anatomy of a Murder*[66] or in Dean Freedman's altruistic sense of commitment,[67] that the client must be armed for effective perjury as well as he would be if he were himself legally trained. To offer anything less is arrogant, elitist, and undemocratic.

It is impossible to guess closely how prevalent this view may be as a practical matter. Nor am I clear to what degree, if any, received canons of legal ethics give it sanction. My submission is in any case that it is a crass and pernicious idea, unworthy of a public profession. It is true that legal training is a source of power, for evil as well as good, and that a wicked lawyer is capable of specially skilled wrongdoing. It is likewise true that a physician or pharmacist knows homicidal devices hidden from the rest of us. Our goals must include means for limiting the number of crooked and malevolent people trained in the vital professions. We may be certain, notwithstanding our best efforts, that some lawyers and judges will abuse their trust. But this is no reason to encourage or facilitate wrongdoing by everyone.

Professional standards that placed truth above the client's interests would raise more perplexing questions. The privilege for client's confidences might come in for reexamination and possible modification. We have all been trained to know without question that the privilege is indispensable for effective representation. The client must know his confidences are safe so that he can tell all and thus have fully knowledgeable advice. We may want to ask, nevertheless, whether it would be an excessive price for the client to be stuck with the truth rather than having counsel allied with him for concealment and distortion. The full development of this thought is beyond my studies to date. Its implications may be unacceptable. I urge only that it is among the premises in need of examination.

If the lawyer is to be more truth-seeker than combatant, troublesome questions of economics and professional organization may demand early confrontation. How and why should the client pay for loyalties divided between himself and the truth? Will we not stultify the energies and

---

[66]R. Traver, *Anatomy of a Murder* (1958). For those who did not read or have forgotten it, the novel, by a state supreme court justice, involved an eventually successful homicide defense of impaired mental capacity with the defendant supplying the requisite "facts" after having been told in advance by counsel what type of facts would constitute the defense.

[67]See text accompanying note 58 *supra*. In M. Freedman, *Lawyers' Ethics in an Adversary System*, ch. 6 (1975), Dean Freedman reports a changed view on this last of his "three hardest questions." He would under some circumstances (including the case in *Anatomy of a Murder*) condemn the lawyer's supplying of the legal knowledge to promote perjury. Exploring whether the Dean's new position is workable would transcend even the wide leeway I arrogate in footnotes.

resources of the advocate by demanding that he judge the honesty of his cause along the way? Can we preserve the heroic lawyer shielding his client against all the world—and not least against the State—while demanding that he honor a paramount commitment to the elusive and ambiguous truth? It is strongly arguable, in short, that a simplistic preference for the truth may not comport with more fundamental ideals—including notably the ideal that generally values individual freedom and dignity above order and efficiency in government.[68] Having stated such issues too broadly, I leave them in the hope that this refinement and study may seem worthy endeavors for the future.

C. A DUTY TO PURSUE THE TRUTH

The rules of professional responsibility should compel disclosures of material facts and forbid material omissions rather than merely proscribe positive frauds. This final suggestion is meant to implement the broad and general proposition that precedes it. In an effort to be still more specific, I submit a draft of a new disciplinary rule that would supplement or in large measure displace existing disciplinary rule 7-102 of the "Code of Professional Responsibility."[69] The draft says:

(1) In his representation of a client, unless prevented from doing so by a privilege reasonably believed to apply, a lawyer shall:

    (a) Report to the court and opposing counsel the existence of relevant evi-

---

[68]Two previous Cardozo Lecturers have been among the line of careful thinkers cautioning against too single-minded a concern for truth. "While our adversary system of litigation may not prove to be the best means of ascertaining the truth, its emphasis upon respect for human dignity at every step is not to be undermined lightly in a democratic state." Botein, "The Future of the Judicial Process," 15 *Record of N.Y.C.B.A.* 152, 166 (1960). See also Shawcross, "The Functions and Responsibilities of an Advocate," 13 *Record of N.Y.C.B.A.* 483, 498, 500 (1958).

[69]The affected portions of DR 7-102 are:

(A) In his representation of a client, a lawyer shall not:

    . . . .

    (3) Conceal or knowingly fail to disclose that which he is required by law to reveal.
    (4) Knowingly use perjured testimony or false evidence.
    (5) Knowingly make a false statement of law or fact.
    (6) Participate in the creation or preservation of evidence when he knows or it is obvious that the evidence is false.
    (7) Counsel or assist his client in conduct that the lawyer knows to be illegal or fraudulent.
    . . . .

(B) A lawyer who receives information clearly establishing that:
(1) His client has, in the course of the representation, perpetrated a fraud upon a person or tribunal shall promptly call upon his client to rectify the same, and if his client refuses or is unable to do so, he shall reveal the fraud to the affected person or tribunal.
(2) A person other than his client has perpetrated a fraud upon a tribunal shall promptly reveal the fraud to the tribunal.

dence or witnesses where the lawyer does not intend to offer such evidence or witnesses.

(b)   Prevent, or when prevention has proved unsuccessful, report to the court and opposing counsel the making of any untrue statement by client or witness or any omission to state a material fact necessary in order to make statements made, in the light of the circumstances under which they were made, not misleading.

(c)   Question witnesses with a purpose and design to elicit the whole truth, including particularly supplementary and qualifying matters that render evidence already given more accurate, intelligible, or fair than it otherwise would be.

(2)   In the construction and application of the rules in subdivision (1), a lawyer will be held to possess knowledge he actually has or, in the exercise of reasonable diligence, should have.

Keywords in the draft, namely, in (1)(b), have been plagiarized, of course, from the Securities and Exchange Commission's rule 10b-5.[70] That should serve not only for respectability; it should also answer, at least to some extent, the complaint that the draft would impose impossibly stringent standards. The morals we have evolved for business clients cannot be deemed unattainable by the legal profession.

Harder questions suggest themselves. The draft provision for wholesale disclosure of evidence in litigation may be visionary or outrageous, or both. It certainly stretches out of existing shape our conception of the advocate retained to be partisan. As against the yielding up of everything, we are accustomed to strenuous debates about giving a supposedly laggard or less energetic party a share in his adversary's litigation property safeguarded as "work product."[71] A lawyer must now surmount partisan loyalty and disclose "information clearly establishing" frauds by his client or others.[72] But that is a far remove from any duty to turn over all the fruits of factual investigation,[73] as the draft proffered here would direct. It has lately come to be required that some approach to helpful disclosures be made by prosecutors in criminal cases; "the suppression by the prosecution of evidence favorable to an accused upon request violates due process where the evidence is material either to guilt or to punishment, irrespective of the good faith or bad faith of the prosecution."[74] One may be permitted as a respectful subordinate to note the awkward placement in the quoted passage of the words "upon request," and to imagine their careful insertion to keep the duty of disclosure within narrow bounds. But even that

[70]17 *C.F.R.* § 240.10B-5 (1974).

[71]See 4 J. Moore, *Federal Practice* para. 26.64 (2d ed. 1974).

[72]See *ABA Code of Professional Responsibility*, DR 7-102(B).

[73]Cf. American College of Trial Lawyers, *Code of Trial Conduct* R. 15(b): A lawyer should not suppress any evidence that he or his client has a legal obligation to reveal or produce. He should not advise or cause a person to secrete himself or to leave the jurisdiction of a tribunal for the purpose of making himself unavailable as a witness therein. However, except when legally required, it is not his duty to disclose any evidence or the identity of any witness.

[74]*Brady v. Maryland,* 373 U.S. 83, 87 (1963).

restricted rule is for the *public* lawyer. Can we, should we, adopt a far broader rule as a command to the bar generally?

That question touches once again the most sensitive nerve of all. A bar too tightly regulated, too conformist, too "governmental," is not acceptable to any of us. We speak often of lawyers as "officers of the court" and as "public" people. Yet our basic conception of the office is of one essentially private—private in political, economic, and ideological terms—congruent with a system of private ownership, enterprise, and competition, however modified the system has come to be.[75] It is not necessary to recount here the contributions of a legal profession thus conceived to the creation and maintenance of a relatively free society. It *is* necessary to acknowledge those contributions and to consider squarely whether, or how much, they are endangered by proposed reforms.

If we must choose between truth and liberty, the decision is not in doubt. If the choice seemed to me that clear and that stark, this essay would never have reached even the tentative form of its present submission. But I think the picture is quite unclear. I lean to the view that we can hope to preserve the benefits of a free, skeptical, contentious bar while paying a lesser price in trickery and obfuscation.

Judge Frankel's Search for Truth

MONROE H. FREEDMAN

The theme of Judge Marvin E. Frankel's Cardozo Lecture is that the adversary system rates truth too low among the values that institutions of justice are meant to serve. Accordingly, Judge Frankel takes up the challenging task of proposing how that system might be modified to raise the truth-seeking function to its rightful status in our hierarchy of values. His proposals, delivered with characteristic intellect, grace, and wit, are radical and, I believe, radically wrong.

Judge Frankel directs his criticism at the adversary system itself and at the lawyer as committed adversary. Challenging the idea that the adversary system is the best method for determining the truth, Judge Frankel asserts that "we know that others searching after facts—in history, geography, medicine, whatever—do not emulate our adversary system."[1] I would question the accuracy of that proposition, at least in the breadth in which it is

---

[75]Cf. Damaska, *supra* note 60, at 565–69, 584–87.

University of Pennsylvania Law Review, 123, No. 5 (May 1975), 1060–66. Reprinted by permission.

[1]Frankel, "The Search for Truth: An Umpireal View," 123 *U. Pa. L. Rev.* 1031, 1036 (1975) [p. 53, above].

stated. Moreover, I think that to the extent that other disciplines do not follow a form of adversarial process, they suffer for it. Assume, for example, a historian bent upon determining whether Edward de Vere wrote the plays attributed to William Shakespeare, or whether Richard III ordered the murder of the princes in the Tower, or even whether it was militarily justifiable for the United States to devastate Nagasaki with an atomic bomb. Obviously, the historian's inquiry would not be conducted in a courtroom, but the conscientious historian's search for truth would necessarily involve a careful evaluation of evidence marshalled by other historians strongly committed to sharply differing views on those issues. In short, the process of historical research and judgment on disputed issues of history is— indeed, must be—essentially adversarial. In medicine, of course, there is typically less partisanship than in historical research because there is less room for the play of political persuasion, and less room for personal interest and bias than in the typical automobile negligence case. Nevertheless, anyone about to make an important medical decision for oneself or one's family would be well advised to get a second opinion. And if the first opinion has come from a doctor who is generally inclined to perform radical surgery, the second opinion might well be solicited from a doctor who is generally skeptical about the desirability of surgery. According to one study, about nineteen percent of surgical operations are unnecessary.[2] A bit more adversariness in the decision-making process might well have saved a gall bladder here or a uterus there.

Moreover, as Professor Black has recently reminded us, it is well established in our law that the extent of due process—meaning adversary procedures—properly varies depending upon the matter at stake in litigation.[3] In medical research, the situation is similar, and recent instances of dishonesty at the Sloan-Kettering Institute and at Harvard illustrate the increasing importance of adversariness in medical research.[4] Prior to World War II, apparently, the material rewards of biological research were small, "scientific chicanery" was extremely limited,[5] and adversariness was of minimal concern, but the stakes have risen since then. Now that publication of discoveries has become essential to professional advancement and to obtaining large grants of money, rigorous verification, as through replication by a skeptical colleague, has become a common requirement.[6]

Having started from what seems to me to be a faulty premise that adversariness is essentially inimical to truth, Judge Frankel concludes his proposal for change with a proposal for fundamental revision of the "Code of Professional Responsibility."[7] Specifically, disciplinary rule 7-102 cur-

[2]*N. Y. Times*, June 19, 1973, at 21, col. 1.

[3]C. Black, *Capital Punishment* 32–35 (1974).

[4]Borek, "Cheating in Science," *N. Y. Times*, Jan. 22, 1975, at 35, col. 2. See also Levine, "Scientific Method and the Adversary Model: Some Preliminary Thoughts," 29 *Am. Psychologist* 661, 669–76 (1974).

[5]Id.

[6]Id.

[7]Frankel, *supra* note 1, at [pp. 61, above].

rently forbids the lawyer from knowingly and actively participating in fraud in the course of representation.[8] Under Judge Frankel's proposed draft of disciplinary rule 7-102, however, an attorney would have an affirmative duty: (a) to report to the court and opposing counsel the existence of relevant evidence or witnesses where the lawyer does not intend to offer such evidence or witnesses; (b) report to the court and opposing counsel any untrue statement, or any omission to state a material fact, even when committed by a client; and (c) to question witnesses "with a purpose and design to elicit the whole truth."[9] Moreover, in order to avoid the traditional sophistry used to evade responsibility in this area,[10] Judge Frankel provides that a lawyer "will be held to possess knowledge he actually has or, in the exercise of reasonable diligence, should have."[11]

To be fair to Judge Frankel—and, at the same time, as part of my attack on his thesis—I should note the repeated expressions of uncertainty with which Judge Frankel puts forth his own proposal. His article, "makes no pretense to be polished or finished wisdom," but is intended "to suggest problems and raise doubts, rather than to resolve confusion; to disturb thought, rather than to dispense legal or moral truth." In sum his effort is only to "sketch" some "tentative lines" along which efforts to reform the adversary system "might" proceed.[12] Those substantial disclaimers are certainly disarming of criticism. At the same time, however, I trust that his audience will be particularly wary about adopting a view to which Judge Frankel has not yet succeeded in persuading himself.

Judge Frankel does not, of course, adopt the simplistic notion that a system for administering justice is concerned solely with truth-seeking. Indeed, it is not even clear that Judge Frankel would make truth the paramount objective. His thesis is more modest—again, disarmingly so. It is not that truth has been denied its rightful place at the apex of our hierarchy of values, but only that it is not "too low" among the values that institutions of justice are meant to serve. One cannot fault Judge Frankel for failing to identify, in his initial and tentative effort, all of the values he might have in mind. However, before we proceed to think any more seriously about substantial modification of our traditional—indeed, constitutional—system for administering justice, I think we ought to know just what values will be rearranged into what order of priorities.

For my own part, I think it is essential that any evaluation of the truth-seeking function of a trial be done in the context of our system of criminal

---

[8]*ABA Code of Professional Responsibility*, DR 7-102. Even that proposition is not as unambiguous as it might seem on first reading. See M. Freedman, *Lawyers' Ethics in an Adversary System*, ch. 3 [1975].

[9]All of the foregoing is subject to the qualifying phrase, "unless prevented from doing so be a privilege reasonably believed to apply." Frankel, *supra* note 1, at [pp. 61f. above]. I am not sure what that clause is intended to mean, but it could, of course, effectively nullify the entire proposal.

[10]See M. Freedman, *supra* note 8, ch. 5.

[11]Frankel, *supra* note 1 at [p. 62 above].

[12]Id. [p. 49, above].

66   *The Adversary System of Justice*

justice[13] and, indeed, the nature of our society and form of government. We might begin, by way of contrast, with an understanding of the role of a criminal defense attorney in a totalitarian state. As expressed by law professors at the University of Havana, "the first job of a revolutionary lawyer is not to argue that his client is innocent, but rather to determine if his client is guilty and, if so, to seek the sanction which will best rehabilitate him."[14] Similarly, a Bulgarian attorney began his defense in a treason trial by noting. "In a Socialist state there is no division of duty between the judge, prosecutor, and defense counsel. . . . The defense must assist the prosecution to find the objective truth in a case."[15] In that case, the defense attorney ridiculed his client's defense, and the client was convicted and executed. Sometime later the verdict was found to have been erroneous, and the defendant was "rehabilitated."[16]

The emphasis in a free society is, of course, sharply different. Under our adversary system, the interests of the state are not absolute, or even paramount. The dignity of the individual is respected to the point that even when the citizen is known by the state to have committed a heinous offense, the individual is nevertheless accorded such rights as counsel, trial by jury, due process, and the privilege against self-incrimination. A trial is, in part, a search for truth; accordingly, those basic rights are most often characterized as procedural safeguards against error in the search for truth. We are concerned, however, with far more than a search for truth, and the constitutional rights that are provided by our system of justice serve independent values that may well outweigh the truth-seeking value, a fact made manifest when we realize that those rights, far from furthering the search for truth, may well impede it. What more effective way is there to expose a defendant's guilt than to require self-incrimination, at least to the extent of compelling the defendant to take the stand and respond to interrogation before the jury? The defendant, however, is presumed innocent, the burden is on the prosecution to prove guilt beyond a reasonable doubt, and even the guilty accused has an "absolute constitutional right to remain silent" and to put the government to its proof.[17]

Thus, the defense lawyer's professional obligation may well be to advise the client to withhold the truth: "[A]ny lawyer worth his salt will tell the suspect in no uncertain terms to make no statement to police under any circumstances."[18] Similarly, the defense lawyer is obligated to prevent the introduction of some evidence that may be wholly reliable, such as a murder weapon seized in violation of the fourth amendment or a truthful

[13]Judge Frankel makes no apparent distinction in his article between criminal and civil cases, and several references in the article indicate clearly that his modifications of the system are intended to reach criminal as well as civil trials.

[14]Berman, "The Cuban Popular Tribunals," 69 *Colum. L. Rev.* 1317, 1341 (1969).

[15]*N. Y. Times*, Dev. 14, 1949, at 9, col. 1, cited in J. Kaplan, *Criminal Justice* 264–65 (1973).

[16]Id. Apr. 4, 1956, at 1, col. 4.

[17]Escobedo v. Illinois, 378 U. S. 478, 491 (1964); *Malloy v. Hogan*, 378 U. S. 1, 8 (1964).

[18] *Watts v. Indiana*, 338 U. S. 49, 59 (1949) (Jackson, J., concurring and dissenting).

but involuntary confession. Justice White has observed that although law enforcement officials must be dedicated to "the ascertainment of the true facts,. . . defense counsel has no comparable obligation to ascertain or present the truth. Our system assigns him a different mission. . . . [W]e . . . insist that he defend his client whether he is innocent or guilty."[19] Such conduct by defense counsel does not constitute obstruction of justice. On the contrary, "as part of the duty imposed on the most honorable defense counsel, we countenance or require conduct which in many instances has little, if any, relation to the search for truth."[20] Indeed, Justice Harlan noted that "the lawyer in fulfilling his professional responsibilities of necessity may become an obstacle to truthfinding,"[21] and Chief Justice Warren has recognized that when the criminal defense attorney successfully obstructs efforts by the government to elicit truthful evidence in ways that violate constitutional rights, the attorney is "exercising. . . good professional judgment. . . He is merely carrying out what he is sworn to do under his oath—to protect to the extent of his ability the rights of his client. In fulfilling this responsibility the attorney plays a vital role in the administration of criminal justice under our Constitution."[22]

Obviously those eminent jurists would not arrive lightly at the conclusion that an officer of the court has a professional obligation to place obstacles in the path of truth. Their reasons go back to the nature of our system of criminal justice and to the fundamentals of our system of government. Before we will permit the state to deprive any person of life, liberty, or property, we require that certain processes which ensure regard for the dignity of the individual be followed, irrespective of their impact on the determination of truth. By emphasizing that the adversary process has its foundations in respect for human dignity, I do not mean to deprecate the search for truth or to suggest that the adversary system is not concerned with it. On the contrary, truth is a basic value and the adversary system is one of the most efficient and fair methods designed for finding it. That system proceeds on the assumption that the best way to ascertain the truth is to present to an impartial judge or jury a confrontation between the proponents of conflicting views, assigning to each the task of marshalling and presenting the evidence for its side in as thorough and persuasive a way as possible. The truth-seeking techniques used by the advocates on each side include investigation, pretrial discovery, cross-examination of opposing witnesses, and a marshalling of the evidence in summation. The judge or jury is given the strongest case that each side can present, and is in a position to make an informed, considered, and fair judgment. Nevertheless, the point that I now emphasize is that in a society that respects the dignity of the individual, truth-seeking cannot be an absolute value, but

[19]*United States v. Wade*, 388 U. S. 218, 256–57 (1967) (White, J., dissenting in part and concurring in part).

[20]Id. at 258.

[21]*Miranda v. Arizona*, 384 U. S. 436, 514 (1966) (Harlan, J., dissenting).

[22]Id. at 480–81 (opinion of the Court).

may be subordinated to other ends,[23] although that subordination may sometimes result in the distortion of the truth.

As indicated earlier, Judge Frankel is neither ignorant of nor insensitive to such concerns. In his Cardozo Lecture, however, he seems to me to give them substantially less than their due, pausing only to note briefly, near the end of his article that it is "strongly arguable . . . that a simplistic preference for the truth may not comport with more fundamental ideals— including notably the ideal that generally values individual freedom and dignity above order and efficiency in government."[24]

One suspects that in minimizing his advertence to that critical aspect of the problem, the umpireal judge was backsliding into a bit of lawyer adversariness. For if we ask, as I think we must, just how strongly arguable is the case for the "more fundamental ideals," we will find either that we are being asked to sacrifice those ideals in some substantial measure, because the case for them is not sufficiently strong, or that Judge Frankel's proposal is wholly impractical, because regard for those ideals precludes a single-minded search for truth. Moreover, if the former be the case, then I think we would be compelled to turn our attention to some fearsome questions thus far elided by Judge Frankel: precisely which parts of the fourth, fifth, and sixth amendments are we being asked to scrap, and how can the requisite amendments to the Bill of Rights be phrased without doing irreparable damage to some of the most precious aspects of our form of government?

In sum, Judge Frankel has succeeded in what he set out to do: He has suggested problems, raised doubts, and disturbed thought. Moreover, he has done so in a way that charms and delights. However, as Judge Frankel warned us at the start of his article, his proposals for radical surgery on the adversary system neither resolve confusion nor dispense truth.

---

[23]See *ABA Project on Standards for Criminal Justice, Standards Relating to the Administration of Criminal Justice* 59–60 (1974). Cf. *Tehan v. United States ex rel. Shott*, 382 U. S. 406, 416 (1966) (Stewart, J.):

> The basic purpose of a trial is the determination of truth. . . . By contrast, the Fifth Amendment's privilege against self-incrimination is not an adjunct to the ascertainment of truth. That privilege, like the guarantees of the Fourth Amendment, stands as a protection of quite different constitutional values. . . . To recognize this is no more than to accord those values undiluted respect.

[24]Frankel, *supra* note 1, at [p. 61, above].

The Zeal of the Civil Advocate

MURRAY L. SCHWARTZ

I. INTRODUCTION

A. Review

A fundamental question for lawyers and those who write about lawyers is the extent to which lawyers are personally accountable for the results they help their clients get. In considering that question in an earlier article,[1] I posited two related principles that, I suggested, express the common understanding of the responsibility and accountability of the criminal and civil advocate in the adversary system.[2] The first, the Principle of Professionalism, states:

> When acting as an advocate, a lawyer must, within the established constraints upon professional behavior, maximize the likelihood that his client will prevail.

The second, the Principle of Nonaccountability states:

> When acting as an advocate for a client according to the Principle of Professionalism, a lawyer is neither legally, professionally, nor morally accountable for the means used or the ends achieved.

The meaning of legal accountability and professional accountability referred to in the Principle of Nonaccountability is evident. Legal accountability means, for example, that the lawyer could be prosecuted criminally or be held civilly liable for damages: professional accountability means that the lawyer could be professionally disciplined for the behavior. The principle states that as long as the lawyer acts within the Principle of Professionalism, he or she cannot be prosecuted, held liable in damages, or disciplined.

What, however, does it mean to say that the lawyer who acts according to the Principle of Professionalism is not morally accountable? I suggest that it means that the lawyer can properly refuse to be called to account with respect to the morality of the means used or ends achieved on behalf of the client.

American Bar Foundation Journal, 1983, (1983), 543–63. Reprinted by permission.

[1]Murray L. Schwartz, "The Professionalism and Accountability of Lawyers," 66 *Calif. L. Rev.* 669 (1978).

[2]Id. at 673.

In procedural terms, the concept of moral accountability is equilvalent to the filing of a demurrer, rather than an answer, to the charge of immorality. In effect, as long as the charge does not allege a violation of the established constraints upon professional behavior, the lawyer is beyond reproof for acting on behalf of the client.[3]

This immunity from accountability, as stated in the Principle of Nonaccountability, was limited in terms to the lawyer acting in accord with the Principle of Professionalism, and that principle applied only to the lawyer acting as an "advocate," that is, as a client representative within the adversary litigation system. Assuming in that essay the validity of the principles, I went on to consider whether lawyers acting on behalf of clients in roles other than that of advocate within the adversary system, such as those of negotiator and counselor, are similarly nonaccountable. I concluded that they should not be: lawyers outside the adversary system, I argued, are as morally accountable as nonlawyers who assist others to achieve their desired results.

I shall not rehearse the full development of that conclusion here. In short, it is based on the assumption that all persons are morally accountable for their behavior, including behavior that helps others achieve their ends. If that is a correct assumption (and of course it does not address the range of exception, close calls, and dilemmas subsumed within the concept), the question to be confronted is whether the nonadvocate lawyer is for some reason exempt. In rejecting such an exemption, I relied heavily on the fact that in our legal system no lawyer need accept any client who seeks his or her legal assistance; accordingly, voluntary acceptance of a client carried with it moral accountability for means and ends employed in that representation.

Inasmuch as lawyers constitute the only group legally permitted to render legal advice to others, clients with lawful ends may thus be deprived of important if not essential assistance. Recognizing this deprivation, I nevertheless concluded that the balance was to be struck on the side of holding lawyers accountable for their assistance. In brief, the special condition of being a nonadvocate lawyer does not alter the personal accountability all bear for their behavior.

This conclusion invites reconsideration of the assumption that the Principle of Nonaccountability does apply to advocates. In the conclusion of that earlier article, I stated, "a more extensive analysis [of the assumptions that underlie the immunity of the advocate] is required than this article undertakes. In short, those matters are left to another day."[4]

This is that "more extensive analysis" and that "other day."

B. Preview

In pursuing the issue of moral accountability of the civil advocate, I shall consider the several dimensions of moral accountability, dimensions

[3]Id. at 673–74.
[4]Id. at 697.

that were not fully explicated in the treatment of the nonadvocate lawyer. The first dimension is personal: the extent to which the lawyer's behavior conforms to his or her own moral standards. The second dimension is societal: the extent to which a society that has not prohibited by law or professional rule the attainment by client of his or her own ends can bring moral censure to bear upon the lawyer who proceeds through civil litigation to help the client achieve those ends. The third dimension is the perspective of the moral philosopher: the extent to which we might regard the lawyer's behavior as immoral even though neither society itself nor the lawyer so regards it.

Once again, for reasons that will appear, I shall limit the scope of the discussion, this time by not disputing that the Principle of Nonaccountability applies to criminal defense lawyers. I shall consider whether the reasons that are usually cited to justify that application of the principle obtain equally in the case of civil advocates. A demonstration that they do not does not of course demonstrate the obverse: that civil advocates are morally accountable. That is a separate undertaking.

The development of these and other themes is as follows:

The structure of the adversary system as it is commonly understood is examined in part II. Subpart A concludes that effective implementation of the system requires that the professional advocate satisfy two postulates: they must be equally competent, and they must be equally adversary. Subpart B inquires into the question whether these two postulates are satisfied in the criminal trial and concludes that they are not. This leads, somewhat surprisingly, to the further conclusion that criminal trial is not an appropriate illustration of the adversary system and that the criminal defense lawyer is not an appropriate model for the lawyer who engages in civil litigation.

Part III examines the civil trial independently of the criminal model and argues that the rules of behavior for civil litigators should be drawn with the primary objective of ascertaining truth.

Part IV is concerned with the moral accountability of the lawyer who attempts to seek immoral though lawful ends for the client in civil litigation. Subpart A concludes that the lawyer cannot properly claim that his or her role as a lawyer provides immunity from acountability. Subpart B [omitted] asks whether a legal system that permits a litigant to seek immoral ends may nevertheless criticize on moral grounds a lawyer who helps a client do so; it concludes that such moral criticism is appropriate. One consequence of this conclusion is that all lawyers should reject on moral grounds the immoral though lawful cause of a client. Since the client will then be unable to obtain a lawyer's professional help to vindicate a legal right, the conflict between a systemic value of representation and the moral repugnance of lawyers must be resolved. The proposed formula for resolving that conflict [involving a balancing of (1) the substantiality of the legal interest involved, (2) the gravity of injury to the party suffering moral wrong, and (3) the adequacy of representation without counsel] . . . is not proposed as an operational principle, but as an algorithm to aid in thinking about whether a court should assign a lawyer to represent a client in a morally repugnant civil cause. Subpart C considers the moral stance of a lawyer who is so assigned.

II. THE ADVERSARY SYSTEM AND THE ADVOCATE

A. The Postulates of the Adversary System

A dispute exists when two (or more) parties disagree, that is, each party believes it should prevail and the other party should not. When they cannot resolve that disagreement by themselves, it is remitted (either voluntarily or involuntarily) to a third party. There are a variety of third-party dispute-resolving processes, of which the adversary system is one.

One essential element of the accepted model of the adversary system is an impartial tribunal. The impartiality has two dimensions: absence of bias, and nonparticipation in prosecution of the cause or in presentation of the evidence and arguments. The nonparticipation of the tribunal is the obverse of another essential element of the adversary system: the parties have the responsibility of prosecuting and presenting their own best cases and of challenging the prosecution and presentation of their opponents.

This assignment of prosecution and presentation to the parties necessitates two postulates, which may be put forward in the following way. Were the presentation and prosecution functions to be lodged in the tribunal, the tribunal would be expected to be evenhanded in its performance; it would be expected to try as hard and ably for one party as for the other. In the system in which the functions are performed not by the tribunal but by the parties, each party believing it should prevail, it would expected that each party will try as hard and ably to prosecute and present its cause as it can. Where the parties have professional representation (e.g., lawyers), those representatives would be expected to try as hard and ably for their principals as they can. That is, each representative—as each party—will attempt to prosecute and present all the evidence and argument thought to support the particular claim and to rebut that which is prosecuted and presented by the other party or its representative. This does not of course say anything about *how* that prosecution and presentation is to take place, that is, the procedural and evidentiary rules. It is to say that each party (or professional representative) will want to put its best foot forward within whatever procedure is in effect.

Because only in rare cases will the parties be equal in their presentational ability, it is not possible to reach the evenhandedness of an impartial tribunal charged with the prosecution and presentation functions. Nevertheless, it is critical that the imbalance be reduced as much as possible, and this can be best accomplished through two postulates relating to the professional representatives: the Postulate of Equal Competence and the Postulate of Equal Adversariness.

The Postulate of Equal Competence is a shorthand way of saying that for the adversary system to function properly, the opposing representatives (advocates) should be roughly equal in their ability to perform their professional functions. The Postulate of Equal Adversariness is a shorthand way of saying that the opposing advocates should also be roughly equal in their dedication to the cause of their principals and in their opposition to the cause of their opponents. The postulates do not—cannot—require true equality; they do assert that there should not be gross disparities in these respects.

It may be argued that whether the two postulates may be properly derived from the model of the adversary system depends on whether the justifications that support the model necessarily imply that an impartial tribunal would be evenhanded were it to proceed without the participation of the parties and their counsel. If the justifications do not imply evenhandedness, there is no basis for concluding that there should be equality between counsel. The postulates then would not be appropriate constraints for the operation of the system.

What are the commonly accepted justifications of the adversary system?[5] One has to do with the outcome of the dispute. It is that the adversary system is the best way to resolve controverted factual issues correctly and the best way to vindicate legal rights,[6] such as the rights to have contracts performed and to receive compensation for tortious injury. On this justification, the basis of the two postulates is that equality of competence and adversariness of the advocates is the best way to ensure correct outcomes.

Several of the leading explicators of the adversary system appear to rely on a different justification: adversary advocacy is itself an intrinsic good.[7] To the extent that this justification is independent of the other, it is more in accord with the postulates than in disagreement with them, for if adversary advocacy is an intrinsic good, it must be equally good for the various parties, and to be equal there must be the equalities demanded by the postulates.

Another often-heard justification that is hard to capture precisely asserts that the adversary system is the best way of preserving human dignity.[8] In one sense, it is the sum of the other justifications. If it differs from that sum, it stands for the proposition that persons involved either voluntarily or involuntarily in an adjudicatory system are entitled, as a matter of self-realization, to untrammeled freedom to present their causes. As I shall attempt to show, this idea has more force in the criminal context than in the civil one. In any event, the postulates apply: a party acting

[5]A primary source for the discussion that follows is David Luban, "The Adversary System Excuse," to appear in David Luban, ed., *The Good Lawyer: Lawyers' Roles and Lawyers' Ethics*, Maryland Studies in Public Philosophy (Totowa, N. J.: Rowman & Allanheld, [1984]). In adumbrating these justifications, as reflected in the literature, my concern is not with their validity or cogency. It is to test whether any militates rejection of the two postulates. In this testing I shall refer only to those justifications that seem to implicate the postulates.

[6]It is possible that a biased tribunal might also arrive at the truth; even that in some cases that bias is essential to overcome other defects in the process. Nevertheless, the position that impartiality is overall necessary for the truth is the most plausible position.

[7]Charles Fried, "The Lawyer as Friend: The Moral Foundations of the Lawyer-Client Relation," 85 *Yale L. J.* 1060 (1976) [below, pp. 236–51]; Monroe H. Freedman, *Lawyers' Ethics in an Adversary System* (Indianapolis: Bobbs-Merrill Co., 1975); David Mellinkoff, *The Conscience of a Lawyer* (St. Paul, Minn.: West Publishing Co., 1973).

[8]See Luban *supra* note 5.

through an advocate is entitled to assume that the advocate will be as competent and as adversary as opposing counsel; otherwise, the party will not be able to preserve his or her dignity to the fullest extent.

In sum, the Postulates of Equal Competence and Equal Adversariness are supported by the several justifications of the adversary system and are inconsistent with none.

B. The Uniqueness of the Criminal Trial

The defense lawyer in the criminal trial is commonly regarded as the archetype of the advocate in the adversary system. Thus, the American Bar Association's Code of Professional Responsibility makes no significant distinction between the criminal defense lawyer and other trial lawyers, and the rhetorical defense of the adversary system more often than not is founded on the criminal trial. Recently, however, serious question has been raised whether the criminal defense lawyer should serve as the model for the civil advocate.[9] And for very good reason.

That criminal trials are significantly different from civil ones in philosophy, procedure, sanction, and role of lawyers needs little exposition. Criminal trials are governed in substantial measure by specific provisions of the Constitution, including the provisions of the Fourth Amendment (search and seizure exclusionary rule), Fifth Amendment (grand jury indictments, double jeopardy), Sixth Amendment (speedy and public trial, impartial jury, local venue, information of nature and cause of accusation, confrontation, compulsory process, assistance of counsel), and Eighth Amendment (excessive bail and fines, and cruel and unusual punishment). Civil trials are expressly governed only by the $20 trial-by-jury provision of the Seventh Amendment. The difference in the burden of proof between criminal and civil trials exemplifies the difference in how the two processes are regarded: The burden of proof on the prosecution in a criminal case is "beyond reasonable doubt"; in the civil case, the burden of proof on the plaintiff is generally "a preponderance of evidence."

Another major difference between the two types of proceedings is the application of the privilege against self-incrimination. Although the privilege may be claimed with respect to specific questions by civil parties as well as by criminal defendants, only the criminal defendant may refuse to take the stand and answer any questions at all. The criminal defendant has thus a substantial shield against discovery proceedings. In parallel fashion, while there may today be a serious constitutional question whether a criminal defense lawyer may even try to prevent his or her client from committing perjury,[10] it is not seriously disputed that the civil attorney must try to prevent his or her client from committing perjury on the stand.[11]

[9]Id. at 9–12.

[10]See *Lowery v. Cardwell*, 575, F.2d 727 (9th Cir. 1978); Charles W. Wolfram, "Client Perjury," 50 *S. Cal. L. Rev.* 809 (1977). [See also *Whiteside v. Scurr*, 744 F.2d 1323 (1984), pp. 297–301, below].

[11]Charles W. Wolfram, "Client Perjury: The Kutak Commission and the Association of Trial Lawyers on Lawyers, Lying Clients, and the Adversary System," 1980 *A.B.F. Res. J.* 964, 977–78.

The structure of the adversary system in the criminal and civil contexts differs in added significant ways. The prosecuting attorney is required by professional rule,[12] if not constitutional mandate,[13] to turn over to the defendant exculpatory evidence that he or she has uncovered but does not intend to introduce. The defendant has no comparable obligation. The prosecuting attorney is to be concerned that the innocent not be convicted[14] The criminal defense attorney has no comparable obligation to ensure that the guilty do not go free. Illustrative is the California State Bar Act: "It is the duty of an attorney. . . [t]o counsel or maintain such actions, proceeding or defenses only as appear to him legal or just, except the defense of a person charged with a public offense."[15]

What accounts for these differences? There is a manifest inequality in resources between the average defendant and the state, necessitating a drastic change of the structural rules to assure that there is some constraint on the ability of prosecution to work its will without significant challenge. It is a commonplace that the majority of defendants are indigent and that the resources available to their court-appointed counsel or public defenders are generally far less than those available to law enforcement authorities.[16] This inequality is exacerbated by the difference in sanctions between criminal and civil trials. The sanctions that attend a criminal conviction are those the society intends to be the most stigmatic and severe. The specter of capital punishment and the often barbaric conditions in our penal institutions in the past and present, as well as the unique stigma of conviction of a crime, have had a profound impact upon the protections accorded the defendant and the freedom of action accorded the defense lawyer in a criminal case.

These functional and structural differences between criminal and civil trials and between the roles of the opposing advocates seriously undermine holding out the criminal defense lawyer as the archetype of the advocate within the adversary system. For both the adversary system itself and the role of the advocate within that system are defined very differently in criminal trials and civil litigation.

What emerges from this analysis is the surprising conclusion that the model of the adversary system is significantly different from the very proceeding most often referred to as its prime illustration: criminal trials. In terms used earlier, the Postulate of Equal Adversariness is not applicable to the criminal trial at all, and the restraints on the prosecuting attorney seem deliberately created to limit that official's performance of the advocate's role to such an extent that the Postulate of Equal Competence may also be largely inapplicable. That there may be good reasons for these differences

[12]*ABA's Model Code of Professional Responsibility* DR 7-103 (B) (Aug. 1980).

[13]See, e.g., *Smith v. Phillips*, 455 U. S. 209 (1982); *United States v. Agurs*, 427 U. S. 97 (1976); *Brady v. Maryland*, 373 U. S. 83 (1963).

[14]*Model Code of Professional Responsibility* DR 7-103(A) (Aug. 1980).

[15]*Cal. Bus. & Prof. Code* § 6068(c) (St. Paul, Minn.: West Publishing Co., 1983).

[16]It is not difficult to think of circumstances in which the distortion is on the other side, as, e.g., a prosecution in a relatively small county against organized crime or wealthy defendants.

between the prosecuting attorney and the criminal defense attorney does not diminish their significance: there is no satisfactory reason to refer to the criminal trial and the prosecuting attorney or defense attorney as models for the civil litigation process or the role of the advocate. The two postulates help distinguish civil from criminal contexts. The differentiation is, however, based on the paradigm cases. It may well be that the fundamental characteristic of some types of civil cases are similar to those of criminal cases and should be treated like them. It may be that some types of criminal cases lack those fundamental characteristics. The discussion that follows does not treat these marginal cases. It is concerned only with the nonmarginal ones.

III. RULES OF PROFESSIONAL BEHAVIOR IN CIVIL TRIALS

The advocate's Principle of Nonaccountability applies both to the means used and to the ends pursued. Much of the concern about the morality of lawyers' behavior has to do with the kinds of techniques lawyers claim are required for effective representation in trials. Illustration of the point does not necessitate reference to such admittedly improper tactics as repressive use of discovery procedures. Illustrations of very proper professional behavior are: cross-examination for the purpose of discrediting the testimony of a witness known to be telling the truth; exploitation of an opponent's evidence known to be false; failure to introduce or advise the opponent of material adverse evidence. Each is a tactic that prima facie impedes the search for truth.

The justifications of such tactics usually appeal to the role of the defense attorney in a criminal trial. Whether those justifications stand up to examiniation in that context is a question not addressed here. Even if it is assumed that such tactics are necessary manifestations of zeal of the criminal defense lawyer, it surely does not follow that they are equally necessary or even appropriate manifestations of the civil litigator.

The issue to be addressed is whether either the conception of adversary system or its implementation demands the use of tactics that by hypothesis impede the ascertainment of truth.[17] In consideration of this issue, two

---

[17]It is important to make clear that what is at issue in the text is the set of "intrasystem" rules, i.e., the set of rules designed to implement the adversary system itself. Rules based on values external to the system may be applied within the system in such a way as to interfere with the ascertainment of truth within the system. The exclusionary rule and the spousal privileged-communication doctrine would be illustrations of such rules, which by excluding probative evidence interfere with the ascertainment of truth. In each such case, the defeating of truth is a recognized cost of the protection of other values, as deterrence of illegal police behavior in the first illustration and the protection of the marriage in the latter. Thus, Marvin Frankel's proposed rules of professional responsibility for the advocate begin: "In his representation of a client, unless prevented from doing so by a privilege reasonably believed to apply." Marvin E. Frankel, "The Search for Truth," 123 *U. Pa. L. Rev.* 1031, 1057 (1975) [p. 61, above]. See text *infra* at note 19. The issue addressed in the text is whether there are intrasystem values that require the subordination of truth.

related but independent issues arise: to what extent rules of behavior under an adversary system are determined by the objective of truth ascertainment, and whether the process is a symmetrical one, that is, whether the rules apply evenhandedly to both parties.

A. The Objective of Truth Ascertainment

Our adjudicatory system is often used to resolve disputes that are based upon a controversy about some prior event, that is, as to what happened. Whatever else may be said about the system's purpose, one of its necessary objectives is to ascertain truth: to reconstruct the past event as accurately as possible. The judicial answer to the question, What should happen now? depends on and is often resolved entirely by the answer to the question, What did happen? The system cannot be indifferent to the task of ascertaining the truth.

No earthly adjudicatory system can be confident of total accuracy. To come as close to that objective as possible, the rules of the system should be designed to maximize the probability of an accurate result. Thus the presumptive answer to the question posed is that neither the idea of the adversary system nor its effectuation requires the use of truth-defeating techniques.

It is important to emphasize the specific assumption on which those conclusions are based: that the particular technique under consideration is one that will defeat the truth—that is, decrease the probability of accurate results. To the extent that a particular practice is defended on the ground that it enhances the truth-seeking function, it should be evaluated on that basis. The cross-examination of a truthful witness might be defended on the ground that no one ever knows whether a witness is telling the truth and the lawyer should not arrogate that determination to himself or herself or, in another form, that it is better for lawyers to challenge witnesses generally without regard to their belief or knowledge of a witness's accuracy to avoid the possibility that lawyers will too easily (and erroneously) conclude that witnesses are telling the truth and thus not expose their errors. Although my own view is that this defense is inadequate, that is not the point. The point is that all such rules of professional behavior should be analyzed and evaluated by reference to their potential for increasing the probability of an accurate result. They should not be approved, for example, because they make the proceeding more "adversary."

B. Symmetry

The previous discussion has tried to develop the point that the criminal trial is not an apt illustration of the adversary system for the very reason that it is not symmetrical. The risks of error as to the outcome are placed almost entirely on the prosecution. The reasons for this symmetry include the political view that the state has an obligation to be concerned about the defendant as well as "itself"; the severity of the sanction, making the risk of error in the direction of conviction more objectionable than in the direction of acquittal; the inordinately greater resources of the state, requiring that something be done to prevent the defendant from being overwhelmed regardless of the merits of the controversy.

On the other hand, the current rules of procedure and professional behavior for the civil trial are, with one exception, symmetrical—that is, neither plaintiff nor defendant is favored. That one exception is the burden of proof, which is presumptively borne by the plaintiff by a "preponderance of the evidence." But that burden is not great, and it is often shifted through the device of presumptions. In reality, it merely resolves the question how to decide when the opposing positions are in equipoise. It does not, as does the burden of proof in criminal cases, shift the scales markedly in the defendant's favor. It does not speak forcefully to the probability of the defendant's accuracy over that of the plaintiff.[18]

The considerations that lead to the asymmetry of the criminal trial are not pertinent in the average civil case: there is no concern about convicting the innocent; there is no reason to favor defendants over plaintiffs or vice versa; in contest are civilians, not the state and an individual. Although the parties in civil litigation are often unequal in resources, the disparity is most often perceived as of a different order from that created by the massing of the state's resources in the criminal prosecution against those of the individual defendant. In a civil contest, what one party gains, another typically loses. There is no comparable "transfer" in a criminal proceeding.

C. Truth-Ascertaining Rules

Accordingly, arriving at as accurate a reconstruction of the past event as is possible is a paramount goal of the civil adjudicatory system. The rules should be constructed with this goal in mind—that is, on the assumption that their basic purpose is to arrive at the truth rather than, as in the criminal proceeding, to avoid one type of error.

1. The correct result   A good start in that direction would be to adopt a set of rules such as those proposed by Marvin Frankel.[19] Those rules would require a lawyer to report to the court and opposing counsel the existence of relevant evidence or witnesses the lawyer does not intend to offer; prevent or, when prevention has proved unsuccessful, report to the court and opposing counsel the making of any untrue statement by client or witness or any material omissions; and question witnesses with purpose and design to elicit the whole truth.

Much of the opposition to those proposals is based on the same arguments that were used in the fight against expanded civil discovery. In a real sense, the question is whether expanded civil discovery rules should be converted into professional ones. To do so would be to take one step further in the attempt to make real the Postulates of Equal Competence and Equal Adversariness. That is, it would provide all parties, regardles of

---

[18]See generally Edward W. Clearly, "Presuming and Pleading: An Essay on Juristic Immaturity," 12 *Stan. L. Rev.* 5 (1959).

[19]Frankel, *supra* note 17 [pp. 61f., above].

their personal resources, with both the favorable and the unfavorable relevant materials for the adjudication.

2. *Vindication of legal rights* Such rules would also maximize that justification of the adversary system concerned with vindicating legal rights. First, a judgment based on a determination of a legal right that is itself predicated on an erroneous factual finding should have no higher standing than the erroneous factual determination itself. Second, misconceptions of the tribunal about what the law is should be eliminated; there is no reason in the civil case to maintain that a party is entitled to a judgment on an erroneous conception of the law. Indeed, professional rules themselves require attorneys to advise the tribunal of material adverse decisions that have not been cited by their opponents.[20]

3. *Protection of human dignity* Implicit—and sometimes explicit—in the discussions of the adversary system is its function in protecting human dignity. In the criminal context, it is undoubtedly caught up in the possible outcome—conviction, with its harsh, degrading, and stigmatizing consequences. In part, it signifies that persons on trial should not be constrained in their efforts to avoid conviction: as previously stated, the full realization of the self depends on untrammeled freedom to challenge the power and resources of the state.

In a civil contest between two civilians, however, the ability to ensure that the state does not become a juggernaut is most often not needed. Cross-examination of truthful witnesses to give the impression that they are telling falsehoods may be justified as a way of keeping the state from overreaching. When neither contestant is the behemoth state, the human dignity argument takes on a different—and lesser—significance.[21]

Subsequently, I shall discuss the extent to which professional representation is an independent value of the adversary system. At this point, it is sufficient to say that if there is such a value, its vindication does not require the kind of tactics apparently deemed appropriate for criminal cases. In the criminal case, the recognized loss of human dignity appears limited to that suffered by the defendant. In the civil case, one party's gain of human dignity may well be outweighed by another's loss. Moreover, a party who is forced to use means he or she deems immoral in order to counter similar means used by the other party who is not so circumspect suffers a loss of human dignity. The net balance of human dignity preserved in a civil trial conducted according to criminal defense lawyer rules may well be negative. Protection of human dignity in civil litigation requires high standards of candor.

[20]E.g., *Model Code of Professional Responsibility* DR 7-106(B)(1) (Aug. 1980).

[21]Of course the fact that the ultimate outcome in both civil and criminal proceedings is a judicial decree does not mean that there is no difference between a criminal and a civil proceeding in the ways in which human dignity is to be preserved. The role of the state as civil judgment enforcer is significantly different from its roles of prosecutor, adjudicator, sentencer, and punisher.

4. Ameliorating impact of the rules If the rules for the behavior of lawyers in civil litigation are drawn with the primary objective of ascertaining truth, the consequences of gross differences in lawyer competence will be ameliorated by greater availability of information to all—one of the intended consequences of discovery. Lawyers will not misleadingly cross-examine truthful witnesses, exploit incorrect testimony adduced by the opposition, or fail to reveal material evidence helpful to the other side. Lawyers may continue to be equally adversary in their partisanship; what will be changed are the kinds of behavior permitted under the partisan banner.

Although all moral challenges to lawyers' behavior will not disappear, at least the aspect of alleged lawyer immorality concerned with procedural and evidentiary tactics will be removed. To the extent that moral problems of procedural or tactical behavior remain, the relationship of the lawyer's zeal to immoral ends must be examined.

IV. THE CIVIL ADVOCATE'S ZEAL AND IMMORAL ENDS.

Unless a pefect correspondence between law and morality obtains, a lawful outcome may be an immoral one. Immorality in this context is not intended to refer to personal behavior that offends social norms; it is not addressed to such questions as prostitution, homosexuality, or drug use. In the present context it includes only unconscionable or overreaching behavior by which one person exploits another. The consequence of this type of behavior is a gain to the exploiter and a concomitant loss—injury or damage—to the person exploited. It may, as will appear, include other types of lawful but harm-inflicting behavior as well.

That there is no perfect correspondence between legal rights and moral rights is manifest. The express terms of the substantive law may produce immoral results; there may be interstices in the substantive law or special factual circumstances that permit them to occur; and there may be procedural rules that, though generally desirable, allow for them.

This lack of perfect correspondence between legal rights and moral rights raises several closely related questions:

Is the civil advocate morally accountable for lawful but immoral ends obtained for a client through representation in civil litigation?

Is a legal system subject to moral criticism if it permits all lawyers to refuse to provide assistance to clients' ends because they believe those ends are immoral?

May a legal system morally require a lawyer to assist a client in achieving lawful but immoral ends?

A. The Moral Accountability of the Civil Advocate

If a lawyer helps a client achieve lawful but immoral ends through representation in civil litigation, is the lawyer morally accountable for that assistance? The narrow focus of this question should be made clear. It does not ask whether the lawyer is behaving immorally; it asks whether the lawyer can be held morally accountable. To answer that a lawyer cannot be held morally accountable is equivalent to giving the lawyer immunity from being forced to respond to questions about the morality of the representational behavior. Under such immunity, the lawyer would not be required to justify the behavior in moral terms; it would be sufficient to answer that he or she is a lawyer and has not acted unlawfully or helped a client achieve unlawful ends.

Further, the question probably touches on relatively few instances of lawyer behavior. In the overwhelming majority of civil cases, there will be no significantly moral issue; the client's ends will be clearly moral ones; or if the moral conclusion is unclear, there will be reasonable arguments on both sides.

Where the client has a morally ambiguous claim, a lawyer may properly take into account another value, the value of professional assistance for the presentation of cases within the adversary system, and represent the client. The only significant cases are those in which the client's lawful ends are unequivocally immoral. For the consideration of such cases, there are two opposing poles of reference.

The first referent is the criminal defense lawyer who, it is here assumed, is not morally accountable for the ends he or she seeks to achieve, as long as those ends are sought in a lawful manner. This assumption is based essentially on concern about the conviction of the innocent, harshness to the defendant of an unfavorable outcome, and disparity between the state and the individual defendant. The antipodal referent is the nonadvocate lawyer, the negotiator or counselor. Elsewhere I have argued that nonadvocate lawyers are as morally accountable as nonlawyer agents for helping their principals, to achieve immoral ends.[22] As long as lawyers are permitted to refuse clients in nonlitigation activities, lawyers—as is true for all voluntary agents—must be morally accountable for that assistance.

Which is the more appropriate referent, the criminal defense lawyer or the nonadvocate lawyer? At first blush, the civil advocate resembles the criminal defense lawyer more closely than he or she resembles the nonadvocate lawyer. Civil and criminal trial lawyers operate on behalf of clients in adjudicatory systems that in apparent form and structure are similar. Yet, as I have attempted to show, the two proceedings are quite dissimilar. Moreover, there is as yet no consensus—as there is with respect to the representation of criminal defendants—that there is a right to have a lawyer appointed in civil matters generally.[23] The special justifications—summarized above—that underlie the assumed immunity of the criminal defense lawyer from moral accountability are not available to the civil advocate.

The calculus of morality for the criminal defense lawyer is simple and straightforward: the primary concern is the defense of the individual against the state. But the civil advocate's moral calculations are more com-

---

[22]Schwartz, *supra*, note 1, at 669.

[23]See *Lassiter v. Department of Social Services*, 452 U. S. 18 (1981).

plex, for a lawful result obtained by the civil advocate may work a moral wrong on the other party. If a moral wrong occurs when a guilty person is acquitted, it is very different from the moral wrong to a private person when he or she loses a civil suit whose result, thought lawful, is immoral.

This difference may be illustrated by comparing the moral implications of an acquittal of a criminal defendant and of a civil verdict that the same criminal defendant is not liable for the harm caused to the victim. The moral issues involved in a lawyer's successful criminal defense of a person who has admittedly committed rape, child beating, or assault of another kind and those involved in a lawyer's successful defense of the same person in a tort action brought by the victim for injuries are very different.[24]

If the criminal process were regarded as an analogue to the civil suit— with the state acting as the victim's surrogate—there would be a persuasive argument that the moral questions would be largely the same. But criminal prosecutions are not analogues of civil suits. They serve different ends. Traditional ends of the criminal law—general deterrence, incapacitation, reformation, even societal retribution—are public ends. The purposes of the civil action only infrequently are similar. However similar in appearance civil and criminal trials may be, the moral accountability of the civil litigator cannot rest on those factors that arguably immunize the criminal defense lawyer from accountability.

Proof that the civil advocate does not share the criminal advocate's nonaccountability does not, of course, decide the extent to which the civil advocate is independently accountable. For this issue, it is necessary to consider the other pole, the essential difference between the nonadvocate lawyer and the civil litigator, the fact that the former does not operate within an adversary system framework. Is that fact sufficient to relieve the civil litigator of moral accountability, even though the nonadvocate lawyer would be morally accountable?

First, such an accountability is already recognized in the expressed rules of professional behavior. Specific provisions accord individual lawyers the discretion, if not the duty, to reject civil clients on moral grounds— for example the previously quoted language of the California State Bar Act: "It is the duty of an attorney . . . [t]o counsel or maintain such actions, proceedings or defenses only as appear to him legal or just, except the defense of the person charged with public offense."[25] Though expressed in less mandatory terms, the American Bar Association's Code of Professional Responsibility made "moral justness" a relevant consideration for lawyer and client.[26]

Second, lawyers in the United States have general discretion to accept or reject clients and causes. It would be anomalous and indeed ironic to deny that discretion only for cases in which the lawyer believes the proposed course of conduct to be immoral. To do so would be to change a discretionary regime to one in which a person who set out to be a lawyer

---

[24]I am not here concerned with problems of res judicata, collateral estoppel, or the like.

[25]See *supra* note 15.

[26]*Model Code of Professional Responsibility* EC 7-8, 7-9 (Aug. 1980).

was thereby forced to forgo moral considerations in representing clients in civil causes (a consequence to which I shall shortly turn).

The assumption on which this discussion has proceeded is that in the civil case the outcome achieved for the client would be immoral—that is, it would work a moral wrong to the other party. No persuasive reason appears as to why the individual lawyer who assists in achieving that outcome should not be morally accountable for it.

* * *

chapter four

THE ATTORNEY AND THE
SYSTEM OF JUSTICE

INTRODUCTION

This chapter will be concerned with those obligations on the part of the attorney and of the legal profession collectively which are, in the most direct sense, obligations to the system of justice. A system of justice will be no system of *justice* at all if it fails to provide some reasonable approximation of equal justice for all members of society. If an adversarial system of justice is in fact to provide some reasonable approximation of justice for all, then it must depend upon the availability to the members of society of competent and honest legal assistance.

Yet despite the fact that the concern for the availability of competent and honest legal assistance seems to be shared by nearly everyone inside and outside of the legal profession, the simple fact has been that legal services have often been unavailable to large groups of people in our society. Moreover, critics of the organized bar, both inside and ouside of the legal profession, critics including the immediate past Chief Justice of the United States, have charged that a significant number of attorneys fail to perform their professional tasks competently.

Availability of Legal Services

The practice of law has historically been limited to a rather tightly closed group. This exclusion has had two central effects. It has reduced competition in the legal market, thereby sustaining high prices and hence placing economic restrictions on the availability of justice. It has also tended to keep minorities out of legal practice. During much of the nineteenth century, for example, many jurisdictions refused to admit women to legal practice. It is infamous that even in our own day Supreme Court Justice Sandra Day O'Connor could get a job only as a legal secretary upon graduation from law school because law firms didn't want to hire women. Blacks, Hispanics, and other ethnic minorities have similarly had precisely the same kinds of problems in being admitted to law schools and the legal profession that they have had in gaining access to most other American institutions. This general restriction of membership in the legal "club" to white males has also tended to limit access to legal services to members of the ethnic majority. Not surprisingly, blacks, Hispanics, and other ethnic minorities have often not been fully convinced that white attorneys would take on the same kind of commitment to their legal interests that those attorneys would have to the legal interests of a white client.

This chapter will start with a selection from *Turner v. American Bar Association*, a case in which the plaintiffs challenge the authority of the courts to restrict legal practice to members of the organized bar. In his opinion, Judge Garza presents a brief history of English and American attempts to ensure a high quality of legal assistance through the restriction of legal practice to members of an organized legal establishment. He then examines what we may reasonably take the term "counsel" to mean in the Sixth Amendment guarantee of a right to "assistance of counsel" in light of both our legal traditions and our concern with a guarantee of competence in legal practice.

The chapter continues with a selection from *Hackin v. Lockwood*, in which the issue is whether Arizona's restriction on membership in its bar to graduates of accredited law schools is "arbitrary, capricious and unreasonable." Circuit Judge Barnes rules that given the state's appropriate concern with a high quality of legal practice, educational requirements such as graduation from an accredited law school are neither arbitrary nor unreasonable.

In "Assisting the Pro Se Litigant: Unauthorized Practice of Law or the Fulfillment of a Public Need?" Moses Apsan starts by taking note of a couple of basic facts. First he notes that the right of a litigant to represent him or herself has been a clearly and unambiguously established part of our legal system at least since the 1975 Supreme Court ruling in *Faretta v. California*. He also notes that the efforts of the organized bar over the past fifty years to combat the unauthorized practice of law reached a point where they tended to serve more the monopolistic interests of the legal profession than their initial purpose of protecting the public from legal incompetence. Apsan notes that there has been some tendency for both the courts and bar associations to reverse their directions and to take note of the fact that the public interest in the widespread availability of legal services may require the presence of forms of nonlegal assistance for the pro se litigant. Apsan argues that the organized bar has a responsibility to help meet this need, taking as its guiding principles both the need of the public to have access to legal processes and the need to be protected from those who would harm the public by providing that access in ways that would damage the public's ability to pursue legal rights with a high level of competence.

The Guilty and Unpopular   A special kind of problem arises in the area of the availability of legal services to the guilty and the unpopular. Wealthy criminals and participants in organized crime have seldom had any problem with the availability of legal services. The mere fact of their wealth has virtually guaranteed that they could find attorneys to represent them. The problem arises more in the case of the drifter, the minority, and the subversive. We might imagine the case in the small town in which there is a drifter whom "everyone knows" brutally raped and murdered a young girl. A member of the local bar is appointed by the court to represent the drifter. That attorney is, we may well imagine, in the following quandary: the client has a constitutional right to an effective defense. Yet the attorney may find the client totally repugnant and deserving of the most severe penalty that the law might render to him. Similarly, the attorney may well know that if he or she does an effective job of representing that client the people of the community may come to identify the attorney with the client's cause (and crime), and the attorney's practice, at least in that community, may be irreparably damaged.

The problem for the minority (or member of any other unpopular group) is perhaps best illustrated by the infamous story of the trials and retrials of the "Scottsboro boys" in the 1930s. At their initial hearing, the trial judge appointed the local bar collectively to provide legal assistance to the defendants. Initially, this would seem to be a highly irregular procedure. As we might expect, the result was that none of the Scottsboro attorneys took any serious responsibility for the defense. Yet we must surely ask ourselves what Southern lawyer in the 1930s, or what lawyer practicing in a small Southern town in the 1980s, would be able to continue practice if he became identified with the cause of seven young blacks accused of raping a white female.

The case of *Johns v. Smyth* provides us with a good illustration of what can happen when the attorney fails to work zealously for his or her client's interests because of the personal repugnance of that client.

Charles Wolfram, in "A Lawyer's Duty to Represent Clients, Repugnant and Otherwise," notes that the duty of the attorney to represent is essentially a variety of duty to rescue. He then goes on to identify the kinds of circumstances that define a duty to rescue, noting such factors as the "necessitousness" of the person in need of rescue, the risk to the rescuer and others, and so forth. Wolfram concludes by noting that the analysis given in his article leaves two classes of people without representation: "those whose representation would impose too great a burden on the lawyer," and those "asserting legal rights to what [Wolfram has] denominated nonessential human needs." Wolfram notes that there may be good reason to regard those exclusions as unacceptable, and that one might conclude that society should provide greater assurance of the availability of legal services to all in need of them. It is this last question that must surely be the most central issue at stake in this entire section of this chapter.

The Poor   When a good attorney charges from $100 to $150 per hour in most areas, one does not have to be poor to be legally poor. The legally poor are those who cannot afford legal services. Perhaps only those whom we would normally regard as poor would have trouble paying for the legal fees connected with a routine, uncontested divorce. As cases become more complex, however, the cost of legal services can place most of the middle class among the legally poor. The average university assistant professor, for example, would have trouble coming up with the $10,000 retainer an attorney might expect before undertaking an anti-discrimination suit against a university.

The problem of the availability of legal services to the poor is a multi-faceted problem. First, it differs considerably in the context of criminal law and that of civil law. In the criminal setting, the indigent criminal defendant can have an attorney appointed by the court. While many attorneys willingly undertake such "pro bono" work, others regard it as a serious infringement on their professional autonomy. Moreover, there is a fair amount of evidence to suggest that criminal defendants with appointed counsel regularly receive a lower quality of legal defense than do those criminal defendants who have retained counsel.

By contrast, the poor are in a far worse situation in trying to obtain counsel for civil litigation. While there are now various legal aid services available to the poor in most large metropolitan areas, such services are badly understaffed, and, of course, even these are unavailable to the poor outside of such metropolitan settings. Yet beyond this, the only way the poor can gain access to civil litigation is to be able to pay an attorney. While one can often find an attorney who will handle a very large case for a client on a contingent basis (working for a percentage of the settlement), in most cases the poor simply cannot afford civil litigation on claims that may very well, to them at least, be very substantial.

One approach to making legal services more available to the poor in certain circumstances has been the advent of group legal services. For a number of reasons, relating to such traditional concerns as client loyalty and solicitation of business, group legal services have met with a good deal of resistance from the organized bar and do raise some serious ethical concerns. A final issue that affects the availability of legal services to the poor is the existence of minimum fee schedules which have often been established by bar associations and sometimes enforced with the threat of disciplinary action against those attorneys who would work for a smaller fee. It has often been argued that such minimum fee schedules constitute an unconsitutional and immoral kind of price-fixing.

Subsection C starts with two legal opinions. *In Re Meizlish* deals with pro bono legal work. Attorney Meizlish is petitioning the court that he should be compensated for pro bono legal work at a rate equal to the bar association's minimum fee schedule. Judge Swainson, for the Supreme Court of Michigan, holds that Meizlish is not entitled to such compensation.

N.A.A.C.P. v. Button is the first great landmark case dealing with group legal services. The Virginia Conference of the N.A.A.C.P. and its

Legal Defense Fund engaged in the practice of holding meetings to find blacks who would be willing to stand as plaintiffs in desegregation cases. This practice ran afoul of the Virginia laws forbidding the solicitation of legal business. In this important case Mr. Justice Brennan, writing for the court, struck down Virginia's blanket disallowal of solicitation.

In the article that concludes the section on availability of legal services, Lester Brickman argues for a "right of universal access to courts and lawyering services." Brickman notes that without such a right of access to the courts all our other rights are without practical value. Accordingly, he argues that the bar should be regarded as a public utility rather than as a collection of private businesses. In the end, Brickman argues that the system for delivery of legal services in American society must be significantly modified so as to lessen the legal profession's monopoly over the performance of legal processes, to eliminate minimum fee schedules, to open itself to the advertising of legal services, and to seek other ways of increasing the efficiency of that delivery system.

Competence

Like every profession, the legal profession includes both competent and incompetent members. The prevalence of incompetents in the profession, however, has been the subject of considerable dispute. What all commentators on the legal profession can agree upon is that any level of incompetence in the profession detracts from the ability of the system of justice to do its job. The simple fact is that the incompetent attorney hurts his or her client and renders the accomplishment of justice less likely by that incompetence.

The issue of competence in the legal profession would seem to be joined at two points: admission to law school and to the bar, and the ongoing maintenance of competence in the attorney's practice. Whether the number of imcompetent attorneys runs as high as the 75 percent of the profession suggested by some judges (according to Mr. Chief Justice Burger's article in this chapter) or only a small fraction of that percentage, presumably society can ensure that people will have their legal affairs well tended only if it attends carefully both to the quality of those admitted to the bar and to their maintenance of the knowledge and skills required for effective legal practice throughout their careers.

One of the controversies that has arisen in recent public debate over competence, not only in the legal profession but in a broad range of occupational areas, is whether the current practice of preferential treatment of women and minorities in both hiring and school admissions has a deleterious effect on the quality of goods or services produced by those institutions that practice such preferential treatment. This section will begin with Mr. Justice Douglas's dissent in the famous case of *DeFunis v. Odegaard*. It is important to note, at the outset, that what Mr. Justice Douglas is dissenting from is the Court's decision not to hear the case.

Marco DeFunis was denied admission to the Law School of the University of Washington, despite the fact that his "Predicted First Year Average" was higher than those of 36 minority applicants who were admitted to that law school. By the time the case got to the United States Supreme

Court, DeFunis had already registered for his final semester of law school and had been assured that, whatever the case's outcome, he would be permitted to graduate. Thus, the Court ruled the case moot.

In this dissent, Mr. Justice Douglas argues that such predictive devices as the University of Washington's "Predicted First Year Average" may well fail to provide an accurate gauge of ability for many, if not most, minority students. Thus, the use of two different standards of admission, one for applicants from the dominant cultural majority and another for minority students, may very well not have the effect of diluting the quality of law school students and the subsequent effect of lowering the level of competence of those emerging from the process of legal education.

I have already mentioned criticisms made by the immediate past Chief Justice of the United States regarding the level of competence in the legal profession. Perhaps the most frequently cited source of the criticism is Mr. Chief Justice Burger's 1973 Fordham University John F. Sonnett Memorial Lecture, "The Special Skills of Advocacy: Are Specialized Training and Certification of Advocates Essential to Our System of Justice?" In that lecture, the Chief Justice argues that skilled advocacy is essential if our system of justice is in fact to accomplish much justice. He argues that the process of education and certification of lawyers does very little to determine whether the lawyer is capable of serving as a competent advocate. Law schools and bar examinations have served primarily to guarantee that prospective attorneys have a knowledge of the law, but not necessarily the skills required to use that knowledge as an effective advocate. Mr. Chief Justice Burger concludes by advocating a fourfold proposal that would, in essence, require that the organized bar develop means of distinguishing, from among all those who are graduated from law school and admitted to the bar, those who are competent to serve as advocates before the courts.

Continuing Competence   The issue of competence in the legal profession does not end with the admission of people with intelligence and skill to the bar. We also find incompetent practice of law where the attorney is simply trying to handle cases outside of his or her competency. An attorney may fail to act competently because he or she fails to keep up with the latest developments in the field, the latest legislation, and the most current definitive decisions. The attorney may also fail to act competently because of simple sloppiness. These problems of continuing competence, after one has been duly admitted to the practice of law, raise a problem quite different from those problems of competence centering around admission to law school and to the bar.

In *United States v. DeCoster*, Chief Judge Bazelon sets forth the minimum requirements which must be met by a criminal defense attorney if the client is to receive his or her constitutionally guaranteed right to effective assistance of counsel. Judge Bazelon notes that the fundamental nature of the right to competent legal representation is that one's failure to receive competent assistance may well affect a person's ability to assert any other legal rights. Given this, it must be clear that the attorney's obligation of competence is an essential condition for the satisfactory operation of the system of justice itself.

Judge James L. Oakes's "Lawyer and Judge: The Ethical Duty of Competency" focuses specifically on the problem of enforcement of the lawyer's obligation to act with competence. Judge Oakes starts out by analyzing the foundations of the duty of competence in the theoretical structure of the adversary system of justice. The difficulty, Judge Oakes notes, has been in the area of enforcement. The strictures on competence in the "Code of Professional Responsibility" are perhaps necessarily, vague. This vagueness has quite naturally led to a "virtually total lack of enforcement." Judge Oakes concludes that, whether or not the problem of imcompetent advocacy is as severe as Chief Justice Burger and some others suggest, the organized bar has a clear obligation to the public to come to a clearer definition and stricter enforcement of the duty of competence. He also examines some proposals that might serve this end.

Honesty

The final section in this chapter is concerned with honesty in the practice of law. At first blush it would seem that this should be the clearest of areas. People, including lawyers, ought to be honest in both their business and personal relationships. Yet in the broad context of adversarial proceedings it is not as clear as one might hope precisely what kind of behavior is required by the lawyer's duty of honesty. It is, for example, clearly not a violation of that duty for a criminal defense attorney to refuse to reveal to the prosecution information that he or she has that might be prejudicial to the client's case. By contrast, the prosecutor seems to have an obligation to reveal certain of his or her evidence to the defense. A more ambiguous case is the situation wherein the defense attorney, through the statements he or she makes to the press prior to trial, intentionally misleads the prosecution as to the main line of defense he or she plans to take.

Clearly the attorney who suborns perjury is in violation of the lawyer's duty of honesty. Yet where that careful line, somewhere between suborning perjury and baring one's case (one's client's soul) to the opposing attorney, should be drawn is difficult to determine.

This section starts with the cases of two attorneys, one prosecutor and one defense attorney, who find themselves on the wrong side of that line, wherever it is to be drawn. *Imbler v. Pachtman* involves the case of a prosecutor who, presumably knowingly, uses perjured testimony to secure a conviction. Imbler, the man who was convicted on the basis of that perjured evidence, brings a civil action for damages against Pachtman, the prosecutor. In this section, both Judge Koelsch's pro curiam opinion and a dissenting opinion by Judge Kilkenny are presented. While both judges agree on the absolute impropriety of Pachtman's behavior, Judge Kilkenny's dissent goes on to argue, contrary to the opinion of the court, that in his use of perjured testimony Pachtman moves outside of the performance of his legitimate judicial function. In so doing, Judge Kilkenny argues, Pachtman also thereby removes himself from the protection traditionally afforded by prosecutorial immunity.

The shoe is on the other foot in *In Re Ryder*. Here Richard Ryder, a criminal defense attorney, attempts to protect two key bits of evidence, some money stolen from a bank and a sawed-off shotgun, from the access of the prosecutor by placing it in his own safety deposit box. He then proceeds to argue that that evidence is protected on the grounds of attorney–client privilege. The court holds that, in actually transferring the evidence to his own safety deposit box, Ryder is going well beyond the limits of attorney–client privilege, is actually making himself a party to his client's criminal acts, and is thus violating his duty of honesty with the court.

Geoffrey Hazard tries to find that careful line mentioned above in "The Lawyer's Obligation to be Trustworthy when Dealing with Opposing Parties." Hazard begins by noting the benefits of trustworthiness. Aside from noting that honesty is a morally esteemed characteristic, he also sees it as "a prime aspect of social maturity." Equally important is the fact that honesty also yields significant economic advantages. When one's opponents in legal dealings can be counted upon to be honest, one can avoid the cost of conducting independent investigations to determine whether the information he or she has given is true. In economic terms, honesty tends to reduce the transaction costs of legal negotiations.

On the other hand, the ability to protect information is also important to the attorney. If the attorney were not able to protect information from opposing parties, then there would be a serious problem gaining information in the first place. Presumably one of the most important tools that the attorney has in gathering information from his or her client is the promise that that information will be kept confidential. There are many situations in which people will reveal information only under the condition that it not fall into the hands of those hostile to their interests.

Hazard goes on to note two different contexts in which the issue of lawyer honesty arises: those transactions that will lead to trial if the negotiations fail; and those transactions that, if successful, will result in some sort of contract. It is clear that honesty is of special importance in the latter type of case, since the mechanisms of the court are not available in the case of the failure of out-of-court negotiation. In the former case, while the requirements of honesty are no less significant, the extent to which honesty may require the attorney to disclose information would seem to be somewhat mitigated by the quite legitimate demands of confidentiality.

This chapter concludes with Edwin H. Auler's "Actions Against Prosecutors Who Suppress or Falsify Evidence." Auler notes the position of the old A.B.A. "Canons of Professional Ethics" on the obligations of prosecuting attorneys, which recognized that the duty of the prosecutor is to obtain justice, not necessarily conviction. As a result of this, the prosecutor is obligated not to suppress evidence that may be favorable to the defendant, much less to fabricate evidence that would be detrimental to the defendant.

Auler goes on to note that the victims of such unscrupulous prosecutorial behavior have (as was the case with Imbler) generally not been able to find remedy through civil tort actions. Auler argues, in much the same manner as the dissenting opinion in *Imbler v. Pachtman*, that civil recovery against such prosecutors should be allowed. However, he shows little optimism that such a remedy is very likely to become available.

Auler argues that, both because of the seriousness of prosecutorial dishonesty, and because of the lack of civil remedy, it becomes especially important for the organized bar to bring disciplinary action against prosecutors who suppress or falsify evidence, and that statutory provisions for the removal of such prosecutors should be used to the fullest extent. He finally notes that, in the extreme case, criminal sanctions are available, under the Civil Rights Act of 1871, against prosecutors who suppress or falsify evidence. While Auler would like to see civil tort liability imposed on prosecutors who thus abuse the power of their office, he concludes that, lacking that form of remedy, it is crucially important for society and the legal profession to use those weapons at their disposal to guarantee the integrity of the prosecutorial function.

section one

AVAILABILITY OF LEGAL SERVICES

A

Openness of the Legal Profession

Turner v. the American Bar Association

407 F. Supp. 451

Actions were filed in the United States District Courts in the States of Texas, Pennsylvania, Indiana, Minnesota, Alabama, and Wisconsin, against members of federal judiciary and others, by plaintiffs claiming a constitutional right to have unlicensed lay counsel assist them in court proceedings. The Chief Justice of the United States Supreme Court and the Chief Justice of the Fifth Circuit designated Reynaldo G. Garza, J., to sit in the cases.

* * *

On May 6, 1975, this Court held a consolidated hearing in the cases of *Turner and Daly v. American Bar Association et al., supra,* and *Turner v. Hunt et al., supra* and *United States v. Turner, supra,* in Lubbock, Texas. Represented at that hearing were the Plaintiffs Turner and Daly appearing *pro se,* and the Defendant Federal Judges, Federal Prosecutors and their agents, the State Bar of Texas and the American Bar Association, all of whom were represented by counsel. The Court listened to all that both sides had to say for several hours and every party was provided an opportunity to explain his views.

While this Court can understand from a professional point of view the judiciary's impatience with these rambling and inartfully drawn complaints which seek billions of dollars in damages from the entire judiciary,[10] the Court must respectfully disagree with those other Courts which believe that these suits are nothing more than a character assassination of the judiciary. This is so for several reasons. First, with regard to the long-winded, inconcise, and, at times, incoherent allegations of the complaint, this Court is under a duty to liberally construe pleadings filed by *pro se*

---

[10]In a case assigned to another Court, *Adams et al. v. American Bar Association et al., supra,* Footnote No. 9, many of the Defendant Judge's wives were also sued.

litigants. *Kelly v. Butler County Board of Commissioners et al.*, 399 F.2d (C.A.3, 1968); *Weaver v. Pate*, 390 F.2d 145 (C.A.7, 1968); *Eaton v. Bibb*, 217 F.2d 446 (C.A.7, 1953), cert. den., 350 U.S. 915, 76 S.Ct. 199, 100 L.Ed. 802 (1955). Second, by virtue of the Lubbock hearing, this Court is of the opinion that the Plaintiffs are sincere in their beliefs and in the questions that they are trying to raise. Third, with regard to the merits of the claims presented, this Court notes that the Plaintiffs have tangentially asserted at least two points of law which the Supreme Court has since recognized: that mandatory minimum fee schedules are violative of the Sherman Antitrust Act, *Goldfarb v. Virginia State Bar*, 421 U.S. 773, 95 S.Ct. 2004, 44 L.Ed.2d 572 (1975), and that a State cannot force counsel on an unwilling criminal defendant, *Feretta v. California*, 422 U.S. 806, 95 S.Ct. 2525, 45 L.Ed.2d 562 (1975).

This Court has read and re-read the complaints in these cases many times, as well as the Plaintiffs' Briefs which have been filed in two of these cases.[11] In the fabric of this nationwide litigation, there is but one thread that is woven and rewoven into the whole with sufficient clarity to delineate a claim: the denial by State and Federal Courts of the plaintiffs' alleged right, springing from the First, Sixth and Fourteenth Amendments, to have spokesmen of their own choice represent them in criminal and civil proceedings in Court.

This Court will consider the Plaintiffs' claim under the Sixth Amendment first. The Sixth Amendment states:

> "In all criminal prosecutions, the accused shall enjoy the right to have the Assistance of Counsel for his defense."

Through its 185-year life, the Sixth Amendment has been interpreted and applied in tens of thousands of criminal prosecutions in State and Federal Courts. Curiously enough, very few of the Appellate decisions have dealt directly with the central question in this litigation.[12] The surprising absence of controlling precedent in this area is best emphasized by the fact that the Supreme Court has just recently recognized for the first time in the history of our country the constitutional right of a defendant to defend himself without counsel in a State prosecution. See *Faretta v. California, supra.* Nor has this Court been aided to any degree by briefs of the various Defendant State Bar Association who are vitally affected by the central issue in this case.

---

[11]*Turner and Daly v. American Bar Association et al.* and *Stockheimer, Daly et al. v. American Bar Association et al.*

[12]This Court has found only two Circuit opinions that directly confronted the issue at bar. In *United States v. Cooper*, 493 F.2d 473 (C.A.5, 1974), the Fifth Circuit held that there was no right to unlicensed lay counsel, especially where the Defendant had twice rejected competent Court-appointed counsel. The fifth Circuit did not cite any authority in support of its holding. In *Guajardo v. Luna*, 432 F.2d 1324 (C.A.5, 1970), a prisoner sought to file a civil suit on behalf of his father, an illiterate who was not in prison. The State Court refused to accept the suit on the ground that only licensed attorneys were allowed to file suit.

In order to understand the concept of "counsel" as it is used in the Sixth Amendment, it is necessary to start with an understanding of the common law system as it existed in England.

The English today and for centuries past have had a bifurcated system of practice where work was divided between barristers and solicitors. The barrister enjoys the monopoly of the right of advocacy in the superior English Courts. A barrister became such by being called to the Bar by one of the Inns of Court. He was later promoted by the Inn to Reader and then to Bencher and was thereafter "selected and tacitly allowed by the Judges to practice in the Courts."[13]

The work of the solicitor most nearly corresponds to the practice of law in the United States today. The solicitor enjoys the right of advocacy in the county and Magistrates' courts, although he may not practice in the superior courts, which are the sole domain of the barrister. As between solicitor and barrister, only the solicitor may have direct contact with the client, and it is the solicitor who instructs the barrister as to the client's wishes.[14] Like the barrister, the solicitor was admitted to practice by way of invitation.

As early as the year 1285, attorneys were allowed to appear for a party as a matter of course,[15] and by 1402, the admission to practice, as to both solicitor and barrister was governed by statute:

> "For sundry Damages and Mischiefs that have ensued before this time to divers persons of the Realm by a great number of attornies, ignorant and not learned in the Law, as they were wont to be before this time; (2) it is ordained and stablished, that all attornies shall be examined by the Justices, and by their Discretions their Names put in the Roll and that they be good and vertuous, and of good Fame, shall be received and sworn well and truly to serve in their Offices, especially that they make no Suit in a foreign Country:"
> 1 Alexander, British Statutes 279 (Coe's Edition 1912).

The above cited statute demonstrates the three-sided relationship between the lawyer, the crown and the public that was the cornerstone of the practice of law in England. The practice was generally controlled by the crown for the public good. The Courts were given the particular responsibility of qualifying lawyers who practice before them on the basis of training and character. Additionally, it should be noted, as is explained in *Brooks v. Laws*, 92 U.S.App.D.C. 367, 208 F.2d 18 (1953), that the whole English process of selecting and qualifying those to practice before the Bar was in the nature of a call, and the judgments rendered thereunder were evaluations as to fitness, and not judicial decisions from which an appeal would lie. Or, stated another way, there was no unqualified right to practice law.

[13]2 Holsworth, *History of English Law* 496 (1936).
[14]Thurman et al., *The Legal Profession*, pp. 196-99 (1970).
[15]*Brasier v. Jeary*, 256, F.2d 474 at 476 (C.A.8, 1958), cert. denied 358 U.S. 867, 79 S.Ct. 97, 3 L.Ed.2d 99 (1958).

Most of the above characteristics of the legal profession were trans-
planted to colonial America and existed, in varying degrees, both prior to
and during the critical years when the Constitution and Bill of Rights were
written and passed.[16] In Massachusetts, admission to the Bar was controlled by each County Court; in Delaware, Rhode Island and Connecticut, the
local Courts controlled the admissions of lawyers, and admission by a local
Court gave the attorneys in these States the right to practice in all of the
State Courts; and in South Carolina, the highest State Appellate Court
controlled the admissions of attorneys. Following the revolution, New York
and all Federal Courts followed the Massachusetts system of admissions,
wherein an attorney had to be admitted separately by each Court wherein
he wished to practice. Later, however, some States switched to the "Delaware" method whereby admission to one State Court gave a right to practice in all State Courts.

All States required that applicants to the Bar must meet some minimal
standards, although the standards were not at all uniform. Some States had
stringent standards for admission, whereas other States eventually eliminated all requirements for admission to the Bar, except good moral
character. Notwithstanding the apparent ease with which one could enter
the practice of law in some States, one did not do so except by permission of
some governing body, and laymen did not practice law. See, generally,
Friedman, *A History of American Law* (1973), pp. 276–277.

The foregoing discussion of the roots of the American lawyer is critical to the understanding of the word "counsel" as used by the framers of
the Sixth Amendment. For centuries prior to the enactment of the Sixth
Amendment, the English forerunner of the American lawyer was called or
invited to practice for a Court only after the Court had satisfied itself that a
person was fit to practice by virtue of his character and/or training. On the
American side of the ocean, this practice continued throughout the colonial, revolutionary and post-revolutionary era of our history. Although
standards for admission were not all uniform and were not always very
stringent, the tradition of admission upon qualification continued to exist
from even the earliest times of the American legal experience. This Court
cannot find even a suggestion in the history of the Common Law after its
primeval inception or in the history of the American lawyer that the word
"counsel," as used in the Sixth Amendment, was meant to include a layman
off the street without qualification as to either training or character.[17]

[16]The graded division between Barristers and Solicitors did not long survive in the
colonies. Friedman, *A History of American Law* (1973), p. 276. Additionally, it should be noted
that American Courts recognized that a Court's decision as to fitness and qualifications to
practice was in the nature of a judicial decision from which an appeal would lie. *Baird v.
Arizona State Bar Association*, 401 U.S. 1, 91 S.Ct. 702, 27 L.Ed.2d 639 (1970); *Ex parte Garland*,
71 U.S. (4 Wall.) 333, 18 L.Ed. 366 (1866).

[17]In *Faretta v. California, supra.* the Supreme Court at Footnote 16, therein, points out
that the very first lawyers were indeed laymen:

> "The first lawyers were personal friends of the litigant, brought
> into court by him so that he might 'take [counsel] with them' before
> pleading. 1 Pollock & Maitland, *History of English Law* 211 (1909).
> Similarly the first 'attorneys' were personal agents, often lacking

This Court's interpretation of the word "counsel" enjoys ample and consistent support of case law. *McKinzie v. Ellis*, 287 F.2d 549 (C.A.5, 1961); *Harrison v. United States*, 128 U.S.App.D.C. 245, 387 F.2d 203 (1967); *Guajardo v. Luna, supra; United States v. Stockheimer*, 385 F.Supp. 979 (W.D. Wisc., 1974). It is recognized that "the practice of law is affected with a public interest and an attorney at law, as distinguished from a layman, has both public and private obligations, being sworn to act with all good fidelity toward both his client and the court." *United States v. Onan*, 190 F.2d 1 (C.A.8, 1951).[18] Although the Supreme Court has refused to pass on the question of whether the practice of law is a right versus a privilege, *Schware v. Board of Examiners*, 353 U.S. 232 at 239, note 5, 77 S.Ct. 752, 1 L.Ed.2d 796 (1957), it has consistently held that the public interest is of sufficient magnitude in this area to allow the legislative arm of the State to prescribe reasonable qualifications for entry into the profession.[19] *Ex parte Garland, supra; Schware v. Board of Examiners, supra; Konigsberg v. State Bar*, 353 U.S. 252, 77 S.Ct. 722, 1 L.Ed.2d 810 (1956); *Baird v. State Bar of Arizona, supra.* There has been sharp conflict as to the limits of reasonable qualification, *Baird v. State Bar of Arizona, supra*, at 2, but this Court has not found any case which has called into the question the centuries-old power of the State in the first instance to set minimal standards for entry into the profession. Indeed, the most recent pronouncement from the Supreme Court solidly reaffirmed the compelling interests that States have in the regulation of the practice of professions within their boundaries. *Goldfarb v. Virginia State Bar, supra.*

Since the beginnings of our nation there has been statutory authority to enforce the rights recognized in the Sixth Amendment. 28 U.S.C.A. § 1654, formerly codified as § 35 of the Judiciary Act of 1789, 1 Stat. 73, 92 and later as 28 U.S.C.A. § 394, provides that:

> "In all of the Courts of the United States, the parties may plead and manage their own causes personally or by the assistance of such counsel or attorneys at law . . ."

This Court has found no case which has interpreted this statute so as to allow an unlicensed layman to represent a party other than himself in a civil or criminal proceeding. Indeed, in a variety of different applications of this

---

any professional training, who were appointed by those litigants who had secured royal permission to carry on their affairs through a representative, rather than personally. Id. at 212-213."

Note, however, that permission of the Crown was still needed. As is apparent from the aforecited English statutes, the requirement of qualification soon became the order of the day.

[18]Cert. denied 342 U.S. 869, 72 S.Ct. 112, 96 L.Ed. 654 (1951).

[19]Because they represent distinct jurisdictions, the State and Federal Courts may have different requirements for admission to the practice of law before them. Generally, however, the Federal Court adopts or defers to the admission requirements of the State in which the Federal Court is located. The following Rule 1 B of The Local Rules of the United States District Court for the Southern District of Texas is typical. [Rule omitted, along with a statement of the corresponding rule for the United States District Court for the Northern District of Indiana.]

statute, the Courts have consistently held that unlicensed individuals may not represent other parties in Federal Court under this Statute. In *In re Looney*, 262 F. 209 (W.D.Tex., 1920), the District Court, on reviewing the decision of a Referee in Bankruptcy to not allow an attorney-in-fact to examine the bankrupt at the first meeting of the creditors, held that the clear implication of the statute excluded from the Court all other agents, attorneys-in-fact and proxies other than attorneys and counselors at law, and that it was a universal practice to exclude such non-licensed people from practicing in court. In *Heiskel v. Mozie*, 65 App.D.C. 255, 82 F.2d 861 (1936), a realty dealer acting as the owner's rental agent for a percentage-of-rent collected filed a *pro se* suit in Municipal Court in Washington, D.C., claiming that the tenant had defaulted and seeking recovery of the premises. The suit was opposed by a "friend of the Court" who moved the complaint be dismissed and the *pro se* Plaintiff be held in contempt of court for violating Local Rule 22 requiring that only members of the Bar of the Supreme Court of the District of Columbia shall be allowed to represent parties in the Court. The *pro se* petitioner was held in contempt and appealed. On appeal, the District of Columbia Circuit held that the petitioner was not, by virtue of his job as a rental agent, a party at interest. Hence, he could not file a *pro se* suit. Additionally, the Court noted that the *pro se* petitioner was not an attorney at law and emphasized that neither his ability nor his character had been examined. The Appellate Court held that he was properly held in contempt, as 28 U.S.C.A. § 1654 allowed only parties at interest or attorneys to litigate in the Federal Courts.

Corporations and partnerships, both of which are fictional legal persons, obviously cannot appear for themselves personally. With regard to these two types of business associations, the long-standing and consistent court interpretation of § 1654 is that they must be represented by licensed counsel. In *S. Stern & Company v. United States*, 331 F.2d 310, 51 C.C.P.A. 15 (1963),[20] the Court of Customs and Patent Appeals held that 12 U.S.C.A. § 1654 would not allow a lay partnership to represent the partnership in a judicial proceeding. Likewise, there is a long line of cases starting with *Osborn v. Bank of the United States*, 9 Wheat, (22 U.S. 738), 6 L.Ed. 204, and continuing through *Commercial & Railroad Bank of Vicksburg v. Slocomb*, 14 Pet. (39 U.S. 60), 10 L.Ed. 354 (1840); *Nightingale v. Oregon Central Railway Company*, 18 Fed.Cas. No 10,264, p. 239; *Brandstein v. White Lamps*, 20 F. Supp. 369 (S.D.N.Y., 1937); *MacNeil v. Hearst Corp.*, 160 F.Supp. 157 (Del., 1958); and *Flora Construction Company v. Fireman's Fund Insurance Company*, 307 F.2d 413 (C.A.10, 1962), which have held that under 28 U.S.C.A. § 1654 and its predecessor statutes a corporation may only be represented by a licensed counsel. Several of these cases, particularly *Nightingale, Hearst,* and *White Lamps,* have emphasized the importance of the centuries-old concept of a Court having a lawyer before it who has been qualified to practice, and who is subject to the Court's control. The long-standing interpretation of § 1654, as applied to partnerships and corporations, is particularly relevant to one of the Plaintiff's claims which is that some of them

---

[20]Cert. denied 377 U.S. 909, 84 S.Ct. 1169, 12 L.Ed.2d 179 (1964).

have speech impediments and are unable to represent themselves . . . . Corporations and partnerships, by their very nature, are unable to represent themselves and the consistent interpretation of § 1654 is that the only proper representative of a corporation or a partnership is a licensed attorney, not an unlicensed layman regardless of how close his association with the partnership or corporation.

The same statute has been given a similar interpretation with regard to *pro se* litigants attempting to represent other litigants. In *McShane v. United States*, 366 F.2d 286 (C.A.9, 1966), a *pro se* petitioner filed what he designated as a Class Action, in which he was appearing for himself and was purporting to act on behalf of all other members of the class. The Ninth Circuit held that while he could act on his own behalf, since he was not an attorney he could not represent anyone else, as the privileges granted to him under § 1654 were personal to him.

From the foregoing analysis of the history of the practice of law, both in England and in the United States, this Court concludes that there is insubstantial historical support for the Plaintiffs' contention that they have a right to have an unlicensed layman assist them under the guise of the Sixth Amendment. This Court further concludes that 28 U.S.C.A. § 1654, which was enacted to enforce the Sixth Amendment's guarantees to right to counsel, only allows for two types of representation: that by an attorney admitted to the practice of law by a governmental regulatory body and that by a person representing himself. The statute does not allow for unlicensed laymen to represent anyone else other than themselves.

The Court wishes to note that the Plaintiffs have themselves wholly failed to provide this Court with any convincing authority, aside from the sincerity of their own beliefs, that the word "counsel," as used in the Sixth Amendment, includes unlicensed laymen within its ambit. The Plaintiffs have by brief (*Turner and Daly v. American Bar Association et al., supra*) argued that what they are seeking is an "assistant" to speak for them in various legal proceedings in Court. As defined in their brief, "assistant" is a person "who assists or serves in a subordinate position as a helper, a person who aids." Brief, p. 30. They argue that a right to have an assistant is also concomitant with the rights to peacefully assemble and to petition the government for redress of grievances as guaranteed by the First Amendment. They have additionally argued that their right has already been recognized by virtue of the ruling of United States District Judge James Doyle in *United States v. Stockheimer*, 385 F.Supp. 979 (W.D.Wisc., 1974). There Stockheimer, a Defendant in a criminal proceeding and a Plaintiff in one of the cases pending before this Court, filed a Motion to have Jerome Daly and Gordon Peterson, two disbarred Minnesota attorneys, assist him in his defense. In a very clearly written opinion, Judge Doyle held that in the absence of any constitutional or federal statutory provision compelling him to either forbid or not to forbid the Defendant such assistance, he would exercise his discretion in the matter and allow Stockheimer the assistance of Gordon Peterson in his criminal trial. Judge Doyle was careful to note that he was not recognizing a right of the Defendant Stockheimer, but was merely, within his discretion, granting the Defendant Stockheimer a request which Judge Doyle did not find was forbidden or prohibited by the Constitution or by Federal statutes.

In the cases at bar, the Plaintiffs, of course, are seeking much more than a discretionary grant of their request; they are seeking to have this Court elevate to the status of a constitutional right their desire to have an unlicensed layman assist them and perform functions in Court ordinarily performed by licensed attorneys.

Furthermore, this Court cannot accept the contention that even if the word "counsel," as used in the Sixth Amendment, does not include unlicensed laymen, a Defendant would still have the right to have an unlicensed lay assistant as an attorney under the banner of conducting one's own defense. Arguably, there is dicta in higher Court opinions, such as the following language from *Adams v. United States ex rel. McCann*, 317 U.S. 269 at 275, 63 S.Ct. 236 at 240, 87 L.Ed. 268 (1942), which plausibly supports Plaintiff's contentions that a litigant may have an unlicensed assistant in the conduct of his own defense: "The short of the matter is that an accused, in the exercise of a free and intelligent choice, . . . may competently and intelligently waive his Constitutional right to assistance of counsel. There is nothing in the Constitution to prevent an accused from [following] the guidance of his own wisdom and not that of a lawyer." Arguably, a knowing and intelligent defendant might think that the best way for him to "manage his own defense" would be to have an unlicensed layman represent him in Court. Such a choice becomes even more attractive if the defendant believes that the members of the Bar are in a conspiracy against him to deprive him of his rights, as well as line their own pockets with their monopolistic profits, as is alleged in the cases at bar. Plaintiff's contention is minimally supported by language in *Faretta, supra*, where the Supreme Court, for the first time, formally recognized that the Sixth Amendment inherently allows the Defendant to manage his own defense: "Although he may conduct his own defense, ultimately to his own detriment, his choice must be honored out of 'the respect for the individual which is the lifeblood of that law.' " 422 U.S. at 834, 95 S.Ct. at 2541.

The problem with this contention is obvious and becomes most apparent when carried to its logical conclusion. Allowing a defendant to have his own unlicensed counsel represent him out of respect for his right to manage his own defense under the Sixth Amendment would amount to a wholesale authorization of the lay practice of law. For the Court to recognize the right of a defendant to defend himself in his own person is one thing. It is quite another thing to allow him to bring unqualified and untrained people off the street to conduct his defense.

In appropriate circumstances, a Federal Judge may, of course, allow a defendant to proceed with a lay assistant or to orally assist his licensed counsel in the presentation of his case, as was done by the undersigned in *United States v. Gaar* . . . . This is so because of the inherent power lodged in a Federal Judge to govern and control the conduct of the trial before him. *Herron v. Southern Pacific Company*, 283 U.S. 91, 51 S.Ct. 383, 75 L.Ed. 857 (1931); *Lefton v. City of Hattiesburg*, 333 F.2d 280 (C.A.5, 1964).

The Plaintiffs have also attempted to couch their right to have unlicensed laymen represent them in Court in terms of the First Amendment guarantees of freedom of association and right to petition their government for redress of grievances. An alliance between a defendant, or plaintiff for that matter, and an unlicensed layman for the purpose of litigation in Court is an association which has as its end the redress of grievances. Hence, the argument goes, the First Amendment guarantees the right of the Plaintiffs to have unlicensed attorneys in Court. In support of their position, they have cited to this Court *NAACP v. Button*, 371 U.S. 415, 83 S.Ct. 328, 9 L.Ed.2d 405 (1963); *Brotherhood of Railway Trainmen v. Virginia State Bar Association*, 377 U.S. 1, 84 S.Ct. 1113, 12 L.Ed.2d 89 (1964); *United Mine Workers v. Illinois State Bar Association*, 389 U.S. 217, 88 S.Ct. 353, 19 L.Ed.2d 426 (1967); and *United Transportation Union v. State Bar of Michigan*, 401 U.S. 576, 91 S.Ct. 1076, 28 L.Ed.2d 339 (1971). These cases did not involve the question of securing redress of grievances in Court by unlicensed counsel. Rather, they held that collective activity undertaken to obtain meaningful access to the Courts is a fundamental right within the protection of the first Amendment, and that a State cannot, under its unauthorized practice of law statutes or solicitation of legal business statutes, prohibit such activity. This Court is not today holding that the Plaintiffs must disband their organization or cease to espouse their cause in the Appellate Courts. Nor is this Court holding that these Plaintiffs may not represent themselves individually in Court. What this Court is holding is that the Constitution of the United States, in particular the First and Sixth Amendments, does not grant to the Plaintiffs the right to have an unlicensed layman represent them in Court proceedings. The corollary of this holding is that unlicensed laymen cannot under the Constitution demand the right to represent other litigants.

The Plaintiffs have cited the case of *Thomas v. Collins*, 323 U.S. 516, 65 S.Ct. 315, 89 L.Ed. 430 (1944), in support of their proposition that the State cannot "license speech." In *Thomas v. Collins*, Thomas, a vice-president of the CIO, was visiting Texas to deliver a speech to the employees of Humble Oil and Refining Company's plant near Baytown, Texas. One of the purposes of the meeting was to encourage non-union members to join a local union which had already organized some employees at the Baytown plant. The Texas Legislature had just passed a law requiring all labor organizers to register with the Secretary of State and obtain an organizer's card prior to conducting any membership activities in the State. The District Court of Travis County issued a Temporary Restraining Order prior to Thomas' speech prohibiting him from giving his speech until he obtained an organizing card. After the Order was served, Thomas addressed a meeting of workers, and at the end of the speech asked persons present to join the union. He was later arrested, held in contempt, fined and sentenced to a short term of imprisonment. The Supreme Court, in striking down Thomas' contempt conviction, held that the State regulation of labor unions, which is a legitimate State interest, in this particular instance partially infringed upon Thomas' First Amendment rights of free speech and free assembly. The facts alone in this case distinguish it from the cases at bar. This case did not involve the right to representation by an unlicensed lay attorney in Court under the guise of free speech or free assembly. In fact, the proposition for which the Plaintiffs are trying to cite this case—the right to conduct the business of unlicensed lay representation of litigants in Court—is directly rebutted by the concurring opinion of Mr. Justice Jackson, wherein he states: "A State may forbid one without license to practice law as a vocation, but I think it could not stop an unlicensed person from making a speech about the rights of man or the rights of labor, or any other kind of right, including recommending that his hearers organize to support his views. Likewise, the state may prohibit the pursuit of medicine as an occupation without its license, but I do not think it could make it a crime publicly or privately to speak urging persons to follow or reject any school of medical thought." *Thomas v. Collins, supra,* at 544, 65 S.Ct. at 329.

Having found that there is no constitutional right to unlicensed counsel, this Court now turns its attention to the various causes of action stated by the Plaintiffs.

In *Perma Life Mufflers v. Intn'l Parts Corp.*, 392 U.S. 134, 88 S.Ct. 1981, 20 L.Ed.2d 982 (1968), the Supreme Court pointed out that the purposes of the antitrust laws are best served by the ever-present threat of private actions. This does not mean, however, that every private citizen may act as a sentinel to the private good by asserting general violations. *SCM Corp. v. RCA*, 407 F.2d 166 (C.A.2, 1969), cert. den. 395 U.S. 943, 89 S.Ct. 2014, 23 L.Ed.2d 577 (C.A.3, 1974).[21] To have standing to sue, the Plaintiff must sufficiently allege and demonstrate that his *legally cognizable business or property* has been injured as a proximate result of the alleged violation of the antitrust laws. *Winckler & Smith Citrus Products v. Sunkist Growers, Inc.*, 346 F.ed 1012 (C.A.9, 1965), cert. den., 382 U.S. 958, 86 S.Ct. 433, 15 L.Ed.2d 362; *Martin v. Phillips Petroleum Co.*, 365, F.2d 629 (C.A.5, 1966), cert. den. 385 U.S. 991, 87 S.Ct. 600, 17 L.Ed.2d 451; *Waldron v. British Petroleum Co.*, 231 F.Supp. 72 (S.C.N.Y., 1964).[22] This Court is convinced that the Plaintiffs wholly lack standing to bring this private antitrust suit for the reason that the Plaintiffs have failed to demonstrate that there is in fact any property or business, present or future, that is deserving of legal protection. The Plaintiffs state that the nature of their business is traveling in interstate commerce to represent each other before agencies of the federal government, and in particular the courts of the United States, as "attorneys" "licensed" only by the people that they will be representing.

As there exists no right or privilege under the First or Sixth Amendments to have an unlicensed layman represent a party in litigation, this Court must conclude that the corresponding "business" of laymen representing litigants in court does not exist or at least is not deserving of the legal protection of the antitrust laws. Consequently, the Plaintiffs lack standing to bring this antitrust action against any of the named Defendants. All of the Defendants' Motions to Dismiss for failure to state a claim upon which relief can be granted, with respect to the antitrust claims, are hereby granted.

[21]Cert. denied 419 U.S. 868, 95 S.Ct. 126, 42 L.Ed.2d 106 (1974).

[22]See also *Jeffrey v. Southwestern Bell*, 518 F.2d 1129 (C.A.5, 1975), and *M.C. Manufacturing Company v. Texas Foundries, Inc.*, 517 F.2d 1059 (C.A.5, 1975).

The Court here wishes to specially note that it is aware of both the numerous allegations concerning fixed legal fees and the recent Supreme Court case of *Goldfarb v. Virginia State Bar, supra*. In *Goldfarb*, the Supreme Court found that mandatory minimum fee schedules for title searches were within the ambit of the antitrust laws and that State regulation of the integrated Virginia State Bar which encouraged the minimum fee system did not in and of itself qualify the Virginia State Bar for the *Parker v. Brown* exemption.[23] Except for *Taylor v. Montgomery et al.*, none of the cases at bar involve any plaintiffs who have alleged sufficiently delineated claims of purchases of legal services at a fixed rate. If anything, the thrust of these complaints is to the contrary: Plaintiffs want to utilize lay counsel who do not operate within the structure of a bar organization. It is elementary that a plaintiff who does not purchase or wish to purchase the goods or services which he claims are being marketed in violation of the antitrust laws lacks standing to assert the alleged violations. *SCM Corp. v. RCA, supra; Rea v. Ford Motor Co., supra*. All of the Plaintiffs, with the exception of Loran Taylor, in the cases at bar are without standing to assert any violation of the antitrust laws flowing from the existence of alleged fixed legal fees.

In *Taylor v. Montgomery*, the Plaintiff Taylor has sufficiently set forth facts which may entitle him to relief under the *Goldfarb* decision. Plaintiff Taylor states that he was forced to purchase legal services from a licensed attorney at an unreasonably high and fixed price. However, in this particular suit the Plaintiff has not sued anyone from which he could obtain relief. In particular he has not sued the lawyer that he hired at a fixed fee nor has he sued any bar association. Consequently, his cause of action based on price fixing must be dismissed for failure to state a claim upon which relief can be granted.[24]

* * *

All requested relief not specifically granted or denied herein is hereby denied.

A judgment is this day being entered dismissing all of the above entitled and numbered lawsuits and dropping them from the docket of the respective Courts.

---

[23]Prior to the Supreme Court's decision in *Goldfarb*, the three integrated Defendant State Bar Associations in these cases, the State Bar of Texas, the Alabama State Bar and the Wisconsin State Bar, could have claimed the *Parker v. Brown* exemption. In light of this Court's resolution of the substantive issues in these cases, it is unnecessary for the Court to determine the present status of the *Parker v. Brown* exemption.

[24]In the other two suits at bar in which Loran Taylor is a Plaintiff, *Taylor and Daly v. American Bar Association et al.* and *Pendell, Pendell and Taylor v. American Bar Association et al.*, the Plaintiff Taylor does not allege that he was forced to purchase legal services at an unreasonably high fixed fee.

Hackin v. Lockwood

UNITED STATES COURT OF APPEALS NINTH CIRCUIT
361 F.2D 499 (1966)

BARNES, Circuit Judge:
This is an appeal from a final judgment of the United States District Court for the District of Arizona, granting appellee's motion to dismiss, and dismissing the cause of action and appellant's complaint and amended complaint as to all appellees.

The dismissal was "for the reasons stated in the Court's opinion of August 2, 1965." That opinion was not published and does not appear in the record before us.

Appellant, appearing in propria persona, is a graduate of a school of law *not* "provisionally or fully approved by the American Bar Association at the time of his graduation." By subdivision 6 of Rule IV of the "Rules Pertaining to Admission of Applicants to the State Bar of Arizona," as amended November 5, 1962, appellant must be a graduate of such an accredited school before he can take the Arizona Bar examinations.

Other restrictions prescribed by the same rules are that each applicant must be:

1.   Over twenty-one years of age.
2.   A bona fide resident of Arizona six months or a graduate of the University of Arizona.
3.   A citizen of the United States.
4.   Of good moral character.
5.   Mentally and phsyically able to engage in active and continuous practice.

* * *

7.   If entitled to practice in another state, in good standing there.

Appellant sued below under Title 28, United States Code, Section 1343(3) which authorizes a civil action in district courts by any person:

> "To redress the deprivation, under color of any State law, statute, ordinance, regulation, custom or usage, of any right, privilege or immunity secured by the Constitution of the United States or by any Act of Congress providing for equal rights of citizens or of all persons within the jurisdiction of the United States."

This court has jurisdiction on appeal. 28 U.S.C. § 1291.

The purpose of the section quoted is to enforce the Fourteenth Amendment to the Constitution (*Davis v. Foreman*, 251 F.2d 421 (7th Cir.), cert. den. 356 U.S. 974, 78 S.Ct. 1137, 2 L.Ed.2d 1148 (1958)), which provides that "No State shall make or enforce any law which shall abridge the privileges * * * of citizens of the United States; nor shall any State deprive any person of * * * property, without due process of law; nor deny to any person * * * the equal protection of the laws."

Appellant urges three questions are involved:

I.   Whether appellant's rights under the Fourteenth Amendment are violated by the aforesaid rules restriction?

II. Whether the United States District Court had jurisdiction to give the relief prayed?

III. Whether the State Bar Committee and the Justices of the Arizona Supreme Court, in promulgating and administering such rules, acted arbitrarily, capriciously, unreasonably, and without factual foundation?

Conceding in his statement of issues that a classification of applicants is permissible, if the basis for such classification be reasonable, appellant contends the classification here made, for the reasons given ("to protect the public against unethical or incompetent practitioners") is unreasonable.

* * *

III

Is subdivision 6 of Rule IV (the admission requirement of graduation from an accredited law school) reasonable, and therefore not violative of the Fourteenth Amendment?

Just as the Supreme Court in *Schware, infra*, refused (353 U.S. at 239 n. 5, 77 S.Ct. at 756) to go into any discussion whether the practice of the law is a "right" or a "privilege," we need not do so. In either event, any restriction on such practice must be valid, i.e., reasonable. (Compare *Lathrop v. Donohue*, 367 U.S. 820, 844 S.Ct. 1826, 6 L.Ed.2d 1191 (1961).)

We agree with appellant that for the requirement to be reasonable it must not be arbitrary; the reason for the prevention of practice must be valid. *Power Manufacturing Co. v. Saunders*, 274 U.S. 490, 493, 47 S.Ct. 678, 71 L.Ed. 1165 (1927).

"A State can require high standards of qualification, such as good moral character or proficiency in its law, before it admits an applicant to the bar, but any qualification must have a rational connection with the applicant's fitness to practice law." *Schware v. Board of Bar Examiners*, 353 U.S. 232, 239, 77 S.Ct. 752, 1 L.Ed.2d 796 (1957).

Any classification can, in a sense, be claimed arbitrary. Is it arbitrary or unreasonable for Arizona to require that an extraordinarily bright legal student, twenty years of age, who has graduated from an accredited law school, wait until he is twenty-one before he can take the examination? We think not. Knowledge may be acquired early by a bright and assiduous student, but the odds are that his judgment will not be so soon acquired. It would be entirely possible, of course, were we to envision a twenty year old law school graduate, that his judgment would be as good or better than one who graduates at twenty-five, but it is probable that it would not.

> "To a wide and deep extent, the law depends upon the disciplined standards of the profession and belief in the integrity of the courts [in prescribing rules of admission]. We cannot fail to accord such confidence to the state process, and we must attribute to its courts the exercise of a fair and not a biased judgment in passing upon the applications of those seeking entry into the profession." Mr. Justice Frankfurter, concurring in *Schware v. Board of Bar Examiners*, 353 U.S. at 249, 77 S.Ct. at 761.

That this high respect for the action of the various State Supreme Courts in determining who should practice law within their respective states is properly a strong factor to be considered in determining whether there has been a Fourteenth Amendment denial of due process and equal protection, is amply demonstrated by the trilogy of 1961 decisions of the Supreme Court of the United States in this field. See the second *Konigsberg* case— *Konigsberg v. State Bar*, 366 U.S. 36, 81 S.Ct. 997, 6 L.Ed.2d 105 (1961); *In re Anastaplo*, 366 U.S. 82, 81 S.Ct. 978, 6 L.Ed.2d 135 (1961); and *Cohen v. Hurley*, 366 U.S. 117, 81 S.Ct. 954, 6 L.Ed.2d 156 (1961).

In the last named case, at 366 U.S. 129, 81 S.Ct. 962, the majority opinion emphasizes:

> "The issue is not, of course, *Whether* lawyers are entitled to due process of law in matters of this kind, but, rather, *what* process is constitutionally due them in such circumstances. We do not hold that lawyers, because of their special status in society, can *therefore* be deprived of constitutional rights assured to others, but only, as in all cases of this kind, that what procedures are fair, what state process is constitutionally due, what distinctions are consistent with the right to equal protection, all depend upon the particular situation presented, and that history is surely relevant to these inquiries.[11]

* * *

11Of course it is not alone the early beginning of the practice of judicial inquiry into attorney practices which is significant upon the reasonableness of what transpired here. Rather it is the long life of that mode of procedure which bears upon that issue, in much the same way that a strong consensus of views in the States is relevant to a finding of fundamental unfairness.

* * *

While none of these cases deal with restrictions based on legal study, we cannot conclude that all educational restrictions are unlawful. We assume that few would deny that a grammar school education requirement, before taking the bar examination, was reasonable. Or that an applicant had to be able to read or write. Once we conclude that *some* restriction is proper, then it becomes a matter of degree—the problem of drawing the line.

In determining whether Arizona's educational requirement is arbitrary, the fact that Abraham Lincoln and Dean Roscoe Pound had no, or little, formal legal schooling is interesting, but not conclusive. Prior to the time restrictions on admission to the bar became almost universal, for every successful lawyer who had had no formal legal training, there have been scores of incompetent lawyers practicing law, to the detriment of the public. No lawyer who has donated his time and effort to bar disciplinary proceedings can conclude otherwise.

Roscoe Pound (the example named by appellant herein as one without *formal* legal education) was himself a member of the 1913 Committee of the American Bar Association that induced the Carnegie Foundation to survey all the law schools of this country, and to evaluate the matter of admission to the bar in the various states of the entire country. Published early in 1921,[2] it had a tremendous effect on the adoption of the American Bar Association's accreditation rule, adopted later in 1921. This was approved by the Association of American Law Schools. In urging its adoption, the Honorable Elihu Root described the vast complications of the then statutory enactments (increased many fold since 1921) as "a wilderness of laws with a wilderness of adjudications that no man can follow—[which] require not less but more ability; not less but more learning; not less but more intellectual training in order to advise an honest man as to what his rights are and in order to get his rights for him.

Even the State of Georgia, long known as the "easiest" state in which to become a lawyer (and the only state where for years no legal or prelegal study was required before a taking of the bar examination), set up the requirement of a high school education or its equivalent, as of July 1, 1952. Approximately one half of the states in the Union have similar if not identical requirements to those of Arizona.

2Training for the Public Profession of the Law (Carnegie Foundation for the Advancement of Teaching, 1921).

But whatever the various states, in their respective wisdom, may require before allowing the taking of bar examinations—so long as they are applicable to every citizen alike, it should be of no concern to the federal courts.[3]

We conclude the funadmental question here is whether Rule IV, Section 6 of the Rules Pertaining to Admission of Applicants to the State Bar of Arizona is "arbitrary, capricious and unreasonable." We conclude an educational requirement of graduation from an accredited law school is not. *Rosenthal v. State Bar Examining Committee*, 116 Conn. 409, 165 S. 211, 87 A.L.R. 991 (1933); *Henington v. State Board of Bar Examiners*, 60 N.M. 393, 291 P.2d 1108 (1956); State ex rel. *Ralston v. Turner*, 141 Neb. 556, 4 N.W.2d 302, 144 A.L.R. 138 (1942).

The judgment of the district court is affirmed.

[3]We refer to Chapter VII, The Accreditation of Law Schools by Homer D. Crotty, Esq., of the Los Angeles Bar Association, appearing in the volume "Bar Examinations and Requirements for Admission to the Bar" (1952).

In it, he quotes from the brilliant 1938 survey of the Law Schools of Tennessee:

> " 'The law is a public profession and, therefore, legal education must be considered from the public, rather than the private, viewpoint. However anxious an individual is to set up a law school, whether for profit or for pleasure or for other reasons, he should not do so unless that school or class or study group can reasonably be expected to turn out products which will be a credit to the profession, having in view the public's interest in it. This means every school should be required to meet reasonable standards such as the court may lay down and which, when announced, should be enforced. Qualifications for admission to the bar as well as standards for law school should be determined by the public interest. If it be said that higher standards in Tennessee would bar some poor boys from becoming lawyers, is not the logical answer that standards for law school and for admission to the bar must be determined on the basis of what is in the public interest and not on the rights of any individual to become a member of any given profession or calling without being adequately prepared to fulfill its obligations? This is the standard which has been applied successfully in the medical profession and it is equally applicable in law. A standard set to meet every possible condition of poverty is no standard at all. No one, rich or poor, should consider himself entitled to admission to any profession without meeting fair professional standards. It is impossible to place a hurdle low enough to accommodate every underprivileged person, and yet place a bar to the unworthy ones who look upon the law as an easy way to a position where one may live by his wits and prey upon the public.' "

Assisting the Pro Se Litigant: Unauthorized Practice of Law or the Fulfillment of a Public Need?

MOSES APSAN

INTRODUCTION

Pro se[1] representation is firmly embedded in American jurisprudence,[2] yet, for a lay person, this conceptual right is but a meaningless truism without the corresponding abilities to see through a legal maze and use the complicated procedural mechanisms necessary to vindicate that right. This dilemma, when accompanied by the spiraling costs of legal services, has created a fertile environment for the emergence of prepublished form packages and services designed to facilitate routine legal matters.[3] In many jurisdictions, however, the availability of inexpensive printed or clerical assistance has been severely limited by bar-initiated litigation brought under statutes proscribing the unauthorized practice of law.[4]

* * *

New York Law School Law Review, 28 (1983), 691, 717–24. Reprinted by permission

[1]Pro se has been defined as ""appearing for oneself, as in the case of one who does not retain a lawyer and appears for himself in court." *Black Law Dictionary*, 1099 (rev. 5th ed. 1979).

[2]In *Faretta v. California*, 422 U.S. 806 (1975), the Supreme Court affirmed the constitutional right of all persons to represent themselves in court proceedings. The Court held that a defendant in a state criminal trial has a constitutional right to proceed without counsel when he voluntarily and intelligently elects to do so. *Id.* at 807. The *Faretta* Court, in emphasizing that an attorney is merely an assistant who helps a citizen protect his legal rights and present his case to the courts, stated that ""(t)he language and spirit of the Sixth Amendment contemplate that counsel, like the other defense tools guaranteed by the Amendment, shall be an aid to a willing defendant— not an organ of the State interposed between an unwilling defendant and his right to defend himself personally." *Id* at 820. The Court further stated that the right of self-representation is supported by the sixth amendment, as well as by the colonial and English jurisprudence from which the amendment emerged. *Id.* at 818. *See Florida Bar v. Brumbaugh*, 355 So. 2d 1186, 1192 (Fla. 1978) (the right to self-representation is constitutionally protected).

[3]One can readily find numerous examples of these form packages and services which are available to the public, by glancing through the newspapers. *See*, e.g., *N.Y. Daily News*, Oct. 29, 1982, at M15, col. 1-2.

[4]*See*, e.g., *Florida Bar v. Furman*, 376 So. 2d 378 (Fla. 1979) (on petition of the Florida Bar, the court permanently enjoined Furman, a nonlawyer, from engaging in the unauthorized practice of law by giving legal advice and by rendering legal services in connection with the sale of "do-it-yourself divorce kits" and adoptions), *appeal dismissed*, 444 U.S. 1066

VI. NON-LEGAL RESOURCES: A RATIONAL APPROACH; THE AMERICAN BAR ASSOCIATION RECOMMENDATION

From 1967, in *New York County Lawyers Association v. Dacey*,[171] to 1978, in *Florida Bar v. Brumbaugh*,[172] courts have systematically modified their earlier decisions to conform to the changing needs of the public. Similarly, the ABA has gone through a parallel phase and recently appointed a special committee to conduct a survey to determine the legal needs of the American population.[173] A "Final Report" was published in 1978, containing a review of empirical data and offering suggestions and conclusions.[174]

Unlike the committee created during the Depression era to prevent flagrant unauthorized practice,[175] this *Final Report* committee recognized that "many kinds of legal problems are amenable to effective resolution through self-help or the use of appropriate resources other than lawyers."[176] A large number of the surveyed members made extensive use of nonlawyer resources such as bankers and real estate brokers because of their presumed superior knowledge in specific areas of law.[177] The committee noted that there is an "essential rationality" in these decisions which "ought to be recognized" and asserted that the ABA has "unduly limited" the effective use of non-legal resources.[178] In view of this the committee made three innovative recommendations: (1) the Bar should put more emphasis on responsibilities that go beyond surveillance of unauthorized

---

(1980); *Florida Bar v. Brumbaugh*, 355 So. 2d 1186 (Fla. 1978) (while one may sell sample legal forms and printed material explaining legal practice and procedure to the public, one may not advise clients as to the various remedies available . . . .)

. . . *In Florida Bar v. Furman*, 376 So. 2d 378 (Fla. 1978), a secretary-paralegal, whose business was to prepare forms for matrimonial dissolution, was found to be engaged in the unauthorized practice of law. The court mandated The Florida Bar Association "to begin immediately a study to determine better ways and means of providing legal services to the indigent." *Id.* at 382. The report, entitled "The Legal Needs of the Poor and Underepresented Citizens of Florida: An Overview," written by the Center for Governmental Responsibility, Holland Law Center, University of Florida, in 1980, displayed concern with the widespread lack of sufficient legal services available to the entire client community. The report suggested alternatives and recommended *increased lay representation* of claimants in administrative hearings as a viable alternative in increasing delivery of services to the poor. 4 NCPR Advance Sheets 5, no. 9 (Sept. 1980) (emphasis added).

In *Florida Bar v. Brower*, 402 So. 2d 1171 (Fla. 1981), respondent prepared, for a fee, legal forms necessary for a dissolution of marriage which his customers would then file. The court noted that respondent held himself out as a lawyer authorized to practice by advising customers as to legal remedies. 6 NCPR Advance Sheets 6, no. 1 (Jan. 1982).

[171]21 N.Y.2d 694, 234 N.E.2d 459, 287 N.Y.S.2d 422 (1967).

[172]355 So. 2d 1186 (Fla. 1978).

[173]Curran, *The Legal Needs of the Public—The Final Report of a National Survey* (1977).

[174]*Final Report, supra* note 83.

[175]*See Hurst, supra* note 44, at 323.

[176]*See Final Report, supra* note 83, at 15.

[177]Id.

[178]Id. at 15–16.

practice;[179] (2) the Bar should aid the consumer in making use of non-lawyer resources when the option is in the public interest;[180] and (3) the definition of "practice of law" should be revised to include those tasks which can safely and satisfactorily be accomplished only by a licensed attorney.[181]

A. Possible Problems and Solutions Suggested

A consideration of the public interest in the practice of law invokes two conflicting concepts: a need for inexpensive and sufficiently available legal assistance, but a required protection from unskilled and unscrupulous practitioners. One commentator has suggested that the relative simplicity of uncontested matrimonial dissolution under the no-fault and similar divorce reform laws creates a relatively small risk of injury;[182] but even where a problem is simple and basic, traps may await the unwary. The ABA's Canon of Ethics explains that legal problems may not be self-revealing and often not timely noticed.[183] This proverbial warning reveals a conflict that has yet to be resolved—if many legal problems may not be apparent, how can the ABA conclude that such legal problems can be resolved without the protection of an attorney?

From the earliest unauthorized practice litigation to the most recent, the activities of both the bar and the courts have been underscored by an emphasis on the potential harm to the public and to the legal profession.[184]

[179]Id. at 16. The committee recommended that the bar should facilitate consumer self-help when that is a feasible mode of dispute resolution. Id.

[180]Id. at 17. The committee recommended that "the bar ought to devise and take steps to help improve the legal problem-solving capacity and expertise of those business and professional persons who are knowledgeable about transactions giving rise to legal problems of types which can be resolved appropriately without the assistance of a lawyer." Id.

[181]Id. The committee, in its proposal stated: "It might also contribute to the more effective prohibition of unauthorized practice of law, which could be refined in definition to be limited to those tasks which can be performed satisfactorily and safely only by a lawyer." Id.

[182]Note, *The Unauthorized Practice of Law and Pro Se Divorce: An Empirical Analysis*, 86 Yale L.J. 104 (1976). This study examined the justifications for reading unauthorized practice prohibitions into uncontested pro se divorce. Principal data was based upon 331 uncontested divorce cases from two counties in Connecticut, questionnaires completed by 106 attorneys, conversations with 99 lawyer-assisted divorce plaintiffs, and 93 "divorce kit" purchasers. The study isolated the discrete functions performed by an attorney in an uncontested divorce and reviewed the arguments marshalled against the propriety of pro se agencies. It then proceeded to test the empirical validity of the arguments and concluded that the unauthorized practice prohibitions had been based upon assumptions unsupported by the data assembled. Id. at 105. The resulting data suggested that an attorney's contribution to ancillary issues is too infrequent and too inconsequential to support justification prohibiting law assistance in form preparation. Id. at 130.

[183]ABA Canons, Preamble.

[184]See *State Bar v. Cramer*, 399 Mich. 116, 249 N.W.2d 1 (1976); *Ayres v. Hodaway*, 303 Mich. 589, 6 N.W.2d 905 (1942) (courts have inherent authority to control participants in courts of the state). See also *Oregon State Bar v. Security Escrows, Inc.*, 233 Or. 80, 87, 377 P.2d 334, 338 (laymen are excluded from the practice of law, whatever the lay practice may be, solely to protect the public). Cf. *Johnson v. Avery*, 393 U.S. 483, 490 n.11 (1969) ("The power of the States to control the practice of law cannot be exercised so as to abrogate federally protected rights.").

B. Injury to the Individual

A necessary initial step to meeting the legal needs of the public is the identification of those legal problems so inherently complex or risky that only a licensed lawyer should be consulted in every case.[185] Four major problems can be initially determined and thereby injury to the individual may be prevented; specifically: (1) possible invalidity of a divorce decree due to the lack of subject matter jurisdiction when proper residency has not been established;[186] (2) a loss of property rights such as an equitable distribution share (i.e., alimony, pension plans, personal or real property) or injury to property rights such as tax liens, credits or contracts (e.g., where one party has co-signed a debt for the other);[187] (3) injury to the family due to conflicts over custody, child support, or visitation rights;[188] and (4) a subtler injury that can result when a pro se litigant does not understand that no attorney will represent him or does not realize that an attorney can be used in conjunction with the services provided by the lay agency.[189] In addition, a justifiable concern has been voiced that the commercial interests of the agency or lay assistant may be placed before the interest of the client and as a result, the client may not be sufficiently warned of the above-mentioned risks.[190]

The procedure recommended by the author to protect pro se litigants who use the services of any type of non-legal resource is a mechanism which will assure full advance disclosure to clients of the nature of the act, the risks involved, and possible alternatives.[191] Specifically, a lay divorce agency should be sure its clients know that their appearance is pro se, how the pro se method operates, what the residency requirements are, that if the parties are in conflict over real property or a real estate transaction is necessary, then the pro se method is not recommended and a lawyer

[185]*Final Report,, supra* note 83, at 16.

[186] *Williams v. North Carolina,* 325 U.S. 266 (1945) (states are entitled to invalidate a divorce decree if a factual determination is made that the decree was granted when the party seeking the foreign divorce was not properly domiciled in the divorce-granting state).

[187]See generally N.Y. Dom. Rel. Law § 234 (McKinney 1977).

[188]See e.g., *Carle v. Carle,* 503 P.2d 1050 (Alaska 1952), illustrating the complex nature of child custody in marital dissolution.

[189]See *Final Report, supra* note 83, at 18. Full advance disclosure will separate those cases capable of resolution through nonlawyer resources and prohibit those cases or aspects of a case that are so inherently risky and complicated that a lawyer must be consulted. Id.

[190]Id. In expressing a concern for the protection of lay persons, the committee suggested that the bar could help by "identify[ing] those situations in which non-lawyers are more likely to have . . . conflicts of interest and [doing] whatever can be done to protect consumers when they turn to non-lawyers for help. . . ."Id.

[191]See e.g., *Model Code of Professional Responsibility* DR 5-101, DR 5-105(c) (1979) (attorneys required to fully disclose to clients any potentially conflicting business interest). The ABA recommends that "the mechanism for controlling the unauthorized practice of law might be adapted so as to permit knowledgeable classes of non-lawyers to render assistance with certain types of legal problems where there has been full disclosure and consumer consent but to prohibit such assistance where appropriate disclosure has not been made." *Final Report, supra* note 83, at 18.

should be consulted instead. If the client does not know an attorney, he should be notified of the availability of the Lawyers Referral Service of the Bar.[192]

The necessary disclosure should be in the form of written notices[193] and should be presented to the client during various phases of the pro se service. The client should first be given notice of the possible risks involved, before he speaks to any of the lay divorce assistants, thereby insuring a type of informed consent as mandated by Canon 5 of the Canons of Ethics.[194] As a result, the individual's need for protection will not be overridden by the lay agency's commercial interest in obtaining new clients.[195]

Once the client has completed the agency's application in long-hand, he affirms his complete understanding of the nature of the process by signing a statement to that effect.[196] In addition to directing the lay divorce agency to copy the application information onto the legal forms, the statement provides that the lay agency did not assist the client in the decisions involved in the preparation of the forms, nor make substantive corrections of errors or omissions unless directed to do so by the court or client. This step will satisfy the *Brumbaugh* requirements[197] by confirming that all information was supplied by the individual.[198]

The last notice should be received by the client after all the forms have been typed. It will state that the lay agent or their employees did not, in conjunction with their business or otherwise, engage in activities in the nature of legal consultation, rendering opinions, advice or other assistance in filling out any part of the forms, in suggesting or advising how the forms should be used in solving the particular customer's marital problems,[199] or in advising customers in any manner as to the various legal remedies available to them. This will provide a self-policing function by reinforcing the essential fact that the lay agency has limited its services to those authorized by law and contracted for by the client, and nothing more.

All notices should be signed and a copy of the original given to the client. If any agency has a substantial amount of non-English speaking clients, appropriate foreign language translation of the English language notices should be used. Pamphlets containing collateral legal information, such as how to use Family Court, the several ways to acquire residence,

---

[192]The Lawyer Referral Service was created around 1950 with the purpose of helping middle-income persons find a lawyer. Referral programs are now available at national, state and local levels. *Final Report, supra* note 83, at 50.

[193]See Appendix for samples of written notices.

[194]*Model Code of Professional Responsibility* EC 5-2, EC 5-3 (1979). See *supra* note 189 and accompanying text.

[195]See Appendix exhibit 1 for sample form.

[196]See Appendix exhibit 2 for sample form.

[197]*Florida Bar v. Brumbaugh,* 355 So. 2d 1186 (Fla. 1978) discussed *supra* notes 155–68 and accompanying text).

[198]See *supra* note 167.

[199]See Appendix exhibit 3 for sample form.

legal grounds for divorce that are acceptable in the state, and how to use the Lawyer Referral Service,[200] should all be made available.

These preventive procedures should protect substantially all the clients, especially in light of the fact that no reported lay divorce agency case has involved any mishap due to the *modus operandi* of the lay agency.[201]

C. Injury to the Integrity of the Bar

Although it is a less obvious problem than that of public injury, there is a very realistic threat of injury to the legal profession and the consuming public in the unauthorized practice of law. Unlike a lawyer, whose license to practice is restricted by the Canons of Ethics and monitored by a grievance committee,[202] a lay agency operates on the basis of *laissez faire* and *caveat emptor*. Thus, if a lay agent is morally corrupt, uneducated or ill-informed, harm to the individual is not only foreseeable, but quite possible as well.[203]

If such injury does occur, the ABA's primary power is presently an injunction, a remedy which is harsh in nature and only practical in extreme cases.[204] When both the public policies involved and the successful integration of non-legal resources in many jurisdictions are considered, a more rational approach is required. A method of regulation instead of enjoinment would be appropriate and should be established. There are various practical options available to the ABA and the judiciary that could be successful in achieving this end. For instance, the bar could establish a new committee to regulate lay agencies and insure that they meet moral criteria

[200]See *Final Report, supra* note 83, at 50. The Lawyer Referral Services, established in order to simplify the lay person's search for a qualified lawyer, are located within the bar association at local, state and national levels. Generally, lawyer involved with the program will charge a low fee for the initial consultation. Clients are referred to lawyers on a rotating basis. Id.

[201]See, e.g., *Florida Bar v. Furman*, 376 So. 2d 378, 379 (Fla. 1980) ("The bar does not contend that . . . her customers suffered any harm as a result of the services rendered, or that she failed to perform the services for which she was paid."), *appeal dismissed*, 444 U.S. 1061 (1980); *Florida Bar v. Brumbaugh*, 355 So. 2d 186, 190 (Fla. 1978) ("This case does not arise out of a complaint . . . as to improper advice or unethical conduct."); *State Bar v. Cramer*, 399 Mich. 116, 128, 249 N.W.2d 1, 14 (1976) (Levin, J., dissenting); *New York County Lawyers Ass'n v. Dacey*, 21 N.Y.2d 694, 234 N.E.2d 459, 287 N.Y.S.2d 422 (1967) (no showing that contested self-help booklet exploited the public); *Oregon State Bar v. Gilchrist*, 212 Or. App. 552, 538 P.2d 913, 918 (1975) (an unsuccessful investigation by the Oregan bar, failing to find any complaints from thousands of clients of lay divorce agents). See also Resh, "More on Do It Yourself Divorce Kits and Services," 37 *Unauth. Prac. News* 59, 69 (1973) (before filing of complaint, Oregon State Consumer Protection Division conducted preliminary investigation of lay divorce agents and found no suggestion of illegality). But see Burke, "New York Divorce Yourself" Enjoined, 37 *Unauth. Prac. News* 22, 27–28 (1973) (citing New York Attorney General's argument that lay divorce kits caused irreparable and immediate injury to the public).

[202]See Hurst, *supra* note 44, at 329–33.

[203]See *Washington State Bar Ass'n v. Washington Ass'n of Realtors*, 41 Wash. 2d 697, 251 P.2d 619 (1952) (court's power to restrict unauthorized practice of law derives from its duty to protect the public from the unskilled).

[204]See *In re Shigon*, 462 Pa. 188, 329 A.2d 235 (1974) (admitted attorney may not be enjoined from the practice of law without reservation, since the right to practice law is constitutionally protected and may not be denied without due process of law).

similar to those required of attorneys. Minimum educational standards could be required, and certification be premised on factors such as completion of a course of studies at an approved paralegal institute,[205] on-the-job training under the supervision of an attorney,[206] or satisfactory completion of a probationary period of work in an "authorized" lay agency. Furthermore, if a staff attorney were permitted to be retained by the lay agency, he could oversee the work, provide needed advice to the lay employees, and serve as a liaison to the local bar association. In order to prevent ethical problems, the attorney should not be allowed to represent any client of the lay agency,[207] nor should he be permitted to refer clients to a particular lawyer, but only to the local bar association's lawyer referral service. The attorney, as an arm of the bar association, would serve as a control over the lay agency. As a final option a licensing requirement could be legislated so that the lay agency would be under the supervision of an administrative agency such as the Department of Consumer Affairs.[208] The ABA could complement the licensing requirement by establishing the scope of the lay agency's "authorized" practice and jointly regulate, with the administrative agency, the lay agency and thereby protect the public from injury.

The employment of any of these options could be used to protect the bar. Lay agents, however, are currently unregulated and the courts and bar, by limiting their regulations of non-legal resources short of injunction, have to rely on the individual lay agency to police itself.[209] This is a very difficult task. Determining the limit of interaction a lay agency may have with an individual before it becomes involved in the "unauthorized practice of law" would be a difficult task even for a seasoned attorney, let alone for a lay person whose legal experience is limited to assisting in the pro se preparation of simple forms, filing the forms, and perhaps following the court docket. If the bar continues to rely on agencies' self-regulation, an innocent error in judgment by the lay agent could prove fatal if the bar moved for an injunction, and no public needs can be satisfied. The *Brumbaugh* criteria[210]

[205]In New York, for instance, there are two institutions dedicated solely to the teaching of paralegal skills, and the New York University School for Paralegal Studies, as well as similar programs at other colleges, offering a curriculum devoted to these skills. *N.Y. Times,* July 22, 1982, at B18, col. 2.

[206]Since the late nineteenth century reading case law has been the prevalent method of learning law. Epstein, "The Classical Tradition of Dialectics and American Legal Education," 31 *J. L. Educ.* 399 (1981). This emphasis, however, has been at the expense of the development of practical lawyering skills. Redlich, "Clinical Education: Stranger in an Elitist Club," 31 *J. L. Educ.* 201 (1981).

[207]Working with nonlawyers may cause ethical problems for the attorney since the Code of Professional Responsibility expressly provides that "a lawyer shall not aid a non-lawyer in the unauthorized practice of law." *Model Code of Professional Responsibility* DR 3-101(a)(1979).

[208]Licensing is a method used to regulate many high risk businesses. See, e.g., N.Y. Real Prop. Law § 440-a (McKinney Supp. 1982) (real estate sales); N.Y. Admin. Code tit. D § 22-2.0 (Supp. 1982) (street vending of food).

[209]*Final Report, supra* note 83, at 16.

[210]*Florida Bar v. Brumbaugh,* 355 So. 2d 1186, 1194 (Fla. 1978) (discussed *supra* notes 155–68 and accompanying text).

might provide a solution to the problem of lay regulation but the terms in those guidelines are general and subject to various interpretations.[211]

It will require more than an uncertain guideline established in one case to devise a set of workable standards. Only when the organized bar accepts the lay agent's role as a corollary to the legal profession, one that supplements and strengthens its efforts to provide sufficient legal services for the public, will the integrity of the bar and the interest of the public be protected.

VII. CONCLUSION

The traditional functions of a lawyer have not included educating lay persons in the exercise of their constitutional right of self-representation. Most lawyers have not provided this service to anyone.[212] For whatever reason, this service has not been provided by the organized bar. If the right of self-representation is to have any meaning, lay people will generally require guidance and assistance.[213]

In conclusion, the implementation of the several steps outlined in this Note will have the effect of substantially increasing the likelihood that an individual who decides not to employ a lawyer for assistance with a legal problem will make that decision knowingly and still be able to resolve his problem to his and the public's satisfaction.

B

Counseling the Guilty and the Unpopular

Johns v. Smyth

UNITED STATES DISTRICT COURT, E.D. VIRGINIA, 1959
176 F.SUP. 949

Walter E. HOFFMAN, District Judge.
    Petitioner is a state prisoner serving a life sentence for the murder of one Melvin Childress in accordance with a final judgment of the Circuit Court of the City of Richmond, Virginia, entered on December 17, 1942.

[211]See *National L.J.*, Feb. 26, 1979, at 2, col. 4.
[212]*State Bar v. Cramer*, 399 Mich. 116, 153, 249 N.W.2d 1, 16 (1976).
[213]Id. at 152–53, 249 N.W. 2d at 16.

Petitioner and Childress were inmates at the State Penitentiary when the killing took place on October 7, 1942. While there is no transcript of the evidence available from the state court, as no court reporter was present, the petitioner's signed statement given on the day following the crime is to the effect that he killed Childress with a knife in the cell of the latter, when Childress took hold of the petitioner and suggested an unnatural sexual act. An investigation by prison authorities points to other motives for the killing but, for the purpose of this proceeding by way of habeas corpus, we are not particularly concerned with the details of the crime.

On some date following the return of an indictment on October 14, 1942, the state court assigned counsel to represent petitioner. The record reveals that the court-appointed attorney had been practicing for a period of approximately fifteen years at the time of petitioner's trial. There is nothing in this proceeding which would reflect that the trial judge or prosecutor were negligent in the performance of their duties with respect to the appointment of the court-assigned counsel and the ensuing trial.

* * *

While the petition alleges several points for consideration, it is only necessary to determine whether petitioner had a fair trial by reason of the actions of court-appointed counsel. All too often the incompetency of counsel is assigned vague allegations which are invariably without merit. It is on the basis of the testimony now given by court-assigned counsel that this court has arrived at the conclusion that petitioner's constitutional rights have been invaded.

One of the cardinal principles confronting every attorney in the representation of a client is the requirement of complete loyalty and service in good faith to the best of his ability. In a criminal case the client is entitled to a fair trial, but not a perfect one. These are fundamental requirements of due process under the Fourteenth Amendment. The same principles are applicable in Sixth Amendment cases (not pertinent herein) and suggest that an attorney should have no conflict of interest and that he must devote his full and faithful efforts toward the defense of his client. *Glasser v. United States*, 315 U.S. 60, 62 S.Ct. 457, 86 L.Ed. 680; *Von Moltke v. Gillies*, 332 U.S. 708, 725, 68 S.Ct. 316, 92 L.Ed. 309.

With this in mind, let us examine the facts to determine (1) whether the representation afforded petitioner at his murder trial was so totally lacking that it cannot be said that he had a fair trial in the usual sense of the word, and (2) whether the court-appointed attorney was so prejudiced and convinced of his client's guilt of *first degree murder* that he was unable to, and did not, give his client the "undivided allegiance and faithful, devoted service" which the Supreme Court has held to be the right of the accused under the Constitution, and (3) whether the attorney's interest in his client was so diverted by his personal beliefs that there existed a conflict in interest between his duty to his client and his conscience.

* * *

The difficulty lies, of course, in ascertaining whether the attorney has been guilty of an error of judgment, such as an election with respect to trial tactics, or has otherwise been actuated by his conscience or belief that his client should be convicted in any event. All too frequently courts are called upon to review actions of defense counsel which are, at the most, errors of judgment, not properly reviewable on habeas corpus unless the trial is a farce and a mockery of justice which requires the court to intervene. *Diggs v. Welch,* 80 U.S.App.D.C. 5, 148 F.2d 667. But when defense counsel, in a truly adverse proceeding, admits that his conscience would not permit him to adopt certain customary trial procedures, this extends beyond the realm of judgment and strongly suggests an invasion of constitutional rights.

Little need to be said of the trial. The accused did not testify. No proposed instructions were submitted to the trial judge in behalf of the defendant, although under the law of Virginia it was possible for the defendant to have been convicted of involuntary manslaughter and received a sentence of only five years. The defense attorney agreed with the prosecutor that the case would be submitted to the jury without argument of counsel. The instructions given by the court were generally acceptable in covering the categories of first and second degree murder, but failed to mention the possibility of a manslaughter verdict.

Standing alone these complaints would have no merit as they may properly be considered as trial tactics. However, when we look at the motivating force which prompted these decisions of trial counsel, it is apparent that "tactics" gave way to "conscience." In explanation of the agreement not to argue the case before the jury, the court-appointed attorney said:

> "I think an argument to the jury would have made me appear ridiculous in the light of evidence that was offered. . . .
> "I had enough confidence in the judgment of the jury to know that they could have drawn an inference, and I would have been a hypocrite and falsifier if I had gone before the jury and argued in the light of what Johns told me that that statement was accurate.

> • • •

> Well, sir, I did not and I wouldn't be dishonest enough to do it in the light of Mr. Johns' statement to me. You can say what the law is and what the record discloses, but if I asked a client, an accused on defense, to explain some such statement as this and he gives me the explanation that Johns gave me, I consider it dishonest. You can talk about legal duty to client all you wish, but I consider it dishonest for me to get up before a jury and try to argue that the statement that came out from the Commonwealth was true when Johns had told me that it wasn't. The explanation that he gave me was very vague.

Immediately thereafter, the following occurred:

> "Q.   That you could not conscientiously argue to the jury that he should be acquitted? A. I definitely could not.
> "Q.   Regardless of what the law is or what your duty to a client is? A. You can talk about law and you can talk about my duty to clients, I felt it

was my—that I couldn't conscientiously stand up there and argue that point in the light of what Johns had told me."

The attorney was then asked whether he ever considered requesting permission to withdraw from the case. He replied in the negative.

No attorney should "frame" a factual defense in any case, civil or criminal, and it is not intimated by this opinion that the attorney should plant the seeds of falsehood in the mind of his client. In the instant case, however, the evidence adduced by the prosecution suggested some provocation for the act through the summary of the statement given by the defendant on the day following the killing. When the defendant was interviewed by his court-appointed attorney, the attorney stated that he had reason to doubt the accuracy of the defendant's statement. It was at this time that the attorney's conscience actuated his future conduct which continued throughout the trial. If this was the evidence presented by the prosecution, the defendant was entitled to the faithful and devoted services of his attorney uninhibited by the dictating conscience. The defendant could not be compelled to testify against himself, and if the prosecution saw fit to use the defendant's statement in aid of the prosecution, the attorney was duty bound to exert his best efforts in aid of his client. The failure to argue the case before a jury, while ordinarily only a trial tactic not subject to review, manifestly enters the field of incompetency when the reason assigned is the attorney's conscience. It is as improper as though the attorney had told the jury that his client had uttered a falsehood in making the statement. The right to an attorney embraces effective representation throughout all stages of the trial, and where the representation is of such low caliber as to amount to no representation, the guarantee of due process has been violated. *Powell v. State of Alabama*, 287 U.S. 45, 53 S.Ct. 55, 77 L.Ed. 158 (1932).

The entire trial in the state court had the earmarks of an *ex parte* proceeding. If petitioner had been without the services of an attorney, but had remained mute, it is unlikely that he would have been worse off. The state argues that the defendant may have received a death sentence. Admitting this to be true, it affords no excuse for lack of effective representation.

Holding that the petitioner was not accorded a "fair trial" in the true sense of the word, because of the motivating forces which dictated the actions and decisions of his court-appointed counsel, we turn to the legal problem which has given this court grave concern. It is a general rule of law that a federal court cannot order the release of a state prisoner, grounded upon the lack of effective counsel in the state court proceeding, unless the incompetence and ineffectiveness of the attorney is so obvious that it becomes the duty of the trial judge or prosecutor (both state officers) to intervene and protect the right of the accused. With this general statement, the court is in accord.

As indicated, there is nothing apparent in this case which would require the trial judge or prosecutor to intervene. But the state of facts here presented indicates that the general rule should not be considered as inflexible. In *Massey v. Moore*, 348 U.S. 105, 75 S.Ct. 145, 99 L.Ed. 135 (1954), the Supreme Court indicated that, on the question of the mental condition of the accused at the time of trial, the presence or absence of affirmative misconduct on the part of the state at the trial was irrelevant.

If it be necessary to engraft an exception on the general rule, it would appear that one is appropriate here, for indeed it would be a dark day in the history of our judicial system if a conviction is permitted to stand where an attorney, furnished to an indigent defendant, candidly admits that his conscience prevented him from effectively representing his client according to the customary standards prescribed by attorneys and the courts.

Counsel for petitioner will prepare an appropriate order granting the writ of habeas corpus and remanding petitioner to the proper authorities of the State of Virginia for further proceedings on the charge of murder.

* * *

A Lawyer's Duty to Represent Clients Repugnant and Otherwise

CHARLES W. WOLFRAM

In the course of a conversation about some differences between legal and moral obligations, my colleague Steven Munzer once offered the example of an executioner in a state that had established the legality of capital punishment. His brief analysis was that the executioner's work could well be regarded as legally appropriate—or at least legally neutral (subject to no legal sanction of disapproval)—but morally objectionable. In some senses it is not overly drastic to substitute the figure of the lawyer for that of the executioner. Indeed, the executioner in a capital punishment jurisdiction can do no grisly work until a prosecutor has employed considerable lawyerly skills and persuasively urged a judge or jury to impose the death penalty. If, then, one supposes that the executioner's act is morally objectionable, although legally permissible, is not the prosecuting lawyer's the same? Or can it be said, as many lawyers would say, that a lawyer enjoys a special moral immunity from judgments about acts taken in behalf of a client?

A lawyer's decision whether or not to represent a prospective client whose objectives are morally objectionable raises two separate issues, the second of which I will pursue here. The first, and extensively debated, issue is whether, once a decision to represent the client has been made, the

Charles W. Wolfram, "A Lawyer's Duty to Represent Clients, Repugnant and Otherwise," from David Luban, ed., *The Good Lawyer: Lawyers' Roles and Lawyers' Ethics* (Totowa, N.J.: Rowman & Allanheld, 1984), pp. 214–20 and 223–35. Reprinted by permission.

lawyer may be tarred with the same brush as the client. Many of the essays in this collection skillfully elucidate various facets of this problem. A time-honored focus of this debate is the conduct of the criminal defense lawyer in defending a person known by the lawyer to be guilty of the crime charged. There are probably disparities between the professional and the "lay" resolutions of this problem. The professional view is that defense of the known guilty person is appropriate in order that the established governmental system, and not private lawyer perceptions, determine guilt and innocence. This professional stance is supported by a principle of professional detachment under which a lawyer is not to be regarded as endorsing the client's political, economic, social, or moral views.[1] The nonprofessional view probably does not so readily or so often put distance between the lawyerly agent and the client principal. Despite the familiarity and attractiveness of the professional view, to my way of thinking the problem remains a troublesome one.

The principle of professional detachment does not claim that in fact all lawyers are innocent of moral views about a client's objectives. It seems instead to assume that a lawyer will typically be willing to sublimate moral repulsion to the requirements of the service function of providing legal assistance, or of the economic function of making a living or living well. But suppose a perhaps unusual case. Suppose that a lawyer in fact feels unwilling, at least at the outset, to set aside personal moral values to further the immoral ends of a prospective client. Is the lawyer nonetheless required to represent the client? A variety of settings suggest themselves. One of the most prominent in recent years was raised by the decision of ACLU lawyers to accept as clients members of the American Nazi party who had been refused permission by local authorities to hold an anti-Jewish parade in Skokie, a predominantly Jewish community near Chicago.[2] Or consider a case in which the operator of a "dirty bookstore" wishes representation to resist efforts of governmental officials or private citizens to limit or altogether ban distribution of pornography. Or consider a lawyer asked by an embattled president of the United States to represent him personally in resisting attempts to force disclosure of potentially damaging materials in the course of an investigation into widespread corruption of the political process.[3] Or consider a lawyer asked to represent a chemical company in resisting the efforts of a governmental agency to restrict its operations

[1]The principle is implicit in Ethical Considerations 7–8 and 7–9 of the *American Bar Association Model Code of Professional Responsibility* and is stated explicitly in the code proposed to replace it—Rule 1.2(b) of ABA Model Rules of Professional Conduct (approved August 1983). See e.g., Murray Schwartz, "The Professionalism and Accountability of Lawyers," *California Law Review* 66 (1978): 609, where the principle of professional detachment is described. The principle, of course, is the subject of telling criticism in other chapters of this volume.

[2]The legal position of the Nazis was ultimately vindicated by the United States Supreme Court. In *National Socialist Party v. Village of Skokie*, 432 U.S. 43 (1977) (per curiam), the Court held that the Illinois Supreme Court had erred when it refused to grant a stay of an Illinois trial court's broad injunction against the petitioners' marching, parading, and distributing pamphlets to incite or promote hatred against Jews. At later points in this paper, I take various liberties with hypothetical variants on the facts of this case.

[3]Transparently, the reference is to *United States v. Nixon*, 418 U.S. 683 (1974).

pending investigations concerning serious public health risks posed by them.

Many lawyers would find it repugnant to support or further in a personal way the cause of the "deserving guilty," Nazis, pornographers, a president who has corrupted the political system, or environmental polluters. The untutored instinct is that the representation of any such client should, at most, be left to the discretion of the lawyer asked to undertake it. On closer examination, however, both the moral and to some extent the legal dimensions of these, I hope, representative and interesting settings give rise to a substantial doubt that a lawyer never is obliged to accept a case of a repugnant client.

But starting with the repugnant client is starting backwards. It must first be established whether or not there is a duty to represent in *any* case, including the much more usual situation in which no strong moral objection to the client's objectives is present. It is clear that if no general duty exists, a duty to represent morally objectionable clients becomes impossible to support.

I will first review briefly the "professional" regulations that lawyers have drafted for themselves. The view apparently reflected there is that no duty exists to represent any client except in a very specialized case: where a court or bar association appoints the lawyer. Beyond the professional obligation, however, it appears that in many other situations lawyers of normal moral sensitivity personally would feel compelled to represent a client whose case they would not otherwise handle. In these situations the necessitous client has a compelling need for legal services that can be satisfied only by the lawyer who is requested by the client to take the case. After this review, I will return to the specialized problem of the repugnant client.

PROFESSIONAL REGULATIONS

At present, under the American Bar Association Code of Professional Responsibility, there is no firm basis for stating that any obligation to represent a client exists that will be enforced by professional discipline, some suggestion that an ethical (nonenforceable) obligation to represent a client exists only if the lawyer is appointed by a court or bar association to defend a person accused of a crime, and some basis for concluding that a lawyer is ethically permitted (but not obliged) to represent any person in any other case. The special problem of the lawyer's moral objections to a client's objectives is mentioned only tangentially.

* * *

In distilled form, under the ABA code a lawyer has professional discretion to accept or reject any proposed representation. Even the obligation to accept a court or bar association appointment is stated only in an Ethical Consideration and thus, at least as far as the code is concerned, is an ethical and not a disciplinary obligation.[5] In exercising that discretion, the lawyer is told by the code not to decline representation lightly and not to reject a client because of the unpopularity of the client or cause unless the lawyer's personal feelings on the matter would prevent effective representation. The code is silent, however, on whether a lawyer whose feelings would not prevent able advocacy may nonetheless decline a representation because of moral qualms about the client's objectives or methods.

The American Bar Association recently replaced the code with a redrafted Model Rules of Professional Conduct.[6] This contains a rule that makes mandatory, and thus a ground for professional discipline, the ethical prescription of the present code that a lawyer accept appointed cases. Rule 6.2 states that "a lawyer shall not seek to avoid appointment" but allows that "good cause" provides an excuse. And Rule 6.2(c) states that good cause includes the fact that "the client or the cause is so repugnant to the lawyer as to be likely to impair the client–lawyer relationship or the lawyer's ability to represent the client." The official commentary to Rule 6.2 states flatly that "a lawyer ordinarily is not obliged to accept a client whose character or cause the lawyer regards as repugnant."[7]

Thus, under the new Model Rules as under the existing code, it appears that a lawyer has professional discretion to accept or reject any case, except for an appointed case. In fact, unlike the code in EC 2-26, the Model Rules and commentary do not suggest that a lawyer in a nonappointment situation must have a reason at all, good or bad, to decline a representation. And there is no requirement that a lawyer represent a repugnant client, in a nonappointment setting, even if the lawyer's feelings would not prevent an adequate relationship and representation.

DIMENSIONS OF A MORAL DUTY TO ACCEPT A CLIENT

Given the present professional regulations, it seems quite unlikely that professional discipline would be visited upon a lawyer for declining to represent a client for any reason aside from court appointments. But that observation does not, of course, end the inquiry, for a lawyer of normal moral instincts will not lead a professional life impelled only by the direct and sanctionable commands of professional regulations. The important

---

[5]Occasional statements can be found of a "duty" to accept unpopular clients or causes on the part of individual lawyers (see, e.g., Justice Marshall, concurring, *In re Primus*, 436 U.S. 412, 470 [1978]) or on the part of the organized bar as an entity (see, e.g., Proceedings of the House of Delegates, *American Bar Association Report* 78 [1953]: 118, 133; Special Committee on Individual Rights as Affected by National Security, "Report," *American Bar Association Report* 78 [1953]: 304). The references seem always to be invoking an ethical, rather than a legal, imperative.

[6]See *ABA Model Rules of Professional Conduct* (approved August 1983).

[7]*ABA Model Rules of Professional Conduct*, Rule 6.2, comment.

question remains: is there a moral duty to represent? Parenthetically, I might add that if one did conclude that a professional regulation with the force of law required a lawyer to accept a representation—for example, as the new Model Rules clearly do in the instance of a court appointment—then, unless the legal duty were morally objectionable, it would create a moral obligation to obey.

The problem of defining and elaborating the moral obligations and prerogatives of a lawyer confronted with a request to represent someone whom he or she is not disposed or legally required to represent calls forth the image, known both to law and to philosophy, of the rescuer. In law, courts in the United States and in other common-law countries generally have rejected a duty to rescue a person in peril unless there exists one of a relatively narrowly defined kind of special pre-existing relationships.[8] But the reasons given for rejecting a general legal duty to rescue have nothing to do with morality. Instead, they are based on a tradition in the common law to find liability only where affirmative acts have caused injury and, more important perhaps, on apprehensions about difficulties in administering a legal duty to rescue.[9] But while denying that the potential rescuer who fails to act may be held liable in damages, judges have left little doubt that they regard the unmoved spectator as a moral derelict.[10] Thus, an adult on a bridge who fails to throw an available rope to a drowning child may escape legal liability but will incur the moral condemnation of almost every lawyer and judge.

The philosophical basis for a duty to rescue is explicable whether one's starting point is a theory based on utilities or one based on rights and obligations that are posited for reasons not related necessarily to consequences. On a utilitarian calculus, at least where the cost to the rescuer is nonexistent or slight and the benefit to the victim is great, a duty clearly stands out.[11] Indeed, because of the importance of protecting the victim and the assumed small cost to the rescuer, the possibly more substantial

---

[8]See, e.g., William Prosser, *Handbook of the Law of Torts*, 4th ed. (St. Paul, Minn.: West Publishing Company, 1971), pp. 340–43; Fowler Harper and Fleming James, *Law of Torts* (Boston: Little, Brown, 1956), pp. 1044–53. The rule of tort law has long been criticized on grounds as diverse as those of morality and of economics. See James Barr Ames, "Law and Morals," *Harvard Law Review* 22 (1908): 97, 110; William M. Landes and Richard A. Posner, "Salvors, Finders, Rescuers, and Other Good Samaritans: An Economic Study of Law and Altruism," *Journal of Legal Studies* 7 (1978): 83, 119–27.

[9]See the critique in Ernest J. Weinrib, "The Case for a Duty to Rescue," *Yale Law Journal* 90 (1980): 247. Henderson, "Process Constraints in Torts," *Cornell Law Review* 67 (1982): 901, 928–43, criticizes Weinrib's failure to account for the "process" difficulties in defining and enforcing a duty to rescue. Henderson concludes that problems with comprehensibility, verifiability, conformability, and manageability of a legally enforceable duty to rescue fully support the refusal of courts to create a general legal duty to rescue.

[10]See, e.g., *Buch v. Amory Mfg. Co.*, 69 N.H. 257, 260, 44 A. 809, 810 (1897) (the nonrescuer "may, perhaps, justly be styled a ruthless savage and moral monster, but he is not liable in damages. . . ."). Prosser, himself given at times to strong statement, recounted that common-law decisions refusing to find liability "are revolting to any moral sense" and noted that "they have been denounced with vigor by legal writers." Prosser, *Handbook*, p. 341.

[11]Weinrib, "The Case for a Duty to Rescue," pp. 280, 283, cites both Bentham and Mill.

intellectual task for the utilitarian is to put meaningful limits on a duty to act benevolently.[12] Philosophical theories based on rights and nonutility-based obligations also recognize a duty to rescue. Concern for the rights of the victim calls forth an obligation on the part of available rescuers to supply aid. Even within individualistic ethical systems that give great attention to the right of the potential rescuer to act on the basis of self-interest, where the inconvenience of rescue to the rescuer is slight or nonexistent, little can be said to resist the intuitive appeal of a duty to rescue.[13]

The generally recognized moral duty of an adult, for example, to save the life of a drowning child by throwing a readily available rope does not immediately translate, of course, into a general duty on the part of every lawyer to lend assistance to every client in need of legal services. Several additional factors remain to be considered: the capacities of the lawyer, the risk that may be incurred by the lawyer or caused to others, and the nature of the client's legal needs.

Capacity to Rescue

No one would suppose that a duty to rescue should be visited upon one who was incapable of discharging it. So a lawyer will not be bound to accept a case in which he or she is not competent to render the kind of legal service that other available lawyers could provide. Indeed, in an era in which specialized knowledge and skills are required for capable performance in many areas of practice, the lawyer's lack of competence strongly operates as a reason not to accept the client. As will be seen, a special problem of competence is presented when the lawyer's personal repugnance to the client is so strong as to preclude effective representation. Yet it is important to note that the "rescue" contemplated need not be a perfect one. That the lawyer may be less competent than other lawyers, none of whom will accept the case, does not mean that the lawyer's assistance will be entirely ineffectual. If the lawyer's assistance would materially aid the client, even if not perfectly, then there might be a duty to give such assistance as is possible. For example, the lawyer may render assistance by helping the potential client to find another lawyer who could handle the case quite competently. Or the lawyer may assist the client by preparing legal documents even though the lawyer would not be permitted to appear in court in the client's behalf because, for example, the lawyer is not admitted to practice before that court.

---

[12]Such an attempt is made by Weinrib, ibid., pp. 218–86. Weinrib finds the necessary limitations upon what otherwise would threaten to become a senselessly broad duty of altruism in a need to avoid reliance upon assistance. This concern generates a postulate that requires that the victim face an emergency. This, in turn, has the effects both of reducing the incidence of the duty and of preventing victim self-generation of a duty to rescue.

[13]Weinrib, ibid., pp. 286–92, relies mainly upon Kant for a deontologically based duty to rescue. Even individualist thinkers are prepared to accept that wrongs can be committed under some circumstances by depriving a victim of assistance. See Charles Fried, *Right and Wrong* (Cambridge, Mass.: Harvard University Press, 1978), p. 114. Truly radical libertarian philosophers may not.

Risk to the Rescuer and Others

A duty to rescue is modulated by the extent to which the potential
rescuer is exposed to risk. To toss a drowning child a rope that lies nearby
is one thing; to plunge into a raging torrent is another. A potential rescuer
may properly take into account the extent of personal risk. Similarly, no
moral fault can be found if the would-be rescuer makes a decision for
morally acceptable reasons to save one drowning child rather than another,
where only one can be saved. This is true as well where the decision is
personalized, or arguably "selfish," as where the child chosen to be saved is
the rescuer's own or even is saved from a significant but lesser danger, for
example, from the risk of a serious crippling injury but not death. The
duty to rescue can be overridden by other compelling duties, loyalties, or
interests.

Yet there are limits on the risks that negate a duty to rescue. Minor
inconvenience, it seems, should not suffice. A casual distaste for young
children or a desire not to soil a fine new pair of gloves on a dirty rope
would not excuse a failure to rescue a drowning child. In the middle range
will be difficult questions of degree in which the normally appropriate
decision will require a careful balancing of the risk that the rescuer would
incur against the certainty and magnitude of the danger confronting the
victim.

Among these difficult, middle-ground problems are issues of economics. To what extent, if any, should a claimed duty to rescue give way
where effecting a rescue would be uneconomical for the potential rescuer?
For example, while morality would not require a sea captain to subject his
or her own ship and crew to certain danger to rescue the crew of another
ship, what if the time required to effect the rescue would merely spoil a
perishable cargo? Or what if the sea captain would become personally liable
for additional days' wages for the crew or would lose additional cargoes
waiting in port that would go to other ships because of the delay? Most
moral systems would conclude that, while rescue under these circumstances is morally correct, even morally heroic, it is not required due to the
sacrifice of the rescuer's own substantial interests that would be involved.
This idea is captured in some of the literature by the concept of the "easy
rescue."[14]

As applied to a lawyer, these ideas imply a duty to accept a case only
where a similar lack of risk to the lawyer or to others would be present. If
there is time in the working day, the task is within the normal competence
of the lawyer, no great financial sacrifice would be required, and no competing professional, family, or personal need would be seriously compromised, then acceptance of the client would seem required—at least in
"necessitous" instances.

* * *

[14]See Weinrib, "The Case for a Duty to Rescue," pp. 279 ff.

A DUTY TO REPRESENT A REPUGNANT CLIENT

Does a Nazi, whose views are repugnant to the lawyer, stand in the lawyer's office in the same posture as any other necessitous client? Or is a lawyer ethically entitled to reject this representation on the ground that Nazi tenets are repugnant? If so in some cases, is this true in all? I believe that the necessitous but repugnant prospective client should be represented in some cases, but only if (1) the client's claim is legally just, (2) the client's claim is a morally important and compelling one, and (3) the client's need for this particular lawyer's services is truly pressing. Overall, my view is that necessitousness should here be considered in a special sense that permits the moral lawyer to take fully into account the precise moral nature of the legal claim that the repugnant client wishes to assert.

Capacity to Represent Effectively

Some lawyers would probably claim that their emotional and philosophical revulsion against Nazism and, to some extent, against one who espoused it was so strong that they could not competently represent such a client. The claim must be taken seriously. The lawyer's role in the United States is typically one in which some significant—at least vicarious, but perhaps more personal—identification occurs between lawyer and client. One need not embrace the ultimate prescription of William Kunstler that he would only represent a client whom he loved. Somewhat less dramatically, many lawyers believe that they function best if they are able to share and agree with the values, beliefs, and goals of the client. This lawyer–client identification is doubtless sometimes feigned. But often it must be real. There is no reason to think that American lawyers as a group—who, as a group, seem so comfortable with their clients' objectives—are particularly good actors or possess in unusual measure the psychological hardihood (or, possibly, even defects of character) that would permit daily work in behalf of persons whose goals and beliefs were sharply divergent from their own.[18]

Much of this follows from the American style—perhaps found nowhere else in such vigor—of intense lawyer loyalty to the client in adversarial representations. Now, as a century ago, a client typically is represented by a lawyer who is expected to, and most often does, throw himself or herself into the representation with little emotional or personal reserve. The "exertions" of an American lawyer in behalf of a client are not merely physical—time spent, energy expended—although these may be substan-

---

[18]This point is made powerfully in Chapter 12 of [David Luban, ed., *The Good Lawyer: Lawyers' Roles and Lawyers' Ethics* (Totowa, N.J.: Rowman and Allanheld, 1984)] by Andreas Eshete, "Does a Lawyer's Character Matter?" part II. In Chapter 13 [of the same volume] Gerald Postema also deals persuasively with the problem of professional character and moral character in his "Self-Image, Integrity, and Professional Responsibility." See also the excellent examination of this problem in his "Moral Responsibility in Professional Ethics," *New York University Law Review* 55 (1980): 60.

tial. More than this, American lawyers and their models (F. Lee Bailey, Percy Foreman, Melvin Belli) often perform with great investments of emotional resources.

Personal repugnance, then, may create a situation in which some lawyers cannot make the customary emotional commitment. As a result, those lawyer's representations might be defective in the normal emotional commitment that those lawyers would make in other representations and that other lawyers—including the lawyer on the other side—would make in the present case. Competence here is not merely a flat-voiced recitation of the leading cases and statutes that support the client's position. It is, if called for, an impassioned plea, and all the rhetorical rest. If it is lacking, then adversaries, judges, jurors, peers, and one's own client might well notice and act upon the difference, and the lawyer's work will not be of the same value to the client as another's would have been.

Nevertheless, if the choice is between this kind of flawed representation and no representation at all, and so long as the client chooses knowingly, it seems that even a representation that may be hobbled by the lawyer's personal rejection may be better than none and, if other criteria are fulfilled, may even be required.

Risk to Rescuer and Others

Would a lawyer be morally justified in refusing legal assistance to a repugnant client because of the harm that might be inflicted upon the lawyer and the lawyer's other clients and family as a result of the representation? Take the decision of the American Civil Liberties Union and its lawyers to represent the American Nazi party in its effort to stage an anti-Jewish march through Skokie. Setting aside any strategic decisions about defending civil liberties, would a duty to represent have existed if one could have foreseen the quite considerable harm that the ACLU suffered as a result of its decision to provide representation?

One with a sensible set of moral values would hesitate a long time before foisting extreme heroism upon ordinary moral agents. A desire not to ruin one's private practice or one's organization, not to impair seriously the extent to which one can make credible arguments in behalf of other clients, not to bring public scorn upon one's family and friends—these and similar concerns are legitimately compelling. And, depending upon the extent of the hypothetical Nazi client's need, they might prevent any duty to represent from arising.

An additional element is that a representation that is forced upon a lawyer necessarily requires the lawyer to compromise or to surrender a considerable measure of personal autonomy. Those who hold, as I do, that individualism, at least in the realm of ideas and beliefs, is an important moral value must take into account the fact that a duty to represent a repugnant client will require the lawyer to suspend, if not to sacrifice, an important part of his or her intellectual and moral freedom. In striking a balance here, some measure of the strength of the prospective client's claim to representation must also be taken into account.

What Counts as Repugnance?

In order to strike a balance the intellectual and moral freedom of a lawyer and the legal needs of a repugnant client, the concept of "repugnance" requires more elaboration than it has thus far received. This is true both with respect to the reasons that legitimately count in generating a characterization of repugnance and with respect to the possible reach of such a characterization.

First, what makes a client "repugnant" and thus serves as a reason for refusing legal assistance to one in need of it? Repugnance may be virtually self-defining for many in the case of representing a Nazi to further the morally objectionable propaganda projects of Nazism. What of a prospective client who is repugnant, not because of an ideology, but because of a different defect of character—for example, a remorseless murderer? Or a grasping entrepreneur who, quite profitably, is engaged in the business of manufacturing "Saturday Night Specials"—small firearms that are used by purchasers chiefly for illegal and often deadly purposes?[19] Or a greedy manipulator who uses legal technicalities to seize the property of the poor?[20] Are all deficient characters to be treated the same? Are remorseless jaywalkers the same as murderers? What of persons of different political parties from the lawyer's? Persons who enjoy popular music or otherwise display unsound aesthetic values?

Second, does a lawyer's moral repugnance legitimately reach only the particular legal matter—the particular morally repugnant project or incident in which the client is involved? Or are some persons—such as a Nazi, a remorseless murderer, a cold-hearted land speculator, and the like—so pervaded by a repugnant characteristic or character that any legal matter brought to a lawyer by such a client would be properly rejectable, regardless of whether or not it was directly related to the source of the lawyer's abhorrence?

Certainly not all possible reasons for differing from another person can count as grounds for "repugnance." Some reasons would have to be rejected as trifling or as the overly judgmental reactions of a senselessly severe moral, political, or aesthetic prudery. To refuse to represent a prospective client, who otherwise would be forced to proceed without a lawyer, on the ground that he or she is a member of another major political party is to demonstrate a failure of ethical judgment, not an abundance of it. Of course, in unusual situations an attorney may have a reasonable conscientious objection to the project that the prospective client has undertaken and for which legal assistance is needed. A lawyer, for example, may conscientiously object to filing suit to block certification of the election of a

---

[19]I take the example from Professor Murray Schwartz's "The Zeal of the Civil Advocate," [David Luban, *The Good Lawyer*].

[20]Some earlier discussion in the symposia that gave rise to these essays involved the example of a real estate operator in a large city who assiduously scouted the tax rolls of the city for tax-delinquent property to buy. The law was assumed to be such that the speculator could quite legally buy up irrevocably the property of a poor person for a small fraction of its real value.

prospective client's political adversary if the lawyer reasonably believes that the law unwisely gives some support to the prospective client's position.[21] On the other hand, if a newspaper illegally refuses to print a political advertisement of a Republican, even a lawyer who disagrees with Republicanism and with the specific message sought to be published would probably feel that this ideological difference is not a sufficient reason to reject a representation that seeks to uphold the values of free expression. The difference from the election suit is that here, presumably, the lawyer has no conscientious scruple with the law protecting free expression and, while differing with it, no strong moral objection to the advertisement.

Repugnance might stem not from ideology but from character defects of the prospective client—such as the remorseless murderer. It is readily imaginable that a lawyer would find that too heavy a sacrifice of his or her reasonably held beliefs about goodness would be entailed by accepting such a representation. Suppose, for example, that a remorseless person has been convicted on overwhelming evidence of a horrible murder. The convicted person wishes the lawyer to handle a discretionary appeal (for which there is no right to a court-appointed lawyer). A lawyer who feels that the conviction was morally justified may reasonably feel strong moral scruples against obtaining release of the deservedly convicted person on possible technical grounds unrelated to the fact of guilt or innocence. Such a lawyer should not be considered to be under a moral obligation to deny those scruples and to accept the representation to file the appeal.

Professor Murray Schwartz argues in ["The Zeal of the Civil Advocate"] that a moral duty to afford representation in civil cases may exist regardless of the immorality of the client's ends. This is said to be true when the client could not function effectively in the legal system without counsel and the client has a legal entitlement to claim a morally objectionable "good." But the moral duty is not borne by individual lawyers. Each remains free in most instances to reject morally repugnant representations. The concept is one of social justice rather than one of individual morality: the moral duty is borne by "the legal system" and not by individual lawyers. But it is not clear to me that a legal system that leaves immoral claimants of legal rights unrepresented (although not preventing them from obtaining counsel if individual lawyers are willing to represent them) is necessarily unjust.

Professor Schwartz is concerned chiefly with a situation in which the manufacturer of "Saturday Night Specials" is threatened with an unlawful attempt by a town council to close his business.[22] Professor Schwartz's formulation attempts to take account of the prospective client's immorality

---

[21]So, under the circumstances in *Brown v. Hartlage*, 456 U.S. 45, 102 S. Ct. 1523, 71 L. Ed. 2d 732 (1982), a lawyer might feel that denial of an otherwise fair election result to a candidate who made a campaign promise to reduce his or her governmental salary if elected, because of a dubious law that might treat such a promise as a "bribe," would be quite unwise and unfair. Indeed, a unanimous Supreme Court held that application of the law on such facts was unconstitutional. My point is that a lawyer may legitimately reject the representation on the ground that the law, whether constitutional or not, would in this instance reach a morally and politically objectionable end.

[22]Schwartz, "The Zeal of the Civil Advocate," p. 165.

and the gravity of the harm to the prospective client, but apparently he is prepared to find these criteria satisfied for this prospective client.

I do not agree that a legal system should be accounted unjust if it leaves unrepresented this particular litigant whom no lawyer will represent because of moral objections. The gun manufacturer, to be sure, will probably lose future profits and might even be unable to shift operations to a morally unobjectionable product and so perhaps will lose the value of the business itself. The injustice of leaving this and similar shady operators to the collective moral judgment of lawyers apparently springs from a perceived defect in a legal system that accords legal rights that are unenforceable because of the seriatim refusal of lawyers to lend their skilled and necessary assistance to enforce them. But why is this society unjust?

The answer does not lie in some assumed categorical supremacy of legal rights over moral claims, for Professor Schwartz is willing to give dominance to some moral claims over some legal entitlements. Nor does his position seem to depend upon some calculus of utilities; we are given no reason to think that the entrepreneur's loss through nonrepresentation would be nonutilitarian. Professor Schwartz's position incorporates a formula from, but is not compelled by, two dicta in decisions of the United States Supreme Court. The first decision rejected a claimed constitutional right to a hearing prior to agency termination of disability benefits; the second rejected a claim of constitutional right to appointed counsel in the case of an impoverished parent whose children were taken away in an uncounseled proceeding.[23] In the course of each decision, the Court majority conceded arguendo that a right to counsel might exist in some civil cases. But the concession, as lawyers know, was quite unnecessary to the decision in the particular cases, and the Court would probably feel free in a future decision to deny that any such right existed in any case.

Instead, the justification for Professor Schwartz's position seems based upon a notion that a right to legal representation is both superior (at times) to moral claims and instincts and is separable from the immorality of the ends to which prospective clients seek to put the imperfect machinery of the law. Representation in this view becomes an end in itself. But legal representation seems without significance apart from the uses to which it is put. It is merely process and is not detachable from the outcomes it produces. If we were to change the hypothetical situation and assume that the morality of the acts of the gun manufacturer is unclear, then the process value of legal representation becomes more compelling. At least then one can say that the resolution of doubtful moral positions should be shouldered by a just society in order to ensure that erroneous moral judgments do not prevent morally deserving claimants of legal rights from obtaining their legal and moral due.[24] But that is a different situation from the one

[23]See *Mathews v. Eldridge*, 424 U.S. 319 (1976); and *Lassiter v. Department of Social Services*, 452 U.S. 18 (1981).

[24]Perhaps this is the basis for Alan Donagan's dictum, upon which Professor Schwartz relies (Schwartz, p. 165), to the effect that a society would be unjust if it "denied" claimants of legal rights a fair opportunity to obtain representation. See Alan Donagan, "Justifying Legal Practice in the Adversary System," Chapter 5, [Luban, *The Good Lawyer*.]

portrayed by Professor Schwartz in which we are to stipulate the moral wrongness of the prospective client's aims.

In any event, for present purposes I assume that the decision on representation confronts an individual lawyer and does not involve a decision about the justness of an entire legal system. I also assume that the lawyer acts reasonably and on adequate information in determining that the prospective client's goals are morally objectionable. Such a lawyer, in my view, is always entitled to take this into account in deciding whether to represent.

Ethical "Shunning"?

What about a legal matter brought to the lawyer in which the client does not seek directly to further goals that the lawyer regards as repugnant? May a lawyer refuse to assist a Nazi, or a remorseless murderer, or a handgun manufacturer, or a grasping land speculator, to buy a personal home? To adopt a child? To defend against an attempt to terminate welfare? Or to defend against the state's attempt to take away parental rights?

Is "ethical shunning" of this kind legitimate? The lawyer could argue that there is no moral obligation to give legal support and comfort to an ethically worthless person. Ethical instincts of this kind seem to inform many people's attitudes and actions in everyday life. Persons with ongoing immoral projects and with prominent immoral acts in their past frequently find themselves avoided by others with whom they might wish to deal.

But one may properly be concerned that such a position might give insufficient regard to the human dignity even of moral reprobates. Ethical shunning is an extreme stance that intuitively seems ligitimate only with respect to extreme instances of unrepentant moral agents. It strikes me that it would be inappropriate if carried to the extent of attempting to legitimize rejection of representation on all unrelated legal matters brought by any person whose representation the lawyer properly may have rejected on another matter. For example, the unrepentant political activist who wishes to take advantage of an unwise law to unseat an elected opponent does not seem to have acted in a way that forfeits his or her claim for legal services on totally unrelated matters. To take a more difficult case, it seems to me that under present social and political conditions in the United States, it goes too far to reject the case of the unrepentant Nazi with unrelated welfare or parental rights problems.

Who Is a "Necessitous" Client

Recall that even in the instance of an unrepugnant prospective client, a duty to represent does not arise for minor legal matters. A duty lies only where the hurt to the client because of the lack of representation threatens to become severe. A fortiori, the loss to a prospective repugnant client normally must be even greater. The problem that remains is to supply more precisely articulated measures of the "weight" to be accorded to different client needs.

At one extreme, consider an innocent Nazi erroneously accused of a serious crime who comes to a competent defense lawyer after being rejected by many other lawyers. Assume that the situation had arisen at a time when there was no right to a court-appointed lawyer in criminal cases. May this lawyer decline the representation on the ground of a strong revulsion against Nazism and its adherents? Even if the prospective client's Nazi beliefs have something to do with the charged offense, still I believe that a duty to represent may exist. For example, if the offense charged was murder and the Nazi had killed the decedent in self-defense against an attack that was caused by the decedent's strong anti-Nazi sentiments, the threatened imprisonment of an innocent would be critical. Even if the Nazi refused to regret the death, even delighted that it was necessary and that a skilled lawyer might obtain an acquittal, still the unwarranted threat to the Nazi's freedom from the impending criminal proceeding would create a duty to rescue.

Suppose, in contrast, that the Nazi seeks the vindication of a right of free speech in order to be able in the future to spread, legally but viciously, Nazi gospel about Jews and blacks. If a lawsuit could protect the right, is a lawyer entitled to refuse the representation, even if this means that the Nazi's legal right to speak will not be vindicated? My conclusion is that no lawyer has any duty to assist such a representation. This situation and that of the innocent Nazi accused of murder are different in several ways. Unlike the murder situation, here the abhorrent ideology of Nazism is central to the proposed course of conduct. With the lawyer's assistance the ideology can be broadcast; without it, it will be suppressed, even if against the legal right of the Nazi to free expression. Critically different from the unjust murder charge, here the Nazi proposes to engage in future elective behavior. Moreover, it is behavior that will impose harm upon the targets of the speech, Jews and blacks, whereas an acquittal of an unjust murder charge will have no "victims." Note that there still is a reason why a lawyer of normal moral instincts might decide to accept the representation: unlawful governmental interference with free speech may encourage more governmental lawlessness. But that threat does not seem so great as to override by itself a lawyer's conscientious scruple against the representation.

Nor do I think that "necessitousness" is present in the following situation. Suppose now that the Nazi wishes to purchase a house, a transaction that, we will assume, requires legal assistance that no other lawyer will provide. As in the criminal defense situation, one could view this as an instance in which the Nazi is sanctioned by the practical need for legal representation and by the refusal of lawyers to provide it. As in the criminal defense situation, moreover, the Nazi is innocent of any wrong that would legally deprive him or her of the entitlement to housing; Nazis are not for that reason barred by law from purchasing houses. And, finally, unlike the free speech situation, here the lawyer's assistance would not have the direct effect of facilitating an act that the lawyer finds reprehensible (publication of Nazi racial views). How, then, can it be that the lawyer is freer in this instance to decline the representation than in the innocent defense situation?

The answer, to my mind, depends less on the nature of the legal rights that might be asserted by the client than upon the sort of human need that vindication of the legal right will fulfill in the particular case. In short, "necessitousness" for our purposes should not take its meaning primarily from legal concepts, but from the needs of human beings. The needs for freedom and dignity are implicated strongly, for example, when an innocent is accused of crime. But basic needs are much less strongly implicated when someone wishes to hold a parade or give a speech (unless all or most other avenues of expression are also closed). Similarly, these needs would typically not be implicated in a Nazi's desire to buy a house, unless, as would be highly unlikely, the purchase were necessary in order to provide essential shelter not available through other common means, such as rental.

Also excluded from the category of necessitousness would be "windfall" situations and certainly those in which vindication of the repugnant client's legal rights would be at another person's expense. Consider a case in which a person convicted of murder on overwhelming evidence is released following an appeal. The appellate court, we will imagine, concludes that the trial was fair and that a guilty verdict was inescapable under the evidence presented. Nonetheless, the court reverses for a reason that has nothing to do with fairness of the proceeding or accuracy of the determination—for example, because the legislature had mistakenly repealed the statute upon which the prosecution was based. The accused, released from all further obligation to stand trial as a defendant in a criminal trial by a legal technicality, comes to a lawyer for assistance in securing an inheritance from the murdered decedent. On the assumption that it would be legally possible for a civil trial to result in granting the murderer the inheritance, the objectionability of such a result, the outrageousness of the murder, and the lack of any compelling need for the inheritance would plainly permit any lawyer to decline the representation, even if this would mean that the murderer was unrepresented in efforts to obtain the inheritance.

In general then, the "rescue" obligation arises only when the prospective client seeks to vindicate a legal right to an essential human need. For anything else, I believe that the lawyer with moral objection to the prospective repugnant client may decline a representation. A fortiori, this means that a lawyer would never be required to undertake a representation in which the client's objective or the client's chosen means were clearly morally objectionable. This follows because the concept of essential human needs includes no right to act immorally or for immoral ends. Thus, a Nazi seeking to protect a legal right to circulate hate literature seeks no basic human right of his or her own. The grasping land speculator seeking to dispossess an impoverished householder seeks through law no basic human need; indeed, the speculator may be seeking to deprive the victim of satisfaction of such a need.

This overall view entails discrimination among various legal rights. For the limited purpose of determining whether a moral obligation to represent a client exists, most legal rights are thus viewed as nonabsolutes whose value and claim for recognition will wax and wane with the circumstances of their expression and with the extent to which they are important in vindicating underlying human needs. Rights of free expression, as I have developed in the example of the Nazi client, thus are not of unitary value. Racial hate (and pornography and other immoral, even if legal, expression) does not stand on the same footing as other forms of expression. Even a right to freedom, if based upon legal technicalities of the kind I have described, is not absolute, but can be ignored by a lawyer who on strong conscientious grounds determines not to represent the "deserving guilty."

The Problem of the "Lawyers' Trump"

Yet the image of an unrepresented client losing a valuable and legally defensible right because all lawyers refuse to lend their aid does not rest entirely comfortably on the mind. The refusal of any lawyer to provide assistance to a morally repugnant client takes on the appearance of an exceptional social policy forced upon a person because of rejection of his or her otherwise lawful or at least legally immune (if immoral) actions. It might be objected that the persistent refusal of lawyers to represent such persons places the seriatim, uniform judgment of lawyers in a position of veto over the considered judgment of public officials—those who promulgated the legal right to free speech regardless of its vicious content or to inherit from one's murdered victim in some circumstances. The resulting "lawyers' trump" replaces official judgments and policies with private moral ones. Unless some mechanism were invented for testing lawyers' opinions by a court of review, we would have to defend the imposition of consequences through a process that is both informal and, arguably, illegitimate in a representational democracy. Nonetheless, I believe that limiting a duty to represent in the way proposed is justifiable.

Perhaps the most telling response to the "lawyers' trump" objection is that it is addressed more to reasons why a society might decide to enact laws requiring lawyers to represent even repugnant clients, or some of them in some situations. It is not an argument that uniformly held moral refusals to provide legal services are necessarily unjust. Political institutions sometimes do enact prophylactic laws because of a legislative suspicion about the process or the product of private judgments. Certain laws dealing with racial discrimination, for example, may be written broadly so as to sanction both morally inappropriate and morally appropriate behavior. A business, for example, will be precluded by law from participating in government contracts unless an announced percentage of the contractor's workforce are members of minority races. That the employer, in good faith and with great effort, has been unable to hire a sufficient number of minority workers may be legally irrelevant. Automobiles are legally constrained to operate at a speed of no higher than 55 miles per hour regardless of the safety of a higher speed at a particular time and regardless of the demonstrably greater gasoline economy of a higher speed for a particular automobile. In law, individuation may be either administratively infeasible or impossible to monitor because intent, motive, or similar internal sentiments may be a significant or the only relevant determinant.

But there should be no moral imperative to act in a particular way solely for the reason that other moral agents might act immorally in the same circumstances. Moral philosophy is all about individual states of mind, about subjective knowledge, intentions, and wishes. And on the level of just social arrangements, many kinds of commonly held moral judgments are not subjected to legal control although, similar to the "lawyers' trump," they can achieve a kind of uniform application that suggests extralegal legislation. Employers might uniformly refuse employment to a Nazi, legally in most jurisdictions as far as I know. Persons who know of a Nazi's beliefs might refuse them their friendship, refuse to greet them on the street, refuse to contract with them, move away from them in public places. We have assumed from the beginning that certain deeply held feelings of repugnance—toward Nazis, murders, grasping entrepreneurs, and others—are entirely defensible on moral grounds. If uniformity in moral judgments produces a de facto kind of extralegal social control, so long as the "shunning" is not itself unlawful, then it would seem that it is morally justified.

Yet a political system well might conclude that universal provision of legal services is still plainly warranted even if not compelled by individual morality. A legal system might determine, for example, that in fact many lawyers are failing in their moral responsibility to provide legal services to clients in need of them. It might be concluded that, regardless of actual immoral practices of lawyers, a legal system should always provide a method of last resort for reasons of appearances—some type of mandatory lawyer appointment—to assure even skeptics that no one has been deprived of a legal right because of a morally indefensible decision by individual lawyers not to provide representation.

Most importantly, the analysis pursued here leaves two very numerous classes of potential clients without representation. The first class is composed of those whose representation would impose too great a burden on the lawyer, most obviously an economic one. The second class is composed of prospective clients asserting legal rights to what I have denominated nonessential human needs. A great many members of both sets will be persons whose lack of lawyer assistance is attributable to poverty. Recent severe restrictions of federal funding for legal services have exacerbated their plight. On my analysis individual lawyers are not required by good morals to make extraordinary efforts in the first case or any effort in the second. But a system that in effect permits access to its justice system to be allocated according to the ability of holders of legal rights to pay might truly be counted unjust. Both justice and sound policy may place demands for income redistribution upon a legal system that are radically different from the demands that morality places upon individuals for voluntary contributions to others who are in need.

C

Counseling the Poor

In re Meizlish

SUPREME COURT OF MICHIGAN, 1972
387 MICH. 228, 196 N.W.2D 129

SWAINSON, Justice.

On February 6, 1969, Fred Clay was convicted in Wayne County Circuit Court, upon a plea of guilty, of breaking and entering a business establishment with intent to commit the crime of larceny.[1] On March 3, 1969, he was sentenced to a term of not less than eight nor more than ten years. Defendant had been represented by Max M. Silverman, of the Defender's office—Legal Aid and Defender Association of Detroit, and that office was initially appointed to represent him for post-conviction and appellate proceedings. However, that office filed a motion to withdraw on the grounds that it could not "objectively review the validity and merits of a plea of guilty in which it participated and which, in the opinion of Max M. Silverman, was providently entered." The motion was granted on May 23, 1969, and on May 28, 1969, Sheldon M. Meizlish was appointed as substitute counsel for post-conviction and appellate proceedings. After a careful and considered review of the matter, Mr. Meizlish concluded that there was no basis for any meaningful challenge of the conviction and, after securing the approval of defendant, filed a motion to withdraw. That motion was granted on September 5, 1969.

The defendant indicated that he still desired to challenge his conviction and in conformity with the requirements of *In re Hoffman* (1969), 382 Mich. 66, 168 N.W.2D 229, the court appointed David Eason as new counsel.

In seeking leave to withdraw, Mr. Meizlish followed the suggested procedure of the U.S. Supreme Court in *Anders v. California*, 386 U.S. 738, 87 S.Ct. 1396, 18 L.Ed.2d 493 (1967), Mr. Meizlish requested a fee for his services and submitted to the court a detailed service voucher showing that he had spent 9¾ hours working on defendant's case.[2] The trial court agreed that the services claimed were reasonable and did not doubt that they were performed.

---

[1]M.C.L.A. §750.110 (Stat. Ann. 1971 Cum. Supp. §28.305).
[2][Record of service voucher omitted.]

Wayne Circuit Court Rule 14.13[3] provides for compensation for assigned counsel. The trial court construed it to allow $50, and this amount was awarded to Mr. Meizlish. Mr. Meizlish was dissatisfied with the award and filed a motion for rehearing. The motion was denied on December 5, 1969. The Court of Appeals denied leave to appeal on April 16, 1970. We granted leave to appeal. 384 Mich. 752.

Appellant states the issue as follows:

> "Did Wayne County Circuit Court Local Rule 14.13 and the award for attorney fees in this case violate the Appellant's rights under the Fourteenth Amendment of the Federal Constitution and Article I, Sections 2 and 17, of the State Constitution, to due process of law and equal protection of laws, and do they violate the right of every indigent defendant, particularly those who desire to institute post-conviction proceedings, to effective assistance of counsel, the right to an effective appeal, due process of law and equal protection of laws in violation of Amendments 6 and 14 of the Federal Constitution and Article I, Sections 2, 17 and 20, of the State Constitution?"

* * *

Appellant contends that the system provided under Wayne Circuit Court Rule 14.13 is irrational and promotes assembly line justice. We cannot agree with this contention. Distinctions are made in the amount of money a lawyer receives if, for example, he conducts a preliminary examination as opposed to waiving a preliminary examination [Rule 14.13 subd. (b)]. Additional fees are granted if a case is appealed to a higher court [Rule 14.13 subd. (k)]. Obviously, lawyers may spend more time on some cases than on others and still receive the same compensation, and certainly in some cases a lawyer will receive far below the minimum bar fees. But, in general, the court rule does provide reasonable compensation for court appointed attorneys for indigents.

Appellant's contention that he has been deprived of due process and equal protection under the U.S. Const. and Mich. Const. 1963 has been discussed and decided adversely to him by numerous courts in this country.[4] In *United States v. Dillon*, 346 F.2d 633 (9 Cir. 1965), certiorari denied 382 U.S. 978, 86 S.Ct. 550, 15 L.Ed.2d 469, the court rejected an attorney's contention that property was taken in violation of due process of law when he was forced to defend an indigent defendant without compensation. The court stated (346 F.2d p. 635):

> "An applicant for admission to practice law may justly be deemed to be aware of the traditions of the profession which he is joining, and to know that one of these traditions is that a lawyer is an officer of the court obligated to represent indigents for little or no compensation upon court order. Thus, the lawyer

[3]The present Wayne Circuit Court Rules became effective on November 1, 1970. At the time this action commenced the applicable rule was 14.5. Present rule 14.13 is identical to the previous rule 14.5.

[4]For a complete collection of these cases, see 21 A.L.R.3d 804, et seq. It appears that only one state, Indiana, has held that the State Constitution requires compensation for an attorney appointed to represent an indigent defendant.

has consented to, and assumed, this obligation and when he is called upon to fulfill it, he cannot contend that it is a 'taking of his services.' "

In *Jackson v. State*, 413 P.2d 488, 490 (Alaska, 1966) the court held that the attorney did not have a constitutional right to compensation for defending an indigent defendant. The court stated:

"The requirement of the attorney's oath and Canon 4 reflect a tradition deeply rooted in the common law—that an attorney is an officer of the court assisting the court in the administration of justice, and that as such he has an obligation when called upon by the court to render his services for indigents in criminal cases without payment of a fee except as may be provided by statute or rule of court. This principle is so firmly established in the history of the courts and the legal profession that it may be said to be a condition under which lawyers are licensed to practice as officers of the court."

Likewise, the courts have uniformly rejected the contention that an attorney is denied the equal protection of laws when he defends an indigent without compensation.

* * *

Appellant has demonstrated the difficult problems that courts face in insuring an efficient administration of criminal justice, combined with the concern for defendants' constitutional rights. Our Court will continue to work for improvement of our present system, agreeing with the appellant that it must be improved.

To this end the State Bar as well as a number of local bar associations have recently petitioned the Court to adopt a rule requiring that court appointed counsel be compensated for their services in accordance with the State Bar Minimum Fee Schedule. Because of these increasingly insistent demands for such a uniform schedule of fees, and in view of the present dialog regarding improved methods of financing the entire judicial system, we shall doubtless review the question again in the future, but for the present we are reluctant to take such action as would plunge the counties into a position of responsibility for the payment of attorneys' fees more than double those presently paid.[5] Such a burden we are not yet prepared to thrust upon them.

Therefore, we hold that Wayne Circuit Court Rule 14.13 is not arbitrary and capricious and does not violate appellant's rights under the due process and equal protection clauses of the United States Constitution or the Michigan Constitution of 1963.

Judgment affirmed.

[5][Supporting data omitted.]

N.A.A.C.P. v. Button

SUPREME COURT OF THE UNITED STATES, 1963
371 U.S. 415, 83 S. CT. 328, 9 L.ED.2D 405

Mr. Justice BRENNAN delivered the opinion of the Court.

This case originated in companion suits by the National Association for the Advancement of Colored People, Inc. (NAACP), and the NAACP Legal Defense and Educational Fund, Inc. (Defense Fund), brought in 1957 in the United States District Court for the Eastern District of Virginia.

* * *

The NAACP was formed in 1909 and incorporated under New York law as a nonprofit membership corporation in 1911.

* * *

The basic aims and purposes of the NAACP are to secure the elimination of all racial barriers which deprived Negro citizens of the privileges and burdens of equal citizenship rights in the United States. To this end the Association engages in extensive educational and lobbying activities. It also devotes much of its funds and energies to an extensive program of assisting certain kinds of litigation on behalf of its declared purposes. For more than 10 years, the Virginia conference [of the NAACP] has concentrated upon financing litigation aimed at ending racial segregation of public schools in the Commonwealth.

The Conference ordinarily will finance only cases in which the assisted litigant retains an NAACP staff lawyer to represent him. The Conference maintains a legal aid staff of 15 attorneys, all of whom are Negroes and members of the NAACP. The staff is elected at the Conference's annual convention. Each legal staff member must agree to abide by the policies of the NAACP, which, insofar as they pertain to professional services, limit the kinds of litigation which the NAACP will assist. Thus the NAACP will not underwrite ordinary damages actions, criminal actions in which the defendant raises no question of possible racial discrimination, or suits in which the plaintiff seeks separate but equal rather than fully desegregated public school facilities. The staff decides whether a litigant, who may or may not be an NAACP member, is entitled to NAACP assistance. The Conference defrays all expenses of litigation in an assisted case, and usually, although not always, pays each lawyer on the case a per diem fee not to exceed $60, plus out-of-pocket expenses. The assisted litigant receives no money from the Conference or the staff lawyers. The staff member may not accept, from the litigant or any other source, any other compensation for his services in an NAACP-assisted case. None of the staff receives a salary or retainer from the NAACP; the per diem fee is paid only for professional services in a particular case. This per diem payment is smaller than the compensation ordinarily received for equivalent private professional work. The actual conduct of assisted litigation is under the control of the attorney, although the NAACP continues to be concerned that the outcome of the lawsuit should be consistent with NAACP's policies already described. A client is free at any time to withdraw from an action.

The members of the legal staff of the Virginia Conference and other NAACP or Defense Fund lawyers called in by the staff to assist are drawn into litigation in various ways. One is for an aggrieved Negro to apply directly to the Conference or the legal staff for assistance. His application is referred to the Chairman of the legal staff. The Chairman, with the concurrence of the President of the Conference, is authorized to agree to give legal assistance in an appropriate case. In litigation involving public school segregation, the procedure tends to be different. Typically, a local NAACP branch will invite a member of the legal staff to explain to a meeting of parents and children the legal steps necessary to achieve desegregation. The staff member will bring printed forms to the meeting authorizing him, and other NAACP or Defense Fund attorneys of his designation, to represent the signers in legal proceedings to achieve desegregation. On occasion, blank forms have been signed by litigants, upon the understanding that a member or members of the legal staff, with or without assistance from other NAACP lawyers, or from the Defense Fund, would handle the case. It is usual, after obtaining authorizations, for the staff lawyer to bring into the case the other staff members in the area where suit is to be brought, and sometimes to bring in lawyers from the national organization of the Defense Fund. In effect, then, the prospective litigant retains not so much a particular attorney as the "firm" of NAACP and Defense Fund lawyers, which has a corporate reputation for expertness in presenting and arguing the difficult questions of law that frequently arise in civil rights litigation.

The meetings are sometimes prompted by letters and bulletins from the Conference urging active steps to fight segregation. The Conference has on occasion distributed to the local branches petitions for desegregation to be signed by parents and filed with local school boards, and advised branch officials to obtain, as petitioners, persons willing to "go all the way" in any possible litigation that may ensue. While the Conference in these ways encourages the bringing of lawsuits, the plaintiffs in particular actions, so far as appears, make their own decisions to become such.[6]

Statutory regulation of unethical and nonprofessional conduct by

---

[6]Seven persons who were or had been plaintiffs in Virginia public school suits did testify that they were unaware of their status as plaintiffs and ignorant of the nature and purpose of the suits to which they were parties. It does not appear, however, that the NAACP had been responsible for their involvement in litigation. These plaintiffs testified that they had attended meetings of parents without grasping the meaning of the discussions, had signed authorizations either without reading or without understanding them, and thereafter had paid no heed to the frequent meetings of parents called to keep them abreast of legal developments. They also testified that they were not accustomed to read newspapers or listen to the radio. Thus they seem to have had little grasp of what was going on in the communities. Two of these seven plaintiffs had been persuaded to sign authorization by their own children, who had picked up forms at NAACP meetings. Five were plaintiffs in the Prince Edward County school litigation in which 186 persons were joined as plaintiffs. See *NAACP v. Patty,* 159 F.Supp. 503, 517 (D.C.E.D.Va. 1958).

attorneys has been in force in Virginia since 1849. These provisions outlaw, inter alia, solicitation of legal business in the form of "running" or "capping." Prior to 1956, however, no attempt was made to proscribe under such regulation the activities of the NAACP, which had been carried on openly for many years in substantially the manner described. In 1956, however, the legislature amended, by the addition of Chapter 33, the provision of the Virginia Code forbidding solicitation of business by a "runner" or "capper" to include, in the definition of "runner" or "capper," an agent for an individual or organization which retains a lawyer in connection with an action to which it is not a party and in which it has no pecuniary right or liability. The Virginia Supreme Court of Appeals held that the chapter's purpose was to strengthen the existing statutes to further control the evils of solicitation of legal business. . . ." 202 Va., at 154, 116 S.C.2d, at 65. The court held that the activities of NAACP, the Virginia Conference, the Defense Fund, and the lawyers furnished by them, fell within, and could constitutionally be proscribed by, the chapter's expanded definition of improper solicitation of legal business, and also violated Canons 35 and 47 of the American Bar Association's Canons of Professional Ethics, which the court had adopted, in 1938. Specifically the court held that, under the expanded definition, such activities on the part of NAACP, the Virginia Conference, and the Defense Fund constituted "fomenting and soliciting legal business in which they are not parties and have no pecuniary right or liability, and which they channel to the enrichment of certain lawyers employed by them, at no cost to the litigants and over which the litigants have no control." 202 Va., at 155; 116 S.E.2d, at 66.

* * *

We reverse the judgment of the Virginia Supreme Court of Appeals. We hold that the activities of the NAACP, its affiliates and legal staff shown on this record are modes of expression and association protected by the First and Fourteenth Amendments which Virginia may not prohibit, under its power to regulate the legal profession, as improper solicitation of legal business violative of Chapter 33 and the Canons of Professional Ethics.

A.

We meet at the outset the contention that "solicitation" is wholly outside the area of freedoms protected by the First Amendment. To this contention there are two answers. The first is that a State cannot foreclose the exercise of constitutional rights by mere labels. The second is that abstract discussion is not the only species of communication which the Constitution protects; the First Amendment also protects vigorous advocacy, certainly of lawful ends, against governmental intrusion. In the context of NAACP objectives, litigation is not a technique of resolving private differences; it is a means for achieving the lawful objectives of equality of treatment by all government, federal, state and local, for the members of the Negro community in this country. It is thus a form of political expression. Groups which find themselves unable to achieve their objectives through the ballot frequently turn to the courts. Just as it was true of the opponents of New Deal legislation during the 1930's[13] for example, no less is it true of the Negro minority today. And under the conditions of modern government litigation may well be the sole practicable avenue open to a minority to petition for redress of grievances.

* * *

C.

* * *

Resort to the courts to seek vindication of constitutional rights is a different matter from the oppressive, malicious, or avaricious use of the legal process for purely private gain. Lawsuits attacking racial discrimination, at least in Virginia, are neither very profitable nor very popular. They are not an object of general competition among Virginia lawyers;[27] the problem is rather one of an apparent dearth of lawyers who are willing to undertake such litigation. There has been neither claim nor proof that any assisted Negro litigants have desired, but have been prevented from retaining, the services of other counsel. We realize that an NAACP lawyer must derive personal satisfaction from participation in litigation on behalf of Negro rights, else he would hardly be inclined to participate at the risk of financial sacrifice. But this would not seem to be the kind of interest or motive which induces criminal conduct.

We conclude that although the petitioner has amply shown that its activities fall within the First Amendment's protections, the State has failed to advance any substantial regulatory interest, in the form of substantive evils flowing from petitioner's activities, which can justify the broad prohibitions which it has imposed. Nothing that this record shows as to the nature and purpose of NAACP activities permits an inference of any injurious intervention in or control of litigation which would constitutionally authorize the application of Chapter 33 to those activities. A fortiori, nothing in this record justifies the breadth and vagueness of the Virginia Supreme Court of Appeals' decree.

* * *

Reversed.

---

[13]Cf. Opinion 148, Committee on Professional Ethics and Grievances, American Bar Association (1935), ruling that the Liberty League's program of assisting litigation challenging New Deal legislation did not constitute unprofessional conduct.

[27]Improper competition among lawyers is one of the important considerations relied upon to justify regulations against solicitation. See Note, "Advertising, Solicitation and Legal Ethics," 7 *Vand L Rev* 677, 684 (1954).

Of Arterial Passageways Through the Legal Process: The Right of Universal Access to Courts and Lawyering Services

LESTER BRICKMAN*

The right of an individual to pursue his legal claims in court is basic to our notions of fair play. Yet for millions of "legally poor" Americans, the high costs involved in litigation effectively foreclose resort to a judicial forum. Professor Brickman examines this high price of justice from both constitutional and policy perspectives. He concludes that the first amendment affords a viable basis for a right of universal access to courts and lawyering services, and that the direct and indirect financial impediments imposed by both the state and the organized bar must be deemed constitutionally suspect.

I

INTRODUCTION

Be it ordeyned and enacted . . . that every pouer persone . . . which have & hereafter shall have cause of accion . . . ayenst any persone . . . shall have . . . writtes originall and writtes of Sub pena . . . therefor nothing paieng to youre Highnes . . . nor to any [other] persone. . . . And that the seid Chaunceller . . . shall assigne suche of the Clerkis which shall doo and use the making and writing of the same writtes . . . and also lerned Councell and attorneyes for the same, without any rewarde taking therefor; And after the said writte . . . be retorned, if it be afore the King in his Benche, the Justices ther shall assign to the same pouer persone . . . Councell . . . which shall geve their Councelles nothing taking for the same, and in like wise the same Justices shall appoynte . . . attorneies for the same pouer persone . . . and all other officers requisite and necessarie to be hadde for the spede of the seid duties without any rewards for their Councelles help. . . .

Statute II Henry VII ch. 12 (1495)[1]

Brickman, Of Arterial Passageways Through the Legal Process: The Right of Universal Access to Courts and Lawyering Services, 48 N.Y.U. L. Rev. 595–97, 617–28, 668 (1973). Reprinted by permisison.

*Professor of Law, University of Toledo College of Law. The author wishes to express his appreciation to Susan Engelman and Alan Lerner, the former having been a research assistant in 1972 and the latter having served in the same capacity in 1973. Ms. Engelman is a graduate of, and Mr. Lerner a third-year student at, the University of Toledo College of Law. This article results from experimental courses and seminars in the legal profession which the author's colleagues at the University of Toledo have been kind enough to allow him to pursue without restraint.

[1]Statutes of the Realm 578, in Maguire, Poverty and Civil Litigation, 36 *Harv. L. Rev.* 361, 373 (1923).

Universal access to the courts and lawyering services is by no means a novel concept. The Romans protected the indigent's access to the judicial system over 2300 years ago.[2] Henry VII's England adopted the statute quoted above in 1495, and engrafted onto our common law the concept that universal access to dispute-solving forums should not be predicated upon an individual's ability to pay for justice. English practice never fully reflected the high ideals espoused by the statute. Even in this country, where the advent of OEO Legal Services has brought the concept nearer to fruition, it is clear that universal access has not become the law of the land. There are, however, a number of legal currents which have brought the issue of universal access to courts and lawyering services to the fore.

The need for expanded access to judicial forums is being generated by new demands for participation in the political process and for sharing in the various forms of governmentally created economic benefits which have become a principal source of wealth in this country.[3] These current developments have increased the resort to courts for resolution of major public policy issues.[4] Consequently, an increased demand for lawyering skills has emerged.[5] However, the plagues of high costs and inefficient delivery of legal services, caused in large part by such restrictive practices as prohibitions against advertising by lawyers, unauthorized-practice-of-law statutes and minimum fee schedules, have priced legal services beyond the means of much of the public.[6]

The impact of this lack of comprehensive legal representation on the quality of justice is incalculable. But surely it cannot be disputed that the lack of equal and open access to the justice-dispensing machinery denies to some segments of the populace one of society's most basic rights. Moreover, since, as will be pointed out, access to the judiciary is meaningless without the assistance of those skilled in the invocation of claims, lack of access to lawyering services is equally damaging to our system of justice.

Despite widespread agreement regarding the foregoing proposition, the Supreme Court has not recognized a fundamental right of universal access under either the due process or equal protection clauses of the

[2]Maguire, *supra* note 1, at 361.

[3]See, e.g., Reich, "The New Property," 73 *Yale L.J.* 733 (1964). See also Address by Wiliam Moore, "A Look to the Future: Occupational Development, to Conference on Paralegals in the United States," 8–9, in Denver, June 25–26, 1971 (copy on file at offices of New York University Law Review).

[4]See, e.g., *Association of Data Processing Serv. v. Camp*, 397 U.S. 150 (1970); *Flast v. Cohen*, 392 U.S. 83 (1968); *Environmental Defense Fund, Inc. v. Hardin*, 428 F.2d 1093 (D.C. Cir. 1970); *Norwalk CORE v. Norwalk Redevelopment Agency*, 395 F.2d 920 (2d Cir. 1968). See also Note, Public Participation in Federal Administrative Proceedings, 120 U. Pa. L. Rev. 702 (1972).

[5]Powell, The President's Annual Address: The State of the Legal Profession, 51 A.B.A.J. 821 (1965).

[6]See B. Christensen, Lawyers for People of Moderate Means 40–81 (1970); Report of the New York State Attorney General Louis J. Lefkowitz on the Non-Availability of Legal Services to Persons of Moderate Income 1–6 (1972; Meserve, "Our Forgotten Client: The Average American," 57 *A.B.A.J.* 1092 (1971). Some commentators have referred to the high prices and inefficient delivery of legal services as the "cost revenue crunch." Sproul, "Use of Lay Personnel in the Practice of Law: Mid-1969," 25 *Bus. Law.* 11, 13–15 (1969); see Strong, "The 'Systems' Approach to Implementing a Program of Lay Assistants for Lawyers" 3, Dec. 15, 1970 (copy on file at offices of New York University Law Review).

fourteenth amendment. However, this article will suggest alternative arguments through which this right may be secured. The primary predicate for such a claim, the first amendment, has already provided protection to newly emerging legal services delivery systems.[7] First amendment protection may serve as the functional equivalent of an outright declaration by the Court of a fundamental right to universal access.

Furthermore, it will also be contended that the organzied bar in its capacity as the effective controller of the practice of law has maintained restrictions that impede access to lawyering services so as to conflict with the first amendment. Subsumed within this argument will be the notion that if lawyers cannot fulfill the needs of the less affluent members of society, then the bar may not wield its monopolistic control to prohibit the dispensation of legal representation by skilled laymen.

It will therefore be the major purpose of this article to analyze the legal arguments supporting the right of the legally poor[8] to be provided with meaningful access to lawyering services and to the judicial process itself, as well as the means of effectuating that right.

* * *

III

ACCESS TO LAWYERING SERVICES

A right of access to the courts is meaningless without concomitant access to lawyering services. Fairness demands that both sides to a dispute have their causes advanced by representatives of relatively equal ability.[118] Furthermore, in view of the importance of litigation to the development of social policy, denial of access to lawyering prevents certain elements of the public from contributing to the creation of new policies that will affect their interests.

Because of the complexity of litigation in modern courts, laymen are incapable of effective and thorough advocacy of their claims.[119] Our judicial system is inundated with technicalities of procedure and nuances of law which present incomprehensible barriers to laymen who seek access to the courts. Our courts do not dispense justice with the simplistic fairness of

---

[7]See *United Transportation Union v. Michigan State Bar*, 401 U.S. 576 (1971); *United Mine Workers v. Illinois State Bar Ass'n*, 389 U.S. 217 (1967); *Brotherhood of R.R. Trainmen v. Virginia ex rel. Virginia State Bar*, 377 U.S. 1 (1964); *NAACP v. Button*, 371 U.S. 415 (1963); text accompanying notes 176–226 infra.

[8]The terms "legally poor" and "legal poverty" will be used in this article to include both indigents and the vast numbers of the middle class who are unable to afford legal services. See note 227 *infra*.

[118]Note, "Trumpets in the Corridors of Bureaucracy: A Coming Right to Appointed Counsel in Administrative Adjudicative Proceedings," 18 *U.C.L.A.L. Rev.* 758, 773 (1971).

[119]"Layman cannot be expected to know how to protect their rights when dealing with practiced and carefully counseled adversaries." *Brotherhood of R.R. Trainmen v. Virginia ex rel. Virginia State Bar*, 377 U.S. 1, 7 (1964).

Solomon; under our system of laws, justice is as often dependent upon the manipulation of complex procedures and symbols as it is on the merits of a cause.[120] The fact that most states require three years of comprehensive legal education before one is allowed to advocate the causes of others attests to the complex matrix within which our courts operate. Moreover, the development of expertise as a litigator requires extensive training, experience and skill beyond the law school education. As a result, it is not surprising that the layman who is unaided by the legal specialist is often lost within our judicial system,[121] for he lacks the skills[122] which are necessary to effectively advocate his position. Consequently, access to the legal process, to courts and to justice itself[123] is dependent upon "the guiding hand of counsel."[124]

[120]An example of the potential complexity of litigation is set out in Brief for Appellant, *Hunt v. Hackett*, Civ. No. 40991 (Cal. Dist. Ct. App.) [hereinafter Brief for Appellant]. In that case, which is presently on appeal, the defendant was successfully sued in an action arising out of a real estate transaction. He had tried to obtain counsel but was unable to afford the retainer. Id. at 2–3. In arguing that civil litigation is no less complex than a criminal proceeding, it was stated:

> As a code-pleading state, California has technical requirements for answers, counter-claims and joinder of parties. Adequate trial preparation frequently will entail interogatories, depositions, inspection of documents and employment of other pre-trial discovery devices. A litigant also must be familiar with demurrers, motions to quash service of process, pleas in abatement, motions for new trial and similar pretrial, trial and posttrial motions available to the litigant. In the instant case, these procedural complexities were compounded by the need to master a matrix of evidentiary rules, possible defenses, contract, property, fraud, negligence and conspiracy principles in order to evaluate and present the case. . . . [T]he testimony of the respondents' expert witness established that the law and facts of this dispute were unusually novel and difficult. . . .

Id. at 13.

[121]Though lawyers thrive on the ambiguities that abound in statutes (which are typically drafted by lawyers), it is well to keep in mind that the statutes are drafted for the typical citizen. How bewildered he must be when lawyers differ sharply as to the interpretation of a statute and the courts are then called upon to decide exactly what the framers of the statute stated or intended. See Dickerson, "Statutory Interpretation: The Users and Anatomy of Context," 23 *Case W. Res. L. Rev.* 353, 367 (1972).

[122]See Lasswell and McDougal, "Legal Education and Public Policy: Professional Training in the Public Interest," 52 *Yale L.J.* 203, 215 (1943)

[123]Empirical data confirm the importance of access to counsel. For example, one study discovered that civil plaintiffs representing themselves were nine times less likely to obtain a settlement, were more likely to have their actions dismissed on the pleadings and were unable either to conduct discovery or reach a trial on the merits. Schmertz, "The Indigent Civil Plaintiff in the District of Columbia," 27 *Fed. B.J.* 235, 243 (1967). In addition, a study of mental hospital commitments conducted by a student publication at the University of Toledo College of Law found that the percentage of unsuccessful commitment proceedings rose from 26.7% to 91.1% when the individuals were represented by counsel. Note, "The Effect of Legal Counsel on the Commitment Decision," *Discovery*, Fall 1973, at 10, 12. See also Wenger and Fletcher, "The Effect of Legal Counsel on Admissions to a State Mental Hospital: A Confrontation of Professions," 10 *J. Health & Soc. Behavior* 66, 69 (1969); Note, "Representation in Child-Neglect Cases: Are Parents Neglected?" 4 *Colum. J.L. & Soc. Prob.* 230, 241 (1968).

[124]*Powell v. Alabama*, 287 U.S. 45, 69 (1932).

Denial of access to lawyering skills is not simply a denial of fairness; it is also a denial of access to the legal process. One of the major components of our lawmaking system is the claim process, through which individuals and groups articulate their demands for a share in society's wealth and for participation in the formulation of society's norms. These demands on our policymaking institutions arise from expectations created by the prior workings of the legal process and reflect values inherent in our social order. The institutional responses to these demands—the resolution of competing claims—are in turn reflected in the statutes, regulations, court decisions and multitude of administrative determinations which govern our collective behavior.[125] Indeed, the law may be regarded as the process of formulation and codification of values and norms which give rise to new expectations which in turn are invoked by new claims. Thus, a dynamic interaction is maintained between claims, the legislative, administrative, executive and judicial responses to the claims, and the expectations given rise to by the responses. The ultimate end of the claim process is a reflection of the expectations of the community. If we are to retain our traditional notions of democracy, all individuals and groups must be able to participate in this lawmaking process.[126]

Those equipped with lawyering skills are the principal evocators in the judicial claim process.[127] If their technical skills are not available, otherwise meritorious claims become vulnerable to evasive tactics which may preclude their just resolution. A motion to dismiss for failure to state a cause of action and its predecessor, the demurrer, are examples of such tactics.[128] It is beyond dispute that many viable claims have never been fully heard because of technical defects in the way in which they were presented. Furthermore, lack of specialized training renders the presentation of novel claims virtually impossible.[129] The ability to read, synthesize, correlate and apply the law to novel situations is a skill that is almost exclusively the province of the lawyer.

In short, the significance of the claim process both to the litigant and to the attainment of democratic values highlights the unique role the lawyer plays in the legal process. It thus becomes clear that access to lawyering skills is a sine qua non of meaningful access to the judicial branch and that denial of access to the skills of advocacy is tantamount to a denial of effective participation in our democratic processes.[130]

[125]See McDougal, "The Comparative Study of Law for Policy Purposes: Value Clarification as an Instrument of Democratic World Order," 61 *Yale L.J.* 915 (1952) [hereinafter McDougal, "Study of Law"].

[126]See generally Lasswell and McDougal, *supra* note 122, at 212; McDougal, "Perspectives for an International Law of Human Dignity," 53 *Am. Soc'y of Int'l L. Proceedings* 107 (1959); McDougal, "Study of Law," *supra* note 125.

[127]See generally Q. Johnstone and D. Hopson, Jr., *Lawyers and Their Work: An Analysis of the Legal Profession in the United States and England* 3 (1967).

[128]See note 120 *supra*.

[129]This problem has been explored by the author in a previous article. See Brickman, *Expansion of the Lawyering Process, supra* note 10, at 1157 n.20.

[130]See, e.g., *NAACP v. Button*, 371 U.S. 415 (1963).

The courts of the United States have recognized the importance of counsel as an essential ingredient of any meaningful right of access to the judicial branch, particularly in the criminal sphere. As early as 1932, in *Powell v. Alabama*,[131] the Supreme Court held that a defendant charged with a capital crime had a right to the assistance of counsel:

> The right to be heard would be, in many cases, of little avail if it did not comprehend the right to be heard by counsel. Even the intelligent and educated layman has small and sometimes no skill in the science of law. If charged with a crime, he is incapable, generally, of determining for himself whether the indictment is good or bad. He is unfamiliar with the rules of evidence. Left without the aid of counsel he may be put on trial without a proper charge, and convicted upon incompetent evidence, or evidence irrelevant to the issue or otherwise inadmissible. He lacks both the skill and knowledge adequately to prepare his defense, even though he may have a perfect one. He requires the guiding hand of counsel at every step in the proceedings against him. Without it, though he be not guilty, he faces the danger of conviction because he does not know how to establish his innocence. If that be true of men of intelligence, how much more true is it of the ignorant and illiterate, or those of feeble intellect. . . .[132]

The proposition that the right to be heard comprehends the right to counsel was reaffirmed and extended in *Gideon v. Wainwright*.[133] Holding that the fourteenth amendment incorporates the sixth amendment right to counsel whenever a defendant is charged with a serious crime, the Supreme Court found that access to lawyering skills is an essential element of our adversarial system of justice.[134] In a subsequent line of cases, the Court has extended this form of protection in two ways. First, defendants have become entitled to the assistance of counsel during the accusatory stages of the criminal process.[135] Second, the protection has been extended to criminal defendants in all cases, misdemeanor and felony, where the possibility of imprisonment exists.[136] It is now evident that a right to be heard in criminal cases is meaningless without a right of access to the "guiding hand of counsel."

Furthermore, the Court has found that where trained attorneys are not available to assist those convicted of criminal offenses, the right of access to lawyering skills is so crucial that it may be secured by consultation with those who have knowledge of the law but no formal training. Thus, in *Johnson v. Avery*,[137] the Court held that the right of access to writs of habeas corpus was denied by a state prison regulation which prohibited inmates

[131]287 U.S. 45 (1932).

[132]Id. at 68–69. Much of the language in *Powell* would seem to apply with equal validity to civil litigation as well.

[133]372 U.S. 335 (1963).

[134]Id. at 344.

[135]See *United States v. Wade*, 388 U.S. 218 (1967); *Miranda v. Arizona*, 384 U.S. 436 (1966); *Escobedo v. Illinois*, 378 U.S. 478 (1964). But see *Kirby v. Illinois*, 406 U.S. 682 (1973).

[136]*Argersinger v. Hamlin*, 407 U.S. 25 (1972).

[137]393 U.S. 483 (1969).

from assisting other inmates in the preparation of petitions for post-conviction relief.[138] Justice Douglas, concurring, emphasized the importance of lawyering skills in this context:

> Where government fails to provide the prison with the legal counsel it demands, the prison generates its own. In a community where illiteracy and mental deficiency is [*sic*] notoriously high, it is not enough to ask a prisoner to be his own lawyer. Without the assistance of fellow prisoners, some meritorious claims would never see the light of a courtroom.[139]

In sum, the right of a criminal defendant to a fair trial, to an opportunity to be heard and to his day in court have been recognized as meaningless without access to lawyering services. The judgment implicit in this line of cases is that the average layman cannot adequately protect his legal interests without the assistance of a skilled advocate. Although the same conclusion may be drawn with respect to litigants in the civil sphere, the right of access to lawyering services is not so well established in this area.

In spite of some viable distinctions between criminal and civil cases,[140] other factors discussed above militate against using these distinctions to deny civil litigants access to the courts.[141] Moreover, persuasive reasons may be advanced to equate access to lawyering skills with meaningful access to civil courts. Civil litigation proceeds in an adversarial context which subsumes the notion of competent representation for all the parties.[142] In addition, some claims which are litigated in the civil branches of our courts closely resemble criminal prosecutions.[143] In such instances, the state hurls the totality of its powers against the civil defendant. Certainly, fairness dictates that one be allowed every available resource to defend oneself in such situations.[144] Indeed, the criminal-civil dichotomy has been entirely

[138]The Court began with the fundamental proposition that "access of prisoners to the courts may not be denied or obstructed." Id. at 485. If the prisoner could not afford to retain paid counsel to prepare his case, then his ability to petition for habeas corpus depended upon the availability of free legal services. If a lawyer was not provided, then laymen who had acquired lawyering skills (so-called "jail-house lawyers") could not be prohibited from assisting the prisoner. Id. at 487. The Court also declared that the state deprived "those unable themselves . . . to prepare their petitions, of access to the constitutionally and statutorily protected availability of the writ of habeas corpus." Id. at 489.

[139]Id. at 496.

[140]See text accompanying notes 70–71 *supra.*

[141]See text accompanying notes 72–75 *supra.*

[142]"[T]here cannot be meaningful access to the judicial process until every serious litigant is represented by competent counsel. . . . [T]he fundamental importance of legal representation in our system of adversary justice is beyond dispute." *Meltzer v. C. Buck LeCraw & Co.*, 402 U.S. 954, 959 (1971) (Black J., dissenting from denial of cert.).

[143]A state-initiated civil suit to deprive parents of custody of their children is an example of such a proceeding. As in criminal prosecutions, the state represents society in such actions. Should the state prevail in the litigation, the consequences for the parents are extremely grave—the loss of their children. Such a proceeding, at least from the point of view of what is at stake, is essentially similar to a criminal prosecution. Id.; see *Danforth v. State Dep't of Health and Welfare.* 303 A.2d 794, 799 (Me. 1973); Note, "Child Neglect: Due Process for the Parent," 70 *Colum. L. Rev.* 465, 477 (1970).

[144]At least two members of the Supreme Court have found this argument compelling. See *Meltzer v. C. Buck LeCraw & Co.*, 402 U.S. 954, 959–60 (1971) (Black, J., dissenting from denial of cert.); id. at 961 (Dougles, J., dissenting from denial of cert.).

discarded in several recent decisions which have held that when the state institutes custody proceedings against an indigent parent, it must supply the parent with counsel unless the right to counsel is knowingly waived.[145]

Furthermore, the unsuccessful litigant in the more mundane civil case may also suffer a "grievous loss."[146] For example, in many states a judgment may be implemented through attachment of wages or bank accounts and execution against an automobile, house or personal property.[147] Collection of judgments by such methods frequently has serious collateral consequences which parallel those of criminal convictions, such as loss of job, impairment of health and disruption of family.[148]

Most fundamentally, the distinction between criminal and civil cases on the basis of rights to liberty as opposed to property is specious. Neither the fifth nor the fourteenth amendment makes such a distinction. Instead, they "guarantee that property, as well as life and liberty, may not be taken from a person without affording him due process of law."[149] Indeed, the Supreme Court has recognized the falsity of the dichotomy between personal liberties and property rights:

> Property does not have rights. People have rights. The right to enjoy property without unlawful deprivation . . . is in truth a "personal" right, whether the "property" in question be a welfare check, a home, or a savings account. In fact, a fundamental interdependence exists between the personal right to liberty and the personal right in property. Neither could have meaning without the other. . . .[150]

The most recent manifestation of the decline of the property–liberty distinction was Justice Powell's concurring opinion in *Argersiner v. Hamlin*,[151] Whereas Justice Douglas' majority opinion applied the *Gideon* rationale to any criminal case where the accused might be deprived of his liberty,[152] Justice Powell argued that the defense of property, as well as

---

[145]*Danforth v. State Dep't of Health and Welfare*, 303 A.2d 794 (Me. 1973); *In re B*. 30 N.Y.2d 352, 285 N.E.2d 288, 334 N.Y.S.2d 133 (1972); *State v. Jamison*, 251 Ore. 114, 444 P.2d 15 (1968). Another recent abandonment case, *In re Murphy*, 7 Clearinghouse Rev. 224 (Cal. Super. Ct. June 29, 1973) (case summary), held that in an action brought by a county to free petitioner's child for adoption, petitioner was entitled to a free copy of transcribed stenographic notes for use on appeal. The progeny of these cases may well constitute an extension of the *Boddie* rationale. Cf. note 154 *infra*.

[146]*Joint Anti-Fascist Refuge Comm. v. McGrath*, 341 U.S. 123, 168 (1951) (Frankfurter, J., concurring). "Often a poor litigant will have more at stake in a civil case than in a criminal case." *Lee v. Habib*, 424 F.2d 891, 901 (D.C. Cir. 1970). "The consequences of a civil judgment can be as devastating as criminal conviction and are often more so, when compared with convictions that result in probation or a fine (or even a short jail sentence)." Brief for Appellant, *supra* note 120, at 18.

[147]See, e.g., Cal. Civ. Pro. Code §§682a, 682.3, 688 (West Supp. 1973).

[148]See 2 D. Caplovitz *Debtors in Default*, ch. 14 (Bureau of Applied Research, Columbia University 1971). The Supreme Court has characterized these social and economic disruptions as "profoundly" affecting a civil litigant's "personal liberty." *Lynch v. Household Fin. Corp.*, 405 U.S. 538, 552 N. 21 (1972).

[149]*Argersinger v. Hamlin*, 407 U.S. 25, 51 (1972) (Powell, J., concurring).

[150]*Lynch v. Household Fin. Corp.*, 405 U.S. 538, 552 (1972).

[151]407 U.S. 25 (1972).

[152]Id. at 33–34.

liberty, might require the provision of legal services for an indigent ligigant. "When the deprivation of property rights and interest is of sufficient consequence, denying the assistance of counsel to indigents who are incapable of defending themselves is a denial of due process."[153]

If unfettered access to courts had been accorded fundamental status under the due process and equal protection clauses, universal access to lawyering services would have been an essential ingredient of that right.[154] Because of the interrelationship between these two rights, the circumscription of the *Boddie* rationale [that, because of the basic position of marriage in "society's hierarchy of values," due process requires access to the courts for the purpose of dissolving a marriage] casts considerable doubt on any claimed right of access to lawyering services. But the problematical status of the claimed right in no way detracts from the clarity of the conclusion that meaningful access to the judiciary is dependent upon access to lawyering skills. Justice entails more than a mere formal hearing of a claim; it requires that the claim be presented by a skilled advocate. The search for an alternative ground on which to premise a fundamental right of access to the legal process implicitly recognizes the symbiotic relationship between these two rights.

IV

BASES FOR A RIGHT OF ACCESS TO LAWYERING SERVICES

The proposition being advanced is simply that there ought to be "Access to the Law for All."[155] In other words, "every individual has a right to legal services as an inherent ingredient of his legal rights and . . . the process which determines his correlative legal duties."[156] This thesis has gained widespread acceptance in virtually every Western nation.[157] For example,

---

[153]Id. at 48.

[154]A New York court has held that the state is required to furnish counsel under the due process clause to all indigent parties in divorce proceedings since access to the court is the exclusive precondition to the termination of a marital relationship. The court distinguished mere presence in court from access to the judicial process, holding that the mere presence of the defendant in court without the representation of counsel did not ripen into access and a meaningful opportunity to be heard under the due process clause. However, the court expressly excluded other civil litigation from the scope of its decision. *Vanderpool v. Vanderpool*, 74 Misc. 2d 122, 344 N.Y.S.2d 572 (Sup. Ct. 1973). New York City is in the process of appealing this decision. 7 Clearinghouse Rev. 205 (1973).

[155]See Transcript of Proceedings of National Conference on Prepaid Legal Services 11 (1972) (address by Leonard Ryan) [hereinafter Transcript].

[156]Pincus, "Programs to Supplement Law Offices for the Poor," 41 *Notre Dame Law.* 887, 892 (1966).

[157]See Cappelletti and Gordley, "Legal Aid: Modern Themes and Variations," 24 *Stan. L. Rev.* 347, 380–86 (1972); Ginsberg, "The Availability of Legal Services to Poor People and People of Limited Means in Foreign Systems," 6 *Int. Law.* 128 (1971). For example, the right to legal assistance in civil litigation was recognized in Germany 500 years ago and was provided through the civil procedure laws of the individual German states. When the second empire

the courts of Switzerland have held that the Swiss equivalent of our equal protection clause[158] requires that a lawyer be provided "in a civil matter where the handling of the trial demands knowledge of the law."[159] A few of our courts have reached similar results.[160]

Nevertheless, the likelihood that courts generally will recognize a right of access in this country remains arguable. As a result, some have advocated the enactment of legislation creating a national system of legal services.[161] Implemented in such a fashion, the nearly 500-year-old stat-

---

was founded in 1871, this right was embodied in the national Code of Civil Procedure which remains in effect today. Klauser and Riegert, "Legal Assistance in the Federal Republic of Germany," 20 *Buffalo L. Rev.* 583, 584–85 (1971). See also Cappelletti, "Fundamental Guarantees of the Parties in Civil Litigation: Comparative, Constitutional, International, and Social Trends," 25 *Stan. L. Rev.* 651 , 692 n.224 (1973); Pelletier, "Legal Aid in France," 42 *Notre Dame Law.* 627 (1967); Stohr, "The German System of Legal Aid: An Alternative Approach," 54 *Calif. L. Rev.* 801 (1966).

[158]"All Swiss are equal before the law. In Switzerland there is neither subjection or privilege of locality, birth, family or person." Constitution fédérale de la Confédération Suisse art. 4 (1874).

[159]O'Brien, "Why Not Appointed Counsel in Civil Cases? The Swiss Approach," 28 *Ohio S.L.J.* 1, 5 (1967).

[160]See *Hotel Martha Washington Management Co. v. Swinick*, 66 Misc. 2d 833, 322 N.Y.S.2d 139 (Sup. Ct. 1971), which held the Constitution and cases such as *Boddie* limited the trial court's statutory discretion not to appoint counsel in appropriate civil cases. See also *Tobak v. Mojica*, 7 Clearinghouse Rev. 167 (N.Y. Sup. Ct. May 11, 1973) (case summary).

[161]For example, William Pincus, one of the most forceful and successful proponents of a right of access to lawyering services, recently stated that:

> The outlines of the required system are certainly clear. What is required is a piece of federal legislation for the legal services scene which would parallel in principle the kind of legislation being considered in regard to national health insurance. Essentially such legislation would guarantee to subsidize out of public funds the cost of legal services, doing so on a sliding scale depending upon a person's income. The services would be provided in most cases by private practitioners, just as they are now for those who can afford to pay the bill under present circumstances. Persons above a certain income level should not receive any subsidy, but in the case of all others the sliding scale of subsidies would apply. Whether a person is poor or not should not be a factor in his or her access to a member of the private practicing bar. The scheme should recognize other forms of practice which provide legitimate legal services and which groups or individuals might prefer. These might include neighborhood law offices, prepaid legal service plans, and group practices such as some labor unions are now organizing for their members. In addition to promulgating overall standards and procedures, the Federal Government's role would be carried out through a system of grants to states whose system for financing legal services would comply with Federal standards. Each state system should provide service on both the civil and the criminal side. Upon approval of a state's system, the Federal Government might provide a minimum of fifty percent of the total cost of providing legal services within the state.

Address by William Pincus, Washburn Law School graduation ceremony at 11, May 3, 1973 (copy on file at New York University Law Review office), to be published in 12 *Washburn L.J.* No. 3 (1973).

utory command of Henry VII's England[162] would take on new life. Although discussion of a national legal services program is becoming more common,[163] the outcome is not sufficiently certain to preclude further analysis of judicial recognition of a right of access. Two possible avenues for judicial consideration, the first policy-oriented and the second derived from precedent, may be usefully examined.

A. The Bar Should Be Regarded as a Public Utility

The provision of access to legal services is accomplished principally by lawyers practicing law. One of the modes of such practice is "lawyering," a term used in this article to mean the invocation of the process of claim, that is, the art of creating and pressing claims to which significant sanctions or value transfers can attach.[164] The means by which lawyering services are conveyed to the public may be generically termed the "legal services delivery system." Control over the various methods of delivering legal services is maintained by the legal profession through its monopoly over the practice of law and its authority over lawyers. However, this monopoly power is subject to implicit limitations that may provide one basis for a right of access to legal services.

The limitations on the bar's exclusive control over legal services are derived from the nature of the services themselves. The practice of law is a public calling. It requires that one assume certain ethical and professional obligations toward other members of society. Furthermore, one may usefully posit the existence of a social contract between the legal profession and the general public, in which the bar receives monopoly power over the legal services delivery system in return for undertaking to deliver those services in an efficient and affordable manner. In view of these factors, a recent book has suggested that the legal profession operates under rules and responsibilities similar to those which attach to a public utility.[165] This analysis leads to the conclusion that the retention of monopoloy control over the legal services delivery is dependent upon the availability of lawyering services for all who desire access to them.[166] A less certain conclusion, which is also advanced here, is that the bar's monopoly control is also dependent upon its making legal services generally available at a reasonable cost.

It is clear that the bar's monopoly enables attorneys to exercise an immoderate degree of control over access to one of our most basic institu-

---

[162]2 Statutes of the Realm 578, in Maguire, *supra* note 1.

[163]A discussion of the Canadian legal aid programs and the potential applicability of provincial funding schemes to the United States will be included on the agenda of a conference on clinical legal education in Canada, sponsored by the Council on Legal Education for Professional Responsibility, Inc. (CLEPR), to take place on November 29–30, 1973 in Montreal, Canada. The conference proceedings will be discussed in a forthcoming issue of the CLEPR Newsletter.

[164]For a discussion of the claim process, see text accompanying notes 125–30 *supra*.

[165]See generally F. Marks, K. Leswing, and B. Fortinsky, *The Lawyer, the Public, and Professional Responsibility* 288–93 (1972) [hereinafter Marks].

[166]Cf. *United Fuel Gas Co. v. Railroad Comm'n of Kentucky*, 278 U.S. 300, 309 (1929).

tions, the judicial forum. As noted above, this access in turn provides individuals and groups with a means of influencing the future development of the law.[167] Our society sets as a foremost goal the widest possible participation in public decisionmaking. Since the bar decides in large part who will participate in the judicial process, it may be concluded as a matter of public policy that the bar's control over the legal profession must be conducted in the public interest.[168] Unfortunately, the bar has for the most part disregarded its public responsibilities.

The grant of a franchise or monopoly power to a public utility is typically justified by the provision of more efficient service to the public. The bar's monopoly over the practice of law requires similar justification. Three assumptions underlie this particular grant of exclusive power: (1) the lawyer performs a socially useful function; (2) the lawyer is a professional who is best equipped to perform that function; and (3) as a professional, the lawyer is capable of self-regulation in the public interest.[169] Yet only the first of these assumptions seems to be grounded in fact; the legal profession is not performing its public function nor is it regulating itself in the public interest.[170] The legal profession allocates its services primarily according to a system of competitive bidding.[171] Only those causes which are sufficiently profitable will win the services of an attorney. Conversely, the claims of the poor and the nonaffluent, as well as many public interest claims, often go unasserted because they are not sufficiently remunerative.

By allocating its services in such a fashion, the bar has ignored its obligations to the public as a whole. As a result, the foundation for its monopoly control over the practice of law has been undermined. The perpetuation of such a dysfunctional monopoly power cannot go unchallenged. Although more drastic remedies may be proposed,[172] it is submitted that the most simple and direct solution is to seek specific perfor-

---

[167]See text accompanying notes 127–30 *supra*. Moreover, the crucial role of lawyers is not limited to the judicial sphere. See text accompanying note 253 *infra*.

[168]Marks, *supra* note 165, at 32–33, 289–90. A useful analogy may be drawn between the bar and the communications media in that both are vehicles which convey essential information and thereby control input into our democratic procedures. The process of claim is an essential component in the system of communicating claims, responses to claims (decisions) and resultant expectations between the public and the decisionmaking institutions. See generally text accompanying notes 125–30 supra. Consequently, lawyers should be treated like licensees under the Federal Communications Act, who are unable to retain their licenses unless they operate in the public interest. See Marks, *supra* at 289–90.

[169]Marks, *supra* note 165, at 288.

[170]"The training and regulating of lawyers still follow the original colonial concept of a small, self-disciplining club. The legal profession is no longer small, and it is arguable if it can still discipline itself." Goldstein, "Legal Ethics and Disbarment," *Wall St. J.*, Aug. 15, 1973, at 10, col. 4. The medical profession's performance in this area is probably superior to that of the legal profession. See note 371 *infra*.

[171]Marks, *supra* note 165, at 291.

[172]It has been suggested that the Government should draft members of the legal profession for public interest work if the cost of legal services remains prohibitive. Id. at 290–91. Moreover, if the bar continues to exclude a great segment of the public from access to its services, the state may have to assume full responsibility for regulating the practice of law and for the cost of lawyering services. Government funding of full legal services has already been proposed. See note 161 *supra*.

mance of the bar's implied contractual obligation to the public. Courts can effectuate this solution by requiring the bar to fulfill its affirmative duty to deliver reasonably priced legal services to all segments of the public.[173] Rules or practices of the legal profession which either prevent the delivery of legal services to the less affluent members of society, or unreasonably raise the costs of legal services, would thus violate the bar's public obligations.[174] Such a course of action is supported by both public policy and the existence of an implied social contract.[175] Enforcing the bar's public duties in such a manner would be the functional equivalent of recognizing a fundamental right of access to lawyering services.

VI

CONCLUSION

The effect of court-related expenses, minimum fee schedules, and prohibitions against advertising, solicitation, specialization, unrestricted group legal services and the unauthorized practice of law, is to bar the legally poor from the formal processes of adjudication and rulemaking in our courts and administrative agencies. These bastions of the legal profession's monopoly over the practice of law have been shown to be constitutionally infirm. Unless a new legal services delivery system, which lacks minimum fees and includes advertising, lay performance of simple legal tasks and the variety of efficiency-increasing techniques, is developed by the bar, the price tag on justice will continue to be unconscionable. Even though the equal protection and due process clauses have failed to provide a basis for successfully challenging impediments to access to the courts and to lawyer-

[173]The duty of a public utility to make its services reasonably available has also been held to apply to quasi-public enterprises. This common law duty requires that public services be rendered without unreasonable discrimination. See *Vaught v. East Tennessee Tel. Co.*, 123 Tenn. 318, 130 S.W. 1050 (1910). Arguably, this duty would enure in such a manner as to prohibit unreasonable discriminations on the basis of wealth. If this construction is adopted, the bar must provide legal services to the public at an affordable price in order to retain its monopoly over the practice of law.

[174]See part V *infra*.

[175]The bar's social contract with the public may be analogized to the common law duty of innkeepers, In exchange for their franchise to operate along the King's highway, innkeepers were required to furnish accommodations to all unobjectionable persons who applied in good faith. See, e.g., Civil Rights Cases, 109 U .S. 3, 25 (1883); *Perrine v. Paulos*, 100 Cal. App. 2d 655, 657, 224 P.2d 41, 42 (1950). The primary rationale for placing an innkeeper under such a duty was that inns were public places and provided the only resting place along the highway. See *Vansant v. Kowalewski*, 28 Del. 92, 96, 90 A. 421, 423 (Super. Ct. 1941).

Similarly, the bar has been granted a franchise to practice law. In return for this grant, the bar must make its services available to the public. Additionally, as is true of innkeepers, the bar's services must be made available in a nondiscriminatory manner. Thus it is arguable that where indigents are excluded from legal assistance, the bar is rendering its services in a discriminatory fashion—the poor of our society are being excluded from the legal services delivery system. The analogy between the innkeeper and the legal profession thus reaffirms the conclusion that the monopoly control exercised by the bar is predicated upon the condition that its services are available to the public without undue restriction.

ing services, the first amendment may prove to be the functional equivalent of a fourteenth amendment guarantee. The bar's practices which prevent segments of our population from participating in the claim process are in jeopardy and ought to so remain until the high ideals espoused by Henry VII's England become a reality in this nation and "every pouer persone . . . shall have . . . [access to courts] and also lerned Councell and attorneyes.[407]

section II

COMPETENCE

A

Law School and Admission to Practice

DeFunis v. Odegaard

Supreme Court of the United States, 1974
416 U.S. 312, 94 S.Ct. 1704, 40 L.Ed.2d 164

Mr. Justice Douglas, dissenting.
    I agree with Mr. Justice Brennan that this case is not moot, and because of the significance of the issues raised I think it is important to reach merits.

I

    The University of Washington Law School received 1601 applications for admission to its first-year class beginning in September 1971. There were spaces available for only about 150 students, but in order to enroll this number the school eventually offered admission to 275 applicants. All applicants were put into two groups, one of which was considered under the minority admissions program. Thirty-seven of those offered admission had indicated on an optional question on their application that their "dominant" ethnic origin was either Black, Chicano, American Indian, or Filipino, the four groups included in the minority admissions program. Answers to this optional question were apparently the sole basis upon which eligibility for the program was determined. Eighteen of these 37 actually enrolled in the law school.
    In general, the admissions process proceeded as follows: An index called the Predicted First Year Average (Average) was calculated for each applicant on the basis of a formula combining the applicant's score on the Law School Admission Test (LSAT) and his grades in his last two years in college. On the basis of its experience with the previous years' applications, the Admissions Committee, consisting of faculty, administration, and students, concluded that the most outstanding applicants were those with

averages above 77; the highest average of any applicant was 81. Applicants with averages above 77 were considered as their applications arrived by random distribution of their files to the members of the Committee who would read them and report their recommendations back to the Committee. As a result of the first three committee meetings in February, March, and April 1971, 78 applicants from this group were admitted, although virtually no other applicants were offered admission this early. By the final conclusion of the admissions process in August 1971, 147 applicants with averages above 77 had been admitted, including all applicants with averages above 78, and 93 of 105 applicants with averages between 77 and 78.

Also beginning early in the admissions process was the culling out of applicants with averages below 74.5. These were reviewed by the Chairman of the Admissions Committee, who had the authority to reject them summarily without further consideration by the rest of the Committee. A small number of these applications were saved by the Chairman for committee consideration on the basis of information in the file indicating greater promise than suggested by the Average. Finally during the early months the Committee accumulated the applications of those with averages between 74.5 and 77 to be considered at a later time when most of the applications had been received and thus could be compared with one another. Since DeFunis' average was 76.23, he was in this middle group.

Beginning in their May meeting the Committee considered this middle group of applicants, whose folders had been randomly distributed to committee members for their recommendations to the Committee. Also considered at this time were remaining applicants with averages below 74.5 who had not been summarily rejected, and some of those with averages above 77 who had not been summarily admitted, but instead held for further consideration. Each committee member would consider the applications competitively, following rough guidelines as to the proportion who could be offered admission. After the Committee had extended offers to admission to somewhat over 200 applicants, a waiting list was constructed in the same fashion, and was divided into four groups ranked by the Committee's assessment of their applications. DeFunis was on this waiting list, but was ranked in the lowest quarter. He was ultimately told in August 1971 that there would be no room for him.

Applicants who had indicated on their application forms that they were either Black, Chicano, American Indian, or Filipino were treated differently in several respects. Whatever their averages, none were given to the Committee Chairman for consideration of summary rejection, nor were they distributed randomly among committee members for consideration along with the other applications. Instead all applications of Black students were assigned separately to two particular committee members: a first-year Black law student on the Committee, and a professor on the Committee who had worked the previous summer in a special program for disadvantaged college students considering application to law school. Applications from among the other three minority groups were assigned to an assistant dean who was on the Committee. The minority applications, while considered competitively with one another, were never directly compared to the remaining applications, either by the subcommittee or by the full committee. As in the admissions process generally, the Committee sought to find "within the minority category, those persons who we thought had the highest probability of succeeding in law school." In reviewing the minority applications, the Committee attached less weight to the Predicted First Year Average "in making a total judgmental evaluation as to the relative ability of the particular applicant to succeed in law school." In its publicly distributed Guide to Applicants, the Committee explained that "[a]n applicant's racial or ethnic background was considered as one factor in our general attempt to convert formal credentials into realistic predictions."

Thirty-seven minority applicants were admitted under this procedure. Of these, 36 had Predicted First Year Averages below DeFunis' 76.23, and 30 had averages below 74.5, and thus would ordinarily have been summarily rejected by the Chairman. There were also 48 nonminority applicants who had Predicted First Year Averages below DeFunis. Twenty-three of these were returning veterans, and 25 others presumably admitted because of other factors in their applications making them attractive candidates despite their relatively low averages.

It is reasonable to conclude from the above facts that while other factors were considered by the Committee, and were on occasion crucial, the Predicted First Year Average was for most applicants a heavily weighted factor, and was at the extremes virtually dispositive. A different balance was apparently struck, however, with regard to the minority applicants. Indeed, at oral argument, the law school advised us that were the minority applicants considered under the same procedure as was generally used, none of those who eventually enrolled at the law school would have been admitted.

The educational policy choices confronting a University Admission Committee are not ordinarily a subject for judicial oversight; clearly it is not for us but for the law school to decide which tests to employ, how heavily to weight recommendations from professors or undergraduate grades and what level of achievement on the chosen criteria are sufficient to demonstrate that the candidate is qualified for admission. What places this case in a special category is the fact that the school did not choose one set of criteria but two, and then determined which to apply to a given applicant on the basis of his race. The Committee adopted this policy in order to achieve "a reasonable representation" of minority groups in the law school. Although it may be speculated that the Committee sought to rectify what it perceived to be cultural or racial biases in the Law School Admission Test or in the candidates' undergraduate records, the record in this case is devoid of any evidence of such bias, and the school has not sought to justify its procedures on this basis.

* * *

III

The Equal Protection Clause did not enact a requirement that Law Schools employ as the sole criterion for admissions a formula based upon the LSAT and undergraduate grades, nor does it proscribe law schools from evaluating an applicant's prior achievements in light of the barriers that he had to overcome. A Black applicant who pulled himself out of the ghetto into a junior college may thereby demonstrate a level of motivation, perseverance and ability that would lead a fairminded admissions committee to conclude that he shows more promise for law study than the son of a rich alumnus who achieved better grades at Harvard. That applicant would not be offered admission because he is Black, but because as an individual he has shown he has the potential, while the Harvard man may have taken less advantage of the vastly superior opportunities offered him. Because of the weight of the prior handicaps, the Black applicant may not realize his full potential in the first year of law school, or even in the full three years, but in the long pull of a legal career his achievements may far outstrip those of his classmates whose earlier records appeared superior by conventional criteria. There is currently no test available to the admissions committee that can predict such possibilities with assurance, but the committee may nevertheless seek to gauge it as best as it can, and weigh this factor in its decisions. Such a policy would not be limited to Blacks, or Chicanos or Filipinos or American Indians, although undoubtedly groups such as these may in practice be the principle beneficiaries of it. But a poor Appalachian white, or a second generation Chinese in San Francisco, or some other American whose lineage is so diverse as to defy ethnic labels, may demonstrate similar potential and thus be accorded favorable consideration by the committee.

The difference between such a policy and the one presented by this case is that the committee would be making decisions on the basis of individual attributes, rather than according a preference solely on the basis of race. To be sure, the racial preference here was not absolute—the committee did not admit all applicants from the four favored groups. But it did accord all such applicants a preference by applying, to an extent not precisely ascertainable from the record, different standards by which to judge their applications, with the result that the committee admitted minority applicants who, in the school's own judgment, were less promising than other applicants who were rejected.

* * *

This consideration of race as a measure of an applicant's qualification normally introduces a capricious and irrelevant factor working an invidious discrimination. Once race is a starting point educators and courts are immediately embroiled in competing claims of different racial and ethnic groups that would make difficult manageable standards consistent with the Equal Protection Clause. "The clear and central purpose of the Fourteenth Amendment was to eliminate all official state sources of invidious racial discrimination in the States." The law school's admission policy cannot be reconciled with that purpose, unless cultural standards of a diverse rather than a homogeneous society are taken into account. The reason is that professional persons, particularly lawyers, are not selected for life in a computerized society. The Indian who walks to the beat of Chief Seattle of the Muckleshoot Tribe in Washington has a different culture than Examiners at Law Schools.

The key to the problem is the consideration of each application *in a racially neutral way*. Since LSAT reflects questions touching on cultural backgrounds, the admissions committee acted properly in my view in setting minority applications apart for separate processing. These minorities have cultural backgrounds that are vastly different from the dominant Caucasian. Many Eskimos, American Indians, Filipinos, Chicanos, Asian Indians, Burmese, and Africans come from such disparate backgrounds that a test sensitively tuned for most applicants would be wide of the mark for many minorities.

The melting pot is not designed to homogenize people, making them uniform in consistency. The melting pot as I understand it is a figure of speech that depicts the wide diversities tolerated by the First Amendment under one flag. Minorities in our midst who are to serve actively in our public affairs should be chosen on talent and character alone, not on cultural orientation or leanings.

I do know, coming as I do from Indian country in Washington, that many of the young Indians know little about Adam Smith or Karl Marx but are deeply imbued with the spirit and philosophy of Chief Robert B. Jim of the Yakimas, Chief Seattle of the Muckleshoots, and Chief Joseph of the Nez Perce which offer competitive attitudes toward life, fellow man, and nature.

I do not know the extent to which Blacks in this country are imbued with ideas of African Socialism. Leopold Senghor and Sekon Torae, most articulate of African leaders, have held that modern African political philosophy is not oriented either to marxism or to capitalism. How far the reintroduction into educational curricula of ancient African art and history has reached the minds of young Afro-Americans I do not know. But at least as respects Indians, Blacks, and Chicanos—as well as those from Asian cultures—I think a separate classification of these applicants is warranted, lest race be a subtle force in eliminating minority members because of cultural differences.

Insofar as LSAT tests reflect the dimensions and orientation of the Organizational Man they do a disservice to minorities. I personally know that admissions tests were once used to eliminate Jews. How many other minorities they aim at I do not know. My reaction is that the presence of an LSAT test is sufficient warrant for a school to put racial minorities into a separate class in order better to probe their capacities and potentials.

The merits of the present controversy cannot in my view be resolved on this record. A trial would involve the disclosure of hidden prejudices, if any, against certain minorities and the manner in which substitute measurements of one's talents and character were employed in the conventional tests. I could agree with the majority of the Washington Supreme Court only if, on the record, it could be said that the law school's selection was racially neutral. The case, in my view, should be remanded for a new trial to consider, *inter alia*, whether the established LSAT tests should be eliminated so far as racial minorities are concerned.

This does not mean that a separate LSAT test must be designed for minority racial groups, although that might be a possibility. The reason for the separate treatment of minorities as a class is to make more certain that racial factors do not militate *against an applicant or on his behalf.*

* * *

The key to the problem is consideration of such applications *in a racially neutral way.* Abolition of the LSAT test would be a start. The invention of substitute tests might be made to get a measure of an applicant's cultural background, perception, ability to analyze, and his or her relation to groups. They are highly subjective, but unlike the LSAT they are not concealed but in the open. A law school is not bound by any legal principle to admit all students by mechanical criteria which are insensitive to the potential of such an applicant which may be realized in a more hospitable environment. It will be necessary under such an approach to put more effort into assessing each individual than is required when LSAT scores and undergraduate grades dominate the selection process. Interviews with the applicant and others who know him is a time-honored test. Some schools currently run summer programs in which potential students who likely would be bypassed under conventional admissions criteria are given the opportunity to try their hand at law courses, and certainly their performance in such programs could be weighed heavily. There is, moreover, no bar to considering an individual's prior achievements in light of the racial discrimination that barred his way, as a factor in attempting to assess his true potential for a successful legal career. Nor is there any bar to considering on an individual basis, rather than according to racial classifications, the likelihood that a particular candidate will more likely employ his legal skills to service communities that are not now adequately represented than will competing candidates. Not every student benefited by such an expanded admissions program would fall into one of the four racial groups involved here, but it is no drawback that other deserving applicants will also get an opportunity they would otherwise have been denied. Certainly such a program would substantially fulfill the law school's interest in giving a more diverse group access to the legal profession. Such a program might be less convenient administratively than simply sorting students by race, but we have never held administrative convenience to justify racial discrimination.

* * *

. . . The Equal Protection Clause commands the elimination of racial barriers, not their creation in order to satisfy our theory as to how society ought to be organized. The purpose of the University of Washington cannot be to produce Black lawyers for Blacks, Polish lawyers for Poles, Jewish lawyers for Jews, Irish lawyers for the Irish. It should be to produce good lawyers for Americans and not to place First Amendment barriers against anyone. That is the point at the heart of all our school desegregation cases, from *Brown v. Board of Education*, 347 U.S. 483, 74 S.Ct. 686, 98 L.Ed. 873 (1954), through *Swann v. Charlotte-Mecklenburg Board of Educ.*, 402 U.S. 1, 91 S.Ct. 1267, 28 L.Ed.2d 554 (1971). A segregated admissions process creates suggestions of stigma and caste no less than a segregated classroom, and in the end it may produce that result despite its contrary intentions.

One other assumption must be clearly disapproved, that Blacks or Browns cannot make it on their individual merit. That is a stamp of inferiority that a State is not permitted to place on any lawyer.

If discrimination based on race is constitutionally permissible when those who hold the reins can come up with "compelling" reasons to justify it, then constitutional guarantees acquire an accordion-like quality. Speech is closely brigaded with action when it triggers a fight, *Chaplinsky v. New Hampshire*, 315 U.S. 568, 62 S.Ct. 766, 86 L.Ed. 1031 (1942), as shouting "fire" in a crowded theatre triggers a riot. It may well be that racial strains, racial susceptibility to certain diseases, racial sensitiveness to environmental conditions that other races do not experience may in an extreme situation justify differences in racial treatment that no fairminded person would call "invidious" discrimination. Mental ability is not in the category. All races can compete fairly at all professional levels. So far as race is concerned, any state sponsored preference to one race over another in that competition is in my view "invidious" and violative of the Equal Protection Clause.

The problem tendered by this case is important and crucial to the operation of our constitutional system; and educators must be given leeway. It may well be that a whole congeries of applicants in the marginal group defy known methods of selection. Conceivably, an admissions committee might conclude that a selection by lot of say the last 20 seats is the only fair solution. Courts are not educators; their expertise is limited; and our task ends with the inquiry whether judged by the main purpose of the Equal Protection Clause—the protection against racial discrimination—there has been an "invidious" discrimination.

We would have a different case if the suit were one to displace the applicant who was chosen in lieu of DeFunis. What the record would show concerning his potentials would have to be considered and weighed. The educational decision, provided proper guidelines were used, would reflect an expertise that courts should honor. The problem is not tendered here because the physical facilities were apparently adequate to take DeFunis in addition to the others. My view is only that I cannot say by the tests used and applied he was invidiously discriminated against because of his race.

I cannot conclude that the admissions procedure of the Law School of the University of Washington that excluded DeFunis is violative of the Equal Protection Clause of the Fourteenth Amendment. The judgment of the Washington Supreme Court should be vacated and the case remanded for a new trial.[24]

[24] For comment, see "Brown to DeFunis—20 Years Later," 3 *Black Law Journal* 221–78 (1974); "DeFunis: The Road Not Taken," 60 *Virginia Law Review* 917–1011 (1974); Redish, "Preferential Law School Admissions and the Equal Protection Clause: An Analysis of the Competing Arguments," 22 *UCLA Law Review* 343 (1974).

The Special Skills of Advocacy: Are Specialized Training and Certification of Advocates Essential to Our System of Justice?

WARREN E. BURGER*

This occasion is one on which friends of John F. Sonnett undertake to pay tribute to him as a person, as an outstanding advocate and as a distinguished public servant. It seems an appropriate occasion, therefore, to raise for the consideration of our profession a problem of large scope and profound importance to all judges, to all lawyers, to the public and, of course, to law schools. I believe that John Sonnett, as a skillful advocate and one deeply committed to our system of justice in all its manifestations, would have shared some of the anxieties I express concerning the quality of advocacy in our courts.

To say we have a "crisis" in the availability of adequate legal services may go too far, but sober, careful and responsible observers of the legal profession have posed the need in almost precisely those terms.[1] My objective in this discussion is not to canvass the swiftly growing need for all kinds of legal services, but to discuss narrowly the need for skilled courtroom advocacy with a special emphasis on the administration of criminal justice. I submit that we can deal with this critical situation if we direct our attention to the causes and think imaginatively about a remedy. We will not lack patterns or precedents.

What I will propose later in this discussion is that some system of certification for trial advocates is an imperative and a long overdue step. Beyond any particular system, however, is the fundamental fact that how lawyers are trained—during and after law school—will determine their skills as advocates and ultimately the quality of our justice. That fundamental fact is nowhere better revealed than in the English experience.

Although our system is a child of the common law, the legal profession has developed in ways that do not parallel England's. Our wide expanses of territory, our heterogeneous and turbulent diversity, and our more than fifty jurisdictions with 150 accredited law schools would make it impossible to transplant the English system here, and I do not suggest it by any means. But simply because we cannot adopt the English system does not mean that we cannot learn much from its operation.

Fordham Law Review, 42 (1973), 227–42. Reprinted by permission.

*Chief Justice of the United States. This article was delivered as the Fourth Annual John F. Sonnett Memorial Lecture on Nov. 26, 1973, at Fordham Law School in New York. The text remains substantially as it was delivered.

[1]H. Packer & T. Ehrlich, *New Directions in Legal Education* 6 (1972).

I

Several aspects of the English legal profession stand out clearly when we look for causes of effective advocacy:

1. England separates its trial lawyers—the barristers—into a separate branch of the profession and they engage exclusively in trial work.[2]
2. Of the 30,000 lawyers in England, 3,000 are barristers.
3. England has about sixty-five lawyers per 100,000 population; the United States has about 160 lawyers per 100,000 population.
4. All English barristers are trained in a centuries-old school conducted by the four Inns of Court. After training in this school of advocacy, a barrister must spend a period of "pupilage," or apprenticeship, with an established barrister.
5. The four Inns of Court occupy quarters in or near the Royal Courts of Justice, and barristers' offices are situated in the same area, thus creating a unique professional community.

I will not try to compare a barrister's productivity with that of an American trial lawyer. That would be unfair in part because the methods and procedures in English courts are generally conducive to speedier justice than we manage to deliver.

Every qualified observer of the English system with whom I have discussed this subject makes the same observation that I have made, drawing on twenty years of rather close contact with the British system, namely, that their trials are conducted in a fraction of the time we expend in the United States for comparable litigation. This is a generalization that has a solid basis and can be readily documented. At once I must note another difference in that, except for libel, fraud and a few other kinds of cases that arise infrequently, civil cases in England are tried without a jury, and judgment is almost invariably rendered forthwith at the close of trial. Appeals are the exception and are only by leave.

Another difference is that judges of trial courts of general jurisdiction are selected entirely from the ranks of the ablest barristers. Thus, there is little or no on-the-job learning for trial judges as is all too often the case in the United States courts, both state and federal. Only the highest qualifications as a trial advocate enter into the selection of English judges. As a result, an English trial is in the hands of three highly experienced litigation specialists who have a common professional background. Each advocate has also served an intensive "apprenticeship" before he or she is permitted to appear in court as lead counsel.[3]

---

[2]Although the majority of barristers are primarily experts in advocacy, there is a good deal of further specialization within their ranks. There are those who confine their practice to the Chancery Division or the Family Division or who do nothing other than criminal work. In addition to these, there are the smaller specialist bars that confine their practice, for example, to taxation, patents, company law, planning or building contracts. A considerable part of the work of members of the smaller specialist bars is concerned with advising on matters that do not result in litigation.

[3]It is widely accepted by England's bench and bar that these factors provide more expeditious determinations without impairing fair and just results. Whether a non-jury system for civil cases would be feasible in a geographically large and diverse country with a heterogeneous society like ours is open to serious question. There is no significant pressure to adopt the English non-jury system and I do not advocate it.

The English training in advocacy places great stress on ethics, manners and deportment, both in the courtroom and in relations with other barristers and solicitors. The effectiveness of this training is reflected in their high standards of ethics and conduct. Discipline is strict, but disciplinary actions for misconduct average about three a year for all of the 3,000 barristers in England. My own personal observation, based on forty years of professional exposure, is that in any multiple-judge American courthouse, there are numerous daily offenses that would bring severe censure if committed by an English barrister. How many serious errors of counsel are made in trials, I would not venture to say.[4]

I have heard it said occasionally by critics of the English legal system that it tends to be "clubby" and "establishment-oriented."[5] For twenty years, I have watched advocates conduct trials in more than a dozen countries, and nowhere have I seen more ardent, more effective advocacy than in the courts of England. English advocacy is generally on a par with that of our best lawyers. I emphasize that their best advocates are no better than our best, but I regret to say that our best constitute a relatively thin layer of cream on top while the quality of the English barristers is uniformly high, albeit with gradations of quality inescapable in any human activity.

What, then, can we learn from the English legal profession? We should first recognize three implicit and basic assumptions about legal training that permeate their system. First: lawyers, like people in other professions, cannot be equally competent for all tasks in our increasingly complex society and increasingly complex legal system in particular; second: legal educators can and should develop some system whereby students or new graduates who have selected, even tentatively, specialization in trial work can learn its essence under the tutelage of experts, not by trial and error at clients' expense; and third: ethics, manners and civility in the courtroom are essential ingredients and the lubricants of the inherently contentious adversary system of justice; they must be understood and developed by law students beginning in law school.

These three basic assumptions are sound and sensible, whether applied to the English system or to our own. Simply because we cannot implement the assumptions in the same manner as the English have done does not mean we cannot recognize their validity. Even though we cannot have, and most emphatically do not want, a small elite, Barrister-like class of lawyers does not mean we cannot take positive steps to promote qualified courtroom advocacy skills in those attorneys who choose to specialize in trial advocacy. Indeed, our failure to do so has helped bring about the low state of American trial advocacy and a consequent diminution in the quality of our entire system of justice. The high purposes of the Criminal Justice

[4]See generally ABA Special Comm. on Evaluation of Disciplinary Enforcement, Problems and Recommendations in Disciplinary Enforcement (Final Draft 1970); and ABA, Report of Special Committee for National Coordination of Disciplinary Enforcement (Aug. 1973).

[5]At one time there was concern among England's solicitors over the exclusivity of the barristers profession, but this has dissipated since transfer from solicitor to barrister was made possible. A prime example is found in the present Lord Chief Justice of England, John Widgery—incidentally the son of a working man—who was a solicitor for many years before transfer to the ranks of barrister, from which he was appointed to the Bench.

Act[6] will be frustrated unless *qualified* advocates are appointed to represent indigents.

For centuries most societies have used performance standards for entry into certain human activities that affect large numbers of people.[7] Standards, varying in effectiveness, have long been used in an attempt to assure qualified teachers, doctors, lawyers, electricians, and a host of others essential to a modern society. Yet, in spite of all the bar examinations and better law schools, we are more casual about qualifying the people we allow to act as advocates in the courtrooms than we are about licensing our electricians. We have no testing or licensing process designed to assure that those engaged to protect and vindicate important rights by trial advocacy are genuinely qualified for their crucial role in society. This is a curious aspect of a system that prides itself on the high place it accords to the judicial process in vindicating peoples' rights.

II

Our failure to inquire into advocates' qualifications—as is done, for example, in separating surgeons from doctors generally—reveals itself in the mounting concern of those who see the consequences of inadequate courtroom performance and look for its causes.

First, and perhaps overriding other causes, is our historic insistence that we treat every person admitted to the bar as qualified to give effective assistance on every kind of legal problem that arises in life, including the trial of criminal cases in which liberty is at stake, civil rights cases in which human values are at stake, and myriad ordinary cases dealing with important private personal interests. It requires only a moment's reflection to see that this assumption is no more justified than one that postulates that every holder of an M.D. degree is competent to perform surgery on the infinite range of ailments that afflict the human animal.

There is no parallel in any other area of life's problems having serious consequence to our naive assumption that every graduate of a law school is, by virtue of that fact, qualified for the ultimate confrontation in a courtroom.[8] No other profession is as casual or heedless of reality as ours. We

[6]18 U.S.C. §3006A (1970).

[7]For example, in the era of sailing vessels, masters and mates were licensed or certified on the basis of their skills in the very difficult task of navigating a ship. The measuring process was quite primitive but highly pragmatic. The traveling public wanted basically the same kind of assurance that we want about today's commercial airline pilots. Today we have more sophisticated and orderly processes to measure the total skills of an airline pilot—his coordination, poise, emotional stability and, of course, technical capacity. The care used as to airline pilots is illustrated by the fact that a graduate of the U.S. Air Force Academy would be required to meet FAA standards before being allowed to operate commercial aircraft. Qualifications are not taken for granted.

[8]Too few lawyers acknowledge the great difference between trial and appellate advocacy as does one leading American trial lawyer who engages a specialist in appellate work to conduct appeals in his cases. On another occasion I hope to discuss the declining quality of appellate advocacy. For now I note that aproximately two-thirds of the lawyers who currently appear before the Supreme Court of the United States are there for the first time—and most of these for the last.

know, however, that the successful law firms do not expose their clients to on-the-job training: they operate their own private "apprentice" or "intern" systems in which the young lawyer who is to engage in litigation is trained by assisting a partner in preparing cases for trial and then by assisting in the second or third chair. If these law firms were to allow the very bright, but inexperienced, young lawyers to roam at large in the courts without close supervision, they would soon lose clients in droves. But, we need shed no tears for the large law firms: necessity has long since forced them to develop their own in-house training comparable to that used in England for Barristers.

So, we see that clients who can afford such lawyers—in the big firms or in the many excellent medium-size firms or indeed among this country's skilled sole practitioners—are well served by lawyers. But this is because those lawyers are not assigned tasks beyond their reach—something that happens regularly on both sides of the table in criminal cases today.

We must acknowledge, I submit, that good advocates are made, much as good airplane pilots are made—by study, by observation of experts and by training with experts. To pursue that analogy, an aspiring pilot who can fly a Piper Cub has learned something about flying, but he is surely not ready to fly large commercial planes or a modern jet airliner. The painful fact is that the courtrooms of America all too often have "Piper Cub" advocates trying to handle the controls of "Boeing 747" litigation. (I should add that by no means are all the "Piper Cub" advocates recent law graduates.)

A second cause of inadequate advocacy derives from certain aspects of law school education. Law schools fail to inculcate sufficiently the necessity of high standards of professional ethics, manners and etiquette as things basic to the lawyer's function. With few exceptions, law schools also fail to provide adequate and systematic programs by which students may focus on the elementary skills of advocacy. I have now joined those who propose that the basic legal education could well be accomplished in two years, after which more concrete and specialized legal education should begin. If the specialty is litigation, the training should be prescribed and supervised by professional advocates cooperating with professional teachers, for both are needed. A two-year program is feasible once we shake off the heritage of our agricultural frontier that the "young folks" should have three months vacation to help harvest the crops—a factor that continues to dominate our education. The third year in school should, for those who aspire to be advocates, concentrate on what goes on in courtrooms. This should be done under the guidance of practitioners along with professional teachers. The medical profession does not try to teach surgery simply with books; more than 80 percent of all medical teaching is done by practicing physicians and surgeons. Similarly, trial advocacy must be learned from trial advocates.

After the third year, those who wish to be advocates should begin a pupilage period, assisting and participating in trials directly with experienced trial lawyers.

Today we spend on the education of a lawyer only a fraction of what is devoted to educating a doctor. If we want an adequate system of justice, we must be prepared to spend more for it—and we cannot train truly effective advocates without spending more.

We know that in the past few years much of what I am suggesting has had small beginnings in some law schools. So-called clinical programs have been developing rapidly, as reflected by the recent survey by the Council on Legal Education for Professional Responsibility. Many of these programs focus on trial advocacy. Recent rules, adopted by a number of state courts and some federal courts, allow students to appear in court as aides to lawyers.[9]

Another development is the growing number of law schools that are finally offering courses in trial advocacy. These are most effective when they provide training which students then use in so-called "clinical" programs. The National Institute for Trial Advocacy has, for the past two summers, offered an intensive training program in trial advocacy designed to channel effective laboratory techniques into law schools as well as into professional circles.[10] The law school, however, is where the groundwork must be laid.

We do not disparage the law as a profession when we insist that, like a carpenter or an electrician, the advocate must know how to use the tools of his "trade." Regrettably the development of these small beginnings in teaching elements of advocacy in law schools is offset somewhat when we see the subject of evidence becomes an *elective* rather than a *required* course. We might, with as much justification, try to make a lawyer without teaching contracts and wills as to omit the law of evidence.

The third cause is the inevitable inability of prosecutor and public defender offices to provide the same kind of apprenticeships for their new lawyers as, for example, the large law firms provide. The prosecution offices and public defender facilities have neither the wealthy clients nor consequent financial resources of the large law firms to enable them to develop whatever skills they need to carry out their mission. Prosecutors and public defenders often learn advocacy skills by being thrown into trial. Valuable as this may be as a learning experience, there is a real risk that it may be at the expense of the hapless clients they represent—public or private. The trial of an important case is no place for on-the-job training of amateurs except under the guidance of a skilled advocate.

[9]For clinical programs, see Council on Legal Education for Professional Responsibility, Inc. (CLEPR), Survey of Clinical Legal Education 1972-1973, May 15 1973. For recent rules permitting student practice in court, see CLEPR, State Rules Permitting The Student Practice of Law: Comparisons and Comments (Including Selected Federal Rules) (2d ed. 1973).

[10]The National Institute for Trial Advocacy is sponsored jointly by the American Bar Association, American College of Trial Lawyers and the Association of Trial Lawyers of America.

The American Bar Association Project on Standards for Criminal Justice has promulgated Standards Relating to The Prosecution Function and The Defense Function (Approved Draft 1971) and the American College of Trial Lawyers had developed a Code of Trial Conduct (Jan. 1963). These are valuable resources to form the basis for training advocates in professional conduct.

III

Time does not allow a recital of the myriad points of substantive law and procedure that an advocate in criminal cases should know in order to perform his or her task. Suffice it to say that in the past dozen or more years a whole range of new developments has drastically altered the trial of a criminal case. To give adequate representation, an advocate must be intimately familiar with these recent developments, most of them deriving from case law.

Whether we measure the recent changes in terms of one decade or three, we see that the litigation volume, particularly in criminal cases, has escalated swiftly. The Criminal Justice Act[11] and the Bail Reform Act, [12] the extension of new federal standards to state courts, rising population, increased crime rates, creation of new causes of action and expanded civil remedies have contributed to the literal flood of cases in state and federal courts.

Whatever the legal issues or claims, the indispensable element in the trial of a case is a minimally adequate advocate for each litigant.[13] Many judges in general jurisdiction trial courts have stated to me that fewer than 25 percent of the lawyers appearing before them are genuinely qualified; other judges go as high as 75 percent.[14] I draw this from conversations extending over the past twelve to fifteen years at judicial meetings and seminars, with literally hundreds of judges and experienced lawyers.[15] It would be safer to pick a middle ground and accept as a working hypothesis that from one-third to one-half of the lawyers who appear in the serious cases are not really qualified to render fully adequate representation. The trial of a "serious" case, whether for damages or for infringement of civil rights, or for a criminal felony, calls for the kind of special skills and experience that insurance companies, for example, seek out to defend damage claims.[16]

Let me try to put some flesh on the bones of these generalizations concerning the function and quality of the advocates. I will try to do this by way of a few examples observed when I sat by assignment as a trial judge, while serving on the U.S. Court of Appeals:

[11] 18 U.S.C. §3006A (1970).

[12] Id. §§3146–52.

[13] Burger, Foreword to L. Patterson and E. Cheatham, *The Profession of Law* at v (1971).

[14] One former colleague of mine on the Court of Appeals, Judge Edward A. Tamm, puts the figure at two percent. Tamm, "Advocacy Can Be Taught—the N.I.T.A. Way," 59 *A.B.A.J.* 625 (1973).

[15] A Sick Profession, Address by then Judge Burger, Winter Convention of the American College of Trial Lawyers, in Hollywood Beach, Fla., Apr. 11, 1967, in 27 *Fed. B.J.* 228 (1967), 5 *Tulsa L.J.* 1 (1968), and 42 *Wis. B. Bull.*, Oct., 1969, at 7.

[16] The techniques of advocacy in appellate courts, before regulatory agencies including tax tribunals, workmen's compensation tribunals and others, present separate and distinct subjects and should not be treated in a discussion of trial advocacy, which usually involves a lay jury.

1. The thousands of trial transcripts I have reviewed show that a majority of the lawyers have never learned the seemingly simple but actually difficult art of asking questions so as to develop concrete images for the fact triers and to do so in conformity with rules of evidence.

2. Few lawyers have really learned the art of cross-examination, including the high art of when not to cross-examine.

3. The rules of evidence generally forbid leading questions, but when there are simple undisputed facts, the leading-questions rule need not apply. Inexperienced lawyers waste time making wooden objections to simple, acceptable questions, on uncontested factual matters.

4. Inexperienced lawyers are often unaware that "inflammatory" exhibits such as weapons or bloody clothes should not be exposed to jurors' sight until they are offered in evidence.

5. An inexperienced prosecutor wasted an hour on the historical development of the fingerprint identification process discovered by the Frenchman Bertillon, until it finally developed that there was no contested fingerprint issue. Such examples could be multiplied almost without limit.

Another aspect of inadequate advocacy—and one quite as important as familiarity with the rules of practice—is the failure of lawyers to observe the rules of professional manners and professional etiquette that are essential for effective trial advocacy.

Jurors who have been interviewed after jury service, and some who have written articles based on their service, express dismay at the distracting effect of personal clashes between the lawyers. There is no place in a properly run courtroom for the shouting matches and other absurd antics of lawyers sometimes seen on television shows and in the movies. From many centuries of experience, the ablest lawyers and judges have found that certain quite fixed rules of etiquette and manners are the lubricant to keep the focus of the courtroom contest on issues and facts and away from distracting personal clashes and irrelevances.[17]

A truly qualified advocate—like every genuine professional—resembles a seamless garment in the sense that legal knowledge, forensic skills, professional ethics, courtroom etiquette and manners are blended in the total person as their use is blended in the performance of the function.

There are some few lawyers who scoff at the idea that manners and

---

[17]For 200 years in this country (and in other civilized countries for much longer), all deliberative processes—the legislative in particular—have recognized that certain rules and formalities must be observed. Indeed, Thomas Jefferson, hardly one to restrain free speech, wrote the original manual of etiquette and behavior for the United States Congress, drawing on the tradition of the English Parliament. See The Necessity for Civility, Address by Chief Justice Burger, ALI Opening Session, in Washington, D.C., May 18, 1971, in 52 *F.R.D.* 211, 216–17 (1971).

From time to time, a Member of the English Parliament or the House or Senate of the United States violates the rules and traditions of those bodies, and when that has happened, various sanctions can be directed against the offending Member. His colleagues may subject him to public scolding on the floor of the house in which he sits, or he may be formally censured after hearings before a committee. These things do not occur often, but frequently enough to remind Members that there are certain lines which may not be crossed with impunity. Unfortunately, in the courts today, for the most part, lines are crossed often and with impunity except in rare instances.

etiquette from any part of the necessary equipment of the courtroom advocate. Yet, if one were to undertake a list of the truly great advocates of the past one hundred years, I suggest he would find a common denominator: they were all intensely individualistic, but each was a lawyer for whom courtroom manners were a key weapon in his arsenal. Whether engaged in the destruction of adverse witnesses or undermining damaging evidence or final argument, the performance was characterized by coolness, poise and graphic clarity, without shouting or ranting, and without baiting witnesses, opponents or the judge. We cannot all be great advocates, but as every lawyer seeks to emulate such tactics, he can approach, if not achieve, superior skill as an advocate.

What is essential is that certain standards of total advocacy performance be established and that we develop means to measure those standards, to the end that important cases have advocates who can give adequate representation. Law school students are adults who can contribute once they are persuaded of the need for training in this area. Rather than being "lectured" on ethics, they should be invited to discuss with the faculty and the best advocates the ethical element in the practice of law so as to impress them with the reality that courtroom ethics and etiquette are crucial to the lawyer's role in society—and indispensable to a rational system of justice. Woven into the seamless fabric of effective advocacy, professional ethics and professional manners are no less important than technical skills.

Lawyers are—or should be—society's peacemakers, problem solvers and stabilizers. The English historian Plucknett suggests that England and America have been largely spared cataclysmic revolutions for two centuries, in part because the common law system lends itself to gradual evolutionary change to meet the changing needs of people. Lawyers can fulfill that high mission only if they are properly trained.

IV

The focus on the inadequacies of advocates has tended to center on the criminal process, and it is plainly correct that this be given close attention and high priority. The first conviction of an accused person may be a determinant that shapes his entire future. Some convicted criminals do not need confinement in prison; neither they nor society can genuinely benefit from it. Effective advocacy can sometimes lead to other alternatives for a first offender—such as a suspended sentence or deferred prosecution.[18]

The contemporary literature tends to focus on the plight of the defendent and the inadequacy of defense counsel. For all too long we grossly neglected the needs of defendants, but the inadequacy of defense counsel is not by any means the whole story. Since we are discussing the problems of a system of justice, it is important to bear in mind that criminal

---

[18]As the ABA Committee on the Standards for Criminal Justice emphasized, the most important role and the most unsatisfactory performance of advocates may be at sentencing. See ABA Project on Minimum Standards for Criminal Justice, Standards Relating to Sentencing Alernatives and Procedures (Approved Draft 1968).

justice is not a one-way street. Judge J. Edward Lumbard observed in a speech about ten years ago that the public is also entitled to due process and justice and that a just conviction is as important to the public interest as a just acquittal.[19]

The enormous demands on criminal courts naturally reflect themselves in the burdens on prosecutors' offices. I observed this in terms of one large prosecution office where the legal staff doubled in five years. The records in appeals handled by that prosecution office, confirmed by personal observations of the judges and experienced trial lawyers, strongly suggested that there was a steady decline in the prosecutors' performance before and after the increase in staff. Countless times in that jurisdiction, a prosecutor, on coming into the courtroom, would ask for a ten-minute recess so he could review a file he had never seen.

In some places it is the observation of judges that the Criminal Justice Act has not brought about improvement in the general quality of criminal defense and the performance has not been generally adequate—either by assigned private counsel or by the public defender office. I am sure that the situation varies from place to place, and the observation of other judges is that the institutionalization of defense work in defender offices holds the best promise for the future. For my part, it is probably too early to reach firm conclusions on the subject, but a choice may be compelled before long.[20]

We have long since institutionalized the prosecution of criminal cases because it best serves the public interest to discharge the function in that way, and the public interest in adequate defense representation is of equal order. Fifteen or twenty years ago, some otherwise sensible people tended to regard the idea of a public defender office as a form of "creeping socialism," but I am confident that attitude no longer has significant acceptance.

However, even placing the defense of indigents largely if not entirely in the jurisdiction of a staff of career public defenders with the necessary auxiliary facilities does not in itself guarantee adequate advocacy skills. In fact, at present, the rapid expansion of both the prosecution offices and public defender facilities has been accompanied by a trend to use either of these functions—or both—as a means for young lawyers to learn how to try cases. It would be instructive to assemble the data on the tenure of staff lawyers in prosecution and public defender offices. To have bright young men and women "flit" in and out of these offices for two or three year apprenticeships may possibly be useful to them and their future clients, but it is a high price to pay if it results in inadequate performance for either

---

[19]Judge Lumbard stressed this point repeatedly in speeches at the time. See in particular "The Administration of Criminal Justice," 35 *N.Y. St. B.J.* 360 (1963); "The Responsibility of the Bar for the Performance of the Courts," 34 *N.Y. St. B.J.* 169 (1962); "The Lawyers' Responsibility for Due Process and Law Enforcement," 12 *Syracuse L. Rev.* 431 (1961).

[20]A detailed overview of this problem is found in Bazelon. "The Defective Assistance of Counsel," 42 *U. Cin. L. Rev.* 1 (1973). We know much less than we should about the comparative quality of assigned and public-defender-office lawyers. An American Bar Foundation-sponsored comparison is L. Silverstein, *Defense of the Poor in Criminal Cases in American State Courts* (1965).

side of a criminal trial. It is a matter of history that some prosecution offices—of which New York is a notable example—have been a proving ground for some of our most outstanding advocates, so I do not disparage the idea of a tour of duty as a prosecutor—or as a public defender.

In our proper concern for criminal justice, we must not forget that the rights and interests of civil litigants should not be brushed under the rug. In nearly eighteen years on the bench and more than twenty years of general practice, I have had occasion to review literally thousands of records—civil, criminal and administrative—and I have observed as many miscarriages of justice in civil cases from inadequacy of counsel as in criminal cases. To borrow some lines from Gray's "Elegy," the injustice in some civil cases becomes part of "the short and simple annals of the poor."[21] In some of those cases, the human tragedy was very real to the principals.

V

If there is substantial validity to this analysis of the problem, what should we do about it?

Some system of specialist certification is inevitable and, as we know, it has been discussed in legal circles for a generation or more. Dean Robert B. McKay of New York University Law School has observed that the legal profession has "marched up the hill of specialist certification only to march right down again in the face of opposition from practitioners not discontent with the absence of regulation."[22] Our commitment to the public and to the system of justice must not let us be marched down that hill any longer.

I see nothing for lawyers, litigants, or courts to fear, and on the contrary I see a great potential gain, by moving toward specialist certification to limit admission to trial practice, beginning in courts of general jurisdiction where the more important claims and rights are resolved. When we have succeeded in that limited area we can then examine broader aspects of specialization. Furthermore, while the legal profession must obviously lead in this effort, the interests of the public dictate that the views of practitioners who are affected cannot be controlling any more than we allow the automobile or drug industry to have complete control of safety or public health standards. There are more than 200 million potential "consumers" of justice whose rights and interests must have protection, and it is the duty of the legal profession to provide reasonable safeguards—unless lawyers prefer regulation from the outside.

Our traditional assumption that every lawyer, like the legendary Renaissance man, is equipped to deal effectively with every legal problem probably had some validity in the day of Jefferson, Hamilton, John Adams and John Marshall, but that assumption has been diluted by the vast changes in the complexity of our social, economic and political structure.

[21] *The Complete Poems of Thomas Gray* 38 (H. Starr & J. Hendrickson ed. 1966).

[22] "Role of Graduate Legal Education in the Development of the Legal Specialist," Dec. 10, 1970, at 2 (paper prepared for symposium of ABA Special Committee on Specialization, New Orleans) (footnote omitted).

The experience of the medical profession affords some guidance in its first step in specialty certification. That step was identifying those doctors genuinely competent to perform serious surgery and limiting access to the operating room to such doctors. Obviously there are and probably always will be sparsely populated areas in which some doctors and lawyers must be jacks-of-all-trades. But, the fact that this is a necessity imposed in some areas of the country by geography and population density does not mean that in the metropolitan centers where courts deal with thousands of cases we need or should tolerate ineffective representation.

The American Bar Association has wisely cautioned that in undertaking certification programs, "it is not desirable for a large number of states to embark upon even experimental programs in specialization before uniform standards can be established lest unnecessarily divergent programs become prematurely crystallized."[23] The ABA committee, however, is carefully monitoring pilot or experimental programs commencing in California and Texas, among others. Those states certify three specialties, and quite appropriately, the one they have in common is criminal law.[24]

It is in this spirit of cautious progress that I urge that we should concentrate where, in the view of most judges, the greatest need exists. For the initial stage, moreover, we should limit ourselves to certification of trial advocates until we learn more about the problems of evaluation and selection. There is danger, as the ABA report stated, in trying to do too much too soon, without knowing enough about the pitfalls. The limited step of certifying trial advocates first will be a large enough task to tax our best efforts. Given the difficulty in terms of dealing with fifty separate state systems, perhaps the prudent thing to do is to begin with the United States

[23]95 *A.B.A. Rep.* 329 (1970). The ABA's Special Committee on Specialization in its 1973 Annual Report cited the avalanche of state projects and once again urged states yet to undertake pilot programs to refrain from doing so until there has been an opportunity to evaluate those already in existence. ABA Report of Special Committee on Specialization 3, 6 (Aug. 1973).

[24]On November 20, 1973, the first 1,182 certificates of specialization were awarded by the State Bar of California under its pilot program in legal specialization. The specialties were divided as follows: criminal law, 391; workmen's compenation, 311; and taxation, 480. The first three certificates, one in each specialty, were issued by ABA President Chesterfield Smith.

One innovative attempt to assure adequate counsel for criminal defendants is under way in the United States District Court for the Southern District of New York, which was started to certify informally those defense attorneys considered eligible for appointment by the court under the Criminal Justice Act, 18 U.S.C. §3006A (1970). A program of certification may not have been intended when this plan was initiated, but it in fact appears to be an important first step toward the certification of trial advocates. Accompanying the court's power to certify Criminal Justice Act attorneys is the power to decertify attorneys for lack of qualifications or refusal to accept three consecutive appointments. The Southern District Committee on the Criminal Justice Act Panel, composed of judges, has established a subcommittee of lawyers to conduct interviews, evaluate applicants' credentials, and then make a recommendation to the committee and to the Chief Judge. The applicants whose paper credentials are sufficient but who lack adequate trial experience are encouraged to serve as assistants to approved Criminal Justice Act attorneys and Legal Aid attorneys for one year and then reapply for certification. This may also be true for those who have the threshold knowledge of criminal litigation but lack trial experience. I am informed by Chief Judge David N. Edelstein that competition for these assignments is rigorous and, interestingly enough, one finds many alumni of the United States Attorney's Office in their ranks.

District Courts. After experimenting in several representative federal districts and in state courts, the Judicial Conferences in the several circuits should consider this problem.

PROPOSAL

What I propose is a broad, four-point program as a first step in specialist certification. We should:

First: Face up to and reject the notion that every law graduate and every lawyer is qualified, simply by virtue of admission to the bar, to be an advocate in trial courts in matters of serious consequence.

Second: lay aside the proposals for broad and comprehensive specialty certification (except where pilot programs are already under way) until we have positive progress in the certification of the one crucial specialty of trial advocacy that is so basic to a fair system of justice and has had historic recognition in the common law systems.

Third: Develop means to evaluate qualifications of lawyers competent to render the effective assistance of counsel in the trial of cases.

Fourth: Call on the American Bar Association, the Federal Bar Association, the American College of Trial Lawyers, the American Association of Law Schools, the Federal Judicial Center, the National Center for State Court and others to collaborate in prompt and concrete steps to accomplish ths [sic] first step in a workable and enforceable certification of trial advocates.

The fate of this proposal, as with any relating to progress in our profession, depends on the members of that "great partnership" of the law made up of lawyers, judges and law teachers—and I have great confidence in that partnership.

SELECTED BIBLIOGRAPHY*

Burger, Warren E., *Counsel for the Prosecution and Defense—Their Roles under the Minimum Standards*, 8 AM. CRIM. L.Q. 2 (1969).
Carlin, Jerome E.; Howard, Jan; and Messinger, Sheldon L., CIVIL JUSTICE AND THE POOR. New York: Russell Sage Foundation. 1967.
Cheatham, Elliott E., A LAWYER WHEN NEEDED. New York: Columbia University Press. 1963.
Cheatham, Elliott E., *The Growing Need for Specialized Legal Services*, 16 VAND L. REV. 497 (1963).
Christensen, Barlow F., LAWYERS FOR PEOPLE OF MODERATE MEANS: SOME PROBLEMS OF AVAILABILITY OF LEGAL SERVICES. Chicago: American Bar Foundation. 1970.
Clark, Tom C., *The Decisional Processes of the Supreme Court*, 50 CORNELL L.Q. 385 (1965).
Derrick, William J., *Specialization in the Law: Texas develops pilot plan for specialization in criminal law, labor law, family law*, 36 TEXAS B.J. 393 (1973).
Finer, Joel J., *Ineffective Assistance of Counsel*, 58 CORNELL L. REV. 1077 (1973).
Greenwood, Glenn and Frederickson, Robert F., SPECIALIZATION IN THE MEDICAL AND LEGAL PROFESSIONS. Mundelein, Ill.: Callaghan & Co. 1964.

*Supplemental to those materials cited in footnotes.

Johnstone, Quintin and Hopson, Dan Jr., LAWYERS AND THEIR WORK: AN ANALYSIS OF THE LEGAL PROFESSION IN THE UNITED STATES AND ENGLAND. Indianapolis: The Bobbs-Merrill Co. 1967.

Joiner, Charles W., *Specialization in the Law: Control It or It Will Destroy the Profession*, 41 A.B.A.J. 1105 (1955).

Joiner, Charles W., *Specialization in the Law? The Medical Profession Shows the Way*, 39 A.B.A.J. 539 (1953).

Jones, William B., *A Trained Trial Bar*, Address at Winter Meeting of the American College of Trial Lawyers, in Los Angeles, Cal., March 16, 1971.

Note, *Effective Assistance of Counsel for the Indigent Defendant*, 78 HARV. L. REV. 1434 (1965).

Note, *The Representation of Indigent Criminal Defendants in the Federal District Courts*, 76 HARV. L. REV. 579 (1963).

Practising Law Institute, CONTINUING LEGAL EDUCATION: A TRANSCRIPT OF THE PROGRAM OF THE PRACTISING LAW INSTITUTE'S FORTIETH ANNIVERSARY CONVOCATION, New York, May 10, 1973.

Sears, Barnabas F., *The Compelling Necessity for Skilled Advocates in the Courts*, 16 TRIAL LAWYER'S GUIDE 87 (1972).

Smith, Chesterfield, *Specialization in the Law—Whither Now?*, 17 NEB. ST. B.J. 123 (1968).

State Bar of California, Committee on Specialization, *Preliminary Report: Results of Survey on Certification of Specialists*, 44 J. OF ST. B. OF CALIF. 140 (1969).

State Bar of California, Committee on Specialization, *Final Report*, 44 J. OF ST. B. OF CALIF. 493 (1969).

State Bar of California, State Board of Legal Specialization, *Standards for Specialization Announced*, 48 J. OF ST. B. OF CALIF. 80 (1973).

TRAINING FOR THE PUBLIC PROFESSIONS OF THE LAW: 1971 (Carrington Report), Part One, Section II of the Proceedings, Association of American Law Schools, 1971 Annual Meeting, in Packer, Herbert L. and Ehrlich, Thomas, NEW DIRECTIONS IN LEGAL EDUCATION 95 et seq. New York: McGraw-Hill Book Co. 1972.

Tweed, Harrison, THE CHANGING PRACTICE OF LAW. New York: The Association of the Bar of the City of New York. 1955.

U.S. Attorney General, REPORT OF THE ATTORNEY GENERAL'S COMMITTEE ON POVERTY AND THE ADMINISTRATION OF FEDERAL CRIMINAL JUSTICE. Washington, D.C. 1963.

Wallace, James E., *The Code of Professional Responsibility—Legislated Irrelevance?*, 48 TEXAS L. REV. 311 (1970).

Waltz, Jon R., *Inadequacy of Trial Defense Representation as a Ground for Post-Conviction Relief in Criminal Cases*, 59 NW. U.L. REV. 289 (1964).

B

Continuing Competence

United States v. DeCoster

UNITED STATES COURT OF APPEALS, DISTRICT OF COLUMBIA CIRCUIT, 1973 487 F.2D 1197

Before BAZELON, Chief Judge, and WRIGHT and MacKINNON, Circuit Judges.

BAZELON, Chief Judge:

The only serious issue in this case is whether appellant was denied his constitutionally guaranteed right to the effective assistance of counsel.

I

The facts are relatively simple. The victim testified that he was accosted by appellant and two accomplices in a parking lot at about 6 P.M. He stated that one of the accomplices held him from behind, while the other stood in front of him with a knife and appellant went through his pockets. The robbers took a wallet containing $110, then fled when the police arrived.

* * *

Between the time of the offense and the time of trial, the victim was in a serious automobile accident, which caused lapses in his memory and damage to his eyesight. At trial, he was unable to identify either appellant or the straight razor taken from Eley.

* * *

DeCoster was convicted by a jury of aiding and abetting in an armed robbery and an assault with a dangerous weapon. He was sentenced to 2–8 years on each count, to be served concurrently.

II

Several events and circumstances suggest that appellant may have been denied his sixth amendment right to the effective assistance of counsel:

(1) Although appellant, who failed to meet bail, was accepted for pretrial custody by Black Man's Development Center on October 12, counsel did not file a bond review motion until November 9. Even then, the motion did not mention the third party custody arrangement, and was filed in the wrong court. On November 13, DeCoster wrote to the court indicating that counsel had promised he would file a motion for his release. On December 8, counsel filed a motion in the proper court and defendant was released.

(2) It appears that defense counsel (who is not counsel on appeal) announced "ready" although he was not prepared to go to trial. [Supporting conversation from the trial record omitted.]

(3) Counsel apparently made no effort to inquire into the disposition of the cases against appellant's two alleged accomplices. In fact, they had both already pled guilty before the same judge who was to sit on DeCoster's case. Thus, counsel agreed to waive a jury trial totally unaware that his client would, as the court pointed out, "be tried by a judge who has heard a portion of this evidence in connection with the other two defendants." (The Government, however, refused to waive a jury trial.)

(4) There were indications of a lack of communication between appellant and his trial counsel. When DeCoster personally requested the court to subpoena his two accomplices, counsel indicated that he had thought of calling them but "we have no address [*sic*] for them." Appellant immediately responded that one of the men was at the D.C. Jail under sentence for the instant offense. The other man had recently been placed

on probation, also for his involvement in the instant offense, by the same judge who was presiding over DeCoster's case. This witness was never called.

Defendant informed the court, first by letter and then at the opening of trial, that he was dissatisfied with his appointed counsel. On the later occasion he pleaded:

Your honor, I feel that this case should be continued because this is, I can't get proper representation that I should be getting.

His request was denied without inquiry into the basis of his claim.[4]

(5) The defense called only two witnesses: appellant and an alleged accomplice who contradicted appellant on a fundamental point. On direct examination, he placed DeCoster at the scene of the crime engaged in a fight with the victim at a time DeCoster himself had testified he was at his hotel. This contradiction confused the defense case and stripped it of its credibility.

*   *   *

IV

Since we remand for a determination of appellant's claim, it is necessary to discuss the governing principles. The effective assistance of counsel is a defendant's most fundamental right "for it affects his ability to assert any other right he may have."[8] The Supreme Court has observed, "if the right to counsel guaranteed by the Constitution is to serve its purpose, defendants cannot be left to the mercies of incompetent counsel."[9]

*   *   *

Since "reasonably competent assistance" is only a shorthand label, and not subject to ready application, we follow the approach adopted by the Fourth Circuit[22] and set forth some of the duties owed by counsel to a client:[23]

[4]An inquiry by the court into the source of defendant's dissatisfaction with his attorney might have been useful to the trial judge in meeting his responsibility "to maintain proper standards of performance by [defense] attorneys," *McMann v. Richardson*, 307 U.S. 759, 771, 90 S.Ct. 1441, 1449, 25 L.Ed.2d 763 (1970), and thereby avoided a later claim of ineffectiveness.

[8]Schaefer, "Federalism and State Criminal Procedure," 70 *Harv.L.Rev.* 1, 8 (1956).

[9]*McMann v. Richardson*, 397 U.S. 759, 771, 90 S.Ct. 1441, 1449, 25 L.Ed.2d 763 (1970). See also *Tollett v. Henderson*, 411 U.S. 258, 93 S.Ct. 1602, 36 L.Ed.2d 235 (1973); cf. *Johnson v. Zerbst*, 304 U.S. 458, 462–463, 58 S.Ct. 1019, 1022, 82 L.Ed. 1461 (1938).

[22][Note omitted.]

[23][Note omitted.]

In General—Counsel should be guided by the American Bar Association Standards for the Defense Function.[24] They represent the legal profession's own articulation of guidelines for the defense of criminal cases.[25]

Specifically—(1) Counsel should confer with his client without delay and as often as necessary to elicit matters of defense, or to ascertain that potential defenses are unavailable.[26] Counsel should discuss fully potential strategies and tactical choices with his client.

(2) Counsel should promptly advise his client of his rights and take all actions necessary to preserve them. Many rights can only be protected by prompt legal action. The Supreme Court has, for example, recognized the attorney's role in protecting the client's privilege against self-incrimination. *Miranda v. Arizona*, 384 U.S. 436 [86 S.Ct. 1602, 16 L.Ed.2d 694] (1966), and rights at a line-up, *United States v. Wade*, 388 U.S. 218, 227 [87 S.Ct. 1926, 18 L.Ed.2d 1149] (1967).[27] Counsel should also be concerned with the accused's right to be released from custody pending trial,[28] and be prepared, where appropriate, to make motions for a pre-trial psychiatric examination[29] or for the suppression of evidence.[30]

(3) Counsel must conduct appropriate investigations, both factual and legal, to determine what matters of defense can be developed. The Supreme Court has noted that the adversary system requires that "all available defenses are raised" so that the government is put to its proof.[31] This means that in most cases a defense attorney, or his agent, should interview not only his own witnesses but also those that the government intends to call, when they are accessible. The investigation should always include efforts to secure information in the possession of the prosecution and law enforcement authorities.[32] And of course, the duty to investigate also requires adequate legal research.[33]

If a defendant shows a substantial violation of any of these requirements he has been denied effective representation unless the government, "on which is cast the burden of proof once a violation of these precepts is

---

[24]American Bar Association Project on Standards for Criminal Justice, Standards Relating to the Defense Function (App.Draft 1971). These standards are the product of a comprehensive study by a distinguished committee chaired by the Chief Justice of the United States, and have been approved by the ABA's House of Delegates.

[25]While the Standards claim that they are not intended "as criteria for judicial evaluation of effectiveness," id. at § 1.1(f), they are certainly relevant guideposts in this largely uncharted area.

[26]*People v. Shells*, 4 Cal.3d 626, 94 Cal.Rptr. 275, 483 P.2d 1227 (1971); cf. *Hawk v. Olsen*, 326 U.S. 271, 66 S.Ct. 116, 90 L.Ed. 61 (1945).

[27]See Amsterdam, Segal, and Miller, *Trial Manual for The Defense of Criminal Cases* §§ 35–37 (1967); cf. *Marshall v. United States*, 141 U.S.App.D.C. 1, 436 F.2d 155 (1970).

[28]See generally, ABA Standards, Pretrial Release (App. Draft 1968).

[29]*United States v. Morgan*, 157 U.S.App.D.C.1975, 482 F.2d 786 (1973); *In re Saunders*, 2 Cal.2d 1033, 88 Cal. Rptr. 633, 472 P.2d 921 (1970) (en banc); *Brooks v. Texas*, 381 F.2d 619 (5th Cir. 1967); *People v. Bennett*, 29 N.Y.2d 462, 329 N.Y.S.ed 801, 280 N.E.ed 637 (1972).

[30]See, e.g., *Government of Canal Zone v. C.*, 479 F.2d 1258 (5th Cir. 1973); *People v. Ibarra*, 60 Cal.2d 460, 34 Cal.Rptr. 863, 386 P.2d 487 (1963).

[31]See *United States v. Ash*, 413 U.S. 300, 93 S.Ct. 2568, 37 L.Ed.2d 619 (1973), * * *

[32]See 18 U.S.C.A. § 3500 (1970) (Jencks Act); Fed.R.Crim.P. 16(c); cf. *Levin v. Katzenbach*, 124 U.S.App.D.C. 158, 363 F.2d 287 (1966); ABA Standards for the Defense Function § 4.1 (App.Draft 1971).

[33]See *People v. Ibarra*, 60 Cal.2d 460, 34 Cal.Rptr. 863, 386 P.2d 487 (1963); *In re Williams*, 1 Cal.3d 168, 81 Cal.Rptr. 784, 460 P.2d 984 (1969).

shown, can establish lack of prejudice thereby." *Coles v. Peyton,* 389 F.2d 224, 226 (4 Cir. 1968).[34] Two factors justify this requirement. First, in our constitutionally prescribed adversary system the burden is on the government to prove guilt. A requirement that the defendant show prejudice, on the other hand, shifts the burden to him and makes him establish the likelihood of his innocence. It is no answer to say that the appellant has already had a trial in which the government was put to its proof because the heart of his complaint is that the absence of the effective assistance of counsel deprived him of a full adversary trial.

Second, proof of prejudice may well be absent from the record precisely because counsel has been ineffective.[35] For example, when counsel fails to conduct an investigation, the record may not indicate which witnesses he could have called, or defenses he could have raised.

V

Much of the evidence of counsel's ineffectiveness is frequently not reflected in the trial record (e.g., a failure to investigate the case, or to interview the defendant or a witness before the trial). As a result, ineffectiveness cases have often evolved into tests of whether appellate judges can hypothesize a rational explanation for the apparent errors in the conduct of the trial.[36] But neither one judge's surmise nor another's doubt can take the place of proof.[37] Thus, when a claim of ineffective assistance is contemplated, it should first be presented to the district court in a motion for a new trial.[38] In such proceeding, evidence *dehors* the record may be submitted by affidavit,[39] and when necessary the district judge may order a hearing or otherwise allow counsel to respond.[40] If the trial court is willing to grant the motion, this court will remand.[41] If the motion is denied, the appeal therefrom will be consolidated with the appeal from the conviction and sentence. The record of any hearing held on the motion, and any documents submitted below, will become part of the record on appeal.

Record remanded.

[34]See *Chapman v. California,* 386 U.S. 18, 87 S.Ct. 824, 17 L.Ed.2d 705 (1967). See also *Moore v. United States,* 432 F.2d 730, 737 (3rd Cir. 1970) (en banc); cf. *United States v. Wade,* 388 U.S. 218, 227, 87 S.Ct. 1926, 1932, 18 L.Ed.2d 1149 (1967); *Glasser v. United States,* 315 U.S. 60. 62 S.Ct. 457, 86 L.Ed. 680 (1942).

[35]See generally *United States v. Thompson,* 155 U.S.App.D.C. 347, 475 F.2d 931 (1973).

[36]Compare *United States v. Benn,* 156 U.S.App.D.C. 180, 476 F.2d 1127, 1133-1136 (1972) (opinion of Chief Judge Bazelon), with id. at 1136–1137 (opinion of Judge Wilkey). See *Plummer v. United States,* 104 U.S.App.D.C. 211, 260 F.2d 729 (1958).

[37]*United States ex rel. Kent v. Maroney,* 435 F.2d 1020 (3rd Cir. 1970).

[38]Fed.R.Crim.P. 33; *United States v. Brown,* 156 U.S. App.D.C. 177, 476 F.2d 933 (1973); *United States v. Thompson,* 155 U.S.App.D.C. 347, 475 F.2d 931 (1973). See *United States v. Smallwood,* 154 U.S.App.D.C. 387, 473 F.2d 98 (1972) (Bazelon, Chief Judge, concurring); *Marshall v. United States,* 141 U.S.App.D.C. 1, 436 F.2d 155, 159 n. 11 (1970).

[39]*United States v. Thompson,* 155 U.S.App.D.C. 347, 475 F.2d 931 (1973).

[40]See ABA Standards for the Defense Function § 8.6(c) (App.Draft 1971). The trial judge might, for example, ask the trial attorney to submit an affidavit in response to the petitioner's allegations before deciding whether a hearing is indicated.

[41]*United States v. Benn,* 156 U.S.App.D.C. 180, 476 F.2d 1127, 1135 (1972); *Smith v. Pollin,* 90 U.S.App.D.C. 178, 194 F.2d 349, 350 (1952).

Lawyer and Judge:
The Ethical Duty of Competency

THE HONORABLE JAMES L. OAKES* JUDGE
UNITED STATES CIRCUIT COURT OF APPEALS, 2D CIRCUIT

I. THE ANALYTICAL UNDERPINNING OF THE ETHICAL DUTY OF COMPETENCY

A. The Adversary System

The adversary system is an analytical basis of the duty of competency. While some have from time to time[17] questioned the utility or value of that system, it is incorporated into the Constitution itself by Article III's case or controversy requirement and by the Bill of Rights on both the criminal[18] and civil[19] sides. Arguably, the adversary model is not the best system for ascertaining truth in the abstract;[20] but abstract truth is, at the least, difficult to attain. Indeed, what was thought to be abstract truth may have produced some of the most unjust trials in the history of the world, those, for example, of Socrates, Jesus, Galileo, and the Salem Witches. Witness also the Bloody Assizes orchestrated by the Stuarts.

Once higher values were thought by our forebears[21] to outweigh the discovery of absolute truth, procedural safeguards for the individual were adopted: general warrants or compelled testimony by the defendant were proscribed; double jeopardy was prohibited. Absolute truth in the form of the tyranny of the majority or the omnipotence of the state has been, indeed, the antithesis of our form of democratic thinking which presup-

Ethics and Advocacy (Washington: The Roscoe Pound-American Trial Lawyers Foundation, 1978), pp. 60–72. Reprinted by permission
*I am indebted to my law clerk, Elliot E. Polebaum, for his editorial suggestions and usual careful parsing of my footnotes.

[17]*See, e.g.*, M. Frankel, *"The Search for Truth: An Umpireal View"*, 123 *U. Pa. L. Rev.* 1031 (1975) [hereinafter Frankel, *"An Umpireal View"*].

[18]U. S. Const. amends. V. & VI.

[19]U. S. Const. amend. VII.

[20]*See* Fuller, *"The Adversary System"* in *Talks on American Law* 30 (Berman ed. 1960); ABA Standards relating to the Prosecution Function and the Defense Function 2–3 (Approved Draft, 1971) [hereinafter ABA Standards]. *But see Brewer v. Williams*, 430 U. S. 387, 426 (1977) (Burger, C. J., dissenting) ("In any event, the fundamental purpose of the Sixth Amendment is to safeguard the fairness of the trial and the integrity of the factfinding process.") (Footnote omitted).

[21]*See* B. Bailyn, *The Ideological Origins of the American Revolution* 176, 187–197 (1967); G. Wood, *The Creation of the American Republic* 536–537, 541–543 (1969).

poses a "creative balance"[22] between the will of the majority and the rights of the minority. Resolution of the dynamic tensions, the achievement of fluid balances, has been largely left in the American form of government to the advocacy system, so that it is a major premise of our Government.[23]

What we have then is, as one well-known advocate has put it, "a form of organized and institutionalized confrontation" leading to "illumination" of "varieties of truth"[24] rather than to revelation of absolute truth. It is a major method—perhaps not the only, but often the ultimate method—of resolving controversy in a democratic society. It differs from an inquisitional system, where the State seeks to ascertain the truth or impose its version of it,[25] and hence helps distinguish our form of government from totalitarian forms. It does not preclude arbitration or settlement of differences; but it invites predefinition of the rules by which the affairs of man- and woman-kind are to be governed. However, where the differences are nonarbitrable, or where, in the myriad relationships that a complex and pluralistic society engenders, the applicability of the preconceived rules or regulations is in doubt, the adversary system provides the ultimate escape valve.

What, it may be asked, does this system posit? First, it needs two parties, the contenders; one may be the State itself.[26] Second, the system requires an advocate for each party. The advocate's relationship with the party is in part that of agent to principal, with all of the duties that implies, but his responsibility is also that of independent contractor, with obligations running to his profession, community, and the court.[27] And third, the system posits an arbiter or judge who, at least for the purpose of finding facts, may rely or may be bound to rely on an independent body of lay people (juries) or experts in a particular field (administrative agencies, a bankruptcy judge), and who is usually subject to further review by three or more appellate judges.

Implicit in the system, if it is to be effective (and by effective I mean fair as well as functional), is that each advocate be competent—that is, able to present her side of the controversy to the arbiter in its best light.[28] Also implicit is that the arbiter or judge be competent to rule and have the temperament, conscience, and sensitivity to rule neutrally and fairly. Whether this implies that he be more than a laissez-faire umpire, that he seek to counterbalance any disequilibrium in the relative competency of the advocates so as to effectuate a balance in the parties' presentation, is a

---

[22]*See* E. Richardson, *The Creative Balance* xxvii–xxviii (1976) (referring to balance between innovation and conservation).

[23]Some would say too major. *See* note 17 *supra. But see Illinois v. Allen*, 397 U. S. 337, 347-348 (1970) (Brennan, J., concurring).

[24]*See* Rifkind, *"The Lawyer's Role and Responsibility in Modern Society"*, in 30 *The Record* 535-536 (1975) (Ass'n of the Bar of the City of N. Y.).

[25]*See* L. Tondel, *The Role of the Private Lawyer in Law and the American Future* 162 (1976).

[26]Upon occasion, both may be the government. *E.g., United States v. United States*, 417 F. Supp. 851 (D.D.C. 1976).

[27]*See* ABA Standards *supra* note 20, at 172–174.

[28]*Id.* at 2–5.

matter only tangential to this paper;[29] the answer turns on the extent to which considerations of real, not abstract, "justice" should offset the sometimes harsh working of the system where the resources of the parties or the skills of their advocates vastly differ.[30] John Rawls and Ronald Dworkin, with the aid of their respectve critics, may address themselves better to this issue than I; we are in accord that we need Dworkin's Hercules as judge if she can be found.

I return then to the advocate—both agent and independent contractor. It is obvious that the system presumes his competency, which encompasses legal knowledge, ability to prepare and to present the client's position, and the capacity to "illuminate," to persuade, and even to "sell." And since it must be a premise of the system that no one can practice unless he is competent, either or both of two things should occur to insure that the advocate does not fall short: sanctions should be imposed against the imcompetent advocate himself, and, at least in the context of the criminal law—where "life" or a "liberty" interest is at stake—a retrial may be ordered. Remember that I am speaking analytically only, and not as to how the system works in fact. The system actually works quite differently: how many disciplinary proceedings for incompetency have been had in your jurisdiction in the past year?[31] How many reversals of conviction for counsel incompetence?

I turn then from the adversary system as a basis of the ethical duty of competence to a specific constitutional foundation of that duty.

B. The Sixth Amendment

The Sixth Amendment provides that "[i]n all criminal prosecutions, the accused shall enjoy the right. . . to have the Assistance of Counsel for his defence." It was not until 143 years after the adoption of the Constitution that this guarantee was translated into *effective* assistance. In the Scottsboro Boys' first case,[32] the Court held that assignment of counsel at a time and under circumstances precluding effective aid violated the Sixth Amendment, applicable to the states by the Due Process clause of the Fourteenth.[33]

Since *Powell* v. *Alabama*, however, the Supreme Court, absent an attorney's conflict of interest, has not set aside a single verdict due to

---

[29]*Compare* Frankel, *"An Umpireal View"*, *supra* note 17, at 1042-1043, *with* Frankel, *"From Private Fights Toward Public Justice,"* 51 *N.Y.U.L. Rev.* 516, 524 (1976). *See Brady v. Maryland*, 373 U. S. 83, 87 & n.2 (1963); *Berger v. United States*, 295 U. S. 78, 88 (1935).

[30]*See* Bazelon, *Realities*, *supra* note 5; Kamisar, *Foreword: Brewer v. Williams—"A Hard Look at a Discomfiting Record"*, 66 *Geo. L. J.* 209 (1977); Kamisar, *"The Right to Counsel and the Fourteenth Amendment: A Dialogue on "the Most Pervasive Right" of an Accused"*, 30 *U. Chi. L. Rev.* 1, 49 (1962).

[31]California disciplines its lawyers for neglect of duties by taking action and printing a report of the disciplinary proceedings. *See* 52 *Calif. St. B. J.* 148 (1977) (reproval for failure to file brief on appeal). *But see* Kaufman, *"Does the Judge Have a Right to Qualified Counsel?"* 61 *A.B.A.J.* 569, 572 (1975).

[32]*Powell v. Alabama*, 287 U. S. 45 (1932).

[33]*Id.* at 68–71.

ineffective counsel.[34] What former Chief Judge Bazelon has called the classic case of "judicial ducking-the-issue"[35] occured in *Chambers* v. *Maroney*,[36] involving a lawyer who met his client for the first time on the way to the courtroom on the morning of the trial. Needless to say, he had "virtually no . . . acquaintance" with the facts of the case and had no trial strategy. The case was not decided on incompetency grounds but on the basis that the defendant did not show that he would have prevailed with an earlier appointment of counsel.[37] True, there is nice language in some of the High Court cases that attorneys are expected to perform "within the range of the competence demanded of attorneys in criminal cases."[38] But, as Mr. Justice Brennan has recently remarked, "it is accurate to assert that most courts, this one included, traditionally have resisted any realistic inquiry into the competency of the trial counsel."[39] The Court has not settled on any standards of competence except to say in dictum that [c]ounsel's failure to evaluate properly facts giving rise to a constitutional claim or his failure properly to inform himself of facts that would have shown the existence of a constitutional claim, might in particular fact situations meet this standard of proof [of incompetent counsel]."[40] This says something, if very little, as to constitutional claims; as to nonconstitutional claims, all we have to go on is a dictum in *McMann* v. *Richardson*: "It has long been recognized that the right to counsel is the right to the effective assistance of counsel."[41]

The lower federal courts have gone little further. While they occasionally reverse convictions for "plain error"[42] where no objection is made, the error is generally an obvious ruling of law—failure to charge an element of the crime,[43] improper admission of prejudicial evidence,[44] or the like.[45] But when it comes to competency, for the most part the courts speak

[34]The Court has of course required counsel to be available for indigents in felony cases, *Gideon v. Wainwright*, 372 U. S. 335 (1963), and in misdemeanors, *Argersinger v. Hamlin*, 407 U.S. 25 (1972). It has also reversed convictions where counsel has a conflict of interest rendering him incapable of providing effective assistance. *Holloway v. Arkansas*, 46 U.S.L.W. 4289 (U. S. Apr. 3, 1978) (no specific showing of prejudice necessary); *Glasser v. United States*, 315 U. S. 60, 76 (1942).

[35]Bazelon, *Defective Assistance, supra* note 5, 21.

[36]399 U. S. 42 (1970).

[37]*But see id.* at 55-60 (Harlan, J., concurring in part and dissenting in part); *cf. Holloway v. Arkansas, supra* (no showing of prejudice necessary where lawyer indicates to court a conflict of interest).

[38]*McMann v. Richardson*, 397 U. S. 759, 771 (1970); *See Tollett v. Henderson*, 411 U. S. 258, 266 (1973).

[39]*Wainwright v. Sykes, supra*, 433 U. S. at 117 (Brennan, J., dissenting) (footnote omitted).

[40]*Tollett v. Henderson, supra* 411 U. S. at 266–267.

[41]*McMann v. Richardson, supra*, 397 U. S. at 771 n. 14 (citations omitted).

[42]Fed. R. Crim. P. 52(b).

[43]E.g., *United States v. Fields*, 466 F.2d 119 (2d Cir. 1972).

[44]E.g., *United States v. Cook*, 530 F.2d 145, 150–151 (7th Cir.), *cert. denied*, 426 U. S. 909 (1976); *United States ex rel. Washington v. Vincent*, 525 F.2d 262 (2d Cir. 1975), *cert. denied*, 424 U. S. 934 (1976).

[45]The reluctance of the courts to reverse for plain error is quite evident. *See* Note, *"The United States Courts of Appeals: 1975-1976 Term Criminal Law and Procedure,"* 65 Geo. L. J. 201, 403, 436–437 (1976) [hereinafter 65 *Geo. L. J.*].

only in generalities, and even the generalities are not particularly meaningful. There is language in the cases that lawyers are presumed to be competent.[46] For a long time most of the circuits followed the District of Columbia Circuit's wholly subjective standard set forth in *Diggs* v. *Welch*[47]—the "farce and mockery of justice" standard under which representation is deemed ineffective only where the trial is such a sham that it shocks the conscience of the court. Under that standard just about anything goes, particularly if the court's conscience is hard to shock. In the Second Circuit, for example, the court's conscience was insufficiently shocked by defense counsel who was seen to be sound asleep during the direct testimony of prosecution witnesses because "the testimony during the periods of counsel's somnolence was not central to [the accused's] case. . . ."[48] Nor in the Sixth Circuit was the court's conscience shocked by defense counsel's misreading of the Michigan statute on commitment as a criminal sexual psychopath and his erroneous advice that it was necessary to plead guilty to be adjudicated as such.[49]

Most federal appellate courts and about half the state courts have abandoned the "farce and mockery" standard,[50] which is merely a restatement of the all too subjective requirements of the Fifth and Fourteenth Amendments' due process clauses[51] and is devoid of Sixth Amendment content. However, these courts have opted for only slightly more stringent standards. One, which was just as vague and almost as subjective as the "farce and mockery" standard, is that the defendant must demonstrate the counsel's "gross incompetence blotted out the essence of a substantial defense."[52] While this may serve to focus upon a specific defense, say an alibi, rather than the whole truth, the showing of prejudice required is so great that the defendant is afforded but little protection.[53] Other courts have adopted a "reasonable competence" standard,[54] but again what is reasonable competence in a federal judge's eyes leaves a lot of room for

---

[46]*See Matthew v. United States*, 518 F.2d 1245, 1246 (7th Cir. 1975); *United States ex. rel. Weber v. Ragen*, 176 F.2d 579, 586 (7th Cir.) (attorney presumed competent as member in good standing of Peoria Bar although he put defendant's first confession in evidence), *cert. denied*, 338 U. S. 809 (1949); *United States ex. rel. Feeley v. Ragen*, 166 F.2d 976, 980 (7th Cir. 1948); *Maye v. Pescor*, 162 F.2d 641, 643 (8th Cir. 1947).

[47]148 F.2d 667 (D. C. Cir.), *cert. denied*, 325 U. S. 889 (1945).

[48]*United States v. Katz*, 425 F.2d 928, 931 (2d Cir. 1970).

[49]*Holnagel v. Kropp*, 426 F.2d 777 (6th Cir.), *cert denied*, 400 U. S. 876 (1970). The court relied upon then Judge Burger's statement in *Harried v. United States*, 389 F.2d 281 (D. C. Cir. 1967), that "[t]he burden on the Appellant to establish his claim of ineffective assistance of counsel is heavy." The Sixth Circuit has since abandoned the farce and mockery standard. *Beasley v. United States*, 491 F.2d 687 (6th Cir. 1974).

[50]*See* Bazelon, *Realities, supra* note 5, at 819–820.

[51]*See Rochin v. California*, 342 U. S. 165, 172 (1952) (stomach pumping held to violate Due Process as "conduct that shocks the conscience").

[52]*Scott v. United States*, 427 F.2d 609, 610 (D. C. Cir. 1970).

[53]*See Harshaw v. United States*, 542 F.2d 455, 457 (8th Cir. 1976); *United States ex rel. Ortiz v. Sielaff*, 542 F.2d 377, 380 (7th Cir. 1976); *United States ex rel. Schultz v. Twomey*, 404 F. Supp. 1300, 1305-1306 (N. D. Ill. 1975). *But see United States ex. rel. Williams v. Twomey*, 510 F.2d 634, 640-641 (7th Cir.), *cert. denied*, 423 U. S. 876 (1975); *United States v. Burks*, 470 F.2d 432, 440–441 (D. C. Cir. 1970).

[54]E.g., *Beasley v. United States, supra*, 491 F.2d at 696; *Herring v. Estelle*, 491 F.2d 125, 127 (5th Cir. 1974).

affirmance. The choice of tests may be little more than a choice of rubrics or catch words. It is now fashionable to say that under neither the farce and mockery nor the reasonable competency standard was incompetence shown.[55] Some courts, including upon occasion my own,[56] still utilize the farce and mockery test and the Supreme Court has yet to resolve the conflict in the circuit courts even though presented with the opportunity to do so.[57] Perhaps the problem is that even if incompetence has been shown, there must also be a showing of prejudice.[58]

At least a few courts have, however, made a break, by spelling out a little what reasonable competence means. In *Coles* v. *Peyton*,[59] the Fourth Circuit has said that, to be effective, counsel must at least prepare. This means conferring with the client early on and, frequently, advising him, investigating the case, and determining and developing the available defense.[60] This has been followed and expanded upon more recently in the District of Columbia Circuit in *United States* v. *DeCoster*.[61] DeCoster incorporated the ABA Standards for the Defense Function and held that a gross violation of the duty to interview possible alibi witnesses shifted the burden of proof to the Government to show harmlessness. Judge Bazelon has put it best: a defendant is entitled to the "reasonable competent assistance of an attorney acting as his diligent and conscientious advocate."[62] And occasionally reversals do occur, as in *United States* v. *Goodwin*, where the defendant's attorney so lacked understanding of the charged offenses that he permitted his client to give testimony amounting to a confession.[63]

Apart from a few exceptions, however, the objective observer must agree with Judge Bazelon's conclusion, seconded by Mr. Justice Brennan, that appellate courts have "papered over" the problem of incompetency, at least insofar as criminal defendants are concerned. The reasons are several; some of them have been discussed elsewhere[64] in greater depth than I

[55]The author has done just that *United States v. Taylor*, 562 F.2d 1345, 1360-1361 (2d Cir. 1977); *see United States v. Williams*, Nos. 77-1454, 77-1501, slip op. 2295, at 2306-2308 (2d Cir. Apr. 6, 1978) (junior associate from well-known firm trying first criminal case and relying on experienced counsel for codefendant); *United States v. Tolliver*, 569 F.2d 724, 731 (2d Cir. 1978).

[56]*United States v. Bubar*, 567 F.2d 192, 201-202 (2d Cir. 1977).

[57]*Rickenbacker v. Warden*, 550 F.2d 62, 67, (2d Cir. 1976) (Oakes, J., dissenting, noting conflict between circuits), *cert. denied*, 46 U.S.L.W. 3215 (U. S. Oct. 4, 1977). It should be noted that occasionally the minimum competence standard leads to reversal. E.g., *United States ex rel. Williams v. Twomey, supra.*

[58]*See McQueen v. Swenson*, 560 F.2d 959 (8th Cir. 1977); *Thomas v. Wyrick*, 535 F.2d 407 (8th Cir. 1976), *cert. denied*, 429 U. S. 868 (1976); *McKenna v. Ellis*, 280 F.2d 592 (5th Cir. 1960); 65 Geo. L. J., *supra* note 45, at 382. But *see United States v. Goodwin*, 531 F.2d 347, 352 (6th Cir. 1976) (per curiam) (no requirement of prejudice once ineffective assistance is shown).

[59]389 F.2d 224, 226 (4th Cir.), *cert. denied*, 393 U. S. 849 (1968).

[60]*See* ABA Standards, *supra* note 20, at §3.2 (204-206), 3.6 (216-219), 4.1 (225-228); Palmer, *"Incompetency and Inadequacy"*, 20 *Sw. L. J.* 136, 137-143 (1966).

[61]487 F.2d 1197 (D. C. Cir. 1973).

[62]*Id.* at 1202.

[63]*United States v. Goodwin, supra*, 531 F.2d at 348.

[64]Bazelon, *Defective Assistance, supra* note 5, at 22-28.

can here. They include a natural disinclination to set aside verdicts, particularly where the defendant is believed guilty.[65] They include a fear perhaps that after every unsuccessful defense the cry of "incompetent counsel" will be heard—the proverbial "open-the-floodgates" syndrome. Or papering over may result from the pragmatic view that if all counsel were truly competent the assembly-line system of criminal justice would simply break down. At least one court would impose a double standard, binding the client by the acts of retained counsel (unless the judge or prosecutor knew of the incompetence) but not by the acts of appointed counsel.[66] Whatever the reasons for overlooking competency, to the extent that they result in a party's unfair treatment, they make a "farce and mockery" of the strident calls for improvement of the bar. It is unfortunate that, while the Chief Justice has been making his plea for such improvement, the Supreme Court has not yet given enlightenment to the concept of lawyer competency.

II. RAMIFICATIONS

The ramifications of pervasive incompetency and concomitant judicial inaction are many. If we have incompetent counsel, on what basis are the convictions of the adversely affected clients left to stand? I have mentioned the utilitarian considerations; the spectre of chaos requires that only in extreme cases and where there is a genuine question of guilt or innocence will counsel be deemed so inadequate as to put the State to the expense and inconvenience of conducting a second trial. The greater good for the greater number in the form of conviction affirmance is permitted to prevail over the individual rights of the accused.[67]

But much deeper problems are evident when one considers that the Court has meanwhile, to a greater extent than at any time in recent decades, subsumed the rights of the criminal defendant into his counsel's control: counsel's action or inaction binds the defendant even without knowledgeable waiver on the latter's part. It is, in short, a long way from *Johnson* v. *Zerbst*,[68] to *Stone* v. *Powell*,[69] *Francis* v. *Henderson*,[70] *Estelle* v.

---

[65]*See Stone v. Powell*, 428 U.S. 465, 491 & n. 30 (1976); *Kaufman v United States*, 394 U.S. 217, 231, 235-236 (1969) (Black, J. dissenting); H. Friendly, *Benchmarks* 260-262 (1967); Y. Kamisar, W. LaFave and J. Israel, *Modern Criminal Procedure* 61 n.b. (4th ed. 1974).

[66]*Fitzgerald v. Estelle*, 505 F.2d 1334, 1336-1337 (5th Cir. 1974) (en banc), *cert. denied* 422 U. S. 1011 (1975). *Contra, Moore v. United States*, 432 F.2d 730, 736 (3d Cir. 1970).

[67]*But see* Cover & Aleinikoff, *"Dialectical Federalism: Habeas Corpus and the Court"*, 86 *Yale L.J.* 1036, 1088-1100 (1977). *See generally* R. Dworkin, *Taking Rights Seriously* ch. 6 (1977).

[68]304 U. S. 458 (1938) (absence of counsel or proper waiver of right of counsel undercuts jurisdiction of trial court, subjecting judgment to collateral review).

[69]428 U. S. 465 (1976) (Fourth Amendment claim precluded on collateral attack where opportunity for full and fair hearing in state court).

[70]425 U. S. 536 (1976) (failure to challenge grand jury composition before trial as required by state procedure precludes collateral attack); see *Davis v. United States*, 411 U. S. 233 (1973) (failure to comply with rule requiring pretrial objection to indictment bars federal prisoner from habeas review, absent showing of cause for failure and prejudice).

Williams,[71] and *Wainwright* v. *Sykes.*[72] To a large extent these latter-day cases cut back heavily on, if they do not overrule, *Johnson* v. *Zerbst* and *Fay* v. *Noia.*[73] In doing so the Court has relied in part on doctrines of agency law.[74] As *Estelle* v. *Williams* said: "Under our adversary system, once a defendant has the assistance of counsel the vast array of trial decisions, strategic and tactical, which must be made before and during trial rests with the accused and his attorney."[75] The Chief Justice would not "rewrite the duties of trial judges and counsel in our legal system."[76] While this concept has a traditional basis,[77] and may be sound on a commerical level, one may question whether it is applicable in the criminal law context where the attorney is often not of the party's choice and where the State not only is a party but is also the licensor and, in the case of indigents, appointer and payor of their counsel. In any case, the reliance on the advocacy system fails to address, or at least leaves unanswered, a basic question: what does the court do when counsel's failure to object is due to ignorance, neglect, or other symptom of incompetency?[78] Leaving aside a defendant's rights under state or federal statutes or well-established decisions are her constitutional rights to be passed over or foreclosed when counsel is incompetent?

To be sure, no one has a right to a perfect trial.[79] But the system, as we have said, presupposes counsel of reasonable competency.[80] The Courts seems to be saying now, as it had not for over a decade, that, whatever the justification—a higher morality, utilitarianism, or, simply, market conditions,[81]—counsel's presumed adequacy will foreclose subsequent collateral attack of a conviction.

Although it is doubtless inconsistent for the Supreme Court to abandon constitutional rights to the winds of presumed competency while at the

[71]425 U. S. 501 (1976) (defendant tried in prison clothes barred from habeas review by counsel's failure to object).

[72]433 U. S. 72 (1977) (failure to object contemporaneously as required by state rule bars habeas review of admission of inculpatory statements made in violation of *Miranda*).

[73]372 U. S. 391, 438–439 (1963) (absent deliberate bypass, *i.e.* a strategic decision to forego assertion of constitutional claims in state courts, defendant may pursue his federal claim in federal court).

[74]*See* Cover and Aleinikoff, *supra* note 67, at 1078–1086.

[75]*Estelle v. Williams, supra,* 425 U. S. at 512.

[76]*Id.* Indeed, he would not permit a defendant to represent himself. *Faretta v. California,* 422 U. S. 806, 836 (1975) (Burger, C. J., dissenting). He relies upon Mr Justice Sutherland's eloquent statement of the layman's inadequacy in *Powell v. Alabama, supra,* 287 U. S. at 69. *See* 422 U. S. at 838–839. And he refers to the "unsupplied demand for competent advocates." *Id.* at 845. He is concerned about the "congestion in the courts" and "the quality of justice" from pro se representation, *id.,* and he is worried lest the defendant will be able to be relieved of his decision to proceed pro se upon appeal. *Id.* at 845–846.

[77]*See* Comment, *"Criminal Waiver; The Requirements of Personal Participation, Competence and Legitimate State Interest",* 54 *Calif. L. Rev.* 1262, 1278–1281 (1966).

[78]*See Wainwright v. Sykes, supra,* 433 U. S. at 100 (Brennan, J., dissenting).

[79]*See Jones v. United States,* 262 F.2d 44, 48 (4th Cir. 1958), *cert. denied,* 359 U. S. 971 (1959).

[80]*See Henry v. Mississippi,* 379 U. S. 443, 451 (1965).

[81]*See* Cover and Aleinkoff, *supra* note 67, at 1081–1082.

same time avoiding the issue of competency directly, it is totally consistent with prevalent doctrine to root out the imcompetents even at the expense of the good feelings of the Bar or the encouragement of public dissatisfaction with lawyers.[82] If limiting a defendant's rights is premised on the adequacy of counsel and counsel are all too often inadequate, then to correct the imbalance one must at least seek to eradicate the inadequacy. Irrespective of where one stands on habeas corpus or wider criminal law concepts, who is there to dispute that this purification is not a desirable end? How then do we state and how do we enforce the constitutional necessity and ethical duty of competency?

III. ENFORCEMENT OF THE DUTY

Monroe Freedman has said that the Code of Professional Responsibility, while sound in concept, is "marred by considerable superficiality, avoidance of difficult issues, and a carry-over of the anti-competitive concerns of the old Canons of Ethics."[83] Anthony Amsterdam has skeptically noted that the Canons "are of as much use to the practising attorney in the courtroom as a Valentine card would be to a heart surgeon in the operating room."[84] Thomas Morgan has pointed out that "[t]he Code is under increasing attack as irrelevant, internally inconsistent, and conspiratorial",[85] and, while he disagrees in part, he concludes that it is "repeatedly biased in the ordering of its priorities"[86] and that "pressure for revision of several basic concepts of professional responsibility is both sound and inevitable.[87]

Two good starting points are Cannon 6, which imposes the ethical duty of competency, and Canon 7, which requires "[a] lawyer [to] represent a client zealously within the bounds of the law."

The virtually total lack of enforcement of Canon 6 may be attributable in part to its vagueness and generality. The "Ethical Considerations" (EC) and "Disciplinary Rules" (DR) under Canon 6 never quite tell us what acting competently is or what competence means. The Ethical Considerations do suggest,[88] to be sure, that what is meant includes being well-informed of changes in the laws and legal procedures pertaining to the matter undertaken,[89] acting with "higher motivation than that arising from fear of civil liability or disciplinary penalty,"[90] and devoting time and

---

[82]*See, e.g., Time Magazine*, Apr. 10, 1978, at 65.

[83]Freedman, *supra* note 2, at 128.

[84]*Quoted in id.* at vii; Norman Dorsen and Leon Friedman attribute this quote to Freedman himself. *Disorder in the Court* 140 and n. 21 (1973). No matter, it a good one. On the vagueness of the Canons, *see id.* at 139-140.

[85]Morgan, *"The Evolving Concept of Professional Responsibility"*, 90 *Harv. L. Rev.* 702, 702 (1977).

[86]*Id.* at 704

[87]*Id.*

[88]ABA Code of Professional Responsibility EC 6-1 & n. 1 [hereinafter ABA Code].

[89]*Id.* EC 6-2.

[90]*Id.* EC 6-5.

energy to being able "to know where to look for the answers, to know how to deal with the problems, and to know how to advise to the best of his legal talents and abilities."[91] But no mention is made in the Ethical Consideraions of investigation and preparation, conferring with the client early and often, ascertaining and developing defenses, or filing appropriate motions to quash, to proceed, to suppress or for discovery—the actions that are called for by minimum standards.[92] No mention is made of trying a case with persuasiveness and zeal, being ready when called to trial, cross-examining with a goal—a goal of testing observation, recollection, variation, interest and bias, or a combination of these goals—and summing up with an aim and with fervor—the things that go into a capable defense, not necessarily a virtuoso performance, but a capable defense. The general considerations of being well-informed of the law, working with higher motivation than that arising from fear of civil liability or disciplinary penalty and knowing how to advise the client are seen, in reality, to be Valentine verses. Specificity in terms of the ethical duty of competency thus becomes of the first order of importance.

Canon 6's Disciplinary Rules are a little more helpful. They require a lawyer (1) not to "[h]andle a legal matter" which he should know that he is "not competent to handle, without associating with him a lawyer who is competent to handle it";[93] (2) not to "[h]andle a legal matter without preparation adequate in the circumstances";[94] or (3) not to "[n]eglect a legal matter entrusted to him."[95] If the term "competent" were spelled out, if "adequate preparation in the circumstances" were made concrete, and if "neglect" were defined to include omission to confer with the client or to keep him informed, we would at least have some rules that would be reasonably enforceable by an appropriate body. Of course, the rules must be enforced. But, as Canon 6 now reads, a charge of unethical incompetency would fail for want of specificity; incompetence is simply not a matter for disciplinary consideration.[96]

Canon 7 is little better––at least it imposes the duty of *zealous* representation, but quickly qualifies that with cautionary "within the bounds of the law." Ethical Consideration 7-1 points out that each individual client is entitled to have his conduct judged in accordance with the law, and to the presentation for adjudication of any lawful issue or defense. EC 7-4 does say that "[t]he advocate may urge any permissible construction of the law favorable to his client without regard to his professional opinion as to the

[91]*Id.* EC 6-1 n. 1, *quoting* Levy and Sprague, *"Accounting and Law: Is Dual Practice in the Public Interest?"* 52 *A.B.A.J.* 1110, 1112 (1966).

[92]*See* ABA Standards, *supra* note 20.

[93]ABA Code, *supra* note 88, at DR 6-101 (A)(1).

[94]*Id.* (A)(2).

[95]*Id.* (A)(3) (footnote omitted).

[96]*Cf. Kentucky State Bar Ass'n v. Taylor*, 482 S. W. 2d 574, 582-583 (1972) ("If the canons of ethics adopted for the legal profession were tested under the void for vagueness' doctrine which has spelled the doom of various breach of peace and disorderly conduct laws through the country it is doubtful that they would survive this case."). *But see Parker v. Levy*, 417 U. S. 733 (1974) (military justice code's proscription against "conduct unbecoming an officer and a gentleman" upheld).

likelihood that the construction will ultimately prevail." And EC 7-6 rather grudgingly states that "[i]n many cases a lawyer may not be certain as to the state of mind of his client, and in those situations he should resolve reasonable doubts in favor of his client." But for the most part the Ethical Considerations under Canon 7 pertain to what is or is not "within the bounds of the law" and they do little to explicate the content of zealous representation.

Canon 7's disciplinary Rules, however, fall even shorter. The only rule requiring positive zeal is DR 7-101, which states only that "[a] lawyer shall not *intentionally*: (1) [f]ail to seek the lawful objectives of his client through reasonably available means permitted by law and the Disciplinary Rules . . .," (2) "[f]ail to carry out a contract of employment . . .," or (3) "[p]rejudice or damage his client during the course of the professional relationship."[97] Proof of intentional neglect would not be easy to marshal. The remainder of these Canon 7 Disciplinary Rules tell what a lawyer should *not* do to further his client's interest, such as to make extrajudicial statements,[98] to engage in undignified conduct toward the tribunal,[99] and the like.

The ambiguities and the emphasis of Canons 6 and 7 are not compatible with the enforcement of any ethical duty of competency whether or not it includes a component of zeal. They are brakes upon over-zealousness, and quite specifically define the limits of what is proper, but they fall short in spelling out the *minimal* requirements that every person who goes into the courts should have to the right to expect.

But even if we had specific, concrete ethical standards of competency, two major questions would remain. How would we enforce those standards and how wise or practical would it be to do so?

The method of enforcement is not easy. Mr. Woytash suggests bar disciplinary committees, perhaps with nonlawyer members:

> Any nonlawyer pressure to put competence failings under the disciplinary system should have plenty of lawyer help. More and more, lawyers understand that professional self-regulation is at the point of evaporating and that it will vanish under government intervention unless it becomes effective in guaranteeing a professionalism from everyone who holds a professional license.[100]

This may or may not be true, but at least it raises the question. Assuming competency were made a subject of investigation by an appropriate disciplinary committee,[101] it is plain that the committee would have to rely extensively upon its trial-oriented members for advice; at least it would be

[97]ABA Code, *supra* note 88, at DR 7-101 (A)(1), (2) and (3).
[98]*Id.* DR 7-107.
[99]*Id.* DR 7-106 (C) (6).
[100]Woytash, *supra* note 15.
[101]This is quite a simplification; the real world environment, it has been persuasively argued, will simply not permit exclusive concentration on a structure set up really to handle only serious attorney deviance. *See* Steele and Nimmer, *"Lawyers, Clients, and Professional Regulation"* 3 Am. Bar Foundation Research J. 917, 1014–1016 (1976).

important that the membership include experienced advocates to lend expertise. And, absent bar action, the courts themselves could establish an appropriate committee.[102] While the Second Circuit did not have the ethical duty of competency specifically in mind, it has recently adopted a set of disciplinary rules and established a Committee on Admissions and Grievances, consisting of distinguished members of the bar and chaired by a distinguished law school dean. Other courts of appeals are doing or have done the same. Trial courts may do likewise, although it would be preferable if the rules were reasonably uniform and established after publication in advance, with opportunity for public comment.[103] There is no reason why such committees could not consider imcompetency complaints and recommend action accordingly.

Who would make the complaints? Presumably clients who felt themselves inadequately represented, subsequently retained counsel, trial judges, or even appellate judges.

Assuming a finding of "incompetency" or "gross incompetency" or whatever were required after an investigation and full due process hearing, what sanctions could be imposed? In most cases mere investigation and advice might suffice—much like a hospital surgical review committee's advice on the conduct of surgery. More serious or repeated instances could result in more serious sanctions: public censure, a severe sanction, one that is used informally and infrequently in England when a barrister steps over the line;[104] suspension, conditioned perhaps upon fulfilling certain continuing education requirements; disbarment from the rolls of the court in question for continued abuse of the privilege to practice—obviously a whole range of possibilities is available.

The ultimate question—the gut question—is whether the problem of incompetency is so great as to require the establishment of a whole new set of rules and procedures to ensure that those practicing now are capable of fulfilling their ethical commitments to be competent and zealous. I am frank to say that despite what I have written I have some doubts, principally because I think that the legal profession engages in a lot of unnecessary self-flagellation; I have never believed that where there is smoke there is necessarily fire—there may be a smoke machine. But I have seen incompetency upon occasion; a fair number of people consider that it is a pervasive problem. Certainly the quality of advocacy needs improvement, though I personally think it more serious among the older than among the newer advocates. We have heretofore proceeded on an assumption of *general* competence, an assumption which simply no longer holds true in the light of the complexities and varieties of modern legal practice. We have also, to a great extent, assumed *perpetual* competence which simply does not hold true in any field,[105] with the possible exception of admiralty and

---

[102]*See* Note, *"Disbarment in the Federal Courts"*, 85 *Yale L. J.* 975 (1976) (urging more active role of federal courts in disciplinary matters and uniform rules therefor).

[103]*See* J. Weinstein, *Reform of Court Rule-Making Procedures* 133–137 (1977).

[104]*See* note 31 *supra.*

[105]Steele and Nimmer note, for these reasons, the "only limited movement toward the mandatory regulation of competence." Steele and Nimmer, *supra* note 101, at 930.

would not hold true even in that hoary specialty were the law to cut loose from the nostalgic days of sailing ships and sealing wax in which it seems to be so deeply ensconced.

Thus I have the feeling that we owe it to the public to ensure that its contacts with our system of advocacy begin to accord with the analytical ideal, that at least some minimal standards of competency are met. I also have the unpleasant feeling, as does Mr. Woytash, that unless we do something about the problem, we will find the legislatures—both state and federal—prescribing inelastic rules or codes. And I suspect that—like the threat of a malpractice action in the medical profession—the very presence of a disciplinary board ready to enforce the ethical duty of competency in advocacy will serve to spur the Bar toward self-improvement. Whether it will deter some from the field is another matter, however, and a serious one, because the additional threat of discipline could be one more factor making the new lawyer lack the confidence that we all know comes only from experience.

It is time then to do something not only about defining but also enforcing the ethical duty of competency. I trust that in coming to this conclusion, rather reluctantly as I have, I have not overlooked the duty of the courts to participate—relieving the injured client from the consequences of his advocate's unreasonable inability to function in his case. To take any other view, where constitutional or minimal supervisory standards are not met, would, I feel, smack of hypocrisy.

section three

HONESTY

Imbler v. Pachtman

500 F.2D 1301
UNITED STATES COURT OF APPEALS, NINTH CIRCUIT, 1974

KOELSCH, Circuit Judge: This matter has a long history. In 1961 plaintiff-appellant Imbler was convicted on a murder charge in Los Angeles Superior Court and sentenced to death. The California Supreme Court affirmed. *People v. Imbler*, 57 Cal.2d 711, 21 Cal.Rptr. 568, 371 P.2d 304 (1962). Thereafter, Imbler's state habeas corpus petition was denied following an evidentiary hearing. *In re Imbler*, 60 Cal.2d 554, 35 Cal.Rptr. 293, 387 P.2d 6 (1963). A subsequent writ set aside the death penalty, *In re Imbler*, 61 Cal.2d 556, 39 Cal.Rptr. 375, 393 P.2d 687 (1964); and when the state declined to prosecute another "penalty trial," Imbler was given a life sentence.

In 1969 the United States District Court, concluding that Imbler's conviction was secured in part by testimony the prosecution knew, or had strong reason to know, was perjured, granted him a writ of habeas corpus. *Imbler v. Craven*, 298 F.Supp. 795, 809 (1969). We affirmed, *Imbler v. Craven*, 424 F.2d 631 (9th Cir. 1970), certiorari denied 400 U.S. 865, 91 S.Ct. 100, 27 L.Ed.2d 104.

Imbler then brought this suit for damages. So far as need be noticed, his allegations in substance are that the defendant Pachtman, the district attorney who prosecuted the criminal charges on behalf of the State of California, had knowingly, maliciously, etc., used perjured testimony to secure a conviction and hence was liable in damages for violation of his, Imbler's, civil rights. The district judge dismissed Imbler's complaint as to Pachtman without leave to amend; he ruled that Pachtman, as a prosecuting attorney, enjoyed an immunity from suit for acts committed "in the performance of duties constituting an integral part of the judicial process . . .," *Marlowe v. Coakley*, 404 F.2d 70 (9th Cir. 1968); see *Robichaud v. Ronan*, 351 F.2d 533 (9th Cir. 1965); and that as a matter of law the acts complained of came within a quasi-judicial prosecutorial function to which immunity attached. Imbler appeals. We affirm.

The district court's dismissal of appellant's claim was consistent with our prior decisions. *Ney v. State of California*, 439 F.2d 1285 (9th Cir. 1971); *Donovan v. Reinbold*, 433 F.2d 738, 743 (9th Cir. 1970); *Marlowe v. Coakley*, *supra*; *Clark v. Washington*, 366 F.2d 678 (9th Cir. 1966); *Robichaud v. Ronan*, *supra*; *Agnew v. Moody*, 330 F.2d 868 (9th Cir. 1964); *Harmon v. Superior*

Court, 329 F.2d 154 (9th Cir. 1964) *Sires v. Cole*, 320 F.2d 877 (9th Cir. 1963). The acts of the defendant which allegedly harmed appellant occurred during prosecutorial activities which can only be characterized as an "integral part of the judicial process."[2] All involved the question of a witness during the 1961 criminal prosecution.[3]

Appellant, in effect, urges us to reject the doctrine of prosecutorial immunity and overrule a long line of this court's decisions. We decline to do so. The protection given a prosecutor acting in his quasi-judicial role protects not simply the prosecutor, but, more importantly, the effective operation of the judicial process, and hence, the "common good." Because both the honest and dishonest are insulated, on occasion an injury without redress inevitably results; but, as well expressed by Judge Learned Hand:

> "It does indeed go without saying that an official, who is in fact guilty of using his powers to vent his spleen upon others, or for any other personal motive not connected with the public good, should not escape liability for the injuries he may so cause; and, if it were possible in practice to confine such complaints to the guilty, it would be monstrous to deny recovery. The jurisdiction for doing so is that it is impossible to know whether the claim is well founded until the case has been tried, and that to submit all officials, the innocent as well as the guilty, to the burden of a trial and to the inevitable danger of its outcome, would dampen the ardor of all but the most resolute, or the most irresponsible, in the unflinching discharge of their duties. Again and again the public interest calls for action which may turn out to be founded on a mistake, in the face of which an official may later find himself hard put to it to satisfy a jury of his good faith. There must indeed be means of punishing public officers who have been truant to their duties; but that is quite another matter from exposing such as have been honestly mistaken to suit by anyone who has suffered from their errors. As is so often the case, the answer must be found in a balance between the evils inevitable in either alternative. In this instance it has been thought in the end better to leave unredressed the wrongs done by dishonest officers than to subject those who try to do their duty to the constant dread of retaliation. Judged as res nova, we should not hesitate to follow the path laid down in the books." *Gregoire v. Biddle*, 177 F.2d 579 (2d Cir 1949).

As indicated earlier, the issue is not "*res nova*" in this circuit.[4] The "balance between the evils inevitable in either alternative" has consistently been struck in favor of protecting honest criminal prosecution, at the expense of those injured by scoundrels,[5] by granting immunity from suit to all prosecutors.[6]

The judgment is affirmed.

[2][Note omitted, summarizing Judge Kilkenny's dissent and arguing that it is inconsistent with the Court's previous rulings.]

[3][Note omitted, dismissing defendant's contention that the prosecutor engaged in non-immune police activity during a particular recess in the trial.]

[4][Note omitted, rejecting the defense's contention that *Scheuer v. Rhodes*, 416 U.S. 232, S.Ct. 1683, 40 L.Ed.2d 90 (1974), undercuts prosecutorial immunity.]

[5]The reference is general and not intended as personal.

[6][Note omitted, regarding the problem of determination of defendant's innocence or guilt.]

KILKENNY, Circuit Judge (dissenting):

Although appellant's 22 page amended complaint, with 23 pages of exhibits, is admittedly repetitious and in places ambiguous, there is no question but that it charges appellee, Pachtman, with knowingly, willfully and maliciously using eight different items of false material testimony in securing appellant's initial conviction. If this is true, I believe that appellee violated appellant's procedural due process rights, and that he should be stripped of his official or representative character and subjected in his person to the consequences of his individual conduct.

*   *   *

To now hold, on our facts, that the knowing, wilful and malicious use of perjured testimony to gain a conviction, even though accomplished during the course of a trial, constitutes an integral part of the judicial process, flies in the fact of the integrity sought to be protected by judicial and quasi-judicial immunity.

The allegations in *Marlowe v. Coakley*, 404 F.2d 70 (CA9 1968) charged the prosecuting attorney with ". . . knowingly and wilfully, *or with gross negligence*, present[ing] perjured testimony to the grand jury . . . ." [Emphasis supplied.] Needless to say, there is a monumental distinction between charging an officer with gross negligence in connection with the presentation of perjured testimony and charging him with knowingly, wilfully and maliciously *using* perjured testimony to obtain a conviction. Consequently, the decision of the *Marlowe* court could well rest on the failure of the complainant to clearly charge wilful misconduct in presenting the perjured testimony. C.f. *Ney v. State of California, supra*, 439 F.2d at 1287. The alternative does not equate with wilful action. I decline to hold that the shield of immunity should rest on the brow of a district attorney who *knowingly, wilfully and maliciously* utilizes perjured testimony to obtain a conviction. This conduct should not be condoned as an *integral part of the judicial process*.

Clark v. State of Washington, 366 F.2d 678 (9 Cir. 1966), recognizes the rule that a prosecuting attorney enjoys immunity under the Civil Rights Act only insofar as his prosecuting functions are concerned. At the risk of being repetitive, I again stress that appellee's acts, as charged in the amended complaint, had nothing to do with his *legitimate* prosecutory functions.

*   *   *

Hilliard v. Williams, 465 F.2d 1212 (6 Cir. 1972), cert. denied 409 U.S. 1029, 93 S.Ct. 461, 34 L.Ed.2d 332 is closely in point. There, the court, in a civil rights action, recognized the general rule that a prosecuting attorney, when acting in his official capacity, is immune from a suit for damages. The court then goes on to hold that the doctrine of quasi-judicial immunity, normally shielding a prosecuting attorney, should not be extended to the situation where a complaint charges that the officer deliberately suppressed material evidence which resulted in the conviction of the appellant.

The court emphasized that such wilful conduct was "... outside [the officer's] quasi-judicial capacity and beyond the scope of 'duties constituting an integral part of the judicial process.' " 465 F.2d at 1218.

On the charges before us, I would hold that appellee acted entirely outside the scope of his jurisdiction and should not be permitted to shelter himself from liability by a plea that he was acting under the immunity of his office. Not to be forgotten is the high responsibility accepted by a prosecuting officer when he enters upon the duties of his office. For example: (1) he is required to recognize that in our system of justice, the accused is to be given the benefit of all reasonable doubt; (2) his decisions during the course of the prosecution must be fair to all, including the defendant; (3) he has a duty of timely disclosure to the defense of all available evidence known to him that tends to help the defendant, and (4) it is his duty to seek justice, not pervert it by placing a conviction above the constitutional rights of the accused. It is time to recognize that prosecutors are not entirely above the law which holds other individuals financially accountable for their *intentional misdeeds*.

Needless to say, I express no opinion as to the merits of appellant's claims. I only say that on the basis of the allegations in the amended complaint, he is entitled to have a full-fledged judicial inquiry.

I would reverse.

In re Ryder

UNITED STATES DISTRICT COURT, E.D. VIRGINIA, 1967
263 F. SUPP. 360
(AFFIRMED PER CURIAM, 381 F.2D 713 (4 CIR. 1967))

Before HOFFMAN, Chief Judge, and Lewis and Butzner, Judges.

MEMORANDUM

PER CURIAM.

This proceeding was instituted to determine whether Richard R. Ryder should be removed from the roll of attorneys qualified to practice before this court. Ryder was admitted to this bar in 1953. He formerly served five years as an Assistant United States Attorney. He has an active trial practice, including both civil and criminal cases.

In proceedings of this kind the charges must be sustained by clear and convincing proof, the misconduct must be fraudulent, intentional, and the result of improper motives. We conclude that these strict requirements have been satisfied. Ryder took possession of stolen money and a sawed-off shotgun, knowing that the money had been stolen and that the gun had been used in an armed robbery. He intended to retain this property pending his client's trial unless the government discovered it. He intended by his possession to destroy the chain of evidence that linked the contraband to his client and to prevent its use to establish his client's guilt.

On August 24, 1966 a man armed with a sawed-off shotgun robbed the Varina Branch of the Bank of Virginia of $7,583. Included in the currency taken were $10 bills known as "bait money," the serial numbers of which had been recorded.

On August 26, 1966 Charles Richard Cook rented safety deposit box 14 at a branch of the Richmond National Bank. Later in the day Cook was interviewed at his home by agents of the Federal Bureau of Investigation, who obtained $348 from him. Cook telephoned Ryder, who had represented him in civil litigation. Ryder came to the house and advised the agents that he represented Cook. He said that if Cook were not to be placed under arrest, he intended to take him to his office for an interview. The agents left. Cook insisted to Ryder that he had not robbed the bank. He told Ryder that he had won the money, which the agent had taken from him, in a crap game. At this time Ryder believed Cook.

Later that afternoon Ryder telephoned one of the agents and asked whether any of the bills obtained from Cook had been identified as part of the money taken in the bank robbery. The agent told him that some bills had been identified. Ryder made inquiries about the number of bills taken and their denominations. The agent declined to give him specific information but indicated that several of the bills were recorded as bait money.

That afternoon Ryder telephoned a former officer of the Richmond Bar Association to discuss his course of action. He had known this attorney for many years and respected his judgment. The lawyer was at home and had no library available to him when Ryder telephoned. In their casual conversation Ryder told what he knew about the case, omitting names. He explained that he thought he would take the money from Cook's safety deposit box and place it in a box in his own name. This, he believed, would prevent Cook from attempting to dispose of the money. The lawyers thought that eventually F.B.I. agents would locate the money and that since it was in Ryder's possession, he could claim a privilege and thus effectively exclude it from evidence. This would prevent the government from linking Ryder's client with the bait money and would also destroy any presumption of guilt that might exist arising out of the client's exclusive possession of the evidence.

Ryder testified:

"I had sense enough to know, one, at that time apparently the F.B.I. did have the serial numbers of the bills. I had sense enough to know, from many, many years of experience in this court and in working with the F.B.I. and, in fact, in directing the F.B.I. on some occasions, to know that eventually the bank—that the F.B.I. would find that money if I left that money in the bank. There was no doubt in my mind that eventually they would find it. The only thing I could think of to do was to get the money out of Mr. Cook's possession. . . . [T]he idea was that I assumed that if anybody tried to go into a safety deposit box in my name, the bank officials would notify me and that I would get an opportunity to come in this court and argue a question of whether or not they could use that money as evidence."

The lawyers discussed and rejected alternatives, including having a third party get the money. At the conclusion of the conversation Ryder was advised, "Don't do it surreptitiously and to be sure that you let your client know that it is going back to the rightful owners."

On Monday morning Ryder asked Cook to come by his office. He prepared a power of attorney, which Cook signed:

"KNOW YOU ALL MEN BY THESE PRESENTS, that I CHARLES RICHARD COOK do hereby make, constitute and appoint, R.R. RYDER as my Attorney at Law and in fact do authorize my said Attorney to enter a safety deposit box rented by me at the Richmond National Bank and Trust Company, 2604 Hull Street, Richmond, Virginia, said box requiring Mosler Key Number 30 to open the same and I further authorize the said Attorney to remove the contents of the said box and so dispose of the said contents as he sees fit and I direct the officials of the said bank to cooperate with my said attorney towards the accomplishment of this my stated purpose."

Ryder did not follow the advice he had received on Saturday. He did not let his client know the money was going back to the rightful owner. He testified about his omission:

"I prepared it myself and told Mr. Cook to sign it. In the power of attorney, I did not specifically say that Mr. Cook authorized me to deliver that money to the appropriate authorities at any time because for a number of reasons. One, in representing a man under these circumstances, you've got to keep the man's confidence, but I also put in that power of attorney that Mr. Cook authorized me to dispose of that money as I saw fit, and the reason for that being that I was going to turn the money over to the proper authorities at whatever time I deemed that it wouldn't hurt Mr. Cook."

Ryder took the power of attorney which Cook had signed to the Richmond National Bank. He rented box 13 in his name with his office address, presented the power of attorney, entered Cook's box, took both boxes into a booth, where he found a bag of money and a sawed-off shotgun in Cook's box. The box also contained miscellaneous items which are not pertinent to this proceeding. He transferred the contents of Cook's box to his own and returned the boxes to the vault. He left the bank, and neither he nor Cook returned.

Ryder testified that he had some slight hesitation about the propriety of what he was doing. Within a half-hour after he left the bank, he talked to a retired judge and distinguished professor of law. He told this person that he wanted to discuss something in confidence. Ryder then stated that he represented a man suspected of bank robbery. The judge recalled the main part of the conversation:

". . . And that he had received from this client, under a power of attorney, a sum [of] money which he, Mr. Ryder, suspected was proceeds of the robbery, although he didn't know it, but he had a suspicion that it was; that he had placed this money in a safety deposit vault at a bank; that he had received it with the intention of returning it to the rightful owner after the case against his client had been finally disposed of one way or the other; that he considered that he had received it under the privilege of an attorney and client and that he wanted responsible people in the community to know of that fact and that he was telling me in confidence of that as one of these people that he wanted to know of it.

"Q. Did he say anything to you about a sawed-off shotgun?

"A. I don't recall. If Mr. Ryder says he did, I would not deny it, but I do not recall it, because the—my main attention in what he was saying was certainly drawn to the fact that the money was involved, but I just cannot answer the question emphatically, but if Mr. Ryder says he told me, why, I certainly wouldn't deny it."

Ryder testified that he told about the shotgun. The judge also testified that Ryder certainly would not have been under the impression that he—the judge—thought that he was guilty of unethical conduct.

The same day Ryder also talked with other prominent persons in Richmond—a judge of a court of record and an attorney for the Commonwealth. Again, he stated that what he intended to say was confidential. He related the circumstances and was advised that a lawyer could not receive the property and if he had received it he could not retain possession of it.

On September 7, 1966 Cook was indicted for robbing the Varina Branch of the Bank of Virginia. A bench warrant was issued and the next day Ryder represented Cook at a bond hearing. Cook was identified as the robber by employees of the bank. He was released on bond. Cook was arraigned on a plea of not guilty on September 9, 1966.

On September 12, 1966 F.B.I. agents procured search warrants for Cook's and Ryder's safety deposit boxes in the Richmond National Bank. They found Cook's box empty. In Ryder's box they discovered $5,920 of the $7,583 taken in the bank robbery and the sawed-off shotgun used in the robbery.

On September 23, 1966 Ryder filed a motion to suppress the money obtained from Cook by the agents on August 26, 1966. The motion did not involve items taken from Ryder's safety deposit box. The motion came on to be heard October 6, 1966. Ryder called Cook as a witness for examination on matters limited to the motion to suppress. The court called to Ryder's attention papers pertaining to the search of the safety deposit boxes. Ryder moved for a continuance, stating that he intended to file a motion with respect to the seizure of the contents of the lockbox.

On October 14, 1966 the three judges of this court removed Ryder as an attorney for Cook; suspending him from practice before the court until further order; referred the matter to the United States Attorney, who was requested to file charges within five days; set the matter for hearing November 11, 1966; and granted Ryder leave to move for vacation or modification of its order pending hearing.

The United States Attorney charged Ryder with violations of Canons 15 and 32 of the Canons of Professional Ethics of the Virginia State Bar. Ryder did not move for vacation or modification of the order, and the case was heard as scheduled by the court en banc. After the transcript was prepared and the case briefed, the court heard the argument of counsel on December 27, 1966.

At the outset, we reject the suggestion that Ryder did not know the money which he transferred from Cook's box to his was stolen. We find that on August 29 when Ryder opened Cook's box and saw a bag of money and a sawed-off shotgun, he then knew Cook was involved in the bank robbery and that the money was stolen. The evidence clearly establishes this. Ryder knew that the man who had robbed the bank used a sawed-off shotgun. He disbelieved Cook's story about the source of the money in the lockbox. He knew that some of the bills in Cook's possession were bait money.

* * *

The money in Cook's box belonged to the Bank of Virginia. The law did not authorize Cook to conceal this money or withhold it from the bank. His larceny was a continuing offense. Cook had no title or property interest in the money that he lawfully could pass to Ryder. The Act of Assembly authorizing the promulgation of the Canons of Ethics in Virginia forbids inconsistency with §18.1-107 Code of Virginia, 1950, which provides:

> "If any person buy or receive from another person, or aid in concealing, any stolen goods or other thing, knowing the same to have been stolen, he shall be deemed guilty of larceny thereof, and may be proceeded against, although the principal offender be not convicted."

No canon of ethics or law permitted Ryder to conceal from the Bank of Virginia its money to gain his client's acquittal.

Cook's possession of the sawed-off shotgun was illegal. 26 U.S.C.A. §5851. Ryder could not lawfully receive the gun from Cook to assist Cook to avoid conviction of robbery. Cook had never mentioned the shotgun to Ryder. When Ryder discovered it in Cook's box, he took possession of it to hinder the government in the prosecution of its case, and he intended not to reveal it pending trial unless the government discovered it and a court compelled its production. No statute or canon of ethics authorized Ryder to take possession of the gun for this purpose.

Canon 15 states in part:

> ". . . [T]he great trust of the lawyer is to be performed within and not without the bounds of law. The office of attorney does not permit, much less does it demand of him for any client, violation of law or any manner of fraud or chicane. He must obey his own conscience and not that of his client."

In helping Cook to conceal the shotgun and stolen money, Ryder acted without the bounds of law. He allowed the office of attorney to be used in violation of law. The scheme which he devised was a deceptive, legalistic subterfuge—rightfully denounced by the canon as chicane.

Ryder also violated Canon 32. He rendered Cook a service involving deception and disloyalty to the law. He intended that his actions should remove from Cook exclusive possession of stolen money, and thus destroy an evidentiary presumption. His service in taking possession of the shotgun and money, with the intention of retaining them until after the trial, unless discovered by the government, merits the "stern and just condemnation" the canon prescribes.

Ryder's testimony that he intended to have the court rule on the admissibility of the evidence and the extent of the lawyer-client privilege does not afford justification for his action. He intended to do this only if the government discovered the shotgun and stolen money in his lockbox. If the government did not discover it, he had no intention of submitting any legal question about it to the court. If there were no discovery, he would continue to conceal the shotgun and money for Cook's benefit pending trial.

Ryder's action is not justified because he thought he was acting in the best interests of his client. To allow the individual lawyer's belief to determine the standards of professional conduct will in time reduce the ethics of the profession to the practices of the most unscrupulous. Moreover, Ryder knew that the law against concealing stolen property and the law forbidding receipt and possession of a sawed-off shotgun contain no exemptions for a lawyer who takes possession with the intent of protecting a criminal from the consequences of his crime.

Canon 15 warns against the reasoning urged in support of Ryder:

> "Nothing operates more certainly to create or to foster popular prejudice against lawyers as a class and to deprive the profession of that full measure of esteem and confidence which belongs to the proper discharge of its duties than does the false claim, often set up by the unscrupulous in defense of questionable transactions, that it is the duty of the lawyer to do whatever may enable him to succeed in winning his client's cause."

We find it difficult to accept the argument that Ryder's action is excusable because if the government found Cook's box, Ryder's would easily be found, and if the government failed to find both Cook's and Ryder's boxes, no more harm would be done than if the agents failed to find only Cook's. Cook's concealment of the items in his box cannot be cited as an excuse by Ryder. Cook's conduct is not the measure of Ryder's ethics. The conduct of a lawyer should be above reproach. Concealment of the stolen money and the sawed-off shotgun to secure Cook's acquittal was wrong whether the property was in Cook's or Ryder's possession.

There is much to be said, however, for mitigation of the discipline to be imposed. Ryder intended to return the bank's money after his client was tried. He consulted reputable persons before and after he placed the property in his lockbox, although he did not precisely follow their advice. Were it not for these facts, we would deem proper his permanent exclusion from practice before the court. In view of the mitigating circumstances, he will be suspended from practice in this court for eighteen months effective October 14, 1966.

Finally, we agree with the amicus curiae and Ryder that in disciplinary proceedings a show cause order generally is preferable to an *ex parte* suspension with leave to apply for reinstatement pending a full hearing. Cf. *Bradley v. Fisher*, 13 Wall. 335, 80 U.S. 335, 20 L.Ed. 646 (1871) and *Laughlin v. Wheat*, 68 App. D.C. 190, 95 F.2d 101 (1937). The difficulties inherent in Ryder's continued representation of Cook require the course followed here. When it became apparent from affidavits for the search warrants and as a result of the hearing on October 6, 1966 that it was Ryder who held concealed in his possession the stolen money and the sawed-off shotgun alleged by the government to be connected with the crime and that he intended to continue his representation of Cook, the three judges of this circuit decided they should act. In the order suspending Ryder and setting a date for hearing, Ryder was afforded an opportunity for an immediate hearing upon motion. We conclude that considering both the substance and the procedure of this case, Ryder was not denied due process of law nor has he suffered prejudice.

The Lawyer's Obligation to Be Trustworthy When Dealing with Opposing Parties

Geoffrey C. Hazard, Jr.*

It is desirable that lawyers be trustworthy in dealing with opposing parties.[1] It is impractical, however, to go very far in formulating rules of professional conduct that require lawyers to be trustworthy.

I. DEFINING TERMS

At the outset, some definition of terms may be useful. By "lawyer" is meant lawyers in the practice of law generally. This includes lawyers in private practice and in public service, in independent firms and in law depart-

South Carolina Law Review, 33, No. 2 (1981), 181–89, 191, and 192–96. Reprinted by permission.

*Baker Professor of Law, Yale University. B. A., Swarthmore College, 1953; L.L.B., Columbia Law School, 1954. Reported, American Bar Association Commission on Evaluation of Professional Standards. This is the text of a lecture prepared for delivery on the occasion of the Fifth Annual Benjamin Adger Hagood Distinguished Lecture before members of the South Carolina Bar, Law Faculty, and Students at the South Carolina Law Center, April 8, 1981.

[1] Kutak, "*Coming: The New Model Rules of Professional Conduct*," 66 A.B.A.J. 47, 48 (1980); Rubin "*A Causerie on Lawyer's Ethics in Negotiations*," 35 La. L. Rev. 577 (1975).

ments, in large organizations and in solo practice; civil and criminal lawyers, specialists and generalists. Lawyers perform a broad range of functions including counseling and advocacy, but this article focuses on those functions that concern direct dealings with opposing parties on behalf of a client.[2] In this analysis, the term "vouching lawyer" refers to a lawyer who is making a representation to an opposing party.

By "opposing parties" is meant those persons, other than clients and officials of a tribunal, with whom vouching lawyers deal during the course of representing clients. Lawyers, of course have special duties of trustworthiness in dealing with tribunals[3] and owe equally exacting and even broader fiduciary duties to their clients.[4] The present analysis focuses on the duty to opposing parties, not in derogation of vouching lawyers' duties to client and court, but for purposes of clarification. The analysis presupposes and holds constant these other duties, particularly duties owed to clients. The term "opposing parties" in its exclusive connotation thus signifies those other than client and court. In its inclusive connotation, the term specifically refers to persons of adverse interest and their legal counsel,[5] including opposite parties in contract or property transactions, formation of partnerships and corporations, negotiations aimed at settling litigation, and negotiation and mediation in interpersonal, interorganizational, interdepartmental, and political or social controversies of all kinds. Adversary relationships are ubiquitous in modern society, and the participation of lawyers in defining and transforming adversary relationships is commonplace. Ordinarily, whenever a lawyer acts for a client, a party of actual or potential opposing interest also exists.

Finally, by "trustworthy" is meant truthfulness in statements made as representations. The definition is limited to "statements made as representations" because conventions governing social intercourse do not require strict truthfulness at all times. On the contrary, those conventions give license to make certain kinds of statements that are literally false.[6] Thus, a lawyer is allowed to say at certain stages of negotiation that his client will not offer or accept a specified sum, concession, or interest when, in fact,

---

[2]*See, e.g.*, Meserve, "*Lawyers in Modern Society*," 49 *N.Y.S.B.J.* 94, 96 (1977); Garrett, "*The Social Responsibility of Lawyers in their Professional Capacity*," 30 *U. Miami L. Rev.* 879, 882 (1976).

[3]*See generally* ABA Code of Professional Responsibility, DR 7-102, -103, -106, -108 to -110 (1977).

[4]*See* ABA Code of Professional Responsibility, DR 4-101 (confidentiality), 5-101 to -107 (avoidance of conflicts of interest) (1977).

[5]For purposes of this analysis, the term "opposing party" includes the party's lawyer. A lawyer's duty of trustworthiness as regards an opposing party should not vary according to whether that party has representation. Indeed, the fact that opposing parties have representation generally makes it easier for vouching lawyers to discharge their own professional obligations. It simplifies communication, for lawyers can communicate in mutually understood jargon. Also, lawyers can generally assume that an opposing party is adequately represented and that an adequately represented party has the narrowest lattitude for subsequently asserting that the transaction was infected by mistake, fraud, or other infirmity. The fact that an opposing party is represented by a lawyer, however, generally changes the potential for effective sanctions against violation of the duty of trustworthiness.

[6]See White, "*Machiavelli and the Bar: Ethical Limitations on Lying in Negotiation*," 1980 *Am. B. Foundation Research J.* 926, 927.

the client is not intransigent. Indeed, the lawyer may so describe the client's position when that position has been taken on the lawyer's advice. A statement that a client will not offer or accept specified terms thus means only that the client will not presently accept such terms and instead wants to extend the risk and cost of nonresolution in the hope of reducing the price he must pay for resolution. Negotiations can reach a point of no return, however, when a party's anticipated gain in a negotiated resolution is less than the anticipated cost of the resolution. When the opposing party's situation begins to approach that point, it is time for the negotiator to shift from chaffering to bargaining in earnest. A lawyer's professional skill should include the ability to project where the points of no return are, both for his client and for the opposing party. The lawyer must also have the ability to signal when his statements are to be taken as representations, that is, when he is vouching for an assertion. Thus, trustworthiness is not simply the moral virtue of veracity but is an amalgam of moral virtue, market sense, and physiological and political discernment. It is the ability to understand what truth is, to understand when the truth is called for, and to instill in others confidence that one has such understanding.

II. THE USES OF TRUSTWORTHINESS

If a lawyer is trustworthy, then a statement made as a representation by the lawyer may be taken by an opposing party as a firm factual component of a transaction. This enables the opposing party to appreciate the situation and recognize what alternative resolutions are practicable. That, in turn, facilitates assessment of the opposing party's interests by the vouching lawyer's client, thereby further clarifying the available alternatives. In the economist's view, the lawyer's voucher, if accepted as such, reduces transaction costs.[7]

This economizing effect of trustworthiness can be more fully appreciated upon consideration of the alternative means for verifying the factual components of a transaction. Two alternatives are available to an opposing party. The party can independently investigate the factual problem in question or employ someone else to investigate the situation. For example, a purchaser of real property can take the word of a seller's lawyer that there are no liens on the property or can obtain an independent title search. A party interested in learning the testimony of a key adverse witness can take the word of the opposing lawyer or can take the witness' deposition. Clearly, independent investigations will in many situations be preferred to reliance on the opposing lawyer. Investigations may be made when there is inadequate confidence in the particular lawyer's trustworthiness or, as in the case of independent title searches, in accordance with a convention calling for an independent investigation so that a particular lawyer's trustworthiness will not have to be put to the test.

Nevertheless, independent investigations are costly. The most defi-

---

[7]*See, e.g.,* Williamson, "*Transaction-Cost Economics: The Governance of Contractual Relations,*" 22 *J.L. & Econ.* 233 (1979).

nitive—and often costliest—form of independent investigation is a trial. By comparison, the cost of a reliable voucher may be slight.

The benfits of trustworthiness may be put in loftier terms by noting that the quality bestows honor upon lawyers in whom it is embodied. Yet thrustworthiness is not only socially esteemed but also socially useful. It is both esteemed and useful in all social transactions—between politicians, business people, bureaucrats, acquaintances, and spouses. It is generally accepted as a prime aspect of social maturity.

Trustworthiness is especially useful for lawyers because of the kinds of transactions into which lawyers are drawn and because of lawyers' peculiar access to the facts. Lawyers are drawn into situations that have a high element of uncertainty about what will happen or what has happened— contracts with serious risk of uncertainties in the future and disputes based on ambiguous evidence of what has occurred in the past. Lawyers are rarely involved in spot market transactions or circumstances in which twenty bishops will testify to an event. By contrast, they are commonly retained in transactions entailing uncertainties over which the parties may choose to litigate. Holding the stakes constant, the relative value of vouching as a means of resolving uncertainties becomes proportionately higher as uncertainty increases. Lawyers' usefulness in vouching to matters that would otherwise remain uncertain is thus greatest in transactions whose uncertainties and stakes make the lawyer useful in the first place.[8]

Lawyers are in a unique position, resulting from their relationships with their clients, to make truthful recommendations and resolve uncertainties. As spokesmen for their clients' interests, lawyers have peculiar access, arising from the lawyer–client relationship, to the facts that surround a given transaction.[9] First, the client is supposed to give the lawyer the whole truth, untempered by pride or pretense. This provides the lawyer with more information than it is ordinarily possible to get under other circumstances—most if not all of the truth as perceived by the client. Second, lawyers have access to documentary and background information and normally to all other sources of information available to their clients. Finally, inquiry is greatly aided by the guarantee of confidentiality.[10] These elements combine to give lawyers a more complete and accurate picture of the facts than that usually possessed by any other person involved in a given transaction.

This store of information is a highly useful resource. Strong justification has been advanced above for making it fully available to opposing parties. A question nevertheless remains whether the rules of professional conduct should *require* that this information be made fully available to opposing parties.

---

[8]Consider the role of lawyers in negotiating the settlement that led to the release of the Americans held hostage by Iran. *See N. Y. Times* Jan. 9, 1981 § A, at 8, col. 1.

[9]The point about a lawyer's peculiar access to the facts was made to me by my esteemed colleague, Professor Arthur Leff.

[10]*See Upjohn v. United States*, 101 S. Ct. 677, 682 (1981); ABA *Code of Professional Responsibility*, EC 4-1 (1977).

III. THE DISCLOSURE PROBLEM

The primary reason why all information available to lawyers should not be disclosed to opposing parties is that the prospect of disclosure would impair the lawyer's investigation in the first instance. This concern is the basis of rules that protect lawyers against disclosure of information acquired in representing clients. The attorney–client privilege provides that lawyers may not be compelled to divulge confidential information supplied by their clients.[11] The work-product rule sharply limits the extent to which an opposing party may compel production of other information acquired by the lawyer in preparation for litigation.[12] Finally, lawyers generally may not disclose on their own initiative information relating to the representation of a client except for the purpose of furthering the client's interests.[13]

The basic rules protecting the confidentiality of information gathered by lawyers while representing clients are taken as working premises for the present discussion. Within the framework of these rules, however, it is possible to argue for the proposition that when a lawyer undertakes to act for a client outside of court, a concurrent duty exists to make full disclosure of relevant facts known.[14] In light of the lawyer's duty of candor inside a courtroom, a question arises whether lawyers should also be required to be fully candid when speaking for a client outside of court. Such a requirement would seem to be a true measure of trustworthiness.

Problems of lawyer trustworthiness can arise in two different contexts. The first, out-of-court transactions to resolve disputes over legal rights, can result in a trial if settlement negotiations fail. The second, out-of-court transactions that comtemplate some type of contract, generally offers no further alternative if negotiations fail.

Transactions that can go to trial upon the failure of negotiations will be examined first. Debate persists over whether greater candor should be required in trials.[15] With regard to disclosure in the forensic setting, the modern rules of discovery[16] expose a considerable portion of lawyers' evidence-gathering to the opposing party. Furthermore, the rule governing the courtroom requires that any representation of fact, as distinct from a statement about what someone else asserts as fact, that is made to the court must be truthful according to the lawyer's knowledge.[17] It has been urged that forensic candor go further. Marvin Frankel argued while on the bench

[11] 101 S. Ct. at 682.

[12] *Hickman v. Taylor*, 329 U. S. 495, 511 (1947). *Accord*, 101 S. Ct. at 686-88.

[13] ABA Code of Professional Responsibility, DR 4-101 (1977).

[14] *See* Rubin, *supra* note 1, at 591.

[15] For a discussion of the benefits and detriments of increased candor before a tribunal, see Frankel, "*The Search for Truth: An Umpireal View*," 123 *U. Pa. L. Rev.* 1031 (1975); Freedman, "*Judge Frankel's Search for Truth*," 123 *U. Pa. L. Rev.* 1060 (1975); Uviller, "*The Advocate, the Truth, and Judicial Hackles: A Reaction to Judge Frankel's Ideas*," 123 *U. Pa. L. Rev.* 1067 (1975).

[16] *See* Fed. R. Civ. P. 26-37.

[17] ABA Code of Professional Responsibility, DR 7-102(A)(5) (1977).

that advocates should be required to disclose everything they know, perhaps excepting communications from clients.[18] That proposal has failed to attract support. Dispute also continues concerning whether lawyers must reveal the fact that their clients' testimony is perjurious when the lawyer knows that is the fact. It is my view that advocates should, to the following limited extent, vouch for their clients' testimony: they should be obliged to vouch that they have not violated their own duty to avoid use of fabricated evidence, even if the evidence is a client's testimony. Conversely, the position is defensible that lawyers should not be required to disclose their clients' perjury, especially in the case of defendants in criminal proceedings.[19]

Forensic disclosure, however, is peripheral to the exploration of truthfulness between opposing parties in negotiation. Trial supplies the factual premises for resolution of a transaction and imposes a resolution based on those premises. Trial is a costly and stressful alternative that can sometimes be avoided by negotiations.[20] The event of a trial shows that the less costly alternative has failed in a particular case.

Trial can thus be viewed as the failure of the parties to stipulate the facts; that is, counsel have been unable to establish the facts by reciprocal representation and must establish them through trial. The causes of this failure have been alluded to: the evidence is not strong enough to enable counsel to induce the client to authorize concessions, counsel lack the competence to recognize that the evidence justifies certain concessions, or one counsel is simply willing to inflict the cost of a trial on the other side, regardless of the evidence. If any one of these conditions exists, a trial results. But if these conditions exist, it seems futile to try to remedy the situation by demanding greater candor at trial. If concessions have not been forthcoming in the relative privacy and repose of pretrial negotiations, what inducements could make them more forthcoming in the more antagonistic circumstances of a trial?

This analysis that shortfall in voluntary disclosure at trial is simply a remanifestation of shortfall in voluntary disclosure before trial. Therefore, consideration of the problem of candor at trial leads to consideration of the problem of trustworthiness in negotiations.

Although negotiations may be categorized as aimed at either settling legal disputes or trying to consummate deals, these two categories of negotiations would collapse into a single type were it not for the availability of a court to which parties could resort upon failure of negotiations concerning a legal dispute. Consider, for example, negotiations in the international situation[21] or negotiation of claims based on moral rights as distinct from those based on legally recognized rights.[22] No trial is available if the nego-

[18]*See* Frankel, *supra* note 15, at 1057-59.

[19]*See* Freedman, *supra* note 15, at 1063-66.

[20]*See* 1 M. Belli, *Modern Trials* § 109 (1954).

[21]See note 8 *supra*.

[22]Negotiations within the legislature may be regarded as negotiations over moral rights. Such negotiations are backed by the parliamentary sanction of resolution through majority vote.

tiations fail. This same situation exists when there is a collapse of negotiations aimed at a deal: the transaction aborts, leaving the parties where they stand. In any event, a trial is an event contingent upon failure of negotiations. Because trial is costly, there is some value in avoiding it. Therefore, even in dispute-settlement negotiations a stage exists at which mutual incentives to avoid trial arise. At that stage, negotiations aimed at settlement are like negotiations aimed at a deal: there is a net value to all parties in a consensual resolution if the facts can be established on which to base that resolution.

The natural conclusion is that every inducement for increased trustworthiness should be fostered. Why then does the law of professional conduct fail to require disclosure on the part of lawyers participating in negotiations?

IV. REGULATION OF TRUSTWORTHINESS

The present regulation of lawyers' trustworthiness is modest. The Code of Professional Responsibility, in DR 7-102(A)(5), provides that "[i]n his representation of a client, a lawyer shall not . . . knowingly make a false statement of law or fact."[23] This provision might be characterized as a minimalist formulation of the law of disclosure. It prohibits only misrepresentation and requires no affirmative disclosure. It is limited to statements of "fact" as distinguished from evidence, indications, portents, opinions, possibilities, or even probabilities of which the lawyer may be aware. It is limited to matters that are false as distinguished from those of which the lawyer is skeptical or even suspicious.

* * *

[The rules on trustworthiness of the American Bar Association Commission of Evaluation of Professional Standards, familiarly know as the Kutak Commission,] do little to alter the status quo as set forth in the Code of Professional Responsibility. Yet the Commission considered and ultimately rejected a more sweeping proposal. Its Discussion Draft of January 30, 1980, included the following formulation:

> 4.2 *Fairness to Other Participants*
> (a) In conducting negotiations a lawyer shall be fair in dealing with other participants.
> (b) A lawyer shall not make a knowing misrepresentation of fact or law, or fail to disclose a material fact known to the lawyer, even if adverse, when disclosure is:
> (1) Required by law or the Rules of Professional Conduct; or
> (2) Necessary to correct a manifest misapprehension of fact or law resulting from a previous representation made by the lawyer or known by the lawyer to have been made by the client. . .[34]

[23]ABA Code of Professional Responsibility, DR 7-102(A)(5) (1977).

[34]ABA Comm'n on Evaluation of Professional Standards, Model Rules of Professional Conduct 88 (Discussion Draft, Jan. 30 1980).

* * *

The idea underlying the Kutak Commission's original proposal was not very complicated: the lawyer, as the instrument of a transaction should be the guardian of its intergrity.[37] The proposal did not purport to hold lawyers strictly liable for the integrity of transactions or even burden them with a duty of reasonable care. Their only duty was to disclose facts of which an opposing party was obviously ignorant and which might affect the integrity of the transaction.[38]

Much more fundamental objections were leveled at the proposal, particularly at the requirement that lawyers be "fair." Many members of the Commission and certainly the Reporter were surprised at the vehemence of the objections. "Vehemence" is the correct word, since much more heat than light was forthcoming in the reaction to the proposal. The Commission's surprise was compounded because the proposal seemed appropriate to the lawyer's role and appeared to reflect one interpretation of the lawyer's duty as established in the decisional law.[39]

Although the explanation of the bar's aversion to the January 1980 proposal is complex, some concerns can be identified. First, many members of the bar do not realize or are unwilling to accept the fact that the law at large applies to lawyers.[40] Perhaps these members of the bar believe an immunity attaches to lawyers against the civil liabilities imposed by the laws on other intermediaries such as real estate brokers or securities underwriters. More subtly, perhaps lawyers recognize that the law at large applies to them but do not wish to be accountable for that obligation in the context of professional discipline.

Still subtler concerns were involved. The fundamental difficulty appears to stem from the lack of a firm professional consensus regarding the standard of openness that should govern lawyers' dealing with others and the lack of settled and homogeneous standards of technique in the practice of law.[41] This lack of consensus indicates that lawyers, at least nationally, do not share a common conception of fairness in the process of negotiation. The lack of this consensus means that lawyers lack the language to express norms of fairness in negotiation and the institutional means to give effect to these norms.

The underlying disagreement about standards of fairness is not difficult to understand. Lawyers' standards of fairness are necessarily derived from those of society as a whole,[42] and subcultural variations are enormous. At one extreme lies the "rural God-fearing standard," so exacting and tedious that it often excludes the use of lawyers. At the other extreme

[37]*See* Rubin, *supra* note 1, at 591.

[38]In this regard, use of the term "material facts" in the January 1980 proposal would have been more precise.

[39]*See* Kutak, *"Evaluating the Proposed Model Rules of Professional Conduct,"* 1980 Am. B. *Foundation Research J.* 1016, 1021 n.22.

[40]*See* Hazard *supra* note 28.

[41]*See* White, *supra* note 6, at 935-37.

[42] *See id.* at 927.

stands "New York hardball," now played in most larger cities using the wall-to-wall indenture for a playing surface. Between these extremes are regional and local standards[43] and further variations that depend on the business involved, the identity of the participants, and other circumstances. Against this kaleidoscopic background, it is difficult to specify a single standard that governs the parties and thus a correlative standard that should govern their legal representatives.

The second area of disagreement concerns professional technique. Lawyers differ widely in the technical sophistication they expect of themselves and of others with whom they deal.[44] As a result, their expectations regarding their own or their opponents' knowledge in the context of a given transaction may vary widely. Among practitioners having a very high level of technique, it is expected that a lawyer has carefully investigated and compiled relevant information, is familiar with recent developments in applicable law, recognizes all tax implications of a transaction, and anticipates secondary transactions likely to be involved in the transaction at hand. At another level of technique, lawyers may use a standard form for a transaction and hope of a satisfactory result.[45]

Professional transactions within any given level of technique proceed according to implicitly understood conventions that allay all but ordinary anxiety on the part of the lawyers. Professional transactions that combine diverse levels of technique pose much greater difficulties. Lawyers accustomed to less sophisticated techniques are understandably fearful that they will be outmatched or even hoodwinked, with the possibility of loss to their clients and humiliation or even worse for themselves.

Lawyers accustomed to more sophisticated techniques have a correlative but perhaps less apparent dilemma. First, signs of bumbling on the other side cannot necessarily be taken at face value; there is such a thing as country-slickering and it occurs even in the city. Second, sophisticated lawyers are at risk precisely because of their technical sophistication. High-level technicians recognize aspects of transactions that lawyers of lesser sophistication may overlook. But what is to be done with that knowledge? If it is withheld, the transaction becomes vunerable to rescission because of the lawyer's nondisclosure. The lawyer's professional competence, if not fully deployed for the benefit of the opposing party, thus becomes a potential infirmity for the transaction.[46] Conversely, if the lawyer's competence is deployed for the benefit of the opposing party, where does the deployment properly stop, short of a takeover of the transaction and assumption of responsibility for the interests of both parties?[47]

[43]These were brought home to me dramatically when I entered the practice of law in Oregon after attending law school in New York City.

[44]*See generally* Laumann and Heinz, "*Specialization and Prestige in the Legal Profession: The Structure of Deference,*" 1977 *Am. B. Foundation Research J.* 155.

[45]*See e.g., Lucas v. Hamm,* 56 Cal. 2d 583, 364 P.2d 685, 15 Cal. Rptr. 821 (1961).

[46]This consideration became pivotal in the Kutak Commission's decision to withdraw proposed Rule 4.1(a) of the Discussion Draft, Jan 30, 1980.

[47]*Cf.* 329 U. S. at 516 (Jackson, J., concurring) ("Discovery was hardly intended to enable a learned profession to perform its functions either without wits or on wits borrowed from the adversary.").

In the ebb and flow of practice, lawyers can and do adjust to these exigencies. The high level technicians deal with each other with circumspection but confidence. Lawyers in other strata of the professional community have their own conventions. When levels are crossed, the less sophisticated lawyer must decide whether to trust the opponent or to associate someone else, research into the night, or perhaps even abort the transaction. The more sophisticated lawyer must decide whether to risk later recriminations about the transaction if the bargain is too hard, whether to make particular disclosures to protect the deal but at the risk also of killing the deal, or whether to handle the transaction for both sides.

This range of possibilities is difficult to govern by regulation. A rule based on the premise that the legal profession is substantially homogeneous in technical sophistication would put the technically sophisticated lawyer in a hopeless dilemma when dealing with an unsophisticated opposing counsel. Such a lawyer could straightforwardly be a partisan of his own client unless it became evident that the other side was inadequately represented. But in that case, the superior technician would have to assist the other side to guard against the risk of a subsequent charge of nondisclosure or fraud. Yet until a transaction is well underway, a lawyer cannot know which course of action is required. At the same time, the lawyer who is unsophisticated or is simply acting according to his idea of the applicable conventions of openness would be in jeopardy of giving away his client's position. Thus, in a situation where the opposing lawyers differ substantially in technical sophistication, a rule requiring reciprocal disclosure could not yield genuine reciprocity.

On the other hand, it would be practically impossible to formulate a general rule that accounts for variations in technical sophistication. Consider the difficulties with the concept of specialization and with the definition of specialization once the concept was accepted,[48] or with the problem of "incompetence" among the trial bar.[49] Could we imagine rules of disclosure that were based on a distinction between Type A Lawyers and Type B Lawyers? Anyone who is sanguine about overcoming these difficulties should try drafting the criteria by which to differentiate the technically sophisticated practitioner from the bar at large.

In light of these constraints, legal regulation of trustworthiness cannot go much further than to proscribe fraud. That is disquieting but not necessarily occasion for despair. It simply indicates limitations on improving the bar by legal regulation.[50]

---

[48]*See e.g.*, Fromson, *"The Challenge of Specialization: Professionalism at the Crossroads,"* 48 *N.Y.S.B.J.* 540, 542 (1976).

[49]*See e.g.*, Smith, *"Peer Review: Its Time Has Come,"* 66 *A.B.A.J.* 451 (1980).

[50]*Compare* Schwartz, *"The Death and Regeneration of Ethics,"* 1980 *Am. B. Foundation Research J.* 953, 960.

Actions Against Prosecutors Who Suppress or Falsify Evidence

EDWIN H. AULER

Canon Five of the American Bar Association's Canons of Ethics states:

> The primary duty of a lawyer engaged in public prosecution is not to convict, but to see that justice is done. The supression of facts or the secreting of witnesses capable of establishing the innocence of the accused is highly reprehensible.[1]

Unfortunately, a few prosecutors have chosen to disregard their professional responsibilities not only by suppressing evidence beneficial to the accused, but also by falsifying evidence for the benefit of the prosecution. Obviously these improper prosecutorial acts damage not only specific defendants but also the public image of justice generally.

An example of extremely reprehensible conduct by a prosecutor is illustrated in *Miller v. Pate*.[2] Defendant proved in a habeas corpus proceeding that a pair of men's underwear which the prosecution had used to convict him of rape were not stained with blood as alleged by the prosecution, but were actually colored with red paint. Defendant also established that the prosecutor, knowing of the false coloration, proceeded to use the evidence at trial. Although the United States Supreme Court held the conviction invalid under the due process clause,[3] no subsequent action was taken against the prosecutor for his misconduct.[4]

47 *Texas Law Review* 642-48 (1969). Reprinted by permission.

[1] ABA Canons of Professional Ethics No. 5

[2] 386 U.S. I (1967).

[3] In similar instances the Supreme Court has reversed convictions on due process grounds because of falsified or suppressed evidence. *See, e.g., Napue v. Illinois*, 360 U.S. 264 (1959) (prosecutor failed to correct the testimony of a witness which he knew was false); *Alcorta v. Texas*, 355 U.S. 28 (1957) (prosecutor told witness not to disclose certain material facts unless specifically asked); *Mooney v. Holohan*, 294 U.S. 103 (1935) (prosecutor knowingly used perjured testimony to obtain a conviction). *See also Berger v. United States*, 295 U.S. 78 (1935).

> [Although the prosecutor] may strike hard blows, he is not at liberty to strike foul ones. It is as much his duty to refrain from improper methods calculated to produce a wrongful conviction as it is to use every legitimate means to bring about a just one.

Id. at 88.

[4] There is conflict between the facts stated in the Supreme Court opinion and the facts disclosed by the Grievance Committee of the Illinois Bar Association two years subsequent to the litigation. According to the report of the Grievance Committee, both blood and paint caused the stain on the underwear, and the prosecutor merely failed to disclose that some of the stains were paint. *See* Illinois State Bar Ass'n Grievance Comm. Rep., May 14, 1968 (unpublished opinion). *See generally* Erlich, "*The Lloyd Eldon Miller, Jr. Case and the U.S. Supreme Court*," 56 *Ill. B.J.* 809 (1968).

A similar case exemplifying a prosecutor's suppression of evidence is *Turner v. Ward*.[5] Defendant was under indictment for rape. Prior to trial, an examining physician discovered that defendant had not raped the victim, but had committed an act of sodomy. Nevertheless, the prosecutor instructed the physician to reveal nothing at the trial unless specifically questioned and encouraged him to testify that the victim had been raped. Defendant was convicted, but in a subsequent habeas corpus proceeding the court of appeals reversed on the ground that due process will not allow the state to suppress material evidence. Again no action was taken against the prosecutor.

Although instances of suppression or falsification of evidence by prosecutors are probably isolated, civil, disciplinary, or criminal actions are needed to deter similar future actions by prosecutors and, if possible, to compensate injured defendants.[6] The purpose of this Comment is to analyze possible remedial actions against prosecutors who suppress or falsify evidence and to examine the relative desirability of available actions.

I. CIVIL ACTIONS

Unfortunately, few common-law tort actions can be used against prosecutors who suppress or falsify evidence. Since tortious actions during trial would be the crux of any civil action for suppression or falsification, tort theories such as malicious prosecution, abuse of process, and false imprisonment that involve pretrial misconduct are not available.[7] The tort action for infliction of distress, however, could conceivably give a remedy against prosecutors who suppress or falsify evidence. Although this action would be difficult to maintain unless a defendant's mental injury is severe,[8] a prosecutor who suppresses or falsifies evidence could be subjected to liability since this conduct might be characterized as "extreme and outrageous" and "calculated to bring about severe emotional stress."[9] Recovery against a prosecutor under this theory, however, would not be possible in several states unless the emotional stress is accompanied by physical injury.[10]

Another possible civil remedy against prosecutors who suppress or

---

[5]321 F.2d 918 (10th Cir. 1963).

[6]A prosecutor who suppresses or falsifies evidence is likely to cause a defendant mental anguish, detention, and financial loss. In the *Miller* litigation, for example, defendant spent ten years attempting to establish his innocence. *See Miller v. Pate*, 386 U.S. 1-3 (1967).

[7]*See generally* 32 *Am. Jur.* 2d *False Imprisonment* §§ 2-4 (1967); 34 *Am. Jur. Malicious Prosecution* §§ 1-3 (1948).

[8]*See generally* W. Prosser, *Torts* § 11, at 43-45 (3d ed. 1964).

[9]These are the elements of a defendant's conduct which need to be proved to maintain an action for infliction of distress. *Id.* at 46-53.

[10]*E.g., Carrigan v. Henderson*, 192 Okla. 254, 135 P.2d 330 (1943); *Duty v. General Fin. Co.*, 154 Tex. 16, 273 S.W.2d 64 (1954); *see* Comment, *"Recovery for Creditor Harassment,"* 46 *Texas L. Rev.* 950-52 (1968).

falsify evidence could be granted by the Civil Rights Act of 1871.[11] This Act in effect allows every person a cause of action against any official who infringes his constitutional rights.[12] Consequently, since suppression or falsification of evidence denies a defendant his constitutional right to a fair trial,[13] prosecutors who indulge in this type of misconduct would seem to be subject to liability under this Act.

Although in theory the tort for infliction of distress and the Civil Rights Act of 1871 would seem available against prosecutors who suppress or falsify evidence, recovery would probably be denied because courts have extended the immunity enjoyed by members of the judiciary for jurisdictional acts[14] to public prosecutors as "quasi-judicial officers."[15] Courts have reasoned that imposition of liability against prosecutors would not only mar the concept of an independent judicial system,[16] but would also deter prosecutors from actively pursuing the administration of justice because of fear of reprisal for errors in judgment.[17] Consequently, a prosecutor is immune from liability for acts done within the scope of his jurisdiction or supervision,[18] regardless of whether the acts are done for a malicious pur-

[11]42 U.S.C. § 1983 (1964).

[12]The Act provides:
Every person who, under color of any statute, ordinance, regulation, custom, or usage, of any State . . . subjects . . . any citizen . . . or other person . . . to the deprivation of any rights . . . secured by the Constitution . . . shall be liable to the party injured . . . .

[13]*See* cases cited note 3 *supra.*

[14]If a judge's act is one of a judicial nature and within his jurisdiction, he is clearly immune from civil liability. *Bradley v. Fisher,* 80 U.S. (13 Wall) 335, 351 (1872). *See also Johnson v. MacCoy,* 278 F.2d 37 (9th Cir. 1960); 73 *U. Pa. L. Rev.* 300 (1925).

[15]*See Bauers v. Heisel,* 361 F.2d 581, 594 (3rd Cir.), *cert. denied,* 386 U. S. 1021 (1966); *Norton v. McShane,* 332 F.2d 855 (5th Cir. 1964); *cert. denied,* 380 U.S. 981 (1965); *Stift v. Lynch,* 267 F.2d 237 (7th Cir. 1959); *Kenney v. Fox,* 232 F.2d 288, 290 (6th Cir.), *cert. denied,* 352 U.S. 855, 856 (1956): *Pritt v. Johnson,* 264 F. Supp. 167 (M.D. Pa. 1967).

[16]*See Tanale v. Sheehy,* 385 F.2d 866, 868 (2d Cir. 1967); cases cited note 15 *supra. See also* 3 W. Blackstone, *Commentaries* 126 (Wendell ed. 1852). "It would be a very great discouragement to the public justice of the kingdom if prosecutors who had a tolerable ground for suspicion were liable to be sued at law whenever their indictment miscarried." *Id.*

[17]*See Gregoire v. Biddle.* 177 F.2d 579, 581 (2d Cir. 1949); *Cooper v. O'Conner,* 99 F.2d 135 (D.C. Cir. 1938); *Smith v. Parma.* 101 Kan. 115, 165 P. 663 (1917); 46 *Colum. L. Rev.* 614 (1946); 66 *Harv. L. Rev.* 1285, 1295 n.54 (1953); 72 *U. Pa. L. Rev.* 300 (1925); cf. *Bradley v. Fisher,* 80 U.S. (13 Wall.) 335 (1872).

[18]*Robichaud v. Ronan,* 351 F.2d 533 (9th Cir. 1965); *Stift v. Lynch,* 267 F.2d 237 (7th Cir. 1959); *Kenney v. Fox,* 232 F.2d 288, 290 (6th Cir.), *cert. denied,* 352 U.S. 855, 856 (1956); *Lewis v. Brautigam,* 227 F.2d 124, 129 (5th Cir. 1955); *Yaselli v. Goff,* 12 F.2d 396 (2d. Cir. 1926), *cert. denied,* 275 U.S. 503 (1927). Since prosecutorial liability normally depends upon whether the alleged acts fall under the prosecutor's jurisdiction, supervision, or scope of office, it has been contended that a means of avoiding immunity for a prosecutor's malicious acts would be to hold them outside the scope of his office. *See Norton v. McShane,* 332 F.2d 855, 858 (5th Cir. 1964), *cert. denied,* 380 U.S. 981 (1965). Application of this reasoning, however, might invite vexatious litigation and confusion. *Id.* Although it may be desirable to limit a prosecutor's immunity to good-faith acts, it should not be done at the expense of confusing a relatively simple test for determining a prosecutor's scope of authority. Moreover, courts that grant immunity to prosecutors for acts done in "excess" of their jurisdiction, but deny immunity for acts "outside" their jurisdiction, merely add confusion to the scope-of-authority test. *See* 42 *N.Y.U.L. Rev.* 160, 162 (1967).

pose.[19] Since production of evidence at trial is a matter within a prosecutor's supervision, it is unlikely that a defendant injured by a prosecutor's suppression or falsification of evidence could recover damages.

Under a more reasonable application of the immunity doctrine prosecutors could be subjected to liability. Immunity is granted to a prosecutor to protect him from honest mistakes made pursuant to the duties of his office.[20] Since suppression or falsification of evidence necessarily involves an evil motive on the part of the prosecutor,[21] recovery for a prosecutor's suppression or falsification of evidence could be granted under either the tort of infliction of distress or the Civil Rights Act of 1871 without subverting the purpose of the doctrine. Moreover, by allowing liability for a prosecutor's bad faith or malicious acts, a new tort action could be created specifically allowing damages to a person injured by a prosecutor's suppression or falsification of evidence.

Civil recovery is the most desirable remedy against prosecutors who suppress or falsify evidence since the injured defendants may obtain compensation for their injuries. Although many authorities have believed that the imposition of civil liability against a prosecutor could result in a large amount of vexatious litigation,[22] this danger could be avoided by limiting civil remedies to injured defendants whose convictions were reversed on appeal.[23] Furthermore, civil liability could deter future similar misconduct without the detrimental publicity of a criminal prosecution. Since any civil recovery against prosecutors seems remote, however, another remedy is needed to deter prosecutors who suppress or falsify evidence.

II. DISCIPLINARY PROCEEDINGS AND REMOVAL

Disciplinary proceedings are another type of remedy that could be used against prosecutors who suppress or falsify evidence.[24] Unlike civil actions,

[19]*See Norton v. McShane*, 332 F.2d 855 (5th Cir. 1964), *cert. denied*, 380 U.S. 981 (1965); *Sires v. Cole*, 320 F.2d 877 (9th Cir. 1963); *Jennings v. Nester*, 217 F.2d 153 (7th Cir. 1954); *Yaselli v. Goff*, 12 F.2d 396 (2d Cir. 1926), *cert. denied*, 275 U.S. 503 (1927); *Lusk v. Hanrahan*, 244 F. Supp. 539, 540 (E.D. Ill. 1965); *Bujaki v. Egan*, 237 F. Supp. 822 (D. Alas. 1965); *Zellner v. Wallace*, 233 F. Supp. 874 (M.D. Ala. 1964): *Prentice v. Berksten*, 50 Cal. App. 2d 344, 123 P.2d 96 (1942); *Schneider v. Sheppard*, 192 Mich. 82, 158 N.W. 182 (1916); *Creelman v. Svenning*, 67 Wash. 2d 882, 410 P.2d 606 (1966); 32 *N.C.L. Rev.* 360, 363 (1954).

[20]*See* authorities cited in notes 16-17 *supra.*

[21]*See* cases cited in note 3 *supra.*

[22]*See* authorities cited in notes 15 and 17 *supra.*

[23]For example, in *Jackson v. Wainwright*, 390 F.2d 288 (5th Cir. 1968), a conviction of rape was remanded for a new trial when it was discovered that the prosecutor had suppressed evidence beneficial to the accused. Assuming liability were available against prosecutors, defendant in *Jackson* should not be allowed to instigate civil proceedings unless he first obtained an acquittal in the new trial. A contrary result might allow vexatious litigation by guilty defendants between the time of remand and the time of the new trial.

[24]Grievance committees of state bar associations are the usual authorities for instituting disciplinary proceedings against an attorney. *See, e.g., In re Phillips*, 17 Cal. 2d 55, 109 P.2d 344 (1941); *Cleveland Bar Ass'n v. Fleck*, 172 Ohio St. 467, 178 N.E.2d 782 (1961). *See generally* Tex. Bar Ass'n, Rules and Canons of Ethics, art. XII, §§ 1-20 (1958).

prosecutors enjoy no immunity from disciplinary sanctions.[25] Consequently, since suppression or falsification of evidence is condemned by canons of ethics,[26] prosecutors who engage in this type of misconduct should be censured, suspended, or disbarred.[27]

In addition to disciplinary proceedings, most states have constitutional or statutory provisions allowing removal of a prosecutor from office.[28] Since grounds for removal are usually expressed as "cause,"[29] "malfeasance,"[30] or "official misconduct,"[31] it seems clear that a prosecutor who intentionally denies a defendant a fair trial by suppression or falsification of evidence could be subject to this procedure.

Although presently available, disciplinary and removal proceedings apparently fail to deter prosecutorial manipulations of evidence. Grievance committees and state officials are understandably hesitant to take action against other state officials which will reveal injustice in the judicial system. It would appear, however, that this reluctance to reprimand a prosecutor often is unjustified.[32] In the Miller case, assuming that the evidence was not falsified,[33] a full disclosure by the prosecuting attorney could have avoided a substantial amount of litigation and damage to the public image of justice without injuring the case against defendant. The Illinois Bar Association, however, failed even to censure the prosecutor. In similar instances the prosecutor's conduct was not even reviewed by the state bar association. Moreover, in no case has a prosecutor been removed from office for suppression or falsification of evidence.

Although discipline or removal of a prosecutor will not compensate a defendant injured by a prosecutor's misconduct, these remedies should deter future improper actions by prosecutors without causing injurious publicity. Since the procedures for discipline and removal of prosecutors are available, they should be used to avoid resort to less desirable remedies.

[25]*E.g., In re McCowan*, 175 Cal. 51, 170 P. 1100 (1917); *In re Truder*, 37 N.M. 69, 17 P.2d 951 (1932); Maginnis's Case, 269 Pa. 186, 112 A. 555 (1921). *Contra, In re Borie*, 166 La. 855, 118 So. 45 (1928).

[26]*E.g.*, ABA Canons of Professional Ethics No. 5; Tex. Bar Ass'n, Rules and Canons of Ethics, canon 5 (1968).

[27]Cf. *In re Taylor*, 300 Ky. 448, 189 S.W.2d 403 (1945); *In re O'Brien*, 95 Vt. 167, 113 A. 527 (1921).

[28]*E.*, Tex. Const. art. IV, § 24; Tex. Const. art. V. § 24; Cal. Gov't Code § 3073 (West 1966); Pa. Stat. Ann. tit. 16, § 450 (1956); Tex. Rev. Civ. Stat. Ann. art. 5970 (1962).

[29]Cause as a basis for removal of an official must relate to reasons of sound public policy. *Lancaster v. Hill*, 136 Ga. 405, 408, 71 S.E. 731, 732 (1911).

[30]Malfeasance as grounds for removal normally means evil conduct. *See State ex rel. Hardie v. Coleman*, 115 Fla. 119, 155 So. 129 (1934).

[31]Official misconduct normally means failure to perform a duty required by law. Tex. Rev. Civ. Stat. Ann. art. 5973 (1962).

[32]In a recent Texas case the court of criminal appeals even refused to acknowledge that a prosecutor's suppression of material evidence was a denial of due process. *See Vessels v. State*, 432 S.W.2d 108 (Tex. Crim. App. 1968).

[33] *See* note 4 *supra.*

III. CRIMINAL SANCTIONS

If censure, disbarment, and removal proceedings are not effectively used against prosecutors who suppress or falsify evidence, a criminal sanction may become necessary. Unlike civil actions in which "quasi-judicial immunity" protects a prosecutor from liability, a prosecutor is subject to criminal sanction for acts committed within or without his jurisdiction.[34] Consequently, criminal liability for a prosecutor's denial to a defendant of a fair trial by suppression or falsification of evidence depends upon whether his misconduct comes within the purview of any criminal statute.

Some existing state criminal sanctions should be applicable to prosecutors who suppress or falsify evidence. A criminal contempt proceeding[35] could be initiated, but its application would necessarily be limited to prosecutorial acts discovered and known to be contemptuous at trial.[36] Although a prosecutor who falsifies evidence is probably not subject to conviction for perjury[37] unless he has taken the requisite oath,[38] he should be subject to conviction for subornation of perjury when he induces witnesses to testify falsely.[39] Also, prosecutors who suppress or falsify evidence to harass a defendant by trial might be convicted of barratry.[40] Moreover, some states allow criminal punishment against persons who offer evidence that they know is fraudulent or forged.[41] No case has been discovered, however, where a prosecutor was convicted for suppression or falsification of evidence under any of these sanctions. Moreover, these remedies would only apply to prosecutors who falsify evidence. Consequently, any state that allows a prosecutor to be convicted for crimes committed under the auspices of his office should draft a statute providing for punishment of a prosecutor who suppresses evidence material to establishing a defendant's innocence.

[34]*See Lusk v. Hanrahan*, 244 F. Supp. 539 (E.D. Ill. 1965); *State v. Winne*, 12 N.J. 152, 96 A.2d 63 (1953); *O'Regan v. Schermerhorn*, 25 N.J. Misc. I, 50 A.2d 10 (Sup. Ct. 1946); *State v. Langley*, 214 Ore. 445, 323 P.2d 301 (1958); *McGinley v. Scott*, 401 Pa. 310, 164 A.2d 424 (1960); *cf. Screws v. United States*, 325 U.S. 91 (1945); *United States v. Classic*, 313 U.S. 299 (1941); *United States v. Ramey*, 336 F.2d 512 (4th Cir. 1964); *Crews v. United States*, 160 F.2d 746 (5th Cir. 1947). *Contra, United States v. Chaplin*, 54 F. Supp. 926, 934 (S.D. Cal. 1944).

[35]Acts that obstruct or embarrass the administration of justice are punishable in criminal contempt proceedings. *See generally* 17 Am. Jur. 2d "Contempt" §§ 2-3 (1964).

[36]*Cf. Ex parte Hudgins*, 249 U.S. 378 (1919); *Nilva v. United States*, 227 F.2d 74 (8th Cir. 1955). It might be desirable, however, to subject a prosecutor who suppresses or falsifies evidence to contempt proceedings regardless of the time the contemptuous acts are discovered since a possible contempt proceeding might discourage prosecutorial misconduct at trial.

[37]Perjury is the willful giving of false testimony under oath. *See generally* 41 Am. Jur. "Perjury" § 2 (1942).

[38]*Id.* § 15, at 10.

[39]*See, e.g.*, Pa. Stat. Ann. tit. 18, § 4332 (1963); Tex. Penal Code Ann. art. 315 (1952).

[40]*See* Cal. Penal Code § 158 (West 1955); Pa. Stat. Ann. tit. 18, § 4306 (1939); Tex. Penal Code Ann. art. 430 (1952).

[41]*See* Ariz. Rev. Stat. Ann. 13-547 (1956); Cal. Penal Code §§ 132-34 (West 1955); Pa. Stat. Ann. tit. 18, § 4328 (1963).

The criminal section of the Civil Rights Act of 1871,[42] which subjects anyone acting "under the color of law" to fine or imprisonment for willfully depriving a person of a constitutionally protected right,[43] could be another criminal sanction against prosecutorial misconduct. A prosecutor who suppresses or falsifies evidence should be acting under "color of law" within the purview of the statute since his acts are made possible by his official position.[44] Although the statute requires that a specific intent to deprive a person of a constitutional right be proved,[45] it should be difficult to meet this requirement. It is clear that the suppression or falsification of evidence necessarily connotes an intent to deny a person the constitutional right to a fair and impartial trial.[46] Consequently, when it can be shown that a prosecutor had knowledge that evidence he introduced was false or that he failed to introduce or make available to the defense evidence he knew was material, that prosecutor should be subject to conviction under the Civil Rights Act of 1871.

Although criminal liability would no doubt deter prosecutors from suppressing or falsifying evidence, it has not been used in the past. It should be used in the future only upon the failure of other remedies since, even though the prosecutor is likely to merit the penalty imposed by statute in flagrant cases, the publicity could be as damaging to the public image of the judicial system as the prosecutor's suppression or falsification itself.

IV. CONCLUSION

Strong deterrent remedies are needed against prosecutors who suppress or falsify evidence. Civil liability against these prosecutors would not only be the most desirable remedy, but could also be granted without destroying the purpose of the immunity doctrine. It is doubtful, however, that courts will allow recovery. Although disciplinary and criminal sanctions will leave injured defendants uncompensated, they must necessarily be used to provide some remedy. Since disciplinary proceedings are more desirable than criminal actions, it is hoped that bar associations will respond to any prosecutorial misconduct with strong sanctions to avoid application of criminal liability to prosecutors.

---

[42]18 U.S.C. § 242 (1964).

[43]The Act provides:

Whoever . . . under color of any law . . . willfully subjects any inhabitant of any State . . . to the deprivation of any rights, privileges, or immunities secured or protected by the Constitution or laws of the United States . . . shall be fined not more than $1,000 or imprisoned not more than one year, or both.

[44]*See United States v. Classic*, 313 U.S. 299, 325 (1941). An officer is acting under the color of law when his acts are made possible by his official position. *Id.*

[45]*Screws v. United States*, 325 U.S. 91, 96 (1945).

[46]*See* cases cited in note 3 *supra*.

chapter five

THE ATTORNEY
AND THE CLIENT

INTRODUCTION

The last chapter examined the obligations of the attorney from the perspective of the attorney's role as a part of the adversarial system of justice. Thus that chapter was concerned with the availability of legal services, which determines the access people have to the system of justice, and hence the real worth of their legal rights. Yet at the heart of the adversarial system of justice lies the belief, whether warranted or otherwise, that the attorney best serves the ideals of justice and truth by serving his or her client. The question that the readings in this chapter should help the reader to address is what it means for the attorney to be a loyal agent to his or her client.

The chapter is divided into three sections. Section I deals with the different faces of loyalty as it applies to a variety of contexts of legal practice. Section II deals with the basis and extent of the attorney's obligation of confidentiality, and Section III deals with the attorney's obligation to handle the client's affairs with competence. Whereas in Chapter Four competence was treated in the context of the attorney's obligation as a part of the system of justice, the treatment of competence in this chapter will focus more on the attorney's liability to the client for failure to act with competence.

Loyalty

The attorney is supposed to be the loyal agent of his or her client, within the bounds set by the law. A number of questions arise in connection with this obligation of loyalty. In addition to the very general questions surrounding the nature of the relationship between the attorney and client and how that relationship may affect the attorney's obligation of loyalty, there are the additional questions involved in identifying the client. In the classic context of legal representation of an individual criminal defendant, the identity of the client is perfectly clear. However, in the multiplicity of contexts in which the contemporary practice of law occurs, there are a number of areas in which the identity of the client presents a significant problem. Among the most perplexing areas in this respect are family practice, corporate practice, and government practice.

This chapter's readings on attorney loyalty start with a case. In *People v. Heirens*, we see a situation in which a criminal defense attorney acted in a manner that surely questions his loyalty to his client. While Heirens's conviction was not overturned as a result of defense counsel's conduct, it is clear from Mr. Justice Klingbiel's opinion that Heirens's attorney did not regard his primary loyalty as due his client. Perhaps the most striking statement cited in the opinion is the claim of the State's Attorney that "The small likelihood of a successful murder prosecution of William Heirens early prompted the State's Attorney's office to seek out and obtain the co-operative help of defense counsel and, *through them* [Schrader's emphasis], that of their client. . . . Without the aid of the defense . . . to this day a great and sincere public doubt might remain as to the guilt of William Heirens. . . ." There is at least the strong suggestion in this statement that defense counsel acted with as much loyalty to what he regarded as the public interest as to his client.

The heart of this first group of readings is Charles Fried's well-known and much-discussed "The Lawyer as Friend: The Moral Foundations of the Lawyer–Client Relation." Fried starts out by examining two criticisms of the traditional view of the attorney's role within the adversary system. First, it is argued that it allows for the misallocation of valuable social resources in allocating the attorney's time and skill for socially unproductive purposes at the expense of more socially productive exercise of those same skills. Second, it is argued that the attorney does positive social harm to the individuals who are unjustly the victims of his or her work on behalf of unworthy clients.

Fried argues that the attorney–client relationship is at bottom basically like a friendship relationship. From a utilitarian point of view, one's relationship with a friend does not, presumably, justify acting differently toward the friend than one is entitled to act toward anyone else. Fried rejects a utilitarian approach to ethics. Adopting instead a deontological framework, Fried argues that the friendship relation justifies behavior on behalf of a friend that would not be justified if performed on behalf of strangers. Often, Fried argues, we are permitted, or even required, to act in defense of a friend in ways that would otherwise be regarded as immoral. Fried views the attorney as what he calls a "special-purpose friend" of his or her client. This friendship relation justifies the complete loyalty which the attorney is supposed to show toward the client.

Loyalty in Family Practice

A whole collection of loyalty-related problems arise in the practice of family law. In the ordinary, hotly contested divorce case with no children involved the situation is quite clear. Each of the two attorneys involved has a client to whom he or she is supposed to be loyal. Yet a great many divorce cases depart from this ideal pattern. There are times when a person may approach an attorney about divorce without yet having formed the resolve to seek a divorce. In some of those cases the marriage in question may be salvageable. The party approaching the attorney may even be interested in salvaging the marriage. Are there ways in which the attorney may, under such circumstances, act in a manner that will bring the marriage partners back together, or does any such attempt involve too serious a potential for conflict of interest or serving an adverse party? Similarly, there are many cases in which a couple may have agreed to get a divorce, have agreed on a mutually fair and agreeable property settlement, and merely need an attorney to handle the legal paper work. In such a case it is to the clear financial advantage of both parties to pay only one attorney. Yet here the attorney is dealing with parties with at least potentially conflicting interests. There is a clear problem of who exactly is the client and where the attorney's loyalty lies.

In *Klemm v. Superior Court of Fresno County* a couple wish to have joint representation in their uncontested divorce action. The couple has no community property, neither seeks any spousal support, and the woman seeks no child support. The County Division of Family Support, however, wants the husband to pay a modest amount of support to the county as reimbursement for A.F.D.C. payments. The county therefore urges separate counsel on the basis of a potential conflict of interest between the husband and wife. The court rules that there is no *actual* conflict of interest between husband and wife and that the real conflict is between the couple on one side and the county on the other. Since the county is not a party to the divorce litigation, there is no reason to forbid joint representation.

The readings on loyalty in family practice continue with Kimberly Taylor Harbinson's article, "Family Law—Attorney Mediation of Marital Disputes and Conflict of Interest Considerations." As the title suggests, Harbinson is concerned with the extent to which the traditional prohibitions against an attorney's representing clients with conflicting interests constrains the role that the attorney may play with respect to clients with marital disputes. She notes that there has been a growing trend, in light of the advent of "no-fault" divorce statutes in most states, toward the use of mediation services and other types of nonadversarial procedures for dealing with marital disputes. To the extent that an attorney becomes party to such processes, that attorney may well be loyally serving the interests of his or her clients yet may also be placing him or herself in a position that carries a serious and significant potential for violation of conflict of interest prohibitions. Harbinson examines the ways in which the organized bar and various state jurisdictions have been trying to shape the parameters of the divorce lawyer's role in order to acknowledge the benefits of nonadversarial approaches to family dispute resolution in certain circumstances while at the same time protecting both attorney and client from the dangers of conflict of interest. She concludes with a bit of practical advice to the attorney who is involved in a family conflict in which nonadversarial mediation may play a useful role, helping the attorney to find a path that will maximize the chance of amicable nonadversarial resolution while protecting the integrity of the attorney's position in the event of failure of that mediation.

Loyalty and the Corporate Lawyer

Among the most difficult problems of loyalty are those encountered by the corporate lawyer. For the corporate attorney the problem of identifying the client to whom loyalty is due can be a virtual nightmare. In principle, of course, the client of the corporate attorney is the corporation itself, the "corporate entity." While that surely sounds clear enough, the problem is in determining whose interests are the interests of the corporate entity. In part this is a question of who speaks for the corporate entity.

Generally, of course, the presumption is that the corporation speaks and expresses its interests through its normal executive channels. There are circumstances, however, in which this assumption clearly cannot be maintained. In many kinds of cases a central issue is whether those executives have indeed acted in the interest of the corporation. In such cases the very executives whose handling of corporate affairs is in question cannot be initially presumed to speak for corporate interests. A further complication is the fact that the corporate executives are the ones who hired and can fire the attorney representing the corporation, whether in-house or outside counsel.

The readings on corporate practice begin with the case of *Hull v. Celanese Corporation*, dealing with the situation of an inside attorney. Donata Delulio was a member of the legal staff of Celanese Corporation. She wished to join Joan Hull, another Celanese employee, as co-plaintiff in a sex-based discrimination suit against the corporation. Celanese was successful in this case in preventing Delulio from joining her case to Hull's and in having Hull's initial choice of counsel disqualified because of its access to confidential material which Delulio gained through her professional legal work on behalf of Celanese.

The material on corporate practice continues with a rather general article by Ronald Rotunda, "Law, Lawyers, and Managers." After noting that the obligation of the corporate attorney, according to the "Code of Professional Responsibility," is to the "corporate entity," Rotunda explores what that means in a number of different contexts. He starts by looking at the corporate attorney's duty in a derivative suit, that is, a suit in which a shareholder brings suit on behalf of the corporation, in a sense. The basic claim of a derivative suit is that the corporation has been harmed by the action of someone inside the corporate structure, someone so positioned

that the corporation will not, through its normal decision-making procedures, bring suit against that person. Rotunda notes that the courts have
not set a uniform standard for the role of corporate counsel in derivative
suits and that the situation is fraught with conflicts of interest and divided
loyalties. Similarly, Rotunda identifies the corporate takeover situation as
another one in which loyalty to the "corporate entity" is no help to the
corporate attorney in identifying his or her concrete obligations. In that
case as well, the interests of different groups of shareholders conflict, and
some of those interests clearly lie at odds with the interests of the current
management.

Rotunda notes a set of additional problems which threaten to compromise the professional independence of the corporate attorney. Service
of an outside corporate counsel on the corporation's board of directors
creates a definite confusion of the attorney's roles as counselor and counseled. The attorney is, in that instance, in part his or her own client. Finally,
Rotunda notes the disturbing tendency of many corporate attorneys to
carry the interests of their clients into their private advocacy of positions in
local and state bar associations and in the public forum more generally.
Such activities again constitute a compromise of professional independent
judgment. The attorney becomes, in this case, not simply the legal counselor and advocate of the corporation, but also its voice in community
controversy, more a corporate public relations person than a corporate
attorney.

Loyalty in Government Practice

Government practice is another area in which the identification of the
attorney's client poses a serious problem. The problem for the government
attorney is very much like that for the corporate attorney. The client of the
corporate attorney is supposed to be the corporation, but, in certain circumstances at least, there is a real question about who speaks for the corporate interests. Similarly, the client of the government attorney is supposed
to be the public, but again there sometimes arises a question about who
speaks for the interests of the public.

Talking about the government attorney is, if anything, even more
complicated than talking about the corporate attorney. The variety of different roles filled by government attorneys is far greater than the variety of
roles filled by corporate attorneys. Perhaps the most obvious role filled by
government attorneys is that of public prosecutor. County Attorneys and
States' Attorneys serve as prosecutors in the criminal cases that come
before the courts, yet beyond this the same County Attorney or Attorney
General whose office acts as a public prosecutor is also called upon to give
legal advice to a wide variety of county and state officials in the performance of their various responsibilities. Perhaps the largest number of
attorneys in public employ are those who work for various governmental
regulatory agencies. These lawyers, often young attorneys recently out of
law school, are usually highly specialized in very narrow fields such as
environmental law, securities law, and so forth. They are involved in the
usual variety of legal activities, investigation, negotiation, litigation, and the

like, but always in a very narrowly defined area of the law. These attorneys build up an impressive degree of specialization and technical knowledge during their tenure of government employment and are in high demand in the business world upon leaving their government work. This situation, as we might anticipate, generates a unique set of conflict of interest issues.

The readings on loyalty in government practice open with a case, *General Motors Corporation v. City of New York*, in which General Motors is seeking to have an attorney, George Reycraft, disqualified as plaintiff's attorney in a class action suit brought against General Motors by the City of New York for violation of antitrust laws. General Motors is seeking to have Reycraft disqualified because of his previous work for the Antitrust Division of the United States Department of Justice on matters substantially related to the issues of the present case. The court's decision in favor of General Motors in this action appears to hinge on two factors. In the first place, the fact that Reycraft is handling the case as a class action suit and on a contingent fee basis constitutes, in the eyes of the court, a "private employment" and not a public employment. Second, Reycraft's particular service in the Antitrust Division on a specific 1956 case was judged by the court to deal with the "same matter" as was in dispute in the current case. These two factors, taken together, led the court to disqualify Reycraft.

This kind of conflict of interest encountered by the former government attorney who leaves government employment for private practice is explored in some detail in Geoffrey Hazard's "The Revolving Door," a chapter from his book, *Ethics in the Practice of Law*. Hazard notes the serious difficulty in applying the principles that we saw at work in *General Motors Corporation v. City of New York*, as the court has to wrestle with the question of what constitutes the "same matter." Given the subtle shading of matter into matter, it would appear that the only easy means of eliminating the present immense potential for conflict of interest would be to make the move between government and private practice more difficult for the attorney. Hazard notes, however, that this "solution" would generate very serious problems of its own. If attorneys were, in effect, locked into either governmental or private practice it would presumably be far more difficult for the government to acquire the level of competence in its legal staff that it presently has; at least it would be difficult to do so without a tremendous increase in public expenditures. Hazard leaves the reader with a dilemma. The present "revolving door" between public and private practice may well be fraught with problems, but the alternatives may, like the alternatives to getting old, be even worse.

Section I concludes with Jack Weinstein's article, "Some Ethical and Political Problems of a Government Attorney." Weinstein moves us to look at a different level of government law practice, that of the County Attorney. He notes the balance that must be drawn between the County Attorney's role as attorney and as elected public official. The County Attorney is not only, and probably not primarily, a public prosecutor. He or she also serves in an important policy-making position in local government, a role that clearly leads to a greater need to be aware of the political dimensions of that office. Yet Weinstein notes that the political dimensions of the position cannot come to dominate totally the work of the County Attorney. For example, corruption cannot be tolerated or covered up even if the well-being of the County Attorney's party, perhaps even his or her own political career, requires doing so. Weinstein argues that, above all, the concern of the County Attorney should be with the administration of law and justice. He illustrates this concern with an examination of two cases of property condemnation. He argues that if the county condemns property and the property owner is willing to sell at an unconscionably low price, the County Attorney may, under certain circumstances have a duty to intervene on behalf of the property owners, to make them aware of the true value of their property. In sum, Weinstein notes that the client of the County Attorney is the people. This situation leaves the County Attorney with divided loyalties as the interests of various constituents diverge. Yet in the end, Weinstein seems to hold, the overriding determinant of the role of the County Attorney must be his or her loyalty to the fundamental long-range interest of the public, the administration of justice.

Confidentiality

While it should be quite apparent that the attorney's obligation of loyalty to the client generates a good many complex questions, there is perhaps no aspect of an attorney's loyalty that generates more ethical controversy than an attorney's obligation to protect the confidences of his or her client. Generally speaking, there is a difficult tension existing between the attorney's obligation to protect the confidences of the client and the attorney's obligation to be candid with the court.

Whiteside v. Scurr presents the central ethical problem of confidentiality in its most striking form. Whiteside killed a drug dealer. Initially he told his attorney that he thought the victim was going for a gun when he stabbed him but that he did not actually see a gun. Whiteside later became convinced that he would fare better in trial if he told the court that he actually saw a gun. When he told his attorney that he planned to present that claim to the court, the attorney threatened that, if Whiteside went through with his planned testimony, the attorney would seek to withdraw from representation and offer himself to the prosecutor's office as a witness against his client in perjury prosecution. While Whiteside's attorney did precisely what the Iowa Bar Association's ethical standards required of him, the United States Court of Appeals (reversed by the Supreme Court in *Nix v. Whiteside*, 80 L. Ed. 2d 123 [1986]) held that the attorney acted so as to create a conflict of interest between himself and Whiteside, thereby violating Whiteside's constitutional right to effective assistance of counsel.

The two articles that follow would support precisely opposing positions on the ethical issue involved in *Whiteside.* John T. Noonan would support the position of the Iowa Bar Association. He starts his article, "The Purposes of Advocacy and the Limits of Confidentiality," by saying that "[t]he privilege of confidentiality between lawyer and client is a significant barrier to the search for truth and the attainment of justice." Noonan's article is basically a response to an earlier article by Monroe Freedman, "Professional Responsibility of the Criminal Defense Lawyer: The Three

Hardest Questions." (64 *Michigan Law Review*, 1469, [1966].) Noonan argues that Freedman's treatment of the attorney's duty of confidentiality as nearly absolute depends on a view of the adversary system as something like a substitute for trial by combat, rather than a system designed to discover truth. Moreover, he maintains that any very strong duty of confidentiality renders the attorney little more than a "mouthpiece" for the client, totally subordinating the individuality, independence, and values of the attorney to those of the client. In particular, Noonan rejects the claim that attorney confidentiality is essential to the operation of the adversary system because it is needed in order to induce the client to reveal to the attorney all the information necessary for the preparation of a case. Noonan's basic position is that the balance between confidentiality and candor with the court should be tilted more in the direction of candor than is presently the case.

In "Perjury: The Criminal Defense Lawyer's Trilemma," a chapter from his book, *Lawyers' Ethics in an Adversary System*, Freedman responds to Noonan's article. The "trilemma" to which Freedman refers is the apparent conflict among the attorney's obligations to: (1) determine all the relevant facts known by his or her client, (2) protect the confidences of his or her clients, and (3) maintain a relationship of candor with the court. The most severe problem area here is in the case where the client insists on testifying and then perjures him or herself. The CPR stipulates that the attorney must not "knowingly use perjured testimony or false evidence." But Freedman notes that the CPR gives the attorney very little help in determining how to carry out this requirement while at the same time protecting the client's confidences. Perjured testimony from one's client may be a bit like the sound of a trumpet—once sounded it can never be unsounded. When the attorney's client perjures him or herself, the attorney would seem to be caught in a dilemma. If the attorney argues on the basis of the client's perjured testimony, then the attorney violates his or her obligation to the court. If the attorney either calls the perjury to the attention of the court, or even conspicuously avoids such testimony in argument, then the attorney violates the confidence of the client by tacitly standing before the court and saying, "My client did it."

Freedman notes that Noonan rests his criticism of Freedman's position on the view that the role of the attorney is to assist the court in reaching a "wise and informed decision." Freedman suggests that Noonan may not quite mean all he says, noting that Noonan would probably be unwilling to sacrifice the constitutional rights of clients in his attempt to make sure the truth was uncovered. Moreover, Freedman argues that Noonan's general position still fails to provide much of a guide to the attorney in the difficult concrete situations encountered in actual criminal defense practice. In the end, Freedman concludes, unlike Noonan, that, while the organized bar has been ambiguous and unhelpful in shaping the conduct of the attorney faced with the "trilemma," the balance between confidentiality and candor with the court must tilt in the direction of confidentiality. Such a tilt is required in order to give full value to fundamental constitutional rights of the client.

Competence

Attorney competence not only is a duty owed to the client, but, as should have been clear from the treatment of that topic in the preceding chapter, is equally a duty to the system of justice itself. For the adversarial system of justice to work as a rational system of discovery, it depends on a reasonably even level of competence in the representation of the competing adversaries. Whenever an attorney fails to represent his or her client competently, the system is less likely to achieve a just result; moreover, all other things being equal, that client stands at a disadvantage before the court. For this reason, the attorney has the strongest of duties to represent the client competently.

Compared with the treatment of the attorney's duty of competence in the last chapter, the discussion in this chapter will focus more narrowly on the lawyer's liability for failure to represent the client competently, that is, on the issue of attorney malpractice liability.

Because of the difference between the criminal and civil contexts of malpractice liability, there will be separate readings on each of those contexts. The readings on malpractice liability in civil practice start out with the very controversial case of *Smith v. Lewis*. In that case an attorney is held liable for his failure to research the clearly debatable (at the time) issue of whether his client might claim her husband's military retirement pension as community property in a divorce settlement. This is a difficult opinion in that the court takes note of the fact that the same attorney had dealt with claims that military pensions were community property prior to his representation of Mrs. Smith. It is difficult to determine what role this fact played in the court's decision to hold Lewis liable for his failure adequately to research the issue and press such a claim on behalf of Mrs. Smith. In any case, the finding in *Smith v. Lewis* proved distressing to a good many within the legal profession, and it has been held by a number of attorneys that the standard of competence set forth in *Smith v. Lewis* is too stringent.

In "Attorney's Negligence and Third Parties," Ellen Eisenberg focuses specifically on the basis of an attorney's duty of competence to those other than clients. Eisenberg notes a number of reasons for extending the attorney's duty to third parties. Some of these reasons are based on considerations of economic efficiency (see the reading by Richard Posner in Chapter Two), while others have to do with the demands of justice. Eisenberg examines the bases on which courts have extended attorney liability for malpractice to third parties, noting the lack of any comprehensive framework to date. In the final section of her article she advocates precisely such a "unifying theory" for attorney liability to third parties. Her "duty theory" rests on identifying harm to a third party as resulting from an "undertaking" of the attorney, and as being a foreseeable result of that undertaking.

The criminal malpractice section opens with the case of *Walker v. Kruse*, a case involving a malpractice action against an appointed criminal defense attorney. The United States Court of Appeals, Seventh Circuit, finds for the attorney, noting several possible grounds for doing so. The court notes that the initial criminal conviction was appealed on grounds of, among other things, inadequate counsel. That appeal was found without merit. The court does, however, note that that would not automatically defeat the malpractice claim. The court also notes the presumed guilt of the defendant as a possible bar to recovery, as well as the fact that the criminal defendant retained the actual control of his own defense rather than simply relying on his attorney. This latter fact presumably involves that defendant in contributory negligence. Finally, the court argues that there are strong policy considerations in favor of making appointed criminal defense counsel free from any liability for professional negligence.

The final article in this chapter is David Potel's "Criminal Malpractice: Threshold Barriers to Recovery Against Negligent Criminal Counsel." Potel examines the various barriers to recovery faced by the plaintiff in a malpractice suit against criminal defense counsel that are not placed against his or her civil counterpart. Several of these issues have already been encountered in *Walker v. Kruse*. Potel argues that each of these added barriers is unjustified and that, to take the extreme case, the guilty criminal whose incompetent counsel leaves him or her with a sentence that is longer than it should have been is no less deserving of recompense than the actually liable defendant in civil litigation whose incompetent counsel leaves him or her with a judgment of monetary liability larger than it should have been.

A

Loyalty to the Client in General

People v. Heirens

SUPREME COURT OF ILLINOIS, 1954 4ILL. 2D 131, 122 N.E. 2D 231

KLINGBIEL, Justice

On September 4, 1946, William Heirens pleaded guilty, in the criminal court of Cook County, to three murder indictments and twenty-six additional indictments charging various burglaries, robberies and assaults. After pronouncing judgments of guilty the court sentenced Heirens to the penitentiary for life on each of the murder indictments, the sentences to run consecutively, and imposed the statutory sentences on the other indictments, the latter to run concurrently with each other but consecutively to the sentences on the murder indictments. On July 8, 1952, Heirens filed a petition under the Post-Conviction Hearing Act, Ill. Rev. Stat. 1953, chap. 38, par. 826 et seq., setting forth a number of respects in which he alleged his constitutional rights had been violated. The State filed an answer and a hearing was had, after which judgment was entered denying the petition. Heirens seeks review by this court on writ of error. We have appointed as *amici curiae* Calvin Sawyer and Arthur R. Seder, Jr., who have filed briefs on behalf of petitioner.

It is contended that police unlawfully searched petitioner's living quarters and seized property found there; that he was subjected to unduly prolonged and continuous questioning by law enforcement authorities; that he was injected with sodium pentothal at their direction and against his consent, to obtain admissions and confessions from him; that he was compelled to submit to a lie-detector test; that adverse newspaper publicity would have prevented him from receiving a fair and impartial trial; that he was subjected to insistent urgings of counsel and parents to plead guilty; that his attorneys, instead of giving him their undivided allegiance, mistakenly conceived it their duty to avoid any action which might result in his return to society; and that the pleas of guilty were not the result of his free and voluntary choice but were induced or compelled by the illegally obtained evidence, his disclosures while under the influence of drugs, the improbability of a fair trial in view of the newspaper publicity, and the pressure exerted by parents and counsel.

* * *

A determination of the questions properly before this court requires consideration of the evidence in some detail. The record discloses that on June 26, 1946, the petitioner, a seventeen-year-old University of Chicago student, was captured by Chicago police officers while prowling in an apartment house on the north side of the city. In the course of a struggle with the officers one of them broke three flower pots over petitioner's head, inflicting severe injuries. He was taken unconscious to a hospital, where he remained as a bed patient for five days. On the day of his arrest police searched his living quarters at the university, and recovered a number of articles later identified as having been stolen. During the following two days petitioner was intermittently questioned in the hospital by police and an assistant State's Attorney, and was subjected to questioning all night of the second day. Petitioner failed to respond coherently, but stared with a vacant expression and behaved in an irrational manner throughout the interrogation.

On the third day the State's Attorney directed a specialist in psychiatry to administer sodium pentothal to petitioner, in order, it is said, to ascertain whether he was malingering. No permission was obtained from petitioner or his parents. Petitioner was injected with sodium pentothal, a so-called "truth serum," which produces a mental state of semi-consciousness wherein the individual is unable to critically survey his responses to questions, or to associate, select and inhibit his remarks. While petitioner was under the influence of this drug, he was questioned about his life and development, and his past and recent experiences. He was asked about specific crimes, particularly the murder of Suzanne Degnan on January 7, 1946. He readily spoke about burglaries, the Degnan murder and other crimes, for which he was subsequently convicted, but attributed them to someone named "George," a person of bad influence who forced Heirens to search out places for him to burglarize. According to Heirens's disclosures while under the influence of the sodium pentothal, "George" was responsible for everything, and Heirens had constantly been trying to prevent him from committing the acts. When Heirens was asked to describe the man he called "George," he described himself exactly. Throughout the examination the State's Attorney, the first assistant State's Attorney, the police commissioner, and a stenographer were present behind screens which had been placed about the bed. The stenographer took notes during the questioning. After petitioner regained an awareness of his surroundings he sat up in bed and asked: "What did I say? What did I say?" to which the first assistant State's Attorney replied: "Why you said all the things that I think we have to know." The examining doctor testified in the present proceedings that "the major factor in the productions which developed under pentothal were not those of a malingerer but those of a mentally sick boy"; that he informed the State's Attorney that petitioner was a disassociated psychotic schizophrenic; and that such affliction is "a mental disease characterized by a splitting of personality, in which very frequently one aspect of the personality may not be aware of the other, and may not be in communication with the other."

After the sodium pentothal interview, questioning by police officers was resumed and continued all night. On June 30, the following day, petitioner was taken to the detective bureau where the police, without obtaining his consent, gave him a polygraph or lie-detector examination. Heirens did not answer the questions but merely repeated each one as it was asked. About 6:30 o'clock that evening, however, he summoned the police captain to the hospital, and said he was going to tell everything. The State's Attorney and his assistant were then called, and Heirens proceeded to give a statement in which he admitted knowledge of the Degnan murder and other crimes but ascribed them to a "George Merman," whom he described as a friend who was always doing the wrong thing and would never listen to him. At the conclusion of this statement he was asked to print out the text of a ransom note involved in the Degnan murder, and he did so, making four copies. On the next day he was told that a handwriting expert found it was his own handwriting on the ransom note, and that in addition the ransom note misspelled two words and Heirens misspelled the same words.

On July 1 Heirens was brought into court on a petition for *habeas corpus* filed on his behalf by attorneys engaged by his parents. Shortly thereafter he was formally charged with a number of burglaries, and some weeks later the murder indictments were presented. One of his attorneys conferred with the prosecuting attorney, who disclosed information tending to connect petitioner with the three murders as well as burglary charges, and subsequently reviewed with petitioner the evidence against him. Petitioner's attorney informed him and his parents that several of the burglary charges could probably be successfully prosecuted; that in view of the publicity the case had received it was doubtful that a jury could be obtained which had not read about it; that it was reasonably certain severe and consecutive sentences would be imposed if the cases were tried on not guilty pleas, with the result that the rest of his life would be spent in the penitentiary; and that even though the possibility of a death penalty for the murders was remote it would be foolish to take the chance. Petitioner had told his attorneys as well as his parents that he committed the murders.

The attorney had conferred with a psychiatrist about the symptoms of mental derangement which Heirens had related to him, and was advised by the psychiatrist that although they showed an abnormality they did not render Heirens unable to distinguish between right and wrong. Several conferences were had between Heirens and his attorney concerning his mental condition and a possible defense of insanity. The attorney concluded there was no available proof that Heirens did not know the difference between right and wrong.

Petitioner's parents and attorneys agreed that the best course to take was to discuss a plea of guilty with the prosecution. The attorney met with the prosecutors, and an arrangement was reached whereby petitioner would plead guilty to the offenses with which he was charged, make a complete confession of the murders, and submit to a psychiatric examination to determine whether he was of sufficient mental soundness to make a plea. In return the prosecutors were to recommend concurrent sentences of life imprisonment.

* * *

On July 30, for the purpose of obtaining his confessions, Heirens was brought to the State's Attorney's office, where a large number of police officials, newspaper reporters and photographers were present. When he was questioned about the crimes, however, Heirens stated he did not remember. His counsel then took him into an adjoining room where Heirens repeated that he did not remember and remarked that he was upset. His parents were called. His attorneys questioned him as to why he did not make the confession, advised him to accept the proposition of the State's Attorney, and talked to him about the newspaper publicity. He was later informed by his attorneys that he should tell them whether he wanted them to continue representing him; that they had expected him to make a confession in the State's Attorney's office on July 30, and did not like to be taken by surprise; and that it appeared likely he would get the electric chair. Petitioner observed that he had no desire to take the chance of being electrocuted, and that he would make a statement.

* * *

Prior to the pronouncement of sentence the prosecutor and the principal defense attorney addressed the court. The State's Attorney in his remarks acknowledged the "co-operative assistance" of defense counsel and observed: "The small likelihood of a successful murder prosecution of William Heirens early prompted the State's Attorney's office to seek out and obtain the co-operative help of defense counsel and, through them, that of their client.* * * Without the aid of the defense we would to this day have no answer for the death of Josephine Ross. Without their aid, to this day a great and sincere public doubt might remain as to the guilt of William Heirens in the killing of Suzanne Degnan and Frances Brown." Petitioner's attorney then proceeded to state to the court the reasons which impelled him and his cocounsel to adopt the course they followed. He remarked in part: "I have no memory of any case, certainly not in my time at the bar, when counsel on both sides were so perplexed as to the mental status of an individual and the causes which motivated him to do certain acts. In those cases we both sought psychiatrists in the hope that they might aid us. I must confess that at this time there exists in my mind many doubts as to this defendant's mental capacity for crime; and I believe doubt must exist in our minds as to just what the relation of cause and effect was, and how he could, in a manner so devoid of feeling, do the acts here charged and upon which the plea has been guilty. On acquiring knowledge, your Honor, of the facts we were further notified at a later date of his mental condition. We were collectively agreed that any thought on the part of the State to cause this man to forfeit his life would be unjust. It would be unfair. By the same token we were collectively agreed that any course on our part which would assist in having him returned to society would be equally unfair."

No contention is made that petitioner was in fact insane at the time the pleas were made, or that he failed to understand the nature and object of the proceedings against him. Nor is it disputed that, in form at least, the usual constitutional safeguards were observed. Petitioner was represented by counsel of recognized ability and experience, and he was advised by the court of his right to trial by jury, he was admonished as to the possible consequences of his pleas. It is insisted, however, that beneath the surface of formal regularity, the combination of circumstances to which petitioner was subjected in effect deprived his of any substantial choice in the matter; and that his attorneys, through a mistaken conception of public duty, failed to take advantage of the defense of insanity, but advised pleas of guilty in order to avoid any chance of petitioner returning to society.

* * *

It is maintained on behalf of petitioner that his counsel at the time of his conviction failed to give him their undivided allegiance; that although they were of undisputed competence and integrity they improperly assumed a public responsibility and acted in part from a desire to protect society from petitioner; that petitioner had a good defense of insanity, but his attorneys, from mistaken motives of public duty, prevailed upon him to plead guilty instead of relying upon said defense; and that petitioner was thereby denied due process of law. The evidence shows that peitioner had four attorneys, selected by his parents and himself; that they were capable and of high integrity; and that they unstintingly devoted time and attention to the case, and conferred frequently with petitioner. It is not contended that they misrepresented the law to petitioner, misinformed him as to his rights, or failed to give him sufficient legal advice. The complaint is merely that their recommendation to plead guilty was made from motives of public duty as well as those of duty to their client, whereas their actions should have been governed only by the latter. Although petitioner was young, emotionally unstable and unusually susceptible to suggestions, he was of normal intelligence and able to make his own decisions. To recognize the responsibility of such a person for his own decisions is not to withhold due process. As a general rule, an accused person who retains counsel of his own selection is responsible if that counsel does not faithfully serve his interest; and he cannot contend, on a post-conviction hearing, that he was denied due process of law because his counsel was incompetent or negligent. *Mitchell v. People*, 411 Ill. 407, 104, N.E.2d 285. Where attorneys frequently consult with the accused, and fully explain his rights and the effect of a plea of guilty does not show inadequacy of representation. *People v. Seger*, 405 Ill. 222, 90 N.E.2d 637.

We have thoroughly examined the record and find no error therein. The judgment of the criminal court of Cook County will be affirmed.
Judgment affirmed.

The Lawyer as Friend: The Moral Foundations of the Lawyer–Client Relation*

CHARLES FRIED†

Advocatus sed non ladro, Res miranda populo . . . .

Medieval anthem
honoring St. Ives

Can a good lawyer be a good person? The question troubles lawyers and law students alike. They are troubled by the demands of loyalty to one's client and by the fact that one can win approval as a good, maybe even great, lawyer even though that loyalty is engrossed by overprivileged or positively distasteful clients. How, they ask, is such loyalty compatible with

Yale Law Journal, 85 (1976), 1060–75 and 1087–89. Reprinted by permission.

*Copyright © 1976 by Charles Fried. This essay is part of a larger work on right and wrong, supported by the National Science Foundation under grant number SOC75-13506. Research assistance and suggestions were provided by Dan Polster and Jerrold Tannenbaum, students at the Harvard Law School. I am grateful for the comments of Gary Bellow, Sissela Bok, Alan Dershowitz, Philip Heymann, Andrew Kaufman, Robert Keeton, Thomas Nagel, Charles Nesson, Albert Sacks, and David Shapiro. I am especially grateful to the editors of the *Yale Law Journal* for their understanding, help, and encouragement. I wonder if any of them agree with what I say here. The National Science Foundation, of course, underwrites only the effort, not the conclusion.

†Professor of Law, Harvard University.

that devotion to the common good characteristic of high moral principles? And whatever their views of the common good, they are troubled because the willingness of lawyers to help their clients use the law to the prejudice of the weak or the innocent seems morally corrupt. The lawyer is conventionally seen as a professional devoted to his client's interests and as authorized, if not in fact required, to do some things (though not anything) for that client which he would not do for himself.[1] In this essay I consider the compatibility between this traditional conception of the lawyer's role and the ideal of moral purity—the ideal that one's life should be lived in fulfillment of the most demanding moral principles, and not just barely within the law. So I shall not be particularly concerned with the precise limits imposed on the lawyer's conduct by positive rules of the law and by the American Bar Association's *Code of Professional Responsibility*[2] except as these provide a background. I assume that the lawyer observes these scrupulously. My inquiry is one of morals: Does the lawyer whose conduct and choices are governed only by the traditional conception of the lawyer's role, which these positive rules reflect, lead a professional life worthy of moral approbation, worthy of respect—ours and his own?

I. THE CHALLENGE TO THE TRADITIONAL CONCEPTION

A. *The Two Criticisms*

Two frequent criticisms of the traditional conception of the lawyer's role attack both its ends and its means. First, it is said that the ideal of

[1]*See, e.g.,* J. Auerbach, *Unequal Justice* (1976); M. Green, *The Other Government* (1975). Lord Brougham stated the traditional view of the lawyer's role during his defense of Queen Caroline:

> [A]n advocate, in the discharge of his duty, knows but one person in all the world, and that person is his client. To save that client by all means and expedients, and at all hazards and costs to other persons, and, among them, to himself, is his first and only duty; and in performing this duty he must not regard the alarm, the torments, the destruction which he may bring upon others. Separating the duty of a patriot from that of an advocate, he must go on reckless of consequences, though it should be his unhappy fate to involve his country in confusion.

2 *Trial of Queen Caroline* 8 (J. Nightingale ed. 1821). A sharply contrasting view was held by law professors at the University of Havanna who said that " the first job of a revolutionary lawyer is not to argue that his client is innocent, but rather to determine if his client is guilty and if so, to seek the sanction which will best rehabilitate him." Berman, "The Cuban Popular Tribunals," 69 *Colum. L. Rev.* 1317, 1341 (1969). And a Bulgarian attorney has been quoted as saying," 'In a Socialist state there is no division of duty between the judge, prosecutor and defense counsel . . . the defense must assist the prosecution to find the objective truth in a case.' " J . Kaplan, *Criminal Justice: Introductory Cases and Materials* 264–65 (1973).

[2]The American Bar Association approved a revised *Code of Professional Responsibility* in 1969. In part that revision was a response to the criticism that the legal profession, by failing to make legal services more widely available, had not met its public responsibilities. J. Auerbach, *supra* note 1, at 285–86. *See also Preface*, ABA Code of Professional Responsibility.

professional loyalty to one's client permits, even demands, an allocation of the lawyer's time, passion, and resources in ways that are not always maximally conducive to the greatest good of the greatest number.[3] Interestingly, this criticism is leveled increasingly against doctors[4] as well as lawyers. Both professions affirm the principle that the professional's primary loyalty is to his client,[5] his patient. A "good" lawyer will lavish energy and resources on his existing client, even if it can be shown that others could derive greater benefit from them. The professional ideal authorizes a care for the client and the patient which exceeds what the efficient distribution of a scarce social resource (the professional's time) would dictate.

That same professional ideal has little or nothing to say about the initial choice of clients or patients. Certainly it is laudable if the doctor and lawyer choose their clients among the poorest or sickest or most dramatically threatened, but the professional ideal does not require this kind of choice in any systematic way—the choice of client remains largely a matter of fortuity or arbitrary choice. But once the client has been chosen, the professional ideal requires primary loyalty to the client whatever his need or situation. Critics contend that it is wasteful and immoral that some of the finest talent in the legal profession is devoted to the intricacies of, say, corporate finance or elaborate estate plans, while important public and private needs for legal services go unmet. The immorality of this waste is seen to be compounded when the clients who are the beneficiaries of this lavish attention use it to avoid their obligations in justice (if not in law) to society and to perpetuate their (legal) domination of the very groups whose greater needs these lawyers should be meeting.[6]

The second criticism applies particularly to the lawyer. It addresses not the misallocation of scarce resources, which the lawyer's exclusive concern with his client's interests permits, but the means which this loyalty appears to authorize, tactics which procure advantages for the client at the direct expense of some identified opposing party. Examples are discrediting a nervous but probably truthful complaining witness[7] or taking advantage of the need or ignorance of an adversary in a negotiation. This second criticism is, of course, related to the first, but there is a difference. The first criticism focuses on a social harm: the waste of scarce resources implicit in a doctor caring for the hearts of the sedentary managerial classes or a lawyer tending to the estates and marital difficulties of the rich. The professional is accused of failing to confer beneifts wisely and efficiently. By the second criticism the lawyer is accused not of failing to benefit the appropriate,

[3]*See* M. Green, *supra* note 1, at 268–269, 285–89.

[4]*See* V . Fuchs, *Who Shall Live?* 60 (1974); Havighurst and Blumstein, "Coping With Quality/Cost Trade-Offs in Medical Care: The Role of PSROs," 70 *Nw. U. L. Rev.* 6, 25–28 (1975). *But see* Fried, "Equality and Rights in Medical Care," 6 *Hastings Center Rep.* 29, 33–34 (1976).

[5]*See* ABA Code of Professional Responsibility Canon 7.

[6]For a description of the growth of such criticisms, see J. Auerbach, *supra* note 1, at 275–88.

[7]For a defense of an attorney's use of such tactics, see M. Freedman, *Lawyers' Ethics in an Adversary System* 43–49 (1975). *See also* Curtis, "The Ethics of Advocacy 4 *Stan L. Rev.* 3 (1951).

though usually unidentified, persons, but of harming his identified adversary.[8]

B. *Examples*

Consider a number of cases which illustrate the first criticism: A doctor is said to owe a duty of loyalty to his patient, but how is he to react if doing his very best for his patient would deplete the resources of the patient's family, as in the case of a severely deformed baby who can only be kept alive through extraordinarily expensive means? Should a doctor prescribe every test of distinct but marginal utility for every patient on public assistance, even if he knows that in the aggregate such a policy will put the medical care system under intolerable burdens?[9] Should he subject his patients to prudent testing of new remedies because he knows that only in this way can medicine make the strides that it has in the past?[10]

---

[8]The point really carries further than the distinction between benefit and harm. In the former case, though some particular person may have benefited had the distribution been efficient, it does not seem correct to say that for that reason this person had a right to the benefit which he was denied, or that this person was wronged by not receiving the benefit. Individuals do not acquire rights under policies which are dictated purely by considerations of efficiency. *See generally* Dworkin, "Hard Cases, 88 *Harv. L. Rev.* 1057, 1058–78 (1975).

Professor Anscombe makes the following suggestive argument: If saving the life of one patient requires a massive dose of a drug that could be divided up and used to save five other people, not one of those five can claim that he has been wronged, that the smaller dose of the drug was owed to him.

> Yet all can reproach me if I gave it to none. It was there, ready to supply human need, and human need was not supplied. So any one of them can say: you ought to have used it to help us who needed it; and so all are wronged. But if it was used for someone, as much as he needed it to keep him alive, no one has any ground for accusing me of having wronged *himself.*—Why, just because he was one of five who could have been saved, is he wronged in not being saved, if someone is supplied with it who needed it? What is *his* claim, except the claim that what was needed go to him rather than be wasted? But it was not wasted. So he was not wronged. So who was wronged? And if no one was wronged, what injury did I do?
>
> . . . .
>
> I do not mean "because they are more" isn't a good reason for helping these and not that one, or these rather than those. It is a perfectly intelligible reason. But it doesn't follow from that that a man acts badly if he doesn't make it his reason. He acts badly if human need for what is in his power to give doesn't work in him as a reason. He·acts badly if he chooses to rescue rich people rather than poor ones, having ill regard for the poor ones because they are poor. But he doesn't act badly if he uses his resources to save X, or X, Y and Z, *for no bad reason*, and is not affected by the consideration that he could save a larger number of people. For, once more: who can say he is wronged? And if no one is wronged, how does the rescuer commit any wrong?

Anscombe, "Who is Wronged?" 5 *Oxford Rev.* 16, 16–17 (1967) (emphasis in original).

[9]*See generally* V. Fuchs, *supra* note 4, at 94–95; Fried, "Rights and Health Care—Beyond Equity and Efficiency," 293 *New England J. Medicine* 241, 244 (1975).

[10]For discussions of this dilemma, see A. Cochrane, *Effectiveness and Efficiency* (1972); C. Fried, *Medical Experimentation: Personal Integrity and Social Policy* (1974).

These problems are analogous to problems which are faced by the lawyer. The lawyer who advises a client how to avoid the effects of a tax or a form of regulation, though it is a fair tax or a regulation in the public interest, is facing the same dilemma and resolving it in favor of his client. So does the public defender who accedes to his client's demands and takes a "losing" case to trial, thereby wasting court time and depleting the limited resources of his organization. We tolerate and indeed may applaud the decision of a lawyer who vigorously defends a criminal whom he believes to be guilty and dangerous.[11] And I for one think that a lawyer who arranges the estate of a disagreeable dowager or represents one of the parties in a bitter matrimonial dispute must be as assiduous and single-minded in fulfilling his obligation to that client as the lawyer who is defending the civil liberties case of the century.

Illustrative of the second criticism (doing things which are offensive to a particular person) are familiar situations such as the following: In a negotiation it becomes clear to the lawyer for the seller that the buyer and his lawyer mistakenly believe that somebody else has already offered a handsome price for the property. The buyer asks the seller if this is true, and the seller's lawyer hears his client give an ambiguous but clearly encouraging response.[12] Another classic case is the interposition of a technical defense such as the running of the statute of limitations to defeat a debt that the client admits he owes.[13]

There is another class of cases which does not so unambiguously involve the lawyer's furthering his client's interests at the direct expense of some equally identified, concrete individual, but where furthering those interests does require the lawyer to do things which are personally offensive to him. The conventional paradigms in the casuistic literature deal with criminal defense lawyers who are asked improper questions by the trial judge ("Your client doesn't have a criminal record, does he?" or "Your client hasn't offered to plead guilty to a lesser offense, has he?"), a truthful answer to which would be damningly prejudicial to the client, but which the lawyer must lie in defense of his client's interests even though lying is personally and professionally offensive to him.[14] The defense lawyer who

[11]*See* M. Freedman, *supra* note 7, at 43–49.

[12]DR 7-102(A)(5) of the *Code of Professional Responsibility* states that a lawyer shall not knowingly make a false statement of law or fact in his representation of a client. The issue is how to apply this admonition in the context of negotiation, where deception is commonplace. *See* M. Meltsner and P. Schrag, *Public Interest Advocacy: Materials for Clinical Legal Education* 231–39 (1974).

[13]For a striking example, see *Zabella v. Pakel*, 242 F.2d 452 (7th Cir. 1957), where the debtor asserting the technical defenses was a savings and loan association president, and the creditor was a man who had worked for him as a carpenter and had lent him money in earlier, less fortunate days.

[14]Although Charles Curtis explicitly denounces lying to the court, his observation that the propriety of lying might depend on whether the question is asked "by someone who has a right to ask it" at least implies a possible qualification in the case of improper questioning by the court. Curtis, *supra* note 7, at 7–9. Monroe Freedman does not specifically address this problem, but his argument that an attorney's duty to safeguard the attorney–client privilege requires the attorney to introduce his client's perjurious testimony would seem to extend to this situation. M. Freedman, *supra* note 7, at 27–41. *Cf.* ABA Comm. on Professional Ethics,

cross-examines a complaining rape victim (whom he knows to be telling the truth) about her chastity or lack thereof in order to discredit her accusing testimony faces a similar moral difficulty. In some respects these cases might be taken to illustrate both principal criticisms of the traditional conception. On the one hand, there is harm to society in making the choice to favor the client's interests: a dangerous criminal may escape punishment or an appropriately heavy sentence. On the other hand, this social harm is accomplished by means of acting towards another human being—the judge, the complaining witness—in ways that seem demeaning and dishonorable.

II. THE LAWYER AS FRIEND

A. *The Thesis*

In this essay I will consider the moral status of the traditional conception of the professional. The two criticisms of this traditional conception, if left unanswered, will not put the lawyer in jail, but they will leave him without a moral basis for his acts. The real question is whether, in the face of these two criticisms, a decent and morally sensitive person can conduct himself according to the traditional conception of professional loyalty and still believe that what he is doing is morally worthwhile.

It might be said that any one whose conscience is so tender that he cannot fulfill the prescribed obligations of a professional should not undertake those obligations. He should not allow his moral scruples to operate as a trap for those who are told by the law that they may expect something more. But of course this suggestion merely pushes the inquiry back a step. We must ask then not how a decent lawyer may behave, but whether a decent, ethical person can ever be a lawyer. Are the assurances implicit in assuming the role of lawyer such that an honorable person would not give them and thus would not enter the profession? And, indeed, this is a general point about an argument from obligation:[15] It may be that the internal logic of a particular obligation demands certain forms of conduct (e.g., honor among thieves), but the question remains whether it is just and moral to contract such obligations.

I will argue in this essay that it is not only legally but also morally right that a lawyer adopt as his dominant purpose the furthering of his client's interests—that it is right that a professional put the interests of his client above some idea, however valid, of the collective interest. I maintain that the traditional conception of the professional role expresses a morally valid

---

Opinions No. 287 (1967) (if attorney for defendant learns of previous criminal record through his communications with his client, he has no duty to correct misapprehension on part of court that client has no record).

[15]That one assumes obligations to persons which cannot always be overridden by the benefits which would accrue from aiding some third person is a standard objection to utilitarianism. *See, e.g.*, W. Ross, *The Right and the Good* 17–19 (1930).

conception of human conduct and human relationships, that one who acts according to that conception is to that extent a good person. Indeed, it is my view that, far from being a mere creature of positive law, the traditional conception is so far mandated by moral right that any advanced legal system which did not sanction this conception would be unjust.

The general problem raised by the two criticisms is this: How can it be that it is not only permissible, but indeed morally right, to favor the interests of a particular person in a way which we can be fairly sure is either harmful to another particular individual or not maximally conducive to the welfare of society as a whole?[16]

The resolution of this problem is aided, I think, if set in a larger perspective. Charles Curtis made the perspicacious remark that a lawyer may be privileged to lie for his client in a way that one might lie to save one's friends or close relatives.[17] I do not want to underwrite the notion that it is justifiable to lie even in those situations, but there is a great deal to the point that in those relations—friendship, kinship—we recognize an authorization to take the interests of particular concrete persons more seriously and to give them priority over the interests of the wider collectivity. One who provides an expensive education for his own children surely cannot be blamed because he does not use those resources to alleviate famine or to save lives in some distant land. Nor does he blame himself. Indeed, our intuition that an individual is authorized to prefer identified persons standing close to him over the abstract interests of humanity finds its sharpest expression in our sense that an individual is entitled to act with something less than impartiality to that person who stands closest to him— the person that he is. There is such a thing as selfishness to be sure, yet no reasonable morality asks us to look upon ourselves as merely plausible candidates for the distribution of the attention and resources which we command, plausible candidates whose entitlement to our own concern is no greater in principle than that of any other human being. Such a doctrine may seem edifying, but on reflection it strikes us as merely fanatical.

This suggests an interesting way to look at the situation of the lawyer. As a professional person one has a special care for the interests of those accepted as clients, just as his friends, his family, and he himself have a very general claim to his special concern. But I concede this does no more than widen the problem. It merely shows that in claiming this authorization to have a special care for my clients I am doing something which I do in other contexts as well.

[16]I have discussed this problem elsewhere. C. Fried, *An Anatomy of Values* 207–36 (1970); C. Fried, *supra* note 10, at 132–37. *Cf.* Schelling, "The Life You Save May Be Your Own," in *Problems in Public Expenditure Analysis* 127, 129–30 (S. Chase ed. 1968) (also discussing our greater concern for known, as opposed to unknown, individuals).

[17]Curtis, *supra* note 7, at 8. Analogizing the lawyer to a friend raises a range of problems upon which I shall not touch. These have to do with the lawyer's benevolent and sometimes not so benevolent tyranny over and imposition on his client, seemingly authorized by the claim to be acting in the client's interests. Domineering paternalism is not a normal characteristic of friendship. This point is due to Jay Katz.

B. The Utilitarian Explanation

I consider first an argument to account for fidelity to role, for obligation, made most elaborately by the classical utilitarians, Mill[18] and Sidgwick.[19] They argued that our propensity to prefer the interests of those who are close to us is in fact perfectly reasonable because we are more likely to be able to benefit those people. Thus, if everyone is mainly concerned with those closest to him, the distribution of social energies will be most efficient and the greatest good of the greatest number will be achieved. The idea is that the efforts I expend for my friend or my relative are more likely to be effective because I am more likely to know what needs to be done. I am more likely to be sure that the good I intend is in fact accomplished. One might say that there is less overhead, fewer administrative costs, in benefiting those nearest to us. I would not want to ridicule this argument, but it does not seem to me to go far enough. Because if that were the sole basis for the preference, then it would be my duty to determine whether my efforts might not be more efficiently spent on the collectivity, on the distant, anonymous beneficiary. But it is just my point that *this* is an inquiry we are not required, indeed sometimes not even authorized, to make. When we decide to care for our children, to assure our own comforts, to fulfill our obligations to our clients or patients, we do not do so as a result of a cost–benefit inquiry which takes into account the ease of producing a good result for our friends and relations.

Might it not be said, however, that the best means of favoring the abstract collectivity is in certain cases not to try to favor it directly but to concentrate on those to whom one has a special relation? This does not involve tricking oneself, but only recognizing the limitations of what an individual can do and know. But that, it seems to me, is just Mill's and Sidgwick's argument all over again. There is no trickery involved, but this is still a kind of deliberate limitation of our moral horizon which leaves us uncomfortable. Do I know in a particular case whether sticking to the narrow definition of my role will *in that case* further the good of all? If I know that it will not further the general good, then why am I acting as the role demands? Is it to avoid setting a bad example? But for whom? I need not tell others—whether I tell or not could enter into my calculation. For myself then? But that begs the question, since if short-circuiting the role-definition of my obligation and going straight for the general good is the best thing to do in that case, then the example I set myself is not a bad example, but a good example. In short, I do not see how one can at the same time admit that the general good is one's only moral standard, while steadfastly hewing to obligations to friends, family, and clients. What we must look for is an argument which shows that giving some degree of special consideration to myself, my friends, my clients is not merely instru-

[18]Mill, "Utilitarianism," in *The Philosophy of John Stuart Mill* 321, 342–44 (M. Cohen ed. 1961).

[19]H. Sidgwick, *The Methods of Ethics* 252 (7th ed. 1907).

mentally justified (as the utilitarians would argue) but to some degree intrinsically so.[20]

I think such an argument can be made. Instead of speaking the language of maximization of value over all of humanity, it will speak the language of rights. The stubborn ethical datum affirming such a preference grows out of the profoundest springs of morality: the concepts of personality, identity, and liberty.

C. Self, Friendship, and Justice

Consider for a moment the picture of the human person that would emerge if the utilitarian claim were in fact correct. It would mean that in all my choices I must consider the well-being of all humanity—actual and potential—as the range of my concern. Moreover, every actual or potential human being is absolutely equal in his claims upon me. Indeed, I myself am to myself only as one of this innumerable multitude. And that is the clue to what is wrong with the utilitarian vision. Before there is morality there must be the person. We must attain and maintain in our morality a concept of personality such that it makes sense to posit choosing, valuing entities— free, moral beings. But the picture of the moral universe in which my own interests disappear and are merged into the interests of the totality of humanity is incompatible with that,[21] because one wishes to develop a conception of a responsible, valuable, and valuing agent, and such an agent must first of all be dear to himself. It is from the kernal of individuality that the other things we value radiate. The Gospel says we must love our neighbor as ourselves and this implies that any concern for others which is a *human* concern must presuppose a concern for ourselves.[22] The human concern which we then show others is a concern which first of all recognizes the concrete individuality of that other person just as we recognize our own.

[20]*See generally* D. Lyons, *Forms and Limits of Utilitarianism* (1965); J. Smart and B. Williams, *Utilitarianism: For and Against* (1973); Harrod, "Utilitarianism Revised," 45 *Mind* 137 (1936); Mabbott, "Punishment," 48 *Mind* 152 (1939).

[21]*See generally* C. Fried, *An Anatomy of Values*, 203–06; Rawls, "The Independence of Moral Theory," 48 *Am. Phil. Ass'n* 17–20 (1975) (Kantian theory, as compared to utilitarianism, takes seriously basic moral fact of primacy of notion of individual personality).

[22]. . . It is written (Lev. xix. 18, Matth. xxii. 39); *Thou shalt love thy neighbor* (Lev. *loc. cit.,—friend) as thyself.* Whence it seems to follow that man's love for himself is the model of his love for another. But the model exceeds the copy.

Therefore, out of charity, a man ought to love himself more than his neighbor.
 . . . .

> We must, therefore, say that, even as regards the affection we ought to love one neighbor more than another. The reason is that, since the principle of love is God, and the person who loves, it must needs be that the affection of love increases in proportion to the nearness to one or the other of those principles.
> . . . .
> . . . As stated above . . , we ought out of charity to love those who are more closely united to us more, both because our love for them is more intense, and because there are more reasons for loving them. . . .

It might be objected that the picture I sketch does not show that each individual, in order to maintain the integral sense of himself as an individual, is justified in attributing a greater value to his most essential interests than he ascribes to the most essential interests of all other persons. Should not the individual generalize and attribute in equal degree to all persons the value which he naturally attributes to himself? I agree with those who hold that it is the essence of morality for reason to push us beyond inclination to the fair conclusion of our premises.[23] It *is* fair conclusion that as my experience as a judging, valuing, choosing entity is crucial to me, I must also conclude that for other persons their own lives and desires are the center of their universe. If morality is transcendent, it must somehow transcend particularity to take account of this general fact. I do not wish to deny this. On the contrary, my claim is that the kind of preference which an individual gives himself and concrete others is a preference which he would in exactly this universalizing spirit allow others to exhibit as well. It is not that I callously overlook the claim of the abstract individual, but indeed I would understand and approve were I myself to be prejudiced because some person to whom I stood in a similar situation of abstraction preferred his own concrete dimensions.

Finally, the concreteness which is the starting point of my own moral sensibility, the sense of myself, is not just a historical, biographical fact. It continues to enter into and condition my moral judgments because the effects which I can produce upon people who are close to me are qualitatively different from those produced upon abstract, unknown persons. My own concreteness is important not only because it establishes a basis for understanding what I and what all other human beings might be, but because in engaging that aspect of myself with the concrete aspects of others, I realize special values for both of us. Quite simply, the individualized relations of love and friendship (and perhaps also their opposites, hatred and enmity) have a different, more intense aspect than do the cooler, more abstract relations of love and service to humanity in general. The impulse I describe, therefore, is not in any sense a selfish impulse. But it does begin with the sense of self as a concrete entity. Those who object to my thesis by saying that we must generalize it are not wholly wrong; they

---

Accordingly we must say that friendship among blood relations is based upon their connection by natural origin, the friendship of fellow-citizens on their civic fellowship, and the friendship of those who are fighting side by side on the comradeship of battle. Wherefore in matters pertaining to nature we should love our kindred most, in matters concerning relations between citizens, we should prefer our fellow-citizens, and on the battlefield our fellow-soldiers. . . .

. . . .

If however we compare union with union, it is evident that the union arising from natural origin is prior to, and more stable than, all others, because it is something affecting the very substance, whereas other unions supervene and may cease altogether.

11 *Thomas Aquinas, Summa Theologica* 1297–1301 (Fathers of the English Dominican Province trans. 1947).

[23]*See* G. Warnock, *The Object of Morality* 79–80 (1971); Nagel, Book Review, 85 *Yale L.J.* 136, 140 (1975).

246 The Attorney and The Client

merely exaggerate. Truly I must be ready to generalize outward all the way. That is what justice consists of. But justice is not all of morality; there remains a circle of intensity which through its emphasis on the particular and the concrete continues to reflect what I have identified as the source of all sense of value—our sense of self.

Therefore, it is not only consonant with, but also required by, an ethics for human beings that one be entitled first of all to reserve an area of concern for oneself and then to move out freely from that area if one wishes to lavish that concern on others to whom one stands in concrete, personal relations. Similarity, a person is entitled to enjoy this extra measure of care from those who choose to bestow it upon him without having to justify this grace as either just or efficient. We may choose the individuals to whom we will stand in this special relation, or they may be thrust upon us, as in family ties. Perhaps we recognize family ties because, after all, there often has been an element of choice, but also because—by some kind of atavism or superstition—we identify with those who share a part of our biological natures.

In explicating the lawyer's relation to his client, my analogy shall be a friendship, where the freedom to choose and to be chosen expresses our freedom to hold something of ourselves in reserve, in reserve even from the universalizing claims of morality. These personal ties and the claims they engender may be all-consuming, as with a close friend or family member, or they may be limited, special-purpose claims, as in the case of the client or patient.[24] The special-purpose claim is one in which the beneficiary, the client, is entitled to all the special consideration *within* the limits of the relationship which we accord to a friend or a loved one. It is not that the claims of the client are less intense or demanding; they are only more limited in their scope. After all, the ordinary concept of friendship provides only an analogy, and it is to the development of that analogy that I turn.

D. Special-Purpose Friends

How does a professional fit into the concept of personal relations at all? He is, I have suggested, a limited-purpose friend. A lawyer is a friend in regard to the legal system. He is someone who enters into a personal relation with you—not an abstract relation as under the concept of justice.

---

[24]This argument is, of course, just a fragment which must be fitted into a larger theory. This larger theory would have to explain, among other things, what the precise contents of the various personal roles might be and how conflicts between personal roles are to be resolved. My later discussion of permissible and impermissible tactics in legal representation deals with this conflict in one context. A complete theory would also have to spell out the relation between personal roles and duties to the larger collectivity. These latter duties to man in the abstract as opposed to concrete persons are the subject of principles of justice. I have no doubt that such abstract duties exist and that they can be very demanding. Roughly , I would adopt something like the principles put forward in J. Rawls, *A Theory of Justice* 54–117 (1971). I would require, however, that these principles of justice leave sufficient scope for the free definition and inviolability of personal relations—to a greater extent perhaps than Rawls allows. These sytematic concerns are the subject of a larger work from which the present essay is drawn. The relation of principles of justice to other aspects of right and wrong is a principal concern of that larger work.

That means that like a friend he acts in your interests, not his own; or rather he adopts your interests as his own. I would call that the classic definition of friendship. To be sure, the lawyer's range of concern is sharply limited. But within that limited domain the intensity of identification with the client's interests is the same. It is not the specialized focus of the relationship which may make the metaphor inapposite, but the way in which the relation of legal friendship comes about and the one-sided nature of the ensuing "friendship." But I do insist upon the analogy, for in overcoming the arguments that the analogy is false, I think the true moral foundations of the lawyer's special role are illuminated and the utilitarian objections to the traditional conception of that role overthrown.

1. The Professional Role as Socially Defined: The Content of the Relation The claims that are made on the doctor or lawyer are made within a social context and are defined, at least in part, by social expectations. Most strikingly, in talking about friendship the focus of the inquiry is quite naturally upon the free gift of the donor; yet in professional relationships it is the recipient's need for medical or legal aid which defines the relationship. So the source of the relationship seems to be located at the other end, that of the recipient. To put this disquiet another way, we might ask how recognizing the special claims of friendship in any way compels society to allow the doctor or the lawyer to define his role on the analogy of those claims. Why are these people not like other social actors designated to purvey certain, perhaps necessary, goods? Would we say that one's grocer, tailor, or landlord should be viewed as a limited-purpose friend? Special considerations must be brought forward for doctors and lawyers.[25]

A special argument is at hand in both cases. The doctor does not minister just to any need, but to health. He helps maintain the very physical integrity which is the contrete substrate of individuality. To be sure, so does a grocer or landlord. But illness wears a special guise: it appears as a critical assault on one's person. The needs to which the doctor ministers usually are implicated in crises going to one's concreteness and individuality, and therefore what one looks for is a kind of ministration which is particularly concrete, personal, individualized. Thus, it is not difficult to see why I claim that a doctor is a friend, though a special purpose friend, the purpose being defined by the special needs of illness and crisis to which he tends.

But what, then, of the lawyer? Friendship and kinship are natural relations existing within, but not declined by, complex social institutions. Illness too is more a natural than social phenomenon. The response here requires an additional step. True, the special situations—legal relations or disputes—in which the lawyer acts as a limited-purpose friend are themselves a product of social institutions. But it does not follow that the role of the lawyer, which is created to help us deal with those social institutions, is defined by and is wholly at the mercy of the social good. We need only

---

[25]This question might be more troubling in a socialist system in which the profit motive is theoretically subordinated to the service of the general good. But my argument is that the needs for which lawyers and doctors provide are significantly different in kind from those met by other economic agents. Therefore, my argument about doctors and lawyers should be general enough to apply in either a free enterprise or a socialist system.

concede that at the very least the law must leave us a measure of autonomy, whether or not it is in the social interest to do so. Individuals have rights over and against the collectivity.[26] The moral capital arising out of individuals' concrete situations is one way of expressing that structure of rights, or at least part of it. It is because the law must respect the rights of individuals that the law must also create and support the specific role of legal friend. For the social nexus—the web of perhaps entirely just institutions—has become so complex that without the assistance of an expert adviser an ordinary layman cannot exercise that autonomy which the system must allow him. Without such an adviser, the law would impose constraints on the lay citizen (unequally at that) which it is not entitled to impose explicitly. Thus, the need which the lawyer serves in his special-purpose friendship may not be, as in the case of the doctor, natural, pre-social. Yet it is a need which has a moral grounding analogous to the need which the physician serves: the need to maintain one's integrity as a person. When I say the lawyer is his client's legal friend, I mean the lawyer makes the client's interests his own insofar as this is necessary to preserve and foster the client's autonomy within the law. This argument does not require us to assume that the law is hostile to the client's rights. All we need to assume is that even a system of law which is perfectly sensitive to personal rights would not work fairly unless the client could claim a professional's assistance in realizing that autonomy which the law recognizes.

2. The Asymmetry of Motive and Duty: The Form of the Relation   The institutional origin of the lawyer-client relationship is not its only characteristic which suggests that the analogy to natural friendship is vulnerable. In natural friendship the ideal relation is reciprocal; in legal friendship it is not. The lawyer is said to be the client's friend insofar as he is devoted to his client's interests, but it is no part of the ideal that the client should have any reciprocal devotion to the interests of his lawyer. Furthermore, I have argued that our right to be a friend to whomever we choose is a product of our individual autonomy. But in legal friendship the emphasis has been on the autonomy of the client, and it is the client who chooses the lawyer;[27] yet it is the lawyer who acts as a friend in the relation. And as a final contrast to natural friendship, the usual motive for agreeing or refusing to provide legal services is money. Indeed, when we speak of the lawyer's right to represent whomever he wishes, we are usually defending his moral title to represent whoever pays.

But recall that the concept of legal friendship was introduced to answer the argument that the lawyer is morally reprehensible to the extent that he lavishes undue concern on some particular person. The concept of friendship explains how it can be that a particular person may rightfully

---

[26]For a recent forceful statement of this conception of rights, see Dworkin, *Taking Rights Seriously*, in *Is Law Dead?* 168 (E. Rostow ed. 1971). *See generally* Dworkin, *The Original Position*, 40 *U. Chi. L. Rev.* 500, 522–28 (1973).

[27]The lawyer is generally free to decline to serve for any or no reason. But even that freedom is qualified; there will be times when there may be a duty to serve, as when a court appoints the lawyer to serve or when his declining may leave a person unrepresented. *See* pp. 1078–79, 1086–87 *infra.*

receive more than his share of care from another: he can receive that care if he receives it as an act of friendship. Although in natural friendship I emphasized the freedom to bestow, surely that freedom must imply a freedom to receive that extra measure of care. And it is the right of the client to receive such an extra measure of care (without regard, that is, to considertaions of efficiency or fairness) as much as the lawyer's right to give it, that I have been trying to explicate. Thus, the fact that the care in legal friendship systematically runs all one way does not impair the argument.

Yet the unease persists. Is it that while I have shown that the lawyer has a right to help the "unworthy" client, I have not shown that whenever the lawyer exercises this right he does something which is morally worthy, entitling him to self-respect? I may have shown that the law is obliged to allow the "unworthy" client to seek legal help and the lawyer to give it. But have I also shown that every lawyer who avails himself of this legal right (his and the client's legal right) performs a *morally worthy* function? Can a good lawyer be a good person?

The lawyer acts morally because he helps to preserve and express the autonomy of his client via-à-vis the legal system. It is not just that the lawyer helps his client accomplish a particular lawful purpose. Pornography may be legal, but it hardly follows that I perform a morally worthy function if I lend money or artistic talent to help the pornographer flourish in the exercise of this right. What is special about legal counsel is that whatever else may stop the pornographer's enterprise, he should not be stopped because he mistakenly believes there is a legal impediment. There is no wrong if a venture fails for lack of talent or lack of money—no one's rights have been violated. But rights *are* violated if, through ignorance or misinformation about the law, an individual refrains from pursuing a wholly lawful purpose. Therefore, to assist others in understanding and realizing their legal rights is always morally worthy. Moreover, the legal system, by instituting the role of the legal friend, not only assures what it in justice must—the due liberty of each citizen before the law—but does it by creating an institution which exemplifies, at least in a unilateral sense, the ideal of personal relations of trust and personal care which (as in natural friendship) are good in themselves.

Perhaps the unease has another source. The lawyer does work for pay. Is there not something odd about analogizing the lawyer's role to friendship when in fact his so-called friendship must usually be bought? If the lawyer is a public purveyor of goods, is not the lawyer–client relationship like that underlying any commercial transaction? My answer is "No." The lawyer and doctor have obligations to the client or patient beyond those of other economic agents. A grocer may refuse to give food to a customer when it becomes apparent that the customer does not have the money to pay for it. But the lawyer and doctor may not refuse to give additional care to an individual who cannot pay for it if withdrawal of their services would prejudice that individual.[28] Their duty to the client or patient to whom they have made an initial commitment transcends the

---

[28]*See* ABA Comm. on Professional Ethics, Opinions 56 (1967) (Informal Opinion No. 334); ABA Code of Professional Responsibility EC 2-31, 2-32. *Compare id.* DR 2-110(C)(l)(f) *with id.* DR 2-110(A)(2).

conventional quid pro quo of the marketplace. It is undeniable that money is usually what cements the lawyer–client relationship. But the content of the relation is determined by the client's needs, just as friendship is a response to another's needs. It is not determined, as are simple economic relationships, by the mere coincidence of a willingness to sell and a willingness to buy. So the fact that the lawyer works for pay does not seriously undermine the friendship analogy.

* * *

CONCLUSION

I do not imagine that what I have said provides an algorithm for resolving some of these perennial difficulties. Rather, what I am proposing is a general way of looking at the problem, a way of understanding not so much the difficult borderline cases as the central and clear ones, in the hope that the principles we can there discern will illuminate our necessarily approximate and prudential quest for resolution on the borderline. The notion of the lawyer as the client's legal friend, whatever its limitations and difficulties, does account for a kind of callousness toward society and exclusivity in the service of the client which otherwise seem quite mysterious. It justifies a kind of scheming which we would deplore on the part of a lay person dealing with another lay person—even if he were acting on behalf of a friend.

But these special indulgences apply only as a lawyer assists his client in his legal business. I do not owe my client my political assistance. I do not have to espouse his cause when I act as a citizen. Indeed, it is one of the most repellent features of the American legal profession—one against which the barrister–solicitor split has to some extent guarded the English profession—that many lawyers really feel that they are totally bought by their clients, that they must identify with their clients' interests far beyond the special purpose of advising them and operating the legal system for them. The defendants' antitrust lawyer or defendants' food and drug lawyer who writes articles, gives speeches, and pontificates generally about the evils of regulation may believe these things, but too often he does so because it is good for business or because he thinks that such conduct is what good representation requires.[39] In general, I think it deplorable that lawyers have specialized not only in terms of subject matter—that may or

---

[39]The implications of this idea are particularly important for the so-called Washington lawyer (wherever he might be) who is hired to represent his client before agencies and legislatures contemplating new law. This may put us on one of the borderlines I do not pretend to resolve definitively, yet I think we can get an idea of how to think about these cases too. To the extent that such representation involves participation in a formal proceeding in which laws or regulations are drafted and technical competence is required, the task is *closer* to the traditional task of the lawyer as I have sketched it, and the legal friend concept is more appropriate. To the extent that the representation involves (wholly lawful) deployment of political pressures, inducements, and considerations, it is closer to being political action, and thus to requiring the kind of overriding concern for the common good that should motivate all political actors. Certainly it is absurd that a man should seek to be insulated from moral judgment of his accomplishments as a political string-puller or publicist by the defense that he was only doing it for money.

may not be a good thing—but in terms of plaintiffs or defendants, in terms of the position that they represent.[40]

There is a related point which cuts very much in the opposite direction. it is no part of my thesis that the *client* is not morally bound to avoid lying to the court, to pay a just debt even though it is barred by the statute of limitations, to treat an opposite party in a negotiation with humanity and consideration for his needs and vulnerability, or to help the effectuation of policies aimed at the common good. Further, it is no part of my argument to hold that a lawyer must assume that the client is not a decent, moral person, has no desire to fulfill his moral obligations, and is asking only what is the minimum that he must do to stay within the law. On the contrary, to assume this about anyone is itself a form of immorality because it is a form of disrespect between persons. Thus in a very many situations a lawyer will be advising a client who wants to effectuate his purposes within the law, to be sure, but who also wants to behave as a decent, moral person. It would be absurd to contend that the lawyer must abstain from giving advice that takes account of the client's moral duties and his presumed desire to fulfill them. Indeed, in these situations the lawyer experiences the very special satisfaction of assisting the client not only to realize his autonomy within the law, but also to realize his status as a moral being. I want to make very clear that my conception of the lawyer's role in no way disentitles the lawyer from experiencing this satisfaction. Rather, it has been my purpose to explicate the less obvious point that there is a vocation and a satisfaction even in helping Shylock obtain his pound of flesh or in bringing about the acquittal of a guilty man.[41]

Finally, I would like to return to the charge that the morality of role and personal relationship I offer here is almost certain to lead to the diversion of legal services from areas of greatest need. It is just my point, of course, that when we fulfill the office of friend—legal, medical, or friend *tout court*—we do right, and thus it would be a great wrong to place us under a general regime of always doing what will "do the most good." What I affirm, therefore, is the moral liberty of a lawyer to make his life out of what personal scraps and shards of motivation his inclination and character suggest: idealism, greed, curiosity, love of luxury, love of travel, a need for adventure or repose; only so long as these lead him to give wise and faithful counsel. It is the task of the social system as a whole, and of all its citizens, to work for the conditions under which everyone will benefit in fair measure from the performance of doctors, lawyers, teachers, and musicians. But I would not see the integrity of these roles undermined in order that the millennium might come sooner. After all, it may never come, and then what would we be left with?

---

[40]In England barristers are regularly hired by the government in all manner of litigation, thereby accomplishing the many-sidedness I call for here. *See* Q. Johnstone and D. Hopson, *Lawyers and Their Work* 374–75 (1967). Why should this not be done in the United States? Perhaps there is fear that this might simply become the occasion for a suspect form of patronage.

[41]This point is due to Albert Sacks and Richard Stewart.

B

Loyalty in Family Practice

Klemm v. Superior Court of Fresno County

CIV. 3543 COURT OF APPEAL, FIFTH DISTRICT DEC. 14, 1977

GEO. A. BROWN, Presiding Justice.

The ultimate issue herein is to what extent one attorney may represent both husband and wife in a noncontested dissolution proceeding where the written consent of each to such representation has been filed with the court.

Dale Klemm (hereinafter "husband") and Gail Klemm (hereinafter "wife") were married and are the parents of two minor children. They separated after six years of marriage, and the wife filed a petition for dissolution of the marriage in propria personna. There was no community property, and neither party owned any substantial personal property. Both parties waived spousal support. The husband was a carpenter with part-time employment.

At the dissolution hearing Attorney Catherine Bailey appeared for the wife. It developed that Bailey is a friend of the husband and wife and because they could not afford an attorney she was acting without compensation. The attorney had consulted with both the husband and wife and had worked out an oral agreement whereby the custody of the minor children would be joint, that is, each would have the children for a period of two weeks out of each month, and the wife waived child support.

The trial judge granted an interlocutory decree and awarded joint custody in accord with the agreement. However, because the wife was receiving aid for dependent children payments from the county, he referred the matter of child support to the Family Support Division of the Fresno County District Attorney's office for investigation and report.

The subsequent report from the family support division recommended that the husband be ordered to pay $25 per month per child (total $50) child support and that this amount be paid to the county as reimbursement for past and present A.F.D.C. payments made and being made to the wife. Bailey, on behalf of the wife, filed a written objection to the recommendation that the husband be required to pay child support.

At the hearing on the report and issue of child support on April 25, 1977, Bailey announced she was appearing on behalf of the husband. She said the parties were "in agreement on this matter, so there is in reality no conflict between them." No written consents to joint representation were filed. On questioning by the court the wife evinced uncertainty as to her position in the litigation. The wife said, "She [Bailey] asked me to come here just as a witness, so I don't feel like I'm taking any action against Dale." The judge pointed out that she (the wife) was still a party. When first asked if she wanted Bailey to continue as her attorney she answered "No." Later she said would consent to Bailey's being relieved as her counsel. She then said she didn't believe she could act as her own attorney but that she consented to Bailey's representing the husband. After this confusing and conflicting testimony and a request for permission to talk to Bailey about it, the judge ordered, over Bailey's objection, that he would not permit Bailey to appear for either the husband or the wife because of a present conflict of interest and ordered the matter continued for one week.

At the continued hearing on May 2, 1977, Bailey appeared by counsel, who filed written consents to joint representation signed by the husband and wife and requested that Bailey be allowed to appear for the husband and wife (who were present in court). The consents, which were identical in form, stated:

"I have been advised by my attorney that a potential conflict of interest exists by reason of her advising and representing my ex-spouse as well as myself. I feel this conflict is purely technical and I request Catherine Bailey to represent me."

The court denied the motion,[1] and the husband and wife have petitioned this court for a writ of mandate to direct the trial court to permit such representation.

Rule 5-102 of the State Bar Rules of Professional Conduct states:

"(A) A member of the State Bar shall not accept professional employment without first disclosing his relation, if any, with the adverse party, and his interest, if any, in the subject matter of the employment. A member of the

[1]The court grounded its ruling upon the following reasons:

"[U]nder our canons of ethics and rules of conduct it would be improper for Miss Bailey to appear in this proceeding on behalf of the respondent where there is not in the court's opinion a theoretical conflict, but an actual conflict of interests in this respect: This proceeding is to determine what amount, if any, the respondent will pay on account of child support to the petitioner Gail Klemm. At this point in time the court is advised and at the April 25th hearing that Mrs. Klemm was receiving public assistance, the end result being that whatever amount ordered paid and in fact paid would be paid to the Family Support Division and would not actually be realized by the petitioner in that such amounts would become a part of the overall monthly grant.

"However, there is obviously a potential if not actual point in time when the petitioner may not be receiving public assistance in which case whatever order, if any, is made to her benefit on account of child support in this proceeding would be the amount subject to modification that she would receive on account of child support at least for some period of time."

254 The Attorney and The Client

State Bar who accepts employment under this rule shall first obtain the client's written consent to such employment.

"(B) A member of the State Bar shall not represent conflicting interests, except with the written consent of all parties concerned." (3B West's Ann. Bus. & Prof. Code (1974 ed., 1977 cum.supp.) foll. & 6076 at p. 65.)²

The California cases are generally consistent with Rule 5-102 permitting dual representation where there is a full disclosure and informed consent by all the parties, at least insofar as a representation pertains to agreements and negotiations prior to a trial or hearing. *(Gregory v. Gregory* (1949) 92 Cal.App.2d 343, 349, 206 P.2d 1122 [marital settlement agreements]: *Davidson v. Davidson* (1949) 90 Cal.App.2d 809, 819, 204 P.2d 71; *Lessing v. Gibbons* (1935) 6 Cal.App.2d 598, 605-606, 45 P.2d 258 [court approved attorney acting for both studio and actress in concluding negotiations and drawing agreements. The court refers to the common practice of attorneys acting for both parties in drawing and dissolving partnership agreements, for grantors and grantees, sellers and buyers, lessors and lessees, and lenders and borrowers].) Where, however, a fully informed consent is not obtained, the duty of loyalty to different clients renders it impossible for an attorney, consistent with ethics and the fidelity owed to clients, to advise one client as to a disputed claim against the other. *(Dettamanti v. Lompoc Union School Dist.* (1956) 143 Cal.App.2d 715, 723, 300 P.2d 78.)

Though an informed consent be obtained, no case we have been able to find sanctions dual representation of conflicting interests if that representation is in conjunction with a trial or hearing where there is an actual, present, existing conflict and the discharge of duty to one client conflicts with the duty to another. (See *Anderson v. Eaton* (1930) 211 Cal. 113, 293 P.788; *Hammett v. McIntyre* (1952) 114 Cal.App.2d 148, 153-154, 249 P.2d 885; *McClure v. Donovan* (1947) 82 Cal.App.2d 664, 666, 186 P.2d 718.) As a matter of law a purported consent to dual representation of litigants with adverse interests at a contested hearing would be neither intelligent nor informed. Such representation would be per se inconsistent with the adversary position of an attorney in litigation, and common sense dictates that it would be unthinkable to permit an attorney to assume a position at a trial or hearing where he could not advocate the interests of one client without adversely injuring those of the other.

However, if the conflict is merely potential, there being no existing dispute or contest between the parties represented as to any point in litigation, then with full disclosure to and informed consent of both clients there may be duel representation at a hearing or trial. *(Burum v. State Compensation Ins. Fund* (1947) 30 Cal.2d 575, 184 P.2d 505; *Lysick v. Walcom* (1968)

---

²Likewise, Rule 4-101 permits the representation of interests adverse to a client or former client with the informed written consent of the client: "A member of the State Bar shall not accept employment adverse to a client or former client, without the informed and written consent of the client or former client, relating to a matter in reference to which he has obtained confidential information by reason of or in the course of his employment by such client or former client." (3B West's Ann.Bus & Prof. Code (1974 ed., 1977 cum.supp.) foll. & 6076 at p. 64.)

258 Cal.App.2d 136, 146-147, 65 Cal.Rptr. 406; see *Arden v. State Bar* (1959) 52 Cal.2d 310, 341 P.2d6.)

In our view the case at bench clearly falls within the latter category. The conflict of interest was strictly potential and not present. The parties had settled their differences by agreement. There was no point of difference to be litigated. The position of each *inter se* was totally consistent throughout the proceedings. The wife did not want child support from the husband, and the husband did not want to pay support for the children. The actual conflict that existed on the issue of support was between the county on the one hand, which argued that support should be ordered, and the husband and wife on the other who consistently maintained the husband should not be ordered to pay support.

While on the face of the matter it may appear foolhardy for the wife to waive child support,[3] other values could very well have been more important to her than such support—such as maintaining a good relationship between the husband and the children and between the husband and herself despite the marital problems—thus avoiding the backbiting, acrimony and ill will which the Family Relations Act of 1970 was, insofar as possible, designed to eliminate. It could well have been if the wife was forced to choose between A.F.D.C. payments to be reimbursed to the county by the husband and no A.F.D.C. payments she would have made the latter choice.

Of course, if the wife at some future date should change her mind and seek child support and if the husband should desire to avoid the payment of such support, Bailey would be disqualified from representing either in a contested hearing on the issue. (Rules of Prof. Conduct, rule 4-101; *Goldstein v. Lees* (1975) 46 Cal.App.3d 614, 120 Cal.Rptr. 253.) There would then exist an actual conflict between them, and an attorney's duty to maintain the confidence of each would preclude such representation. (*Industrial Indem. Co. v. Great American Ins. Co.* (1977) 73 Cal.App.3d 529, 140 Cal. Rptr. 806).

The conclusion we arrive at is particularly congruent with dissolution proceedings under the Family Law Act of 1970, the purpose of which was to discard the concept of fault in dissolution of marriage actions (Civ.Code, §§ 4506, 4509), to minimize the adversary nature of such proceedings and to eliminate conflicts created only to secure a divorce. (*In re Marriage of Cary* (1973) 34 Cal.App.3d 345, 109 Cal.Rptr. 862 (disapproved on other grounds in *Marvin v. Marvin* (1976) 18 Cal.3d 660, 665 134 Cal.Rptr. 815, 557 P.2d 106); *The End of Innocence: Elimination of Fault in California Divorce Law* (1970) 17 *UCLA L.Rev.* 1306). It is contrary to the philosophy of that act to create controversy between the parties where none exists in reality.

We hold on the facts of this case, wherein the conflict was only potential, that if the written consents were knowing and informed and given

---

[3]It is to be noted that the parties' agreement that the children should not receive support would not prevent the court from awarding child support either at the hearing or at some time subsequent thereto. Therefore, the children's rights are not in issue nor are they jeopardized. (*Elkind v. Byck* (1968) 68 Cal.2d 453, 67 Cal.Rptr. 404, 439 P.2d 316; *Krog v. Krog* (1948) 32 Cal.2d 812, 198 P.2d 510.)

after full disclosure by the attorney, the attorney can appear for both of the parties on issues concerning which they fully agree.

It follows that if we were reviewing the order of the trial court after the first hearing held on April 25, 1977, the petition for mandate would have to be denied on the ground that no written consents to joint representation had been procured at that time. Moreover, as a result of the judge's questioning of the wife, he could have reasonably concluded that the wife's consent was not given after a full disclosure and was neither intelligent nor informed.

The order before us, however, is the order entered after the second hearing held on May 2, 1977, at which time the written consents of both the husband and wife, dated that date, were received by the judge without further inquiry of the clients or of the attorney. It could well have been that between April 25 and May 2 and before signing the written consents the parties became apprised of sufficient information to make the written consents intelligent and informed. The situation on May 2 was not necessarily the same as it was on April 25. The record of the May 2 hearing reflects no inquiry whatsoever as to whether the written consents were knowing, informed and given after full disclosure. Thus it appears the trial judge failed to exercise his discretion in accordance with proper legal principles. Accordingly, the cause must be returned to the trial court to make the determination of whether the consents were knowing, informed and given after a full disclosure.

A word as to procedure. Initially, the trial court is entitled to accept properly executed written consents to joint representation at their face value. The judge is entitled to presume the attorney is familiar with the law and code of professional ethics and has complied with the proper standards. However, if the judge has any question regarding whether the proper standards have been observed, it is his duty to either require counsel to inquire further or inquire himself regarding the circumstances of the execution of the written consents and the state of mind of the clients for the purpose of making the necessary factual determination in this regard.[4]

Finally, as a caveat, we hasten to sound a note of warning. Attorneys who undertake to represent parties with divergent interests owe the highest duty to each to make a full disclosure of all facts and circumstances which are necessary to enable the parties to make a fully informed decision regarding the subject matter of the litigation, including the areas of potential conflict and the possibility and desirability of seeking independent legal advice. (*Ishmael v. Millington* (1966) 214 Cal.App.2d 520, 50 Cal.Rptr. 592.) Failing such disclosure, the attorney is civilly liable to the client who suffers loss caused by lack of disclosure. (*Lysick v. Walcom*, supra, 258 Cal.App.2d

---

[4]A trial court has the inherent and statutory power to intervene on its own initiative to inquire into any appearance of impropriety, control the proceedings to remedy the effect, and even disqualify an attorney if that appears necessary. (Code Civ.Proc., & 128; *People v. Superior Court (Greer)* (1977) 19 Cal.3d 255, 261, 137 Cal.Rptr. 476, 561 P.2d 1164, fn. 4; *Meehan v. Hopps* (1955) 45 Cal.2d 213, 215, 288 P.2d 267.) *Cloer v. Superior Court* (1969) 271 Cal.App.2d 143, 76 Cal.Rptr. 217 is not inconsistent with the above cases because the trial court exceeded these powers by disqualifying an attorney where no impropriety existed in the proceeding before it.

136, 65 Cal.Rptr. 406.) In addition, the lawyer lays himself open to charges, whether well founded or not, of unethical and unprofessional conduct. (*Arden v. State Bar, supra,* 52 Cal.2d 310, 341 P.2d 6.) Moreover, the validity of any agreement negotiated without independent representation of each of the parties is vulnerable to easy attack as having been procured by misrepresentation, fraud and overreaching. (*Gregory v. Gregory* (1949) 92 Cal.App.2d 343, 206 P.2d 1122.) It thus behooves counsel to cogitate carefully and proceed cautiously before placing himself/herself in such a position.

As was said in *Anderson v. Eaton, supra,* 211 Cal. 113, 116, 293 P. 788,789:

> "It is also an attorney's duty to protect his client in every possible way, and it is a violation of that duty for him to assume a position adverse or antagonistic to his client without the latter's free and intelligent consent given after full knowledge of all the facts and circumstances. [Citation.] By virtue of this rule an attorney is precluded from assuming any relation which would prevent him from devoting his entire energies to his client's interests. Nor does it matter that the intention and motives of the attorney are honest. The rule is designed not alone to prevent the dishonest practitioner from fraudulent conduct, but as well to preclude the honest practitioner from putting himself in a position where he may be required to choose between conflicting duties, or be led to an attempt to reconcile conflicting interests, rather than to enforce to their full extent the rights of the interest which he should alone represent. [Citation.]"

We have considered respondent's other contentions and find them to be without merit.

It is ordered that a preemptory writ of mandate issue directing the trial court to reconsider Bailey's motion to be allowed to represent both husband and wife, that the court determine if the consent given by each was knowing and informed after a full disclosure by the attorney, and to decide the motion in accordance with the principles set forth in this opinion.

Petitioners shall recover costs.

Family Law—Attorney Mediation of Marital Disputes and Conflict of Interest Considerations

Kimberly Taylor Harbinson

A recent trend toward the increasing use of mediation services and nonadversarial proceedings in the resolution of marital disputes has raised a serious question as to whether attorney mediation of domestic disputes violates the ethical "conflict of interest" standards of the legal profession. This note will examine this concern in light of the need for flexibility in dealing with an often already tragic situation. As a result of the adoption of no-fault divorce legislation in the majority of American jurisdictions[1] it has become increasingly unnecessary to consider fault in divorce actions. Under current divorce laws, fault issues are usually raised only in conjunction with questions of spousal support, property division, and child custody.[2] Though the adversary system is still necessary in a no-fault divorce action when a couple is unable or unwilling to reach a voluntary settlement agreement, frequently an adversarial approach operates against the best interests of the parties by creating conflicts that did not exist originally.[3] Often the parties agree on the desirability of obtaining a divorce and wish to end the marriage in the most expeditious manner possible. They prefer to settle their differences out of court because they both fear the strangeness and formality of the courtroom and wish to avoid the high cost and embarrassment of litigation.[4]

[1]As of October 1980 forty-eight states had adopted no-fault divorce laws. Currently only Illinois and South Dakota require fault grounds for divorce. Freed and Foster, "Divorce in the Fifty States: An Outline." 11 *Fam. L.Q.* 297, 300 (1977); Ill. Ann. Stat. ch. 40 § 401 (Smith-Hurd (1980) 23 Pa. Cons. Stat. Ann. § 201(c) (Purdon 1980 Cum. Supp.) (allowing no-fault divorce): S.D. Compiled Laws Ann. § 25-4-2 (1976).

[2]For a discussion of fault as a consideration in alimony, spousal support, and property division awards pursuant to a no-fault divorce, see Annot. 86 A.L.R.3d 1116 (1978): Freed and Foster, *supra* note 1. at 305-10.

When no-fault divorce statutes fail to specify whether fault is a proper consideration in determining issues of alimony, spousal support, and property division, the matter has been left to judicial determination. E.g., *Huggins v. Huggins*, 57 Ala. App. 691, 331 So. 2d 704 (1976): *Juick v. Juick.* 21 Cal. App. 3d 421, 427, 98 Cal. Rptr. 324. 329 (1971).

[3]Buttenweiser. Horan, Strauss and Williams, "Professional Responsibility in the Practice of Family Law," in *Professional Responsibility of the Lawyer* 73, 74–75 (N. Galsioc ed. 1977). Pickrell and Bendheim. "Family Disputes Mediation—A New Service for Lawyers and Their Clients," 7 *Barriser* 27–28 (1980): Note, Non-Judicial Resolution of Custody and Visitation Disputes. 12 U. Cal. D.L. Rev. 582. 583–84 (1979) [hereinafter cited as Non-Judicial Resolution].

[4]"Meroney, Mediation and Arbitration of Separation and Divorce Agreements." 15 *Wake Forest L. Rev.* 467, 469 (1979).

The public's desire for an alternative to courtroom resolution of marital conflicts has resulted in the increasing use of mediation services. In the mediation process the couple meets with a neutral third party who takes an active part in the discussion of issues and makes affirmative suggestions for the resolution of disagreements.[5] The mediator's objectives in a separation or divorce case are to aid the parties in reaching an acceptable compromise of their positions and to facilitate a voluntary settlement.[6]

In order for the mediation process to be successful, the mediator must encourage the couple to assess their demands realistically and to accommodate their differences, rather than to magnify them. The parties must be willing to communicate and to arrive at a fair settlement without consideration of fault.[7] Theoretically, parties who voluntarily and maturely have reached their own agreement, rather than a court-imposed one, are more likely to be satisfied with the results and less likely to avoid compliance or to engage in repetitive and costly litigation.[8]

Public demand for these mediation services has developed for several reasons. Mediation of the uncontested divorce reduces the artificially created hostility which can be a by-product of adversarial proceedings.[9] Mediation also reduces the financial burden of a contested divorce case.[10] This burden can be extremely debilitating to individuals who are suddenly responsible for the maintenance of two households instead of one. Additionally, a mediated custody agreement is preferable to a court-imposed settlement in several ways. It is evident that in most cases the parents are the individuals who have the greatest understanding of the needs of their children. They are, therefore, most capable of determining what is in the "best interests of the child."[11] When the parents resolve custody matters privately, they are no longer at the mercy of a judge who often has little knowledge of the needs and interests of the particular family.[12] The chil-

[5]"Mediation" is to be distinguished from "conciliation" in which the neutral third party takes a more passive role, analogous to that of a marriage counselor. The conciliator merely creates a situation that will be conducive to the objective discussion of issues. He does not attempt to interject personal suggestions for compromise. Meroney, *supra* note 4, at 470. The mediator may alternate between the roles of conciliator and mediator, depending on the course of the discussion. Id. at 470–71. n. 21. In both mediation and conciliation the third party promotes negotiation, while in arbitration the neutral third party serves in a quasi-judicial role. The parties have submitted to arbitration with a prior agreement to accept as final and binding the decision of the arbitrator. Id: Pickrell and Bendheim, *supra* note 3.

[6]Id.; Meroney. *supra* note 4. at 470.

[7]Meroney, *supra* note 4, at 486; Steinberg. "The Therapeutic Potential of the Divorce Process," 62 *A.B.A.J.* 617, 619 (1976).

[8]Steinberg, *supra* note 7, at 620.

[9]See authorities cited in note 3 and accompanying text *supra*.

[10]This is particularly true in a contested custody case which may involve expert witness fees for psychologists and social workers as well as lenghty depositions and high legal fees. See Non-Judicial Resolution at 585–86.

[11]See Spencer and Zammit, "Mediation-Arbitration: A Proposal for Private Resolution of Disputes Between Divorced or Separated Parents," 1976 *Duke L.J.* 911, 932–33.

[12]Id. at 916–17, 939.

dren are not subjected to the psychologically damaging strain of an adversarial procedure.[13] They are not put in the difficult position of determining which parent with whom to live.[14] Instead these decisions are made by the parents through the give-and-take of the mediation process.

Mediation of the uncontested divorce also promotes the important public interest of relieving crowded court dockets[15] by reducing the number of contested divorce cases going to court, specifically child custody cases. When the parties are able to resolve custody disputes during the mediation process there is no necessity for a prolonged initial custody hearing.[16] Furthermore, if the parties have reached their own custody agreement they will feel responsible for its success and will be less prone to litigate matters of custody and visitation after the marriage is dissolved.[17]

Despite public demand for mediation services[18] many lawyers are reluctant, for several reasons, to act as mediators in marital disputes. The role of neutral mediator is quite different from the attorney's traditional role as an advocate who acts as a "hired gun" for his client.[19] Attorneys may believe they lack sufficient training in this form of client counseling.[20] They may fear that attorney mediation of domestic disputes violates the ethical standards of the legal profession.[21] In addition, many mediation services prefer not to employ attorneys as mediators on the assumption that legal training is inconsistent with the tempering of client demands necessary to make the mediation process successful.[22] Thus attorneys are not currently involved in mediation in large numbers.

In part because of the unavailability of attorney mediators, divorcing spouses have turned to mediation and conciliation services organized or funded by state legislatures,[23] judicial systems,[24] and privately operated

[13]See Non-Judicial Resolution, *supra* note 3, at 584–85.

[14]See Simons, "The Invisible Scars of Children of Divorce." 7 *Barrister* 14 (1980). Simons states that the number of children affected by divorce is increasing. In 1956, 361,000 children's parents became divorced. That number has tripled to approximately one million children a year currently. Id. at 15.

[15]See note 24 *infra*.

[16]Non-Judicial Resolution. *supra* note 3, at 584.

[17]Id. at 593–95.

[18]See text accompanying notes 9–17 *supra*.

[19]G. Hazard. *"Ethics in the Practice of Law"* 80 (1978): Pick, "The Go-Between," 8 *Student Law* 39, 55 (1980).

[20]See O. Coogler, *Structured Mediation in Divorce Settlement* 85 (1978); Shaffer. "Lawyers, Counselors. and Counselors at Law". 61 *A.B.A.J.* 854, 855 (1975).

[21]See notes 37–44 and accompanying text *infra*: Note. Simultaneous Representation: Transaction Resolution in the Adversary System. 28 *Case W. Res. L. Rev.* 86, 87 (1977).

[22]Pack, *supra* note 19, at 58–59. According to Pick, lawyer-mediators comprise only 15% of the national total. Id. at 59. Lawyers who work as mediators with the American Arbitration Association are not permitted to give legal advice or function as attorneys. Pickrell and Bendheim, *supra* note 3. at 28. But see Non-Judicial Resolution. *supra* note 3. at 596 n. 78. Under the Family Law Mediator Program, established by the San Fernando Valley Bar Association in California, family law attorneys volunteer to act as mediators in family law matters. Id.

[23]The New York Court Act provides for informal conciliation services available on the petition of one of the parties. N.Y. Jud. Law §§ 911-26 (McKinney 1975). See Blum, "Concilia-

organizations.[25] Most of these services are staffed by mediators who are trained in the behavioral sciences or who have received specialized training as mediators in their employment.[26] Apparently, however, the nonattorney mediator is not allowed to give any type of legal advice because of state statutes prohibiting the unauthorized practice of law.[27] The parties, consequently, may agree on issues of property settlement, support and

---

tion Courts: Instruments of Peace," 41 *J. St. B. Cal.* 33 (1966) for a description of conciliation courts in California. See also Jenkins. "Divorce California Style." 9 *Student Law.* 31 (1981) for a discussion of mandatory conciliation procedures in California.

    The Dispute Settlement Center in Chapel Hill. N.C. received $7,000.00 funding from the North Carolina General Assembly in 1979 and $27,000.00 funding for the year ending June 30. 1981. Interview with Evelyn Smith, Program Coordinator of the Dispute Settlement Center of Chapel Hill, N.C., (Oct. 1, 1980). There are predictions that the New York and Florida legislatures will provide similar funding for neighborhood dispute resolution centers in the near future. Pick, *supra* note 19, at 59.

    [24]Judicial mediation was attempted in 1979 in a superior court in Riverside County, California because of a severe backlog of civil cases. A judge was removed from his regular caseload and assigned to handle settlement conferences exclusively. The program resulted in the settlement of 614 cases in ten months and in the elimination of the backlog. Rich, "Personal Viewpoint: An Experiment with Judicial Mediation." 66 *A.B.A.J.* 530 (1980).

    The Domestic Relations Department of the Los Angeles Superior Court in California is another example of judicially sponsored mediation. This Department refers parties to the Center for Legal Psychiatry at U.C.L.A. for in-depth divorce counseling. Non-Judicial Resolution. at 596 n. 79.

    [25]There are private mediation services throughout the United States. The American Arbitration Association, Family Dispute Services, provides mediators for marital disputes. Pickrell and Bendheim, *supra* note 3, at 28; Non-Judicial Resolution. *supra* note 3, at 592.

    The Family Mediation Association, a nonprofit organization located in Winston-Salem, N.C., provides mediators to couples at an hourly fee. The association also provides the facilities for mediation sessions. For a description of the procedure used by the Family Mediation Association, see O. Coogler, *supra* note 20, at 23–29, 31–38. 131–44, Meroney, *supra* note 4, at 476.

    Labor management negotiators in New York City began the Institute for Mediation and Conflict Resolution in New York in 1969. The Institute now supervises two dispute settlement centers in New York. Standord, "Gentle Art of Settling Family Disputes," *Charlotte Observer*, Sept. 14, 1980. *(Parade Magazine)* at 7-8.

    [26]O. Coogler, *supra* note 20, at 75–78. American Arbitration Association mediators undergo approximately 35 hours of training with the AAA. Pick, *supra* note 19, at 39. Mediators for the Dispute Settlement Center in Chapel Hill originally received approximately forty hours of training from the Community Relations Service of the U.S. Justice Department. Currently the Center administers its own weekend training sessions. Interview with Evelyn Smith, *supra* note 23.

    [27]For a summary of state statutes and cases dealing with the unauthorized practice of law see Chicago American Bar Foundation, *Unauthorized Practice Handbook* (J. Fischer and D. Lachman eds. 1972).

    The Unauthorized Practice of Law Committee of the North Carolina State Bar determined in 1980 that the preparation of a contract by a nonattorney mediator constituted the unauthorized practice of law. Apparently the basis for the decision was that the contract contained terms "whereby a husband and wife agree to give up rights and remedies under the divorce, alimony, and other statutes by substituting binding arbitration for these rights." Council Action/Committee Reports, Unauthorized Practice of Law. 27 N.C. St. B.Q. 4, 5 (1980). The Committee further decided that advice by the organization as to the "advisability of and legal effect of entering into such an agreement also constitutes the unauthorized practice of law." Id. at 7.

child custody with no knowledge of the legal rights that they are relinquishing or of the tax advantages that they are foregoing.[28]

Because legal advice is frequently desirable prior to entering into a final separation agreement, it is often necessary for the parties to employ an attorney outside the mediation process in order to ensure the legal validity of their agreement.[29] Even at this stage a single attorney may be reluctant to handle the case for both parties.[30] The couple, therefore, incurs the previously avoided expense of hiring separate attorneys, along with the risk that the lawyer's assumption of an adversarial role will cause hostilities that were hoped to be averted.[31]

The need for attorney mediators is growing because of a combination of factors. The increasing demand for mediation services in general[32] has surpassed the availability of nonattorney mediation services.[33] Furthermore, legal advice is vital in any mediation process aimed at settling property and custody disputes. In light of this developing trend, attorneys should consider whether hesitation to serve as mediators is justified.

There are two major reasons for attorney reluctance to become involved in mediation. The first is a belief by the individual attorney that he lacks sufficient counseling skills to adequately control discussions with such potential for emotional volatility. It is relatively easy, however, to remedy a deficiency in counseling skills. The attorney who lacks training or experience with mediation counseling could participate in training sessions similar to those attended by lay mediators.[34] Co-mediation with a trained counselor could also be used to supplement the skills of the inexperienced attorney, although this may increase the cost of mediation.[35]

[28]Under Family Mediation Association (FMA) procedure the couple selects an "advisory attorney" from a panel of attorneys who have applied for membership in the FMA. The couple may also choose a nonpanel attorney if the attorney agrees to abide by FMA rules and procedures. The selected attorney supervises the drafting and execution of the final settlement agreement, impartially explains terms of the agreement to each party, and gives advice—including tax advice—concerning the legal implications of the agreement. O. Coogler, *supra* note 20, at 86, 142, 172, 193–202.

[29]American Arbitration Association mediators draft a "Memorandum in Mediation" for the parties. The couple then takes the agreement to an attorney who drafts the final separation agreement. Pickrell and Bendheim *supra* note 3, at 28.

[30]See notes 45–53 and accompanying text *infra.*

[31]See generally G. Hazard, *supra* note 19, at 80.

[32]Mediation services are expected to spread to smaller cities as a result of the popularity of mediation in urban areas. Pick, *supra* note 19, at 59.

[33]See Steinberg, *supra* note 7, at 618.

[34]See note 26 and accompanying text *supra.* Merder, "The Need for an Expanded Role for the Attorney in Divorce Counseling." 4 *Fam. L.Q.* 280, 288 (1970); Mussehl, "From Advocate to Counselor: The Emerging Role of the Family Law Practitioner," 12 *Gonz. L. Rev.* 443, 448 (1977); Non-Judicial Resolution, *supra* note 3, at 597–98.

See New York State Trial Lawyers' Association Code of Professional Responsibility. [1975] I Fam. L. Rep. (BNA) 3115. Section 6(a) of the Code states, "(t)he matrimonial lawyer shall encourage, counsel and advise negotiation toward the settlement of marital and/or family problems by agreement before litigation." Id. at 3116.

[35]Interview with Susan Lewis, a private practitioner in Durham and Chapel Hill, North Carolina. (Oct. 8, 1980). Ms. Lewis has practiced marital mediation for three years and occasionally works in conjunction with a psychologist. She suggests that any attorney who is

The second major factor inhibiting attorney involvement in mediation services pertains to ethical considerations. The most significant ethical dilemma arising out of attorney mediation of domestic disputes is posed by the "conflict of interest" provisions of the American Bar Association (ABA) Code of Professional Responsibility.[36] The applicable provision, Disciplinary Rule (DR) 5-105(A), requires that a lawyer decline employment if the employment will adversely affect his judgment or if he will be required to represent different interests.[37] The purpose of the restriction on multiple representation is to maintain the lawyer's independent professional judgment and to ensure adequate representation of the interests of each client.[38] Under a separate provision of the Code, DR 5-105(C), however, a lawyer may represent multiple clients if three conditions are met. First, it must be *obvious* that he can adequately represent the interests of each client. Second, each client must *consent* to the joint representation. Third, the consent of each client must be given *after full disclosure* of the possible effect of multiple representation on the exercise of the lawyer's independent professional judgment.[39] The lawyer is instructed to "resolve all doubts against the propriety of the representation" if the clients have "potentially differing interests."[40]

The presence or absence of litigation is a factor in determining the propriety of representing multiple clients. The lawyer is advised that he should *never* represent in litigation multiple clients with differing interests.[41] This rule has been applied even when both parties have consented

---

inexperienced in mediation consider working with a trained counselor to provide the counseling necessary in the mediation process. Even after obtaining sufficient counseling skills, the attorney may wish to work with a psychologist in cases in which the parties are highly emotional. See Steinberg, *supra* note 7.

To avoid a violation of Disciplinary Rule (DR) 3-102(A) of the ABA Code of Professional Responsibility, the attorney should refrain from sharing legal fees with the nonlawyer. American Bar Association, Code of Professional Responsibility, DR 3-102(A) (1979), reprinted in T. Morgan and R. Rotunda. 1979 Standards Supplement to Problems and Materials on Professional Responsibility 25 (1979) [hereinafter cited as ABA Code]. The attorney should also avoid forming a partnership with the nonlawyer to prevent a violation of DR 3-103(A). Id. at 3-103(A).

[36]E.g., ABA Code, *supra* note 35, at Ethical Consideration (EC) 5-14, 5-15, 5-16, 5-19, 5-20. DR 5-105(A)-(C).

[37]Id. at DR 5-105(A). The text of DR 5-105(A) reads:

A lawyer shall decline proffered employment if the exercise of his independent professional judgment in behalf of a client will be or is likely to be adversely affected by the acceptance of the proffered employment, or if it would be likely to involve him in representing different interests, except to the extent permitted under DR 5-105(C).

[38]Id. at EC 5-14, DR 5-105(C). The ABA has stated that the underlying view for precluding the attorney from representing conflicting interests is that "a client is entitled to the benefit of his lawyer's undivided judgment, unfettered by commitments or loyalty to others." ABA Comm. on Professional Ethics Informal Opinions, No. 1233 (1972).

[39]ABA Code, *supra* note 35, at DR 5-105(C).

[40]Id. at EC 5-15.

[41](Emphasis added.) See, e.g., *Klemm v. Superior Court*, 75 Cal. App. 3d 893. 142 Cal. Rptr. 509 (1977); *Greene v. Greene*, 47 N.Y.2d 447, 391 N.E.2d 1355, 418 N.Y.S.2d 379 (1979); *Jedwabny v. Philadelphia Transp. Co.*, 390 Pa. 231, 135 A.2d 252 (1957).

to multiple representation after full disclosure of potential undesirable consequences.[42]

When no litigation is involved, the attorney must balance factors that indicate the potential harm to clients from joint representation against those favoring the employment of only one attorney. Some of the factors to be considered include the degree to which the client's interests potentially differ, the possibility of increased hostility and expense resulting from the employment of separate attorneys, the desire of the parties to have the attorney serve in a neutral capacity as opposed to taking an adversarial role, and the ability of the clients to protect their interests with only limited representation.[43] The attorney must bear in mind the possibility that an initially uncontested divorce may escalate into an action requiring litigation. If this should occur the attorney would be required to withdraw from representation of either party, resulting in hardship to the clients.[44]

If the attorney accepts multiple employment in a divorce action, and his decision is later found to have been erroneous, the penalties could be severe. A party alleging injury caused by the conflict of interest may bring a civil malpractice action against the attorney,[45] who could be sanctioned by a legal ethics committee,[46] and the divorce decree could be subject to collateral attack by a party alleging fraud, duress, or overreaching.[47]

[42]See cases cited in note 41 *supra*. A possible explanation for this distinction is that the "obvious" standard of DR 5-105(C) creates a per se rule under which multiple representation can never be undertaken when the parties are opponents in litigation. Kaufman, "A Critical First Look at the Model Rules of Professional Conduct," 66 *A.B.A.J.* 1074, 1079 (1980). The "conflict of interest" provision of the Model Rules of Professional Conduct omits the "obvious" requirement of the current Code. Discussion Draft of ABA Model Rules of Professional Conduct § 1.8, reprinted in [1980] 26 Crim. L. Rep. (BNA) (Supp. Feb. 20, 1980) [hereinafter cited as Model Rules of Professioal Conduct]. See note 72 *supra*.

Another rationale for the distinction is that withdrawal of the attorney due to an increase in conflict will normally have less detrimental effect on the clients if the matter is not currently in litigation. R. Wise, *Legal Ethics* 77–78 (2d ed. 1970); ABA Code, *supra* note 35, at EC 5-15.

[43]Morgan, "The Evolving Concept of Professional Responsibility," 90 *Harv. L. Rev.* 702, 727 (1977), Weddington, "A Fresh Approach to Preserving Independent Judgment—Canon 6 of the Proposed Code of Professional Responsibility," *Ariz. L. Rev.* 31, 35–6 (1969).

[44]ABA Code, *supra* note 35, at EC 5-15; "Non-Judicial Resolution," *supra* note 3, at 597-99. Note, *supra* note 21, at 94.

[45]E.g., *Woodruff v. Tomlin*, 593 F.2d 33 (6th Cir. 1979); *Lysick v. Walcom*, 258 Cal. App. 2d 136, 65 Cal. Rptr. 406 (1968); *Ishmael v. Millington*, 241 Cal. App. 2d 520, 50 Cal. Rptr. 592 (1966); *Kelly v. Greason*, 23 N.Y.2d 368, 244 N.E.2d 456, 296 N.Y.S.2d 937 (1968).

The consent of the parties to joint representation would not bar recovery in a malpractice action if the attorney has violated the ordinary standard of care by the initial acceptance of multiple employment by failing to maintain a neutral position with the parties or by failing to adequately disclose the limited nature of joint representation. *Ishmael v. Millington*, 241 Cal. App. 2d 520. 50 Cal. Rptr. 592 (1966); Note, *supra* note 21, at 94.

[46]E.g., *People v. Selby*, 156 Colo. 17, 396 P.2d 598 (1964); *In re Opacek*. 257 Minn. 600. 101 N.W.2d 606 (1960). See Annot. 17 A.L.R.3d 835, 844-45 (1968).

[47]E.g., *Jensen v. Jensen*, 97 Idaho 922, 557 P.2d 200 (1976); *Holmes v. Holmes*, 145 Ind. App. 52, 248 N.E.2d 564 (1969). See *Smith v. Price*, 253 N.C. 285, 116 S.E.2d 733 (1960). Note, "Possible Effect of Conflict of Interests in a Divorce Action Arising from Only One Attorney Obtaining the Divorce Decree," 15 *Ala. L. Rev.* 502, 507 (1963).

But see *Brosie v. Stockton*, 105 Ariz. 574, 468 P.2d 933 (1970) (court refused to set aside a property settlement because plaintiff failed to allege damages resulting from joint representation): *Todd v. Rhodes*, 108 Kan. 64, 193 P. 894 (1920) (when husband employed the same

Although the Code leaves open the possibility of multiple representation, some jurisdictions absolutely preclude multiple representation in a divorce action, even where no-fault and dissolution-of-marriage statutes have been adopted.[48] The four principal reasons given for this rule are: (1) the existence of inherently differing interests between the spouses that may later become the subject of adversary litigation.[49] (2) the existence of obstacles that prevent a lawyer representing both spouses from obtaining the information necessary for the adequate representation of the parties;[50] (3) the need to avoid an appearance of impropriety,[51] and (4) the interest of the state in child custody, settlement of property rights and the marital status of the parties.[52]

Before one concludes that an attorney should *never* represent both parties in an uncontested divorce action, it should be noted that such representation is permissible in many jurisdictions if the parties have previously resolved all conflicts and if the attorney has obtained the consent of both clients after full disclosure of the implications of common representation.[53] Furthermore, there are valid policy reasons for allowing the attorney to act as a mediator.[54]

In mediation, the parties enter the process with the intent to resolve conflicts and to avoid litigation.[55] Although the interests of the couple diverge in some areas, they are not yet "conflicting" because the parties have not decided to pursue them aggressively.[56] The attorney can inform the clients from the outset that he is not acting as an advocate for either

---

attorney to represent both parties to the divorce he could not subsequently attack the divorce on grounds of joint representation); *Halvorsen v. Halvorsen*, 3 Wash. App. 827, 479 P.2d 161 (1970) (court refused to set aside property settlement because joint representation by one attorney was proper under the circumstances).

[48]Ohio Bar Ethics Committee, Formal Opinion No. 30, reprinted in [1975] 1 Fam. L. Rep. (BNA) 3109, N.Y. County Law. Ass'n Comm. on Professional Ethics. Opinion No. 258 (1972) reprinted in 2 Opinions of the Committee on Professional Ethics of the Association of the Bars of the City of New York and New York County Lawyers' Association (1980) [hereinafter cited as N.Y. Opinions]: Note, *supra* note 21, at 95.

[49]Ohio Bar Ethics Comm., *supra* note 48, at 3109; N.Y. Opinions, *supra* note 48.

[50]Ohio Bar Ethics Comm., *supra* note 48, at 3110; Note, *supra* note 21, at 99. Obstacles include the reluctance of the parties to disclose all relevant information because they fear that harmful disclosures may be used later by the opposing spouse in a contested action. It is a general rule of evidence that the attorney-client privilege does not extend to a communication made by a joint client if it is relevant to the common interests of the parties and is offered in an action between the clients. Uniform Rule of Evidence 502(d)(5) reprinted in Federal Judicial Center, Federal Rules of Evidence for United States Courts and Magistrates 253, 269 (1975) [hereinafter cited as Rules of Evidence]. See text accompanying notes 86–87 infra.

[51]Note, *supra* note 21, at 99. See Note, *supra* note 47, at 507.

[52]Note *supra* note 21, at 98. See *Greene v. Greene*, 47 N.Y.2d 447, 391 N.E.2d 1355, 418 N.Y.S.2d 379 (1979); Mich. St. B.A. Comm. on Professional Ethics Opinion No. 85 (1945), reprinted in 38 Mich. St. B.J. 112 (1959). This argument is somewhat outdated by current divorce laws that allow the couple, by voluntary agreement, to deal with the incidents of marriage in any reasonable manner. See note I and accompanying text *supra*.

[53] *Klemm v. Superior Court of Fresno County*, 75 Cal. App. 3d 893, 142 Cal. Rptr. 509 (1977). See [1977] 3 Fam. L. Rep. (BNA) 2633; Note, *supra* note 21, at 95–109.

[54]See notes 9–17 and accompanying text *supra*.

[55]See text accompanying note 17 *supra*.

[56]G. Hazard, 78–79.

party. Consequently there is little possibility that either spouse will rely on the attorney for adversarial advice. Since the attorney does not hold himself out as being the representative of each party in an adversarial situation, any appearance of impropriety is lessened. In a sense the mediator is acting as the attorney for the mediation process rather than for the individual clients.[57] He must, therefore, inform the clients that he will withdraw from the representation of either party prior to the subsequent divorce action, whether it is contested or not.[58]

Although the attorney-mediator has a fiduciary duty to give correct and appropriate advice on tax matters and on the possible legal effects of any agreement, he should not propose a specific plan for the terms of the agreement.[59] These decisions ultimately are left to the discretion of the couple. Upon entering mediation the parties have usually decided that they have the emotional maturity and independence necessary to protect their own interests and to conduct their own negotiations. A client, however, who is insecure about his or her ability to make an independent decision should be advised to employ an outside attorney for advice on choosing a particular course of action.[60] If the attorney determines that one of the parties is particularly vulnerable to domination by the other spouse, or is willing to give up everything to "get it all over with," he should advise the dominated party to retain separate counsel, and the attorney-mediator should seriously consider total withdrawal from mediation.[61]

* * *

[An] examination of the ethical guidelines for attorneys indicates that attorney-mediation is a permissible option. The interests of both the attorney-mediator and the mediating couple, however, require the following precautions to be taken if an attorney assumes the mediation role. First, the attorney should ascertain whether the couple's goal on entering mediation is to reach a fair settlement without consideration of fault. He should be certain that both spouses are capable of making informed and independent decisions about support, property, and custody matters. If either party appears unable to make such decisions, he or she should be advised to retain outside counsel for advice during the mediation process.[94]

Second, in order to comply with the disclosure provisions of DR 5-105(C), the attorney should hold an initial information session with the

[57]Id. at 58–68.

[58]See ABA Code, *supra* note 35, at EC 5-20; N.Y. Opinions, *supra* note 48, 258; Code of Professional Responsibility of the North Carolina State Bar, N.C. Gen. Stat. App. VII, EC 5-20, at 337 (1979 Cu. Supp.) [hereinafter cited as N.C. Code].

[59]Interview with Susan Lewis, *supra* note 35; see Non-Judicial Resolution, *supra* note 3, at 598.

[60]Interview with Susan Lewis, note 35 *supra*.

[61]See Steinberg, *supra* note 7, at 619; Note, *supra* note 21, at 100.

[94]The parties may also be permitted to have outside counsel present during mediation sessions. Before accompanying a client into mediation, the attorney should be fully informed of the client's wish to reach a settlement through a nonadversarial approach. The attorney should participate in the session only to the extent of advising her client on the consequences of the particular courses of action.

parties to disclose the possible adverse effects of mediation. This disclosure should include a warning that mediation sessions may not be confidential in an action between the parties,[95] a warning that the attorney would be required to withdraw from mediation if hostilities increase,[96] and a warning that the attorney is not acting as an advocate for either party. The attorney should then obtain a written and informed consent from each spouse to prevent later allegations of fraud, duress, or undue influence.[97]

Third, if litigation is underway prior to the commencement of mediation, the parties should be required to dismiss or suspend the court action. If the parties decide to resort to litigation during the mediation process, the attorney-mediator should withdraw from further involvement.[98]

Finally, if the couple reaches a mutually acceptable settlement, the attorney should draft the agreement and fully explain its provisions to both parties. He should then terminate his representation of either spouse in any matter concerning their marital relationship. He is precluded from representing either party in a subsequent divorce action, even if uncontested.[99]

Attorney mediation is a permissible and desirable alternative to the adversarial approach in reaching divorce settlements in many jurisdictions. Although an attorney-mediator must be fully aware of his ethical responsibilities and willing to sharpen his counseling skills, the opportunity to fill a need is great. The individual and societal benefits[100] of providing mediation as an alternative to litigation in divorce cases makes it an option worth pursuing.

[95]The couple may be asked to sign a confidentiality agreement stating that each party agrees to forego his or her right to subpoena the mediator or mediation work product in any subsequent legal action. The agreement should also state that all statements made during mediation are considered client confidences and secrets, and are for the purpose of compromise. See notes 81-93 and accompanying text *supra.*

[96]See note 58 and accompanying text *supra.* Section 5.2 of the Model Roles of Professional Conduct require withdrawal of the attorney-mediator if: 1) either of the clients requests his withdrawal; 2) if any of the conditions for mediation listed in Section 5.1 cannot be met; or 3) if it becomes apparent that a mutually advantageous adjustment of interests cannot be made. Model Rules of Professional Conduct, *supra* note 42, at 23.

[97]Note *supra* note 21, at 103-04. Disclosure standards may be different for different types of clients. With a less informed or educated client the lawyer must take greater care to ascertain whether the client comprehends the full implications of mediation. See *In Re Farr,* 264 Ind. 153, 340 N.E.2d 777 (1976); *Holmes v. Holmes,* 145 Ind. App. 52, 248 N.E.2d 208 (1969); *In Re Dolan,* 76 N.J. I, 384 A.2d 1076 (1978).

[98]ABA Code, *supra* note 35, at EC 5-15.

[99]Id. at EC 5-20.

[100]See notes 9–17 and accompanying text *supra.*

C

Loyalty and the Corporate Lawyer

Hull v. Celanese Corporation

UNITED STATES COURT OF APPEALS, SECOND CIRCUIT, 1975 513
F.2D 568

TENNEY, * District Judge. This Court todays hears the appeal from an
order of disqualification of plaintiff's counsel, the law firm of Rabinowitz,
Boundin & Standard ("the Rabinowitz firm"). The question at issue is
whether a law firm can take on, as a client, a lawyer for the opposing party
in the very litigation against the opposing party. Factually, the case is novel
and we approach it mindful of the important competing interests present.
* * *

The complaint in this action was brought by plaintiff-appellant Joan
Hull ("Hull"), an employee of Celanese Corporation ("Celanese") against
Celanese alleging sex-based discrimination in employment in violation of
Title VII of the Civil Rights Act of 1964, 42 U.S.C.A. & 2000e et seq. In its
answer, Celanese denied the material allegations of the complaint. Thereafter, the Rabinowitz firm filed a motion seeking leave for five other
women to intervene as plaintiffs in the action. One of the proposed inter-
venors was Donata A. Delulio, an attorney on the corporate legal staff of
Celanese. Celanese opposed the proposed intervention and additionally
sought the disqualification of the Rabinowitz firm based on the risk that
confidential information received by Delulio as Celanese's attorney might
be used by the Rabinowitz firm against Celanese in the prosecution of the
joint Hull-Delulio claims.

The trial court denied Delulio's motion to intervene and subsequently
ordered the disqualification of the Rabinowitz film.

Judge Owen premised the denial of intervention on the fact that
Delulio had been active in the defense of this very action, thus raising a
serious risk of disclosure of confidential information. He found the opportunity for even inadvertent disclosure to be ever-present.

In granting the motion to disqualify the Rabinowitz firm, Judge Owen
clearly recognized three competing interests: (1) Hull's interest in freely
selecting counsel of her choice, (2) Celanese's interest in the trial free from
the risk of even inadvertent disclosures of confidential information, and (3)
the public's interest in the scrupulous administration of justice. In balanc-

* United States District Judge for the Southern District of New York, sitting by designation.

ing these competing interests, the trial court acknowledged the right of Hull to counsel of her choice, but held the interests of Celanese and the public to be predominant. Based upon the relationship between Delulio and the Rabinowitz firm, the preparation by the Rabinowitz firm on the motion to intervene, supporting affidavits, and amended complaint, and the contents of those documents, Judge Owen concluded:

> "The foregoing contents of affidavits prepared by Delulio and the Rabinowitz office are some evidence, in my opinion, of the possibility that Delulio, unquestionably possessed of information within the attorney-client privilege, did in fact transmit some of it to the Rabinowitz firm, consciously or unconsciously."

The trial court felt that the continued retention of the Rabinowitz firm would create at least the appearance of impropriety due to the on-going possibility for improper disclosure.[1] For the reasons stated *infra*, we must affirm.

The unusual factual situation presented here bears repetition in some detail. Hull's employment by Celanese began in 1963; Delulio's employment there began in July 1972. In September of 1972, Hull filed charges with the Equal Employment Opportunity Commission ("EEOC") against Celanese alleging sex-based discrimination in employment. Delulio was assigned to work on the defense of the *Hull* case in February of 1973 and her work on the case continued until September 1973.[2] In the interim, the complaint herein was filed.[3]

It was during September of 1973 that Hull and Delulio met socially for the first time. Two months later Delulio approached Hull to ascertain the name of the law firm representing Hull. As a result of this conversation, Delulio contacted the Rabinowitz firm on November 9, and on November 15, 1973 the Rabinowitz firm filed sex discrimination charges on behalf of Delulio with the EEOC. Delulio thereafter consulted with the Association of the Bar of the City of New York regarding, *inter alia*, the propriety of

[1]Judge Owen initially considered holding a hearing to determine whether there had been actual disclosures, but decided in the negative. He concluded that "a hearing would be self-defeating since it would be necessary to reveal to the Rabinowitz firm in some specificity the extent of Celanese's disclosures to Miss Delulio in the course of ascertaining to what extent, if any, that information reached them.

[2]Delulio characterized her work on the *Hull* case as follows:

> "During the six months that I worked on that case I studied the general regulations of the Equal Employment Opportunities Commission, its procedures and the law on sex discrimination generally. I obtained specific information from the personnel department at the division concerning salaries and hiring practices. I attended on [sic] interview of the employee's [Hull's] superior, and attended one interview of another division employee. I participated in a conference with outside consultants hired by the corporation to prepare statistical information regarding employment within the division. I obtained inter-office memoranda and prepared a memorandum myself regarding the case."

[3] Filed on August 27, 1973.

her intervention in the *Hull* action. By letter dated March 12, 1974, the Association of the Bar of the City of New York advised Delulio against intervention. Subsequently, the motion herein seeking intervention on behalf of Delulio and four other women was filed. Two weeks later Celanese cross-moved to deny intervention and to disqualify the Rabinowitz firm.

* * *

The Rabinowitz firm argues that they had never worked for Celanese and therefore never had direct access to any confidence of Celanese. They maintain that they carefully cautioned Delulio not to reveal any information received in confidence as an attorney for Celanese, but rather to confine her revelations to them to the facts of her own case. This, they contend would avoid even an indirect transferal of confidential information. They conclude that since they never got any information either directly or indirectly, they could not use the information either consciously or unconsciously.

This argument, somewhat technical in nature, seems to overlook the spirit of Canon 9 as interpreted by this Court in *Emle*. We credit the efforts of the Rabinowitz firm to avoid the receipt of any confidence. Nonetheless, *Emle* makes it clear that the court need not "inquire whether the lawyer did, *in fact*, receive confidential information. * * *" Emle Industries, Inc. v. Patentex, Inc., *supra*, 478 f.2d at 571. Rather, "where 'it can reasonably be said that in the course of the former representation the attorney *might* have acquired information related to the subject matter of his subsequent representation,' *T. C. Theatre Corp., supra* [113 F. Supp.], at 269 (emphasis supplied), it is the court's duty to order the attorney disqualified." Id at 571. The breach of confidence would not have to be proved; it is presumed in order to preserve the spirit of the Code.

The Rabinowitz firm had notice that Delulio had worked on the defense of the *Hull* case and should have declined representation when approached. Had Delulio joined the firm as an assistant counsel in the *Hull* case, they would have been disqualified. Here she joined them, as it were, as a client. The relation is no less damaging and the presumption in *Emle* should apply.

Our holding herein is distinguishable from the result reached in *Meyerhofer v. Empire Fire and Marine Insurance Co.,* 497 F.2d 1190 (2d Cir.), certiorari denied 419 U.S. 998, 95 S.Ct. 314, 42 L.Ed. 2d 272 (1974). There it was held that disqualification was unnecessary since the lawyer had acted properly in defending himself "against 'an accusation of wrongful conduct.' " Id. 497 F.2d at 1194-95.

The novel factual situation presented here dictates a narrow reading of this opinion. This decision should not be read to imply that either Hull or Delulio cannot pursue her claim of employment discrimination based on sex. The scope of this opinion must, of necessity, be confined to the facts presented and not read as a broadbrush approach to disqualification.

The preservation of public trust both in the scrupulous administration of justice and in the integrity of the bar is paramount. Recognizably important are Hull's right to counsel of her choice and the consideration of the judicial economy which could be achieved by trying these claims in one lawsuit. These considerations must yield, however, to considerations of ethics which run to the very integrity of our judicial process.

Accordingly, the order of the district court is affirmed.

Law, Lawyers, and Managers

Ronald D. Rotunda

* * *

The learning and practice of legal ethics should be more than a stab in the dark. This is not to say that the area of black and white is greater than the area of murky gray; but it does assert that the tools of legal analysis, which seek to bring some order to areas of corporate law, apply equally well to legal ethics and to the law of professional responsibility for corporate lawyers and managers. Since ethical issues always arise in a context, abstract discussion of them without reference to that context is unproductive. I would therefore like to identify several complex areas of corporate legal ethics (focusing in particular on some conflicts-of-interest issues within the corporate entity) in order to determine how corporate managers and lawyers may help one another to fulfill their ethical and professional obligations.

By way of caveat to the layman it should be noted that the following examples represent complex issues of law. Yet in every case, the relationship to corporate ethical behavior is important, and the mode and resolution of the technical legal problem has a bearing on the style and substance of corporate ethics.

First I will consider some examples of corporate lawyers and managers trying to represent the diverse interests within a corporation. Then I shall turn to some of the lawyer's and manager's duties to interests outside the corporate entity; duties of loyalty to the public, and how these duties place limits on one's loyalty to the corporation.

CONFLICTS OF INTERESTS WITHIN THE CORPORATE ENTITY

We all know that the corporation is considered a legal "entity" and that, much like our own souls, it has no body. While it cannot be seen, it exists legally apart from its constituencies of officers, board, stockholders, cred-

Clarence Walton, ed., *The Ethics of Corporate Conduct* (The American Assembly, Columbia University, 1977), pp.128–34 and 137–41. Reprinted by permission of Prentice-Hall, Inc., Englewood Cliffs, N. J.

itors, and so on. Such a multifaceted client creates special problems of conflicts of interest for the corporate manager and lawyer.

To deal with such problems for lawyers the American Bar Association has promulgated a Code of Professional Responsibility, which most states have adopted as law with varying modifications. This code is divided into Canons (axiomatic norms and disciplinary rules which are mandatory in character) and Ethical Considerations which suggest the aspirations that properly motivate the ethical lawyer. Canon 5 of this code deals primarily with the lawyer who confronts conflicts-of-interest situations. Recognizing the special problem of the *corporate entity* in its Ethical Consideration 5-18, the code announces that a corporation lawyer "owes his allegiance to the entity and not to a stockholder, director, officer, employee, representative, or other persons connected with the entity."

It is the entity's interests which the code insists must be kept "paramount." While the code applies only to lawyers, its entity theory is not a novel one. Corporate managers as well owe their legal duty to the corporation and not to themselves or to certain factions.

Sometimes (perhaps too rarely) the law offers mechanical tests to solve legal problems. There are, of course, a few problematic issues where the entity theory is useful in solving corporate ethical problems, but such problems are not the difficult ones. For example, if a competitor sues a corporate client alleging an antitrust violation, it is easy to conclude that the corporate lawyer does not represent a shareholder of defendant who is also a shareholder of plaintiff; rather, the lawyer represents the corporation as an entity. Similarly the corporate manager owes no duty of loyalty to another corporation simply because one of its shareholders is also a shareholder of the manager's corporation.

Derivative Suits

Aside from such rather simple problems, the entity theory proves less helpful. A good example occurs with the problem of so-called "derivative" suits. When a shareholder sues his corporation, the action may be classified as either an individual or a derivative action. If the complaint is that the corporation has individually injured him as a stockholder—by unlawfully refusing to pay mandatory dividends or by not allowing him his right to inspect corporate books—the action is called an individual action. Its characteristics are those of an ordinary lawsuit, and we expect corporate counsel to defend the corporation in the action. If the corporation loses, it must pay money or give some right to the plaintiff-shareholder.

The situation is more complex in a derivative action. In such cases the shareholder is suing because he claims that the corporation is injured. The shareholder may believe the directors have breached their duty to the corporation by mismanagement or by theft of corporate assets. If a third party stole from the corporation we could expect it to sue to recover the proceeds. But if insiders stole, the corporation may be reluctant to sue since these insiders are in control. The law thus allows the shareholders to sue on behalf of the corporation. If a money recovery is sought and recovered, the insider-defendants must normally pay that judgment to the corporation, not to the plaintiff-shareholder. To motivate shareholders to become, in effect, private attorneys-general, the courts will grant attorney fees to the plaintiff's lawyer if the suit is successful. And, as we might surmise, the expectation of attorney fees encourages frivolous lawsuits.

Role of Counsel

If the corporate directors are sued derivatively, what is the proper role of the law firm which is counsel to the corporation? Which issues may the corporation raise in defense of the derivative suit and which issues may it not? Is the lawyer in an impossible conflict-of-interest situation if he represents both the corporate insiders as well as the entity? If he represents only the corporate entity, what is his proper role?

Some court decisions and bar association ethical opinions have tried to decide these issues, supposedly by using the test of the entity theory of a corporation. But the proper resolution of most questions is still very much open. The corporation counsel's role in cases where insiders are sued derivatively—insiders who have been advised in their actions by the same counsel representing the corporation—is a particularly awkward one. In the case law we can find examples of the corporation in some instances aiding the plaintiffs suing derivatively; in other instances, the corporation has resisted the action and aided the real defendants by raising procedural defenses, such as a lack of proper service or misjoinder of causes of action, or moving to require security for costs. If these procedural hurdles have been passed, and settlement is being discussed, how does the corporate attorney advise the entity to bargain in a settlement conference of a derivative suit when some, or all, of the defendants are also insiders of the corporation? After all, if the derivative plaintiff bargains successfully, the reluctant corporation, aligned as a defendant, may find more money added to its coffers.

In all aspects of the derivative litigation the corporate lawyer's ethical response is complicated by the fact that he may represent, or appear to be controlled by, the alleged inside wrongdoers. This appearance is fortified by the lawyer's natural incentive to favor the corporate officers and directors with whom he has dealt and advised. A lawyer who ignores this fact by trying to represent only the incorporeal entity may find himself dismissed by the flesh-and-blood insiders who actually hired him.

The Lewis Case

In one leading federal case, *Lewis v. Shaffer Stores Co.* (1963), where the regular corporate counsel was also defending the officers and directors, the district judge ordered the entity "to retain independent counsel, who have no previous connection with the corporation, to advise it as to the position which it should take" in the derivative suit. But these new lawyers, selected pursuant to court order, are not in an enviable position. The same insiders who are being sued may be influential in selecting new counsel. This same court voiced no concern that "the selection of such independent counsel will necessarily be made by officers and directors who are defendants." And if the newly selected counsel for the corporation becomes too independent-minded, he may then be dismissed by the interested insiders. Such insiders need not be corrupt or evil men. From their perspective—a self-interested perspective to be sure—they may view the particular derivative suit against them as a frivolous one.

In those cases where the corporation is aligned as a defendant with its insiders, a rule could require the corporation to raise no defenses or otherwise participate. It would be passive though, in theory, a defendant. In such cases, the law might instead, allow the real defendants having their own counsel to assert the corporate and individual defenses. But this rule would completely deprive the shareholders of their corporation's participation in important litigation that could significantly affect it.

To expect the court to allow the insider-defendants initially to choose counsel (with the court subsequently engaging in constant monitoring of the representation process) is not realistic. It may cause excessive entanglement between one of the litigants and the impartial judge. The directors who are not being sued derivatively could choose counsel, but all directors might be sued. Or the court might find that they are influenced by the other directors who actually are defendants. The judge could choose independent counsel for the corporation only in those cases where he thinks the suit is not frivolous, but the question of frivolity really goes to the merits of the case and ought not be decided by the court in a preliminary hearing.

*   *   *

CORPORATE TAKEOVERS

The entity theory is perhaps even less helpful in a takeover situation. Assume that a larger corporation plans a takeover attempt of a carefully selected target. Corporate counsel for the target must represent it as an entity. Therefore the attorney does not represent the significant number of minority shareholders of the target which now controls the corporate offeror or "raider" and approve [sic] of the takeover. Nor does the lawyer represent the board or officers of the target who are expected to fight the takeover.

What is the lawyer's role in such a case? What if the lawyer thinks that a takeover would probably be better for the corporation's stockholders? Perhaps he is persuaded that the raider can run the target better than the mismanagement revealed by the present board. Recall that the lawyer for the corporation is to keep that entity's interest "paramount." The board of the target, by way of defense, may suggest a charter amendment which would make it very difficult for any takeover attempt to succeed. How does the lawyer's loyalty to the "entity" resolve his possible conflicts between the interests of the present management and the present or future stockholders? Is it ethical for management to propose and urge adoption of such a charter amendment? Does duty or loyalty to the corporation require them to resist a takeover attempt? Or is their judgment to fight obviously clouded by their own self-interest?

One lawyer who specializes in defending targets of takeover attempts told me that he resolves his dilemma in defending targets by delaying tactics. He has opposed charter amendments which make takeovers virtually impossible because he believes they pave the way for less favorable legislation. But the delay, he feels, is beneficial to the shareholders of the target because it allows other offerors time to come in and bid up the offer. If a corporation is really ripe for a takeover, these other offerors will assure stockholders a better price. Perhaps the managers' role should be similarly limited to the blitzkreig situation—simply to assure that, procedurally, the takeover attempt is not so sudden that all sides cannot present their best case to the shareholders. This proposal, while it may solve one problem, raises another—the ethical issue of delay, particularly the calculated use of tactics for delay. This area will be considered toward the end of this essay.

These examples have considered the problem of an attorney for a public corporation, but the issue of representing a corporate entity may not be lessened in the closely held, family corporation situation. If there are various, fighting factions of a closely held corporation, the lawyer for the "entity" can have his hands full. Does he primarily represent the faction that controls? The faction that is more interested in corporate officers or jobs? Or the faction that is more interested in dividends?

* * *

LAWYERS AS DIRECTORS

Related to this issue of true independence of outside counsel is the problem of lawyers who also serve as board members of their corporate clients. While I believe that corporate lawyers should be guaranteed an audience with the directors, it does not follow that the corporation's attorney should also be a member of the board. Lawyers who are directors of their clients justify this role by insisting that they are more carefully listened to in this capacity than in the capacity of an outside counsel invited to speak to the board or who insists on speaking to the board. They often feel that not only are they less likely to lose the client to another firm, but that, as lawyers, they bring an added dimension of expertise and a broader perspective to board decisions.

But there is a deficit side to this ledger. From the perspective of his own self-interest, the lawyer had better be right because he will be judged as a director with legal expertise. More importantly, from an ethical standpoint there are other difficulties. The lawyer may be motivated to serve as a director because the position allows him to attract new clients more readily and to hold old ones. Such an individual has subordinated his duty to the corporate entity to a greater loyalty to his own firm.

Tightening the Rules

The attorney's independence may also be compromised by becoming a member of the client. One distinguished New York attorney, Paul Cravath, believes that "in most cases the client is best advised by a lawyer who maintains an objective point of view and such objectivity may be impeded by a financial interest in the client's business or any participation in its management." His partner, Robert T. Swaine, wrote in the *American Bar Association Journal* of 1949 "most of us would be greatly relieved if a canon of ethics were adopted forbidding a lawyer in substance to become his own client through acting as a director or officer of a client." But he resignedly lamented that "the practice is too widespread to permit any such expectation."

In spite of Cravath's personal beliefs he himself served as chairman of Westinghouse and, at the insistence of clients, other "Cravath" partners wound up on important corporate boards. Perhaps the ultimate solution will be these prophylactic rules: *Lawyers should not be on the boards of their clients. Nor should corporate clients employ, as their outside counsel, a law firm that has one of its partners on the Corporate Board.* Corporate managers should consider the advantages of implementing such a rule. Attorneys could continue to serve on boards so long as they are not also counsel to the client.

CONFLICTS OF INTEREST AS WEAPONS

Some corporate law firms, by specializing in an extremely narrow range of legal problems, develop a national reputation which enables them to attract corporate clients from around the country. Some corporate clients, in an unusual behavioral twist are now using as a weapon against these firms the professional rules relating to conflicts of interest. One example suffices. Let us imagine a firm which specializes in representing target companies or raiders in takeover at attempts. A prospective raider-client—through one of its corporate officers—*deliberately* telephones this law firm and talks to a partner about possible representation on a takeover fight. He discusses possible theories of action, discloses some facts, and so on. But the prospective client never follows through by retaining the firm. Now the raider telephones other law firms similarly situated, proceeds in the same fashion, and does not hire any of them either. By this technique the ruthless raider can keep its regular firm as counsel. Yet, it has also been able to disqualify other firms from representing the target company since disqualification of one partner or associate is imputed to the entire firm. The Code of Professional Responsibility creates the "conflicts" rules but does not reckon with their use as a weapon. There is not merely economic harm to law firms in lost business; more importantly, a sophisticated and ingenious lay person can use such rules to limit his opponent's choice of attorneys.

It would not be sufficient for the code to explicitly prohibit the practice because the code applies only to lawyers. Certainly the ethical manager would not seek to abuse the attorneys' professional code in such a manner. But if the opponent is not ethical and does not use them, how can the ethical manager fight back? Should the Code of Professional Responsibility create a defense to such activity? If so, how would that defense work? The client will not be happy with a rule of law which requires a lawyer to spend a half year or more making preliminary motions just to establish his defense to a conflicts-of-interest charge. After all, the legal time meter keeps running throughout the entire period.

The legal conflicts problem could be significantly reduced if we allowed the presently "disqualified" law firm to take the case on the proviso that it would insulate its disqualified member. Under such a role we would not impute to the entire firm the conflict of one of its partners or associates. But this "walling-off" technique would not be satisfactory to the opponents who may always suspect leaks from a poorly insulated wall.

THE CORPORATE LAWYER AND THE PUBLIC

Corporate Lawyers in Public Capacities

The expertise of corporate lawyers often leads to their involvement in special bar association projects or other public service activities. A city or state bar association may wish to invite a particular corporate lawyer to sit on one of its major committees in order to bring to it a special knowledge. In such situations, lawyers often confuse their roles by acting as advocates rather than as advisers.

The Code of Professional Responsibility does not forbid lawyers to shed their client's interests in such "nonrepresentational" situations. Its Ethical Consideration (8-1) specifically encourages lawyers to propose and support legislative programs "to improve the system, without regard to the general interests or desires of clients or former clients." The code further states:

> The obligation of loyalty to his client applies only to a lawyer in the discharge of his professional duties and implies no obligation to adopt a personal viewpoint favorable to the interests or desires of his clients. While a lawyer must act always with circumspection in order that his conduct will not adversely affect the rights of a client in a matter he is then handling, he may take positions on public issues and *espouse legal reforms he favors without regard to the individual views of any client.* (Ethical Consideration 7-17; emphasis added)

Later the code states:

> When a lawyer purports to act on behalf of the public he should espouse those changes which he conscientiously believes to be in the public interests. (Ethical Consideration 8-4)

But lawyers, in fact, do often try to "sell" their clients' positions in such situations. Sometimes this selling flows naturally from their coming to identify with client needs, but realism requires recognition of the fact that, at other times, it may be due to fear of losing clients with whom they actually disagree.

In language relating to a lawyer who "purports to act on the basis on the public . . ." the code suggests that disclosure of the lawyer's interests may be all that is required. But disclosure is not an adequate remedy in all such situations for two reasons: (1) a lawyer is not appointed to a bar committee or to any other professional group in order to represent his clients but is expected to share his professional experiences and to bring his technical knowledge to help solve various legal problems. To exploit his position, to promote client interests at the expense of his own convictions is to breach faith with those who brought him to the committee in the first place. (2) Committee members themselves are not privileged to allow use of public-service membership as a forum to lobby for a particular client or group. When committee members assent to partisan advocacy, they too are behaving unethically. They are also suggesting that in future assignments of a similar nature they too should be allowed to act as advocates of their clients.

The lawyer should divorce personal and professional beliefs from clients' interests. Yet some do treat such appointments to professional or public service committees as another advocacy opportunity. And, *a fortiori*, the attorney ought not to bill the private clients for professional time; nor should a lawyer use client resources to support public-service functions. Separation of these public and private capacities is a basic ethical necessity. Mere disclosure is not enough. Ethical corporate managers, should in turn, expect such separation of roles and never pressure an attorney in these situations.

* * *

D

The Move Between Government and Private Practice

General Motors Corporation v. City of New York

UNITED STATES COURT OF APPEALS, SECOND CIRCUIT, 1974 501 F.2D 639

IRVING R. KAUFMAN Chief Judge:

* * * In this case, brought by the City of New York [City], which alone has a $12,000,000 claim, as a class action alleging that General Motors Corporation [GM] has violated the antitrust laws principally by monopolizing or attempting to monopolize the nationwide market for city buses, we face appeals by GM from interlocutory orders deciding two bitterly contested pretrial, although unrelated, motions. * * * the second, GM's unsuccessful motion to have the City's privately retained counsel, George D. Reycraft, disqualified for breach of the ethical precepts embodied in Canon 9 of the Code of Professional Responsibility.[1] * * * With respect to the motion to disqualify counsel, however, we conclude, without intending to suggest any actual impropriety on the part of Reycraft, that his disqualification is required to "avoid even the appearance of professional impropriety."[2] Accordingly, the court's order denying disqualification of Reycraft is reversed.

* * *

According to Reycraft's affidavit, filed in opposition to the disqualification motion, he was asked by the Office of the Corporation Counsel, sometime in July 1972, to assist in the preparation of the complaint. When approached by the Corporation Counsel, then J. Lee Rankin, Reycraft responded by informing Rankin of his prior and substantial involvement in an action brought by the United States against GM, under Section 2 of the Sherman Act, based on GM's alleged monopolization of a nation-wide market for the manufacture and sale of city and intercity buses. *United States v. General Motors* (No. 15816, E.D. Mich.1956) [1956 *Bus* case].

In his affidavit, Reycraft described his participation in the 1956 *Bus* case, and his work for the Antitrust Division of the Department of Justice, in these words:

> I was employed as an attorney for the Antitrust Division of the Department of Justice from the end of December, 1952 through the end of December, 1962. From sometime during the middle of 1954 through the end of 1962 I was employed in the Washington Office of the Antitrust Division. My initial assignment in the Washington Office of the Antitrust Division in 1954 was as a trial attorney in the General Litigation Section.
>
> One of my first assignments as a member of the General Litigation Section was to work on an investigation of alleged monopolization by General Motors of the city and intercity bus business. The chief counsel in that matter from at least 1954 until the case was settled by Consent Decree in 1965 was Walter D. Murphy. At no time was I in active charge of the case. *That investigation culminated in the Complaint filed on July 6, 1956 which I signed and in the preparation of which I participated substantially.*
>
> In 1958 I became Chief of the Special Trial Section of the Antitrust Division and no longer had any direct or indirect involvement with the 1956 *Bus* case. Subsequently in 1961 I became Chief of Section Operations of the Antitrust Division and had technical responsibility for all matters within the Washington Office of the Antitrust Division, including the 1956 *Bus* case. I have no recollection of any active participation on my part in the 1956 *Bus*

---

[1] Canon 9 of the Code of Professional responsibility provides that "A lawyer should avoid even the appearance of professional impropriety." More particularly, Disciplinary Rule [DR] 9-101(B), prohibits "a lawyer * * * [from accepting] private employment in a matter in which he had substantial responsibility while he was a public employee."

[2] Canon 9, *supra* note 1.

case from 1958 through the time I departed from the Antitrust Division in December of 1962. The case was in the charge of Walter D. Murphy from its inception and he continued in charge until the Consent Decree was entered on December 31, 1965. (emphasis added)

In light of his substantial involvement as an employee of the Department of Justice in a matter which, at the very least, was similar to the dispute for which his retention was sought, Reycraft initially consulted his partners in the firm of Cadwalader, Eickersham & Taft and, subsequently, requested the advice of the Antitrust Division on the applicability of the Federal conflict of interest statute.[3] That Statute, we note, is penal in nature and its prohibitory rules, only two in number, must therefore be specifically defined and strictly construed. With that in mind, the Justice Department had little difficulty in concluding that the statute placed no bar on Reycraft's employment by the City. Its response to Reycraft states, in pertinent part:

> It is clear that section 207(b) [which applies for only one year after separation from government employ] has no bearing on your case. As for section 207(a) [which applies only where the United States is a party or has a direct and substantial interest in the matter], although it appears that you participated personally and substantially in the case brought by the United States against General Motors, the Antitrust Division advises us that the United States will not be a party to or have a direct and substantial interest in the private antitrust suit by the City of New York against General Motors.

Therefore, section 207(a) has no application. Accordingly, with Cadwalader's approval and the absence of any barrier posed by federal law, Reycraft agreed to represent the City on a contingent fee basis, a not infrequent arrangement in actions where recovery is at the same time uncertain but potentially great.

* * *

It is undisputed that Reycraft had "substantial responsibility" in initiating the Government's Sherman § 2 claim against GM for monopolizing or attempting to monopolize the nationwide market for city and intercity buses. Thus, we are left to determine whether the City's antitrust suit is the same "matter" as the Government's action and whether Reycraft's contingent fee arrangement with the City constitutes "private employment."

Directing our attention to the simpler question first, we are convinced beyond doubt that Reycraft's and, indeed, his firm's opportunity to earn a substantial fee for Reycraft's services is plainly "private employment" under DR9-101(B). The district judge apparently grounded his contrary decision on the rationale that Reycraft "has not changed sides"—i.e. "there is nothing antithetical in the postures of the two governments in the actions in question. * * *" But, as we have already noted, Opinion No. 37 of the ABA Commission on Professional Ethics unequivocally applies the ethical

[3]18 U.S.C.A. § 207.

precepts of Canon 9 and DR9-101(B) irrespective of the side chosen in private practice.[4] And see *Allied Realty of St. Paul v. Exchange Nat. Bank of Chicago*, 283 F.Supp. 464, 466 (D.Minn.1968). We believe, moreover that this is as it should be for there lurks great potential for lucrative returns in following into private practice the course already charted with the aid of governmental resources. And, with such a large contingent fee at stake, we could hardly accept "pro bono publico" as a proper characterization of Reycraft's work, simply because the keeper of the purse is the City of New York or other governmental entities in the class.

It is manifest also, from an examination of the respective complaints (see the appendix to this opinion), that the City's antitrust action is sufficiently similar to the 1956 *Bus* case to be the same "matter" under DR 9-101(B). Indeed, virtually *every* overt act of attempted monopolization alleged in the City's complaint is lifted *in haec verba* from the Justice Department complaint. We cite, merely by way of illustration, paragraphs appearing in both complaints alleging the withdrawal of more than 20 companies from bus manufacturing, the coincidence of directors on the boards of GM and another bus manufacturer, the Flexible Company, and GM's acquisition of a controlling stock interest in Yellow Coach in 1925.

* * *

The City maintains, in the end, that if we reverse the court below and disqualify Reycraft, we will chill the ardor for Government service by rendering worthless the experience gained in Government employ. Indeed, the author of this opinion is hardly unaware of this claim, * * * Kaufman, *supra*, 70 *Harv.L.Rev.* 15 668. But, in that commentary, and the case upon which it was based (*United States v. Standard Oil Co.* (N. J.), 136, F.Supp. 345 (S.D.N.Y. 1955)-Esso Export Case), the accommodation between maintaining high ethical standards for former Government employees, on the one hand, and encouraging entry into Government service, on the other, was struck under far different circumstances. Unlike the instant case, in which Reycraft's "substantial responsibility" in the *Bus* case is undisputed, the writer of this opinion concluded in *Esso Export* that the lawyer:

> never investigated or passed upon the subject matter of the pending care * * * never rendered or had any specific duty to render any legal advice in relation to the regulations involved in the litigation.

Kaufman, *supra*, 70 *Harv.L.Rev.* at 664. More to the point, therefore, is another admonition voiced in that article:

> If there was a likelihood that information *pertaining* to the pending matter

---

[4]Indeed, the question of "side-switching," and of the conflict of interest which is almost certain to arise when counsel changes sides, is one addressed by Canon 4 and not Canon 9. Compare *Emle Industries, Inc. v. Patentex, Inc., supra*. The ethical problem raised here, we repeat, does not stem from the breach of confidentiality bred by a conflict of interest but from the possibility that a lawyer might wield Government power with a view toward subsequent private gain.

reached the attorney, although he did not investigate" or "pass upon" it, * * * there would undoubtedly be an appearance of evil if he were not disqualified.

Id. at 665 (emphasis added)

Esso Export unquestionably presented a case for the cautious applica- tion of the "appearance-of-evil doctrine," because the former Government lawyer's connection with the matter at issue was the tenuous one of mere employment in the same Government agency. If, for example, Reycraft had not worked on the 1956 *Bus* case, but was simply a member of the Antitrust Division at that time, a case not unlike *Esso Export* would be before us. To the contrary, however, Reycraft not only participated in the *Bus* case, but he signed the complaint in that action and admittedly had "sub- stantial responsibility" in its investigatory and preparatory stages. Where the overlap of issues is so plain, and the involvement while in Government employ so direct, the resulting appearance of impropriety must be avoided through disqualification.

Accordingly, we dismiss the appeal from the order granting class action status, and reverse the court's order denying disqualification of Reycraft.

* * *

The Revolving Door

GEOFFREY C. HAZARD, JR.

It is recurrently asserted that a lawyer employed by the government should not be allowed to enter private practice involving the kinds of things he did while in government service. It is also often questioned whether a govern- ment agency should employ a lawyer from private practice who has repre- sented clients that are subject to the agency's jurisdiction. These are aspects of a personnel practice of long standing sometimes called the "revolving door."

Many lawyers who work for the government, particularly the federal government, in time leave to join private law firms. Young lawyers often begin their careers with the government because the government pays competitive salaries at lower position levels and gives their incumbents far greater responsibilities than those entrusted to professionals of comparable age and experience in the private sector. The careers of many experienced lawyers—those in their 30s and 40s—are often punctuated with a term of high level service in the government, at least if the tide of political fortune

Ethics in the Practice of Law (New Haven: Yale University Press, 1978), pp. 107–19. Reprinted by permission.

coincides with their own inclinations and availability. A stint in Washington, or at the cabinet level of state government, provides an experienced lawyer opportunity to do some interesting things he cannot do in private practice—make public policy, participate openly in political power struggles, and be rid of his clients for a while. And a few lawyers become statesmen, returning in their senior years to help run the government and make history.

So far as it involves experienced lawyers, this pattern is not new. At the highest levels of appointment, it is a concomitant of electoral politics. In an elective system, policy makers by definition hold office on a temporary basis, being subject to ouster when the mandate changes. With regard to lower level appointments, what has been called the revolving door has an historical antecedent in the system of political patronage, which supplied not only warm places near the fire for the party's faithful subalterns but also professional positions, particularly in law. In the present day, those who circulate in and out of government, whether neophytes or seasoned professionals, include economists, scientists, and managers.

The practice has persisted despite recurrent attacks on its legitimacy and integrity. It has been defended on inconsistent grounds. Those who accepted the patronage system have asserted that government jobs were such that almost anyone could do them and hence nothing was lost by having them done by friends of the regime. (The validity of this theory is implicitly reaffirmed by some of the appointments of every new administration.) Reformers of all political persuasions assert that government jobs at the professional level entail such broad discretionary powers that only professionals sympathetic to the elected administration can be entrusted to hold them. Indeed, it can be argued that political-professionals are as necessary to the effectiveness of the presidential system of administration as political-ministers are necessary in a cabinet system. Whether this theory has validity is perhaps arguable. What is important, however, is that the theory is believed to have validity. In any event, experienced professionals are attracted to upper and near-upper echelon positions in part by the prospect of accomplishing something; younger ones are attracted to lower level positions by the prospect of demonstrating professional precocity.

The problem is whether the system involves conflicts of interest that should be regarded as unethical and, if so, what should be done about them. A further problem is whether lawyers who move in and out of government stand in any different position from other kinds of professionals, such as technical people who are associated with defense production or the regulated industries.

There are legal controls on the revolving door. Although the precise terms of the rules have varied and will no doubt be revised in the future, they are of two basic types. One is a rule that a government employee upon leaving government service may not be employed for a specified period by a private company that sold goods or services to the department with which the employee was associated. This kind of rule most often affects professionals who in the private sector have salaried positions with suppliers of hard- and software to the government. The other is a rule that a former government employee may not involve himself on behalf of a private employer in any matter for which he had responsibility while in government service. This type of rule most often affects professionals such as lawyers, who in the private sector are typically engaged in consultative or advisory practice.

It is common ground that a lawyer who has acted for the government in a matter may not upon leaving the government represent a private party in the same matter. It does not make any difference that the positions of the government and the subsequent client appear wholly compatible. Thus, a lawyer who has prosecuted a government antitrust action cannot upon leaving the government represent a private party allegedly injured by the conduct in question. Even in this situation there is potential incompatibility between the interests of the government and the private client. It is in the private client's interest that a government suit be pressed to conclusion, so that the defendant's liability is established, while from the government's viewpoint the suit is only one of many that compete for attention. The risk is that the government's prosecutorial effort would be deflected to benefit the prosecutor's prospective private client. Still more clearly would it be improper for a former government lawyer to represent a private client having an antagonistic interest in a matter for which the lawyer was previously responsible.

The difficult problems are more subtle. One of these concerns the definition of "a matter." It is easy enough to identify the subject of the government lawyer's professional work when one is talking about a lawsuit or a contract negotiation. But what about development of policy or regulations that affect a whole industry, or drafting and lobbying an administration's legislative program? There are also problems of duration of responsibility. Is a legal draftsman of defense procurement regulations barred from ever representing a defense contractor as long as those regulations are still in effect?

The concept of "a matter" is similarly complicated when the subject concerns the responsibilities of a lawyer serving as an agency's general counsel or in a cabinet or subcabinet administrative position. Such an officer is in some sense involved in every transaction of his agency during his tenure. Does it follow that he may not thereafter properly represent any private client in a transaction that was within the agency's jurisdiction in that period? The answer might well be that he should be so disqualified. However, if this is the proper answer, and if it is also true that a lower echelon legal draftsman should not be permanently disqualified from dealing with the subject of his draftsmanship, distinctions have to be drawn between types of involvement for purposes of future disqualification. Drawing such distinctions is not easy, given that the types of involvement run from being attorney general to being a research assistant who sometimes is given a chance to carry another lawyer's briefcase.

Another dimension to the problem arises from the principle of imputation. The principle is that a lawyer's relationship to a client is imputed to his professional associates and hence determines their disqualifications as well. Thus, if a lawyer has represented the government in a matter, and then leaves the government to join a law firm, that firm cannot thereafter represent a private client in that matter, for the disqualification of the lawyer should extend to the other lawyers in his firm. But as applied in the stages of next remove, the principle of imputation can have broad sweep. In one direction, there can be imputation among the lawyers working for a single government agency. For example, a lawyer for an antitrust agency who works on a case against company A may have close working relations with another lawyer in the same agency who is in charge of a case against company B; under a principle of imputation, the first lawyer would be disqualified from subsequently representing not only company A but also company B. In the other direction, if the first lawyer were to join a private firm, not only would all those associated with that firm be disqualified from representing company A, but, if double imputation is applied, the firm is also disqualified from representing company B. Finally, if application of the principle is pushed to the next degree, it follows that any other lawyer associated with the firm when the exgovernment lawyer joined it would carry the disqualification with him, like an infectious disease. If such a lawyer then left the firm and joined another, the latter would also be disqualified from representing company A. There is no logical stopping place, only a practical one.

The impact of the disqualification rule, especially when applied with its imputation corollary, can be very severe for a lawyer who has neither an independent income nor an academic base to return to. A lawyer who has held a high level position may have to reenter practice as a solo practitioner, lest he contaminate a whole firm. Former Attorney General Herbert Brownell followed this course after his service in the Eisenhower administration, for example. Although such a solution seems extreme, it apparently does not deter senior lawyers from serving the government in high office. Not only are the responsibilities and prestige of high office a compelling inducement in themselves, but the lawyers eligible for these positions have sufficient professional stature that they could make a living even if their practice were limited to purely nongovernment transactions. But the problem is quite different for lawyers considering government service at a somewhat lower level and for newly admitted law graduates who might seek a position with the government as their first job.

If the rule of disqualification were rigorously applied, younger lawyers would have to consider that service with the government might entail severely restricted reentry into the private professional market. Setting up a solo practice or forming a new firm is generally not a realistic alternative for a lawyer who has no well established position in the private market. Only a few can find their way into the academic world and not all of them would want to follow that path. To be sure, employment can be found in some other line of work but that would involve at least temporary retirement from the profession. Thus, the suitable alternative employment for a lawyer working for the government is a law firm, preferably one with a practice involving the government. Unless there is leeway in application of the disqualification rule, however, that alternative is closed and the attractiveness of government professional employment thereby diminished.

Leeway has been provided through the practice of waiver of the disqualification. The waiver procedure assumes the existence of a broad rule of disqualification, so that all former government lawyers are prima facie debarred from anything having to do with their previous work with the government. However, upon a disclosure of the intended practice affiliation, waiver is then sought from the government with such specific limitations on clientele as seem fitting in the circumstances. Under current practice, waiver is routinely granted on these terms. The procedure parallels that used for dealing with conflict of interest among private clients—consent of the client after full disclosure.

Another proposal for dealing with the problem is "walling off." The idea is that the firm could still represent a client after the former government lawyer joined it, even in matters in which he had participated while in government, but that he would be "walled off " from the firm's work for the client. As an arrangement for handling specific situations, the idea is no different from the waiver procedure. As an arrangement to be adopted as a general rule, it seems to be the epitome of naive legalism. No one who is anxious about the fidelity of former government lawyers will regard such a rule as adequate; and everyone who thinks the problem is primarily one of an individual's trustworthiness will regard the rule as obnoxious. "Walling off " is thus like the alleged New England practice of bundling, having neither the credibility of real prophylaxis nor the dignity of real self-control.

Recently, a movement has been initiated to terminate the waiver procedure. The argument is that the waiver procedure cannot be impartially administered. This is because the waiver procedure is administered by the lawyers still in the government, and they are predisposed to administer it liberally because they want to keep the professional exists open for themselves. The proposal to abolish the waiver procedure has been forestalled at least temporarily, but if nothing else it has rekindled debate about the propriety of revolving door law practice for the government.

As many lawyers familiar with the Washington scene have said, abolition of the waiver procedure would make it much more difficult for the government to attract young lawyers of high competence and would have some adverse effect on recruitment of upper echelon professionals. The government would not have difficulty finding bodies to fill its positions and might actually come out ahead in middle range positions, where career service government lawyers now suffer the frustration of being passed over in favor of outsiders. But the range of competence is very great among lawyers having the same formal qualifications and the government service in general does not offer incentives, certainly not in money and often not in responsibility, to hold able people in the face of private market blandishment. If the available choices were life-time government service or private practice, government service is unlikely to fare well among really competent professionals. Reduction of mobility in and out of the government would therefore probably cost the government a good deal in terms of the technical proficiency of its legal staff.

If the problem is looked at in longer term perspective, the implications of eliminating easy mobility in and out of government seem more complex. As a point of beginning it can be said that if the government were regarded as simply another client, serving it with revolving door lawyers would simply not be countenanced. One cannot imagine a multinational corporation maintaining a legal staff headed by the former counsel of one of its chief competitors and comprised of juniors bound in a few years to join the service of other competitors. A professional personnel policy that is at least arguably desirable for the government is thus unarguably undesirable for a private enterprise. This might suggest that the government should obviously stop the revolving door. But equally it suggests that there may be unexplored reasons that make it inappropriate to treat the government like a private enterprise in this respect.

One way to explore these reasons is to describe a model of a government legal staff governed by a rigid restriction on "revolving." The rule could be that a lawyer who left the government could not for three years appear before the agency in which he served and could not be associated with a client who had a matter before the agency during the lawyer's tenure.

For practical purposes this would mean that a lawyer leaving government would have to pursue a practice in some other area of law than the one in which he was involved when in the government. For very young lawyers, those in the first two years or so of practice, this would not be much of a burden. The elementary skills mastered in this phase of professional development—researching, writing, speaking, dealing effectively with opposite numbers—are readily transferable to other types of practice. Beyond this apprenticeship stage, however, the lawyer becomes a specialist in whatever he is doing, particularly if he is employed by a client with problems such as a government agency. Specialization involves more than mastery of the present law in a subject. It also involves the mastery of the subject's history and politics, the structure of power in which it is administered, and the character and abilities of the principal players in the field. That kind of knowledge is not readily transferable to other fields and becomes rapidly obsolete. A lawyer leaving the government after five or six years of service with an agency would therefore have to abandon the most valuable part of his intellectual capital, unless he was one of the few who could sell it in the academic marketplace.

A lawyer entering government service at the beginning of his career would thus have to plan an exit after three or four years, or anticipate then having to decide to stay on for the rest of his professional life. A lawyer entering government service after his apprenticeship would have to assume he was committing himself to a more or less permanent career change.

If this schema is correct, the government's legal staff under the regime of a strict limitation on mobility would have a somewhat different composition than it has now. It would be essentially a career service, occasionally augmented by visiting professors. The middle echelons and above would be career staff because individuals having reached that level could not afford to leave for private practice. Private practitioners could make lateral entry into the system only on a permanent basis, and even that kind of movement would probably be eliminated by political pressure from the permanent staff to require that its members be given preference in all higher position openings. The government would no longer be an attractive first employer for young lawyers who wanted positions of responsibility, because reaching those positions would lock them out of the private sector. The government could not afford to hire youngsters merely for an apprenticeship, however, and so would discourage terms of service that were less than three years. As a result, most of those entering at the bottom would be intent upon making government service a career.

In this scenario, cabinet level officers presumably would change with administrations. Below this, however, and certainly in offices of agency general counsel, there would be relatively little of the infiltration from the private sector that is now characteristic of government service. The staff would resemble the legal departments of some large corporations and the core of the legal staffs of most government agencies. It would replicate the legal departments of most European governments and those of state and local governments in this country that have civil service systems.

It is not at all clear that such an arrangement would be better than what we have now. It would eliminate the most commonly voiced objection to revolving door service, that of conflicts of interest. It would end the valuable on-the-job training now afforded by government employment. (What critics of the present system may find most galling is that a professional in temporary service gets advanced training at government expense.) It would result in a staff that would be strong in department expertise, in loyalty to the agency and the government generally, in personal probity, and in bureaucratic street wisdom.

Possibly such a system would be preferable to a purely patronage system on the model attributed to President Jackson. But it would have limitations of its own. Staff would be composed of people preferring a government career to the viscissitudes of the private sector, and therefore on the average likely to be more conservative, more cautious, and more "technical" than their legal counterparts in the private sector. The ties of the legal staff to the agency would be more intimate and would involve less self-criticism. Dependency on the pleasure of Congress would be greater and hence also the susceptibility to legislative pressure. The policy of an agency so staffed could not be redirected by infiltration of operating personnel but through the much more difficult procedure of orders from above or outside. In short, the legal departments of government in general might well look like those of, say, the Corps of Engineers and the Food and Drug Administration, rather than the Justice Department or the Securities and Exchange Commission.

If this analysis of the purist alternative is anywhere near accurate, the conclusion can be drawn that it leaves a lot to be desired from the viewpoint of the government. A career staff lawyer is a lawyer who has only one client all of his professional life. Lawyers with such a background necessarily lack the professional range of a more heterogeneous staff. They are more isolated from the professional fraternity, for whatever that might be worth. Perhaps most important, their definition of loyalty to client could well be of a kind that is not an unalloyed virtue, for proper loyalty to the client is modified by obligations to others and faithfulness to some external mandate that we may call professional duty. What seems clear is that real sensitivity to these conflicts is the product of experiencing them, repeatedly and in endlessly varying form. Putting aside all other questions, it is difficult to believe that government career staff would have equivalent opportunity to share that experience.

As things now stand, government legal staffs are a mixture of political appointments at the top, career people in the middle, and younger people of unresolved ambition at the bottom. It would be a mistake to assume that this arrangement is perfect in balance though fortuitous in origin. Of course, one could hope for a more fundamental change. One could hope that the government service, not only in law but in other disciplines, could be made so attractive that the professionals of highest ability would be drawn into government careers. Doing so would require the professionals to be given higher salaries, greater autonomy (especially from the influence of Congress), and distinct identity—endowments now provided only to the federal judiciary, the Foreign Service, the military, and perhaps a few other government establishments. This would make government professionals in law much like their counterparts in a Ministry of Justice in the European model or the Civil Service in Britain, an elite not beholden to the marketplace or to partisan politics.

The gains to be had in such a service could be substantial, but the possibility of its being established in this country seem remote. The public attitude toward high pay and high status for public officials is not sympathetic, to put it mildly. Perhaps critics of the present situation have in mind a service made up of dedicates like Ralph Nader, but that is a style that few people seem to sustain after age 35. It seems more realistic to expect that the choice is between something like the present revolving door system and one in which the government legal service is composed essentially of professional technicians, with both positive and negative connotations of that term. Given that we expect government agencies to originate policy as well as to execute it, and given that policy making is strongly influenced by legal staff, the present system may well be superior. At any rate, it would be a mistake to assume that private lawyers now usually enter government so that they can fix things for their clients. And it surely cannot be all bad that, under the present system, many members of the private bar at one time have had the responsibility for enforcing the law.

Some Ethical and Political Problems of a Government Attorney

JACK B. WEINSTEIN

II. SINGLE LEGAL PROFESSION

There is a core of knowledge and skills common to lawyers, whether they are practitioners, government officials, law teachers, or judges. One of the great joys of our profession is that our training permits us to advise diverse clients in disparate fields and to move from government to private work with comparative ease. We can learn what we need of economics to try an antitrust suit, of psychiatry to try a homicide case, and of bureaucracy to help our clients get reelected.

In many respects, the work of the government attorney is similar to that of a law teacher. He finds himself revising and writing documents; explaining his policies to his subordinates, and to others in county government and to the public; and trying to teach judges and juries—often with as little success as he has in class.

I shall only note here that my experience in government has convinced me of the importance of theoretical training in the law school. The lawyers who are essential when a new and difficult legal problem is presented are those who have been trained to think critically—not necessarily those with the greatest practical experience. Most intelligent lawyers can learn rather quickly the detailed practice in special fields. I do not undervalue, of course, the sense of proportion and knowledge of alternatives that come with maturity and experience. The Nassau County Attorney's office was, fortunately, nicely balanced with sound, experienced men aware of the limitations of government authority, and bright young law graduates who thought anything was possible.

Naturally, as a teacher, I am somewhat biased in my view. But our experiences in the Nassau County Attorney's office in providing summer programs for second- and third-year student law-interns convinced me that good practice and good law school training are closely correlated.[12] Training in thinking as lawyers makes a difference long after the student has graduated, when he is sure to have forgotten almost all the detailed

Maine Law Review, 18 (1966), 157–60 and 168–72. Reprinted by permission.

[12]The summer interns did professional work including research and brief writing under the supervision of the county attorney or deputy. Twice each week they attended two hour seminars on legal problems such as brief writing and condemnation practice and local governmental problems such as budgeting and organization of the police department; guided tours included such places as the county clerk's offices, the health laboratories and the jail.

rules he learned at law school—and those that he has not forgotten have probably been modified by statute or case law.

A general practitioner's skills are, in the main, those skills a government attorney must rely upon. Both must be habituated to view their client's disasters with equanimity.

III. SPECIAL PROBLEMS OF THE GOVERNMENT ATTORNEY

What I would like to speak about primarily tonight are some of the special problems of judgment presented by a local government practice.

The bothersome problems of a government attorney are not so much the legal-technical ones of what can be done, or how to do it, but what should be done. As Edmund Burke put it in his plea to Parliament on behalf of the American colonies in 1775, "The question with me is . . . not what a lawyer tells me I may do, but what humanity, reason, and justice tells me I ought to do."[13]

Three aspects of the government attorney's work have particularly intrigued me. They are first, the deep political dimension that almost all important governmental legal questions have; second, the necessity of integrating the government's law office with other government departments; and third, the difficult problems of judgment and ethics created by the government lawyer's multiplicity of clients.

A. Political Dimensions of a Law Officer's Decisions

A report, *The Survey of the Legal Profession* by the American Bar Association, declared in black letter: "To Inspire Confidence, It is required that Public Legal Positions Shall be Conducted and Opinions Rendered According to Law and Not to Please Politicians."[14]

If this statement means that political bosses should not be permitted to rig legal opinions and activities of a government law office for private benefit, the statement must be endorsed. If it means, however, that the legal position of a government office should be taken without considering its political or policy implications, it is wrong.

The chief government law officer must and should attempt to please some politicians: he is, by virtue of his position, a political or policymaking figure, a member of a government administration which achieved office by a political-governmental program. He has a responsibility to consider what effect his actions will have in developing and executing what he conceived to be sound public policy, in inducing confidence of the public in govern-

---

[13]Niles, *Chronicles of the American Revolution* 115 (Vaughan ed. 1965).

[14]Seasongood, *"Public Service by Lawyers in Local Government,"* 2 *Syracuse L. Rev.* 210, 222 (1951). *Cf.* Cowen, *"The Need for County Legal Departments,"* 31 *American County Government* 43, 44 (1966) (suggesting that if the office becomes "embroiled in politics" properly qualified lawyers may avoid the position).

ment, and in strengthening elected officials so that they can continue to control the governments machinery in achieving the ends he supports.

Governments and their attorneys have a duty to help individuals and to try to build a better society.[15] The persnickety law official who keeps his shoes clean by stepping around the mudholes of politics and public policy neglects the most important and exciting aspect of his office. He conceives of his office as a slot machine handing out opinions and acting with mechanical exactitude; he fails to grasp its more useful, complex and flexible function in meeting social problems.

Let me somewhat narrow the limits of the problem as I see it. It is wrong to exercise favoritism toward an individual dealing with the government. If a man, for example, is seeking a license or an award for tort or condemnation damages, or defending against a prosecution by the government, his treatment should be completely independent of whom he knows, who are his relatives, or what are his political connections. Boss Flynn, in his biography, illustrated what he conceived to be one of the advantages of political connections when he noted: "At times business concerns are cited for minor violations. Where discretion is indicated, having a friend at court harms no one."[16] I would submit that such an attitude does grievous harm to the whole governmental fabric because the average citizen then knows he is not getting equal treatment with the politically well connected.

The rule in my office with respect to what might be called the service aspect of the government attorney's work was flat and absolute. No discrimination was tolerated. It is utterly and outrageously wrong to differentiate among citizens because of their political connections. Every member of the legal staff should be aware of undeviating policy that no one's political background should have any significance in the way claims are processed. Members of the public are entitled to, and must receive, the assurance that their claims and business with the County—or any other governmental unit—will be decided solely on the merits. Any person walking into the office should be confident that there are no back doors for the politicians.

One way of making this rule clear to the staff is to enforce a policy within the office of assigning work, pay increases and promotions strictly on the basis of work product and achievement in the office. This policy reduces somewhat the pressure on individual lawyers to help themselves by helping influential people. It does not completely eliminate pressures since there is always the possibility of advancement outside the office whether in other branches of public service or through lucrative private practice. The example of the head of the office, and the express threat that anyone

---

[15]See, *e.g.*, Mr. Justice Stanley Reed: "Democracy has a right to expect that the members of the Bar . . . shall show their appreciation of the benefits conferred upon them by a conscious effort to make that Democracy effective." *"The Bar's Part in the Maintenance of American Democratic Ideals,"* 24 *A.B.A.J.* 622, 623 (1938), cited in Mathews, *"The Communication of Professional Values,"* 26 *Ohio St. L.J.* 89, 96 (1965); see also Countryman, *"The Scope of the Lawyer's Professional Responsibility,"* 26 *Ohio St. L.J.* 66, 71-82, 84-87 (1965). *Cf.,* Paige, *"The Professor and Politics,"* 52 *Am. Ass'n of Univ. Profs. Bull.* 52 (1966) (estimates five thousand academic consultants to government in the Cambridge, Massachusetts area).

[16]Flynn, *"You're the Boss"* 25 (1947).

caught succumbing to such temptation will be fired, help guard against this pervasive danger.

There is one unavoidable exception to the rule against discrimination. In dealing with individuals, the government lawyer will, naturally, get a sense for who can and cannot be trusted. A private lawyer with a good reputation has an easier time because his word can be relied upon in instances where another lawyer might be pressed to produce hard evidence. But this factor, it seems to me, is perfectly legitimate—a lawyer's reputation is, after all, his chief stock in trade. Here social and political connections may have a slight bearing. Having observed a man repeatedly, you may have more faith in him than in a stranger. This psychological verity needs to be controlled to avoid abusive use of government office to favor cronies. My own experience has not indicated any party monopoly of rectitude. In the case of some—including members of both parties—to know them is to distrust them. Most lawyers are, of course, completely trustworthy, and a presumption to that effect is properly applied in any government office.

One more matter should be excluded from the field of proper political activities. If there is wrongdoing in government, it must be exposed. The law officer has a special obligation not to permit a cover-up of illegal activity on the ground that exposure may hurt his party. His duty to the people, the law, and his own conscience requires disclosure and prosecution. In point of fact, it has always seemed to me that any failure to prosecute members of a party in power is a political as well as an ethical mistake. In this respect, the public lawyer is assisted by the view of the more sophisticated modern political leaders that "good government is good politics." It is far better for any party to clean its own house than to leave the issue of corruption to an opposing party.

* * *

C. Conflicts of Interest Among Clients

I have already suggested in my remarks some of the ethical difficulties of the county attorney caused by the heightened responsibility he has as a lawyer for reform of the administration of justice and law. Let me now emphasize one further aspect of this problem caused by the multiplicity of services he renders, the many departments he represents, and the fact that he represents the people as well as government. The private lawyer can, within broad limits, attempt to get the best possible result—from his single client's point of view—letting the adversary system provide justice. What, however, of the public attorney?

He is torn in a number of ways. Let me give you some examples. Shortly after I took office, one of our negotiators presented me with a proposed settlement in a condemnation case, which was approximately one-third of the value of the land we had taken as indicated by our appraiser's reports. The condemnees were not represented by an attorney. What should I have done? I talked to them on the telephone and discovered that they were an elderly couple who had bought their property many years before and who had no idea of how much it had increased in value. In an extended conversation, I finally convinced them that they were entitled to much more than they wanted. But should I have insisted on paying more than I had to?

In another case, the award of the court seemed to me to be too large by several millions of dollars. The condemnation resolutions adopted by the Board of Supervisors, our local legislative body, were exceedingly and unusually favorable to the condemnee, but there was no evidence of fraud. A reversal on the ground of excessiveness of the award was unlikely. What was a proper course of action? I instituted an extensive collateral attack on the award on the ground that the favorable provision was illegal, over the opposition of our Board of Supervisors. We used every procedural device in the book and some created especially for the case. It was clear that we would throw all the County's enormous resources into this litigation. After numerous motions and appeals, when it became obvious that the dispute might go on for many years, the matter was settled with a saving to the county of some million dollars. Once I told my classes procedure should never be used for delay. Now I wonder, are there exceptions?

Somewhere in between those two cases lie the bulk of matters where we insisted that the claimant take somewhat less than our appraisals showed the land to be worth. Condemnees settled and waived interest in order to avoid a long delay before trial and receipt of their money. Is this technique justified even though it saves the taxpayers money? A more appropriate procedure, in my opinion, would be for the County to obtain more thorough and reliable appraisals; they should be revealed to the condemnee, and he should then be tendered the full appraised value plus interest as a matter of due. If the condemnee wants more, he should receive almost the entire appraised value as an advance payment. We should, I believe, also pay—as we now do not—for loss of good will.[41]

While I was County Attorney I commissioned a study of our condemnation procedures by Professor Curtis Berger of Columbia Law School and Professor Patrick Rohan of St. John's Law School. They studied over a thousand of our condemnation awards of the last few years, and I hope their recommendations will be followed to provide a fairer condemnation system. Already we have made a number of improvements, as in the payment of relocation allowances and interest on settled cases. A new system will cost the county more money, but it will be more just.

The same problem of fairness applies in the area of torts. Here the matter is more complicated because it is harder to obtain an objective

---

[41]See, *e.g.*, "'Just Compensation' and the Small Businessman," 2 *Columbia Journal of Law and Social Problems*, March 21, 1966, p. 1 and authorities cited. It is paradoxical that the courts of England and Canada, which have no fourteenth amendment to protect against deprivation of property without just compensation, reach a contrary conclusion under statutes which do not specifically require compensation for good will and value of a going concern. 10 Halsbury, *Laws of England* §§ 281–287 (3d ed.); loss of business, goodwill, costs of removal, value of fixtures, and losses incurred until suitable premises obtained must be taken into account in assessing compensation. *Id.* at § 284; Annot., 1 *D.L.R.* 1027–30, 1033–37 (1952) (compensation for similar items). See also Orgel, *Valuation Under the Laws of Eminent Domain* § 75 (2d ed. 1953).

valuation of permanent injuries, or of causal connection, or of negligence. One way of avoiding the problem is to have the county buy insurance so that the insurance company's lawyers will carry on the unpleasant business of minimizing recoveries. As self-insurers, however, Nassau County saved several hundreds of thousands of dollars each year. Our operation was much the same as that of any insurance company. Our lawyers took pride in getting the lowest possible settlements and in securing defendants' verdicts in close cases. In a number of instances we won dismissals against widows and orphans who should, under any sensible system, have obtained some award. But in each one of these cases, we did offer a substantial amount in settlement, and I suppose that the onus must rest upon the attorney for the plaintiff who decided to go for broke. I would be much happier with a system such as that suggested by Professor Keeton of Harvard with respect to guaranteed payment for injuries. So long as we are playing this game by present rules I suppose we owe it to the taxpayer to play to win. And I must confess that the negligence litigation game has a pleasure and piquancy all its own. The cost to society and to individuals of our fun and games in tort law may, however, be too high.

In some instances our office defended cases I would have refused were I in private practice. But our client was bound to us by statute and his position was not so clearly wrong that we could turn him out of our office. For example, our District Attorney seized the whole edition of a magazine as obscene although it seemed to me to have less appeal to prurient interest that the average brassiere or perfume advertisement. But when the county was sued before a federal three-judge court for $100,000 and an injunction, my office defended. We had a good procedural defense—the matter should have been left to the state criminal courts. While we lost in the three-judge court, we were able to settle the case when a long stay by Mr. Justice Harlan became a possibility. As a result, the magazines were released with favorable publicity, the district attorney received publicity he considered favorable because it indicated he was against obscenity, an unreversed opinion makes such seizures in the future much less likely, the county was saved a judgment for damages, and I lost some friends in the civil liberties movement who could not understand that a government official is entitled to counsel even if his lawyer is not enthusiastic about the merits of the government position.

There are instances where the postion of one of the departments is completely contrary to the position that the attorney feels is legally defensible. In such cases the county attorney should, I believe, represent the side he considers to be correct. Special independent counsel should be provided to represent the other side. Such an appointment was made by Chief Justice Stone when he was Attorney General of the United States; he himself argued against the special counsel.[42]

In some instances the government attorney should confess error in a case in which his government is a defendant. This is the position we took in the state reapportionment cases, for example.[43] The County Executive was

---

[42]Mason, *Harlan Fiske Stone, Pillar of the Law* 167–68 (1956).

[43]*WMCA, Inc. v. Lomenzo,* 377 U.S. 633 (1964).

sued as one of the defendants in the New York reapportionment case because our county was malapportioned and he participates in fixing lines for the state assembly. The Attorney General of the state defended the suit so that it was not necessary to appoint special counsel.

It was in part because I felt more comfortable with an attorney on the other side that, although I was by statute the sole legal representative of the Board of Supervisors, I did not object to the board's utilizing its own counsel much more extensively than our county charter intended. The fact that the Republican Board of Supervisors had an honorable counsel, Harold Collins, one I could deal with on an adversarial basis, eliminated many of the possible conflicts of interest and ethical problems that otherwise would have proven most troublesome. Indeed, more often than not we assisted each other in moderating our clients' positions so that they could, together, move forward in the exciting and essential job of providing good local government.

One of the most important functions of the government's lawyer is to provide a bridge or neutral meeting ground between opposing forces so that the viable compromises which are the hallmark of a functioning democracy can be developed. If the government's attorney is to fulfill this role, there must be no doubt in anyone's mind about his good faith and integrity.

IV. CONCLUSION

I conclude by repeating that, while the government's attorney is a political figure, he operates within a framework of professional and ethical responsibility that limits what he can and should do. There is no inconsistency between sound ethics and good politics. Indeed, government service, while it furnishes some of the hardest ethical problems, affords a lawyer many of the greatest opportunities for professional fulfillment.

CONFIDENTIALITY

Whiteside v. Scurr No. 83-1015 744 F.2d 1323(1984)

UNITED STATES COURT OF APPEALS, EIGHTH CIRCUIT

McMILLIAN, Circuit Judge.

Emmanuel Charles Whiteside appeals from a final judgment entered in the District Court for the Southern District of Iowa denying his petition for writ of habeas corpus. For reversal appellant argues the district court erred in holding that counsel's threats to seek to withdraw, disclose confidential discussions and testify against him did not deny him due process and effective assistance of counsel. For the reasons discussed below, we reverse the judgment of the district court and remand for further proceedings consistent with this opinion.

A state court jury convicted appellant of second degree murder for the stabbing death of Calvin Love in 1977. Appellant was sentenced to forty years imprisonment. Appellant and two companions had gone to Love's apartment to get some marijuana. During an argument about the marijuana, appellant stabbed Love as Love was moving toward him. Appellant's theory of defense was self-defense. According to appellant, Love had been reaching for a gun beneath a pillow when appellant stabbed him. When questioned by defense counsel in preparation for trial, appellant stated that he had not actually seen the gun, but that he thought that he had seen a gun and was convinced that Love had one because Love had a reputation for carrying a gun. Counsel questioned appellant's two companions and Love's girlfriend about the gun. They denied actually seeing a gun, although appellant's companions believed that Love probably did have a gun. Counsel also learned that the police had found no gun during a quick search of the room where the stabbing occurred. Nor had the apartment manager found a gun. Counsel personally searched the room for the gun without success. During the course of his investigation, however, counsel discovered that several hours after the stabbing, Love's girlfriend and his family had forced the police padlock on the apartment and had removed everything from the apartment.

Appellant was anxious about the success of this theory of self-defense if the gun was not found. Counsel had earlier advised appellant that the gun itself was not essential to his theory of self-defense and that the defense would be successful if the jury was convinced that appellant reasonably believed that Love had had a gun. Shortly before trial, appellant told counsel that he had seen something "metallic" in Love's hand just before the stabbing. This discrepancy precipitated the disagreement between appellant and counsel that underlies this appeal. Counsel told appellant that if he insisted upon testifying that he saw a gun, then he (counsel) would move to withdraw, advise the state trial judge that the testimony was perjurious and testify against him.

At trial appellant testified only that he thought Love had a gun and that he had acted to protect himself from an assault by Love with the gun. Appellant was found guilty of second degree murder. On appeal to the state supreme court appellant argued that counsel's threats to withdraw, advise the state trial judge about his testimony and testify against him prevented him from presenting his defense and thus denied him a fair trial. The state supreme court rejected this argument, finding that "counsel was convinced with good cause to believe [appellant's] proposed testimony would [have been] deliberately untruthful" and that, consistent with the Iowa Code of Professional Responsibility for Lawyers, "[c]ounsel properly refused to be a partner in such a dishonest and deceitful scheme." *State v. Whiteside*, 272 N.W.2d 468, 471 (Iowa 1978). The state supreme court commended counsel for the "high ethical manner" in which the matter was handled. Id.

In 1981 appellant filed a petition for writ of habeas corpus alleging that counsel's threats to withdraw, advise the state trial judge and testify against him denied him the right to effective assistance of counsel, the right to present a defense and due process in violation of the fifth, sixth and fourteenth amendments. The district court found that the state courts' finding that appellant would have committed perjury was fairly supported by the record and that appellant had failed to establish by convincing evidence that this finding was erroneous. *Whiteside v. Scurr*, No. Civil-81-246-C, slip op. at 2 (S.D.Iowa Dec. 7, 1982). The district court noted the constitutional right to testify did not include perjury and concluded that appellant was not denied due process or effective assistance of counsel because counsel prevented him from testifying falsely. Id. The district court denied the petition and this appeal followed.

* * *

Our discussion begins with the following observation: our analysis does not deal with the ethical problem inherent in appellant's claim. We are concerned only with the constitutional requirements of due process and effective assistance of counsel. As the ABA Model Rules 3.3 comment, appendix B, states, the Constitution prevails over rules of professional ethics, and a lawyer who does what the sixth and fourteenth amendments command cannot be charged with violating any precepts of professional ethics. This is a very controversial matter and we commend counsel for conscientiously attempting to address the problem of client perjury in a manner consistent with professional responsibility.

Appellant first argues that counsel improperly acted on the basis of mere suspicion that appellant would testify falsely. The reason why counsel believes that the defendant intends to testify falsely is an important threshold question because "'[w]here ... the veracity or falsity of the defendant's testimony is conjectural, the ethical dilemma does not arise.'" *Butler v. United States*, 414 A.2d at 850, *citing Johnson v. United States*, 404 A.2d at 164. Both ABA Model Rule 3.3 and ABA Proposed Defense Function Standard 4-7.7 presuppose that defense counsel *knows* that the defendant's testimony will be false on the basis of either independent investigation or prior discussions with the defendant or both. Mere suspicion of inconsistent statements by the defendant alone are insufficient to establish that the defendant's testimony would have been false. See *Butler v. United States*, 404 A.2d at 164 (inconsistency between two proffered defenses); *Commonwealth v. Wolfe*, 447 A.2d at 310 n. 7 (suspicion). Counsel must act if, but only if, he or she has "a firm factual basis" for believing that the defendant intends to testify falsely or has testified falsely. See *United States ex rel. Wilcox v. Johnson*, 555 F.2d at 122. It will be a rare case in which this factual requirement is met. Counsel must remember that they are not triers of fact, but advocates. In most cases a client's credibility will be a question for the jury.

In the present case the state supreme court found that "counsel was convinced with good cause to believe [appellant's] proposed testimony would be deliberately untruthful," and that counsel had based this belief upon an independent investigation and prior discussions with appellant. 272 N.W.2d at 471. This factual determination is fairly supported by the record and is therefore presumptively correct. See *Sumner v. Mata*, 449 U.S. 539, 544, 101 S.Ct. 764, 7677, 66 L.Ed.2d 722 (1980). For purposes of our analysis, we presume that appellant would have testified falsely. We recognize, of course, that the criminal defendants' privilege to testify in their own defense does not include the right to commit perjury. See *Harris v. New York*, 401 U.S. 222, 225, 91 S.Ct. 643, 645, 28 L.Ed.2d 1 (1971). However, the fact that appellant would have committed perjury does not mean that appellant has waived his right to a fair trial, due process or effective assistance of counsel. Cf. *Lowery v. Cardwell*, 575 F.2d at 730 (examination of defendant ceased abruptly and was followed by counsel's in camera motion to withdraw and refusal to state the reason for the motion; only rational conclusion to be drawn by judge as fact-finder was that defendant had testified falsely; held denial of due process). The "remedy" for appellant's perjury is prosecution for perjury.

* * *

In the present case counsel's actions in threatening to withdraw, advise the state trial judge and testify against appellant if appellant testified falsely, impermissibly compromised appellant's right to effective assistance of counsel. Despite counsel's legitimate ethical concerns, counsel's actions were inconsistent with the obligations of confidentiality and zealous advocacy. See *Lowery v. Cardwell*, 575 F.2d at 732 (Hufstedler, J., specially concurring). See generally Freedman, "Professional Responsibility of the Criminal Defense Lawyer: The Three Hardest Questions", 64 *Mich.L.Rev.* at 1475–78. Counsel's actions, in particular the threat to testify against appellant, indicate that a conflict of interest had developed between counsel and appellant, even though this conflict was admittedly precipitated by appellant's intention to testify falsely. At this point counsel had become a potential adversary and ceased to serve as a zealous advocate of appellant's interests. "No matter how commendable may have been counsel's motives, [counsel's] interest in saving himself [or herself] from potential violation of the canons [or the ABA Model Rules of Professional Conduct] was adverse to [the] client, and the end product was [counsel's] abandonment of a diligent defense." *Lowery v. Cardwell*, 575 F.2d at 732 (Hufstedler, J., specially concurring).

* * *

Conflicts of interest necessarily implicate breach of counsel's duty of loyalty, which is "perhaps the most basic of counsel's duties." *Strickland v. Washington*, 104 S.Ct. at 2067. Here the breach of loyalty arose from counsel's threat to testify against appellant. Such threats undermine the fundamental trust between lawyer and client that can exist only if the lawyer "can convince the client that full and confidential disclosure . . . will never result in prejudice to the client by any word or action of the lawyer." Freedman, "Professional Responsibility of the Criminal Defense Lawyer: The Three Hardest Questions", 64 *Mich.L.Rev.* at 1473. Thus, threats like the one here are presumptively prejudicial to the defense.

We recognize the difficulties created when the duty to render effective assistance, imposed by the sixth and fourteenth amendments, is not completely congruent with the relevant code of professional ethics. We wish to stress that our task is not at all to determine whether counsel behaved in an ethical fashion. That question is governed solely by the Iowa Code of Professional Responsibility, as it was in effect at the time of the trial in this case, and as it has been authoritatively interpreted by the Supreme Court of Iowa. The Supreme Court of Iowa is the last word on all questions of state law, and the Code of Professional Responsibility is a species of state law. It nevertheless remains our duty to determine what the sixth amendment requires. In doing so, we are at liberty to consider, purely as guidelines and not as governing rules, the views of authorities on legal ethics, including views set forth in various proposed standards and codes of professional conduct. In this connection, we note that counsel here fell short not only under the strict Freedman approach, but also under the ABA Proposed Defense Function Standards. Even the ABA Model Rules of Professional Conduct do not appear to sanction a threat by defense counsel actually to take the stand and to testify as a prosecution witness on rebuttal. Our holding is no broader than necessary to dispose of the perhaps unique fact situation presented here. In particular, we express no view on the sixth amendment implications of a lawyer's simply moving to withdraw, with or without informing the trial court of the reason. Surely a lawyer who actually testified against his own client could not be said to be rendering effective assistance. The same is true, we think, of a lawyer who threatens to testify against his own client.

Here, counsel went so far in his (at least initially) commendable zeal to avoid deceiving the court that he became an adversary to his own client. In this situation, we believe that appellant did not receive the effective assistance of counsel.

Accordingly, the judgment of the district court is reversed and the case is remanded to the district court with directions to grant the petition for writ of habeas corpus if the state does not begin new trial proceedings within a period to be determined by the district court.

The Purposes of Advocacy and the Limits of Confidentiality

JOHN T. NOONAN, JR.*

The privilege of confidentiality between lawyer and client is a significant barrier to the search for truth and the attainment of justice. Since bankers, accountants, psychiatrists, and confessors are not entitled at common law to confidentiality in their relationships with those with whom they deal, one may well inquire why lawyers possess such an extraordinary privilege. In the early English case which established the lawyer-client privilege, counsel offered several justifications: (1) A "gentleman of character" does not disclose his client's secrets. (2) An attorney identifies himself with his client, and it would be "contrary to the rules of natural justice and equity" for an individual to betray himself. (3) Attorneys are necessary for the conduct of business, and business would be destroyed if attorneys were to disclose their communications with their clients.[1]

None of the above justifications seems very persuasive today. Gentlemen of character have no legally recognized immunity from testifying about their friends' secrets. The identification of lawyer and client is, at best, only a metaphor, indicating an underlying policy justification for the privilege. Finally, attorneys are no more essential to the conduct of general business than are accountants, bankers, and secretaries, who do not enjoy the privilege. The suspicion arises that the legal profession has carved out for itself a privilege which it is reluctant to grant to other equally necessary and honorable men merely because the privilege is good for the legal business.

However, the secrecy of information communicated by a client to a lawyer may have a more rational justification than those discussed above when the information is divulged in preparation for a trial. The purpose of

*Professor of Law, University of Notre Dame.—Ed. [of *Michigan Law Review*] I am indebted to the suggestions of my colleague, Professor G. Robert Blakey.

[1] *Annesley v. Anglesey,* 17 *How. St. Tr.* 1140, 1223–26, 1241 (Ex. 1743).

employing a trial lawyer is to assert one's rights in a lawsuit; this purpose might be defeated if a relevant secret were available to one side merely by calling the opposing counsel to testify. Therefore, if the essential function of lawyers is to conduct trials, they must be able to receive relevant information and keep it confidential.

To say that a lawyer's function is to conduct a trial, however, does not suffice, for one must inquire into the purposes of a trial and of trial advocacy. If one agrees with Charles Curtis that a trial is an irrational process—a substitute for trial by battle which gives the litigant the satisfaction of having "his day in court"[2]—one may conclude that the function of the advocate is to be a friendly champion who, by his wholehearted devotion to the cause, is able to satisfy his client's desire for a day in court. It is hard to deny that many trials of the past, and some of the present, suggest the appropriateness of such an analysis. If this theory of the purposes of a trial and of advocacy is accepted, there is no reason why the solutions proposed by Professor Monroe Freedman to his three hypothetical cases should be rejected. Since many trial lawyers believe, perhaps subconsciously, that the Curtis view is an accurate reflection of what actually happens in a trial, it is easy to understand why Professor Freedman's solutions seem plausible, if not mandatory; he has merely expressed as a norm what is, in fact, current practice for some practitioners. Indeed, the merit of Professor Freedman's exposition is that he candidly exposes the working principles of many lawyers at the same time that he makes those principles vital by showing how they would govern particular cases. This scholarly explication of what is often taken for granted serves a very useful function.

Professor Freedman's analysis, however, presupposes that the Curtis theory, or something approximating it, is a correct description of the trial process. Yet, Curtis' description of the system obscures three important points. First, although a trial may be a battle, not only is physical violence excluded, but some purely peaceful tactics such as the subornation of perjury and the introduction of faked documents are discouraged; the system gives each litigant his day in court, but it also excludes obviously false information. Second, the satisfaction the client receives depends not on his sense of the friendly atmosphere of the court, but rather on his feeling that justice is being done, insofar as he is being heard, for the client will usually believe that once he is heard, truth will prevail. Third, the truth-discovering techniques of Anglo-American law have developed from such crude devices as trial by battle to more refined and more ample procedures such as detailed interrogatories and discovery procedures under the Federal Rules; this evolution must be taken into consideration in any analysis of purposes of the system.

A second, perhaps more appropriate view of a trial and of the adversary system is the view endorsed in 1958 by the Joint Conference on Professional Responsibility of the Association of American Law Schools and the American Bar Association. It is a modern view in that it looks less at the way in which trials have been conducted in the past than at the way in which

[2]Curtis, *It's Your Law* 17–21 (1954).

they may be conducted in the future. A trial is seen as a process "within which man's capacity for impartial judgment can attain its fullest realization,"[3] and the function of the advocate is to assist the trier of fact in making this impartial judgment. In a non-adversary system, the tribunal would do its own investigating, have its own theory of the case, and possibly decide the issues too quickly. On the other hand, the adversary system permits the tribunal to remain uncommitted while a case is explored from opposing viewpoints, thus requiring the liability or guilt to be demonstrated publicly to a neutral tribunal. In this view of the system, "the advocate plays his role well when zeal for his client's cause promotes a wise and informed decision of the case."[4]

Evidently, if the Joint Conference's approach is taken, distinctions must be made in answering Professor Freedman's three hypotheticals. As to the first problem,[5] it could be argued that the sole function of an advocate is to produce a wise and informed *ultimate* judgment. In the process of assisting the trier in attaining this final result, counsel therefore may properly obscure or impugn testimony which, while true, would not be relevant to the determination of guilt but rather would merely create an erroneous impression.[6] For example, a defense lawyer could attempt to impair the credibility of a witness who testified truthfully before a jury of Negroes that the defendant was a member of the Ku Klux Klan. By destroying the true but irrelevant testimony, it is argued, the advocate would, in fact, contribute to a wise ultimate result. This reasoning, however, does not seem persuasive. Rather, it resembles the paternalism which is so often invoked as an excuse for not trusting others with the truth. Instead of attempting to destroy the testimony it would be better to refrain from impeaching the truthful witness and to trust the trier of fact to draw the right conclusions. The law itself provides mechanisms for excluding irrelevant and prejudicial evidence; where evidence is not clearly irrelevant, a lawyer should not attempt to exclude it at the cost of attacking a truthful witness. Repeated acts of confidence in the rationality of the trial system are necessary if the decision-making process is to approach rationality.

The second hypothetical[7] is easier than the first to solve in terms of the Joint Conference's theory. To permit a client who will commit perjury to take the stand does not contribute to a wise and informed decision. It is difficult to differentiate among forging documents, suborning another witness, and calling one's own client with the knowledge that he will lie. An impartial, informed, and wise decision presupposes that the person deciding a case has been given the truth. To furnish him with a lie is to mock impartiality, to mislead rather than to inform, and to stultify the decisional

[3] "*Professional Responsibility: Report of the Joint Conference*," 44 A.B.A.J. 1160–61 (1958).
[4] *Ibid.*
[5] Freedman, "*Professional Responsibility of the Criminal Defense Lawyer: The Three Hardest Questions*," 64 *Mich. L. Rev.* 1469 (1966).
[6] Professor Freedman uses a slightly different rationale to reach the same conclusion. See *id.* at 1474–75.
[7] *Id.* at 1469.

304 The Attorney and The Client

process rather than to make it an exploration leading to mature judgment.

The third hypothetical[8] would seem to be answerable, in part, the same way under both Professor Freedman's analysis and that of the Joint Conference. A lawyer should not be paternalistic toward his client, and cannot assume that his client will perjure himself. Furthermore, a lawyer has an obligation to furnish his client with all the legal information relevant to his case; in fulfilling this duty to inform his client, a lawyer would normally not violate ethical standards. Motives may properly be given their weight after the legal consequences of an act are known by the client, for a human being rarely acts with a completely undivided heart. Although the courts have made a generous allowance for this multiplicity of human motivations, there is a point, however, at which it becomes brute rationalization to claim that the legal advice tendered to a client is meant to contribute to wise and informed decision-making. For example, a lawyer may, in substance, be suggesting perjury rather than giving legal advice when the lawyer knows that the facts are completely contrary to the defense which he outlines to his client. In *Anatomy of a Murder*, Paul Biegler won his case, but lost his fee.[9] Possibly this result reflects the author's own conception of a just reward for Biegler's manipulative use of the system. Professor Freedman seems to feel that to refuse to tell a client of a defense which is not supported by the facts would penalize truth-telling clients; the answer is that truth sometimes has unfortunate consequences.

Thus, if one considers that the function of the advocate is to assist in the formulation of wise and informed decisions, there is a limit to the confidentiality of communication between client and trial counsel. The partisanship involved in keeping a communication confidential must be restricted when it leads to conduct which destroys the truth or presents perjury to the fact-finder. Indeed, in some instances, courts may even compel a lawyer to testify about confidential information revealed to him by a client. The communication of an intention to commit a crime is not privileged;[10] neither does the privilege exist if a lawyer has a pre-existing duty which precludes him from acting for a client.[11] Some courts have held that only relevant information is privileged[12] and that information may not remain confidential after the client's death.[13] All of these qualifications present difficult questions which a naïve client, believing his communications were truly free from disclosure by his lawyer, would not anticipate.[14]

---

[8]*Ibid.*

[9]Traver, *Anatomy of a Murder* (1958).

[10]*E.g., United States v. Bob*, 106 F.2d 37, 39–40 (2d Cir. 1939).

[11]*E.g., Prichard v. United States*, 181 F.2d 326 (6th Cir. 1950).

[12]*E.g., Snow v. Gould*, 74 Me. 540, 543 (1883).

[13]*In re Graf's Estate*, 119 N.W.2d 478 (N.D. 1963).

[14]In the ancient civil case first recognizing the privilege, the issue was whether an earl's solicitor could disclose his client's intent to arrange the judicial hanging of a rival for his estate. The court, while recognizing the privilege, ordered disclosure of the information. One ground of the decision was that the communication was not relevant to the earl's legal business, although in fact it bore very heavily on the earl's willingness to settle certain lawsuits in which the solicitor was involved. *Annesley v. Anglesey*, 17 *How. St. Tr.* 1140, 1223–26, 1241 (Ex.

Thus, it appears that neither confidentiality nor the adversary system is an absolute; each is justified pragmatically by its ability to serve certain social needs. Professor Freedman repeatedly treats a privileged communication as an absolute which takes precedence over all other values. He justifies this by asserting that complete lawyer–client confidentiality is necessary to the adversary system. Yet such confidentiality is necessary to the adversary system only if the system exists as Professor Freedman views it. Asserted as a standard by which to measure the lawyer's conduct in all situations, absolute confidentiality is inimical to a system which has as its end rational decision-making.

It might, however, be objected that I have not sufficiently considered the requirements of a criminal trial. In criminal trials, the privilege against self-incrimination has a far more significant impact on the procedure than it does in civil trials. Dominant among the multiple purposes of this constitutional privilege are the creation of some balance between the government and the individual and the assurance of respect for the person of the defendant.[15] It may be asserted that the objective of displaying respect for the humanity of a defendant cuts across and limits the truth-discovering purpose of a trial should be absolute. This approach can be persuasive, especially if the tendency to expand the meaning and scope of the constitutional privilege against self-incrimination is interpreted as a series of advances in the protection of the person.[16] Nevertheless, truth-discovering may still be a dominant purpose of a criminal trial.

The criminal process operates in such a way that a large number of convictions are obtained by admissions; in this decade, roughly five sixths of those convicted in the federal courts have pleaded *nolo contendere* or guilty.[17] Recent decisions have resulted in a marked lessening of the adversary role of the prosecutor, who is now compelled to respond to the broad discovery rights of the defendant,[18] is prohibited from suppressing evidence helpful to the defendant,[19] and is required to make the names of the material witnesses available to the defendant.[20] While this trend could be considered another series of advances in the protection of the individual, it could also be interpreted as an effort to eliminate those characteristics of a trial which have made trials appear to be somewhat of a game.[21] The

---

1743). Randolph Paul says that "in some instances taxpayers are unaware of the safety inherent in the confidential relationship which exists between tax clients and their attorneys." Paul, *"Responsibilities of the Tax Adviser,"* 63 *Harv. L. Rev.* 377, 383 (1950). He apparently does not point out to them that this privilege is limited; if the client reveals an intent to continue a plan of tax evasion, there is no judicially recognizable confidentiality attending the communication.

[15]See Wigmore, *Evidence* § 2251 (McNaughton rev. 1961); Note, 78 *Harv. L. Rev.* 426 (1964).

[16]See, *e.g.*, *Malloy v. Hogan*, 378 U.S. 1 (1964).

[17]Director of the Administrative Office of the United States Courts, Ann. Rep. 132 (1963).

[18]*Campbell v. United States*, 373 U.S. 487 (1963); *Bowman Dairy v. United States*, 341 U.S. 214 (1951).

[19]*Brady v. Maryland*, 373 U.S. 83, 87 (1963); Note, 34 *Geo. Wash. L. Rev.* 92, 103 (1965).

[20]*United States ex rel. Meers v. Wilkins*, 326 F.2d 135 (2d Cir. 1964).

[21]*Curran v. Delaware*, 259 F.2d 707, 711 (3d Cir. 1958), *cert. denied*, 358 U.S. 948 (1959).

adversary system is not eliminated by such changes, but its irrational aspects are diminished, and if the trend is truly one of eliminating the irrational, it may be expected that the irrational elements favoring the defendant will also be reduced. In the new Federal Rules of Criminal Procedure, the courts are given the power to condition discovery by a defendant on the defendant's giving the government a limited right to discovery.[22] It may be expected that if the government prosecutor cannot present a doubtful witness without calling the defendant's attention to his lack of credibility,[23] the defendant's lawyer may be asked to observe the same standard as to his witnesses. Should there be any difference if the witness is the defendant himself? Is it really an enhancement of the rights of the person or a protection of the defendant's dignity to permit him to commit perjury with his lawyer's acquiescence? These questions are raised because it is difficult to believe that the defense of human rights depends upon a deliberate avoidance of the rational.

Extensive subordination of the lawyer's interests to those of his client also has an effect on the lawyer himself. Professor Freedman is concerned about the rights of the client; but what of the rights of the lawyer? Professor Freedman's chief authorities are the Canons of Professional Ethics of the American Bar Association, Opinion 287 interpreting Canons 29 and 37,[24] and the case of *Johns v. Smyth*.[25] While the Canons, which were adopted at the beginning of this century, do not offer as clear or as rational a view of the advocate's function as is found in the report of the 1958 Joint Conference, they are significant in so far as they are the work of a professional group which refused to let professional requirements be the ultimate norm. The Canons do not say that the man is to be subordinated to the advocate or that a lawyer, *qua* lawyer, is to be less than human. On this cardinal point, the Canons are squarely in disagreement with the extraordinary dictum in *Johns v. Smyth*.[26] Under the heading, "How far may a lawyer go in supporting a client's cause," the Canons recognize the need for "warm zeal" in the maintenance of a client's rights, but they conclude flatly that the lawyer "must obey his own conscience and not that of his client."[27]

It is inconceivable that Professor Freedman would endorse a system in which a lawyer is merely the willing tool, mouthpiece, or technician for his client. Only a moral idealist would so uncompromisingly proclaim his position as Professor Freedman has done. Only a moral absolutist would

---

[22]*Fed. R. Crim. P.* 16b, 16c, as amended Feb. 28, 1966, to take effect July 1, 1966.

[23]*Curran v. Delaware*, 259 F.2d 707, 711 (3rd Cir. 1958), *cert. denied*, 358 U.S. 948 (1959).

[24]Opinion 287, Committee on Professional Ethics and Grievances of the American Bar Association (1953).

[25]176 F. Supp. 949 (E.D. Va. 1959). [Above, pp. 116-20.]

[26]*Id.* at 953: "[T]he defendant was entitled to the faithful and devoted services of his attorney uninhibited by the dictating conscience." The lawyer, when he could not conscientiously proceed with the defense, should have offered his client the option of seeking other counsel. In failing to do so, he deprived his client of the basic right to choose a lawyer who was willing to act for him. *But see* Orkin, *"Defense of One Known To Be Guilty,"* 1 *Crim. L.Q.* 170, 174 (1958).

[27]American Bar Association, Canons of Professional Ethics, Canon 15 (1908).

say that a criminal's plea of not guilty is a lie.[28] Professor Freedman is so strongly in favor of candor and idealism that he in effect exposes the working principles of some lawyers by spelling out explicitly their assumptions and the consequences of those assumptions. Like many idealists, however, he is so candid that he may be mistaken for a cynic by the unenlightened. His position is not cynical, but it does seem to ignore the dangers inherent in defining the lawyer's role without broader consideration of the demands of human personality and of society. I would hope that reflection on the nature of the moral automatons which lawyers would logically become under Professor Freedman's view might cause him to reconsider his premises.

A lawyer should not impose his conscience on his client; neither can he accept his client's decision and remain entirely free from all moral responsibility, subject only to the restraints of the criminal law. The framework of the adversary system provides only the first set of guidelines for a lawyer's conduct. He is also a human being and cannot submerge his humanity by playing a technician's role. Although the obligation to be candid is not so absolute that it cannot be affected by context, both the seeking and stating of truth are so necessary to the human personality and so demanded by broad social values that the systematic presentation of falsehood is both personally demeaning and socially frustrating. Moreover, the adversary system itself does not demand active suppression of truth. As a free person, cooperating with another free person—his client—to prove the client's innocence in a way which will also lead to the revelation of truth, the lawyer must act with regard for the requirements of the adversary system and with concern for his own standards as a human person, as well as with regard for the requirements of the society which the system serves.

[28]Professor Freedman posits a "moralist" who will tell lawyers that they lie in entering such a plea. However, the obligation to tell the truth is seen today as dependent on the duty to respond. Moreover, words have no absolute significance. The plea "not guilty," as used in the context of a court proceeding, is understood by everyone to mean, "I cannot be proved guilty of the charge by the ordinary process of law."

Perjury: The Criminal Defense Lawyer's Trilemma†

MONROE H. FREEDMAN

Is it ever proper for a criminal defense lawyer to present perjured testimony?

One's instinctive response is in the negative. On analysis, however, it becomes apparent that the question is an exceedingly perplexing one. My own answer is in the affirmative.

At the outset, we should dispose of some common question-begging responses. The attorney, we are told, is an officer of the court, and participates in a search for truth. Those propositions, however, merely serve to state the problem in different words: As an officer of the court, participating in a search for truth, what is the attorney obligated to do when faced with perjured testimony? That question cannot be answered properly without an appreciation of the fact that the attorney functions in an adversary system of criminal justice which, as we have seen in the two previous chapters, imposes special responsibilities upon the advocate.

First, the lawyer is required to determine "all relevant facts known to the accused,"[1] because "counsel cannot properly perform their duties without knowing the truth."[2] The lawyer who is ignorant of any potentially relevant fact "incapacitates himself to serve his client effectively," because "an adequate defense cannot be framed if the lawyer does not know what is likely to develop at trial."[3]

Second, the lawyer must hold in strictest confidence the disclosures made by the client in the course of the professional relationship. "Nothing is more fundamental to the lawyer–client relationship that the establishment of trust and confidence."[4] The "first duty" of an attorney is "to keep the secrets of his clients."[5] If this were not so, the client would not feel free to confide fully, and the lawyer would not be able to fulfill the obligation to ascertain all relevant facts. Accordingly, defense counsel is required to

---

Lawyers' Ethics in an Adversary System (Indianapolis: The Bobbs-Merrill Company, 1975), pp. 27–43. Reprinted by permission.

†Professor Freedman has amplified his views in "Personal Responsibility in a Professional System," 27 *Cath. U.L. Rev.* 19 (1978) (Pope John XXIII Lecture)

[1]American Bar Association, Standards Relating to the Defense Function, § 3.2(a) (1971) [hereinafter cited as ABA Standards].

[2]American Bar Association, Committee on Professional Ethics and Grievances, Opinion 23 (1930).

[3]ABA Standards, Commentary a, at 204–05.

[4]ABA Standards, Commentary a, at 201.

[5]*Id.*, quoting *Taylor v. Blacklow*, 3 Bing. N.C. 235, 249, 132 Eng. Rep. 401, 406, C.R. (1836).

establish "a relationship of trust and confidence" with the accused, to explain "the necessity of full disclosure of all facts," and to explain to the client "the obligation of confidentiality which makes privileged the accused's disclosures."[6]

Third, the lawyer is an officer of the court, and his or her conduct before the court "should be characterized by candor."[7]

As soon as one begins to think about those responsibilities, it becomes apparent that the conscientious attorney is faced with what we may call a trilemma—that is, the lawyer is required to know everything, to keep it in confidence, and to reveal it to the court. Moreover, the difficulties presented by those conflicting obligations are particularly acute in the criminal defense area because of the presumption of innocence, the burden upon the state to prove its case beyond a reasonable doubt, and the right to put the prosecution to its proof.

Before addressing the issue of the criminal defense lawyer's responsibilities when the client indicates to the lawyer the intention to commit perjury in the future, we might note the somewhat less difficult question of what the lawyer should do when knowledge of the perjury comes after its commission rather than before it. Although there is some ambiguity in the most recent authorities, the rules appear to require that the criminal defense lawyer should urge the client to correct the perjury, but beyond that, the obligation of confidentiality precludes the lawyer from revealing the truth.

In an opinion of major importance under the old Canons, an eminent panel of the American Bar Association Committee on Professional Ethics and Grievances, headed by Henry Drinker, held that if the client falsely tells the judge that he has no prior record, the lawyer should remain silent despite knowledge to the contrary.[8] The majority of the panel distinguished the situation in which the attorney has learned of the client's prior record from a source other than the client. William B. Jones, then a trial lawyer and now a judge in the United States District Court for the District of Columbia, wrote a separate opinion in which he asserted that in neither event should the lawyer expose the client's lie.

The relevant provision of the new Code of Professional Responsibility[9] is DR 7-102(B)(1). As originally drafted, in 1969, that provision is in two clauses—a main clause and an "and if" clause. The main clause provides that when the lawyer learns that a client has "perpetrated a fraud upon a person or tribunal," the lawyer "shall promptly call upon his client to rectify" the fraud. The second clause reads: ". . . and if his client refuses or is unable to do so, he shall reveal the fraud to the affected person or tribunal." Thus, the American Bar Association at first appeared to take a

[6]ABA Standards, § 3.1(a).

[7]American Bar Association, Canons of Professional Ethics, Canon 22 (1908).

[8]American Bar Association, Committee on Professional Ethics and Grievances, Opinion 287 (1953).

[9]American Bar Association, Code of Professional Responsibility (1970) [hereinafter cited as The Code].

position in favor of disclosure by the lawyer contrary to the client's interest and in violation of confidentiality.

The District of Columbia was the first jurisdiction in the United States in which the practicing bar focused upon that particular provision and passed judgment upon it specifically. On my motion, DR 7-102(B)(1) was amended when the Code was adopted in the District, so as to delete the "and if " clause entirely. On a mail referendum of the bar, the amendment carried by 74 percent of the vote, or virtually three to one. Similarly, the Quebec Bar Association, which has adopted substantial portions of the ABA Code, has rejected DR 7-102(B).[10] In addition, the Law Society, which oversees the conduct of solicitors in England, has taken the position that a solicitor must maintain confidentiality even upon learning from the client after the conclusion of a civil case that a witness has been paid by the client to commit perjury.[11] Finally, the American Bar Association itself recognized the impropriety of requiring a breach of confidentiality. In 1974, the ABA added a third clause to DR 7-102(B)(1), so that the attorney is called upon to reveal the client's fraud "except when the information is protected as a privileged communication."

Of course, DR 7-102(B) is not limited to perjury in the context of criminal litigation. Indeed, the bar of the District of Columbia was advertising specifically to the obligations of the civil practitioner in a divorce case or a tax case.[12] Entirely apart from any consensus of the bar relative to civil practice, however, divulgence by the defense attorney in a criminal case would be controlled by such constitutional provisions as the right to counsel, the privilege against self-incrimination, the right to trial by jury, and the right to due process. Thus, the ABA Standards, referring to the original draft of DR 7-102(B)(1), state flatly that that provision "is construed as not embracing the giving of false testimony in a criminal case."[13] That is, even in those jurisdictions that may not yet have adopted the ABA's amendment to DR 7-102(B), that clause does not apply to the criminal defense lawyer.

With respect to the case where the lawyer has foreknowledge of the perjury, another section of the Code appears, at first reading, to be unambiguous. According to DR 7-102(A)(4), a lawyer must not "knowingly use perjured testimony or false evidence."[14] The difficulty, however, is that the Code does not indicate how the lawyer is to go about fulfilling that obligation. What if the lawyer advises the client that perjury is unlawful and,

---

[10]Bar of Quebec, Code of Ethics (Revised Draft, 1974).

[11]T. Lund, *A Guide to the Professional Conduct of Solicitors* 105 (1960).

[12]The argument for the amendment stated in part: "The effect of the Code provision can be illustrated by a divorce case. At the husband's deposition he produces his tax return and testifies that it is complete and accurate. Through confidential communications from his client, the husband's attorney learns that the husband has additional, unreported income. The attorney urges him to correct his false testimony, and he refuses to do so. The proposed DR subjects the attorney to discipline if he does not reveal the unreported income to the wife and her attorney, to the court, and to the IRS. . . ."

[13]ABA Standards, Supplement, at 18.

[14]*See also*, DR 7-102(A)(5), (7) and (8); EC 7-26.

perhaps, bad tactics as well, but the client nevertheless insists upon taking the stand and committing perjury in his or her own defense? What steps, specifically, should the lawyer take? Just how difficult it is to answer that question becomes apparent if we review the relationship between lawyer and client as it develops, and consider the contexts in which the decision to commit perjury may arise.

If we recognize that professional responsibility requires that an advocate have full knowledge of every pertinent fact, then the lawyer must seek the truth from the client, not shun it. That means that the attorney will have to dig and pry and cajole, and, even then, the lawyer will not be successful without convincing the client that full disclosure to the lawyer will never result in prejudice to the client by any word or action of the attorney. That is particularly true in the case of the indigent defendant, who meets the lawyer for the first time in the cell block or the rotunda of the jail. The client did not choose the lawyer, who comes as a stranger sent by the judge, and who therefore appears to be part of the system that is attempting to punish the defendant. It is no easy task to persuade that client to talk freely without fear of harm.

However, the inclination to mislead one's lawyer is not restricted to the indigent or even to the criminal defendant. Randolph Paul has observed a similar phenomenon among a wealthier class in a far more congenial atmosphere. The tax adviser, notes Mr. Paul, will sometimes have to "dynamite the facts of his case out of unwilling witnesses on his own side—witnesses who are nervous, witnesses who are confused about their own interest, witnesses who try to be too smart for their own good, and witnesses who subconsciously do not want to understand what has happened despite the fact they they must if they are to testify coherently."[15] Mr. Paul goes on to explain that the truth can be obtained only by persuading the client that it would be a violation of a sacred obligation for the lawyer ever to reveal a client's confidence. Of course, once the lawyer has thus persuaded the client of the obligation of confidentiality, that obligation must be respected scrupulously.

Assume the following situation. Your client has been falsely accused of a robbery committed at 16th and P Streets at 11:00 P.M. He tells you at first that at no time on the evening of the crime was he within six blocks of that location. However, you are able to persuade him that he must tell you the truth and that doing so will in no way prejudice him. He then reveals to you that he was at 15th and P Streets at 10:55 that evening, but that he was walking east, away from the scene of the crime, and that, by 11:00 P.M., he was six blocks away. At the trial, there are two prosecution witnesses. The first mistakenly, but with some degree of persuasiveness, identifies your client as the criminal. At that point the prosecution's case depends upon that single witness, who might or might not be believed. The second prosecution witness is an elderly woman who is somewhat nervous and who wears glasses. She testifies truthfully and accurately that she saw your client at 15th and P Streets at 10:55 P.M. She has corroborated the erroneous

[15]Paul, *"The Responsibilities of the Tax Adviser,"* 63 *Harv. L. Rev.* 377, 383 (1950).

testimony of the first witness and made conviction extremely likely. However, on cross-examination her reliability is thrown into doubt through demonstration that she is easily confused and has poor eyesight.* Thus, the corroboration has been eliminated, and doubt has been established in the minds of the jurors as to the prosecution's entire case.

The client then insists upon taking the stand in his own defense, not only to deny the erroneous evidence identifying him as the criminal, but also to deny the truthful, but highly damaging, testimony of the corroborating witness who placed him one block away from the intersection five minutes prior to the crime. Of course, if he tells the truth and thus verifies the corroborating witness, the jury will be more inclined to accept the inaccurate testimony of the principal witness, who specifically identified him as the criminal.

In my opinion, the attorney's obligation in such a situation would be to advise the client that the proposed testimony is unlawful, but to proceed in the normal fashion in presenting the testimony and arguing the case to the jury if the client makes the decision to go forward. Any other course would be a betrayal of the assurances of confidentiality given by the attorney in order to induce the client to reveal everything, however damaging it might appear.

A frequent objection to the position that the attorney must go along with the client's decision to commit perjury is that the lawyer would be guilty of subornation of perjury. Subornation, however, consists of willfully procuring perjury, which is not the case when the attorney indicates to the client that the client's proposed course of conduct would be unlawful, but then accepts the client's decision.† Beyond that, there is a point of view, which has been expressed to me by a number of experienced attorneys, that the criminal defendant has a "right to tell his story." What that suggests is that it is simply too much to expect of a human being, caught up in the criminal process and facing loss of liberty and the horrors of imprisonment, not to attempt to lie to avoid that penalty. For that reason, criminal defendants in most European countries do not testify under oath, but simply "tell their stories." it is also noteworthy that subsequent perjury prosecutions against criminal defendants in this country are extremely rare. However, the judge may well take into account at sentencing the fact that the defendant has apparently committed perjury in the course of the defense.[16] That is certainly a factor that the attorney is obligated to advise the client about whenever there is any indication that the client is contemplating perjury.

The discussion thus far has focused only on the lawyer's obligation when the perjury is presented by the client. Some authorities indicate a distinction between perjury by the criminal defendant, who has a right to

*The question of the propriety of cross-examining an accurate and truthful witness is considered in Chapter 4 *infra*.

†The analysis at pp. 5–6 *supra*, regarding the applicability of criminal statutes generally to the lawyer–client relationship, is also applicable here.

[16]*Cf. United States v. Hendrix*, Docket No. 74-1603 (2d Cir., Sept. 15, 1974).

take the stand, and perjury by collateral witnesses.[17] I agree that there is an important distinction, and that the case involving collateral witnesses is not at all as clear as that involving the client alone. In one case, however, a new trial was ordered when the trial court discovered that the defendant's attorney had refused to put on the defendant's mother and sister because the attorney was concerned about perjury.[18] Certainly a spouse or parent would be acting under the same human compulsion as a defendant, and I find it difficult to imagine myself denouncing my client's spouse or parent as a perjurer and, thereby, denouncing my client as well. I do not know, however, how much wider that circle of close identity might be drawn.

In a criticism of my position, Professor John Noonan of Boalt Hall argued that the true function of the advocate is to assist the trier of fact to reach a "wise and informed decision."[19] Upon analysis, however, that proposition only compounds the problem. For example, I have suggested that a criminal defendant is privileged to lie to the court in pleading "not guilty" even when the defendant knows that the plea is contrary to fact. Professor Noonan responded that the not-guilty plea, as used in the context of a court proceeding, is not a lie, because it is understood by everyone to mean: "I cannot be proved guilty of the charge by the ordinary process of law."[20] The "ordinary process of law," however, unquestionably includes the constitutional right to suppress relevant and truthful evidence that has been obtained in violation of constitutional rights—even though a wise and informed judgment might thereby be sacrificed. Thus, in order to justify or rationalize the false plea of not guilty, Professor Noonan is thrown back to a recognition of those aspects of the system that are inconsistent with his rationale. Certainly it is unlikely that Professor Noonan would suggest that attorneys should relinquish their client's constitutional rights where those rights conflict with truth-seeking. Yet he does argue that attorneys should forego long-accepted trial tactics (e.g., cross-examination of the relevant and truthful witness), because: "Repeated acts of confidence in the rationality of the trial system are necessary if the decision-making process is to approach rationality."[21] That seems to mean that the fortunes, liberty, and lives of today's clients can properly be jeopardized for the sake of creating a more rational system for tomorrow's litigants.

Moreover, Professor Noonan's general proposition does not decide specific cases. Like other critics who express disapproval of the idea that a lawyer might knowingly present perjured testimony, Professor Noonan does not suggest what a lawyer should do, as a practical matter, in the course of conferring with the client and presenting the case in court. For

---

[17]*See, e.g.*, DR 7-102(B); ABA Standards, Commentary a to § 7.5; Bowman, *Standards of Conduct for Prosecution and Defense Personnel: An Attorney's Viewpoint*," 5 *Am. Crim. L. Q.* 28, 30 (1966).

[18]*See, Washington Post*, Oct. 31, 1971, § D, at 3.

[19]Noonan, "*The Purposes of Advocacy and the Limits of Confidentiality*," 64 *Mich. L. Rev.* 1485 (1966). [Above, pp. 301-7.]. Professor Noonan drew his rationale from "*Professional Responsibility: Report of the Joint Conference*," 44 *A.B.A.J.* 1160–61 (1958).

[20]*Id.* [Above, p. 307, n. 28.]

[21]*Id.* [Above, p. 303.]

example, how would Professor Noonan's proposition resolve the following case? The prosecution witness testified that the robbery had taken place at 10:15, and identified the defendant as the criminal. However, the defendant had a convincing alibi for 10:00 to 10:30. The attorney presented the alibi, and the client was acquitted. The alibi was truthful, but the attorney knew that the prosecution witness had been confused about the time, and that his client had in fact committed the crime at 10:45. (Ironically, that same attorney considers it clearly unethical for a lawyer to present the false testimony on behalf of the innocent defendant in the case of the robbery at 16th and P Streets.) Should the lawyer have refused to present the honest alibi? How could he possibly have avoided doing so? Was he contributing to wise and informed judgment when he did present it?

The most obvious way to avoid the ethical difficulty is for the lawyer to withdraw from the case, at least if there is sufficient time before trial for the client to retain another attorney. The client will then go to the nearest law office, realizing that the obligation of confidentiality is not what it has been represented to be, and withhold incriminating information or the fact of guilt from the new attorney. In terms of professional ethics, the practice of withdrawing from a case under such circumstances is difficult to defend, since the identical perjured testimony will ultimately be presented. Moreover, the new attorney will be ignorant of the perjury and therefore will be in no position to attempt to discourage the client from presenting it. Only the original attorney, who knows the truth, has that opportunity, but loses it in the very act of evading the ethical problem.

The difficulty is all the more severe when the client is indigent. In that event, the client cannot retain other counsel, and in many jurisdictions it is impossible for appointed counsel or a public defender to withdraw from a case except for extraordinary reasons. Thus, the attorney can successfully withdraw only by revealing to the judge that the attorney has received knowledge of the client's guilt,* or by giving the judge a false or misleading reason for moving for leave to withdraw. However, for the attorney to reveal knowledge of the client's guilt would be a gross violation of the obligation of confidentiality, particularly since it is entirely possible in many jurisdictions that the same judge who permits the attorney to withdraw will subsequently hear the case and sentence the defendant.[22] Not only will the judge then have personal knowledge of the defendant's guilt before the trial begins, but it will be knowledge of which the newly appointed counsel for the defendant will very likely be ignorant.

Even where counsel is retained, withdrawal may not be a practical solution either because trial has begun or it is so close to trial that withdrawal would leave the client without counsel, or because the court for other reasons denies leave to withdraw.[23] Judges are most reluctant to

---

*The typical formula is for the attorney to advise the judge of "an ethical problem." The judge understands that to mean that the client is insisting upon a perjured alibi over the lawyer's objections. In one case, the judge incorrectly drew that inference when the lawyer's ethical concern was with the fact that the client wanted to enter a guilty plea despite the fact that he was innocent.

[22]*"Accord,"* ABA Standards, at 12.

[23]ABA Standards, at 275. *See also,* Freedman, *"Professional Responsibility of the Criminal Defense Lawyer: The Three Hardest Questions,"* 64 *Mich. L. Rev.* 1469, 1476–77 (1966).

grant leave to withdraw during the trial or even shortly before it because of the power that that would give to defendants to delay the trial date or even to cause a series of mistrials.

Another solution that has been suggested is that the attorney move for leave to withdraw and that, when the request is denied, the attorney then proceed with the case, eliciting the defendant's testimony and arguing the case to the jury in the ordinary fashion. Since that proposal proceeds on the assumption that the motion will be denied, it seems to me to be disingenuous. If the attorney avoids the ethical problem, it is only by passing it on to the judge. Moreover, the client in such a case would then have grounds for appeal on the basis of deprivation of due process and denial of the right to counsel, since the defendant would have been tried before, and sentenced by, a judge who had been informed by the defendant's own lawyer that the defendant is guilty both of the crime charged and of perjury. The prejudice inherent in such a situation is illustrated by a federal appellate case in which the majority voted to remand the case to determine whether the defendant had been denied certain due process rights. One judge dissented, however, expressly basing his opinion in part on incriminating information that had been put into the record by the defendant's own counsel.*

Another unsuccessful effort to deal with the problem appears in the ABA Standards Relating to the Defense Function. The Standards first attempt to solve the problem by a rhetorical attack, unsupported by practical analysis or verifiable research, upon those who are concerned with maintaining confidentiality. Thus, the Standards state that it has been "universally rejected by the legal profession" that a lawyer may be excused for acquiescing in the use of known perjured testimony on the "transparently spurious thesis" that the principle of confidentiality requires it. While "no honorable lawyer" would accept that view and "every experienced advocate can see its basic fallacy as a matter of tactics apart from morality and law," the "mere advocacy" of such an idea "demeans the profession and tends to drag it to the level of gangsters and their 'mouthpiece' lawyers in the public eye." The Standards conclude that that concept is "universally repudiated by ethical lawyers," although that fact does not fully repair the "gross disservice" done by the few who are "unscrupulous" enough to practice it.[24]

One hundred thirty-two pages later, however, the Standards express a very different assessment of lawyer's attitudes regarding perjury by the client. Although "some lawyers" are said to favor disclosure of the perjury, the Standards recognize that other attorneys (not characterized in the

Holmes v. United States, 370 F.2d 209, 212 (D.C. Cir. 1966) (Danaher, J.):
"Finding the Holmes testimony at variance from the opening statement made by his trial attorney, the latter in the absence of the jury addressed the court: 'For purposes of the record, Your Honor, about half of what the defendant said on the stand was a complete surprise to me.'
"He added that in the course of numerous interviews' the appellant had 'consistently told me' a different story. The attorney asked Holmes no further questions.
"*From the foregoing, some idea can be gleaned as to why I do not join my colleagues in thinking there even possibly could have been prejudice.*' " (Emphasis added.)

[24]ABA Standards, at 142.

pejorative terms of the earlier passage) hold that the obligation of confidentiality does not permit disclosure of the facts learned from the client. To disclose the perjury, it is noted, "would be inconsistent with the assurances of confidentiality which counsel gave at the outset of the lawyer-client relationship."[25] Thus, the Standards acknowledge a genuine "dilemma" in the forced choice between candor and confidentiality.[26]

Since there are actually three obligations that create the difficulty—the third being the attorney's duty to learn all the facts—there is, of course, another way to resolve the difficulty. That is, by "selective ignorance." The attorney can make it clear to the client from the outset that the attorney does not want to hear an admission of guilt or incriminating information from the client.* That view, however, puts an unreasonable burden on the unsophisticated client to select what to tell and what to hold back, and it can seriously impair the attorney's effectiveness in counselling the client and in trying the case.

For example, one leading attorney, who favors selective ignorance to avoid the trilemma, told me about one of his own cases in which the defendant assumed that the attorney would prefer to be ignorant of the fact that the defendant had been having sexual relations with the chief defense witness. As a result of the lawyer's ignorance of that fact, he was unable to minimize its impact by raising it with potential jurors during jury selection and by having the defendant and the defense witness admit it freely on direct examination. Instead, the first time the lawyer learned about the illicit sexual relationship was when the prosecutor dramatically obtained a reluctant admission from the defense witness on cross-examination. The defense attorney is convinced that the client was innocent of the robbery with which he had been charged, but the defendant was nevertheless found guilty by the jury—in the attorney's own opinion because the defendant was guilty of fornication, a far less serious offense for which he had not been charged.

The question remains: what should the lawyer do when faced with the client's insistence upon taking the stand and committing perjury? It is in response to that question that the Standards present a most extraordinary solution. If the lawyer knows that the client is going to commit perjury, Section 7.7 of the Standards requires that the lawyer "must confine his examination to identifying the witness as the defendant and permitting him to make his statement." That is, the lawyer "may not engage in direct examination of the defendant . . . in the conventional manner." Thus, the client's story will become part of the record, although without the

---

[25]*Id.* at 276.

[26]*Id.*

*The ABA Standards again employ harsh rhetoric in criticizing a viewpoint of which they disapprove: "The most flagrant form of the practice of 'intentional ignorance' on the part of defense lawyers is the tactic, occasionally advocated by unscrupulous lawyers both in private and in practice manuals and seminars, of advising the client at the outset not to admit anything to the lawyer which might handicap the lawyer's freedom in calling witnesses or in otherwise making a defense." According to the Standards, that tactic is "most egregious" and constitutes "professional impropriety." ABA Standards Relating to the Defense Function, Commentary b to § 3.2 at 205.

attorney's assistance through direct examination. The general rule, of course, is that in closing argument to the jury "the lawyer may argue all reasonable inferences from the evidence in the record."[27] Section 7.7 also provides, however, that the defense lawyer is forbidden to make any reference in closing argument to the client's testimony.

There are at least two critical flaws in that proposal. The first is purely practical: The prosecutor might well object to testimony from the defendant in narrative form rather than in the conventional manner, because it would give the prosecutor no opportunity to object to inadmissible evidence prior to the jury's hearing it. The Standards provide no guidance as to what the defense attorney should do if the objection is sustained.

More importantly, experienced trial attorneys have often noted that jurors assume that the defendant's lawyer knows the truth about the case, and that the jury will frequently judge the defendant by drawing inferences from the attorney's conduct in the case.[28] There is, of course, only one inference that can be drawn if the defendant's own attorney turns his or her back on the defendant at the most critical point in the trial, and then, in closing argument, sums up the case with no reference to the fact that the defendant has given exculpatory testimony. As held by a federal court:

> . . . The failure to argue the case before the jury, while ordinarily only a trial tactic not subject to review, manifestly enters the field of incompetency when the reason assigned is the attorney's conscience. *It is as improper as though the attorney had told the jury that his client had uttered a falsehood in making the statement.* The right to an attorney embraces effective representation throughout all stages of the trial, and where the representation is of such low caliber as to amount to no representation, the guarantee of due process has been violated.[29]

Similarly, Professor Addison Bowman of Georgetown Law Center (an experienced trial lawyer, and a member of the Legal Ethics Committee of the District of Columbia Bar) has stated: "I do not believe it is proper for defense counsel to present the defendant's testimony in a fashion that may lead the jury to conclude that counsel does not believe his client."[30] Ironically, the Standards reject any solution that would involve informing the judge,[31] but then propose a solution that, as a practical matter, succeeds in informing not only the judge but the jury as well.

It would appear that the ABA Standards have chosen to resolve the trilemma by maintaining the requirements of complete knowledge and of candor to the court, and sacrificing confidentiality. Interestingly, however, that may not in fact be the case. I say that because the Standards fail to

---

[27]ABA Standards, § 7.8.

[28]*See,* Burger, "*A Sick Profession?*," 27 *Fed. B. J.* 228, 229–30 (1967).

[29]*Johns v. Smyth,* 176 F. Supp. 949, 953 (E.D. Va. 1959) [above, p. 119] (emphasis added) (cited, The Code, at 29, n. 3).

[30]Bowman, *supra* note 16, at 28, 30.

[31]ABA Standards, at 12, 227.

answer a critically important question: Should the client be told about the obligation imposed by Section 7.7? That is, the Standards ignore the issue of whether the lawyer should say to the client at the outset of their relationship: "I think it's only fair that I warn you: If you should tell me anything incriminating and subsequently decide to deny the incriminating facts at trial, I would not be able to examine you in the ordinary manner or to argue your untrue testimony to the jury." The Canadian Bar Association, for example takes an extremely hard line against the presentation of perjury by the client, but it also explicitly requires that the client be put on notice of that fact.[32] Obviously, any other course would be a betrayal of the client's trust, since everything else said by the attorney in attempting to obtain complete information about the case would indicate to the client that no information thus obtained would be used to the client's disadvantage.[33]

On the other hand, the inevitable result of the position taken by the Canadian Bar Association would be to caution the client not to be completely candid with the attorney. That, of course, returns us to resolving the trilemma by maintaining confidentiality and candor, but sacrificing complete knowledge—a solution which, as we have already seen, is denounced by the Standards as "unscrupulous," "most egregious," and "professional impropriety."[34]

Thus, the Standards, by failing to face up to the question of whether to put the client on notice, take us out of the trilemma by one door only to lead us back by another.

Earlier in this chapter we noted that the Code appears to be unambiguous in proscribing the known use of perjured testimony, but that the Code does not indicate how the lawyer is to go about fulfilling that obligation. Analysis of the various alternatives that have been suggested shows that none of them is wholly satisfactory, and that some are impractical and violate basic rights of the client. In addition the ABA Standards rely upon unsupported assertions of what lawyers "universally" think and do. It is therefore relevant and important to consider the actual practices of attorneys faced with the ethical issue in their daily work.

A survey conducted among lawyers in the District of Columbia is extremely revealing. The overall conclusion is that "less than 5% of practicing attorneys queried consistently acted in a manner the legal profession claims that members of the Bar act, and, under the new Code of Professional Responsibility, demands that they act."[35] Specifically, when asked what to do when the client indicates an intention to commit perjury, 95%

[32]Canadian Bar Association, Code of Professional Conduct, Ch. VIII, ¶9, at 59–60, 62–64 (Special Committee on Legal Ethics, Preliminary Report, June, 1973).

[33]*See,* Orkin, *"Defence of One Known to be Guilty,"* 1 *Crim. L. Q.* 170, 174 (1958). Unless the lawyer has told the client at the outset that knowledge of guilt will require the lawyer to withdraw, "it is plain enough as a matter of good morals and professional ethics" that the lawyer should not withdraw on that ground. American Bar Association, Committee on Professional Ethics and Grievances, Opinion 90 (1932).

[34]*See,* [p. 316] *supra.*

[35]Friedman, *"Professional Responsibility in D.C.: A Survey,"* 1972 *Res Ipsa Loquitur* 60 (1972).

indicated that they would call the defendant, and 90% of those attorneys responded that they would question the witness in the normal fashion.[36]*

That striking discrepancy between published standards and professional action is perhaps best explained by attorneys' reactions to being asked to participate in the survey. Virtually all of the attorneys personally interviewed refused to make an on-the-record statement, although without exception they were willing to participate in an anonymous interview.[37] Senior partners of two of Washington's most prestigious law firms, after refusing to allow the circulation of the questionnaire among the firm's members, permitted personal interviews on the condition that neither their names, names of the other members in the firm interviewed, nor the name of their firm would be published. Both attorneys, after apologizing for their insistence upon anonymity, explained that many of the local judges with whom they dealt daily would not look favorably upon their true views about the role of the defense attorney in a criminal case, especially if aired publicly. Their reason for not complying with the ABA's rules relating to the presentation of perjury was that those standards would compromise their role as advocates in an adversary system.[38]

In view of those findings, which stem in substantial part from the impracticality of the published standards, we might return to the relevant provisions of the Code with a somewhat more critical eye to consider whether the rules really mean what they appear at first reading to say.†

The cases cited by the codifiers provide important clues as to what is intended. The strongest of the cases against confidentiality is *In re Carroll,*[39] which held that an attorney "should not sit by silently and permit his client to commit what may have been perjury, and which certainly would mislead the court and the opposing party." Two important observations can be made about that case. First, it was not a criminal case, but involved a divorce. Second, the husband, whom the attorney represented, testified that he did not own certain property, but the same attorney had been authorized by the husband to claim ownership of the property in another judicial proceeding. Thus, the bond of confidentiality had already been loosened by the client's authorization. Third, assuming that *Carroll*

---

[36]*Id.* at 81.

*The attorneys in the survey reflected, as a group, an ambivalence similar to that expressed above at p. 313 regarding the propriety of putting on a perjurious witness other than the defendant. Only a bare majority (52%) answered in the affirmative, although a substantial number of those in the negative responded on tactical, not ethical, grounds. Friedman, *infra* note 34, at 69, 82. Unfortunately, the question was not broken down to distinguish between testimony by a spouse or parent as against, say, a casual acquaintance.

[37]*Id.* at 60.

[38]*Id.* at 60, n. 3.

†DR 7-102(A)(4), which deals with the use of perjured testimony, turns upon whether the lawyer acts "knowingly." As we will see in a later chapter, that word is a term of art—or, put less charitably, a term of evasion—in the area of legal ethics. There are those who say that the lawyer never "knows" that the client is guilty or lying. For those lawyers the ethical question never arises, and the provisions of the Code and the Standards therefore never come into play.

[39]244 S.W.2d 474 (Ky. Ct. App. 1951).

does stand as unqualified authority on behalf of divulgence, it is significant that the case is cited as a footnote to an Ethical Consideration (which is only "aspirational in character") and not a Disciplinary Rule (which is "mandatory in character," stating a "minimum level of conduct below which no lawyer can fall without being subject to disciplinary action").[40]

The case citation to the applicable Disciplinary Rule, DR 7-102, is significantly different. That case, *Hinds v. State Bar*,[41] also involved a divorce rather than a criminal matter. Most important, the attorney had participated in preparing the perjured affidavit that was at issue. (Also, the attorney was shown to have altered the client's deed to make the attorney's daughter a grantee, and apparently perjured himself in testifying in connection with the disciplinary proceeding.) Putting the *Carroll* and *Hinds* cases together, therefore, we may infer that the rule—in civil cases—is that an attorney is urged (by an Ethical Consideration) to divulge the client's fraud on the other party, at least when the client has authorized disclosure of the truth for other purposes, but the attorney is required to divulge the client's perjury, under sanction of a Disciplinary Rule, only when the attorney has participated in creation of the perjury.

There is another relevant citation in the notes to Canon 7. That case is *Johns v. Smyth*,[42] which, unlike the other two cases in point, is a criminal case. *Johns* is in a note to the opening sentence of EC 7-1, which reads: "The duty of a lawyer, both to his client and to the legal system, is to represent his client zealously *within the bounds of the law, which includes Disciplinary Rules.* . . . "[43] The case held that a defendant's constitutional rights had been violated because the attorney, believing his client to be guilty, did not argue the case in the ordinary manner.

Taking into account, therefore, the lack of practical guidance in the Code, the practical and constitutional difficulties encountered by any of the alternatives to strict maintenance of confidentiality, the consensus and the practice of the Bar, and the implications of *Carroll, Hinds* and *Johns*, which are the three key cases cited in the notes to Canon 7, I continue to stand with those lawyers who hold that "the lawyer's obligation of confidentiality does not permit him to disclose the facts he has learned from his client which form the basis for his conclusion that the client intends to perjure himself."[44] What that means—necessarily, it seems to me—is that the criminal defense attorney, however unwillingly in terms of personal morality, has a professional responsibility as an advocate in an adversary system to examine the perjurious client in the ordinary way and to argue to the jury, as evidence in the case, the testimony presented by the defendant.

---

[40]The Code, Preliminary Statement.

[41]19 Cal. 2d 87, 119 P.2d 134 (1941).

[42]176 F. Supp. 949 (E.D. Va. 1959). [Above, pp. 116-20.]

[43]Emphasis added.

[44]ABA Standards Commentary to § 7.7, at 276.

section three

COMPETENCE

A

Civil Malpractice

Smith v. Lewis

SUPREME COURT OF CALIFORNIA, 1975

MOSK, J. Defendant Jerome R. Lewis, an attorney, appeals from a judgment entered upon a jury verdict for plaintiff Rosemary E. Smith in an action for legal malpractice. The action arises as a result of legal services rendered by defendant to plaintiff in a prior divorce proceeding. The gist of plaintiff's complaint is that defendant negligently failed in the divorce action to assert her community interest in the retirement benefits of her husband.

Defendant principally contends, inter alia, that the law with regard to the characterization of retirement benefits was so unclear at the time he represented plaintiff as to insulate him from liability for failing to assert a claim therefore on behalf of his client.[1] We conclude defendant's appeal is without merit, and therefore affirm the judgment.

In 1943 plaintiff married General Clarence D. Smith. Between 1945 and his retirement in 1966 General Smith was employed by the California National Guard. As plaintiff testified, she informed defendant her husband "was paid by the state * * * it was a job just like anyone else goes to." For the first 16 years of that period the husband belonged to the State Employees' Retirement System, a contributory plan.[2] Between 1961 and

---

[1]Defendant alternatively contends the state and federal military retirement benefits in question cannot properly be characterized as community property, and hence his advice to plaintiff was correct. As will appear, the contention is manifestly untenable in light of recent decisions by this court. (*In re Marriage of Fithian*, 10 Cal.3d 592 [111 Cal.Rptr. 369, 517 P.2d 440 (1974); *Waite v. Waite*, 6 Cal.3d 461 [99 Cal.Tptr. 325, 492 P.2d 13 (1972)]; *Phillipson v. Board of Administration*, 3 Cal.3d 32 [89 Cal.Tptr. 61, 473 P.2d 765 (1970)].)

[2]A contributory plan is one in which the member contributes to his retirement fund, normally through payroll deductions. A noncontributory plan is one in which no such contributions are made.

The State Employees' Retirement System is now referred to as the Public Employees' Retirement System (West's Ann.Cal.Gov.Code § 20000 et seq.).

the date of his retirement he belonged to the California National Guard retirement program, a noncontributory plan. In addition, by attending National Guard reserve drills he qualified for separate retirement benefits from the federal government, also through a noncontributory plan. The state and federal retirement programs each provide lifetime monthly benefits which terminate upon the death of the retiree. The programs make no allowance for the retiree's widow.

On January 1, 1967, the State of California began to pay General Smith gross retirement benefits of $796.26 per month. Payments under the federal program, however, will not begin until 1983, i.e., 17 years after his actual retirement, when General Smith reaches the age of 60. All benefits which General Smith is entitled to receive were earned during the time he was married to plaintiff.

On February 17, 1967, plaintiff retained defendant to represent her in a divorce action against General Smith. According to plaintiff's testimony, defendant advised her that her husband's retirement benefits were not community property. Three days later defendant filed plaintiff's complaint for divorce. General Smith's retirement benefits were not pleaded as items of community property, and therefore were not considered in the litigation or apportioned by the trial court. The divorce was uncontested, and the interlocutory decree divided the minimal described community property and awarded Mrs. Smith $400 per month in alimony and child support. The final decree was entered on February 27, 1968.

On July 17, 1968, pursuant to a request by plaintiff, defendant filed on her behalf a motion to amend the decree, alleging under oath that because of his mistake, inadvertence, and excusable neglect (Code Civ. Proc., § 473) the retirement benefits of General Smith had been omitted from the list of community assets owned by the parties, and that such benefits were in fact community property. The motion was denied on the ground of untimeliness. Plaintiff consulted other counsel, and shortly thereafter filed this malpractice action against defendant.

Defendant admits in his testimony that he assumed General Smith's retirement benefits were separate property when he assessed plaintiff's community property rights. It is his position that as a matter of law an attorney is not liable for mistaken advice when well informed lawyers in the community entertain reasonable doubt as to the proper resolution of the particular legal question involved. Because, he asserts, the law defining the character of retirement benefits was uncertain at the time of his legal services to plaintiff, defendant contends the trial court committed error in refusing to grant his motions for nonsuit and judgment notwithstanding the verdict and in submitting the issue of negligence to the jury under appropriate instructions.[3]

[3]The jury was instructed as follows:

"In performing legal services for a client in a divorce action an attorney has the duty to have that degree of learning and skill ordinarily possessed by attorneys of good standing, practicing in the same or similar locality and under similar circumstances.

"It is his further duty to use the care and skill ordinarily exercised in the like

* * *

We recognize, of course, that an attorney engaging in litigation may have occasion to choose among various alternative strategies available to his client, one of which may be to refrain from pressing a debatable point because potential benefit may not equal detriment in terms of expenditure at time and resources or because of calculated tactics to the advantage of his client. But, as the Ninth Circuit put it somewhat brutally in *Pineda v. Craven*, 424 F.2d 369, 372 (9 Cir. 1970): "There is nothing strategic or tactical about ignorance **." In the case before us it is difficult to conceive of tactical advantage which could have been served by neglecting to advance a claim so clearly in plaintiff's best interest, nor does defendant suggest any. The decision to forego litigation on the issue of plaintiff's community property right to a share of General Smith's retirement benefits was apparently the product of a culpable misconception of the relevant principles of law, and the jury could have so found.

Furthermore, no lawyer would suggest the property characterization of General Smith's retirement benefits to be so esoteric an issue that defendant could not reasonably have been expected to be aware of it or its probable resolution. (*Lucas v. Hamm, supra,* 56 Cal.2d 583, 15 Cal.Rptr. 821, 364 P.2d 685 (1961).) In *Lucas* we held that the rule against perpetuities poses such complex and difficult problems for the draftsman that even careful and competent attorneys occasionally fall prey to its traps. The situation before us is not analogous. Certainly one of the central issues in any divorce proceeding is the extent and division of the community property. In this case the question reached monumental proportions, since General Smith's retirement benefits constituted the only significant asset available to the community.[4] In undertaking professional representation of plaintiff, defendant assumed the duty to familiarize himself with the law defining the character of retirement benefits; instead, he rendered erroneous advice contrary to the best interests of his client without the guidance through research of readily available authority.

Regardless of his failure to undertake adequate research, defendant through personal experience in the domestic relations field had been exposed to community property aspects of pensions. Representing the wife of a reserve officer in the National Guard in 1965, defendant alleged as one of the items of community property "the retirement benefits from the

---

cases by reputable members of his profession practicing in the same or a similar locality under similar circumstances, and to use reasonable diligence and his best judgment in the exercise of his skill and the accomplishment of his learning, in an effort to accomplish the best possible result for his client.

"A failure to perform any such duty is negligence.

"An attorney is not liable for every mistake he may make in his practice; he is not, in the absence of an express agreement, an insurer of the soundness of his opinions."

[4]It is undisputed that the only assets the parties had to show as community property after 24 years of marriage, aside from General Smith's retirement benefits, were an equity of $1,800 in a house, some furniture, shares of stock worth $2,800, and two automobiles on which money was owing.

Armed Forces and/or the California National Guard." On behalf of the husband in a 1967 divorce action, defendant filed an answer admitting retirement benefits were community property, merely contesting the amount thereof. In 1965 a wife whom he was representing was so insistent on asserting a community interest in a pension, over defendant's contrary views, that she communicated with the state retirement system and brought to defendant correspondence from the state agency describing her interest in pension benefits. And representing an army colonel, defendant filed a cross-complaint for divorce specifically setting up as an item of community property "retirement benefits in the name of the defendant with the United States Government." It is difficult to understand why defendant deemed the community property claim to pensions of three of the foregoing clients to deserve presentation to the trial court, but not the similar claim of this plaintiff.

In any event, as indicated above, had defendant conducted minimal research into either hornbook or case law, he would have discovered with modest effort that General Smith's state retirement benefits were likely to be treated as community property and that his federal benefits at least arguably belonged to the community as well. Therefore, we hold that the trial court correctly denied the motions for nonsuit and judgment notwithstanding the verdict and properly submitted the question of defendant's negligence to the jury under the instructions given. (See fn. 3, ante.) For the same reasons, the trial court correctly refused to instruct the jury at defendant's request that "he is not liable for being in error as to a question of law on which reasonable doubt may be entertained by well informed lawyers." Even as to doubtful matters, an attorney is expected to perform sufficient research to enable him to make an informed and intelligent judgment on behalf of his client.[5]

Having concluded the issue of negligence was properly placed before the jury, we now consider defendant's claims that the verdict was excessive and unsupported by the evidence and that the trial court used an incorrect measure of damages in making a unitary award of $100,000.

*   *   *

A court of law, however, has no power to duplicate the variety of remedies available to a divorce court sitting in equity. In an action at law for

---

[5]The principal thrust of the dissent is its conclusion that "even assuming that defendant was negligent in failing to research the pension questions, the record does not furnish a balance of probabilities that his negligence—rather than the uncertain status of the law * * * caused plaintiff to lose $100,000." Whether defendant's negligence was a cause in fact of plaintiff's damage—an element of proximate cause—is a factual question for the jury to resolve. (*Valdez v. Clark* (1959) 173 Cal.App.2d 476, 478-479 [343 P.2d 281]; *Land v. Gregory* (1959) 168 Cal.App.2d 15, 19 [335 P.2d 141]; *Hill v. Matthews Paint Co.* (1957) 149 Cal.App.2d 714, 723 [308 P.2d 865]; Rest. 2d Trusts, & 434.) Here the jury was correctly instructed that plaintiff had the burden of proving, inter alia, that defendant's negligence was a proximate cause of the damage suffered, and proximate cause was defined as "a cause which, in natural and continuous sequence, produces the damage, and *without which the damage would not have occurred.*" (Italics added.) Under the strict standards governing appellate review of disputed questions of fact we see no reason on the present record to disturb the jury's implied finding of proximate cause.

malpractice, as in any negligence suit, the court is limited in its remedy to one award of money damages because it lacks the equitable power of contempt to enforce its judgment. Accordingly, the sum in this case was necessarily derived from an actuarial projection of the accumulated damage suffered by plaintiff now and in the future. By this method, the trial court was best able to approximate within its acknowledged powers the value of the claim lost to plaintiff through defendant's negligence.[6]

* * *

The judgment is affirmed.

Attorney's Negligence and Third Parties

ELLEN S. EISENBERG

INTRODUCTION

Attorneys generally owe a duty of care solely to their clients,[1] and courts therefore seldom hold them liable for negligence resulting in injury to third parties.[2] The historical requirement of privity still bars recovery in many states.[3] Although some courts have abolished the requirement[4] and

[6]As with all actuarial projections, it is likely that General Smith will not live the precise number of years estimated in the calculation. However, the possibility he will live less than that number is no greater than the possibility he will live more. Thus, as is true of all tort awards computed on a lump-sum basis, the chances of windfall are equally distributed.

Note, Attorney's Negligence and Third Parties, 57 *N.Y.U.L. Rev.* 126–31, 138, 139, 141, 142, 144–145, 152, 155–57 (1982). Reprinted by permission.

[1]See, e.g., *Savings Bank v. Ward,* 100 U.S. 195, 200 (1879) (seller's attorney did not owe duty of care to buyer of property); *Pelham v. Griesheimer,* 93 Ill. App. 3d 751, 757, 417 N.E.2d 882, 887 (1981) (attorney representing spouse in divorce action does not owe duty of care to minor children); *Clagett v. Dacy,* 47 Md. App. 23, 30, 420 A.2d 1285, 1287–89 (1980) (attorneys conducting foreclosure sale are not liable to high bidders for failure to follow procedures that twice resulted in setting aside the sale); *Victor v. Goldman,* 74 Misc. 2d 685, 685–86, 344 N.Y.S.2d 672, 673–74 (1973) (attorney not liable to beneficiary of will because of privity bar), aff'd, 43 A.D.2d 1021, 351 N.Y.S.2d 956 (1974).

[2]In this Note, third parties shall include persons other than the client who are injured through the attorney's negligence.

[3]See, e.g., *Bloomer Amusement Co. v. Eskenazi,* 75 Ill. App. 3d 117, 119, 394 N.E.2d 16, 18 (1979) (Illinois); *Victor v. Goldman,* 74 Misc. 2d 685, 685–86, 344 N.Y.S.2d 672, 673–74 (1973) (New York), aff'd 43 A.D.2d 1021, 351 N.Y.S.2d 956 (1974); *Goerke v. Vojvodich,* 67 Wis. 2d 102, 205–06, 226 N.W.2d 211, 212–14 (1975) (Wisconsin). The Supreme Court first applied the privity bar to attorneys in *Savings Bank v. Ward,* 100 U.S. 195 (1879); see text accompanying notes 36–43 *infra.*

[4]See, e.g. *Fickettt v. Superior Court,* 27 Ariz. App. 793, 794–95, 558 P.2d 988, 990 (1976) (Arizona); *Heyer v. Flaig,* 70 Cal. 2d 223, 226–27, 449 P.2d 161, 163, 74 Cal. Rptr. 225, 227 (1969) (California); *Guy v. Liederbach,* 421 A.2d 333, 335 (Pa. Super. Ct. 1980) (Pennsylvania).

some allow exceptions,[5] they have yet to develop a negligence standard tailored to the attorney–third party relationship. As a result, two interrelated harms have ensued—third party plaintiffs have been denied compensation and attorney misconduct has not been deterred.

Currently, third parties must bear the burden of attorneys' negligence by absorbing the costs of the injuries inflicted. Third parties have been harmed both through direct dealing with attorneys and through the attorney's discharge of obligations to the client.[6] Yet they are generally less blameworthy[7] than the attorney and less capable of spreading the costs of attorney negligence.[8] Since attorneys' avoidance costs are lower than those of third parties, imposing the burden on attorneys is the more economically efficient and logical choice.[9]

Denying compensation to third parties also removes an effective tool for policing attorney misconduct. Without such a sanction, attorneys have little incentive to conform their conduct toward third parties to a standard of reasonable care.[10] Third parties' lack of recourse in the courts leaves a void in the enforcement of professional standards that bar association grievance committees and clients' malpractice suits are incapable of filling.[11]

This Note argues that attorneys owe a duty of care to third parties foreseeably injured by their negligence.[12] It begins by demonstrating the need to extend attorney liability. Next, after tracing the historical role of privity, this Note examines the four theories that courts have used in bypassing privity analysis to hold attorneys to a standard of reasonable care toward third parties. It concludes that these theories do not adequately cover all the situations in which attorneys should owe a duty of care to third parties. Finally, this Note proposes a framework for assessing attorneys' duties that will compensate third party plaintiffs and enforce professional standards without unduly burdening attorneys.

[5]Florida, for example, creates an exception in will-drafting cases. See *Drawdy v. Sapp,* 365 So. 2d 461, 462 (Fla. Dist. Ct. App. 1978).

[6]See, e.g., id. at 462 (attorney could not be liable for negligent preparation of a deed for client's wife as part of divorce settlement); *Metzker v. Slocum,* 272 Or. 313, 315, 537 P.2d 74, 76 (1975) (attorney not liable to child for failure to perfect adoption papers).

[7]See text accompanying notes 13–16 *infra.*

[8]See text accompanying notes 17–19 *infra.*

[9]See text accompanying notes 21–27 *infra.*

[10]See text accompanying notes 28–30 *infra.*

[11]See text accompanying notes 31–35 *infra.*

[12]This Note focuses primarily on the duty requirement. Before attorneys can be held liable to a third party, they must be found to have breached a standard of care, and their conduct must be found the proximate cause of the injury. The analysis of these issues would not differ from the analysis in general negligence cases.

I

NECESSITY TO EXTEND ATTORNEYS' DUTIES TO THIRD PARTIES

Historically, the law of negligence has considered moral "fault" in distributing risks among parties.[13] The traditional view defines blameworthiness as a failure to exercise forethought.[14] Attorneys generally have greater expertise and easier access to information than third parties and thus not only are better able to prevent the injury, but also can be considered more "responsible." Further, it is their lack of foresight and care that causes the injury. For instance, beneficiaries of a will have lost their bequest due to an attorney's negligence, but have been denied recourse in the courts.[15] There is little question that a fault analysis would mandate shifting the cost to the attorney. Thus, under this moral view, the blameworthy attorney should compensate the third party.[16]

Another way of allocating risks between attorneys and third parties is to consider how the cost of injury can best be spread.[17] The usual justification for cost-spreading is that by taking a series of small sums of money from many people rather than taking a large sum of money from one person, economic dislocation and the resultant social costs can be minimized.[18] Attorneys are better situated than third parties to insulate themselves from the prospect of a heavy loss by procuring insurance, both because their skill and knowledge puts them in a better position to assess risks and because most have ready access to insurance.[19] Insurance may operate to spread loss since the costs of the extra insurance are passed along to the attorneys' clients.[20] Therefore, if the costs are to be spread, attorneys should bear the risks of their negligent conduct and compensate injured third parties.

Goals of economic efficiency also dictate that attorneys compensate third party plaintiffs. Influential commentators have maintained that tort

[13]See O. W. Holmes, *The Common Law* 75–120 (1881); G. White, *Tort Law in America* 13, 38, 164 (1980).

[14]O. W. Holmes, *supra* note 13, at 100.

[15]*Victor v. Goldman*, 74 Misc. 2d 685, 685–86, 344 N.Y.S.2d 672, 673–74 (1973), aff'd, 43 A.D.2d 1021, 351 N.Y.S.2d 956 (1974).

[16]This Note advances a traditional negligence standard and thus adopts a type of "fault" analysis. To the extent that attorneys are not at fault, they should not be forced to compensate third parties for the injuries received. See text accompanying notes 169–96 *infra*.

[17]G. Calabresi, *The Costs of Accidents* 39 (1970).

[18]Id.

[19]Insurance policies that cover attorneys against liability from suit are readily available. Jericho and Coultas, "Are Lawyers an Insurable Risk?" 63 *A.B.A.J.* 832, 834 (1977). The amount of coverage and the deductible will vary from policy to policy, and "umbrella" or "special excess" policies providing additional coverage are also available. Id.

[20]G. Calabresi, *supra* note 17, at 45–50.

law should encourage economic efficiency when allocating risk.[21] Under this view, courts should place the costs of a particular injury on the party who would have the lowest avoidance costs so that the aggregate sum of accident and avoidance costs is minimized.[22] As the following examination of the costs of avoiding injury in the attorney-third party situation suggests, the attorney's avoidance costs are lower than those of the third party.

Some injuries in the attorney–third party situation flow from actions requested by a client.[23] In these circumstances, an attorney's negligence consists either of performing a task poorly or of failing to complete a task. When an attorney performs a task poorly, the cost of avoiding the injury is the cost of instituting better procedures for performing the task, the cost of taking more time to do the task properly,[24] or the cost of having someone else—another lawyer, a paralegal, or a secretary—look over the work. When the attorney just fails to complete a task, the cost of avoiding injury is the cost of completion.

The third party's cost of avoidance is the cost of hiring an attorney to do the job properly, since hiring his own attorney is typically the way in which a third party possibly could avoid injury. Although the third party's avoidance cost would always be the cost of the performance of the total task, the attorney either will have initiated the task or accumulated enough information so that his costs for completing the task competently would be less than those of the third party.

Furthermore, in many situations in which injuries flow from actions pursued at a client's request, the third party may be unable to avoid the injury at all. For instance, will beneficiaries may not know that they are named in the will until the testator dies, when it is too late to prevent injury. In addition, third party minors may be unable to avoid injury since they may lack access to their own attorneys.[25] Thus, when the attorney's performance of a task for a client harms a third party, the attorney should compensate that third party.

The attorney's avoidance costs are even less when the attorney directly deals with the third party.[26] In these circumstances, the attorney's costs of avoidance are the costs of not undertaking the task at all. Because attorneys undertake tasks for many reasons, these costs may vary. The cost might be loss of goodwill, or, if the task is undertaken to help the client indirectly, the cost of the extra time needed to perform the task properly.

---

[21]Calabresi and Melamed, "Property Rules, Liability Rules, and Inalienability," 86 *Harv. L. Rev.* 1089, 1096–97 (1972); Posner, "A Theory of Negligence," 1 *J. Legal Stud.* 29, 39–40 (1972). For a critique of the economic approach, see Steiner, "Economics, Morality, and the Law of Torts," 26 *U. Toronto L.J.* 227, 242–43 (1976).

[22]Calabresi and Melamed, *supra* note 21, at 1096–97; Posner, *supra* note 21, at 39–40.

[23]See, e.g., *Metzker v. Slocum*, 272 Or. 313, 315, 537 P.2d 74, 76 (1979) (child sued attorney for injury resulting from failure to perfect adoption papers).

[24]This type of cost would have the greatest effect on attorneys who charge a set fee for drafting various documents and depend therefore on high volume and quick turnover, If the additional time required forced substantial changes in operation, the current quality is probably so poor that the change is for the better.

[25]See notes 201, 209 *infra*.

[26]See, e.g., *Stewart v. Sbarro*, 142 N.J. Super. 581, 362 A.2d 581 (1976) (attorney directly undertook to obtain signatures to perfect mortgage).

In comparison, the cost to the third party will always be greater since it is the cost of hiring her own attorney to perform the task completely. Therefore, as the lowest cost avoider, the attorney should compensate the third party.

Not only should third parties gain compensation, but society would be better off as a whole if the attorney's negligence were deterred.[27] As a threshold question, it should be asked what is the need for deterring the negligent conduct. Apart from moral reasons, deterring misconduct would result in greater economic efficiency. Attorneys will avoid activities that result in harm[28] as long as the costs of avoidance are less than the costs of the injury—the economically efficient result.[29]

Arguably, the availability of insurance may reduce the economic effectiveness of the imposition of monetary sanctions as a deterrent. But insurance does not completely remove the influence of these sanctions, because a rise in insurance rates provides at least an attenuated monetary sanction.[30] Furthermore, malpractice actions tarnish professional reputations and act as a deterrent without the immediate threat of pecuniary loss. Despite the existence of insurance, therefore, placing the costs of injury upon negligent attorneys by forcing them to compensate injured third parties encourages attorneys to avoid these injuries.

Methods of deterring attorney misconduct other than tort liability have not been altogether successful. Bar association grievance committees alone cannot sufficiently police attorney misconduct. They lack the funding, the power, and the inclination to stalk attorney incompetence.[31] Nor

[27]Making attorneys responsible for injuries to third parties which occur through direct dealing may lead to a reduction in the information that the attorney offers to third parties. The extent to which attorneys will actually refrain from dispensing information, advice, or other aid will depend largely upon the benefits their actions will create for their clients. Even if the attorney is in fact deterred from advising third parties, the third parties will still benefit in the long run. Because of potential carelessness, the third party will have lost very little and may even have gained since he is encouraged to rely upon his own attorney.

[28]This change in conduct occurs because reasonable people change their behavior to avoid cost. See G. Calabresi, *supra* note 17, at 73–75; Steiner, *supra* note 21, at 229–30.

[29]The costs of injury are generally the probability of occurrence multiplied by the severity of the injury, see *United States v. Carroll Towing Co.*, 159 F.2d 169, 173 (2d Cir. 1947) (L. Hand, J.). Thus, an attorney's cost of injury can be higher than the cost of avoidance when, for example, the attorney certifies title to property as collateral for a large loan without adequately checking the facts. An incomplete check makes the probability of injury quite high while the severity of the injury is potentially the amount of the loan that the third party stands to lose. By comparison, the cost of avoidance is the cost of attorney work hours to research the requisite information. The cost of avoidance, therefore, will be less than the cost of injury, and the attorney should alter her conduct to avoid the loss.

[30]T. Ison, *The Forensic Lottery* 80–82 (1967).

[31]Few state bar associations adequately finance their disciplinary agencies. Garbus and Seligman, "Sanctions and Disbarment: They Sit in Judgment," in *Verdicts on Lawyers* 51 (R. Nader and M. Green eds. 1976). Seventeen state bar associations make no specific budgetary allowances for grievance committees. P. Stern, *Lawyers on Trial* 91 (1980). Without funds, no systematic review of behavior is possible. Garbus and Seligman, *supra* at 51. Records have not been kept, and thorough investigation is therefore unlikely. Id. In addition, many bar association grievance committees lack any power to compel production of documents. In some states, the bar association grievance committees may not issue subpoenas. Id. at 51–52. The lack of access to information obviously impedes investigation. See id. Furthermore, committees cannot compel attorneys to testify against themselves. *Spevack v. Klein.* 385 U.S. 511, 514 (1967).

do malpractice suits by clients adequately serve to deter attorney negligence. Clients may not have sufficient interest to bring suit—they may be untouched by the attorney's conduct,[32] they may be bankrupt,[33] or they may even have benefitted from the attorney's negligence.[34] The client may have died by the time the negligence is discovered, as when an attorney negligently prepares a will.[35] In these situations, attorneys need not worry about the possibility of suits from clients. Even when attorneys consciously attempt to avoid malpractice suits, they may fail to consider the ramifications of their acts on third parties. Therefore, allowing courts to find that attorneys have a duty to third parties puts attorneys on notice that they must consider the impact of their actions on third parties even if the client is not likely to bring suit.

As this section of the Note has demonstrated, the law currently fails to compensate third parties for their injuries even though doing so would place the burden on the blameworthy party, spread the costs more evenly, aid economic efficiency, and help enforce minimum standards of competency.

* * *

III

INROADS INTO PRIVITY

Although privity still acts as a bar in many states, some courts have recognized the need to extend attorneys' duties.[82] Even so, the law regarding

---

Finally, friendship and professional camaraderie among attorneys make it difficult for attorneys to discipline one another, especially when the attorneys may worry about their own potential liability. Garbus and Seligman, *supra*, at 56. This self-protective impulse turns into an overriding concern for preserving public image rather than enforcing standards. See J. Carlin, *Lawyer's Ethics* 170 (1966).

This Note recognizes that other alternatives may exist in order to police attorney misconduct. For instance, informal community grievance centers could be established and joint attorney-layperson commissions, analogous to the Better Business Bureau, could be created. Yet these alternatives have some of the same drawbacks as the bar association grievance committees; they would lack both access to information and effective sanctions.

[32]For example, although a husband's divorce attorney negligently prepared a title deed for the ex-wife who later finds that she cannot sell the property, the husband is not harmed by her inability to sell. See *Drawdy v. Sapp*, 365 So. 2d 461, 462 (Fla. Dist. Ct. App. 1978).

[33]See *Schwartz v. Greenfield, Stein and Weisinger*, 90 Misc. 2d 882, 884-86, 396 N.Y.S.2d 582, 583–85 (1977), in which a borrower's attorney negligently perfected a security agreement after telling his client that he would do so. The bankruptcy of the borrower was the immediate cause of the lender's injury. Since the borrower corporation went bankrupt, it had little interest in the security agreement and was unlikely to sue the attorney. The money it would have gained would only have paid off creditors.

[34]For example, in *McEvoy v. Helikson*, 277 Or. 781, 786–89, 562 P.2d, 543–44 (1977), an attorney violated a divorce stipulation when he returned the client's passport, and the client benefitted from the negligence by subsequently fleeing the country with her son.

[35]See *Victor v. Goldman*, 74 Misc. 2d 685, 344 N.Y.S.2d, 672, aff'd 43 A.D.2d 1021, 351 N.Y.S.2d 956 (1974).

[82]Especially in suits by will beneficiaries against testators' attorneys, courts have expanded duty, recognizing that only the beneficiary could sue to enforce the will's purpose. See, e.g., *Heyer v. Flaig*, 70 Cal.2d 223, 228, 449 P.2d 161, 165, 74 Cal. Rptr. 225, 229 (1969); *Licata v. Spector*, 26 Conn. Supp. 378, 382, 225 A.2d 28, 30 (1966).

third party suits against attorneys has neither adequately addressed the needs of compensating plaintiffs and deterring negligent conduct, nor led to a coherent framework for assessing duties to third parties. Courts have utilized at least four different theories of duty: (1) a third party beneficiary theory;[83] (2) a fiduciary or agency theory;[84] (3) a theory based upon the policy factors set forth in *Biakanja*;[85] and (4) a theory based on assumption of the duty.[86] This Note * * * concludes in the next section that the assumption of the duty theory holds the most promise.

A. Third Party Beneficiary Theory

Third party beneficiary theory derives from contract law.[87] When two parties enter a contract intending to deliver some material benefit to a third party, the third party can sue on the contract despite the lack of privity. The promise creates a duty in the promisor to the intended beneficiary.[88] The third party's right to sue on the contract rests on three policies: (1) allowing the suit recognizes that the contract may induce reliance in the third party;[89] (2) permitting the third party to enforce the contract satisfies the promisee's expectations;[90] and (3) barring the suit prevents any redress whatever.[91]

* * *

B. Relationship Theories

Escrow agency and fiduciary theories have also been offered to support a finding that attorneys have duties to third parties.[104] A special relationship between attorney and third party gives rise to a duty of care despite the lack of privity.

* * *

C. *Biakanja* Factor Theory

An attempt to provide a more comprehensive framework for assessing attorneys' third party liability has been made based on general negligence principles. Some courts have held that attorneys owe a duty of care

---

[83]See text accompanying notes 87–103 *infra*.

[84]See text accompanying notes 104–13 *infra*.

[85]See text accompanying notes 114–31 *infra*.

[86]See text accompanying notes 132–96 *infra*.

[87]See 4 A. Corbin, *supra* note 70, §§772–781, at 1–75.

[88]Restatement (Second) of Contracts §304 (1981). According to the Restatement, an intended beneficiary should be able to sue "if recognition of a right to performance in the beneficiary is appropriate to effectuate the intention of the parties and . . . the circumstances indicate that the promise intends to give the beneficiary the benefit of the promised performance." Id. §302; see also 4 A. Corbin, *supra* note 70, §775, at 8–14.

[89]4 A. Corbin, *supra* note 70, §775, at 8–14.

[90]Id.

[91]J. Murray, *Murray on Contracts* §276, at 562 (1974).

[104]E.g., *Stewart v. Sbarro*, 142 N.J. Super. 581, 593, 362, A.2d 581, 588 (1976) (fiduciary theory offered as alternative theory); *McEvoy v. Helikson*, 277 Or. 781, 785–86, 562 P.2d 540, 542–43 (1977) (escrow agency theory offered as alternative theory).

to third parties using a balance of factors similar to those listed in *Biakanja*:[114] (1) the extent to which the transaction was intended to affect the plaintiff; (2) the foreseeability of harm to the plaintiff; (3) the degree of certainty that the plaintiff suffered injury; (4) the closeness of the connection between the defendant's conduct and the injuries suffered; (5) the moral blame attached to the defendant's conduct; and (6) the policy of preventing future harm. The widest acceptance of these factors has come in suits by will beneficiaries,[115] the situation in which the test originated.[116] In other situations, however, applying the test has proved more problematic.

*   *   *

IV

ESTABLISHING A UNIFYING THEORY

This Note suggests that attorneys should owe a duty of reasonable care to third parties in order to compensate deserving plaintiffs and to promote attorney competence.[132] The framework for determining the duties of attorneys should reflect these underlying concerns. The third party beneficiary theory, the relationship theories, and the *Biakanja* factors neither provide a framework broad enough to compensate deserving plaintiffs nor adequately enforce standards for professional care. Although the relationship theories presuppose an established relationship between attorneys and third parties, the other theories focus too narrowly on the attorney–client transaction rather than the surrounding circumstances. Resting the theory upon the attorney–client contract itself ignores both the quality and frequency of attorney contacts with third parties.

Assumption of the duty theory avoids these limitations. The theory does not turn on the existence or nonexistence of a contract or special relationship, but on action: "[O]ne who assumes to act, even though gratuitously, may thereby become subject to the duty of acting carefully, if he acts at all."[133] Courts have applied the theory in circumstances as different as automobile accidents[134] and the failure to file a claim for a rebate,[135]

---

[114]49 Cal.2d 647, 650, 320 P.2d 16, 19 (1958); see text accompanying notes 66–68 *supra*.

[115]E.g., *Heyer v. Flaig*,, 70 Cal. 2d 223, 226–29, 449 P.2d 161, 163–65, 74 Cal. Rptr. 225, 227–29 (1969); *Licata v. Spector*, 26 Comm. Supp. 378, 382–84, 225 A.2d 28, 31 (1966); *Guy v. Liederbach*, 421 A.2d 333, 335 (Pa. Super. Ct. 1980).

[116]See text accompanying note 67 *supra*.

[132]See text accompanying notes 13–35 *supra*.

[133]*Glanzer v. Shepard*, 233 N.Y. 236, 239–40, 135 N.E. 275, 276 (1922).

[134]E.g., *Haralson v. Jones Truck Lines*, 223, Ark. 813, 816–17, 270 S.W. 2d 892, 895 (1954); *Schwartz v. Helms Bakery Ltd.*, 67 Cal. 2d 232, 238, 430 P.2d 68, 72 60 Cal. Rptr. 510, 514 (1967).

[135]E.g., *Carr v. Maine Cent. R.R.*, 78 N.H. 502, 503, 102 A. 532, 532–33 (1917); cf. *Hyde v. Moffat*, 16 Vt. 271, 279 (1844) (failure to record a deed).

thus covering situations both of physical and economic harm. The broad range of application reflects social policies of compensating innocent victims and preventing lack of care in the performance of an act.

The theory can therefore stand as the foundation for a proper duty analysis. It recognizes that because of the nature of services provided by attorneys, their actions foreseeably affect parties not in privity. When attorneys undertake an action that foreseeably affects a third party, they owe a duty of care to that individual. A unified approach in determining the duty of attorneys to third parties serves the policy goal of deterrence. It apprises attorneys of the criteria for establishing duties to third parties. Attorneys can therefore examine the task that they are about to undertake with a view towards the liability that could result.[136] Without any limitations, however, the theory could result in liability of too wide a scope.[137] Consequently, the general notion of assumption of the duty should be tailored to the attorney–third party situation. This section will explore the theory in an effort to articulate the criteria for determining whether an attorney owes a duty of care to a third party.

* * *

B. Foreseeability

An undertaking forms the basis for duty. The attorney's representation, assurance, or action signals that an attorney will bring professional competence to bear on the task at hand. Yet in attorney–third party situations, the number of people affected by the undertaking could be indeterminate. A written evaluation of a transaction made at a client's behest could affect countless investors or employees. Extending a duty to all affected by the attorney's negligence might not only "chill" an attorney's effective representation of clients, but lead to compensating "undeserving" plaintiffs as well.[169] Therefore, duties flowing from an "undertaking" should be circumscribed by a standard of foreseeability. Without foreseeability, liability resulting from a breach of duty would not act as a deterrent, since an attorney could not adjust his or her actions to prevent an unforeseeable

---

[136]Based on economic efficiency, attorneys would then theoretically avoid any potential harm inflicted. See text accompanying notes 21–25 *supra*.

[137]Voluntary assumption of duty through affirmative conduct is a simple requirement to meet. Prosser indicates that the 'undertaking' is commonly found in minor acts, of no significance in themselves and without any effect of their own upon the plaintiff's interests," W. Prosser, *supra* note 47, §56, at 345. For discussion of the proper limitations on the assumption of duty concept, see text accompanying notes 166–96 *infra*.

[169]See text accompanying notes 186–96 *infra*. Any overly broad extension would allow plaintiffs to recover even though their own behavior was unreasonable. This notion is akin to that of contributory negligence—conduct on the part of plaintiffs falling below the standard to which they are expected to conform for their own protection. See Restatement (Second) of Torts §§463, 464, 466 (1965); see also *Mroz v. Dravo Corp.*, 429 F.2d 1156, 1163 (3rd Cir. 1970); *Cincotta v. United States*, 362 F. Supp. 386, 403 (D. Md. 1973). In some states, contributory negligence may bar recovery. See, e.g., *Lopez v. Deatrich Leasing Corp.*, 237 So. 2d 284, 285 (Fla. Dis. Ct. App. 1970); *Marean v. Petersen*, 259 Iowa 557, 567, 144 N.W. 2d 906, 912 (1966).

occurrence.[170] Three conditions of foreseeability must be met—the plaintiffs must be foreseeable, their reliance must be foreseeable, and the resulting harm must fall within the zone of risk foreseen. Thus, in order to demonstrate that the attorney assumed a duty of care, third parties must show that the attorney undertook a task that foreseeably affected their interests.

* * *

2. Role of reasonable reliance   Foreseeability depends on more than just the identification of potential plaintiffs; it also depends on the likelihood that third parties will rely on the attorney's action. Custom, then, plays a crucial role.[185] For instance, if buyers and sellers in real estate transactions both customarily retain their own attorney's, the seller's attorney cannot foresee that the buyer would rely on his title search or drafting of the agreement.[186] Of course, the situation differs if the seller's attorney directly makes assurances to the buyer.[187] Similarly, an attorney's confidential memorandum analyzing the antitrust ramifications of a merger does not customarily reach third parties. The client's subsequent disclosure of the analysis to the investing public does not circumvent the foreseeability requirement. If the attorney's action does not usually affect anyone besides the client, and if the attorney has no special knowledge that his work will influence a party not in privity, then no duty should exist.

Custom, however, can cut the other way. Attorneys perform tasks for clients that they know will directly affect third parties. Drafting a will is the classic situation;[188] establishing a trust fund is another.[189] Foreseeability can also be demonstrated by showing that the attorney should have known that the third parties did not have access to their own attorneys. Perfecting

[170]If the injury is not foreseeable, then it does not serve economic efficiency to impose a duty on the attorney. The assumption underlying economic efficiency theory is that a person will structure his conduct to avoid potentially higher injury costs, see note 28 *supra*. Without foreseeability the assumption fails. Furthermore, the attorney who causes an unforeseeable injury is not blameworthy since she was never on notice that her actions violated any standard of care.

[185]Custom can be defined as the usual conduct of others in the community under similar circumstances. W. Prosser, *supra* note 47, §33, at 166.

[186]Model Code of Professional Responsibility EC 5-14 (1980) implies that one attorney may not represent both sides in a sale transaction. Thus, at least in many communities, custom would seem to run strongly against a buyer's reliance on the seller's attorney, even if a buyer fails to hire his own attorney. See *Adams v. Chenowith*, 349 So. 2d 230, 231 (Fla. Dist. Ct. App. 1977). Thus, the unreasonableness of reliance would make the harm unforeseeable.

[187]See *Stewart v. Sbarro*, 142 N.J. Super. 581, 362 A. 2d 581 (1976), which holds that a cause of action would lie against a buyer's attorney. The attorney allegedly failed to advise the sellers' attorney that he had not obtained signatures even though he had directly assured the sellers that he would do so. Id. at 593, 362 A.2d at 588.

[188]Wills affect beneficiaries as well as the client. See *Heyer v. Flaig*, 70 Cal. 2d 223, 228, 449 P.2d 161, 165, 74 Cal. Rptr. 225, 229 (1969) ("[I]n some ways, the beneficiary's interests loom greater than those of the client.").

[189]Trust funds affect trust beneficiaries. Restatement (Second) of Trusts §3(4) (1959).

adoption papers[190] or handling the estate of an incompetent[191] are useful illustrations. Attorneys can foresee that despite the absence of privity the prospective adoptee in the one case and the ward in the other will rely on their professional expertise. The lack of access to an attorney in these situations suggests that third parties foreseeably and reasonably rely on attorneys with whom they are not in privity. Custom, then, can help determine whether the unidentified plaintiff would reasonably rely upon an attorney and therefore would be foreseeably harmed by the attorney's negligent conduct.

    3. Type of harm foreseen   To satisfy the foreseeability standard, plaintiffs must also demonstrate that the injury suffered was of the same type as that foreseen.[192] Otherwise, attorneys would suffer liability even when they were not on notice that failure to conform to a standard of reasonable care could result in a specific injury. For instance, if an attorney negligently perfected a security agreement on a loan, such as a lien on machinery, the harm foreseen by delay in perfection is loss of priority for the creditor.[193] Suppose, instead, that the loss of the entire sum including that in the secured assets caused the creditor to lose a contract because he could not demonstrate to a bank that he had enough liquid assets to post the bonds required to obtain an award of a public contract.[194] Although the attorney's negligence might be a "but for" cause of the creditor's loss of a contract, loss of priority was the most probable result of the negligence. The attorney should not be liable unless loss of the contract fell within the zone of risk foreseen.

    If the type of harm falls within the zone of risk,[195] however, the injury should be considered foreseeable. Suppose the borrower sells the

---

    [190]Since one of the purposes of adoption is to establish the child's rights to support, inheritance, and survivor rights, see note 208 *infra*, improper perfection of adoption clearly may harm the prospective adoptee.

    [191]See *Ficket v. Superior Court*, 27 Ariz. App. 793, 794–95, 558 P.2d 988, 990 (1976) (in which access to court was through conservator).

    [192]Foreseeable harm generally is an injury of a character which a reasonable person would view as likely to occur. While the harm must be one of the kind of consequences expected, the exact form or nature of the particular injury need not have been anticipated. See, e.g., *Griggs v. Firestone Tire & Rubber Co.*, 513 F.2d 851, 861 (8th Cir.) (with failure of manufacturer to warn of dangers of mismatching components, intervening cause of mismatch of wheel rim components was foreseeable), cert. denied, 423 U.S. 865 (1975); *Pinkerton-Hays Lumber Co. v. Pope*, 127 So. 2d 441, 442–43 (Fla. 1961) (inability to call fire department due to destruction of telephone line not type of harm foreseen); *Phelan v. Santelli*, 30 Ill. App. 3d 657, 663–64, 334 N.E.2d 391, 395–96 (1975) ("[T]he first wrongdoer . . . reasonably should have anticipated the negligent conduct of the second in reaction as a probable and natural result of his own negligence."). See generally W. Prosser, *supra* note 47, §44, at 287.

    [193]U.C.C. §9-302 provides for perfection of security interests by filing. Holders of valid, enforceable, and perfected Article 9 interests can defeat the claims of most other parties who assert rights to the asset involved. See generally J. White and R. Summers, Uniform Commercial Code 1030–42 (2d ed. 1980).

    [194]See, e.g., Mich. Comp. Laws §§129.201 to .203 (1976) (requiring a contractor to post a performance and payment bond before a contract may be awarded).

    [195]See W. Prosser, *supra* note 47, ch.7.

machinery before the creditor's lien is filed. The creditor, then, would not have obtained a secured interest in his loan. The harm to the creditor is not specifically a loss of priority, but is within the zone of risk foreseen—the loan remains unsecured.[196] The attorney knows that the resulting harm is one possible outcome of negligent conduct. Thus, if the injury falls within the zone or risk foreseeably created by the attorney's negligence, the type of injury is foreseeable.

* * *

CONCLUSION

Attorneys should owe a duty of care to third parties foreseeably affected by their actions. Whether the action arises by direct dealing with a third party or in discharging obligations to a client, an attorney's actions must not fall below a standard of professional care. Adopting an assumption of the duty theory, applied under the framework presented in this Note, would put attorneys' on notice that they must fulfill professional roles competently or subject themselves to liability. As a result, the proposal advances the underlying aims of tort law by deterring tortious conduct and remunerating deserving plaintiffs regardless of their technical status as third parties.

B

Competence and Criminal Defense

Walker v. Kruse

UNITED STATES COURT OF APPEALS, SEVENTH CIRCUIT, 1973
484 F.2D 802

STEVENS, Circuit Judge.

Plaintiff appeals from an order dismissing his malpractice action against a lawyer who was appointed to provide him with legal advice in defending a charge of attempted murder and aggravated battery. Plaintiff was found guilty in November, 1969, and sentenced to the Illinois State Penitentiary for a term of 16 to 20 years. In this litigation he accuses the

[196]A security interest is perfected when it has attached and when all steps required for perfection, including filing, are completed. U.C.C. §§9-302, 303(1).

defendant of negligence in failing to carry out various requests which plaintiff made before, during, and after the criminal trial. After deciding preliminary motions, the district court dismissed the complaint, holding that civil action questioning the competency of defendant's professional services should not go forward until plaintiff had exhausted state procedures, including habeas corpus, whereby his criminal conviction might be overturned on that ground. In effect, the district court dismissed the complaint on abstention grounds.

We believe the lower court should not have abstained. Jurisdiction is based on diversity of citizenship, and the complaint raises only issues of state law. Except in extraordinary situations, federal courts should not abstain from deciding state law issues in diversity cases.

Moreover, after the district court's decision, the Illinois Supreme Court affirmed plaintiff's conviction and denied his petition for writ of habeas corpus. *Walker v. Pate*, 53 Ill.2d 485, 292 N.E. 2d 387 (1973). Therefore, even if the basis for the district court's action were correct, there no longer is any reason why this matter should not be decided. We are convinced that the Illinois courts would dismiss this action on any of several grounds.

We are assured by counsel that the competency of counsel question was raised on appeal, but the Supreme Court's exhaustive opinion never specifically addressed it. Apparently the court saw no merit in it whatsoever: "There are other contentions which the defendant makes, but the clear want of merit in them warrants our not formally discussing them in detail in this already lengthy opinion." Id. at 399. This holding by the Illinois Supreme Court might very well bar relief in plaintiff's malpractice action. Plaintiff correctly observes that the standard of proof in a malpractice action might not be as strenuous as it is when questioning the constitutional adequacy of counsel. However, there is sufficient similarity that an Illinois civil court might dismiss the complaint when the Supreme Court has found a "clear want of merit" in the contention.

Alternatively, the Illinois courts might require an allegation of innocence. On the record before us we must assume that plaintiff is in fact guilty of the crime of which he was convicted. He does not allege otherwise; he primarily contends that his conviction might have been avoided if the defendant had complied with certain tactical requests relating to the possible suppression of incriminating evidence. In these circumstances, it is questionable whether the Illinois courts would conclude that the defendant's alleged professional shortcomings proximately caused an injury to the plaintiff which entitled him to damages. An Illinois court might well hold, as a matter of law, that a criminal conviction cannot support a malpractice claim unless the plaintiff is able to establish his actual innocence.[1]

Illinois also has a firmly established policy of requiring the plaintiff

---

[1] In *Olson v. North*, 276 Ill.App. 457 (2d Dist. 1934), on which appellant relies, the plaintiff did allege his own innocence as well as the fact that third persons had confessed to the crime for which he was tried. See 276 Ill.App. at 461-465. Indeed, in this connection, the Illinois courts could require plaintiff to obtain post-conviction relief as a prerequisite to civil relief.

advancing a negligence claim to plead and prove his own freedom from contributory negligence.[2] In view of the rather unusual relationship between plaintiff and defendant during the criminal proceedings, it is doubtful that plaintiff could satisfy this requirement. The references to the criminal trial which are before us make it quite plain that plaintiff retained control of his own defense and utilized defendant's assistance only as he pleased; he did not entrust responsibility for the conduct of the trial to counsel, and therefore cannot properly claim that counsel served in a typical fiduciary capacity.[3] Since the complaint, as illuminated by the various exhibits and attachments in the record, makes it clear that plaintiff participated significantly in, and interfered with, the conduct of the trial, an Illinois court might well conclude, as a matter of law, that plaintiff's own contribution to the ultimate outcome should foreclose any recovery on a negligence theory.

Moreover, there are strong reasons of policy which might persuade the Illinois courts to hold that a lawyer, who has been appointed to serve without compensation in the defense of an indigent citizen accused of crime, should be immune from malpractice liability. Requiring such lawyers to defend charges such as this can only make it more difficult for the Bar to discharge its professional responsibilities which have recently been so greatly enlarged by the Supreme Court's holding in *Argersinger v. Hamlin*, 407 U.S. 25, 92, S.Ct. 2006, 32 L.Ed.2d 530 (1972). The reasoning which provides immunity for various public officials, see, e.g., *Pierson v. Ray*, 386 U.S. 547, 553-554, 87 S. Ct. 1213, 18 L.Ed.2d 288 (1967), is also applicable to the performance by private citizens of public services which play such a significant role in the administration of justice.

In a diversity action it is our duty to decide the case as we believe an Illinois court would decide it. In the absence of Illinois precedent precisely in point, we must estimate, as best we can, what an Illinois tribunal would do with this case. Although we are not sure of the theory on which a state court would base its decision, we are convinced that an Illinois court would dismiss this complaint for failure to state a cause of action. The district court is therefore directed to vacate its order of February 22, 1972, and to enter judgment dismissing the complaint with prejudice.

Vacated and remanded with directions.

---

[2]See, e.g., *Williams v. Rock River Savings and Loan Ass'n*, 51 Ill.App.2d 5, 200 N.E.2d 848 (2d Dist. 1964).

[3]The order appointing defendant in the criminal trial reads as follows:

> "ON MOTION of the Defendant, acting as Attorney for himself,
> "IT IS HEREBY ORDERED AND DECREED that EARL JOSEPH KRUSE, a duly qualified practicing attorney of the State of Illinois, be and he is hereby appointed as counsel for the defendant, DANIEL WALKER, limited in scope as heretofore indicated on the record by the defendant, but subject to further direction of defendant as may from time to time be expressed on the record hereafter."

The foregoing order was entered by Judge Carey on August 29, 1969, and approved by plaintiff Walker pro se.

Criminal Malpractice: Threshold Barriers to Recovery Against Negligent Criminal Counsel

DAVID H. POTEL

In the past decade the number of malpractice suits brought against attorneys by their former clients increased dramatically.[1] Most of these cases were civil malpractice actions, involving claims that arose out of an attorney's handling of a civil matter.[2] Some suits, however, were actions for criminal malpractice—legal malpractice in the course of representing a criminal defendant.[3] Although criminal malpractice suits are relatively uncommon, they are becoming increasingly attractive to convicted criminal defendants.[4]

Civil and criminal malpractice actions involve many of the same issues, and courts generally treat them in a similar manner. The basic

Duke Law Journal, 1981 (1981), 542–43, 546–52, 556–61, and 563–64. Reprinted by permission.

[1]*See* R. Mallen and V. Levit, Legal Malpractice § 6 (1977).

[2]State malpractice claims may sound in tort or contract, and the analysis is similar in either situation. *See* R. Mallen and V. Levit, supra note 1, § 71. Several convicted criminal defendants also have brought actions against their attorneys under 42 U.S.C. § 1983 (1976). *See, e.g., Smith v. Clapp*, 436 F.2d 590 (3d Cir. 1970). These actions are outside the scope of this comment, which deals only with malpractice actions based on state law.

[3]Kaus and Mallen, "*The Misguiding Hand of Counsel—Reflections on 'Criminal Malpractice.'*" 21 *U.C.L.A. L. Rev.* 1191, 1191 n.2 (1974).

[4]Two-thirds of the reported cases have been decided since 1970. *See Ferri v. Ackerman*, 444 U.S. 193 (1979); *Jackson v. Salon*, 614 F.2d 15 (1st Cir. 1980); *Myers v. Butler*, 556 F.2d 398 (8th Cir.), *cert. denied*, 434 U.S. 956 (1977); *Walker v. Kruse*, 484 F.2d 802 (7th Cir. 1973), *Sullens v. Carroll*, 446 F.2d 1392 (5th Cir. 1971); *Hunt v. Bittman*, 482 F. Supp. 1017 (D.D.C. 1980), *Tasby v. Peek*, 396 F. Supp. 952 (W.D. Ark. 1975); *Sanchez v. Murphy*, 385 F. Supp. 1362 (1) Nev. 1974); *Malloy v. Sullivan*, 387 So. 2d 169 (Ala. 1980); *Bradshaw v. Pardee*, Civ. No. 15444 (Cal. Ct. App. Mar. 13, 1978); *Martin v. Hall*, 20 Cal. App. 3d 414, 97 Cal. Rptr 730 (1971); *Spring v. Constantino*, 168 Conn. 563, 362 A.2d 871 (1975); *Henzel v. Fink*, 340 So. 2d 1926 (Fla. Dist. Ct. App. 1976); *Hughes v. Malone*, 146 Ga. App. 341, 247 S.E.2d 107 (1978). *Talley v. Yonan*, 72 Ill. App. 3d 851, 391 N.E.2d 79 (1979); *Ochoa v. Maloney*, 69 Ill. App. 3d 689, 387 N.E.2d 852 (1979); *Geddie v. St. Paul Fire & Marine Ins. Co.*, 354 So. 2d 718 (La. Ct. App). *writ denied*, 356 So. 2d 1011 (La. 1978); *Jepson v. Stubbs*, 555 S.W.2d 307 (Mo. 1977)(en banc); *Vavolizza v. Krieger*, 33 N.Y.2d 351, 308 N.E.2d 439, 352 N.Y.S.2d 919 (1974); *Weaver v. Carson*, 62 Ohio App. 2d 99, 404 N.E.2d 1344 (1979); *Gaito v. Matson*, 228 Pa. Super. Ct. 288, 323 A.2d 753, *cert. denied*, 419 U.S. 1092 (1974); *Garcia v. Ray*, 556 S.W.2d 870 (Tex. Civ. App. 1977).

The earlier criminal malpractice cases are: *Underwood v. Woods*, 406 F.2d 910 (8th Cir. 1969); *Lamore v. Laughlin*, 159 F.2d 463 (D.C. Cir. 1947); *Vance v. Robinson*, 292 F. Supp. 786 (W.D.N.C. 1968); *Olson v. North*, 276 Ill. App. 457 (1934); *Miller v. Ginsberg*, 134 Minn. 397, 159 N.W. 950 (1916); *Cleveland v.Cromwell*, 128 A.D. 237, 112 N.Y.S. 643 (1908); *Cleveland v. Cromwell*, 110 A.D. 82, 96 N.Y.S. 475 (1905); *Malone v. Sherman*, 49 N.Y. Super. 530 (1883); *Heathman v. Hatch*, 13 Utah 2d 266, 372 P.2d 990 (1962).

elements of both actions are identical.[5] Criminal malpractice cases, however, present unique threshold issues. If the plaintiff does not prevail on these threshold issues, a court may bar his claim without hearing the merits of his case.

*   *   *

[T]his comment examines four threshold obstacles the criminal malpractice plaintiff may have to overcome. First, a requirement of innocence:[6] a court may hold that a plaintiff who cannot demonstrate his actual innocence of the underlying criminal charges cannot recover for the malpractice of his defense attorney. Second, a unique application of the doctrine of collateral estoppel:[7] a client[8] who raised and lost a claim of ineffective assistance of counsel in the underlying criminal case may be estopped from attacking the performance of the attorney in a subsequent criminal malpractice action. Third, the potential immunity of a court-appointed attorney:[9] courts occasionally hold that a court-appointed defense counsel or a public defender is immune from malpractice liability. Finally, a trial lawyer, whether civil or criminal, may be granted immunity from malpractice liability for any errors of judgment he makes in the conduct of litigation.[10] After examining each of these potential bars, this comment concludes that a plaintiff seeking to recover for the malpractice of his criminal defense attorney should have to overcome no greater initial burden than his civil malpractice counterpart.

*   *   *

II. THE REQUIREMENT OF INNOCENCE

Several courts have indicated that a criminal defendant who is actually guilty[24] of a crime for which he was convicted cannot recover in a malprac-

---

[5]*Compare Bradshaw v. Pardee*, Civ. No. 15444, slip op. at 3 (Cal. Ct. App. Mar. 13, 1978) *with Budd v. Nixen*, 6 Cal. 3d 195, 200, 491 P.2d 433, 436, 98 Cal. Rptr 849, 852 (1971). See notes 11–23 *infra* and accompanying text.

[6]See notes 24–48 *infra* and accompanying text.

[7]See notes 49–74 *infra* and accompanying text.

[8]Denoting a particular party is invariably confusing because criminal malpractice involves two distinct actions: the actual malpractice suit and the underlying criminal trial. In this comment the term "client" will be used to refer to the plaintiff in the malpractice suit who was the defendant in the underlying criminal action. Similarly, the "attorney" represented the client in the criminal trial and is the defendant in the criminal malpractice suit.

[9]See notes 75–102 *infra* and accompanying text.

[10]See notes 103–16 *infra* and accompanying text.

[24]The criminal law is designed to punish legal guilt. Actual guilt is a term of art.

> First, its antonym, "innocence," merely means innocence of the crime of which the client has been convicted. Thus, in the context of a claim that the lawyer's negligence caused the client to be convicted of murder, guilt of manslaughter is the equivalent of innocence.

tice action for his attorney's negligent failure to use a technical defense to win his release.[25]

The client must prove his actual innocence of the underlying charge or his claim will be barred. No comparable burden exists in civil malpractice suits,[26] and no reason justifies imposing this burden on criminal malpractice plaintiffs.

In *Bradshaw v. Pardee*[27] the defendant in a criminal proceeding had confessed his guilt to law enforcement officials and pleaded guilty on advice of counsel. He then brought a criminal malpractice suit, charging that his sentence was the proximate result of his attorney's negligent advice. He alleged that if his attorney had properly performed his legal duties, the criminal charges would have been reduced or dismissed or, alternatively, his sentence would have been less severe. The California Court of Appeals held that the client could not maintain the action, reasoning that if a criminal defendant was actually guilty of the crime for which he was convicted, his prison sentence was proximately caused by his guilt and not by the alleged negligence of his attorney.[28]

Had the *Bradshaw* court used the terms guilt or innocence in their legal sense, its holding would have been entirely correct. A client who is legally guilty cannot satisfy his burden of proximate cause (his "suit within a suit" requirement); he cannot show that, but for the negligence of his attorney, the result in the criminal case would have differed.[29] The court, however, imposed a requirement of actual innocence. It relied on two facts

---

Second, "actual guilt" does not mean actual guilt. No system of procedure and proof can infallibly determine the client's guilt or innocence. By "actual guilt" we merely mean guilt provable at the malpractice trial—a civil proceeding—with the aid of all then available evidence admissible in such a trial.

Kaus and Mallen, *supra* note 3, at 1200 n.25; *cf.* Friendly, *"Is Innocence Irrelevant? Collateral Attacks on Criminal Judgments,"* 38 *U. Chi. L. Rev.* 142, 160 (1970) (defining a colorable showing of innocence in the context of collateral attack on a criminal conviction).

[25]*See, e.g., Walker v. Kruse,* 484 F.2d 802, 804 (7th Cir. 1973); *Bradshaw v. Pardee,* Civ. No. 15444, slip op. at 4–5 (Cal. Ct. App. Mar. 13, 1978); *Garcia v. Ray,* 556 S.W.2d 870, 872 (Tex. Ct. App. 1977). *See also Hughes v. Malone,* 146 Ga. App. 341, 347, 247 S.E.2d 107, 112 (1978)

[26]*See* Kaus and Mallen, *supra* note 3, at 1203:

In the context of civil malpractice, when a [defendant's] lawyer is sued for permitting an action on a debt to go by default, the client need only show that he would have prevailed had the case been defended on the merits. We do not ask him to prove in addition that he did not actually owe the debt.

[27]Civ. No. 15444 (Cal. Ct. App. Mar. 13, 1978).

[28]*Id,* slip op. at 5–7. The court indicated that the client's actual guilt undercut his ability to establish proximate cause: "Since plaintiff was indeed guilty, as he pleaded after being 'advised at length about the consequences of the guilty plea' and having 'fully understood the nature of the proceedings,' his prison sentence was caused by such guilt and not by defendant's alleged negligence." *Id,* slip op. at 5. (footnote omitted).

[29]*Id,* slip op. at 4–5.

in reaching its decision: the confession and the guilty plea.[30] Neither demonstrates legal guilt. A confession does not preempt a legal defense, for a layman may not know what defenses are provided by the law. One of the functions of the attorney is to present legal defenses not apparent to the layman. Certainly the guilty plea does not prove legal guilt; the essence of the client's claim is that he was negligently advised to plead guilty when he was in fact legally innocent.[31] *Bradshaw*, however, holds that an actually guilty client cannot establish proximate causation.

The court's reasoning is flawed. A client who is actually guilty can establish proximate causation by showing that he had a legal defense that his attorney neglected to raise.[32] For example, an actually guilty client cannot be convicted once the statute of limitations has expired. In such a situation the defendant is legally innocent and it is his attorney's duty to raise that defense.[33] If the attorney does not, and the client is convicted, the attorney's negligence is the proximate cause of the conviction. In *Bradshaw* the requirement of innocence barred a potentially valid claim even though there was no proof that the client was legally guilty.

Although an actually guilty client may not be legally guilty, he may be morally culpable. The expiration of the statute of limitations makes him legally innocent, but it does not restore his virtue. Nevertheless, a defendant who is convicted because his attorney neglected to raise a technical defense, such as the statute of limitations, should recover damages. The criminal law imposes no requirement of actual innocence; no reason exists to use actual guilt as a bar to civil recovery for professional negligence. As a tort action, criminal malpractice should focus on the activity of the alleged tortfeasor, not on the conduct of the victim.[34]

The criminal courts, though affording defendants greater procedural safeguards than civil courts,[35] do not impose a requirement of actual guilt

[30]See note 18 *supra* and accompanying text.

[31]Of course, that a client is legally guilty of a lesser crime does not affect the negligent nature of advice to plead guilty to a more serious offense.

[32]*See Martin v. Hall*, 20 Cal. App. 3d 414, 97 Cal. Rptr. 730 (1971); Kaus and Mallen, *supra* note 3, at 1226–31.

[33]*See* ABA Project on Standards for Criminal Justice, *supra* note 13, at 148 ("[counsel's] role as advocate permits and requires that he press all points legally available, even if he must subordinate his personal evaluation of the client's conduct"); ABA Model Code of Professional Responsibility and Code of Judicial Conduct, Canon 7, n.3 (1980) (quoting ABA Canons of Professional Ethics No. 5).

[34]Under conventional tort theory the doctrines of contributory negligence and assumption of risk place the plaintiff's behavior at issue, but neither of these doctrines is relevant to a requirement of innocence. Being guilty of the original crime does not constitute contributory negligence to the malpractice tort. When the client robs a liquor store, he is not increasing the risk that his lawyer will be incompetent. *See generally* W. Prosser, *Law of Torts*, § 65 (4th ed. 1971). The contributory negligence defense may be available to the attorney, however, if the defense is premised on client conduct that took place during the course of the trial, rather than on conduct that occurred beforehand.

To apply the doctrine of assumption of the risk suggests that the client, by committing the criminal act, has recognized the risk of malpractice and has relieved the attorney, in advance, of his duty to use ordinary skill and knowledge. *See id.* § 68.

[35]The Constitution guarantees criminal defendants many rights, including the right to counsel, the right to plead not guilty, and the right to be tried in a courtroom presided over by

when they identify and punish criminal behavior. Because it is impossible to ascertain moral culpability conclusively, the criminal justice system is designed to punish only legal guilt. If an actually guilty client has a viable defense to the criminal charge—for example, that the statute of limitations has expired—the law considers him innocent for reasons of public policy despite his moral culpability.[36]

Dividing criminal malpractice claims into two categories more clearly demonstrates the inappropriateness of considering actual guilt in a tort action. The first category includes those cases in which the client was legally guilty but, through the negligence of his attorney, was either sentenced more heavily than the legal maximum or was convicted of a more serious crime than was legally appropriate. In this situation the attorney's negligence caused the client to suffer an excessive penalty.[37] Actual innocence is irrelevant;[38] the client pays his debt to society in any event. He is merely asking for damages for the excess penalty.

The second category includes those cases in which the client was legally innocent of any crime,[39] but was convicted because of his attorney's failure to raise an appropriate defense. If an actually guilty client may recover damages for an excess penalty, it follows that a client may recover damages if he should never have been convicted at all. Even an actually guilty client is entitled to all appropriate defenses,[40] and is entitled to damages if his attorney neglects to present these defenses.

It may seem wrong for an actually guilty client to recover from his attorney for failure to assert a technical defense on his behalf. Some defenses, such as alibi, self-defense, and, in some cases, insanity, are related to the question of a defendant's actual criminal guilt. Other defenses reflect

---

a judge. *Rideau v. Louisiana*, 373 U.S. 723, 726–27 (1963). Comparable rights are not necessarily afforded in civil actions. *See, e.g., Watson v. Moss*, 619 F.2d 775, 776 (8th Cir. 1980). *See generally Chambers v. Florida*, 309 U.S. 227, 235–38 (1940).

[36]*See American Pipe & Constr. Co. v. Utah*, 414 U.S. 538, 554 (1974); *Order of R.R. Telegraphers v. Railway Express Agency, Inc.*, 321 U.S. 342, 348–49 (1944). The criminal law will not penalize the client after the statute has run because the passage of time makes the evidence unreliable. Once the client proves his legal innocence in a civil proceeding by showing that the limitations period has expired, it is irrational to require him to prove his actual innocence as well; the evidence has not become more reliable by virtue of the civil forum. *But cf. Kaufman v. United States*, 394 U.S. 217, 234 (1969) (Black, J., dissenting) (probable or possible innocence should be given weight in determining whether judgment should be open to collateral attack); Friendly, *supra* note 24 (a colorable showing of innocence should be prerequisite to collateral attack on a criminal conviction).

[37]The court in *Geddie v. St. Paul Fire & Marine Ins. Co.*, 354 So. 2d 718 (La. Ct. App.) *writ denied*, 356 So. 2d 1011 (La. 1978), coined the term "excessive incarceration" to designate the time spent in prison beyond the legal maximum. 354 So. 2d at 719.

[38]*See* R. Mallen and V. Levit, *supra* note 1, § 248.

[39]For simplicity, the text deals with a plaintiff who claims he is legally innocent of any crime and was convicted solely due to malpractice. Alternatively, a plaintiff might admit his guilt of a lesser crime, but bring suit because the malpractice caused his conviction on a more serious charge. *See Geddie v. St. Paul Fire & Marine Ins. Co.*, 354 So. 2d 718 (La. Ct. App.) *writ denied*, 356 So. 2d 1011 (La. 1978). The rationale is the same in both cases: if the plaintiff can establish that the criminal courts would have found him legally innocent of the crime for which he was convicted, the civil courts should not demand additional proof of his innocence.

[40]*See* text accompanying notes 46–47 *infra*.

policies of the criminal justice system unrelated to the actual guilt of the defendant. Examples of this kind of defense include the exclusionary rule,[41] the statute of limitations,[42] and the rule against improper grand jury selection.[43] Because the policies behind these technical defenses are not directly aimed at the defendant's actual guilt, it may be argued that a criminal defendant should not recover from an attorney who negligently fails to assert such a defense.[44]

The criminal law provides these technical defenses, however, for valid policy reasons.[45] Defense attorneys owe a duty to their clients to assert all reasonable defenses.[46] An attorney who fails to raise a valid technical defense is just as negligent as one who overlooks a viable truth-related defense.[47] Moreover, the policies behind technical defenses are ill served if defense attorneys can freely choose whether to raise them. The tort law of malpractice would subvert the criminal system if it shielded attorneys from liability for failing to raise a technical defense.

[41]The purpose of the exclusionary rule is to deter police from making unreasonable searches and seizures. *See Terry v. Ohio*, 392 U.S. 1, 12 (1968); *Linkletter v. Walker*, 381 U.S. 618, 629–35 (1965).

[42]See note 36 *supra*.

[43]Discrimination in the selection of grand jurors "strikes at the fundamental values of our judicial system and our society as a whole . . ." *Rose v. Mitchell*, 443 U.S. 545, 556 (1979).

[44]In *Stone v. Powell*, 428 U.S. 465 (1976), the Supreme Court held that a criminal defendant may not seek habeas corpus relief on the basis of a state's denial of his fourth amendment rights if he had a full and fair opportunity to assert his constitutional claim in the state court. *Id.* at 494. The Court suggested that federal habeas corpus relief may be unavailable to defendants with claims unrelated to their actual guilt. *Id.* at 489–90, 491 n.31. In *Rose v. Mitchell*, 443 U.S. 545 (1979), however, the Court permitted collateral review of the defendant's claim of racial discrimination in the selection of a state grand jury, despite the fact that the claim was unrelated to the defendant's guilt. Similarly, in *Cuyler v. Sullivan*, 446 U.S. 335, 342–44 (1980), the Court held that federal habeas corpus relief could be available to a state prisoner claiming that his retained counsel failed to provide him with effective assistance. Because the court of appeals award of such relief was based, in part, upon an improper weighing of the evidence of conflict-of-interest, the Supreme Court vacated the decision. Thus, the Court is responding not only to *Stone's* guilt-related standard but to other policies as well in determining the availability of collateral review. *See "The Supreme Court, 1978 Term,"* 93 *Harv. L. Rev.* 1, 203–05 (1979).

The guilt-related standard is inappropriate in criminal malpractice cases. *Stone* requires deference to a state court's adjudication of a constitutional claim, but *Rose* allows collateral review when the asserted constitutional claim impinges directly on the state court's ability to determine the claim fairly. For discussion of *Rose*, see Duker, *"Rose v. Mitchell and Justice Lewis Powell: The Role of Federal Courts and Federal* Habeas," 23 *How. L.J.* 279, 281 (1980); *"The Supreme Court, 1978 Term,"* 93 *Harv. L. Rev.* 1, 199–209 (1979). Federal deference to the competence of state courts is not at issue in the context of criminal malpractice. Criminal malpractice is a state law claim, often brought in state court. Moreover, the outcome of a criminal malpractice action has no bearing on the finality or integrity of the prior criminal proceeding. While habeas corpus relief results in the release of a state prisoner, malpractice results only in a damages award against his defense attorney. The malpractice action is entirely separate from the underlying criminal proceeding, and therefore the policies involved are those of tort law, not of federalism or criminal procedure.

[45]See notes 41–43 *supra*.

[46]See note 33 *supra*.

[47]Cf., *Christy v. Saliterman*, 288 Minn. 144, 179 N.W.2d 288 (1970) (an attorney held liable in civil malpractice for neglecting to raise the technical statute of limitations defense).

Even if a criminal malpractice plaintiff establishes all the elements of his claim, few juries would award substantial damages to a criminal who, they believe, received an appropriate sentence.[48] Thus, even without a judicially imposed requirement of innocence, an actually guilty client will rarely recover damages for criminal malpractice. Nevertheless, a client suing his criminal defense attorney for malpractice should be required to prove only that he was legally innocent of the charges against him, and should not have to prove his actual innocence.

III. COLLATERAL ESTOPPEL

The doctrine of collateral estoppel[49] is a potential defense to any legal malpractice action. One application of the doctrine, however, is unique to criminal malpractice suits. A client who has unsuccessfully raised the constitutional claim of ineffective assistance of counsel in the underlying criminal action[50] is estopped from relitigating identical issues in a subsequent malpractice action against his defense attorney.[51] This estoppel defense is inapplicable in civil malpractice actions; a party to a civil suit has no opportunity to challenge the competence of his attorney during the initial civil action because attorney incompetence is not a basis for appeal.

[48]*See* Kaus and Mallen, *supra* note 3, at 1203:

> [W]hat would be the result of . . . this question: "Should a lawyer have to pay damages to a guilty client because he negligently fails to secure an acquittal?" Surely a very substantial percentage of those polled would say that the guilty client is not entitled to damages since—God works in mysterious ways—"justice" was done. Would the public really tolerate the thought of a prisoner, who is precisely where he ought to be, receiving substantial damages for not being on the street planning to rob another bank?

[49]Collateral estoppel precludes relitigation of issues actually litigated and determined in a prior suit, regardless of whether both suits involve the same cause of action. *Lawlor v. National Screen Serv. Corp.*, 349 U.S. 322, 326 (1955). *See* Polasky, *"Collateral Estoppel Effects of Prior Litigation,"* 39 *Iowa L. Rev.* 217, 222 (1954). Although the doctrine usually precludes relitigation of issues of fact, it may also bar issues of law. Vestal, *"Preclusion/Res Judicata Variables: Nature of the Controversy,"* 1965 *Wash. U.L.Q.* 158, 171. *See generally* 1B *Moore's Federal Practice* ¶0.441 (2d ed. 1948 & Supp. 1980).

[50]U.S. Const. amend. VI provides: "In all criminal prosecutions, the accused shall enjoy the right . . . to have . . . the Assistance of Counsel for his defence." The right to counsel is the right to effective assistance of counsel. *McMann v. Richardson*, 397 U.S. 759, 771 n.14 (1970); *Reece v. Georgia*, 350 U.S. 85, 90 (1955). *See generally* Note, *"Identifying and Remedying Ineffective Assistance of Criminal Defense Counsel: A New Look After United States v. Decoster,"* 93 *Harv. L. Rev.* 752, 753–58 (1980). Any post-conviction proceeding in which the client seeks relief on the ground that his defense counsel provided inadequate representation can form the basis for estoppel in this context. *See Vavolizza v. Krieger*, 33 N.Y.2d 351, 351, 308 N.E.2d 439, 439, 352 N.Y.S.2d 919, 919 (1974).

[51]*See Walker v. Kruse*, 484 F.2d 802, 803–04 (7th Cir. 1973); *Vavolizza v. Krieger*, 33 N.Y.2d 351, 355–56, 308 N.E.2d 439, 441–42, 352 N.Y.S.2d 919, 922–23 (1974); *Garcia v. Ray*, 556 S.W.2d 870, 872 (Tex. Civ. App. 1977). In *Walker* and *Garcia* the prior proceeding was a direct appeal of the client's criminal conviction. In *Vavolizza* the client had previously challenged his attorney's conduct in a collateral review proceeding.

Applying this form of estoppel in a criminal malpractice action is justified only in certain circumstances. First, the issue barred from relitigation must be identical to an issue necessarily decided or actually adjudicated. in the prior proceeding.[52] Second, the party against whom the defense is asserted must have had a full and fair opportunity to litigate the issues in the prior proceeding.[53] In the context of criminal malpractice actions the second requirement generally presents no problem. The client had his day in court when his claim of ineffective assistance of counsel was litigated in the underlying criminal action. The first requirement, however—that the issues be identical—is not so easily satisfied.

* * *

IV. IMMUNITY FOR COURT-APPOINTED COUNSEL

A client who was represented in the underlying criminal action by court-appointed counsel may face a third threshold barrier to recovery for malpractice. Several federal courts[75] have held that a public defender[76] or court-appointed attorney[77] enjoys immunity from suit, including immunity from criminal malpractice claims.[78] In *Ferri v. Ackerman*,[79] however, the Supreme Court unanimously held that federal law does not protect

---

[52]Alabama Farm Bureau Mut. Cas. Ins. Co. v. Moore, 349 So. 2d 1113, 1116 (Ala. 1977); *People v. Taylor*, 12 Cal. 3d 686, 691, 527 P.2d 622, 625, 117 Cal. Rptr. 70, 73 (1974) (en banc); *Vavolizza v. Krieger*, 33 N.Y.2d 351, 356, 308 N.E.2d 439, 442, 352 N.Y.S.2d 919, 923 (1974); 1B *Moore's Federal Practice* ¶0.443[2] (2d ed. 1948 & Supp. 1980).

[53]*Parklane Hosiery Co. v. Shore*, 439 U.S. 322, 328 (1978); *Blonder—Tongue Laboratories, Inc. v. University of Ill. Foundation*, 402 U.S. 313, 329 (1971); *Johnson v. United States*, 576 F.2d 606, 614 (5th Cir. 1978); *Borland v. Gillespie*, 206 Neb. 191, 199, 292 N.W.2d 26, 31 (1980); *Hicks v. De La Cruz*, 52 Ohio St. 2d 71, 74, 369 N.E.2d 776, 778 (1977). An actual hearing is not required. An issue that is submitted and determined on a motion for summary judgment, for example, will be precluded from relitigation. *Restatement (second) of Judgments* § 68, Comment d (Tent. Draft No. 4, 1977).

[75]Because state malpractice actions have been rare until recently, most claims against appointed counsel have arisen under 42 U.S.C. § 1983 (1976). Some of these decisions held that a court-appointed attorney enjoys judicial immunity from suit, and dismissed the claim. *E.g., Brown v. Joseph*, 463 F.2d 1046, 1049 (3d Cir. 1972), *cert. denied*, 412 U.S. 950 (1973). A case involving this issue is currently before the Supreme Court. *See Dodson v. Polk County*, 628 F.2d 1104 (8th Cir. 1980), *cert. granted*, 49 U.S.L.W. 3635 (U.S. Mar. 3, 1981) (No. 80-824). Other courts have reasoned that appointed counsel do not act under color of state law. *E.g., Page v. Sharpe*, 487 F.2d 567 (1st Cir. 1973); *Espinoza v. Rogers*, 470 F.2d 1174 (10th Cir. 1972).

[76]*Robinson v. Bergstrom*, 579 F.2d 401, 411 (7th Cir. 1978), *Miller v. Barilla*, 549 F.2d 648, 649–50 (9th Cir. 1977); *Brown v. Joseph*, 463 F.2d 1046 (3d Cir. 1972), *cert. denied*, 412 U.S. 950 (1973).

[77]*Minns v. Paul*, 542 F.2d 899 (4th Cir. 1976), *cert. denied*, 429 U.S. 1102 (1977); *see Walker v. Kruse*, 484 F.2d 802, 804–05 (7th Cir. 1973).

[78]In *Sullens v. Carroll*, 308 F. Supp. 311 (M.D. Fla. 1970), *aff'd*, 446 F.2d 1392 (5th Cir. 1971), the plaintiff brought a malpractice action against his court-appointed attorney in federal court under 42 U.S.C. § 1983 (1976). The district court dismissed on the ground that an attorney appointed by a federal court does not act under color of state law. The plaintiff then brought his claim as a diversity suit for criminal malpractice. The Court of Appeals for the Fifth Circuit held the court-appointed attorney to be immune from malpractice liability. *See Sullens v. Carroll*, 446 F.2d 1392, 1392–93 (5th Cir. 1971).

[79]444 U.S. 193 (1979).

court-appointed counsel from state criminal malpractice claims. Two recent state court decisions found that no such immunity derives from state law.[80]

Ferri was indicted by a federal grand jury on a conspiracy charge. The district court appointed Ackerman as Ferri's counsel pursuant to the Criminal Justice Act of 1964.[81] After being convicted of conspiracy, Ferri sued Ackerman for malpractice. The state trial court dismissed the complaint, and the Pennsylvania Supreme Court affirmed.[82] The state supreme court considered itself bound by federal law and held that federal principles of immunity were properly extended to court-appointed counsel.[83]

The Supreme Court reversed. It concluded that federal law did not immunize court-appointed attorneys from civil liability for malpractice. The Court recognized that a state may provide such immunity as a matter of state law, but that a state was under no federal compulsion to do so.[84] The *Ferri* Court rejected the argument that by providing compensation to court-appointed attorneys through the Criminal Justice Act of 1964, Congress intended to immunize such counsel from civil liability. Nothing in the language of the statute, nor in its legislative history, suggested such an intent.[85]

The Court then considered whether, apart from the statute, the federal doctrines of official or judicial immunity extend to counsel appointed to represent an indigent criminal defendant in federal court. It found that court-appointed attorneys did not warrant such immunity. The court reasoned that judges and prosecutors enjoyed such immunity because "[a]s public servants, they represent the interest of society as a whole."[86] The conduct of their official duties affects many individuals, each of whom may be a source of future controversy. The law confers immunity on these officials to provide them with the maximum ability to "deal fearlessly and impartially with the public."[87] In contrast, a court-appointed lawyer, like a privately retained attorney, represents only his client. His conduct does not directly affect the public at large, and immunity should not extend to him.[88]

Proponents of immunity for appointed counsel advance several policy

[80]*Spring v. Constantino*, 168 Conn. 563, 362 A.2d 871 (1975); *Reese v. Danforth*, 486 Pa. 479, 406 A.2d 735 (1979). *Spring* involved a criminal malpractice claim against a public defender. *Reese* was a negligence action against a public defender who had represented the plaintiff in involuntary commitment proceedings. In each case the court arrived at the same conclusion: once the attorney is assigned to a client, his function does not differ from that of a private attorney. 168 Conn. at 567, 362 A.2d at 875; 486 Pa. at 486, 406 A.2d at 739.

[81]18 U.S.C. § 3006A (Supp. II 1978).

[82]*Ferri v. Ackerman*, 483 Pa. 90, 394 A.2d 553 (1978), *rev'd*, 444 U.S. 193 (1979).

[83]483 Pa. at 99, 394 A.2d at 558.

[84]444 U.S. at 198.

[85]*Id.* at 199.

[86]*Id.* at 202–03.

[87]*Id.* at 203.

[88]*Id.* at 204. *See generally Imbler v. Pachtman*, 424 U.S. 409, 420–29 (1975); Note, "Remedies Against the United States and Its Officials," 70 *Harv. L. Rev.* 827, 833–38 (1957); 30 *U. Fla. L. Rev.* 810 (1978).

arguments in support of their position.[89] First, they cite "the need to encourage counsel in the full exercise of professionalism."[90] Appointed attorneys need to have the discretion "to decline to press the frivolous, to assign priorities between indigent litigants, and to make strategic decisions [in the course of litigation] . . . ."[91] This argument presents valid concerns that could be resolved by a grant of immunity. The problem of professional discretion is faced by all attorneys, however, not merely by appointed counsel. Retained and court-appointed attorneys perform identical duties. Each requires freedom to exercise professional discretion, and appointed counsel merit no special treatment.

A second argument in favor of immunity, based on the public's interest in avoiding repetitive litigation,[92] exhibits a similar weakness. To establish a malpractice claim a client must prove that, but for the attorney's negligence, he would have been acquitted, convicted of a lesser crime, or given a less severe penalty. A client can make this showing of proof only when a criminal case that has been settled is retried in a civil court. The argument contends that judicial finality would be undermined by this practice.[93] This argument, like the first, fails to explain why appointed counsel should be granted unique protection. Any malpractice action based upon underlying litigation involves to some extent the retrial of a closed case. Under this rationale, both retained criminal defense counsel and attorneys who litigate civil cases also should be immunized.[94]

Several significant distinctions, however, exist between appointed attorneys and privately retained counsel. First, an appointed attorney cannot choose his clients; he cannot "assay the likelihood that the frustrations of a client's case may lead to recriminations and, ultimately, litigation. . . .[95] Nor does the client have the opportunity to select an attorney with whom

---

[89]*See Reese v. Danforth*, 486 Pa. 479, 495, 406 A.2d 735, 743 (1979) (Manderino, J., dissenting); *Rondel v. Worsley*, [1969] 1 A.C. 191 (H.L.); Mallen, *"The Court-Appointed Lawyer and Legal Malpractice—Liability or Immunity?"* in *Professional Liability of Trial Lawyers: The Malpractice Question* 36 (1979).

[90]*Minns v. Paul*, 542 F.2d 899, 901 (4th Cir. 1976), *cert. denied*, 429 U.S. 1102 (1977).

[91]*Id. Accord, Reese v. Danforth*, 486 Pa. 479, 485–86, 406 A.2d 735, 739 (1979). Lord Pearce best expressed this view in *Rondel v. Worsley*, [1969] 1 A.C. 191 (H.L.), when he wrote:

> It is impossible to expect an advocate to prune his case of irrelevancies against his client's wishes if he faces an action for negligence when he does so. Prudence will always be prompting him to ask every question and call every piece of evidence that his client wishes, in order to avoid the risk of getting involved [in a malpractice action].

Id. at 273.

[92]*Reese v. Danforth*, 486 Pa. 479, 495, 406 A.2d 735, 743 (1979) (Manderino, J., dissenting). Kaus and Mallen, *supra* note 2, at 1192 n.5. *See Rondel v. Worsley*, [1969] 1 A.C. 191, 230 (H.L.).

[93]*Rondel v. Worsley*, [1969] 1 A.C. 191, 230 (H.L.).

[94]Some authorities advocate immunity for all trial lawyers for their errors of judgment in the conduct of litigation. See notes 104–06 *infra* and accompanying text.

[95]*Reese v. Danforth*, 486 Pa. 479, 494, 406 A.2d 735, 743 (1979) Manderino, J., dissenting).

he feels comfortable. Consequently, the attorney–client relationship may commence in an atmosphere of suspicion and hostility and, if the client is convicted, end in bitterness.[96] Furthermore, because he does not pay for the lawyer's services, an indigent is more likely to urge his counsel to press frivolous appeals and raise meritless defenses.[97] If the attorney refuses to comply, the client may believe he is entitled to damages for malpractice.[98] Finally, many courts cite the need to recruit able lawyers to represent indigent defendants.[99]

Appointed attorneys may be particularly vulnerable to malpractice actions, but all attorneys are vulnerable in some degree to such suits. Retained lawyers may handle cases that carry equal or greater risks of client dissatisfaction. A convicted defendant facing a long prison term may feel bitter regardless of whether his attorney was retained or appointed. Attorneys who litigate civil matters also are vulnerable, and if the stakes are high enough, the losing party may try to recover his loss in a malpractice suit. Most attorneys are not immune from suit; they protect themselves by more conventional methods, such as malpractice insurance. The appointed attorney can protect himself in the same way.[100]

A court discriminates against indigent clients when it permits retained but not appointed attorneys to be held liable for their negligence.[101] Poor clients become doubly disadvantaged: they may neither choose their lawyer nor recover damages if the appointed attorney is negligent. Far from improving the quality of indigent representation, immunity for appointed counsel will reduce the quality of representation available to the poor. Paid less than private attorneys and insulated from malpractice liability, court-appointed counsel will almost certainly render less effective representation. Finally, even if the proponents of immunity are correct, the question

[96]*See Ferri v. Ackerman*, 444 U.S. 193, 200 n.17 (1979).

[97]*See Brown v. Joseph*, 463 F.2d 1046, 1049 (3d Cir. 1972), *cert. denied*, 412 U.S. 950 (1973). The *Brown* court noted that complaints under section 1983 are usually pro se, 42 U.S.C. § 1983 (1976). An indigent plaintiff pays nothing to file a section 1983 claim; thus an indigent receiving a court-appointed attorney would be more likely to bring such a claim than would the client of a privately retained attorney, who would pay to press his section 1983 suit. The *Brown* court used this logic to grant immunity to a court-appointed attorney. 463 F.2d at 1049. Because the attorney in *Ferri* was appointed by a federal court, the decision does not necessarily preclude an attorney appointed by a state court and sued under 42 U.S.C. § 1983 (1976) from claiming immunity. The Supreme Court has recently granted certiorari to decide whether state court-appointed attorneys are amenable to suit under section 1983. *See Dodson v. Polk County*, 628 F.2d 1104 (8th Cir. 1980), *cert. granted*, 49 U.S.L.W. 3635 (U.S. Mar. 3, 1981) (No. 80-824).

[98]An attorney may always request the court's permission to withdraw from the case. The procedure may be time consuming, *see Anders v. California*, 386 U.S. 738, 744 (1967), and if the court denies permission the attorney–client relationship will almost certainly have deteriorated. Certainly, the attorney may decide to take the extra appeal or make the extra argument rather than to go through an unsuccessful withdrawal procedure.

[99]*See, e.g., Minns v. Paul*, 542 F.2d 899, 901 (4th Cir. 1976), *cert. denied*, 429 U.S. 1102 (1977); *Brown v. Joseph*, 463 F.2d 1046, 1049 (3d Cir. 1972); *Reese v. Danforth*, 486 Pa. 479, 486, 406 A.2d 735, 739 (1979).

[100]R. Mallen and V. Levit, *supra* note 1, § 175; Mallen, *supra* note 89, at 43.

[101]*Ferri v. Ackerman*, 483 Pa. 90, 100-01, 394 A.2d 553, 559 (1978) (Roberts J., dissenting), *rev'd*, 444 U.S. 193 (1979).

is better suited to legislative than judicial determination.[102] A state legislature may decide that public policy demands such immunity for appointed counsel, and confer it by statute. In the absence of legislative action, however, the judiciary should not extend immunity to court-appointed attorneys.

V. IMMUNITY FOR ERRORS OF JUDGMENT IN THE CONDUCT OF LITIGATION

A court may grant an attorney immunity from liability for any errors in the conduct of civil or criminal litigation.[103] This immunity is grounded in two independent theories. First, trial attorneys should not be liable for mere errors of judgment.[104] Decisions of trial tactics are within an attorney's professional discretion and errors of judgment should not result in liability. This argument, however, does not justify absolute immunity for a negligent trial attorney.[105]

The second argument for trial-attorney immunity is that regardless of the existence of negligence, a malpractice plaintiff rarely can establish conclusively the element of proximate cause.[106] Causation is obvious when an attorney negligently omits a defense which, had it been asserted, would have resulted in a favorable judgment in the initial proceeding as a matter of law.[107] Causation is not obvious, however, when the malpractice plaintiff alleges that the omitted defense would have prevailed, not as a matter of law, but because it would have persuaded the jury to reach a more favorable result.[108]

[102]*Ferri v. Ackerman,* 444 U.S. 193, 205 (1979).

[103]*See Woodruff v. Tomlin,* 423 F. Supp. 1284, 1288 (W.D. Tenn. 1976), *rev'd,* 593 F.2d 33 (6th Cir. 1979), *aff'd in part, rev'd in part on rehearing en banc,* 616 F.2d 924 (6th Cir.), *cert. denied.* 101 S. Ct. 246 (1980); *Stricklan v. Koella,* 546 S.W.2d 810, 814 (Tenn. Ct. App. 1976). *See generally* Beckham, *"Trial Lawyer's Liability for Judgmental Decisions,"* in *Professional Liability of Trial Lawyers: The Malpractice Question* 157 (1979); Haskell, *"The Trial Lawyer's Immunity from Liability for Errors of Judgment,"* in *Professional Liability of Trial Lawyers: The Malpractice Question* 141(1979); Thomason, *"A Plea for Absolute Immunity for Errors in Trial Judgment,"* 14 *Willamette L.J.* 369 (1978).

[104]*Dorf v. Relles,* 355 F.2d 488, 492 (7th Cir. 1966); *Woodruff v. Tomlin,* 423 F. Supp. 1284, 1288 (W.D. Tenn. 1976), *rev'd,* 593 F.2d 33 (6th Cir. 1979), *aff'd in part, rev'd in part on rehearing en banc,* 616 F.2d 924 (6th Cir.), *cert denied,* 101 S. Ct. 246 (1980); *Baker v. Beal,* 225 N.W.2d 106, 112 (Iowa 1975). *See* R. Mallen and V. Levit, *supra* note 1, § 111.

[105]*Siegel v. Kranis,* 29 A.D.2d 477, 479, 288 N.Y.S.2d 831, 834 (1968); R. Mallen and V. Levit, *supra* note 1, § 111; Beckham, *supra* note 103, at 160.

[106]*See Woodruff v. Tomlin,* 423 F.Supp. 1284, 1288 (W.D. Tenn. 1976), *rev'd,* 593 F.2d 33 (6th Cir. 1979), *aff'd in part, rev'd in part on rehearing en banc,* 616 F.2d 924 (6th Cir.), *cert denied,* 101 S. Ct. 246 (1980); *Stricklan v. Koella,* 546 S.W.2d 810, 813 (Tenn. Ct. App. 1976); Haskell, *supra* note 103, at 141–42; Thomason, *supra* note 103, at 383.

[107]*See Better Homes, Inc. v. Rodgers,* 195 F. Supp. 93, 97 (N.D.W. Va. 1961). For example, there is no difficulty in establishing causation if the defense attorney neglects to raise a valid statute of limitations defense.

[108]Negligence is assumed for the purposes of the present discussion. Naturally, the decision not to assert a defense, which might have led to a more favorable result, would not be a basis for malpractice if the attorney exercised ordinary skill and knowledge in making his decision. See note 104 *supra* and accompanying text.

* * *

Courts should allow criminal malpractice plaintiffs to demonstrate causation by satisfying the same burden of proof as in the underlying criminal case. If this theory of causation seems speculative, a court should not overreact by providing absolute immunity. Rather, it should accept the more conclusive causal link provided by the margin-of-error proposal. This system is imperfect; because the causation burden in the malpractice case is higher than in the underlying criminal case, many clients who would have been acquitted with adequate representation will be unable to recover for the negligence of their attorneys. Nevertheless, the margin-of-error proposal is fairer to the client than a system of absolute immunity.

VI. CONCLUSION

A criminal malpractice plaintiff, like other tort victims, may attempt to prove his case unless a substantial public policy reason justifies a threshold barrier to recovery. A criminal malpractice plaintiff should not face harsher threshold requirements than his civil counterpart. A man who is wrongfully imprisoned is no less deserving of restitution than a man who has wrongly suffered a money judgment. A concept such as the requirement of innocence suggests that the court is focusing not on the alleged injury, but on whether the victim deserves protection. Tort law is not concerned with the conduct of the victim in that sense because the morality of the plaintiff is not an element of the cause of action.

No reason exists to preclude a potentially valid criminal malpractice claim as a threshold matter. Considering the rarity of such suits, the extra expenditure of judicial resources will not unduly burden the courts. Collateral estoppel and the different types of immunity are valid concepts if exercised prudently, but neither is universally appropriate. Collateral estoppel should be applied to criminal malpractice claims only after the particular facts of each case have been examined. The concept of immunity should not bar otherwise valid claims unless the equities are overwhelming. The rule of law is that liability follows the tort, and immunity is only the exception.[117] Such exceptions to criminal malpractice recovery are unjustified.

[117]*Reese v. Danforth*, 486 Pa. 479, 487, 406 A.2d 735, 739 (1979).

INDEX

INDEX OF CASES

GENERAL INDEX